The Human Encounter

SECOND EDITION

THE HUMAN ENCOUNTER
Readings in Education

SHELDON PTASCHEVITCH STOFF
Adelphi University

HERBERT SCHWARTZBERG
Queens College of the City University of New York

HARPER & ROW, Publishers
New York, Evanston, San Francisco, London

THE HUMAN ENCOUNTER: READINGS IN EDUCATION, Second Edition

Copyright © 1969, 1973 by Sheldon Stoff and Herbert Schwartzberg.

Harper & Row, Publishers, Inc.   10 East 53rd Street, New York, N.Y. 10022

Standard Book Number: 06-046452-6
Library of Congress Catalog Card Number: 72-9406

TO MATTHEW, JESSE, AND JOSHUA.

May theirs be an education and a life in balance;
may they see clearly and wholely
the things that are ever changing
and the things that never change.

Contents

Preface to the Second Edition

The first edition of *The Human Encounter* emphasized the basic issues of our times: man's freedom and philosophy, as corner stones on which to build and evaluate educational issues and decisions.

Since the publication of that edition it has become increasingly clear that freedom is the focal point of our age. Man will be free! It is essential that he understand the meaning of that concept and develop his philosophy, life style, and education in accordance with the most significant concept of freedom available to our time.

A misunderstanding of the nature of freedom could well bring about an age of egoism and anarchy. It could usher in an era of morality without responsibility. The significance of a fulfilling "partnership" relationship should not be lost in the search for the ever important "I."

It also remains for a balanced and broad scientific view to understand and support a concept of the free man, at home with himself and others, freely dedicated in the service of mankind.

S.P.S.
H.S.

Preface to the First Edition

One of the primary functions of the education of teachers today is to challenge students to develop the rationale and the insights necessary for making significant decisions. Beyond mere thinking and acting, students must be brought to a deep-seated sense of responsibility for their actions. They must become sensitive to the relationships among people and to the complex of interactions that make community living possible. They must become aware of what is truly human and richly rewarding in a world that too often is fearful, sterile, and mechanical. They must commit themselves to the most important career in our social order, one that is exciting, demanding, and dangerous. They must look forward to a lifetime of change and growth in a revolutionary era that they will help to shape.

With these considerations in mind, we have attempted to vitalize teacher education through a series of informative and provocative positions and papers. Some are classical and historical, by way of background; others deal with the realities of the contemporary scene. Their analysis in the college classroom will help the teacher-to-be to visualize the relationship of theory to practice in an atmosphere of immediacy and directness.

Two main goals are sought here: one, an awareness of those values that make for rich, warm, human living and learning; and, two, the development of the powers and the skills necessary to react positively and wholeheartedly to the management of the tasks of education. There are no "right" or "wrong" answers to the issues and the problems posed here; rather, there are fundamental questions to which the learner may consider relevant alternatives. Out of the resolution of these alternatives, decision will come.

Confrontation of the problem itself may call for exploration and information-gathering beyond the scope of this volume. Almost certainly, it will demand intense self-scrutiny. In time, there will be a response marked by wholeness and spontaneity. The learner's feelings of commitment and responsibility are free to take shape and direction. The end product is a consistent and characteristic way of acting and of being, a "life style." There is no longer need to vacillate, to "flounder."

Each chapter affects the other and carries implications for the other. However, all of the chapters are manageable in terms of a concept of man as uniquely individual and completely human.

S.P.S.
H.S.

PART ONE Basis for Action

CHAPTER 1 Freedom

Can we compromise freedom in any of its forms—freedom of thought, of expression, of movement, of choice—the freedom of students, of teachers, of the "deprived" and the "disadvantaged"—and still maintain that "freedom" is a dominant goal of the social organism?

Consideration of the concept of freedom in education raises many questions. Can students at all levels of the educational process live freely so that they can learn the modes and habits of free adults? Do teachers possess the freedom to deal fully and frankly with controversial issues so that students will learn the ways of inquiry and investigation and the habit of using knowledge at the cutting edge of intelligence? Is freedom to change built into the educational structure? Do schools cherish diversity of thought and nonconformity in all of its manifestations? What does it mean to be free? Do we mean to be free?

In the American educational scene today, freedom is too often misunderstood, too often abused and denied. Students doubt their rights, or are unaware that they have any rights. Teachers, perhaps more than any other group, are under tremendous pressure to exchange their freedom for security and advancement. Academic freedom is discovered to be no more or less than the freedom of the community at large.

The concept of freedom is central to all that is said in this chapter. Hopefully, a sharper insight into the complex nature of freedom will evolve out of consideration of the various issues presented here. If man is to be "free," if freedom can command a heartfelt dedication, man must understand what freedom signifies. For teachers, the future of freedom is a charge upon them.

JOHN DEWEY What Is Freedom?

The place of natural fact and law in morals brings us to the problem of freedom. We are told that seriously to import empirical facts into morals is equivalent to an abrogation of freedom. Facts and laws mean necessity we are told. The way to freedom is to turn our back upon them and take flight to a separate ideal realm. Even if the flight could be successfully accomplished, the efficacy of the prescription may be doubted. For we need freedom in and among actual events, not apart from them. It is to be hoped therefore that there remains an alternative; that the road to freedom may be found in that knowledge of facts which enables us to employ them in connection with desires and aims. A physician or engineer is free in his thought and his action in the degree in which he knows what he deals with. Possibly we find here the key to any freedom.

What men have esteemed and fought for in the name of liberty is varied and complex—but certainly it has never been a metaphysical freedom of will. It seems to contain three elements of importance, though on their face not all of them are directly compatible with one another. (1) It includes efficiency in action, ability to carry out plans, the absence of cramping and thwarting obstacles. (2) It also includes capacity to vary plans, to change the course of action, to experience novelties. And again (3) it signifies the power of desire and choice to be factors in events.

Few men would purchase even a high amount of efficient action along definite lines at the price of monotony, or if success in action were bought by all abandonment of personal preference. They would probably feel that a more precious freedom was possessed in a life of ill-assured objective achievement that contained undertaking of risks, adventuring in new fields, a pitting of personal choice against the odds of events, and a mixture of success and failures, provided choice had a career. The slave is a man who executes the wish of others, one doomed to act along lines predetermined to regularity. Those who have defined freedom as ability to act have unconsciously assumed that this ability is exercised in accord with desire, and that its operation introduces the agent into fields previously unexplored. Hence the conception of freedom as involving three factors.

Yet efficiency in execution cannot be ignored. To say that a man is free to choose to walk while the only walk he can take will lead him over a precipice is to strain words as well as facts. Intelligence is the key to freedom in act. We are likely to be able to go ahead prosperously in

From *Human Nature and Conduct: An Introduction to Social Psychology* by John Dewey. Copyright, 1922, by Holt, Rinehart and Winston, Inc. Copyright, 1950, by John Dewey. Reprinted by permission of Holt, Rinehart and Winston, Inc.

the degree in which we have consulted conditions and formed a plan which enlists their consenting cooperation. The gratuitous help of unforeseen circumstance we cannot afford to despise. Luck, bad if not good, will always be with us. But it has a way of favoring the intelligent and showing its back to the stupid. And the gifts of fortune when they come are fleeting except when they are made taut by intelligent adaptation of conditions. In neutral and adverse circumstances, study and foresight are the only roads to unimpeded action. Insistence upon a metaphysical freedom of will is generally at its most strident pitch with those who despise knowledge of matters-of-fact. They pay for their contempt by halting and confined action. Glorification of freedom in general at the expense of positive abilities in particular has often characterized the official creed of historic liberalism. Its outward sign is the separation of politics and law from economics. Much of what is called the "individualism" of the early nineteenth century has in truth little to do with the nature of individuals. It goes back to a metaphysics which held that harmony between man and nature can be taken for granted, if once certain artificial restrictions upon man are removed. Hence it neglected the necessity of studying and regulating industrial conditions so that a nominal freedom can be made an actuality. Find a man who believes that all men need is freedom *from* oppressive legal and political measures, and you have found a man who, unless he is merely obstinately maintaining his own private privileges, carries at the back of his head some heritage of the metaphysical doctrine of free-will, plus an optimistic confidence in natural harmony. He needs a philosophy that recognizes the objective character of freedom and its dependence upon a congruity of environment with human wants, an agreement which can be obtained only by profound thought and unremitting application. For freedom as a fact depends upon conditions of work which are socially and scientifically buttressed. Since industry covers the most pervasive relations of man with his environment, freedom is unreal which does not have as its basis an economic command of environment.

I have no desire to add another to the cheap and easy solutions which exist of the seeming conflict between freedom and organization. It is reasonably obvious that organization may become a hindrance to freedom; it does not take us far to say that the trouble lies not in organization but in over-organization. At the same time, it must be admitted that there is no effective or objective freedom without organization. It is easy to criticize the contract theory of the state which states that individuals surrender some at least of their natural liberties in order to make secure as civil liberties what they retain. Nevertheless there is some truth in the idea of surrender and exchange. A certain natural freedom is possessed by man. That is to say, in some respects harmony exists between a man's energies and his surroundings such that the latter support and execute his purposes. In so far he is free; without such a basic natural support, conscious contrivances of legislation, administration and deliberate human institution of social arrangements cannot take place. In this sense natural freedom is prior to political freedom and is its condition. But we cannot trust wholly to a freedom thus procured. It is at the mercy of accident. Conscious agreements among men must supplement and in some degree supplant freedom of action which is the gift of nature. In order to arrive at these agreements, individuals have to make concessions. They must consent to curtailment of some natural liberties in order that any of them may be rendered secure and enduring. They must, in short, enter into an organization with other human beings so that the activities of others may be permanently counted upon to assure regularity of action and far-reaching scope of plans and courses of action. The procedure is not, in so far, unlike surrendering a portion of one's income in order to buy insurance against future contingencies, and thus to render the future course of life more equably secure. It would be folly to maintain that there is no sacrifice; we can however contend that the sacrifice is a reasonable one, justified by results.

Viewed in this light, the relation of individual freedom to organization is seen to be an experimental affair. It is not capable of being settled by abstract theory. Take the question of labor unions and the closed or open shop. It is folly to fancy that no restrictions and surrenders of prior freedoms and possibilities of future freedoms are involved in the extension of this particular form of organization. But to condemn such organization on the theoretical ground that a restriction of liberty is entailed is to adopt a position which would have been fatal to every advance step in civilization, and to every net gain in effective freedom. Every such question is to be judged not on the basis of antecedent theory but on the basis of concrete consequences. The question is to the balance of freedom and security achieved, as compared with practicable alternatives. Even the question of the point where membership in an organization ceases to be a voluntary matter and becomes coercive or required, is also an experimental matter, a thing to be decided by scientifically conducted study of consequences, of pros and cons. It is definitely an affair of specific detail, not of wholesale theory. It is equally amusing to see one man denouncing on grounds of pure theory the coercion of workers by a labor union while he avails himself of the increased power due to corporate action in business and praises the coercion of the political state; and to see another man denouncing the latter as pure tyranny, while lauding the power of industrial labor organizations. The position of one or the other may be justified in particular cases, but justification is due to results in practice not to general theory.

Organization tends, however, to become rigid and to limit freedom. In addition to security and energy in action, novelty, risk, change are ingredients of the freedom which men desire. Variety is more than the spice of life; it is largely of its essence, making a difference between the free and the enslaved. Invariant virtue appears to be as mechanical as uninterrupted vice, for true excellence changes with conditions. Unless character rises to overcome some new difficulty or conquer some temptation from an unexpected quarter we suspect its gain is only a veneer. Choice is an element in freedom and there can be no choice without unrealized and precarious possibilities. It is this demand for genuine contingency which is caricatured in the orthodox doctrine of a freedom of indifference, a power to choose this way or that apart from any habit or impulse, without even a desire on the part of will to show off. Such an indetermination of choice is not desired by the lover of either reason or excitement. The theory of arbitrary free choice represents indeterminateness of conditions grasped in a vague and lazy fashion and hardened into a desirable attribute of will. Under the title of freedom men prize such uncertainty of conditions as give deliberation and choice an opportunity. But uncertainty of volition which is more than a reflection of uncertainty of conditions is the mark of a person who has acquired imbecility of character through permanent weakening of his springs of action.

Whether or not indeterminateness, uncertainty, actually exists in the world is a difficult question. It is easier to think of the world as fixed, settled once for all, and man as accumulating all the uncertainty there is in his will and all the doubt there is in his intellect. The rise of natural science has facilitated this dualistic partitioning, making nature wholly fixed and mind wholly open and empty. Fortunately for us we do not have to settle the question. A hypothetical answer is enough. *If* the world is already done and done for, if its character is entirely achieved so that its behavior is like that of a man lost in routine, then the only freedom for which man can hope is one of efficiency in overt action. But *if* change is genuine, if accounts are still in process of making, and if objective uncertainty is the stimulus to reflection, then variation in action, novelty and experiment, have a true meaning. In any case the question is an objective one. It concerns not man in isolation from the world but man in his connection with it. A world that is at points and times indeterminate enough to call out deliberation and to give play to choice to shape its future is a world in which will is free, not because it is inherently vacillating and unstable, but because deliberation and choice are determining and stabilizing factors.

Upon an empirical view, uncertainty, doubt, hesitation, contingency and novelty, genuine change which is not mere disguised repetition, are facts. Only deductive reasoning from certain fixed premises creates a bias in favor of complete determination and finality. To say that these things exist only in human experience not in the world, and exist there only because of our "finitude" is dangerously like paying ourselves with words. Empirically the life of man seems in these respects as in others to express a culmination of facts in nature. To admit ignorance and uncertainty in man while denying them to nature involves a curious dualism. Variability, initiative, innovation, departure from routine, experimentation are empirically the manifestaton of a genuine nisus in things. At all events it is these things that are precious to us under the name of freedom. It is their elimination from the life of a slave which makes his life servile, intolerable to the freeman who has once been on his own, no matter what his animal comfort and security. A free man would rather take his chance in an open world than be guaranteed in a closed world.

These considerations give point to the third factor in love of freedom: the desire to have desire count as a factor, a force. Even if will chooses unaccountably, even if it be a capricious impulse, it does not follow that there are real alternatives, genuine possibilities, open in the future. What we want is possibilities open in the *world* not in the will, except as will or deliberate activity reflects the world. To foresee future objective alternatives and to be able by deliberation to choose one of them and thereby weight its chances in the struggle for future existence, measures our freedom. It is assumed sometimes that if it can be shown that deliberation determines choice and deliberation is determined by character and conditions, there is no freedom. This is like saying that because a flower comes from root and stem it cannot bear fruit. The question is not what are the antecedents of deliberation and choice, but what are their consequences. What do they do that is distinctive? The answer is that they give us all the control of future possibilities which is the crux of our freedom. Without it, we are pushed from behind. With it we walk in the light.

The doctrine that knowledge, intelligence rather than will, constitutes freedom is not new. It has been preached by moralists of many a school. All rationalists have identified freedom with action emancipated by insight into truth. But insight into necessity has by them been substituted for foresight of possibilities. Tolstoi for example expressed the idea of Spinoza and Hegel when he said that the ox is a slave as long as he refuses to recognize the yoke and chafes under it, while if he identifies himself with its necessity and draws willingly instead of rebelliously, he is free. But as long as the yoke is a yoke it is impossible that voluntary identification with it should occur. Conscious submission is then either fatalistic submissiveness or cowardice. The ox accepts in fact not the yoke but the stall and the hay to which the yoke is a necessary incident. But if the ox foresees the consequences of the use of the yoke, if he anticipates the possibility of harvest, and identifies himself not with the yoke but with the realization of its possibilities, he acts freely, voluntarily. He hasn't accepted a necessity as unavoidable; he has welcomed a possibility as a desirability.

Perception of necessary law plays, indeed, a part. But no amount of insight into necessity brings with it, as such, anything but a consciousness of necessity. Freedom is the "truth of necessity" only when we use one "necessity" to alter another. When we use the law to foresee consequences and to consider how they may be averted or secured, then freedom begins. Employing knowledge of law to enforce desire in execution gives power to the engineer. Employing knowledge of law in order to submit to it without further action constitutes fatalism, no matter how it be dressed up. Thus we recur to our main contention. Morality depends upon events, not upon demands and ideals alien to nature. But intelligence treats events as moving, as fraught with possibilities, not as ended, final. In forecasting their possibilities, the distinction between better and worse arises. Human desire and ability cooperates with this or that natural force according as this or that eventuality is judged better. We do not use the present to control the future. We use the foresight of the future to refine and expand present activity. In this use of desire, deliberation and choice, freedom is actualized.

DISCUSSION QUESTIONS

1. What is the relationship between freedom and education?
2. How does Dewey's view on variety of life fit into his trifold criteria for freedom?
3. Is modern man's freedom inevitably curtailed by the increasing mechanization and stratification of the age of technology?
4. What does Dewey's concept of freedom mean when applied to the current civil rights struggles of minority groups?
5. Is man the sum of his desires?
6. If one accepts Dewey's concept of freedom, is it possible then to be free in an environment that is unfree? In your concept of freedom, does such a possibility exist?
7. Do you accept power and efficiency as the heart of your concept of freedom?

A. S. NEILL   The Free Child

Self-regulation means the right of a baby to live freely, without outside authority in things psychic and somatic. It means that the baby feeds when it is hungry; that it becomes clean in habits only when it wants to; that it is never stormed at nor spanked; that it is always loved and protected.

It all sounds easy and natural and fine, yet it is astounding how many young parents, keen on the idea, manage to misunderstand it. Tommy, aged four, bangs the notes of a neighbor's piano with a wooden mallet.

Reprinted from A. S. Neill, *Summerhill* (New York: Hart, 1960), pp. 105–111, with permission of the publisher.

His fond parents look on with a triumphant smile which means, "Isn't self-regulation wonderful?"

Other parents think that they ought never to put their baby of eighteen months to bed, because that would be interfering with nature. No, baby must be allowed to stay up; when he is tired out, mother will carry him to his cot. What actually happens is that baby gets increasingly tired and cross. He cannot say that he wants to go to sleep, because he cannot verbalize his need. Usually, the weary and disappointed mother lifts him and carries him screaming to bed. Another young couple came to me rather apologetically, and asked if it would be wrong for them to put up a fireguard in a baby's nursery. All these illustrations show that any idea, old or new, is dangerous, if not combined with common sense.

Only a fool in charge of young children would allow unbarred bedroom windows or an unprotected fire in the nursery. Yet, too often, young enthusiasts for self-regulation come to my school as visitors, and exclaim at our lack of freedom in locking poison in a lab closet, or our prohibition about playing on the fire escape. The whole freedom movement is marred and despised because so many advocates of freedom have not got their feet on the ground.

One such protested to me recently because I shouted sternly at a problem boy of seven who was kicking my office door. His idea was that I should smile and tolerate the noise until the child should live out his desire to bang doors. It is true that I spent a good few years of my life patiently tolerating the destructive behavior of problem children, but I did this as their psychological doctor and not as their fellow citizen.

If a young mother thinks that her child of three should be allowed to paint the front door with red ink on the ground that he is thereby expressing himself freely, she is incapable of grasping what self-regulation means.

I remember sitting with a friend in the Covent Garden theater. During the first ballet, a child in front of us talked loudly to her father. At the end of the ballet, I found other seats. My companion said to me, "What would you do if one of your kids from Summerhill did that?"

"Tell him to shut up," I said.

"You wouldn't need to," said my friend; "he just wouldn't act that way." And I don't think any of them would.

Once a woman brought her girl of seven to see me. "Mr. Neill," she said, " I have read every line you have written; and even before Daphne was born, I had decided to bring her up exactly along your lines."

I glanced at Daphne who was standing on my grand piano with her heavy shoes on. She made a leap for the sofa and nearly went through the springs. "You see how natural she is," said the mother. "The Neillian child!" I fear that I blushed.

It is this distinction between freedom and license that many parents cannot grasp. In the disciplined home, the children have *no* rights. In the spoiled home, they have *all* the rights. The proper home is one in which children and adults have equal rights. And the same applies to school.

It must be emphasized again and again that freedom does not involve spoiling the child. If a baby of three wants to walk over the dining table, you simply tell him he must not. He must obey, that's true. But on the other hand, you must obey him when necessary. I get out of small children's rooms if they tell me to get out.

There has to be a certain amount of sacrifice on the part of the adult if children are to live according to their inner nature. Healthy parents come to some sort of a compromise agreement; unhealthy parents either become violent or they spoil their children by allowing them to have all the social rights.

In practice, the divergence of interests between parents and children can be mitigated, if not solved, by an honest give and take. Zoë respected my desk, and showed no compulsion to play with my typewriter and papers. In turn, I respected her nursery and playthings.

Children are very wise and soon accept social laws. They should not be exploited as they too often are. Too often a parent calls out, "Jimmy, get me a glass of water," when the child is intent on an engrossing game.

A great amount of naughtiness is due to the wrong method of handling. Zoë, when a little over a year old, went through a period of great interest in my glasses, snatching them off my nose to see what they were like. I made no protest, showed no annoyance by look or tone of voice. She soon lost interest in my glasses and never touched them. No doubt, if I had sternly told her not—or worse, spanked her little hand—her interest in my glasses would have survived, mingled with fear of me and rebellion against me.

My wife let her play with breakable ornaments. The child handled them carefully and seldom broke anything. She found things out for herself. Of course, there is a limit to self-regulation. We cannot allow a baby of six months to discover that a lighted cigarette burns painfully. It is wrong to shout in alarm in such a case; the right thing to do is to remove the danger without any fuss.

Unless a child is mentally defective, he will soon discover what interests him. Left free from excited cries and angry voices, he will be unbelievably sensible in his dealing with material of all kinds. The harassed mother standing at the gas stove, frantic about what the children are doing, is she who has never trusted her children in their activities. "Go and see what baby is doing and tell him he mustn't" is still a phrase applying to many homes today.

When a mother writes asking me what she should do with children messing things up while she is busy cooking the dinner, I can only reply that perhaps she has brought them up that way.

One couple read some of my books and were conscience-stricken when they thought of the harm they had done in bringing up their children. They summoned the family to a conference and said, "We have brought you up all wrong. From now on, you are free to do what you like." I forget how much they said the breakage bill came to, but I can recall that they had to summon a second conference and rescind the previous motion.

The usual argument against freedom for children is this: *Life is hard, and we must train the children so that they will fit into life later on. We must therefore discipline them. If we allow them to do what they like, how will they ever be able to serve under a boss? How will they compete with others who have known discipline? How will they ever be able to exercise self discipline?*

People who protest the granting of freedom to children and use this argument do not realize that they start with an unfounded, unproved assumption—the assumption that a child will not grow or develop unless forced to do so. Yet the entire thirty-nine years of experience of Summerhill disproves this assumption. Take, among one hundred others, the case of Mervyn. He attended Summerhill for ten years, between the ages of seven to seventeen. During those ten years, Mervyn never attended a single class. At age seventeen, he hardly knew how to read. Yet when Mervyn left school and decided to become an instrument maker, he quickly taught himself how to read and absorbed in a short time through self-study all the technical knowledge he needed. Through his own efforts, he made himself ready for his apprenticeship. Today, this same chap is thoroughly literate, commands a good salary, and is a leader in his community. As to self-discipline, Mervyn built a good part of his house with his own hands and he is bringing up a fine family of three boys from the fruits of his daily labors.

Similarly, each year boys and girls at Summerhill who up to then have rarely studied, decide to enter college; and of their own accord, they then begin the long and tiresome grind of preparing themselves for college entrance examinations. Why do they do it?

The common assumption that good habits that have not been forced into us during early childhood can never develop in us later on in life is an assumption we have been brought up on and which we unquestioningly accept merely because the idea has never been challenged. I deny this premise.

Freedom is necessary for the child because only under freedom can he grow in his natural way—the good way. I see the results of bondage in new pupils coming from prep schools and convents. They are bundles of insincerity, with an unreal politeness and phony manners.

.   .   .

Possibly the greatest discovery we have made in Summerhill is that a child is born a sincere creature. We set out to let children alone so that we might discover what they were like. It is the only possible way of dealing with children. The pioneer school of the future must pursue this way if it is to contribute to child knowledge and, more important, to child happiness.

The aim of life is happiness. The evil of life is all that limits or destroys happiness. Happiness always means goodness; unhappiness at its extreme limits means Jew-baiting, minority torture, or war.

DISCUSSION QUESTIONS

1. Should children have freedom? If so, what kind?
2. Is Neill's concept of freedom possible in the public schools? Does any of it apply to the public schools? Should it apply?
3. Given a choice between your past education and education at Summerhill, which would you choose? Defend your choice.

B. F. SKINNER   Freedom

Almost all living things act to free themselves from harmful contacts. A kind of freedom is achieved by the relatively simple forms of behavior called reflexes. A person sneezes and frees his respiratory passages from irritating substances. He vomits and frees his stomach from indigestible or poisonous food. He pulls back his hand and frees it from a sharp or hot object. More elaborate forms of behavior have similar effects. When confined, people struggle ("in rage") and break free. When in danger they flee from or attack its source. Behavior of this kind presumably evolved because of its survival value; it is as much a part of what we call the human genetic endowment as breathing, sweating, or digesting food. And through conditioning similar behavior may be acquired with respect to novel objects which could have played no role in evolution. These are no doubt minor instances of the struggle to be free, but they are significant. We do not attribute them to any love of freedom; they are simply forms of behavior which have proved useful in reducing various threats to the individual and hence to the species in the course of evolution.

A much more important role is played by behavior which weakens harmful stimuli in another way. It is not acquired in the form of conditioned reflexes, but as the product of a different process called operant conditioning. When a bit of behavior is followed by a certain kind of consequence, it is more likely to occur again, and a consequence having this effect is called a reinforcer. Food, for example, is a reinforcer to a hungry organism; anything the organism does that is followed by the receipt of food is more likely to be done again whenever the organism is hungry. Some stimuli are called negative reinforcers; any response which reduces the intensity of such a stimulus—or ends it—is more likely to be emitted when the stimulus recurs. Thus, if a person escapes from a hot sun when he moves under cover, he is more likely to move under cover when the sun is again hot. The reduction in temperature reinforces the behavior it is "contingent upon"—that is, the behavior it follows. Operant conditioning also occurs when a person simply avoids a hot sun—when, roughly speaking, he escapes from the *threat* of a hot sun.

Negative reinforcers are called aversive in the sense that they are the things organisms "turn away from." The term suggests a spatial separation—moving or running away from something—but the essential relation is temporal. In a standard apparatus used to study the process in the laboratory, an arbitrary response simply weakens an aversive stimulus or brings it to an end. A great deal of physical technology is the result of this kind of struggle for freedom. Over the centuries, in erratic ways, men have constructed a world in which they are relatively free of many kinds of threatening or harmful stimuli—extremes of temperature, sources of infection, hard labor, danger, and even those minor aversive stimuli called discomfort.

Escape and avoidance play a much more important role in the struggle for freedom when the aversive conditions are generated by other people. Other people can be aversive without, so to speak, trying: they can be rude, dangerous, contagious, or annoying, and one escapes from them or avoids them accordingly. They may also be "intentionally" aversive—that is, they may treat other people aversively because of what follows. Thus, a slave driver induces a slave to work by whipping him when he stops; by resuming work the slave escapes from the whipping (and incidentally reinforces the slave driver's behavior in using the whip). A parent nags a child until the child performs a task; by performing the task the child escapes nagging (and reinforces the parent's behavior). The blackmailer threatens exposure unless the victim pays; by paying, the victim escapes from the threat (and reinforces the practice). A teacher threatens corporal punishment or failure until his students pay attention; by paying attention the students escape from the threat of punishment (and reinforce the teacher for threatening it). In one form or another intentional aversive control is the pattern of most social coordination—in ethics, religion, government, economics, education, psychotherapy, and family life.

A person escapes from or avoids aversive treatment by behaving in ways which reinforce those who treated him aversively until he did so, but he may escape in other ways. For example, he may simply move out of range. A person may escape from slavery, emigrate or defect from a government, desert from an army, become an apostate from a religion, play truant, leave home, or drop out of a culture as a hobo, hermit, or hippie. Such behavior is as much a product of the aversive conditions as the behavior the conditions were designed to evoke. The latter can be guaranteed only by sharpening the contingencies or by using stronger aversive stimuli.

Another anomalous mode of escape is to attack those who arrange aversive conditions and weaken or destroy their power. We may attack those who crowd us or annoy us, as we attack the weeds in our garden, but again the struggle for freedom is mainly directed toward intentional controllers—toward those who treat others aversively in order to induce them to behave in particular ways. Thus, a child may stand up to his parents, a citizen may overthrow a government, a communicant may reform a religion, a student may attack a teacher or vandalize a school, and a dropout may work to destroy a culture.

It is possible that a man's genetic endowment supports this kind of struggle for freedom: when treated aversively people tend to act aggressively or to be reinforced by signs of having worked aggressive damage. Both tendencies should have had evolutionary advantages, and they can easily be demonstrated. If two organisms which have been coexisting peacefully receive painful shocks, they immediately exhibit characteristic patterns of aggression toward each other. The aggressive behavior is not necessarily directed toward the actual source of stimulation; it may be "displaced" toward any convenient person or object. Vandalism and riots are often forms of undirected or misdirected aggression. An organism which has received a painful shock will also, if possible, act to gain access to another organism toward which it can act aggressively. The extent to which human aggression exemplifies innate tendencies is not clear, and many of the ways in which people attack and thus weaken or destroy the power of intentional controllers are quite obviously learned.

What we may call the "literature of freedom" has been designed to induce people to escape from or attack those who act to control them aversively. The content of the literature is the philosophy of freedom, but philosophies are among those inner causes which need to be scrutinized. We say that a person behaves in a given way because he possesses a philosophy, but we infer the philosophy from the behavior and therefore cannot use it in any satisfactory way as an explanation, at least until it is in turn explained. The literature of freedom, on the other hand, has a simple objective status. It consists of books, pamphlets, manifestoes, speeches, and other verbal products, designed to induce people to act to free themselves from various kinds of intentional control. It does not impart a philosophy of freedom; it induces people to act.

The literature often emphasizes the aversive conditions under which people live, perhaps by contrasting them with conditions in a freer world. It thus makes the conditions more aversive, "increasing the misery" of those it is trying to rescue. It also identifies those from whom one is to escape or those whose power is to be weakened through attack. Characteristic villains of the literature are tyrants, priests, generals, capitalists, martinet teachers, and domineering parents.

The literature also prescribes modes of action. It has not been much concerned with escape, possibly because advice has not been needed; instead, it has emphasized how controlling power may be weakened or destroyed. Tyrants are to be overthrown, ostracized, or assassinated. The legitimacy of a government is to be questioned. The ability of a religious agency to mediate supernatural sanctions is to be challenged. Strikes and boycotts are to be organized to weaken the economic power which supports aversive practices. The argument is strengthened by exhorting people to act, describing likely results, reviewing successful instances on the model of the advertising testimonial, and so on.

The would-be controllers do not, of course, remain inactive. Governments make escape impossible by banning travel or severely punishing or incarcerating defectors. They keep weapons and other sources of power out of the hands of revolutionaries. They destroy the written literature of freedom and imprison or kill those who carry it orally. If the struggle for freedom is to succeed, it must then be intensified.

The importance of the literature of freedom can scarcely be questioned. Without help or guidance people submit to aversive conditions in the most surprising way. This is true even when the aversive conditions are part of the natural environment. Darwin observed, for example, that the Fuegians seemed to make no effort to protect themselves from the cold; they wore only scant clothing and made little use of it against the weather. And one of the most striking things about the struggle for freedom from intentional control is how often it has been lacking. Many people have submitted to the most obvious religious, governmental, and economic controls for centuries, striking for freedom only sporadically, if at all. The literature of freedom has made an essential contribution to the elimination of many aversive practices in government, religion, education, family life, and the production of goods.

The contributions of the literature of freedom, however, are not usually described in these terms. Some traditional theories could conceivably be said to define freedom as the absence of aversive control, but the emphasis has been on how that condition *feels*. Other traditional theories could conceivably be said to define freedom as a person's condition when he is behaving under nonaversive control, but the emphasis has been upon a state of mind associated with doing what one wants. According to John Stuart Mill, "Liberty consists in doing what one desires." The literature of freedom has been important in changing practice (it has changed practices whenever it has had any effect whatsoever), but it has nevertheless defined its task as the changing of states of mind and feelings. Freedom is a "possession." A person escapes from or destroys the power of a controller in order to feel free, and once he feels free and can do what he desires, no further action is recommended and none is prescribed by the literature of freedom, except perhaps eternal vigilance lest control be resumed.

The feeling of freedom becomes an unreliable guide to action as soon as would-be controllers turn to nonaversive measures, as they are likely to do to avoid the problems raised when the controllee escapes or attacks. Nonaversive measures are not as conspicuous as aversive and are likely to be acquired more slowly, but they have obvious advantages which promote their use. Productive labor, for example, was once the result of punishment: the slave worked to avoid the consequences of not working. Wages exemplify a different principle; a person is paid when he behaves in a given way so that he will continue to behave in that way. Although it has long been recognized that rewards have useful effects, wage systems have evolved slowly. In the nineteenth century it was believed that an industrial society required a hungry labor force; wages would be effective only if the hungry worker could exchange them for food. By making labor less aversive—for instance, by shortening hours and improving conditions—it has been possible to get men to work for lesser rewards. Until recently teaching was almost entirely aversive: the student studied to escape the consequences of not studying, but nonaversive techniques are gradually being discovered and used. The skillful parent learns to reward a child for good behavior rather than punish him for bad. Religious agencies move from the threat of hellfire to an emphasis on God's love, and governments turn from aversive sanctions to various kinds of inducements, as we shall note again shortly. What the layman calls a reward is a "positive reinforcer," the effects of which have been exhaustively studied in the experimental analysis of operant behavior. The effects are not as easily recognized as those of aversive contingencies because they tend to be deferred, and applications have therefore been delayed, but techniques as powerful as the older aversive techniques are now available.

A problem arises for the defender of freedom when the behavior generated by positive reinforcement has deferred aversive consequences. This is particularly likely to be the case when the process is used in intentional control, where the gain to the controller usually means a loss to the controllee. What are called conditioned positive reinforcers can often be used with deferred aversive results. Money is an example. It is reinforcing only after it has been exchanged for reinforcing things, but it can be used as a reinforcer when exchange is impossible. A counterfeit bill, a bad check, a stopped check, or an unkept promise are conditioned reinforcers, although aversive consequences are usually quickly discovered. The archetypal pattern is the gold brick. Countercontrol quickly follows: we escape from or attack those who misuse conditioned reinforcers in this way. But the misuse of many social reinforcers often goes unnoticed. Personal attention, approval, and affection are usually reinforcing only if there has been some connection with already effective reinforcers, but they can be used when a connection is lacking. The simulated approval and affection with which parents and teachers are often urged to solve behavior problems are counterfeit. So are flattery, back-slapping, and many other ways of "winning friends."

Genuine reinforcers can be used in ways which have aversive consequences. A government may prevent defection by making life more interesting—by providing bread and circuses and by encouraging sports, gambling, the use of alcohol and other drugs, and various kinds of sexual behavior, where the effect is to keep people within reach of aversive sanctions. The Goncourt brothers noted the rise of pornography in the France of their day: "Pornographic literature," they wrote, "serves a Bas-Empire . . . one tames a people as one tames lions, by masturbation."

Genuine positive reinforcement can also be misused because the sheer quantity of reinforcers is not proportional to the effect on behavior. Reinforcement is usually only intermittent, and the schedule of reinforcement is more important than the amount received. Certain schedules generate a great deal of behavior in return for very little reinforcement, and the possibility has naturally not been overlooked by would-be controllers. Two examples of schedules which are easily used to the disadvantage of those reinforced may be noted.

In the incentive system known as piece-work pay, the worker is paid a given amount for each unit of work performed. The system seems to guarantee a balance between the goods produced and the money received. The schedule is attractive to management, which can calculate labor costs in advance, and also to the worker, who can control the amount he earns. This so-called "fixed-ratio" schedule of reinforcement can, however, be used to generate a great deal of behavior for very little return. It induces the worker to work fast, and the ratio can then be "stretched"—that is, more work can be demanded for each unit of pay without running the risk that the worker will stop working. His ultimate condition—hard work with very little pay—may be acutely aversive.

A related schedule, called variable-ratio, is at the heart of all gambling systems. A gambling enterprise pays people for giving it money—that is, it pays them when they make bets. But it pays on a kind of schedule which sustains betting even though, in the long run, the amount paid is less than the amount wagered. At first the mean ratio may be favorable to the bettor; he "wins." But the ratio can be stretched in such a way that he continues to play even when he begins to lose. The stretching may be accidental (an early run of good luck which grows steadily worse may create a dedicated gambler), or the ratio may be deliberately stretched by someone who controls the odds. In the long run the "utility" is negative: the gambler loses all.

It is difficult to deal effectively with deferred aversive consequences because they do not occur at a time when escape or attack is feasible—when, for example, the controller can be identified or is within reach. But the immediate reinforcement is positive and goes unchallenged. The problem to be solved by those who are concerned with freedom is to create immediate aversive consequences. A classical problem concerns "self-control." A person eats too much and gets sick but survives to eat too much again. Delicious food or the behavior evoked by it must be made sufficiently aversive so that a person will "escape from it" by not eating it. (It might be thought that he can escape from it only before eating it, but the Romans escaped afterward through the use of a vomitorium.) Current aversive stimuli may be conditioned. Something of the sort is done when eating too much is called wrong, glutonous, or sinful. Other kinds of behavior to be suppressed may be declared illegal and punished accordingly. The more deferred the aversive consequences the greater the problem. It has taken a great deal of "engineering" to bring the ultimate consequences of smoking cigarettes to bear on the behavior. A fascinating hobby, a sport, a love affair, or a large salary may compete with activities which would be more reinforcing in the long run, but the run is too long to make countercontrol possible. That is why countercontrol is exerted, if at all, only by those who suffer aversive consequences but are not subject to positive reinforcement. Laws are passed against gambling, unions oppose piece-work pay, and no one is allowed to pay young children to work for them or to pay anyone for engaging in immoral behavior, but these measures may be strongly opposed by those whom they are designed to protect. The gambler objects to antigambling laws and the alcoholic to any kind of prohibition; and a child or prostitute may be willing to work for what is offered.

The literature of freedom has never come to grips with techniques of control which do not generate escape or counterattack because it has dealt with the problems in terms of states of mind and feelings. In his book *Sovereignty*, Bertrand de Jouvenel quotes two important figures in that literature. According to Leibnitz, "Liberty consists in the power to do what one wants to do," and according to Voltaire, "When I can do what I want to do, there is my liberty for me." But both writers add a concluding phrase: Leibnitz, ". . . or in the power to want what can be got," and Voltaire, more candidly, ". . . but I can't help wanting what I do want." Jouvenel relegates these comments to a footnote, saying that the power to want is a matter of "interior liberty" (the freedom of the inner man!) which falls outside the "gambit of freedom."

A person wants something if he acts to get it when the occasion arises. A person who says "I want something to eat" will presumably eat when something becomes available. If he says "I want to get warm," he will presumably move into a warm place when he can. These acts have been reinforced in the past by whatever was wanted. What a person *feels* when he feels himself wanting something depends upon the circumstances. Food is reinforcing only in a state of deprivation, and a person who wants something to eat may feel parts of that state—for example, hunger pangs. A person who wants to get warm presumably feels cold. Conditions associated with a high probability of responding may also be felt, together with aspects of the present occasion which are similar to those of past occasions upon which behavior has been reinforced. Wanting is not, however, a feeling, nor is a feeling the reason a person acts to get what he wants. Certain contingencies have raised the probability of behavior and at the same time have created conditions which may be felt. Freedom is a matter of contingencies of reinforcement, not of the feelings the contingencies generate. The distinction is particularly important when the contingencies do not generate escape or counterattack.

The uncertainty which surrounds the countercontrol of nonaversive measures is easily exemplified. In the 1930's it seemed necessary to cut agricultural production. The Agricultural Adjustment Act authorized the Secretary of Agriculture to make "rental or benefit payments" to farmers who agreed to produce less—to pay the farmers, in fact, what they would have made on the food they agreed not to produce. It would have been unconstitutional to *compel* them to reduce production, but the government argued that it was merely inviting them to do so. But the Supreme Court recognized that positive inducement can be as irresistible as aversive measures when it ruled that "the power to confer or withhold unlimited benefit is the power to coerce or destroy." The decision was later reversed, however, when the Court ruled that "to hold that motive or temptation is equivalent to coercion is to plunge the law into endless difficulties." We are considering some of these difficulties.

The same issue arises when a government runs a lottery in order to raise revenue to reduce taxes. The government takes the same amount of money from its citizens in both cases, though not necessarily from the same citizens. By running a lottery it avoids certain unwanted consequences: people escape from heavy taxation by moving away or they counterattack by throwing a government which imposes new taxes out of office. A lottery, taking advantage of a stretched variable-ratio schedule of reinforcement, has neither of these effects. The only opposition comes from those who in general oppose gambling enterprises and who are themselves seldom gamblers.

A third example is the practice of inviting prisoners to volunteer for possibly dangerous experiments—for example, on new drugs—in return for better living conditions or shortened sentences. Everyone would protest if the prisoners were forced to participate, but are they really free when positively reinforced, particularly when the condition to be improved or the sentence to be shortened has been imposed by the state?

The issue often arises in more subtle forms. It has been argued, for example, that uncontrolled contraceptive services and abortion do not "confer unrestricted freedom to reproduce or not to reproduce because they cost time and money." Impoverished members of society should be given compensation if they are to have a truly "free choice." If the just compensation exactly offsets the time and money needed to practice birth control, then people will indeed be free of the control exerted by the loss of time and money, but whether or not they then have children will still depend upon other conditions which have not been specified. If a nation generously reinforces the practices of contraception and abortion, to what extent are its citizens free to have or not to have children?

Uncertainty about positive control is evident in two remarks which often appear in the literature of freedom. It is said that even though behavior is completely determined, it is better that a man "feel free" or "believe that he is free." If this means that it is better to be controlled in ways which have no aversive consequences, we may agree, but if it means that it is better to be controlled in ways against which no one revolts, it fails to take account of the possibility of deferred aversive consequences. A second comment seems more appropriate: "It is better to be a conscious slave than a happy one." The word "slave" clarifies the nature of the ultimate consequences being considered: they are exploitative and hence aversive. What the slave is to be conscious of is his misery; and a system of slavery so well designed that it does not breed revolt is the real threat. The literature of freedom has been designed to make men "conscious" of aversive control, but in its choice of methods it has failed to rescue the happy slave.

One of the great figures in the literature of freedom, Jean-Jacques Rousseau, did not fear the power of positive reinforcement. In his remarkable book *Émile* he gave the following advice to teachers:

Let [the child] believe that he is always in control, though it is always you [the teacher] who really controls. There is no subjugation so perfect as that which keeps the appearance of freedom, for in that way one captures volition itself. The poor baby, knowing nothing, able to do nothing, having learned nothing, is he not at your mercy? Can you not arrange everything in the world which surrounds him? Can you not influence him as you wish? His work, his play, his pleasures, his pains, are not all these in your hands and without his knowing? Doubtless he ought to do only what he wants; but he ought to want to do only what you want him to do; he ought not to take a step which you have not foreseen; he ought not to open his mouth without your knowing what he will say.

Rousseau could take this line because he had unlimited faith in the benevolence of teachers, who would use their absolute control for the good of their students. But, as we shall see later, benevolence is no guarantee against the misuse of power, and very few figures in the history of the struggle for freedom have shown Rousseau's lack of concern. On the contrary, they have taken the extreme position that all control is wrong. In so doing they exemplify a behavioral process called generalization. Many instances of control are aversive, in either their nature or their consequences, and hence all instances are to be avoided. The Puritans carried the generalization a step further by arguing that most positive reinforcement was wrong, whether or not it was intentionally arranged, just because it occasionally got people into trouble.

The literature of freedom has encouraged escape from or attack upon all controllers. It has done so by making any indication of control aversive. Those who manipulate human behavior are said to be evil men, necessarily bent on exploitation. Control is clearly the opposite of freedom, and if freedom is good, control must be bad. What is overlooked is control which does not have aversive consequences at any time. Many social practices essential to the welfare of the species involve the control of one person by another, and no one can suppress them who has any concern for human achievements. We shall see later that in order to maintain the position that all control is wrong, it has been necessary to disguise or conceal the nature of useful practices, to prefer weak practices just because they can be disguised or concealed, and—a most extraordinary result indeed!—to perpetuate punitive measures.

The problem is to free men, not from control, but from certain kinds of control, and it can be solved only if our analysis takes all consequences into account. How people feel about control, before or after the literature of freedom has worked on their feelings, does not lead to useful distinctions.

Were it not for the unwarranted generalization that all control is wrong, we should deal with the social environment as simply as we deal with the nonsocial. Although technology has freed men from certain aversive features of the environment, it has not freed them from the environment. We accept the fact that we depend upon the world around us, and we simply change the nature of the dependency. In the same way, to make the social environment as free as possible of aversive stimuli we do not need to destroy that environment or escape from it; we need to redesign it.

Man's struggle for freedom is not due to a will to be free, but to certain behavioral processes characteristic of the human organism, the chief effect of which is the avoidance of or escape from so-called "aversive" features of the environment. Physical and biological technologies have been mainly concerned with natural aversive stimuli; the struggle for freedom is concerned with stimuli intentionally arranged by other people. The literature of freedom has identified the other people and has proposed ways of escaping from them or weakening or destroying their power. It has been successful in reducing the aversive stimuli used in intentional control, but it has made the mistake of defining freedom in terms of states of mind or feelings, and it has therefore not been able to deal effectively with techniques of control which do not breed escape or revolt but nevertheless have aversive consequences. It has been forced to brand all control as wrong and to misrepresent many of the advantages to be gained from a social environment. It is unprepared for the next step, which is not to free men from control but to analyze and change the kinds of control to which they are exposed.

DISCUSSION QUESTIONS

1. Do you believe that "behavior is completely determined"?
2. Do you agree with Skinner that "the problem is to free men, not from control, but from certain kinds of control"?

SHELDON PTASCHEVITCH STOFF ## The Currency of Freedom

Receive the child in reverence,
Educate him in love,
Send him forth in freedom.

Rudolf Steiner

Freedom—I love its flashing face:
it flashes forth from the darkness
and dies away, but it has made the
heart invulnerable. I am devoted
to it, I am always ready to join
in the fight for it, for the appear-
ance of the flash, which lasts no
longer than the eye is able to
endure it. I give my left hand to
the rebel and my right to the
heretic: forward! But I do not
trust them. They know how to
die, but that is not enough.

Martin Buber

In the Garden of Eden, man began his quest to know "good and evil," to be free of external demands, to be free even from his Creator. Yet today, though he wields unlimited power, he still appears to be controlled by instinctive and environmental forces and therefore unfree. All the more determinedly he seeks to solve the riddle of freedom, as though he must succeed now or never. The time has surely come to search out the concept of freedom as a forerunner of social reform. They are related, for the first condition of freedom is the will to self-improvement: a social action that begins with changes within each individual.

It is possible, of course, even in the midst of war, uncertainty and deprivation, that man can by inner effort rise above his troubles. His thoughts can soar, regardless of external circumstances, into the pure air of freedom. The many examples of noble thought conceived in concentration camps and ghettos attest to this ability of man to transcend physical conditions. It can even be observed that poverty is generally more favorable than wealth as the matrix for the burning ideal of liberty. Wealth and ease often depress and corrupt the human spirit to a greater extent than poverty and suffering. To be truly free is to be master of outer conditions, whether favorable or adverse. It is to be oneself. We may or may not be able to be free outwardly, but we are impregnable if we are inwardly free.

When is a man free to be himself? He is master in his own house when he has achieved harmony among his own faculties of will, feeling and thinking. If he responds automatically to a stimulus, he acts without control of his own will; and obviously there is very little of the man himself in such response. Yet human behavior is still being explained by current psychology in terms of the stimulus-response theory. This theory may suit automatons but it denies the very premise of human freedom: namely, that man himself shall intervene (to chose and to decide) *between* stimulus and response. It ignores the real man and his climb toward lasting values. In its undue emphasis on externals it loses sight of the inner quest, the fateful encounter of a man with himself, his primary need for self-conquest.

The finest guides in man's quest for his higher self, the only self whose will truly suits the individual and fits the world, have always been found in the self-forgetting concepts of sacrifice and active service to mankind. Without the willingness to sacrifice his limited advantage for the whole that he holds dearer than self, man is doomed to pursue the kind of self-aggrandizement that always ends in self-defeat. Throughout history the great religions have sought to lead communities of men to the light and power of such ideals as that of rebirth through the giving of self. Today, as individuals, we must discover these ideals anew if will-lessness is not to drown us in inertia, or willfulness destroy us through violence.

Unchecked emotions also can rob a man of freedom of choice by denying him his rationality. His feeling response then becomes as automatic and unthinking as a reflex action. Both are "programmed." Compulsive loathing and hatred or attraction and desire deny a man his conscious self-direction. Serving such emotions, he loses his unique individuality. True feeling is not compulsive. It does not dominate the will but reinforces it. Its warmth does not obliterate reason but enriches it, giving it power of comprehension. There can be no dialogue without warmth; man or nature can be rightly known only through warm encounter. The "I" must be bound in warmth of heart to the "Thou."

To think in freedom is to overcome stereotype and tradition: regionalism, nationalism, and peer pressure. It is to consider how the pure ideal can be imaginatively, efficiently realized in action. It is to overcome one's bias of self-love in order to truly know oneself. With the help of the free insights thus achieved, man can execute the bidding of his higher self; he can do that which is knightly and just.

On this rung of experience our intuition is awakened. The one using only intellect is alienated from the world about him, simply a spectator of life. His thinking freezes into rigid patterns, and his coldness is the beginning of decay. Such a man stands in the wings of life's drama with little zest to play his part. But when intellect and intuition combine, their balance brings wisdom, freedom, love and creativeness—all that guarantee human achievement.

A society of free individuals, capable of rising at critical moments above inner as well as outer compulsions, must be the goal of enlightened civilization. This achievement would be the completion of the task begun in Eden. Today it is the goal of many who dare to question. To question is to seek perspective, to look for beginnings and endings. The individual who searches comes to feel the pain and joy of the hour's claim on his soul: he begins to chart his own course and to shoulder social responsibility.

Ours is the beginning of an age when freedom is attainable. The external restraints of family, religion, and societal codes are crumbling. In such a situation man has the possibility of making his own decisions. He is called upon to walk the thin ridge of freedom that rises between the abyss of self-abandonment on the one side and the abyss of self-immersion on the other. But the mastery of freedom requires a deep understanding, and this can only follow from a far more significant education than society is now providing.

How are free human beings to be educated? Surely the extensive use of the teaching machine will have to be avoided. Those behaviorists who favor the machine do not accept even the hope of a free man able to neutralize and transcend his environment. They would prefer to program all behavior to their conception of the good life, denying both opportunity and responsibility. Whether this conditioning is to be accomplished by programming or by drugs, it can never awaken, encourage, nor permit what is essentially human; namely the free act. To ease ourselves of the burden of choice is to become something between man and machine.

Opposed yet strongly linked with programmed instruction is another new impulse in education: the open classroom. Its appeal is to the best in teachers. It has wisely removed harsh authority in education but it offers no systematic understanding of the interrelatedness of knowledge. It is often based on concepts of freedom that may be dangerously false because only half-true. Though it involves the emotions it does not see beyond the traditional intellectualistic brand of knowledge that has, in the end, always deeply disappointed children. It does not point children to a distant horizon nor does it help them with an understanding of the higher as opposed to the lower nature of man and existence.

By confusing freedom with movement and by preferring knowledge as a tool of power to knowledge as the gateway to insight and love it does not usher the child to the portal of deep wonder and gratitude. By viewing all knowledge in terms of selfish usage it may develop a subjective bias. This unwise subjectivism is as harmful to the best interests of the objective world as behavioristic objectivism is deadly to the human soul.

Superficial warmth, fired by sentimentalism, does not lead to true self-awareness. The appeal of the open classroom is to self-satisfaction rather than to self-trandscendance. Yet, as we have seen, to do what one wants to do is not freedom. To do what is right and true, in devotion, comes closer to the mark.

Programmed learning and open education lack the qualities needed to educate the free man. A better beginning will have to be made with an education that can show us how freedom arises from love of the world and the desire to serve it.

A first step must be to see that education at all levels is filled with reverence from man and nature alike. In the words of Abraham Heschel, "The beginning of awe is wonder, and the beginning of wisdom is awe." Every act of learning must open the heart to appropriate feeling. An education of the head alone is a distortion of reality. If feeling is to grow it must spring from the deeper recesses of a heart that knows the brotherhood of man with man and man with nature.

To provide an example: One could teach arithmetic in the first grade by counting objects that reveal no meaning either to the teacher or the children. On the other hand, the teacher who is trying to stir a child's mind and heart might begin his arithmetic lesson with an orange. To the lively imagination of teacher and class, however, it is not longer just an orange. It becomes a representation of the world and of a unified humanity. The teacher peels the orange—with drama. Its halves represent the hemispheres: the number "two" is introduced as the whole is parted. And finally the segments of the orange are disengaged, each one representing a nation. The segments are real and separate, yet the orange is clearly made to be one. Men are individualized, yet they should remain brothers. Such an arithmetic lesson can satisfy a child's heart as well as his mind. The teaching is simple and practical, yet it has also deeper levels of meaning.

The fairy tale is especially effective in satisfying a child's longing for experience that touches the heart. It opens him to inner beauty and the world's hidden meaning. While the teacher can utilize such stories for teaching reading, they also provide the basis for unlimited experiences in drawing, painting, drama, and dance. Fable and myth deal with the inward realities of human life; they awaken moral discrimination and foster dedication to the good. In the education of children of all backgrounds, fairly tale, fable, myth, and legend are an essential ingredient, a step toward the development of freedom.

Another step in the education of free individuals would be achieved through the training of the will, as we mentioned earlier. If the will is to develop, it must be based on a childhood regard for wholesome authority. The child should grow strong in the presence of teachers who are able to perform their tasks and able to say "no" when necessary. The teacher must serve as more than a passive guide; rather, he must be almost a hero, inspiring his students with enthusiasm and love for the day's labor. Such childhood experience will later support in a man the strength to stand up to his duty, to practice the self-control adult responsibilities require of him. If the experience of authority is missed in childhood, the possibility for self-direction in maturity become slim. The child wants outside authority as a model preparing him for the development of obedience to his own innermost promptings. He comes to a later self-discipline only through an earlier discipleship. Schools should not attempt, in their striving for "democracy" in all things, to duplicate the politics of an adult world designed for far different purposes. Student control in education is not the answer to present problems; a nourishing education is more the way.

The final aspect of an education for freedom lies in the development of independent thought. The secondary schools and colleges must not be afraid to confront the ultimate questions: Who am I? Why am I here? What is the meaning of life on earth? It may well be that the most relevant challenge the student can face is the time-honored one of learning to know himself. He makes progress in this as he comes to understand the activities of mankind, as he draws lessons from his encounters. Out of clear thinking he must determine where he ought to go and what he ought to do. The student must experience himself as both sacred and commonplace. His consciousness must expand until all about him comes alive and declares itself. The world is symbol, and the symbolic is to be penetrated. Life is to be known! When intuition joins intellect in the complete act of thought, a realization of the wonder, sacredness, and beauty of the earth becomes the joy of the free man.

Today it is vital that the militant weight his actions. He must evaluate his passion. Action based on hatred or lust is obviously reaction. It is never free; it can never favor the cause of man. Buddha's words are as true today as when first spoken:

"He abused me, he beat me, he defeated me"—in those who harbor such thoughts hatred will never cease.
"He abused me, he beat me, he defeated me, he robbed me,"—in those who do not harbor such thoughts hatred will cease.
For never does hatred cease by hatred here below: hatred ceases by love; this is an eternal law.

The individual must understand his motives. His action must result from the balance of feeling and thinking if it is to be a forward step. Without such balance, confusion, frustration, and violence are inevitable. The conquest of one's lower self is the painful, laborious task of our time. It is also the gateway to the upward climb.

Let us understand that it is with clear thinking, permeated by love, fulfilled in consecrated action, that man can reach his moments of freedom. Today's man, heeding the voice of his better self, mastering life, can truly accomplish the quest for freedom begun so long ago. To fail in this quest is to miss the meaning of our time. To fail in this quest is also to guarantee individual and social disaster.

DISCUSSION QUESTIONS

1. Is Stoff's concept of freedom attainable or is it just fantasy?
2. What does Stoff include in his concept that Dewey, Neill, and Skinner ignore?
3. Can man experience "freedom"? Compare the concepts of Dewey, Skinner, and Stoff.

WILLIAM F. O'NEILL   # Existentialism and Education for Moral Choice

> *... what there is of free will in individual determination begins only on a rather high human level. ... The broadly developed intelligence is needed to ponder moral problems, to have moral problems, and only he who feels ethics as a continuous problem is a person to whom ethics is a real concern,—just as the only blasphemers or near-unbelievers, like Job, Kierkegaard, Hopkins, Dostoievsky, Kafka, Simone Weil, are the only ones to deal deeply with religion. The Prussian king Frederick II, an atheist, was the*

Reprinted from *Phi Delta Kappan*, Vol. XLVI, No, 2 (October 1964), pp. 48–53, with permission of the publisher.

only one among his devout dynasty who took
religion quite seriously.

Erich Kahler, "The Tower and Abyss"

We have values, and we judge values. Of course,
having them is not an intellectual or cognitive
process; but judging is. . . . The rational man is
one who values only what evaluation reveals to be
worthy of it. A value judgment is not a mere
expression of the fact that we then and there
find something satisfying, but a hypothesis that
it will prove to be satisfactory; not merely that
we are interested in it, but that indeed it is our
interest.

Abraham Kaplan, "New World of Philosophy"

To sum up, *good in humanistic ethics is the*
affirmation of life, the unfolding of man's powers.
Virtue is responsibility toward his own existence.
Evil constitutes the crippling of man's powers;
vice is irresponsibility toward himself.

Erich Fromm, "Man for Himself"

In the last ten or fifteen years educators have become increasingly
aware of just how little they know, not only about ethics in general, but
about the whole process of education for the development of moral character. It is probably true that to some degree this discomfiting sense of
disorientation stems from a radical new sense of urgency with respect
to the whole question of human values which has in part grown out of
the activities of a relatively small group of intellectuals who are frequently referred to as "the existentialists."

Existentialism is a difficult term to define. In perhaps the most basic
sense, it is a sort of metaphysical first principle which holds that all
meaning is a product of direct personal experience. Existentialism at its
broadest does not necessarily imply any particular concepts of value. On
the other hand, most existentialist philosophers have clearly developed
their theories beyond the bare assertion that "existence precedes essence" and most are in fundamental agreement on what might be termed
a sort of minimum existentialist theory of value. In a very general sense,
this theory can be reduced to three basic principles:

1. Man exists—experiences the world—through the medium of choice.
2. His moral standards are also choices, by means of which he regulates his responsibility with respect to others.
3. A *good* choice (including a good *moral* choice), is one which has
been derived "authentically"—that is, on the basis of active, conscious
and self-determined experience.[1]

[1] The existentialists hold that man is "free"—that he is capable of "free choice,"
which is actually a sort of epistemological self-selection.

Virtually all of the existentialist philosophers have developed some ethical point of view which encompasses these basic assumptions. The fundamental differences between these theories are those which exist between the *theistic* (religious) existentialists, who are perhaps best represented by such individuals as Kierkegaard and, more recently, Jaspers, Tillich, Marcel, and Buber, and the *non-theistic* (agnostic and/or atheistic) existentialists such as Heidegger and Sartre.

It goes without saying that there are vast and significant differences between the fully developed ethical viewpoints expressed by these men and particularly, of course, by the viewpoints which characterize the extreme poles of existentialist thought. On the other hand, there are certain general assumptions which the major representatives of the existentialist point of view hold in common and which, supplemented by the more recently developed views of the existentialist psychologists and psychoanalysts such as Frankl and May, seem to represent a reasonably reliable source of warrantable assertions with respect to the more general position which most existentialists share with respect to the problems posed by moral education. This position, while it has never been explicitly developed by any of the major representatives of the existentialist point of view, is, on the whole, implied by the theories developed by the major existentialists and may be summarized in the following six basic points.

1. Man is potentially autonomous.[2] The only value which applies categorically to all men *as men* is the actualization of the self as a free agent. This is the so-called value of "authenticity," or "authentic existence." A man who lives authentically exists in the autonomous mode. Such an individual is capable of choosing his own acts and is, in a sense, the author of his own destiny.

2. The basic function of the school is normative. It should act to encourage the maximum development of individual autonomy, or free choice. The fundamental problem confronted by the school is, as Heidegger states, *"Wie man wird, was man ist*—how one becomes what one is."[3]

Developing the capacity for free choice encompasses two basic steps: (1) cultivating the *ability* to make free and rational decisions and (2) developing the *inclination* to make such decisions in the first place. Of these, the latter is clearly the more important phase. The basic aim of existentialist education is to develop a sense of commitment to free

---

[2] The question of how and to what extent man is autonomous is a point of argument even among the existentialists themselves. All would seem to hold to the position that man is at least *capable* of free choice. Some would go so far as to assert that man is *absolutely free* and is, therefore, incapable of augmenting his free choice through any sort of volitional activity whatsoever.

[3] Martin Heidegger, *Being and Time.* As quoted in Rollo May, Ernest Angel, and Henri F. Ellenberger, eds., *Existence: A New Dimension in Psychiatry and Psychology.* New York: Basic Books, Inc., 1958, p. 31.

choice. The existentialist agrees that dullness is generally an achievement and not a gift.[4] The aim of existentialist education is not simply to help the individual *cope* with his existence. Its primary purpose is to help him to *experience his existence* by confronting it with a sense of defined purpose. For the existentialist, the proper outcome of education is a certain sort of attitude toward life. Such an attitude includes more than "openness," however; it also implies an "eagerness." The educated man is characterized not only by what he *knows* but also, and perhaps even more, by what he is *capable of knowing and experiencing*. In a basic sense, then, the hallmark of an existentialist education is not knowledge as such but rather "educability."

The existentialist advocates "education for choice" because he has a clear awareness that the most basic educational problem pertains to the criteria for selecting appropriate knowledge and not with the techniques for disseminating knowledge as such. The existentialist is concerned, above all, with the "habit of growth." He focuses on values precisely because he recognizes that values are directive and, therefore, determinative of more subsequent knowledge.

3. The school should be basically concerned with "moral education" —that is, with developing not only the *capacity* for but also the *inclination toward* moral choice—and not with "moral training"—that is, the conditioning of "acceptable behavior" as such.[5] From the existentialist point of view it is far more important that a child be taught to be "moral"—that he become capable of moral *choice*, and hence, become fully "human"—than that he be "right" in the sense of conforming to the established dictates of society.

This position is based on two underlying assumptions about the nature of moral choice: (a) A "moral act" is necessarily an autonomous act, and (b) an autonomous (authentic) act may be either good *or* bad, but is in any event preferable to an inauthentic "non-act," which can be *neither* good nor bad, since it is never really "chosen" at all but merely "performed" on a more or less unreflective basis.

In a general sense, then, existentialism is more concerned with developing the capacity for *moral choice* than with the moral nature—i.e., the goodness and badness—of the choice made. For the existentialist there can be morality without goodness, but there cannot be goodness without morality.

As a general rule, then, the existentialist takes the position that we

[4] Earl Kelley, *In Defense of Youth*. New York: Spectrum, 1963, p. 129.
[5] This is not to suggest that "moral education" and "moral training" are in any sense mutually exclusive. In many instances they are mutually reinforcing. As Ryle points out, the capacity to appreciate a performance is generally, if qualifiedly, one in type with the capacity to execute it. (Gilbert Ryle, *The Concept of Mind*. New York: Barnes and Noble, 1949, p. 56.) On the other hand, the fact that moral education may expedite moral training and vice versa does not mean that they are the same thing.

should not try to anticipate all moral problems in an attempt to pre-formulate decisions to every conceivable sort of moral conflict but should seek to produce the sort of individual who is capable of impro-vising enlightened solutions to various moral questions as they emerge. The existentialist would not say that lying, for example, is *not* a moral problem. He would, however, characteristically take the position that *whether* lying is or is not a moral problem for any particular person de-pends upon three basic conditions: (a) whether that individual is capable of making a real moral choice—that is, of making a decision in the ra-tional-autonomous mode; (b) whether truthfulness is a value which is logically required by the goal of autonomous behavior as such (i.e., whether it is a condition necessary for autonomous choice to take place); and (c) whether truthfulness is otherwise logically implied by any addi-tional value-commitments which have been made. In all events, for the existentialist the basic moral question involved would not be whether one should or should not lie, but, rather, whether one is willing and able to decide *whether* one should lie or not—that is, whether one is capable of making a moral choice with respect to the advisability of lying in the first place.

4. There is no basic and irreconcilable conflict between self-interest and the interests of others. A concern for others is a logical develop-ment of self-interest clearly conceived, since personal autonomy requires a complex set of supportive social conditions, including a fully function-ing democratic process and a high degree of civil liberty. Real autonomy precludes license and, to be effective,

... every pupil must be convinced that discipline is the best way of attaining the aims of the community. ... A logic of ... discipline confirms that discipline places each individual personality in a position of greater security and free-dom. Children easily understand the apparent paradox that discipline means freedom. ...[6]

5. Any real commitment to free choice as an educational goal both implies and entails a certain type of self-discipline on the part of the stu-dents themselves. If the school succeeds in making rational self-deter-mination a dominant value, two important consequences arise: (a) Most of the more traditional ethical objectives of the school, such as honesty and responsibility, tend to emerge automatically as conditions necessary for the full realization of rational-autonomous behavior, and (b) the need for the usual sort of externalized discipline is largely precluded.

The existentialist would tend to agree that "a single moral principle hammered out in discussion and applied to real situations is worth tons

[6] Anton S. Makarenko, *The Road to Life*. As quoted in National Society for the Study of Education: The Fifty-fourth Year Book, Part I. Nelson B. Henry, ed., *Modern Philosophies and Education*. Chicago: University of Chicago Press, 1955, p. 209.

of affirmed values which are never put to a natural test."[7] It is best that a few really significant ideas, a few truly generative principles, should be developed and reinforced through direct practice over a period of time than that the really significant issues should be obscured behind a multiplicity of trivial and legalistic rules.

These values (with the possible exception of the value of autonomy itself) are available to common sense and can be affirmed on the basis of relatively undirected and informal experience. Once autonomous behavior has been allowed to develop, other types of moral behavior tend to emerge more or less spontaneously out of the natural process of trial-and-error experience and are either confirmed or denied on the basis of their own natural consequences.[8]

This position deviates from the traditional Rousseauistic concept of "negative education" in two basic respects. First, existentialism precludes any naive concept of goodness as an innate quality (although some existentialists would take the position that man's basic capacity for rational self-determination, in conjunction with his preinclination to conform to such a constructive potential, predisposes him toward "goodness"). Second, the existentialist is ordinarily little inclined to the idea that the individual recapitulates the history of the race in his natural development. Most existentialists are, if anything, somewhat *anti*historical in inclination, frequently taking the position that much, if not most, past knowledge is actually noncontributive and possibly even dysfunctional with respect to the fulfillment of basic human freedom. Their fundamental objection would seem to center on the idea that much of what presently passes for "education" is simply an attempt to obscure

[7] T. V. Smith and Eduard C. Lindeman, *The Democratic Way of Life.* New York: New American Library, 1951, p. 134.

[8] It goes more or less without saying that this is a controversial position. What so many existentialists are suggesting is essentially (a) that there are actually very few categorical (intercontextual) problems which are shared by all men (b) that the "answers" to those that do exist are for the most part (and providing the situation remains uncontaminated by gratuitous theory) relatively self-evident on the basis of common-sense trial-and-error experience conducted in the sort of learning situation which makes such experience possible. Perhaps the best example of this point of view in action is A. H. Neill's well-known school, Summerhill, where all moral training is allowed to evolve as a product of direct experience in response to practical problems encountered in what approximates a life-like learning situation. It should be noted that Neill does not take the position that there are no errors under such a procedure but rather that all learning requires practice; that all practice involves error or at least the possibility of error; and that to eliminate error (or at least *significant* error) is to curb learning drastically. He does not, in other words, say, "This is the ideal way in which it is possible to conceive of learning taking place," but rather, "This is the way learning *does* take place whether we like it or not." Much of progressive pedagogy was, of course, based upon much the same point of view—that is, not that you cannot teach *more*, but that children can only learn so much effectively, based upon the necessary conditions for any sort of responsible learning.

the real (existential) problems relating to the *human condition* behind a great deal of irrelevant or erroneous data about the past and present *human situation.*

The schools have traditionally made the error of trying to change behavior directly, that is, of trying to make children do and say those things which would ostensibly alter their values in an immediate and observable manner. Unfortunately, and as the great educational theorists have observed repeatedly for many centuries, the most effective way to change belief and behavior is not to deal with belief and behavior as such, but rather to use the "seed crystal effect"—that is, to concentrate upon the values which make any given individual susceptible to certain kinds of experience rather than others.

James once said that it is nonsense to suppose that every step in education *can* be interesting.[9] He might well have added, however, that those things which are not interesting in and of themselves can at least be made *necessary* and, hence, turned into a source of secondary interest when they have been implicated in the total life-process through a sense of overriding purpose. In other words, intellectual knowledge conduces to change only by being transmuted into emotional knowledge. As Wiener has indicated, ". . . it is not the quantity of information sent that is important for action, but rather the quantity of information which can penetrate into a communication and storage apparatus sufficiently to serve as a trigger for action."[10]

Moral education, properly developed, is self-corroborating. It channels perception into prescribed routes and generates the kind of moral training compatible with its own underlying presuppositions. As Comenius said as far back as the beginning of the 17th century,

Most teachers are at pains to place in the earth plants instead of seeds, and trees instead of shoots, since, instead of starting with the fundamental principles, they place before their pupils a chaos of diverse conclusions or the complete texts of authors.

. . .

Hitherto the schools have not taught their pupils to develop their minds like young trees from their own roots, but rather to deck themselves with branches plucked from other trees, and, like Aesop's crow, to adorn themselves with the feathers of other birds; they have taken no trouble to open the fountain of knowledge that is hidden in the scholars, but instead have watered them with water from other sources.[11]

Certain types of moral choice cannot be forced. The young child is

[9] William James, *Talks to Teachers on Psychology: and to Students on Some of Life's Ideals.* New York: W. W. Norton and Company, 1958, p. 51.

[10] Norbert Wiener, *The Human Use of Human Beings: Cybernetics and Society.* Garden City, N.Y.: Doubleday Anchor Books, 1950, p. 94.

[11] Comenius, *The Great Didactic.* Trans. by M. W. Keatings. Quoted in Ronald Gross, *The Teacher and the Taught.* Now York: Dell Publishing Company, 1963, p. 38.

incapable of undertaking a meaningful sort of religious commitment for the simple reason that he is incapable of comprehending the various options involved in any but the most superficial sense. Premature education is shallow because it tends toward empty verbalization. A fact which few educators have ever really faced up to is that much significant learning simply cannot be acquired during the school years at all because it is totally unrelated to the needs and problems of school children. Every year we manage to distort, obscure, and otherwise mishandle a great deal of religion, philosophy, and literature by force-feeding it to children who haven't the foggiest notion of what it really *means* and whose only adequate defense lies in either total indifference or naive misinterpretation. It is simply not true, as many high school students would be willing to testify, that *Moby Dick* is actually an excellent sea story even if its real meaning is overlooked or that *Hamlet* is basically an exciting mystery in addition to everything else. The sad fact that *Moby Dick* is a pretty dull sea story unless it is understood as precisely the intellectually provocative and deeply intense moral and psychological drama it was intended to be in the first place and that *Hamlet* doesn't really hold a candle to the average paperback thriller in the eyes of the typical adolescent.

6. Moral *content* cannot be separated from the moral *procedures* that are used to establish and maintain classroom discipline. The development of free choice is incompatible with arbitrary or externalized control. Autonomy is not derived through a system characterized by habituation to unquestioning obedience. Authoritarian control, regardless of how ostensibly "efficient" it may seem to be, undermines the basic human values which should motivate the entire educational process and even serves to subvert the basic goal of student *self*-determination. As Edgar Friedenberg indicates with reference to the contemporary high school,

... the consequence of continuing through adolescence to submit to diffuse authority that is not derived from the task at hand—as a doctor's orders or the training regulations of an athletic coach, for example, usually are—is more serious than political incompetence or weakness of character.[12]

It is difficult to elicit a real enthusiasm for solving problems and making choices where the problems and choices with which one is habitually confronted are essentially *fait accompli* which have been disseminated from above and in which professed and real values are perceived to be clearly incompatible. As Erich Fromm suggests,

"Liberal" or "progressive" systems of education have not changed this situation as much as one would like to think. Overt authority has been replaced by anonymous authority, overt commands by "scientifically" established form-

[12] Edgar Z. Friedenberg, "The Modern High School: A Profile," *Commentary*, November, 1963, p. 379.

ulas; "don't do this" by "you will not like to do this." In fact, in many ways, this anonymous authority may be even more oppressive than the overt one. The child is no longer aware of being bossed (nor are the parents of giving orders), and he cannot fight back and thus develop a sense of independence. He is coaxed and persuaded in the name of science, common sense, and co-operation—and who can fight against such objective principles?[13]

Or as philosopher T. V. Smith comments,

A few years after graduation from high school we expect students to be mysteriously transformed into citizens. When they reach the magic age of twenty-one, they are expected to participate. But the sad truth is that in our last national elections only slightly more than one-half of the legal voters took the trouble to cast their ballots. They had not acquired the habit of participation.[14]

. . .

Democracy may be defended on battlefields but it can become a way of life worth defending only through intelligent practice.[15]

The existentialist takes the point of view that moral choice cannot be taught didactically. The danger with vicarious morality is, as Wendell Johnson has suggested, that while waiting for Moses to lead them into the promised land, the children may forget how to walk.[16]

One of the most astonishing sights to be seen all too often in our schools is a teacher of civics or political science conducting a class in democratic government" with the pupils sitting in neat rows dutifully giving answers prescribed by the teacher and the book. A dictator can't teach democracy. It just can't be taught with a hickory stick any more than it can be taught with a bayonet. It can only be taught by a good listener.[17]

Certainly one of the great but virtually incomprehensible truths of all times is that which holds that formative moral principles can only be acquired through direct personal experience. Basic moral truths may be *communicated* verbally, but they can never acquire any full and personal *significance* in this way. As Kierkegaard has said, genuine moral insight is always a profoundly personal thing which can only be shared with others who have also come to experience it as a profoundly intimate sort of *self*-discovery.

Whatever the one generation may learn from the other, that which is genuinely human no generation learns from the foregoing. . . . Thus, no generation has learned from another to love, no generation begins at any other point than at the beginning, no generation has a shorter task assigned to it than had the previous generation. . . . In this respect every generation begins primitively, has no different task from that of every previous generation, nor does it get further, except insofar as the preceding generation shirked its task and deluded itself.[18]

[13] Erich Fromm, *Man for Himself*. New York: Rinehart, 1947, p. 156.
[14] T. V. Smith and Eduard C. Lindeman, *The Democratic Way of Life*. New York: New American Library, 1951, p. 151.
[15] *Op. cit.*, p. 154.
[16] Wendell Johnson, *People in Quandaries*. New York: Harper, 1946, p. 342.
[17] *Op. cit.*, pp. 480–81.
[18] Soren Kierkegaard, *Fear and Trembling*. As quoted in Rollo May, Ernest Angel,

There is, however, something about a man that does not love a paradox—even one that has been amply confirmed by the best psychological evidence. We insist on holding tight to our Euclidean certainties in a post-Euclidean age. Stubbornly, we continue to confuse the "logic of discover" with the "logic of presentation," overlooking the fact that "trials terminate in verdicts, they do not consist of them."[19] Unwilling to accept the conclusions of our own best research, we continue to reject the fact that learning is a highly devious, indirect, and complex phenomenon and persist in placing our reliance on the all too easy, if frequently misleading, techniques of traditional "telling" in which morality is conceived to emerge through a sort of spontaneous combustion out of the friction arising from repeated moral admonition.

For the existentialists, autonomy is not a *fact* to be learned but a *process* to be mastered. A system of moral education based upon the unreflective assimilation of the conclusions of others unfortunately provides no basis for deriving one's own conclusions. Rational assent is an insufficient basis for authentic existential commitment.

DISCUSSION QUESTIONS

1. Should education have as a basic aim the development in the individual of "a sense of commitment to free choice"?
2. If so, how would you accomplish this goal in your classroom?
3. What is your "defined purpose" in life? How helpful was your schooling in arriving at this definition?
4. What is "authentic existential commitment"? What is its relationship to freedom?

SIDNEY HOOK Student Revolts Could Destroy
Academic Freedom

COLLEGES SHOULD NOT YIELD TO MILITANTS' BLACKMAIL, PROFESSOR WARNS; ONLY COURAGE TAMES FANATICS

I began my college career in the fall of 1919, almost a half century ago. My academic lifetime spans half a dozen revolutions in American education. But have no fear, I am not going to reminisce. I want to stay young, at least in spirit, and I learned from my teacher John Dewey,

Reprinted from *The New York University Alumni News*, May 1968, with permission of the publisher.

and Henri F. Ellenberger (eds.), *Existence: A New Dimension in Psychiatry and Psychology*. New York: Basic Books, Inc., 1958, p. 70.
[19] Gilbert Ryle, *The Concept of Mind*. New York: Barnes and Noble, 1949, pp. 298–99.

whom I observed closely for the last 25 years of his life, what the secret of staying young is, and that is *not* to reminisce about the past. Actually, I never heard John Dewey reminisce until he was in his nineties, and that was as a reluctant response to my deliberate prodding in order to extract biographical data from him.

However, there is a way of talking about the past that is not merely reminiscence or idle reverie. It occurs when we make comparisons of the past and present for the sake of a present purpose or for the sake of finding a new way out of present difficulties.

Fifty years ago when I began my college studies, it would be no exaggeration to say that the belief in academic freedom was regarded as faintly subversive even in many academic circles. The AAUP [American Association of University Professors], organized by two philosophers, Arthur Lovejoy and John Dewey, was in its infancy without influence or authority. Today, except in some of the cultural and political backwaters of the U.S., academic freedom, although not free from threats, is firmly established. In some regions it has the support of law.

Fifty years ago, the power of the chief university administrator was almost as unlimited as that of an absolute monarch. Today the administrator is a much harried man with much less power and authority among faculty, and especially students, than his forebears. Today there may be temperamentally happy administrators but their present life is an unhappy one. There seems to be an open season on them, and to such a degree that for the first time in history there is an acute shortage of candidates for the almost 300 vacant administrative posts in institutions of higher learning. When I did my graduate work at Columbia, Nicholas Murray Butler was both the reigning and ruling monarch. I don't believe that in his wildest dreams he could have conceived of the Columbia scene today. The strongest argument I know against the resurrection of the body is that if it were within the realm of possibility, Nicholas Murray Butler would have risen from his grave and would now be storming Morningside Heights.

Having been an administrator in a small way myself, I have learned what an ungrateful job it is, and at the same time how necessary. Without administrative leadership, every institution (especially universities, whose faculties are notoriously reluctant to introduce curricular changes) runs downhill. The greatness of a university consists predominantly in the greatness of its faculty. But faculties, because of reasons too complex to enter into here, do not themselves build great faculties. To build great faculties, administrative leadership is essential. In the affairs of the mind and in the realm of scholarship, the principles of simple majority rule or of "one man, one vote" do not apply. The most "democratically" run institutions of learning are usually the most mediocre. It takes a big man to live comfortably with a still bigger man under him, no less to invite him to cast his shadow over the less gifted.

Targets of Abuse

The paradox today is that as administrative power decreases and becomes more limited, the greater the dissatisfaction with it seems to grow. The memory of favors or requests denied remains much stronger than the memories of requests granted. Faculties are fickle in their allegiance. Overnight the most beloved of administrators can become the target of abuse, a figure of obloquy in the eyes of the very faculty, or a large section of it, which he himself has helped to build. In the very year that Clark Kerr received the Meikeljohn medal for academic freedom, the faculty at the University of California campus at Berkeley panicked in consequences of the events resulting from the *fourth* student sit-in.

In effect it repudiated him by adopting a set of resolutions that made him the scapegoat for the student lawlessness that it conspicuously refused to condemn. The faculty even voted down a motion that would have given the students complete freedom of speech except to urge the commission of *immediate acts* of force and violence. Another example: Vice President Truman of Columbia University was vigorously applauded at Columbia's commencement last June for, among other things, opening new avenues of communication with students. Only a few days ago he was roundly booed by a section of the Columbia faculty.

Why any scholar (and administrators are largely recruited from the ranks of scholars) should want to become a *full-time* administrator has always puzzled me. The duties, sacrifices and risks seem altogether disproportionate to the rewards. In speaking of administrators, one is tempted to characterize them with the words Lecky used in his great history of European morals about the fallen women of Europe . . . "The eternal priestesses of humanity blasted for the sins of their people." Well, university administrators are no longer priests, but whenever a crisis arises they are sure to be damned if they do and damned if they don't.

Synthetic Storms

One thing seems clear. In the crisis situations shaping up throughout the country, administrators are not going to enjoy a peaceful life. Their prospect of weathering the storms that will be synthetically contrived for them depends upon their ability and willingness to win the faculty for whatever plans and proposals they advance in the name of the university. For if they permit students or any other group to drive a wedge between them and the faculty, they will discover the sad fact of academic life that in such rifts the faculty will either play a neutral role or even assume a hostile one.

Not only on good educational grounds, therefore, but on prudential ones as well, the administration must draw the faculty into the formulation of institutional educational policy. I say this with reluctance because it means the proliferation of committee meetings, the dilution of scholarly interest, and even less time for student. But this a small price to pay for academic freedom and peace.

In talking about academic freedom, nothing signifies the distance we have come in the space of my lifetime so much as the fact that we now are concerned with the academic freedom of *students*. For historical reasons I cannot now explore, academic freedom in the United States meant *Lehrfreiheit*, freedom to teach. *Lernfreiheit*, freedom to learn, has only recently been stressed. It does not mean the same as it meant under the German university system that presupposed the all-prescribed curriculum of studies of the *Gymnasium*. If academic freedom for students means freedom to learn, then two things should be obvious. There is no academic freedom to learn without *Lehrfreiheit* or academic freedom to teach. Where teachers have no freedom to teach, students have obviously no freedom to learn, although the converse is not true.

Second, students' freedom to learn was never so widely recognized, was never so pervasive in the United States as it is today—whether it be construed as the freedom to attend college or not, or the freedom to select the *kind* of college the student wishes to attend or his freedom of curricular choice *within* the kind of college he selects. Above all, if academic freedom for students means the freedom to doubt, challenge, contest and debate within the context of inquiry, American students are the freest in the world, and far freer than they were when I attended college.

I recall an incident when I was a student in a government class at CCNY. The teacher conducted the class by letting the students give reports on the themes of the course. All he contributed was to say "next" as each student concluded. But when in reporting on the Calhoun-Webster debates, I declared that it seemed to me that Calhoun had the better of the argument, that his logic was better than Webster's although his *cause* was worse, the instructor exploded and stopped me. After emotionally recounting his father's services in the Civil War, he turned wrathfully on me and shouted: "Young man! When you're not preaching sedition, you are preaching secession!" Whereupon he drove me from the class. (The "sedition" was a reference to an earlier report on Beard's economic interpretation of the Constitution that he had heard with grim disapproval.) And this was at CCNY in 1920! The incident wasn't typical, but that it could happen at all marks the profundity of the changes in attitudes toward students since then. John Dewey's influence has made itself felt even in the colleges today.

Moral Premise

Of course, there is still a large group of potential college students who are deprived of freedom to learn because of poverty or prejudice or the absence of adequate educational facilities. And as citizens of a democratic society whose moral premise is that each individual has a right to that education that will permit him to achieve his maximum growth as a person, our duty is to work for, or support, whatever measures of reconstruction we deem necessary to remove the social obstacles to freedom of learning. It is perfectly legitimate to expect the university to study these problems and propose solutions to them. All universities worthy of the name already do. This is one thing. But to therefore conclude that these problems must become items not only on the agenda of study but for an agenda of action is quite another.

For it therewith transforms the university into a political action organization and diverts it from its essential task of discovery, teaching, dialogue and criticism. Since there are profound differences about the social means necessary to achieve a society in which there will be a maximum freedom to learn, the university would become as partisan and biased as other political action groups urging their programs on the community. Its primary educational purpose or mission would be lost. It would be compelled to silence or misrepresent the position of those of its faculty who disagreed with its proposals and campaigns of action. Class and group conflicts would rend the fabric of the community of scholars in an unceasing struggle for power completely unrelated to the quest for truth.

Objectivity Imperiled

If the university is conceived as an agency of action to transform society in behalf of a cause, no matter how exalted, it loses its *relative* autonomy, imperils both its independence and objectivity, and subjects itself to retaliatory curbs and controls on the part of society on whose support and largesse it ultimately depends.

This is precisely the conception of a university that is basic to the whole strategy and tactics of the so-called Students for a Democratic Society. I say "so-called" because their actions show that they are no more believers in democracy than the leaders of the so-called Student Non-Violent Coordinating Committee are believers in non-violence. And indeed the leaders of SDS make no bones about that fact. In manifesto after manifesto they have declared that they want to use the university as an instrument of revolution. To do so, they must destroy the university as it exists today.

I wish I had time to list some of the clever stratagems they have devised to focus their opposition. On every campus there are always some grievances. Instead of seeking peacefully to resolve them through existing channels of consultation and deliberation, the SDS seeks to inflame them. Where grievances don't exist, they can be created. In one piece of advice to chapter members, they were urged to sign up for certain courses in large numbers, and then denounce the university for its large classes!

Freedom of dissent, speech, protest is never the real issue. They are, of course, always legitimate. But the tactic of the SDS is to give dissent the immediate form of violent action. The measures necessarily adopted to counteract this lawless action then become the main issue, as if the original provocation hadn't occurred. Mario Savio admitted after the Berkeley affair that the issue of "free speech" was a "pretext"—the word was his—to arouse the students against the existing role of the university in society.

Seek To Destroy

One of the leaders of the SDS at Columbia is reported to have said: "As much as we would like to, we are not strong enough as yet to destroy the United States. But we are strong enough to destroy Columbia!" He is wrong about this, too—the only action that would destroy Columbia would be faculty support of the students!—but his intent is clear.

Actually, the only thing these groups, loosely associated with the New Left, are clear about is what they want to destroy, not what they would put in its stead. In a debate with Gore Vidal, Tom Haydon, one of the New Left leaders, was pointedly asked what his revolutionary program was. He replied: "We haven't any. First we will make the revolution, and *then* we will find out what for." This is truly the politics of absurdity.

The usual response present-day academic rebels make to this criticism is that the university today is nothing but an instrument to preserve the status quo, and therefore faithless to the ideals of a community of scholars. Even if this charge were true, even if the universities today were bulwarks of the status quo, this would warrant criticism and protest, not violent and lawless action in behalf of a contrary role, just as foreign to their true function. But it is decidedly *not* true!

There is no institution in the country in which dissent and criticism of official views, of tradition, of the conventional wisdom in all fields, is freer and more prevalent than in the university. The very freedom of dissent that students today enjoy in our universities is in large measure a consequence of the spirit of experiment, openness to new ideas, absence of conformity and readiness to undertake new initiatives found among them.

Arrogant Claim

The first casualty of the strategy of the campus rebels is academic freedom. It is manifest in their bold and arrogant claim that the university drop its research in whatever fields these students deem unfit for academic inquiry and investigation. This note was already sounded in Berkeley. It is focal at Columbia. It is a shameless attempt to usurp powers of decision that the faculty alone should have. After all, it is preposterous for callow and immature adolescents who presumably have come to the university to get an education to set themselves up as authorities on what research by their teachers is educationally permissible.

Unless checked, it will not be long before these students will be presuming to dictate the conclusions their teachers should reach, especially on controversial subjects. This is standard procedure in totalitarian countries in which official student organizations are the political arm of the ruling party. Already there are disquieting signs of this. At Cornell a few weeks ago—*before* the martyrdom of Dr. King—a group of Black Nationalist students invaded the offices of the chairman of the economics department and held him captive in order to get an apology from a teacher whose views on African affairs they disagreed with. Only yesterday, another group at Northwestern demanded that courses in "black literature" and "black art" be taught by teachers approved by the Negro students.

And there are spineless administrators and cowardly members of the faculty who are prepared to yield to this blackmail. Under the slogans of "student rights" and participatory democracy" the most militant groups of students are moving to weaken and ultimately destroy the academic freedom of those who disagree with them.

Let us not delude ourselves. Even when these militant students fail to achieve their ultimate purpose, they succeed in demoralizing the university by deliberately forcing a confrontation upon the academic community that it is not prepared to face and the costs of which it is fearful of accepting. In forcing the hand of the academic community to meet force with force, the citadel of reason becomes a battlefield. The students glory in it, but the faint of heart among their teachers turn on their own administrative leaders. These militants succeed in sowing distrust among students who do not see through their strategy. They also succeed in dividing the faculties.

Embitter Relations

There is always a small group—a strange mixture of purists and opportunists desirous of ingratiating themselves with students—who will *never* condemn the violence of students but only the violence required to stop it. These students succeed, even when they fail, in embittering relations between the administration and some sections of the faculty. They succeed, even when they fail, in antagonizing the larger community of which the university is a part, and in arousing a vigilante spirit that demands wholesale measures of repression and punishment that educators cannot properly accept.

How is it possible, one asks, for events of this character to happen? There have always been extremist and paranoidal tendencies in academic life, but they have been peripheral—individuals and small groups moving in eccentric intellectual orbits. But not until the last four or five years has the norm of social protest taken the form of direct action, have positions been expressed in such ultimatistic and intransigent terms, have extremist elements been strong enough to shut down great universities even for a limited time.

There are many and complex causes for this. But as I see it, the situation in the university is part of a larger phenomenon, viz., the climate of intellectual life in the country. I do not recall any other period in the last 50 years when intellectuals themselves have been so intolerant of each other, when differences over complex issues have been the occasion for denunciation rather than debate and analysis, when the use of violence —in the right cause, of course!—is taken for granted, when dissent is not distinguished from civil disobedience, and civil disobedience makes common cause with resistance, and readiness for insurrection. A few short years ago, anti-intellectualism was an epithet of derogation. Today it is an expression of revolutionary virility.

Fanaticism Rampant

In the fifties I wrote an essay on "The Ethics of Controversy," trying to suggest guidelines for controversy among principled democrats no matter how widely they differed on substantive issues. Today I would be talking into the wind for all the attention it would get. Fanaticism seems to be in the saddle. That it is a fanaticism of conscience, of self-proclaimed virtue, doesn't make it less dangerous. This past year has presented the spectacle of militant minorities in our colleges from one end of the country to another, preventing or trying to prevent representatives of positions they disapprove of from speaking to their fellow-students wishing to listen to them.

The spectacle shows that we have failed to make our students understand the very rudiments of democracy, that to tolerate active intolerance is to compound it. If we judge commitment by action, the simple truth is that the great body of our students is not firmly committed to democracy or to the liberal spirit without which democracy may become the rule of the mob.

I do not know any sure way or even a new way of combatting the dominant mood of irrationalism, especially among students and even among younger members of the faculty whose political naiveté is often cynically exploited by their younger, yet politically more sophisticated, allies. What is of the first importance is to preserve, of course, the absolute intellectual integrity of our classrooms and laboratories, of our teachings and research against any attempt to curb it. We must defend it not only against the traditional enemies, who still exist even when they are dormant, but also against those who think they have the infallible remedies for the world's complex problems, and that all they need is sincerity as patent of authority. Fanatics don't lack sincerity. It is their long suit. They drip with sincerity—and when they have power, with blood—other people's blood.

We need more, however, than a defensive strategy, safeguarding the intellectual integrity of our vocation against those who threaten it. We need—and I know this sounds paradoxical—to counterpose to the revolt of the emotionally committed the revolt of the rationally committed. I do not want to identify this with the revolt of the moderates. There are some things one should not be moderate about. In the long run, the preservation of democracy depends upon a passion for freedom, for the logic and ethics of free discussion and inquiry, upon refusal to countenance the measures of violence that cut short the processes of intelligence upon which the possibility of shared values depends.

These are old truths but they bear repeating whenever they are denied. Even tautologies become important when counterposed to absurdities.

We as teachers must make our students more keenly aware of the centrality of the democratic process to a free society and of the centrality of intelligence to the democratic process. Democracy has our allegiance because of its cumulative fruits, but at any particular time the process is more important than any specific program or product. He who destroys the process because it does not guarantee some particular outcome is as foolish as someone who discards scientific method in medicine or engineering or any other discipline because of its failure to solve altogether or immediately a stubborn problem.

Courage Needed

There is one thing we cannot deny to the intransigent and fanatical enemies of democracy. That is courage. Intelligence is necessary to overcome foolishness. But it is not sufficient to tame fanaticism. Only courage can do that. A handful of men who are prepared to fight, to bleed, to suffer and, if need be, to die, will always triumph in a community where those whose freedom they threaten are afraid to use their *intelligence* to resist and to fight, and ultimately to take the same risks in action as those determined to destroy them.

Yes, there is always the danger that courage *alone* may lead us to actions that will make us similar to those who threaten us. But that is what we have intelligence for—to prevent that from happening! It is this union of courage and intelligence upon which the hope of democratic survival depends.

DISCUSSION QUESTIONS

1. Do you agree with Hook that "in the affairs of the mind and in the realm of scholarship, the principles of simple majority rule ... do not apply"?
2. What does "freedom to learn" mean to you? What is your concept of "freedom to teach"? Do they imply a contradiction?
3. Are you in sympathy with Hook's evaluation of Students for a Democratic Society?
4. Who should decide on what research is to be conducted at a university?

5. Should students have the power to "approve" who should teach specific courses?
6. Is Hook's contention true that "we have failed to make our students understand the very rudiments of democracy"? How would you bring about an understanding of true democracy in students?

DONALD S. SECKINGER Freedom and Responsibility
in Education

The terms freedom and responsibility can be made to mean different things to different people. Educational philosophers often have sought to make terms such as these meaningful, in order to clarify educational discourse. Propagandists of education, however, whether attacking or apologizing for the schools, treat freedom and responsibility as slogans, meaningless in theory and irrelevant in practice.

This is not to say that educational propaganda is worthless. The schools are dependent on many publics for support and, moreover, are particularly vulnerable to the pressures of special interest groups and the demagoguery of all manner of critics. Propaganda from within education serves to mobilize its friends and neutralize unfounded attacks or severe cutbacks in school programs. This function of educational propaganda often is buttressed by the defense of schools in terms of actual cash value, and there is no doubt that education is an investment in future productivity.

Educational propaganda, nevertheless, does have its limitations, and these appear all too clearly when arguments about the schools shift from cash values to the aims and content of instructional programs. It is at this point that propagandists and philosophers part company, and here that many educators, unfortunately, settle for the slogans, rather than the meanings, of freedom and responsibility.

Slogans usually are safe from public criticism, but meanings often are controversial. Consider the following: "Freedom must be earned by those mature enough to understand and accept the responsibilities it involves. The schools will teach controversial issues, but only at the appropriate level of maturity and understanding." This would be perfectly acceptable propaganda for most school systems. It enables the schools to affirm their faith that, *all in good time*, the students in their charge will be inducted into the responsibilities of citizenship.

In the meantime, what are the schools doing to develop individual initiative and responsibility? Most often the school program involves the organization and transmission of information, which then is fed

Reprinted from *School and Society,* vol. XCV1:2308 (Summer, 1968), with permission of the publisher, The Society for the Advancement of Education, Inc.

back to the teacher through recitations, examinations, and performances of one sort or another. It is an open question as to how much is retained, but one suspects that a great deal is forgotten, even as the process is repeated in a variety of guises up through the systems of schooling.

Freedom, in this situation, is the freedom to learn the informational cues of grade getting, by which the teacher reveals what he expects, and to learn the codes of conduct enforced by the peer group. The individual's responsibility to himself is blurred in this situation, as his judgments must stand public scrutiny and verification in the eyes of teacher and classmates.

This is the price exacted of teachers and students in schools where socially acceptable propaganda suffices for individual decision. The school is a training ground for occupational and social skills, and the development of the individual is seen in terms of learning the roles appropriate to these skills. All protestations to the contrary, the individual is treated as an object in a social system.

In the light of protestations and slogans about freedom and responsibility, there is a curious relationship between propaganda and philosophy in education. Frequently, educators look on propaganda as a useful tool for blunting criticism, enlisting support, and getting on with the job of keeping school. Philosophy, in contrast, is viewed as an impractical, visionary enterprise, far removed from everyday learning situations with real students in real schools.

Yet, it is the propaganda of education which treats the individual as an object by abstracting him into a typical learner. Genuine philosophizing in education, on the contrary, insists on dealing with concrete, and often paradoxical, ethical and moral situations faced by real human beings, and with the obligations of schools to face these situations.

The propagandist follows the conventional wisdom; he is frightened at the idea of taking risks with ideas. The philosopher demands the human right to make mistakes for the sake of discovering what it is to be human, to be responsible for making one's own judgments. The learner may have to break with the conventional wisdom to find himself, to experience commitment, to march to the beat of his own distant drummer.

Not surprisingly, programs of instruction based on the propaganda of education are geared to the same safe averages and norms, the same social expectations, as is the propaganda itself. These programs must stress the comfortable and the conformable. They must purvey knowledge which is prepackaged and procedures where the getting of this knowledge, as a commodity to be stored and fed back to the school on demand, are spelled out. Rewards and punishments also are spelled out and skillful teachers are encouraged to exploit social pressures in the name of individual freedom.

This freedom to conform to intellectual cues and social expectations is, of course, no freedom at all; it is coercion, packaged in the benevolent rationale of education as socialization, framed in the lofty rhetoric of education for excellence. Responsibility is not to the society through the self, but through a social situation which presumes to define the self, to treat it as a classifiable item of social data.

Freedom in education demands occasions for learning. These occasions require teachers who are open to the intellectual risks involved in sharing discoveries in knowledge with their students. Freedom involves students in the uncoerced appropriation of knowledge that may lead on to self-discovery and the awareness that one is responsible for his own decisions.

We live in a time of social unrest and social progress, of technological achievement which sees us poised between unprecedented material well-being and a new age of incredible barbarism and suffering. In such a time, the desire for escape is understandable, but there is no escape.

For the educator, there is no tuning out of society, whatever its imperfections, nor is there any really comfortable retreat from freedom in the conformities of educational propaganda. There is only the facing of freedom, the responsibility to answer for oneself, and the obligation we have as educators to provide the occasions wherein others may seek their own commitments to themselves and to the world.

DISCUSSION QUESTIONS

1. How would you design a curriculum to accomplish Seckinger's goals?
2. What changes would you have wished in your past education "to develop [your] individual initiative and responsibility"?

RONALD D. GOBEN The Case of the Good Teacher

By most standards, W. Ron Jones would be considered an outstanding teacher. His classes are so popular he doesn't need to take attendance because he knows no one will cut them. Students find the classes so stimulating they shout interruptions and often carry over discussions into their next class. Administrators have generally given him high marks as a teacher.

But Jones has been ousted after three years as a social-studies teacher at Cubberley High School in Palo Alto, Calif. Technically, he resigned.

Reprinted from *Changing Education* (Fall, 1969), with permission of the publisher, The American Federation of Teachers.

In reality, he was fired on a list of bizarre charges that included those listed above as assets: his failure to take attendance and the overly stimulated behavior of his students.

The students insist they know better. Jones is gone, they say, because of his ultra-liberal political beliefs—beliefs that led him to show films on the Black Panther Party and to open his classes to speakers such as David Harris, former Stanford University student body president who is now facing jail for his refusal to accept induction into the armed forces.

These same students, however, insist that Jones went out of his way to present both sides of all controversial issues. And among his staunchest supporters are student members of the extremely conservative Young Americans for Freedom.

Students, in fact, were almost unanimously for Jones. Most of the more than 700 names on a petition seeking his retention were students, and there are only 1,250 students at Cubberley. Those who didn't sign simply didn't know Jones. During two months of bitter controversy over his impending ouster, not one student spoke publicly against him.

Almost no teachers spoke publicly against him, either, but privately, it was a different matter. In fact, one of the puzzling aspects of the case was the virulence Jones seemed to generate in some of his fellow teachers—generally older teachers (Jones is 29).

Jones and the administration had appeared to be getting along well until the past year. He had begun teaching at Cubberley as an intern while still at Stanford University, and then had spent three full-time years on the Cubberley staff. His attorney later insisted that in three years under former principal Scott Thomson, Jones had received laudatory evaluations. The first derogatory evaluation, the attorney said, came during the 1968–69 school year under new principal David Stanard, who was himself 29 and possibly the youngest administrator of a major secondary school in California.

It was Stanard who initiated the action against Jones, but whether he acted on his own or under pressure will probably never be known. One frequently repeated version was that the pressure came from a group of senior faculty members.

Whatever the pressures, Stanard did recommend to Superintendent of Schools Harold Santee that Jones not be rehired for the 1969–70 school year. The timing is significant because Jones was completing three full-time years at Cubberley and his rehiring for the fall semester would automatically have assured him of tenure.

Jones was formally notified on March 15 (in accordance with the California Education Code) that he would not be rehired. Then he hired attorney Jerry E. Berg of San Jose and immediately demanded an open hearing. Any teacher in a similar situation in California has the same right, but few ask for even a closed hearing—and fewer still ever win.

No one could remember any Palo Alto teacher ever asking for an open hearing before.

It was more than a month before the hearing opened, and it was a busy month for the students. They circulated petitions, wrote letters to the editor of the *Palo Alto Times* and prepared a series of leaflets outlining the case (or lack of a case) against Jones.

The student supporters formed a highly unlikely coalition, ranging from the radical United Student Movement on the left to the YAF on the right. The USM support was predictable—Jones had been the organization's faculty sponsor and many of his political views were along the same lines as the USM—but the YAF backing was dramatic evidence of his popularity throughout the student body. The reason for the YAF support, according to member Mike Mayer, was that, although Jones was "very liberal," he was also "very fair" and made it clear when he was presenting his own views that they were just one man's opinions.

Conservative students may have been for Jones, but conservative adults were emphatically against him. A right-wing group called Citizens for Excellence in Education had been organized primarily to fight a novel Palo Alto venture in "multicultural" education, and members readily joined the campaign against Jones by contributing letters to the editor and telephone calls to Santee. Few had any personal knowledge of Jones, but they were prepared to dislike him simply for his liberal views. Liberal adults, on the other hand, lined up solidly behind him.

Teacher reaction was less clear-cut. The young, so-called "new breed" teachers were on Jones' side—but they were in the minority at Cubberley. The others posed another puzzle. A majority probably disliked Jones, but none said so publicly. And those silently against him included some teachers normally classified as liberal. Clearly, the left-right split evident in the outside community was not the only reason for the difference in teacher attitudes.

During the weeks before the hearing, students repeatedly branded the charges against Jones as ridiculous and in their leaflets listed some of his alleged offenses. Because the offenses appeared to be of a minor nature, it semed probable there was omission or distortion on the part of the student pamphleteers. However, when the hearing finally started on April 21, the students' pipeline proved to be astoundingly accurate. They had forecast almost all of the charges that the district revealed as the hearing opened. The full list of charges:

Jones had played a "B" squad basketball player who was ineligible under rules of the Interscholastic Athletic League.

He told girls they could wear slacks during the semester examination week in violation of the district's dress code. (The code was subsequently altered to allow girls at all schools to wear slacks at all times.)

He observed a student smoking on the school grounds "and did nothing to prevent it."

He encouraged student leafleting on the Cubberley campus in violation of district rules. (This charge, possibly the most serious, was challenged by attorney Berg on the grounds it allegedly happened April 11, long after the complaint against Jones was supposed to be filed.)

Jones repeatedly took students from school on unauthorized field trips.

He failed to return films to the film department on time.

He failed to "maintain and deliver timely and accurate attendance reports for classes."

He requisitioned films "not previously authorized by the district."

He acquired 200 copies of the ACLU's "Academic Freedom in the Secondary School" without authorization.

He incurred a debt to the Institution of Nations in Berkeley without proper authorization.

He failed to issue passes to students when they were excused from class, as required.

He failed to "control the noise level of his class and the conduct of students," which resulted in distracting adjoining classes.

He solicited reaction from fellow faculty members to the district action against him by distributing copies of his confidential evaluation form and asking for their comments.

He sought support and backing from students in his "confrontation" with the district.

Those were the official charges, but the unofficial charges were what concerned the students. Those were listed in one sentence in a USM publication, _Serve the People,_ that said: "Ron brings in too many films about ghettos, smog, war, China, poverty, and grapes [a reference to the California grape boycott], plus guest speakers on everything from apartheid to socialism."

A "compromise" was worked out with the trustees after the first day of the hearing, but the details were not learned until the hearing reopened on April 23—and closed after a 75-word statement from Berg. The district, he said, had agreed to rehire Jones for the fall but on a probationary status, minus tenure, and not for Cubberley. He would be assigned to one of the two other Palo Alto high schools. Then, Berg added that Jones had decided to resign from the district, effective June 30, meaning that he was dropping the hearing.

Shouts of "no, no" from students mingled with the applause of conservative adults in the audience as Berg made his announcement. There were several bitter shouting matches between angry students and pleased adults (few, if any, of whom were parents of Cubberley students), and the students headed back to the campus for an all-school meeting.

Jones, meanwhile, said he had decided to drop the hearing because "it would have torn the school apart . . . it would have degraded a lot of people—students and faculty." That afternoon, his voice breaking, he addressed about 800 Cubberley students and said: "If you go into the arena with them, you bloody your own hands."

Stanard had said the students could use the school gymnasium for their meeting as long as they wished. After dozens of speakers had finished praising Jones and damning Stanard and Santee, about 200 students decided to stay in the gym all night. Some parents stayed with them, however, and, as sit-ins go, it was remarkably quiet and orderly. Students appeared to be saving themselves for the public meetings yet to come.

The big meeting was held two days later, on Friday, May 25, at Cubberley. The school board met at Cubberley to formally receive Jones' resignation, but Stanard provided a surprise by submitting his own resignation. The trustees accepted both resignations, then turned the microphone over to the audience. Students, faculty members, and parents all testified on Jones' behalf. Not a single speaker criticized him.

John Marion, speaking on behalf of the Palo Alto Federation of Teachers, accused the district of violating due process in the case against Jones, charging him falsely, and being guilty of "cruel manipulation." He urged the board to rescind its acceptance of Jones' resignation.

At the end of two hours of oratory, Board President Bernard Oliver thanked the speakers and told them, "I assure you the board has been moved." He said the trustees would schedule additional meetings during the following two weeks to consider the case.

The board held at least two meetings, but they were closed, as is normal in personnel matters. On Friday, May 2, the board members issued a brief statement taking note of the "eloquent outpouring of support" for Jones and the "voluminous correspondence" that had "revealed the range and intensity of feelings both for and against his continuation at Cubberley." Then it added:

"Even the ability of the teacher to motivate students must be examined, for the good teacher appeals to the intellect, not just the emotions.

"After weighing all the evidence, the board unanimously endorses the position taken by the superintendent, which led to Mr. Jones' resignation. Our inquiry in this case has reaffirmed our confidence in the administration's judgment and we consider the Jones case closed."

However students didn't consider the case closed. Some 200 marched on the board meeting the following Monday night.

The board statement also prompted Jones to change his position and seek to have the case reopened. He took out a half-page advertisement in the *Palo Alto Times* to display an open letter to Santee and the board.

"I resigned from the Palo Alto Unified School District to open communication, not to close it," he said. "I demand an immediate public review of your 'recent' accusations or an immediate apology and reinstatement to Cubberley High School."

In one last attempt to reopen the case, Jones appeared at the school board meeting of May 20 along with student supporters. "You are demonstrating your arrogance of power," he told the trustees. "Other teachers will be up here and you know it . . . I tried to bring you new qualities, new priorities. I'm sorry that you didn't listen."

David Wyle, a Cubberley junior, zeroed in on perhaps the most vulnerable action of the administration: the offer to allow Jones to teach at another school.

He said the administration was "intellectually dishonest" in offering Jones the alternative. "If they truly conceived of him as being as bad and as dangerous as they have, then how could they dare to release him upon the unsuspecting innocents of those two schools?" Wyle asked.

But the trustees had made their decision, and they stuck to it. They listened politely and attentively, but is was clear they were not going to reverse themselves when at the end of Jones' presentation, Chairman Oliver said only, "Thank you, Mr. Jones."

Jones remained in his classroom until school ended in June, although the district did make a futile attempt to have him turn the classes over to a substitute. The classes were as lively and enthusiastic as ever. Once, he turned a class over to a visiting reporter, told the students to respond frankly to any questions, and walked out. The closest any of the students came to criticizing Jones was a suggestion from one boy that he did too much research for students—supplying them with reading material that they might more profitably learn to dig up themselves. The students stressed the fact that Jones had spent hundreds of dollars of his own money for classroom films and reading material.

Some of that money was returned to Jones in a collection taken by students and parents to help pay for his advertisement in the *Times*. Jones had some of the money left after paying for the advertisement and, typically, spent it on the students. He rented a series of off-beat films and sponsored a film festival open to the public.

Then it was the end of the school year and he was gone from Cubberley—but not from Palo Alto. Although he was reportedly offered an educational research job in the East, Jones decided to remain in Palo Alto, at least temporarily, to push for the kind of education he and his student followers still believed in. He put together a prospectus for a "Palo Alto Community School" that would stress the kind of flexibility and imagination he tried to bring to his own classroom.

Jones estimated he would need $86,000 for a one-year pilot program and went seeking foundation support. At the time this was written he was optimistic, but not certain, that he would get the support. At any rate, it did seem certain that he would keep searching for some method of presenting his educational ideas.

DISCUSSION QUESTIONS

1. Should students have a voice in deciding who shall teach and how he shall go about it?
2. How shall power be distributed to provide an equitable balance among students, faculty, and administration?
3. Should the community have a voice in the running of a high school?
4. Why is Ron Jones such a threat to the conservative forces in Palo Alto? Is he justified in raising any topic in class as long as he presents all sides of the issue?

PART TWO The Issues

CHAPTER 2 Goals of Education

Education in any social order arises out of the need to perpetuate that society, to provide continuity in its ways of thinking, doing, and behaving, to reinforce its value structure, and to establish conformity to those norms that it sees as consequential and sustaining. At the same time, to insure its viability in a changing, demanding, and challenging modern world setting, it must seek to redirect and reconstruct the social order to meet the needs of the future.

Education in a democratic society is of a particular hue and tone. It is infused with a certain vision of man, of what he is and what he may become. It subscribes to ends that are describable in words such as *freedom*, *justice* and *equality*. It is charged with the responsibility for translating these words and the concepts for which they stand into reality. It must determine the means by which this will be achieved. In its mind's eye, it must picture clearly the person who is the tangible embodiment of the democratic concepts and ideals. Education has meaning only in terms of human flesh and blood. Individuality is clearly the focus of concern.

No teacher can operate without a philosophy of education. To have a philosophy, one must be a philosopher, a "lover of wisdom," as Sawyer has pointed out. The two key words, *love* and *wisdom*, are particularly applicable to education at this point in its history; they seem seldom to have been heard less frequently.

Quite deliberately, to encourage the adoption of a stance, the positions offered in this chapter demand scrutiny of a variety of goals for education, some broad, some narrow; some pragmatic, some poetic. Working through to a philosophy of education means to see education whole, to have the insights, the sentiments and the convictions that enable one to react unhesitatingly and truthfully to all situations in a manner in tune with one's being.

Having clearly in mind the goals of education places what follows in subsequent chapters in clearer perspective. This perspective makes the history of education the bearer of insights and the source of object lessons. It causes contemporary problems to become alive and challenging and, out of breadth of vision, capable of resolution.

The informed and militant educator of today no longer simply follows the lead of others; he accepts the responsibility for speaking out in a strong, clear voice in educational decision-making. He is deeply committed to a posture that challenges the past. He insists upon the purposes of education and the role of the educator. He is an activist who is willing to pay the price for being "where the action is." He is determined to help channel the direction in which the action goes.

The American High School Today

In the half-century that has elapsed, there have been no drastic changes in the basic pattern of education in either Europe or the United States. But in two respects the American pattern has diverged even more from that to be found in other countries; certain unique characteristics have been emphasized, so to speak. The percentage of youth attending a college or university has jumped from 4 to 35, and, at the same time, the percentage enrolled in grades eleven to twelve of the high school has about doubled. In 1910, only 35 per cent of the seventeen-year-olds were in school; today, the corresponding figure is over 70 per cent. These changes could easily have been predicted in 1900 by a student of American Education. He would already have seen how enormous was the power of the twin ideals of equality of opportunity and equality of status; it was evident that the American people had come to believe that more education provided the means by which these ideals were to be realized. But two other factors also played a role. First, there was the urge for institutional expansion—the drive for larger faculties and student bodies in the colleges and universities; fifty years ago expansion was more than welcomed. Second, there was a radical change in the picture regarding the employment of youth. When this century began, approximately half of the boys and girls fifteen years of age were not attending school; many were at work. Thirty years later the percentage of this group attending school had reached 85. This alteration was not a consequence of state laws raising the school-leaving age; the laws were rather a consequence of profound economic and social changes. To explore adequately the background of this shift in the American scene would require many pages; suffice it to remind the reader that in the second decade of this century the campaign against child labor was being pushed vigorously at the state and national levels. Today, as a result of laws affecting employment, as well as the attitude of management and labor, it is difficult for boys even at the age of seventeen to obtain many types of jobs. In European countries three quarters or more of the youth go to work at fourteen or fifteen years of age. (pp. 6–7)[1]

Thousands of comprehensive high schools of considerable size exist throughout the United States. Though generalization about American public education is highly dangerous (and I shall avoid it as far as possible in this report), I believe it accurate to state that a high school accommodating all the youth of a community is typical of American public

---

Reprinted from James B. Conant, *The American High School Today* (New York: McGraw-Hill Book Co., 1959), pp. 6–77 *passim*, with permission of the author and the Educational Testing Service.

[1] Page numbers cited throughout this selection refer to pages in the original text.

education. I think it safe to say that the comprehensive high school is characteristic of our society and further that it has come into being because of our economic history and our devotion to the ideals of equality of opportunity and equality of status.

THE QUESTION TO BE ANSWERED

As I indicated in Section I of this report, the comprehensive high school is an American development of this century. It has no equivalent, so far as I am aware, in any European country. If the high school is of sufficient size and located in a community where parental pressure for preparing for college is not overriding, those boys and girls who desire to pursue education beyond the high school level will be in a minority. The question arises whether, being in a minority, such students can obtain an adequate education. Stating it another way, one can raise the question whether, under one roof and under the same management, it is possible for a school to fulfill satisfactorily three functions: Can a school at one and the same time provide a good general education for all the pupils as future citizens of a democracy, provide effective programs for the majority to develop useful skills, and educate adequately those with a talent for handling advanced academic subjects—particularly foreign languages and advanced mathematics? The answer to this question would seem to be of considerable importance for the future of American education. If the answer were clearly in the negative, then a radical change in the structure of American public secondary education would be in order. If the students in a given geographic area who have the ability to profit from the study of foreign languages and advanced mathematics on the high school level cannot obtain an adequate education in a comprehensive high school, then one can argue that separate high schools for these students should be maintained, as is now the case in some of the large eastern cities. On the other hand, if the answer is in the affirmative, then no radical change in the basic pattern of American education would seem to be required. (pp. 14–15)

AN EXAMINATION OF COMPREHENSIVE HIGH SCHOOLS IN EIGHTEEN STATES

To repeat, the three main objectives of a comprehensive high school are: *first*, to provide a general education for all the future citizens; *second*, to provide good elective programs for those who wish to use their acquired skills immediately on graduation; *third*, to provide satisfactory programs for those whose vocations will depend on their subsequent education in a college or university. If one could find a single comprehensive high school in the United States in which all three objectives were reached in a highly satisfactory manner, such a school might be taken as a model or pattern. Furthermore, unless there were some especially favorable local features which enabled such a school to attain these three objectives, the characteristics found might be developed in all the other schools of sufficient size in the United States. (p. 17)

ELIMINATION OF THE SMALL HIGH SCHOOL—A TOP PRIORITY

Most of the schools visited by me and my staff during this past year have had graduating classes of one-hundred or more. From what I observed in these schools, in the two schools noted with graduating classes of less than one hundred, and in a much smaller school I visited, I am convinced small high schools can be satisfactory only at an exorbitant expense. The truth of this statement is evident if one considers the distribution of academic talent in the school which serves all the youth of a community. It will be a rare district where more than 25 per cent of a high school class can study with profit twelfth-grade mathematics, physics, and a foreign language for four years (assuming that standards are maintained). If a school has a twelfth grade of only forty and if indeed only a quarter of the group can handle the advanced subjects effectively, instruction in mathematics, science, and foreign languages would have to be provided for a maximum of ten students. If the girls shy away from the mathematics and science as they do in most of the schools I visited, the twelfth-grade mathematics classes may be as small as six or seven. To provide adequate teachers for specialized subjects is extremely expensive. Furthermore, to maintain an interest in academic subjects among a small number is not always easy. (p. 37)

There are three requisites for the successful operation of a high school: *first*, a school board composed of intelligent, honest, devoted citizens who understand that their function is policy-making and not administration; *second*, a first-rate superintendent; *third*, a good principal. Without a good school board the situation is almost hopeless. If members of a school board become involved in the appointment of teachers and in other matters of patronage, the maintenance of good morale in the teaching staff becomes almost impossible, however excellent may be the superintendent and the principal. Given a good school board and strong leadership by the superintendent and principal, an excellent group of teachers will be recruited, and it is hardly necessary to emphasize that on the quality of the teachers (assuming wise leadership) the quality of the education must ultimately depend.

Probably one of the most important factors in determining whether a high school is providing adequately for the education of the academically talented is the attitude of the community. Too much emphasis on basketball, football, and marching bands may affect the decisions of the school board, the administrators, and the teachers; and, often equally important, community activities may take up too much of the students' time. (pp. 38–39)

RECOMMENDATION 1: THE COUNSELING SYSTEM

There should be one full-time counselor (or guidance officer) for every two hundred fifty to three hundred pupils in the high school. The counselors should have had experience as teachers but should be devoting virtually full time to the counseling work; they should be familiar with the use of tests and measurements of the aptitudes and achievement of pupils. (p. 44)

RECOMMENDATION 2: INDIVIDUALIZED PROGRAMS

It should be the policy of the school that every student has an individualized program; there would be no classification of students according to clearly defined and labeled programs or tracks such as "college-preparatory," "vocational," "commercial." (p. 46)

RECOMMENDATION 3: REQUIRED PROGRAMS FOR ALL

General Education

The requirements for graduation for all students should be as follows:

four years of English, three or four years of social studies—including two years of history (one of which should be American history—and a senior course in American problems or American government—one year of mathematics in the ninth grade (alegebra or general mathematics), and at least one year of science in the ninth or tenth grade, which might well be biology or general physical science. (p. 47)

RECOMMENDATION 4: ABILITY GROUPING

In the required subjects and those elected by students with a wide range of ability, the students should be grouped according to ability, subject by subject. (p. 49)

RECOMMENDATION 5: A SUPPLEMENT TO A HIGH SCHOOL DIPLOMA

The awarding of a diploma is evidence only that a student has (1) completed the required work in general education to the best of his ability, and (2) had finished satisfactorily a certain sequence of elective courses. In addition to the diploma, each student should be given a durable record of courses studied in four years and the grades obtained. The existence of such a record should be well publicized. (p. 50)

RECOMMENDATION 6: ENGLISH COMPOSITION

The time devoted to English composition during the four years should occupy about half the total time devoted to the study of English. Each student should be required to write an average of one theme a week. (p. 50)

RECOMMENDATION 7: DIVERSIFIED PROGRAMS FOR THE DEVELOPMENT OF MARKETABLE SKILLS

Programs should be available for girls interested in developing skills in typing, stenography, the use of clerical machines, home economics, or a specialized branch of home economics which through further work in college might lead to the profession of dietitian. Distributive education should be available if the retail shops in the community can be persuaded to provide suitable openings. If the community is rural, vocational agriculture should be included. For boys, depending on the community, trade and industrial programs should be available.

As stated in Recommendation 3, the students enrolled in programs which develop marketable skills should also be enrolled in English, social studies, and other courses required for graduation. Furthermore, efforts should be made to prevent isolation from the other students. (pp. 51–52)

RECOMMENDATION 8: SPECIAL CONSIDERATION FOR THE VERY SLOW READERS

Those in the ninth grade of the school who read at a level of the sixth grade or below should be given special consideration. These pupils should be instructed in English and the required social studies by special teachers who are interested in working with such students and who are sympathetic to their problems. Remedial reading should be part of the work, and special types of textbooks should be provided. The elective programs of these pupils should be directed toward simple vocational work, and they should be kept out of the regular vocational programs for boys, the distributive education program, and the regular commercial program for girls. These students should not be confused with mentally retarded students. The education of the mentally retarded is a special problem which in some states is also handled in the regular high school through special instruction and the use of special state funds. (p. 55)

RECOMMENDATION 9: THE PROGRAMS OF THE ACADEMICALLY TALENTED

Four years of mathematics, four years of one foreign language, three years of science, in addition to the required four years of English and three years of social studies; a total of eighteen courses with homework to be taken in four years. This program will require at least fifteen hours of homework each week. (p. 57)

RECOMMENDATION 10: HIGHLY GIFTED PUPILS

For the highly gifted pupils some type of special arrangement should be made. These pupils of high ability, who constitute on a national basis about 3 per cent of the student population. . . . (p. 62)

RECOMMENDATION 11: THE ACADEMIC INVENTORY

In order to provide meaningful statistics about the education of the academically talented, a school board through the superintendent should ask the principal each year to provide an academic inventory. As explained earlier, the academic inventory summarizes the programs of the academically talented students in the senior class without giving their names. (pp. 63–64)

RECOMMENDATION 12: ORGANIZATION OF THE SCHOOL DAY

The school day should be so organized that there are at least six periods in addition to the required physical education and driver education which in many states occupy at least a period each day. (p. 64)

RECOMMENDATION 13: PREREQUISITES FOR ADVANCED ACADEMIC COURSES

Standards in advanced courses should be such that those who enroll in each successive course of a sequence have demonstrated the ability required to handle that course. (p. 65)

RECOMMENDATION 14: STUDENTS SHOULD NOT BE GIVEN A RANK IN CLASS ACCORDING TO THEIR GRADES IN ALL SUBJECTS

In many schools, it is customary to designate a rank in class on graduation as determined by the marks received; the position of valedictorian is usually held by the student whose rank is number one. The ranking is calculated by averaging the grades in all subjects taken during the four years. I have found that in many schools the desire to rank high has led bright students to elect easy courses in order to obtain high grades. (p. 66)

RECOMMENDATION 15: ACADEMIC HONORS LIST

At the end of each marking period, a list should be published of the students who had elected courses recommended for the academically talented and had made an average grade of B. On graduation a notation might be made on the diploma if a student had placed on the academic honors list in all four years.

In order to provide an incentive for the election of a meaningful non-academic sequence, those students whose achievement was outstanding in the courses that are usually labeled "commercial" or "vocational" should receive some special recognition. (p. 67)

RECOMMENDATION 16: DEVELOPMENTAL READING PROGRAM

A school should have the equipment for a developmental reading program. (p. 67)

RECOMMENDATION 17: SUMMER SCHOOL

The school board should operate a tuition-free summer school in which courses are available not only for students who have to repeat a subject, but also for the bright and ambitious students who wish to use the summer to broaden the scope of their elective programs. (p. 68)

RECOMMENDATION 18: FOREIGN LANGUAGES

The school board should be ready to offer a third and fourth year of a foreign language, no matter how few students enroll. (p. 69)

RECOMMENDATION 19: SCIENCE COURSES

All students should obtain some understanding of the nature of science and the scientific approach by a required course in physical science or biology. This course should be given in at least three sections grouped by ability. (p. 73)

RECOMMENDATION 20: HOMEROOMS

For the purpose of developing an understanding between students of different levels of academic ability and vocational goals, homerooms should be organized in such a way as to make them significant social units in the school. (p. 74)

RECOMMENDATION 21: TWELFTH-GRADE SOCIAL STUDIES

In the twelfth grade a course on American problems or American government should be required. (p. 75)

THE SMALL HIGH SCHOOL

The enrollment of many American public high schools is too small to allow a diversified curriculum except at exorbitant expenses. The prevalence of such high schools—those with graduating classes of less than one hundred students—constitutes one of the serious obstacles to good secondary education throughout most of the United States. I believe such schools are not in a position to provide a satisfactory education for any group of their students—the academically talented, the vocationally oriented, or the slow reader. (p. 77)

DISCUSSION QUESTIONS

1. Do you agree with Conant's objectives for a comprehensive high school, in view of the goals that you would set for our democratic society?
2. Are Conant's objectives stated clearly enough to furnish a workable guide?
3. Would Conant's program fulfill his objectives?
4. Do you believe that Conant's program would promote intergroup understanding and fluidity?

MARTIN BUBER The Education of Character

I

Education worthy of the name is essentially education of character. For the genuine educator does not merely consider individual functions of his pupil, as one intending to teach him only to know or be capable of certain definite things; but this concern is always the person as a whole, both in the actuality in which he lives before you now and in his possibilities, what he can become. But in this way, as a whole in reality and potentiality, a man can be conceived either as personality, that is, as a unique spiritual-physical form with all the forces dormant in it, or as character, that is, as the link between what this individual is and the sequence of his actions and attitudes. Between these two modes of conceiving the pupil in his wholeness there is a fundamental difference. Personality is something which in its growth remains essentially outside the influence of the educator; but to assist in the moulding of character is his greatest task. Personality is a completion, only character is a task. One may cultivate and enhance personality, but in education one can and one must aim at character.

However—as I would like to point out straightaway—it is advisable not to over-estimate what the educator can even at best do to develop character. In this more than in any other branch of the science of teaching it is important to realize, at the very beginning of the discussion, the fundamental limits to conscious influence, even before asking what character is and how it is to be brought about.

If I have to teach algebra I can expect to succeed in giving my pupils an idea of quadratic equations with two unknown quantities. Even the slowest-witted child will understand it so well that he will amuse himself by solving equations at night when he cannot fall asleep. And even one with the most sluggish memory will not forget, in his old age, how to play with x and y. But if I am concerned with the education of character, everything becomes problematic. I try to explain to my pupils that envy is despicable, and at once I feel the secret resistance of those who are poorer than their comrades. I try to explain that it is wicked to bully the weak, and at once I see a suppressed smile on the lips of the strong. I try to explain that lying destroys life, and something frightful happens: the worst habitual liar of the class produces a brilliant essay on the destructive power of lying. I have made the fatal mistake of giving instruction in ethics, and what I said is accepted as current coin of knowledge; nothing of it is transformed into character-building substance.

But the difficulty lies still deeper. In all teaching of a subject I can announce my intention of teaching as openly as I please, and this does not interfere with the results. After all, pupils do want, for the most part, to learn something, even if not overmuch, so that a tacit agreement becomes possible. But as soon as my pupils notice that I want to educate their characters I am resisted precisely by those who show most signs of genuine independent character: they will not let themselves be educated, or rather, they do not like the idea that somebody wants to educate them. And those, too, who are seriously labouring over the question of good and evil, rebel when one dictates to them, as though it were some long established truth, what is good and what is bad; and they rebel just because they have experienced over and over again how hard it is to find the right way. Does it follow that one should keep silent about one's intention of educating character, and act by ruse and subterfuge? No; I have just said that the difficulty lies deeper. It is not enough to see that education of character is not introduced into a lesson in class; neither may one conceal it in cleverly arranged intervals. Education cannot tolerate such politic action. Even if the pupil does not notice the hidden motive it will have its negative effect on the actions of the teacher himself by depriving him of the directness which is his strength. Only in his whole being, in all his spontaneity can the educator truly affect the whole being of his pupil. For educating characters you do not need a moral genius, but you do need a man who is wholly alive and able to communicate himself directly to his fellow beings. His aliveness streams out to them and affects them most strongly and purely when he has no thought of affecting them.

The Greek word *character* means impression. The special link between man's being and his appearance, the special connexion between the unity of what he is and the sequence of his actions and attitudes is impressed on his still plastic substance. Who does the impressing? Everything does: nature and the social context, the house and the street, language and custom, the world of history and the world of daily news in the form of rumors, of broadcast and newspaper, music and technical science, play and dream—everything together. Many of these factors exert their influence by stimulating agreements, imitation, desire, effort; others by arousing questions, doubts, dislike, resistance. Character is formed by the interpenetration of all those multifarious, opposing influences. And yet, among this infinity of form-giving forces the educator is only one element among innumerable others, but distinct from them all by his will to take part in the stamping of character and by his consciousness that he represents in the eyes of the growing person a certain selection of what is, the selection of what is "right," of what should be. It is in this will and this consciousness that his vocation as an educator finds its fundamental expression. From this the genuine educator gains two things: first, humility, the feeling of being only one element amidst the fullness of life; only one single existence in the midst of all the tremendous inrush of reality on the pupil; but secondly, self-awareness, the feeling of being therein the only existence that wants to affect the whole person, and thus the feeling of responsibility for the selection of reality which he represents to the pupil. And a third thing emerges from all this, the recognition that in this realm of the education of character, of wholeness, there is only one access to the pupil: his confidence. For the adolescent who is frightened and disappointed by an unreliable world, confidence means the liberating insight that there is human truth, the truth of human existence. When the pupil's confidence has been won, his resistance against being educated gives way to a singular happening: he accepts the educator as a person. He feels he may trust this man, that this man is not making a business out of him, but is taking part in his life, accepting him before desiring to influence him. And so he learns to ask.

The teacher who is for the first time approached by a boy with somewhat defiant bearing, but with trembling hands, visibly opened-up and fired by a daring hope, who asks him what is the right thing in a certain situation—for instance, whether in learning that a friend has betrayed a secret entrusted to him one should call him to account or be content with entrusting no more secrets to him—the teacher to whom this happens realizes that this is the moment to make the first conscious step towards education of character; he has to answer, to answer under a responsibility, to give an answer which will probably lead beyond the alternatives of the question by showing a third possibility which is the right one. To dictate what is good and evil in general is not his business. His business is to answer a concrete question, to answer what is right and wrong in a given situation. This, as I have said, can only happen in an atmosphere of confidence. Confidence, of course, is not won by the strenuous endeavour to win it, but by direct and ingenuous participation in the life of the people one is dealing with—in this case in the life of one's pupils—and by assuming the responsibility which arises from such participation. It is not the educational intention but it is the meeting which is educationally fruitful. A soul suffering from the contradictions of the world of human society, and of its own physical existence, approaches me with a question. By trying to answer it to the best of my knowledge and conscience I help it to become a character that actively overcomes the contradictions.

If this is the teacher's standpoint towards his pupil, taking part in his life and conscious of responsibility, then everything that passes between them can, without any deliberate or politic intention, open a way to the education of character: lessons and games, a conversation about quarrels in the class, or about the problems of a world-war. Only, the teacher must not forget the limits of education; even when he enjoys confidence he cannot always expect agreement. Confidence implies a break-through from reserve, the bursting of the bonds which imprison an unquiet heart. But it does not imply unconditional agreement. The teacher must never forget that conflicts too, if only they are decided in a healthy atmosphere, have an educational value. A conflict with a pupil is the supreme test for the educator. He must use his own insight wholeheartedly; he must not blunt the piercing impact of his knowledge, but he must at the same time have in readiness the healing ointment for the heart pierced by it. Not for a moment may he conduct a dialectical manoeuvre instead of the real battle for truth. But if he is the victor he has to help the vanquished to endure defeat; and if he cannot conquer the self-willed soul that faces him (for victories over souls are not so easily won), then he has to find the word of love which alone can help to overcome so difficult a situation.

II

So far I have referred to those personal difficulties in the education of character which arise from the relation between educator and pupil, while for the moment treating character itself, the object of education, as a simple concept of fixed content. But it is by no means that. In order to penetrate to the real difficulties in the education of character we have to examine critically the concept of character itself.

Kerschensteiner in his well-known essay on *The Concept and Educa-*

tion of Character distinguished between "character in the most general sense," by which he means "a man's attitude to his human surroundings, which is constant and is expressed in his actions," and real "ethical character," which he defines as "a special attitude, and one which in action gives the preference before all others to absolute values." If we begin by accepting this distinction unreservedly—and undeniably there is some truth in it—we are faced with such heavy odds in all education of character in our time that the very possibility of it seems doubtful.

The "absolute values" which Kerschensteiner refers to cannot, of course, be meant to have only subjective validity for the person concerned. Don Juan finds absolute and subjective value in seducing the greatest possible number of women, and the dictator sees it in the greatest possible accumulation of power. "Absolute validity" can only relate to universal values and norms, the existence of which the person concerned recognizes and acknowledges. But to deny the presence of universal values and norms of absolute validity—that is the conspicuous tendency of our age. This tendency is not, as is sometimes supposed, directed merely against the sanctioning of the norms by religion, but against their universal character and absolute validity, against their claim to be a higher order than man and to govern the whole of mankind. In our age values and norms are not permitted to be anything but expressions of the life of a group which translates its own needs into the language of objective claims, until at last the group itself, for example a nation, is raised to an absolute value—and moreover to the only value. Then this splitting up into groups so pervades the whole of life that it is no longer possible to re-establish a sphere of values common to a mankind, and a commandment to mankind is no longer observed. As this tendency grows the basis for the development of what Kerschensteiner means by moral character steadily diminishes. How, under these circumstances, can the task of educating character be completed?

At the time of the Arab terror in Palestine, when there were single Jewish acts of reprisal, there must have been many discussions between teacher and pupils on the question: Can there be any suspension of the Ten Commandments, i.e. can murder become a good deed if committed in the interest of one's own group? One such discussion was once repeated to me. The teacher asked, "When the commandment tells you 'Thou shalt not bear false witness against thy neighbour,' are we to interpret it with the condition, 'provided that it does not profit you'?" Thereupon one of the pupils said, "But it is not a question of my profit, but of the profit of my people." The teacher: "And how would you like it, then, if we put our condition this way: 'Provided that it does not profit your family'?" The pupil: "But family—that is still something more or less like myself; but the people—that is something quite different; there all question of I disappears." The teacher: "Then if you are thinking, 'we want victory,' don't you feel at the same time, 'I want victory'?" The pupil: "But the people, that is something infinitely more than just the people of to-day. It includes all past and future generations." At this point the teacher felt the moment had come to leave the narrow compass of the present and to invoke historical destiny. He said: "Yes, all past generations. But what was it that made those past generations of the Exile live? What made them outlive and overcome all their trials? Wasn't it that the cry 'Thou shalt not' never faded from their hearts and ears?" The pupil grew very pale. He was silent for a while, but it was the silence of one whose words threatened to stifle him. Then be burst out: "And what have we achieved that way? This!" And he banged his fist on the newspaper before him, which contained the report on the British White Paper. And again he burst out with "Live? Outlive? Do you call that life? We want to live!"

I have already said that the test of the educator lies in conflict with his pupil. He has to face this conflict and, whatever turn it may take, he has to find the way through it into life, into a life, I must add, where confidence continues unshaken—more, is even mysteriously strengthened. But the example I have just given shows the extreme difficulty of this task, which seems at times to have reached an impassable frontier. This is no longer merely a conflict between two generations, but between a world which for several millennia has believed in a truth superior to man, and an age which does not believe in it any longer—will not or cannot believe in it any longer.

But if we now ask, "How in this situation can there be any education of character?" something negative is immediately obvious: it is senseless to want to prove by any kind of argument that nevertheless the denied absoluteness of norms exists. That would be to assume that the denial is the result of reflection, and is open to argument, that is, to material for renewed reflection. But the denial is due to the disposition of a dominant human type of our age. We are justified in regarding this disposition as a sickness of the human race. But we must not deceive ourselves by believing that the disease can be cured by formulae which assert that nothing is really as the person imagines. It is an idle undertaking to call out, to a mankind that has grown blind to eternity: "Look! the eternal values!" To-day host upon host of men have everywhere sunk into the slavery of collectives, and each collective is the supreme authority for its own slaves; there is no longer, superior to the collectives any universal sovereignty in idea, faith, or spirit. Against the values, decrees and decisions of the collective no appeal is possible. This is true, not only for the totalitarian countries, but also for the parties and party-like groups in the so-called democracies. Men who have so lost themselves to the collective Moloch cannot be rescued from it by any reference, however eloquent, to the absolute whose kingdom the Moloch has usurped. One has to begin by pointing to that sphere where man himself, in the hours of utter solitude, occasionally becomes aware of the disease through sudden pain: by pointing to the relation of the individual to his own self. In order to enter into a personal relation with the absolute, it is first necessary to be a person again, to rescue one's real personal self from the fiery jaws of collectivism which devours all selfhood. The desire to do this is latent in the pain the individual suffers through his distorted relation to his own self. Again and again he dulls the pain with a subtle poison and thus suppresses the desire as well. To keep the pain awake, to waken the desire—that is the first task of everyone who regrets the obscuring of eternity. It is also the first task of the genuine educator in our time.

The man for whom absolute values in a universal sense do not exist cannot be made to adopt "an attitude which in action gives the preference over all others to absolute values." But what one can inculcate in him is the desire to attain once more to a real attitude, and that is, the desire to become a person following the only way that leads to this goal to-day.

But with this the concept of character formulated by Kerschensteiner and deriving, as we know, from Kant is recognized to be useless for the specifically modern task of the education of character. Another concept has to be found if this task is to be more precisely defined.

We cannot conceal from ourselves that we stand to-day on the ruins of the edifice whose towers were raised by Kant. It is not given to us living to-day to sketch the plan for a new building. But we can perhaps begin by laying the first foundation without a plan, with only a dawning image before our mind's eye.

According to Kerschensteiner's final definition character is "fundamentally nothing but voluntary obedience to the maxims which have been moulded in the individual by experience, teaching, and self-reflection, whether they have been adopted and then completely assimilated or have originated in the consciousness through self-legislation." This voluntary obedience "is, however, only a form of self-control." At first, love or fear of other people must have produced in man "the habit of self-conquest." Then, gradually, "this outer obedience must be transformed into inner obedience."

The concept of habit was then enlarged, especially by John Dewey in his book, *Human Nature and Conduct*. According to him character is "the interpenetration of habits." Without "the continued operation of all habits in every act" there would be no unified character, but only "a juxtaposition of disconnected reactions to separated situations."

With this concept of character as an organization of self-control by means of the accumulation of maxims, or as a system of interpenetrating habits, it is very easy to understand how powerless modern educational science is when faced by the sickness of man. But even apart from the special problems of the age, this concept can be no adequate basis for the construction of a genuine education of character. Not that the educator could dispense with employing useful maxims of furthering good habits. But in moments that come perhaps only seldom, a feeling of blessed achievement links him to the explorer, the inventor, the artist, a feeling of sharing in the revelation of what is hidden. In such moments he finds himself in a sphere very different from that of maxims and habits. Only on this, the highest plane of his activity, can he fix his real concept of character which is his concern, even though he might not often reach it.

For the first time a young teacher enters a class independently, no longer sent by the training college to prove his efficiency. The class before him is like a mirror of mankind, so multiform, so full of contradictions, so inaccessible. He feels "These boys—I have not sought them out; I have been put here and have to accept them as they are—but not as they now are in this moment, no, as they really are, as they can become. But how can I find out what is in them and what can I do to make it take shape?" And the boys do not make things easy for him. They are noisy, they cause trouble, they stare at him with impudent curiosity. He is at once tempted to check this or that trouble-maker, to issue orders, to make compulsory the rules of decent behaviour, to say No, to say No to everything rising against him from beneath: he is at once tempted to start from beneath. And if one starts from beneath one perhaps never arrives above, but everything comes down. But then his eyes meet a face which strikes him. It is not a beautiful face nor particularly intelligent; but it is a real face, or rather, the chaos preceding the cosmos of a real face. On it he reads a question which is something different from the general curiosity: "Who are you? Do you know something that concerns me? Do you bring me something? What do you bring?"

In some such way he reads the question. And he, the young teacher, addresses this face. He says nothing very ponderous or important, he puts an ordinary introductory question: "What did you talk about last in geography? The Dead Sea? Well, what about the Dead Sea?" But there was obviously something not quite usual in the question, for the answer he gets is not the ordinary schoolboy answer; the boy begins to tell a story. Some months earlier he had stayed for a few hours on the shores of the Dead Sea and it is of this he tells. He adds: "And everything looked to me as if it had been created a day before the rest of creation." Quite unmistakably he had only in this moment made up his mind to talk about it. In the meantime his face has changed. It is no longer quite as chaotic as before. And the class has fallen silent. They all listen. The class, too, is no longer a chaos. Something has happened. The young teacher has started from above.

The educator's task can certainly not consist in educating great characters. He cannot select his pupils, but year by year the world, such as it is, is sent in the form of a school class to meet him on his life's way as his destiny; and in this destiny lies the very meaning of his life's work. He has to introduce discipline and order, he has to establish a law, and he can only strive and hope for the result that discipline and order will become more and more inward and autonomous, and that at last the law will be written in the heart of his pupils. But this real goal which, once he has well recognized it and well remembers it, will influence all his work, is the great character.

The great character can be conceived neither as a system of maxims nor as a system of habits. It is peculiar to him to act from the whole of his substance. That is, it is peculiar to him to react in accordance with the uniqueness of every situation which challenges him as an active person. Of course there are all sorts of similarities in different situations; one can construct types of situations, one can always find to what section the particular situation belongs, and draw what is appropriate from the hoard of established maxims and habits, apply the appropriate maxim, bring into operation the appropriate habit. But what is untypical in the particular situation remain unnoticed and unanswered. To me that seems the same as if, having ascertained the sex of a new-born child, one were immediately to establish its type as well, and put all the children of one type into a common cradle on which not the individual name but the name of the type was inscribed. In spite of all similarities every living situation has, like a new-born child, a new face, that has never been before and will never come again. It demands of you a reaction which cannot be prepared beforehand. It demands nothing of what is past. It demands presence, responsibility; it demands you. I call a great character one who by his actions and attitudes satisfies the claim of situations out of deep readiness to respond with his whole life, and in such a way that the sum of his actions and attitudes expresses at the same time the unity of his being in its willingness to accept responsibility. As his being unity, the unity of accepted responsibility, his active life, too, coheres into unity. And one might perhaps say that for him there rises a unity out of the situations he has responded to in responsibility, the indefinable unity of a moral destiny.

All this does not mean that the great character is beyond the acceptance of norms. No responsible person remains a stranger to norms. But the command inherent in a genuine norm never becomes a maxim and the fulfilment of it never a habit. Any command that a great character takes to himself in the course of his development does not act in him as part of his consciousness or as material for building up his exercises, but remains latent in a basic layer of his substance until it reveals itself to him in a concrete way. What it has to tell him is revealed whenever a situation arises which demands of him a solution of which till then he had perhaps no idea. Even the most universal norm will at times be recognized only in a very special situation. I know of a man whose heart was struck by the lightning flash of "Thou shalt not steal" in the very moment when he was moved by a very different desire from that of stealing, and whose heart was so struck by it that he not only abandoned doing what he wanted to do, but with the whole force of his passion did the very opposite. Good and evil are not each other's opposites like right and left. The evil approaches us as a whirlwind, the good as a direction. There is a direction, a "yes," a command, hidden even in a prohibition, which is revealed to us in moments like these. In moments like these the command addresses us really in the second person, and the Thou in it is no one else but one's own self. Maxims command only the third person, the each and the none.

One can say that it is the unconditioned nature of the address which distinguishes the command from the maxim. In an age which has become deaf to unconditioned address we cannot overcome the dilemma of the education of character from that angle. But insight into the structure of great character can help us to overcome it.

Of course, it may be asked whether the educator should really start "from above," whether, in fixing his goal, the hope of finding a great character, who is bound to be the exception, should be his starting-point; for in his methods of educating character he will always have to take into consideration the others, the many. To this I reply that the educator would not have the right to do so if a method inapplicable to these others were to result. In fact, however, his very insight into the structure of a great character helps him to find the way by which alone (as I have indicated) he can begin to influence also the victims of the collective Moloch, pointing out to them the sphere in which they themselves suffer—namely, their relation to their own selves. From this sphere he must elicit the values which he can make credible and desirable to his pupils. That is what insight into the structure of a great character helps him to do.

A section of the young is beginning to feel today that, because of their absorption by the collective, something important and irreplaceable is lost to them—personal responsibility for life and the world. These young people, it is true, do not yet realize that their blind devotion to the collective, e.g. to a party, was not a genuine act of their personal life; they do not realize that it sprang, rather, from the fear of being left, in this age of confusion, to rely on themselves, on a self which no longer receives its direction from eternal values. Thus they do not yet realize that their devotion was fed on the unconscious desire to have responsibility removed from them by an authority in which they believe or want to believe. They do not yet realize that this devotion was an escape. I repeat, the young people I am speaking of do not yet realize this. But they are beginning to notice that he who no longer, with his whole being, decides what he does or does not, and assumes responsibility for it, becomes sterile in soul. And a sterile soul soon ceases to be a soul.

This is where the educator can begin and should begin. He can help the feeling that something is lacking to grow into the clarity of consciousness and into the force of desire. He can awaken in young people the courage to shoulder life again. He can bring before his pupils the image of a great character who denies no answer to life and the world, but accepts responsibility for everything essential that he meets. He can show his pupils this image without the fear that those among them who most of all need discipline and order will drift into a craving for aimless freedom: on the contrary, he can teach them in this way to recognize that discipline and order too are starting-points on the way towards self-responsibility. He can show that even the great character is not born perfect, that the unity of his being has first to mature before expressing itself in the sequence of his actions and attitudes. But unity itself, unity of the person, unity of the lived life, has to be emphasized again and again. The confusing contradictions cannot be remedied by the collectives, not one of which knows the taste of genuine unity and which if left to themselves would end up, like the scorpions imprisoned in a box, in the witty fable, by devouring one another. This mass of contradictions can be met and conquered only by the rebirth of personal unity, unity of being, unity of life, unity of action—unity of being, life and action together. This does not mean a static unity of the uniform, but the great dynamic unity of the multiform in which multiformity is formed into unity of character. Today the great characters are still "enemies of the people," they who love their society, yet wish not only to preserve it but to raise it to a higher level. To-morrow they will be the architects of a new unity of mankind. It is the longing for personal unity, from which must be born a unity of mankind, which the educator should lay hold of and strengthen in his pupils. Faith in this unity and the will to achieve it is not a "return" to individualism and collectivism. A great and full relation between man and man can only exist between unified and responsible persons. That is why it is much more rarely found in the totalitarian collective than in any historically earlier form of society; much more rarely also in the authoritarian party than in any earlier form of free association. Genuine education of character is genuine education for community.

In a generation which has had this kind of upbringing the desire will also be kindled to behold again the eternal values, to hear again the language of the eternal norm. He who knows inner unity, the innermost life of which is mystery, learns to honour the mystery in all its forms. In an understandable reaction against the former domination of a false, fictitious mystery, the present generations are obsessed with the desire to rob life of all its mystery. The fictitious mystery will disappear, the genuine one will rise again. A generation which honours the mystery in all its forms will no longer be deserted by eternity. Its light seems darkened only because the eye suffers from a cataract; the receiver has been turned off, but the resounding ether has not ceased to vibrate. To-day, indeed, in the hour of upheaval, the eternal is sifted from the pseudo-eternal. That which flashed into the primal radiance and blurred the primal sound will be extinguished and silenced, for it has failed before the horror of the new confusion and the questioning soul has unmasked its futility. Nothing remains but what rises above the abyss of today's monstrous problems, as above every abyss of every time: the wing-beat of the spirit and the creative word. But he who can see and hear out of unity will also behold and discern again what can be beheld and discerned eternally. The educator who helps to bring man back to his own unity will help to put him again face to face with God.

DISCUSSION QUESTIONS

1. What is Buber's definition of "character"? How does this differ from the "character" with which the schools are concerned?
2. Does the concept of mass education, with the establishment of norms and the mechanization of learning, make possible the development of character that Buber sees as the main goal of education?
3. To what "universals of idea, faith, and spirit" do the members of our society subscribe? For which of these are we prepared to die?

JOHN DEWEY Education as Growth

THE CONDITIONS OF GROWTH

In directing the activities of the young, society determines its own future in determining that of the young. Since the young at a given time will at some later date compose the society of that period, the latter's nature will largely turn upon the direction children's activities were given at an earlier period. This cumulative movement of action toward a later result is what is meant by growth.

The primary condition of growth is immaturity. This may seem to be a mere truism—saying that a being can develop only in some point in

Reprinted with permission of The Macmillan Company from *Democracy and Education* by John Dewey. Copyright 1916 by The Macmillan Company, renewed 1944 by John Dewey.

which he is undeveloped. But the prefix "im" of the word immaturity means something positive, not a mere void or lack. It is noteworthy that the terms "capacity" and "potentiality" have a double meaning, one sense being negative, the other positive. Capacity may denote mere receptivity, like the capacity of a quart measure. We may mean by potentiality a merely dormant or quiescent state —a capacity to become something different under external influences. But we also mean by capacity an ability, a power; and by potentiality potency, force. Now when we say that immaturity means the possibility of growth, we are not referring to absence of powers which may exist at a later time; we express a force positively present—the *ability* to develop.

Our tendency to take immaturity as mere lack, and growth as something which fills up the gap between the immature and the mature is due to regarding childhood *comparatively*, instead of intrinsically. We treat it simply as a privation because we are measuring it by adulthood as a fixed standard. This fixes attention upon what the child has not, and will not have till he becomes a man. This comparative standpoint is legitimate enough for some purposes, but if we make it final, the question arises whether we are not guilty of an overweening presumption. Children, if they could express themselves articulately and sincerely, would tell a different tale; and there is excellent adult authority for the conviction that for certain moral and intellectual purposes adults must become as little children.

The seriousness of the assumption of the negative quality of the possibilities of immaturity is apparent when we reflect that it sets up as an ideal and standard a static end. The fulfillment of growing is taken to mean an *accomplished* growth: that is to say, an Ungrowth, something which is no longer growing. The futility of the assumption is seen in the fact that every adult resents the imputation of having no further possibilities of growth; and so far as he finds that they are closed to him mourns the fact as evidence of loss, instead of falling back on the achieved as adequate manifestation of power. Why an unequal measure for child and man?

Taken absolutely, instead of comparatively, immaturity designates a positive force or ability—the *power* to grow. We do not have to draw out or educe positive activities from a child, as some educational doctrines would have it. Where there is life, there are already eager and impassioned activities. Growth is not something done to them; it is something they do. The positive and constructive aspect of possibility gives the key to understanding the two chief traits of immaturity, dependence and plasticity. (1) It sounds absurd to hear dependence spoken of as something positive, still more absurd as a power. Yet if helplessness were all there were in dependence, no development could ever take place. A merely impotent being has to be carried, forever, by others. The fact that dependence is accompanied by growth in ability, not by an ever increasing lapse into parasitism, suggests that it is already something constructive. Being merely sheltered by others would not promote growth. For (2) it would only build a wall around impotence. With reference to the physical world, the child is helpless. He lacks at birth and for a long time thereafter power to make his way physically, to make his own living. If he had to do that by himself, he would hardly survive an hour. On this side his helplessness is almost complete. The young of the brutes are immeasurably his superiors. He is physically weak and not able to turn the strength which he possesses to coping with the physical environment.

1. The thoroughgoing character of this helplessness suggests, however, some compensating power. The relative ability of the young of brute animals to adapt themselves fairly well to physical conditions from an early period suggests the fact that their life is not intimately bound up with the life of those about them. They are compelled, so to speak, to have physical gifts because they are lacking in social gifts. Human infants, on the other hand, can get along with physical incapacity just because of their social capacity. We sometimes talk and think as if they simply happened to be *physically* in a social environment; as if social forces exclusively existed in the adults who take care of them, they being passive recipients. If it were said that children are themselves marvelously endowed with *power* to enlist the coöperative attention of others, this would be thought to be a backhanded way of saying that others are marvelously attentive to the needs of children. But observation shows that children are gifted with an equipment of the first order for social intercourse. Few grown-up persons retain all of the flexible and sensitive ability of children to vibrate sympathetically with the attitudes and doings of those about them. Inattention to physical things (going with incapacity to control them) is accompanied by a corresponding intensification of interest and attention as to the doings of people. The native mechanism of the child and his impulses all tend to facile social responsiveness. The statement that children, before adolescence, are egotistically self-centered, even if it were true, would not contradict the truth of this statement. It would simply indicate that their social responsiveness is employed on their own behalf, not that it does not exist. But the statement is not true as matter of fact. The facts which are cited in support of the alleged pure egoism of children really show the intensity and directness with which they go to their mark. If the ends which form the mark seem narrow and selfish to adults, it is only because adults (by means of a similar engrossment in their day) have mastered these ends, which have consequently ceased to interest them. Most of the remainder of children's alleged native egoism is simply an egoism which runs counter to an adult's egoism. To a grown-up person who is too absorbed in his own affairs to take an interest in children's

affairs, children doubtless seem unreasonably engrossed in *their* own affairs.

From a social standpoint, dependence denotes a power rather than a weakness; it involves interdependence. There is always a danger that increased personal independence will decrease the social capacity of an individual. In making him more self-reliant, it may make him more self-sufficient; it may lead to aloofness and indifference. It often makes an individual so insensitive in his relations to others as to develop an illusion of being really able to stand and act alone—an unnamed form of insanity which is responsible for a large part of the remediable suffering of the world.

2. The specific adaptability of an immature creature for growth constitutes his *plasticity*. This is something quite different from the plasticity of putty or wax. It is not a capacity to take on change of form in accord with external pressure. It lies near the pliable elasticity by which some persons take on the color of their surroundings while retaining their own bent. But it is something deeper than this. It is essentially the ability to learn from experience; the power to retain from one experience something which is of avail in coping with the difficulties of a later situation. This means power to modify actions on the basis of the results of prior experiences, the power to *develop dispositions*. Without it, the acquisition of habits is impossible.

It is a familiar fact that the young of the higher animals, and especially the human young, have to *learn* to utilize their instinctive reactions. The human being is born with a greater number of instinctive tendencies than other animals. But the instincts of the lower animals prefect themselves for appropriate action at an early period after birth, while most of those of the human infant are of little account just as they stand. An original specialized power of adjustment secures immediate efficiency, but, like a railway ticket, it is good for one route only. A being who, in order to use his eyes, ears, hands, and legs, has to experiment in making varied combinations of their reactions, achieves a control that is flexible and varied. A chick, for example, pecks accurately at a bit of food in a few hours after hatching. This means that definite coördinations of activities of the eyes in seeing and of the body and head in striking are perfected in a few trials. An infant requires about six months to be able to gauge with approximate accuracy the action in reaching which will coordinate with his visual activities; to be able, that is, to tell whether he can reach a seen object and just how to execute the reaching. As a result, the chick is limited by the relative perfection of its original endowment. The infant has the advantage of the *multitude* of instinctive tentative reactions and of the experiences that accompany them, even though he is at a temporary disadvantage because they cross one another. In learning an action, instead of having it given readymade, one of necessity learns to vary its factors, to make varied combinations of them, according to change of circumstances. A possibility of continuing progress is opened up by the fact that in learning one act, methods are developed good for use in other situations. Still more important is the fact that the human being acquires a habit of learning. He learns to learn.

The importance for human life of the two facts of dependence and variable control has been summed up in the doctrine of the significance of prolonged infancy.[1] This prolongation is significant from the standpoint of the adult members of the group as well as from that of the young. The presence of dependent and learning beings is a stimulus to nurture and affection. The need for constant continued care was probably a chief means in transforming temporary cohabitations into permanent unions. It certainly was a chief influence in forming habits of affectionate and sympathetic watchfulness; that constructive interest in the well-being of others which is essential to associated life. Intellectually, this moral development meant the introduction of many new objects of attention; it stimulated foresight and planning for the future. Thus there is a reciprocal influence. Increasing complexity of social life requires a longer period of infancy in which to acquire the needed powers; this prolongation of dependence means prolongation of plasticity, or power of acquiring variable and novel modes of control. Hence it provides a further push to social progress.

HABITS AS EXPRESSIONS OF GROWTH

We have already noted that plasticity is the capacity to retain and carry over from prior experience factors which modify subsequent activities. This signifies the capacity to acquire habits, or develop definite dispositions. We have now to consider the salient features of habits. In the first place, a habit is a form of executive skill, of efficiency in doing. A habit means an ability to use natural conditions as means to ends. It is an active control of the environment through control of the organs of action. We are perhaps apt to emphasize the control of the body at the expense of control of the environment. We think of walking, talking, playing the piano, the specialized skills characteristics of the etcher, the surgeon, the bridge-builder, as if they were simply ease, deftness, and accuracy on the part of the organism. They are that, of course; but the measure of the value of these qualities lies in the economical and effective control of the environment which they secure. To be able to walk is to have certain properties of nature at our disposal—and so with all other habits.

Education is not infrequently defined as consisting in the acquisition of those habits that effect an adjustment of an individual and his environment. The definition expresses an essential phase of growth. But it

[1] Intimations of its significance are found in a number of writers, but John Fiske, in his *Excursions of an Evolutionist*, is accredited with its first systematic exposition.

is essential that adjustment be understood in its active sense of *control* of means for achieving ends. If we think of a habit simply as a change wrought in the organism, ignoring the fact that this change consists in ability to effect subsequent changes in the environment, we shall be led to think of "adjustment" as a conformity to environment as wax conforms to the seal which impresses it. The environment is thought of as something fixed, providing in its fixity the end and standard of changes taking place in the organism; adjustment is just fitting ourselves to this fixity of external conditions.[2] Habit as *habituation* is indeed something *relatively* passive; we get used to our surroundings—to our clothing, our shoes, and gloves; to the atmosphere as long as it is fairly equable; to our daily associates, etc. Conformity to the environment, a change wrought in the organism without reference to ability to modify surroundings, is a marked trait of such habituations. Aside from the fact that we are not entitled to carry over the traits of such adjustments (which might well be called *accommodations*, to mark them off from active adjustments) into habits of active use of our surroundings, two features of habituations are worth notice. In the first place, we get used to things by *first* using them.

Consider getting used to a strange city. At first, there is excessive stimulation and excessive and ill-adapted response. Gradually certain stimuli are selected because of their relevancy, and others are degraded. We can say either that we do not respond to them any longer, or more truly that we have effected a persistent response to them—an equilibrium of adjustment. This means, in the second place, that this enduring adjustment supplies the background upon which are made specific adjustments, as occasion arises. We are never interested in changing the *whole* environment; there is much that we take for granted and accept just as it already is. Upon this background our activities focus at certain points in an endeavor to introduce needed changes. Habituation is thus our adjustment to an environment which at the time we are not concerned with modifying, and which supplies a leverage to our active habits.

Adaptation, in fine, is quite as much adaptation *of* the environment to our own activities as of our activities *to* the environment. A savage tribe manages to live on a desert plain. It adapts itself. But its adaptation involves a maximum of accepting, tolerating, putting up with things as they are, a maximum of passive acquiescence, and a minimum of active control, of subjection to use. A civilized people enters upon the scene. It also adapts itself. It introduces irrigation; it searches the world for plants and animals that will flourish under such conditions; it improves, by careful selection, those which are growing there. As a consequence,

[2] This conception is, of course, a logical correlate of the conceptions of the external relation of stimulus and response, and of the negative conceptions of immaturity and plasticity noted in this chapter.

the wilderness blossoms as a rose. The savage is merely habituated; the civilized man has habits which transform the environment.

The significance of habit is not exhausted, however, in its executive and motor phase. It means formation of intellectual and emotional disposition as well as an increase in ease, economy, and efficiency of action. Any habit marks an *inclination*—an active preference and choice for the conditions involved in its exercise. A habit does not wait, Macawber-like, for a stimulus to turn up so that it may get busy; it actively seeks for occasions to pass into full operation. If its expression is unduly blocked, inclination shows itself in uneasiness and intense craving. A habit also marks an intellectual disposition. Where there is a habit, there is acquaintance with the materials and equipment to which action is applied. There is a definite way of understanding the situations in which the habit operates. Modes of thought, of observation and reflection, enter as forms of skill and desire into the habits that make a man an engineer, an architect, a physician, or a merchant. In unskilled forms of labor, the intellectual factors are at minimum precisely because the habits involved are not of a high grade. But there are habits of judging and reasoning as truly as of handling a tool, painting a picture, or conducting an experiment.

Such statements are, however, understatements. The habits of mind involved in habits of the eye and hand supply the latter with their significance. Above all, the intellectual element in a habit fixes the relation of the habit to varied and elastic use, and hence to continued growth. We speak of *fixed* habits. Well, the phrase may mean powers so well established that their possessor always has them as resources when needed. But the phrase is also used to mean ruts, routine ways, with loss of freshness, openmindedness, and originality. Fixity of habit may mean that something has a fixed hold upon us, instead of our having a free hold upon things. This fact explains two points in a common notion about habits: their identification with mechanical and external modes of action to the neglect of mental and moral attitudes, and the tendency to give them a bad meaning, an identification with "bad habits." Many a person would feel surprised to have his aptitude in his chosen profession called a habit, and would naturally think of his use of tobacco, liquor, profane language as typical of the meaning of habit. A habit is to him something which has a hold on him, something not easily thrown off even though judgment condemn it.

Habits reduce themselves to routine ways of acting, or degenerate into ways of action to which we are enslaved just in the degree in which intelligence is disconnected from them. Routine habits are unthinking habits: "bad" habits are habits so severed from reason that they are opposed to the conclusions of conscious deliberation and decision. As we have seen, the acquiring of habits is due to an original plasticity of our natures: to our ability to vary responses till we find an appropriate and efficient way of acting. Routine habits, and habits that possess us instead of our possessing them, are habits which put an end to plasticity. They mark the close of power to vary. There can be no doubt of the tendency of organic plasticity, of the physiological basis, to lessen with growing years. The instinctively mobile and eagerly varying action of childhood, the love of new stimuli and new developments, too easily passes into a "settling down," which means aversion to change and a resting on past achievements. Only an environment which secures the full use of intelligence in the process of forming habits can counteract this tendency. Of course, the same hardening of the organic conditions affects the physiological structures which are involved in thinking. But this fact only indicates the need of persistent care to see to it that the function of intelligence is invoked to its maximum possibility. The short-sighted method which falls back on mechanical routine and repetition to secure external efficiency of habit, motor skill without accompanying thought, marks a deliberate closing in of surroundings upon growth.

THE EDUCATIONAL BEARINGS OF THE CONCEPTION OF DEVELOPMENT

We have had so far but little to say in this chapter about education. We have been occupied with the conditions and implications of growth. If our conclusions are justified, they carry with them, however, definite educational consequences. When it is said that education is development, everything depends upon *how* development is conceived. Our net conclusion is that life is development, and that developing, growing, is life. Translated into its educational equivalents, that means (*i*) that the educational process has no end beyond itself; it is its own end; and that (*ii*) the educational process is one of continual reorganizing, reconstructing, transforming.

1. Development when it is interpreted in *comparative* terms, that is, with respect to the special traits of child and adult life, means the direction of power into special channels: the formation of habits involving executive skill, definiteness of interest, and specific objects of observation and thought. But the comparative view is not final. The child has specific powers; to ignore that fact is to stunt or distort the organs upon which his growth depends. The adult uses his powers to transform his environment, thereby occasioning new stimuli which redirect his powers and keep them developing. Ignoring this fact means arrested development, a passive accommodation. Normal child and normal adult alike, in other words, are engaged in growing. The difference between them is not the difference between growth and no growth, but between the modes of growth appropriate to different conditions. With respect to the development of powers devoted to coping with specific scientific and

economic problems we may say the child should be growing in manhood. With respect to sympathetic curiosity, unbiased responsiveness, and openness of mind, we may say that the adult should be growing in childlikeness. One statement is as true as the other.

Three ideas which have been criticized, namely, the merely privative nature of immaturity, static adjustment to a fixed environment, and rigidity of habit, are all connected with a false idea of growth or development—that it is a movement toward a fixed goal. Growth is regarded as *having* an end, instead of *being* an end. The educational counterparts of the three fallacious ideas are first, failure to take account of the instinctive or native powers of the young; secondly, failure to develop initiative in coping with novel situations; thirdly, an undue emphasis upon drill and other devices which secure automatic skill at the expense of personal perception. In all cases, the adult environment is accepted as a standard for the child. He is to be brought up *to* it.

Natural instincts are either disregarded or treated as nuisances—as obnoxious traits to be suppressed, or at all events to be brought into conformity with external standards. Since conformity is the aim, what is distinctively individual in a young person is brushed aside, or regarded as a source of mischief or anarchy. Conformity is made equivalent to uniformity. Consequently, there are induced lack of interest in the novel, aversion to progress, and dread of the uncertain and the unknown. Since the end of growth is outside of and beyond the process of growing, external agents have to be resorted to to induce movement toward it. Whenever a method of education is stigmatized as mechanical, we may be sure that external pressure is brought to bear to reach an external end.

2. Since in reality there is nothing to which growth is relative save more growth, there is nothing to which education is subordinate save more education. It is a commonplace to say that education should not cease when one leaves school. The point of this commonplace is that the purpose of school education is to insure the continuance of education by organizing the powers that insure growth. The inclination to learn from life itself and to make the conditions of life such that all will learn in the process of living is the finest product of schooling.

When we abandon the attempt to define immaturity by means of fixed comparison with adult accomplishments, we are compelled to give up thinking of it as denoting lack of desired traits. Abandoning this notion, we are also forced to surrender our habit of thinking of instruction as a method of supplying this lack by pouring knowledge into a mental and moral hole which awaits filling. Since life means growth, a living creature lives as truly and positively at one stage as at another, with the same intrinsic fullness and the same absolute claims. Hence education means the enterprise of supplying the conditions which insure growth, or adequacy of life, irrespective of age. We first look with impatience upon immaturity, regarding it as something to be got over as rapidly as possible. Then the adult formed by such educative methods looks back with impatient regret upon childhood and youth as a scene of lost opportunities and wasted powers. This ironical situation will endure till it is recognized that living has its own intrinsic quality and that the business of education is with that quality.

Realization that life is growth protects us from that so-called idealizing of childhood which in effect is nothing but lazy indulgence. Life is not to be identified with every superficial act and interest. Even though it is not always easy to tell whether what appears to be mere surface fooling is a sign of some nascent as yet untrained power, we must remember that manifestations are not to be accepted as ends in themselves. They are signs of possible growth. They are to be turned into means of development, of carrying power forward, not indulged or cultivated for their own sake. Excessive attention to surface phenomena (even in the way of rebuke as well as of encouragement) may lead to their fixation and thus to arrested development. What impulses are moving toward, not what they have been, is the important thing for parent and teacher. The true principle of respect for immaturity cannot be better put than in the words of Emerson: "Respect the child. Be not too much his parent. Trespass not on his solitude. But I hear the outcry which replies to this suggestion: Would you verily throw up the reins of public and private discipline; would you leave the young child to the mad career of his own passions and whimsies, and call this anarchy a respect for the child's nature? I answer—Respect the child, respect him to the end, but also respect yourself. . . . The two points in a boy's training are, to keep his *naturel* and train off all but that; to keep his *naturel*, but stop off his uproar, fooling, and horseplay; keep his nature *and arm it with knowledge in the very direction in which it points*." And as Emerson goes on to show, this reverence for childhood and youth instead of opening up an easy and easy-going path to the instructors, "involves at once, immense claims on the time, the thought, on the life of the teacher. It requires time, use, insight, event, all the great lessons and assistances of God; and only to think of using it implies character and profoundness."

SUMMARY

Power to grow depends upon need for others and plasticity. Both of these conditions are at their height in childhood and youth. Plasticity or the power to learn from experience means the formation of habits. Habits give control over the environment, power to utilize it for human purposes. Habits take the form both of habituation, or a general and persistent balance of organic activities with the surroundings, and of active capacities to readjust activity to meet new conditions. The former furnishes the background of growth; the latter constitute growing. Active habits involve thought, invention, and initiative in applying capacities to new aims. They are opposed to routine which marks an arrest of growth. Since growth is the characteristic of life, education is all one with growing; it has no end beyond itself. The criterion of the value of school education is the extent in which it creates a desire for continued growth and supplies means for making the desire effective in fact.

DISCUSSION QUESTIONS

1. Evaluate your own childhood education against the criterion of Dewey's concept of "growth."
2. Is the concept of "growth" precise enough to furnish workable guidelines for a teacher?
3. Do modern innovations in education, such as programmed learning and teaching machines, fit into Dewey's definition of education?
4. Must mass education necessarily result in the kind of conformity that Dewey sees as antithetical to the development of "humanness"?
5. Is education its own end?

FRANZ WINKLER   The Three Dimensions of Reality

The plight of modern man, torn between materialistic thought habits and an innate spiritual longing, is at last finding growing recognition in sermons, appeals, and publications. Many eminent personalities, such as Toynbee, Myers, and Du Noüy have devoted their lives to proving that science and religion need not contradict each other. Much has been achieved, and yet the general trend toward materialism, with all its dire consequences, is still gaining, and drawing additional strength from many and varied sources. There are powerful political interests determined to further their own objectives by making use of man's unfulfilled spiritual longing; there are well-intended but confusing philosophical doctrines hiding errors in logic behind a screen of unintelligible terms; and there is the deep-rooted intellectual conceit in the minds of the too highly specialized. But the greatest obstacle blocking the way to inner security is man's ignorance of basic psychological principles which could serve as keys to the crucial problems of humanity.

Without such keys the countless well-meant efforts to bring man back to a more spiritual understanding of life are of theoretical rather than of

From pp. 33–49 "The Three Dimensions of Reality" from *Man: The Bridge Between Two Worlds* by Franz Winkler. Copyright © 1960 by Franz E. Winkler. By permission of Harper & Row, Publishers, Inc.

practical value; for they are likely to show the goal without pointing out the path which leads to it.

Current religious endeavors can be roughly divided into two categories. They work predominantly either on man's emotions or on his intellect.

The emotional approach finds its expression in revival movements as well as in many sermons and admonitions. Yet exhortations "to be more spiritual" somewhat resemble a doctor's advice to his patient to hurry up and get well. If the doctor has made the correct diagnosis and selected the right remedies, such an appeal may be very helpful; if not, it can bring only temporary relief, often followed by frustration and despair. Sermons and exhortations are of great value to those who seek them; they can do little for the growing number of people who accept guidance only from the intellect. Nor can they really heal the ever-widening rift between faith and reason, a rift which threatens even the deeply religious.

Although in the free world a resurgent interest in religion and an unprecedented rise in the membership of churches exist, we must not forget that religion today is still confined to the realm of emotions and has little influence on the trend of materialistic thinking and the conduct of everyday life. If someone were tactless enough to stand up in church to protest the unscientific attitude of the Bible with its references to angels, visions, and supernatural interferences, a storm of indignation would arise and put the offender in his place. But what would happen if on an ordinary weekday a faithful parishioner were confronted by a stranger who believed without question in the existence of angels, archangels, and supernatural events? Would he not consider the man feeble-minded, to say the least? Yet such an attitude reduces his Sunday consciousness to the level of hypocrisy or superstition, and thus widens the split in the subconscious reaches of his own mind.

On the other hand, intellectual efforts to reconcile modern thought habits with religion vary greatly in usefulness and understanding. Some of them are rather naïve, some highly scientific and elaborate, but almost all try to subordinate spiritual concepts to the dictates of present-day thinking, and to fit them into the scope of an intellectual world picture.

True, modern man has reached a state of evolution in which the voice of faith must be corroborated by reason, but this cannot be attained by despiritualization of the spirit; nor can it be achieved by setting up our limited intelligence as the final measure of truth. Unfortunately, this is exactly what so many intellectual religionists try to do. Even theologians, professing deepest reverence for the spiritual giants of the past, unwittingly reduce them to the level of charlatans by implying that they used medical or other scientific means to trick their less educated fellow men into believing in miracles. It is ironical that the same type of materialistic reasoning, so strongly opposed to the acceptance of ancient miracles, seems only too ready to expect divine influence on modern man's material life. There are reports of businessmen who expect greater prosperity to result from the practice of taking Bibles to their offices, and similar reports of executives gathering for weekly meetings, under a clergyman's guidance, to pray for good business. Steps of this sort are frequently hailed as indications of a religious renaissance but, in our opinion, it would be better to reject religion entirely than to make it a servant of egotistic aims. Surely subservient and diluted spirit is not spirit at all; it is a slow-acting but deadly poison. And the use of spiritual forces for selfish reasons may prove an extremely poor investment in the end.

Many otherwise highly intelligent personalities have shown themselves more inclined to reduce religion to the level of our present-day intellect rather than to make an all-out effort to raise the standard of thinking to the heights of spiritual reality. Yet it is helpful to know that a growing number of truly great scientists find nothing in modern science which contradicts their own religious convictions. "To pursue science is not to disparage the things of the spirit. In fact, to pursue science rightly is to furnish a framework on which the spirit may rise."[1]

Science of history is founded on acceptance of the records of various original sources so far as these recorded events can be verified by traceable effects on the evolution of consciousness. It is scarcely honest to accept historical evidence only as far as it confirms one's own predilections and, regardless of our intentions, the practical results of such inconsistency have proved disastrous to modern education. This is not surprising; for if we imply that metaphysical traditions are merely a residue of an ignorant past and permit the average man to take on the responsibility of modifying or rejecting some or all of them, he will hardly refrain from censoring God Himself. Remodeled and reshaped, even God will become man's creation rather than his creator: a deity habitually in accord with oneself and one's own views, but a stern judge of others. The Nazi philosophy with its concept of a deity favoring the physically strong is just one example of the dangerous potentialities of this approach to truth.

The dilemma which confronts us is not easily solved. For if we accept all religious tradition as unalterable truth, we may discover in our soul an unbridgeable chasm between faith and reason. If we admit that part or all of such tradition is untenable in the light of modern knowledge, we destroy the very foundation of a building whose erection has taken millenniums of labor and suffering. Should this building fall, all that is left of inner security will fall too, and man's inherent longing for the spirit will flow into entirely subjective channels. Then the gates will be

[1] Vannevar Bush, in an address at M.I.T., Oct. 5, 1953.

opened even wider to the victory of half-mystical, half-political ideologies whose triumph might seal the fate of man.

Yet the dilemma can be solved. Its clue lies in a quest for truth that may and must be undertaken by every man. It lies in thought. Unquestionably there must be leaders, men who have the time and the ability to prepare the ground for an edifice of thought accessible not only to professional philosophers but to all who are endowed with common sense. But these leaders should not be accepted on authority alone, nor by virtue of an awe-inspiring, unintelligible language. What we need today is a common-sense philosophy accessible to all who search for truth.

In earlier periods of civilization the attitude of intelligent people toward their great philosophers and prophets was subtly but significantly different from ours. They knew better than we that even the most profound words of wisdom are but inadequate symbols. Differences in doctrines seemed as natural to them as various images of the same object, seen through different mediums. If the system and the teachings of a philosopher made a particular appeal to a man, he was more than willing to cross half the known world to become his pupil; seeking not infallible answers, but help in attaining a greater capacity for cognition.

Today we are still willing to accept ideologies, provided their phraseology is complicated enough to give us a valid excuse for not reading them, their conclusions simplified enough to be learned without effort, and their truth guaranteed by the social or academic position of their authors. We are inclined to forget that it is the struggle for knowledge, rather than knowledge itself, which gives wisdom. Modern man, in fact, does not like to think; he prefers to pay others to do his thinking for him. Overly impressed by the importance of material objects, he does not really consider the world of ideas essential for his well-being on earth.

Yet there he is mistaken. Ideas *do* exert a tremendous influence on our lives; even in world politics their power is greater than force of arms or economic strength. During the critical periods of the past, Americans have often blamed themselves for military unpreparedness and lack of political vigilance, but they could have traced their real failure to an almost contemptuous attitude toward ideas, and to an unwillingness to formulate for their own benefit and for the good of the world the basic principles of an American philosophy. Removal of trade barriers, political leadership, and, at times, even military interference by the world's greatest nation are necessary. Still all material help is deeply resented as an offense against human dignity unless it is matched by spiritual contributions; and so far our spiritual gifts to a world starving for ideals have been meager indeed. The public is so disinterested in ideas and diffident as to their significance that it has become possible for a handful of men to label as "American" those concepts which are diametrically opposed to all this nation stands for. While Americans have proved time and again that they would not only spend their wealth lavishly, but fight and die for the sake of ideas, their spokesmen have convinced the world that this nation believes in nothing but material values.

And still we neither can nor should silence our philosophers. We cannot even blame them for obvious mistakes, for all human beings err; it is we ourselves, the average citizens, who are not truly awake. For the time is long past when the public could leave the quest for truth to a few seekers. Half the world's population has already lost its freedom, owing to such mental apathy: Hitler rose to power, and communism gained sway over hundreds of millions, not on the strength of superior weapons but on that of blindly accepted doctrines. The fate of democracy itself hinges on the independent thinking of the greatest possible number of individuals.

True, there are many intelligent people who have fully realized the significance of ideas, but they are in the minority. While some do not feel competent to struggle with the complicated terms and the bizarre ways of philosophy, other are too deeply impressed by the undeniable achievements of great personalities to weigh and evaluate their opinions. Here much harm has been done, for greatness in itself is not proof against error.

Regardless of whether a man is great or not, whether he is liked or disliked, and regardless of the quality of his achievements, his ideas must be accepted or rejected solely on the strength of their own merits. A human being who refuses to assume full responsibility for his own independent judgment in dealing with ideas is actually destroying the groundwork of his freedom. Purely emotional acceptance or rejection of any ideology, even one of apparently little significance, weakens the power of discrimination and makes the individual an easy victim of political dialectics.

By way of example, let us consider the champion of progressive education. We know that John Dewey liberated pedagogy from its lingering medieval confinements and brought joy and light into stuffy schoolrooms. It was primarily he and his pupils who freed the artistic abilities of the child, and opened the eyes of many a teacher to dormant talents that might have been doomed by abstract educational methods. Yet, while this modern method of education has given freedom of expression to the small child, its philosophy has weakened the very foundation of freedom for the adult. For if we accept the views of John Dewey, who states that "habits . . . are the sole agents of observation, recollection, foresight, and judgment, and that a mind or consciousness or soul in general which performs these operations is a myth,"[2] we may as well abandon all belief in man's capacity for freedom.

None can doubt that attainment of good habits is highly beneficial to

[2] John Dewey, *Human Nature and Conduct*, p. 176.

any form of community life; but even the best of habits are no more than casts into which man's will may flow. Essentially rigid, and truly useful only as props for the routine affairs of social life, they must be overcome—regardless of whether they are good or bad—whenever an act of freedom is required. Beings actually governed by habits could no more conceive of freedom than could robots.

Freedom is lost not by political upheaval but by uncritical acceptance of prefabricated concepts which paralyze individual thinking and thus prepare the way for dictators. The citizen of the still free world is dimly aware of such danger and mistrusts ideas altogether. Furthermore, he has all but stopped reading, and thus remains blissfully unconcerned with the quickly changing philosophic trends of his time. He is unaware that every single ideology, known or unknown to him, is capable of exerting a subtle but decisive influence on his personal life; and he does not realize that, in today's crucial struggle between freedom and slavery, every individual must take an active part in shaping a world concept for his age.

Failing in this participation, he will eventually become no more than a puppet, controlled by a small group of puppeteers. Lack of initiative in thinking creates a mental vacuum into which alien concepts flow unchallenged. In newspapers, radio, television, movies, and popular-science magazines, our time has countless channels through which such concepts can enter a person's subconscious mind, evading his mental defenses; thus thought habits could indeed become "the sole agents of foresight and judgment," and thereby replace man's ego in the shaping of his destiny.

Whether the concepts determining our cultural life are correct or not is scarcely the point; for, right or wrong, such views are manifestations of someone's longing for truth or enmity against it. What matters is the manner in which they are absorbed. Every piece of information we receive, be it factual or conceptual, is but a challenge to our innate sense of truth. This sense may be warped, but can, if persistently exercised, become a reliable means of experiencing reality.

Yet, does reality exist at all, and if so, is it accessible to the human mind? As we all know, a battle has been raging on this issue with devastating results on the ideological, political, and psychological life of the last centuries. But to us such a philosophical conflict appears as futile as the "Schoolman's" famous dispute on how many angels find room on a needle's point. Since an angel is by definition a supernatural being and a needle a material object, it is hard for modern men to understand how it was possible for brilliant minds to waste their intelligence on such an illogical question. But our own philosophical squabbles on truth and reality are no less foolish, for they try to prove or disprove intellectually what is accessible only to intuitive perception. Such perception has always existed in man, and is responsible for all his great religions and ideas. Today it has grown faint and needs training if it is to fulfill its all-important mission in human existence.

Such training, however, can be successful only if based on a threefold quest: the quest for self-knowledge, for scientific penetration of the outer, and for intuitive insight into the inner world. "Know thyself" was the inscription over the portals of ancient temples. The world of the spirit was a perceptible reality not only to the seers and prophets of old, but also to the greatest philosophers of all times. Thales, Plato, Aristotle, Hippocrates, Plotinus, Thomas Aquinas, Jacob Boehme, and Johannes Kepler are only a few of the many who never doubted that man is a spiritual being and that a world of intangible realities exists which, however elusive, has never been entirely inaccessible.

Yet our ancestors, though far more interested in the supersensible than we are today, rarely denied the realities present in the world of the senses, to which the human organism belongs. Even Plato, the greatest idealist, who saw ultimate truth only in the world of ideas, did not minimize the significance of earthly life. To him, the world of matter was the reflection of a higher truth; although inferior to it, it was nonetheless patterned according to the eternal laws of the intangible. This Platonic philosophy has no intrinsic similarity to later forms of idealism denying the very existence of an external world (acosmism or immaterialism) which weakened man's hold on the physical reality without stemming the tide of materialism.

It is true that the sources of modern skepticism and philosophical defeatism can be traced far back in history, even to the fifth and fourth centuries B.C., but they must not be sought in the systems of the great masters of philosophy. Trends of this kind were usually born in schools not too much concerned with the search for truth, but devoted to ulterior motives—such as the Sophists' desire to train young people for fast and easy political careers.

In his search for truth, ancient man did not have the problems of our day. Although we may deem his intellectual outlook on life less advanced than ours, we must remember that at least he knew his spiritual origin to be divine rather than biological. This knowledge has faded from consciousness during the course of history. Modern man, while discovering the secrets of his own physical organism—as well as that of the world—has almost lost himself. Today he has awakened to his plight; and all the conceit and self-assurance of the last century have given way to fear.

How can he rediscover himself without losing the fruits of intellectual evolution? By starting his search at the only solid base available to him: at his own nature as it manifests itself in the routine conduct of ordinary life.

What are the basic principles on which life is carried on? One is an unquestioning belief in the existence of physical realities. The food we eat and the money we earn are real to us, as are our physical gains and deprivations. We may find a second principle in our trust in the existence of intangible realities: love, friendship, loyalty, even hatred and lust for power. And the third basic principle in life is our self- or ego-consciousness. Even the philosopher-to-be starts in the second or third year of his life to refer to himself by the unique term, "I," and from then on remains aware of his selfhood.

Any form of philosophic speculation denying the reality-in-principle of any of these three points of psychological orientation does not understand earthly man as he is and acts, but refers to a being of an abnormal mentality. Such speculations, influencing modern habits, undermine even further the already badly shaken balance of the human mind.

Let us consider a few examples of that conflict between the demands of daily life and the powerful philosophic undercurrents which influence our thinking.

We all agree that our time calls for the development of strong, self-assured individualities—of people who can judge and act for themselves, as well as defend themselves against mental and moral hazards. In a time when mental illnesses have reached an unprecedented peak, when the disintegration of personality, obsessions, amnesia, and unmotivated, compulsive acts have become daily occurrences, man's discovery of himself as an individual spiritual entity should be more than ever the goal of mental hygiene and education. Here, indeed, lies the only protection against the mental and moral dissolution brought home to us day after day in the never-ending reports of crimes, increasing alcoholism, and drug addiction. Yet our present educational system, challenged as it is by an ominous increase in juvenile delinquency and youthful schizophrenia, is inclined to undermine rather than to strengthen the human self. It still holds, if no longer to the methods, so at least to the ideology of a system which has unwittingly undermined the very foundation for spiritual self-affirmation. John Dewey, referring to the basic functions of human psychological behavior, writes: "The doctrine of a single, simple, and dissoluble soul was the cause and the effect of failure to recognize that concrete habits are the means of knowledge and thought."[3]

Then there is the problem presented by intangible realities. Politically, we are pledged to defend our freedom at any price, even at the risk of total destruction; but, while we are raising a generation which may have to sacrifice its physical existence for the sake of an idea, we are turning our whole civilization into a cult of material values.

Paradoxically, this cult does not prevent us from doubting the very reality of our sensual world. Whether or not the well-known reasons

[3] *Ibid.*, p. 176.

for such doubts are valid, will be discussed later. From the viewpoint of practical pychology such ideologies as post-Kantian idealism, acosmism, immaterialism, et cetera, are extremely harmful since, unobserved and unchallenged by individual consciousness, they have penetrated into present-day intellectual life to add further to modern man's growing sense of bewilderment. Living in a world of movies, television, advertisements, and propaganda, all designed "make-believe," he has come dangerously close to losing all ability to distinguish between fact and illusion. And unless modern youth is given the strong conviction that there are basic realities in the physical world, as there are in the world of ideas and in the human self, the trend toward instability will grow still further.

Some optimists feel that no great harm can come from such doctrines which, while denying reality in one sphere, stress its existence in another and thus balance their ultimate effect on human psychology. Unfortunately, this is not so; for it is much easier to destroy convictions than to create them. Moreover, in all radical doctrines there is one common factor capable of a cumulative effect on human thought life, and that is doubt. Whether such skepticism concerns the physical world or the reality of ideas is of less importance than the spreading conviction that nothing is real except the satisfaction of personal desires. For example, pure idealism did nothing to stem the tide of materialism: it helped only to liberate modern man from his sense of moral responsibility to his physical surroundings. Craving for power and sensual enjoyments is not diminished by a denial of physical realities, but the feeling of responsibility toward one's fellow creature definitely is.

Man is a spiritual as well as a physical being. He lives in a world of ideas and in a world of tangible objects. If he loses confidence in the reality of one of them, he automatically destroys the validity of the other. What remains is chaos.

The purpose of this study is not to evaluate individual philosophical systems but to search everywhere for the fragments of truth which are dispersed all through the various doctrines. There seems to be a strong urge to separate such fragments from the whole, to appropriate them, and build around them edifices of speculation that serve self-glory and the establishment of ideological factions. Any attempt to collect those dispersed building-stones for the eventual erection of an edifice of truth faces not only opposition from ideological fanatics, but also the frustrating influence of speculative skepticism which poses as the voice of science. Too many of our modern skeptics not only know little of modern science, but are prone to neglect the primary rules of logic whenever these interfere with their own inclinations.

True, an absolute proof for the existence of any reality is impossible. Yet so is proof for the very existence of human consciousness, without which man could not reason at all. Lacking consciousness, no human being can either prove or disprove anything whatever; and still—

Consciousness cannot be defined; we may be ourselves fully aware what consciousness is, but we cannot, without confusion, convey to others a definition of what we ourselves clearly apprehend. The reason is plain. Consciousness lies at the root of all knowledge. Consciousness is itself the one highest source of all comprehensibility and illustration![4]

There are some fundamentals in human psychology which must be accepted as archphenomena, subject neither to proof nor disproof. Just as it is impossible for a photoelectric cell to disprove the reality of the light whose presence or absence it registers, so is it logically untenable for the human mind to *deny the laws under which it operates*. As human beings we are endowed with certain primary gifts which are our only available tools for cognition. We cannot make use of them for the purpose of denying their existence. In doing so we would unwittingly destroy the postulates necessary to reach a logically valid conclusion. Any human being making a statement proves by his very action his belief in reality. For if he were actually convinced of the nonexistence of reality, why would he state his views which, according to his own reasoning, could hold no truth? The materialist who preaches the nonexistence of absolute truth and of God, seems unaware of the fact that in so doing he himself is making metaphysical statements which he, too, considers as absolute truth. Only the person who has never expressed an opinion at all may be an honest skeptic. Unfortunately, we are in no position to know his views.

To protect the sanity of his generation and to assert his own freedom of thought, the average individual must become capable of defending the principles of common sense against ideological indoctrination. Common sense cannot survive, however, unless the individual can maintain the fundamentals of mental existence: trust in inner and outer realities, and in his own self. For what holds true in the actual conduct of everyday life must be reflected in the philosophical outlook of man; otherwise the already existing rift in the human soul will be widened.

In personal life, sincere doubts regarding the existence of reality constitute a symptom of mental illness. A person losing the conviction of his own self-existence is as ill as the patient to whom objects of the outer world appear unreal. In political life, doubts concerning the existence of absolute realities are conducive to the introduction of "subjective science" on the one hand, and to interference with religious freedom on the other. The political history of nazism and communism should at least convince the world of the powerful effects that philosophical ideologies may exert on the lives and liberties of millions.

As was said before, many people may never have heard of philosophical systems which deny the existence of objective reality in the world of the senses or in the world of intuition. Nevertheless, philosophical skep-

[4] Sir William Hamilton, *Lectures on Metaphysics*, Lecture XI, p. 132.

ticism has penetrated through countless channels into the conscious and subconscious minds of all. We have also mentioned the paralyzing effect which philosophical indoctrination has on the development of free thinking. Its effect is even worse when a whole generation is brought up in a pedagogical system whose underlying philosophy denies the existence of metaphysical reality. For here not only freedom of thought is endangered, but also freedom of moral decision.

In any serious moral conflict the voice of our intangible conscience is hard put to overcome the vivid sensations of aroused emotions. Unless education succeeds in implanting into the child a deep respect for, and an acute awareness of, spiritual reality, the scales will automatically tip in favor of desire, hate, lust for revenge, or other forms of immoral satisfaction. Even if the fear of reprisal or punishment should suffice to prevent action of a criminal nature, such restraint in behavior would not represent a moral achievement.

If morality is nothing but "an endeavor to find for the manifestation of impulse in special situations an office of refreshment and renewal,"[5] why should not crime be committed when the result appears more refreshing to the criminally inclined? In his *Psychology* John Dewey writes:

He [man] will have himself good. The reason that he will is, that he will. Only the ideal of himself as good will satisfy him. If we ask why this ideal alone is satisfactory, we can get no other answer than this: he wills to be satisfied in that, and in that alone. It is willed because it is satisfactory because it is willed as that the man would be.[6]

This rather involved statement leaves no room for moral choice since it degrades morality into a quest for satisfaction not much different from an animal's search for its appropriate food. Moreover, since some obviously find satisfaction in evil, such a concept would divide men into different species, some of them harmless—or good, if we chose to call them so—others ferocious. Nor is it likely that habits could actually change "bad" people into "good" ones, since centuries of civilization, not to mention decades of "progressive" education, have failed to check the increase in criminal trends.

Only when we stop speculating and simply observe the archphenomena of our own psychological attitude toward life can we see that every single one of our mental activities depends on unquestioning acceptance of three categories of reality: one material, the second intangible, and the third which is part of both and a bridge between them.

For centuries philosophical arguments have raged over the nature of man's consciousness: whether it depends on sense perception in its relation to the outer world, or consists of man's awareness of his selfhood and the world of ideas. Monism and dualism have been the battle cries

[5] Dewey, *Human Nature and Conduct*, p. 169.
[6] Dewey, *Psychology*, p. 410.

of whole generations, and their conflict has had tremendous effects on the history of culture and on the evolution of science. Yet the chasm between them, now possibly wider than ever, is not due to an actual incompatibility between two opposing realities, but to man's tedious habit of drawing party lines where they are least appropriate—in the sphere of cognition.

Leaving aside all the countless forms and aspects of those two conflicting world concepts, and turning only toward what is experienced, we must admit that at the first glance man appears as a twofold being. His body consists of matter; his primitive instincts are animal-like, and his very existence depends on the same natural factors which sustain the life of other creatures. Thus he unquestionably belongs to a world ruled by the laws of matter and of biological processes.

Man is also a spiritual being. His thoughts may depend for their manifestation on the structure of his brain, but neither their origin nor their contents lies in the realm of matter or physical energy. Still, however intangible they may be, thoughts are realities. Often defying biological purposes, they can cause man to sacrifice his life, the life of his offspring, and even the life of his whole race, for the sake of ideas.

So long as only these two aspects of human nature are considered, a dualistic world concept is prone to emerge. However, the dualist makes the mistake of disregarding his own selfhood which closes the gap between the world of senses and the world of ideas, the realm of biology and the realm of the spirit. He fails to see that man's ego, his unique capacity for merging physical and spiritual consciousness into the oneness of self-awareness, closes the apparent rift of dualism and confirms the world concept of monism, which believes in only one fundamental reality. And yet a human being cannot comprehend himself and his greatest gift, freedom, unless he learns to contemplate the oneness of creation in its various aspects, which in man are threefold.

Actually, the history of human consciousness could be rewritten from the viewpoint of man's attitude toward the three aspects of reality—the intuitive, the sensual, and the bridge between them: his ego. During the classical eras of some nations, especially of ancient Greece, there were great personalities, the artists among them in particular, who knew that human culture must rest on these three facets of reality, which find their expression in religion, science, and individual freedom. What they built survived the ages and added lasting values to the spiraling course of historical evolution. Yet the classical periods were short-lived and not really rooted in the consciousness of the masses. Thus every historic epoch labored to build the edifice of its culture on one single aspect of human nature, while neglecting the others. No wonder that none of them could withstand the tempests of history for long. Necessary as it was for civilizations to die, the fruits of their labors could have survived better had their foundations been firmer.

But as it was, cultures predominantly rooted in mysticism paid scant attention to the physical needs of men, and fell into fanaticism and unworldliness.

Eras like ours, preoccupied with materialistic science, inevitably misdirect man's unfulfilled longings into pseudo-religious ideologies, powerful enough to threaten civilization as a whole.

Civilizations overemphasizing individualism only too often neglect spiritual aims and physical realities, and consequently become easy victims of self-worshiping tyrants. Only when man will learn to be less one-sided, and to build his life and that of his nation on the principles of individualism, spiritual values, and physical realism alike, will the edifice of human culture grow until it spans the world.

DISCUSSION QUESTIONS

1. Do you subscribe to Winkler's view of man as "the bridge between two worlds"?
2. If you were seeking to educate the balanced individual, how would you go about it?
3. What is the school's concern with intuition? How could this be developed?

CHARLES E. SILBERMAN **The Liberal Education of Teachers**

> The great men of culture are those who have a passion for diffusing, for making prevail, for carrying from one end of society to the other, the best knowledge, the best ideas of their time; who have laboured to divest knowledge of all that was harsh, uncouth, difficult, abstract, professional, exclusive; to humanize it, to make it efficient outside the clique of the cultivated and learned, yet still remaining the best knowledge and thought of the time, and a true source, therefore, of sweetness and light.
>
> Matthew Arnold,
> *Culture and Anarchy,* 1899

I

In the end, we come back to the teacher. "Our most pressing educational problem," as Philip Jackson keeps reminding us, is "learning how to create and maintain a humane environment in our schools." Techno-logical aids—film strips, programmed instruction, instructional television, computer-assisted instruction—"may help in the process, but they will not substitute for a firm sense of direction and a commitment to the preservation of human values. Only people come equipped with these qualities."[1] Hence the teacher's indispensability.

And hence the indispensability of a thorough-going reform of teacher education, to make sure that teachers are equipped with a firm sense of direction and a commitment to the preservation and enlargement of human values as well as with the ability to transmit that commitment and sense of direction to their students. "Education is too significant and dynamic an enterprise to be left to mere technicians," Lawrence Cremin writes, urging that we "begin now the prodigious task of preparing men and women who understand not only the substance of what they are teaching but also the theories behind the particular strategies they employ to convey that substance. A society committed to the continuing intellectual, esthetic, and moral growth of all its members can ill afford less on the part of those who undertake to teach." If . . . it is fruitless to reform teacher education without simultaneously trying to reform the schools in which the teachers will teach, the reverse is also true. The re-making of American public education requires, and indeed will not be possible without, fundamental changes in the education of teachers— without, in a sense, the creation of a new breed of teacher-educator, educated to self-scrutiny and to serious thought about purpose.

The task is huge: it is not possible to reform the education of teachers without reforming higher education as a whole. For one thing, three-quarters of the nation's colleges and universities are in the business of preparing teachers. Only a handful of teachers now receive their education in single-purpose normal schools or teachers colleges. On the basis of data collected for James Conant's study of teacher education, Merle Borrowman, dean of the School of Education at the University of California at Riverside, estimates that 90 percent now receive their education in multi-purpose institutions—municipal, private, and state colleges and universities—each of which prepares more than one hundred teachers a year.[2] Borrowman's estimate may be somewhat high, since he classifies an institution as multi-purpose if 20 percent or more of its graduates are prepared for a field other than education.

But changing the definition would not alter the order of magnitude or change the basic point, namely, that the overwhelming majority of teachers now receive their education in colleges and universities for

[1] Philip W. Jackson, *The Teacher and the Machine*, Pittsburgh, Pa.: University of Pittsburgh Press, 1968.
[2] Merle L. Borrowman, "Liberal Education and the Professional Preparation of Teachers" in M. L. Borrowman, ed., *Teacher Education in America*. New York: Teachers College Press, 1965.

which teacher education is only one of a number of educational missions. Many of these institutions, to be sure, began as normal schools or single-purpose teachers colleges, and some remain teachers colleges in function and spirit, if not in title. Most, however, have become, or are rapidly becoming, full-fledged colleges and universities. Of the twenty-five largest "producers" of teachers, for example, half began as single purpose institutions. But as Table 1 indicates, eighteen of the twenty-five now award more than half their degrees to students preparing for fields other than education.

As the figures in Table 1 also suggest, teacher education is a gigantic enterprise. (There were another 98 colleges and universities which pre-

TABLE 1. Number of Initially Certified Teachers, 1967

Institution	Total Certified	Proportion of Total Degrees Granted
Michigan State University	2,102	27.7
Western Michigan University	1,837	48.7
Indiana University	1.661	26.1
Arizona State University	1,441	44.4*
Ohio State University	1,426	20.4
Illinois State University	1,358	68.0*
University of Puerto Rico	1,354	43.8*
Eastern Michigan University	1,338	56.2
Pennsylvania State University	1,302	23.5
Wayne State University	1,290	28.8
Bowling Green State University (Ohio)	1,179	56.9
Kent State University (Ohio)	1,171	53.1*
University of Michigan	1,153	14.1
East Carolina University (North Carolina)	1,139	83.8
Ball State University (Indiana)	1,133	43.7
Central Michigan University	1,132	64.9
Boston University	1,124	28.2*
Brigham Young University (Utah)	1,064	33.0
Miami University (Ohio)	1,054	46.7*
Mankato State College (Minnesota)	1,026	59.4
Morehead State University (Kentucky)	1,026	n.a.
Southern Illinois University	1,019	34.5
CUNY—Brooklyn College	993	30.0
CUNY—Queens College	993	40.5
San Jose State College (California)	983	23.2

Source: American Association of Colleges for Teacher Education, *Teacher Productivity—1967.*
Note: * means proportion estimated by the author, from Otis A. Singletary, ed., *American Universities and Colleges*, 10th Edition (Washington, D.C.: American Council on Education, 1968).
n.a.—not available.

pared 500 or more teachers each.) In 1967, for example, the nation's colleges and universities turned out nearly 207,000 students eligible for initial certification as teachers, 192,000 of them recipient of bachelor's degrees, the rest receiving Master of Arts in Teaching (M.A.T.) degrees or its equivalent. This represented 35 percent of all bachelor's and first professional degrees—a ratio that has been remarkably stable in recent years. Since the number of college graduates is increasing, the number of graduates certified for teaching rose to nearly 260,000 in 1969, and may exceed 300,000 by 1975. Not all of these graduates, of course, go on to teach. In recent years, between 70 and 75 percent of those completing their preparation for teaching have entered the classroom in the year following graduation; of the remainder, some continue their studies, some enter the armed services, some get married and stay out of the labor force, some take other jobs; many simply are not accounted for.[3]

The public colleges and universities account for the bulk of the teacher education. According to an American Council on Education study of freshmen entering college in the fall of 1967, 22.4 percent of the freshmen at *all* institutions, but 42.2 percent of those at public four-year colleges, were planning to go into elementary or secondary teaching (for female students only, the corresponding ratios were 36.4 percent at all institutions and 59.4 percent at public colleges). Fewer than half of these students, however—10.5 percent of the students at all institutions, 18.2 percent of those at public four-year institutions—were planning to major in education, a division roughly corresponding to the proportions interested in elementary versus secondary school teaching. The typical (though by no means invariant) pattern is that only students planning to teach at the elementary level major in education and/or register in the school of education. Students planning to teach at the secondary level, on the other hand, typically major in an academic subject and register in the appropriate liberal arts college or department, although they are generally required to take some specified minimum number of courses in the school or department of education.

Thus, teacher education is a major responsibility of the academic departments of most colleges and universities, and not just their schools or departments of education.

ITEM: At Michigan State University, some 2,000 students are enrolled in the College of Education, all of them students planning to become elementary school teachers. Twice as many undergraduates are enrolled in the College of Arts and Letters—students majoring in his-

[3] National Education Association, *Teacher Supply and Demand in Public Schools,* 1968, Washington, D.C.: NEA Research Report 1969–R4; U.S. Office of Education, *Education in the Seventies,* U.S. Government Printing Office, 1968 (U.S. Department of Health, Education and Welfare Planning Paper 68–1); The American Association of Colleges for Teacher Education, *Teacher Productivity—1967,* Washington, D.C.: The American Association of Colleges for Teacher Education, 1968.

tory, English, philosophy, Romance languages, music, and art. Curious as to what its students did after graduation, the College of Arts and Letters made a survey which turned up the startling fact that 70 percent of its students went on to become secondary school teachers.

The situation varies, of course, from institution to institution. But whether students major in education or in an academic subject, they take the bulk of their course work—as a rule, two-thirds to three-quarters—in the academic departments. This is true whether they attend a teachers college or a large university. In comparing the requirements of a group of prestigious colleges and universities with a group of teachers colleges, for example, Dr. Conant could not find any differences in the time allocated to academic as opposed to professional or technical education courses. Some teachers colleges, in fact, required more academic preparation than some of the liberal arts institutions.[4]

Thus, if American school teachers are poorly educated it is the liberal arts professors, not just the educationists, who are to blame. Scholarly critics of the schools have not always acknowledged this fact, preferring to place the blame on that easy, if well-deserved, target, the professor of education. Addressing the 1966 annual meeting of the Council for Basic Education, for example, Dr. Glenn T. Seaborg of the California Institute of Technology (at the time, chairman of the Atomic Energy Commission), described the state of science instruction in the schools at the beginning of the decade of curriculum reform:

Although there were prominent weaknesses in our instructional materials and facilities, perhaps the greatest deficiencies were due to our programs for teacher training and our somewhat one-sided philosophy of education. In educating our teachers we had emphasized courses on pedagogy and method to the detriment of preparing them in the subjects they were supposed to teach. Often it seemed that school science had been swallowed up by the prevalent goal of "life adjustment." There had grown up—regrettably—a rigid estrangement between scientists and science educators, so that science courses for prospective teachers were commonly taught in departments or colleges of education, while professors in the scientific departments often tended to discourage their better students from considering careers as school science teachers.[5]

But "science courses for prospective teachers" are *not* "commonly taught in departments or colleges of education"—nor were they in the 1930s or 1940s. To be sure, elementary school teachers in that period frequently did receive a limited education, but this is hardly relevant to Seaborg's point; before the middle or late 1950s, science was not taken seriously in the elementary schools, nor did any scientist propose that it

[4] James B. Conant, *The Education of American Teachers*, New York: McGraw-Hill Paperbacks, 1964.
[5] Glenn T. Seaborg and Jacques Barzun, *The Sciences and the Humanities in the Schools After a Decade of Reform*, Washington, D.C.: Council for Basic Education, Occasional Paper No. 13.

should be. If Seaborg's critique has any point of reference, it can only be the high school curriculum. But the "life adjustment" movement, which began around the end of World War II, had no impact on the preparation of high school science teachers. On the contrary, the high school physics or chemistry teacher typically took his bachelor's degree in physics or chemistry, not education; in all probability, he would have twenty courses in physics or chemistry, several courses in other sciences, and perhaps a half-dozen courses in education, together with some practice teaching. If he didn't know his chemistry, it was the chemistry department's, not the education department's fault.

Lest there be any misunderstanding, let this point be made clear: to insist that the academic departments bear a large part of the blame for what James Koerner referred to as "The Miseducation of American Teachers" is in no way to exonerate the departments and schools of education. On the contrary, they deserve most of the opprobrium which critics like Koerner, Seaborg, and Arthur Bestor have heaped upon them. But they deserve praise as well, for fulfilling, however imperfectly, a responsibility which the liberal arts faculties simply refused to accept and indeed disparaged. As Seaborg concedes in the passage just quoted, the arts and sciences faculties not only refused responsibility for teacher education, they actively discouraged their students from careers in the public schools. Thus, Arthur Bestor, one of the severest but fairest critics of teacher education writes: "The training of teachers for the public schools is one of the most important functions of the American university. It ought always to be treated as a function of the university as a whole. In recent decades it has not been so treated. The blame rests squarely upon the faculties of liberal arts and sciences, who have simply abdicated their responsibilities. By refusing to take seriously the problem of setting up sound and appropriate curricula for the education of teachers, scholars and scientists have left a vacuum into which the professional educationists have moved."[6]

II

The problem runs deeper still. As we have argued repeatedly . . . , what is wrong with elementary and secondary education—or for that matter, higher education, journalism, television, social work, and so on—has less to do with incompetence or indifference or venality than with mindlessness.

If this be so, the solution must lie in infusing the schools, and the other educating institutions, with purpose—more important, with thought about purpose, and about the ways in which techniques, content, and organization fulfill or alter purpose. Given the tendency of institutions to

[6] Arthur Bestor, *The Restoration of Learning*, New York: Alfred A. Knopf, 1955.

confuse day-to-day routine with purpose, to transform the means into the end itself, the infusion cannot be a one-shot affair. The process of self-examination, or "self-renewal," must be continuous. We must find ways of stimulating educators—public school teachers, principals, super-intendents, and schood board members, as well as college professors, deans, and presidents; radio, television, and film directors and pro-ducers; newspaper, magazine, and TV journalists and executives—to think about what they are doing, and why they are doing it. There is a measure of romantic exaggeration, to be sure, but a larger measure of truth, in Harold Taylor's insistence that "preparing to become a teacher is like preparing to become a poet. The preparation begins in a decision to become something, a commitment made about one's own life and the purpose of it."[7]

But that commitment is rarely made, for the sense of purpose is rarely cultivated. What is wrong with the way teachers and administrators (or journalists, filmmakers, TV directors, et al.) are educated has less to do with the fact that they are given inadequate mastery of the techniques of teaching (or writing, directing, filmmaking, etc.) than with the fact that they are not trained to think about either the purposes or the pro-cesses, the ends or the means, of education. Men or women who are going to be teaching elementary school children need some preparation that is different from those who will be teaching graduate students; and prospective journalists or TV directors need some preparation different from those who will teach.

They all need an education that equips them to ask why, to think seriously and deeply about what they are doing—which is to say that they all need a liberalizing and humanizing education. "Men are men before they are lawyers, or physicians, or merchants, or manufacturers, and if you make them capable and sensible men," John Stuart Mill ob-seved in his Inaugural Address at the University of St. Andrew, "they will make themselves capable and sensible lawyers or physicians"—or teachers. "The education of teachers," Mark van Doren has written (and his words apply equally well to the education of journalists, law-yers, college professors, et al.), "is an education in the liberal arts. When this education is good and falls on the right ground, it produces persons with usable intellects and imaginations who know both what and why they are teaching."

In short, the weakness of teacher education is the weakness of liberal education as a whole; if teachers are educated badly, that is to say, it is in large measure because almost everyone else is educated badly, too. For in the last analysis, we are *all* educators—of our wives or husbands, our children, our friends and colleagues—and ourselves. "The purpose

[7] Harold Taylor, *The World and the American Teacher*, Washington, D.C.: The American Association of Colleges for Teacher Education, 1968.

of education at Chicago," the catalogue of that university's College states, "is to free students to explore, for a lifetime, the possibilities and limits of the human intellect. Though we cannot promise to produce educated men and women, *we do endeavor to bring each student . . . to a point beyond which he can educate himself."* [Emphasis added] And this, after all, is what liberal education is all about—what liberal education has always been about.

This much we have argued before, and we have attempted at several points to indicate of what the capacity to educate oneself consists. What distinguishes education at the college level from that which precedes it is not simply its greater complexity and intensity, but its greater self-consciousness as well. To be educated to the point where one can educate himself, or others, means not only to think seriously about the means and ends of education (one's own, and others'), but about the *consequences* of education as well—about the way education shapes and molds the people being educated.

This in turn means that to be educated—to be an educator—is to understand something of how to make one's education effective in the real world. It means to know something of how to apply knowledge to the life one lives and the society in which one lives it—in a word, to know what is relevant—and how to make knowledge relevant, which is to say, effective.

And the most direct and immediate way of finding out what it is one really knows and how it can be applied—of finding the purpose and testing the human relevance of what one has learned—is to teach it to someone else. In this sense, teaching is the ultimate liberal art—something many of the rebellious college students understand better than many of their professors. One of the ways in which some college students have sought relevance and purpose in recent years, one of the ways they have tried to relate education to life, has been to go out and teach—in the urban slums and ghettos, in the underdeveloped nations of Africa, Asia, and Latin America or the underdeveloped rural areas of the United States.

.   .   .

What these "new" students understand, far better than their parents, is that the choice of a career involves far more than a choice of how to earn a livelihood. They understand, viscerally if not intellectually, that the question, "What shall I do?" really means "What shall I do with myself?" or rather, "What shall I make of myself?" And that means asking "Who am I?" "What do I want to be?" "What values do I want to serve?" "To whom and to what, do I want to be responsible?" As Drucker rightly observes, "These are existential questions, for all that they are couched in secular form and appear as choices between a job in government, in business, or in college teaching."[8] That the students' answers are not always relevant is less important than the fact that they are forcing us to confront the most fundamental questions of value and purpose.

Part of what we must confront is the fact that many of the young are rejecting values, goals, and identities we have always taken for granted —values, goals, and identities we have regarded as intrinsic parts of the social fabric. What is new it must be understood, is not the generational conflict itself; four thousand years before Christ, an Egyptian priest carved in stone what contemporary parents are lamenting: "Our earth is degenerate . . . children no longer obey their parents." Nor is there anything new in college protests—not even in the violent ones. The first, and most successful, "student power" movement was organized at the University of Bologna in the twelfth and thirteenth centuries, and student riots were endemic to the medieval university.[9] In eighteenth- and nineteenth-century American colleges, too, students were constantly waging war with the faculty, whom they generally viewed as the enemy, and violence was almost commonplace. "Among the victims of the collegiate way," Frederick Rudolph writes, "were the boy who died in a duel at Dickinson, the students who were shot at Miami in Ohio, the professor who was killed at the University of Virginia, the president of Oakland College in Mississippi who was stabbed to death by a student, the president and professor who were stoned at the University of Georgia, the student who was stabbed at Illinois College, the students who were stabbed and killed at the University of Missouri and the University of North Carolina."[10] Large-scale student rebellions took place, moreover, at Princeton, Miami University, Amherst, Brown, University of South Carolina, Williams, Georgetown, University of North Carolina, Harvard, Yale, Dartmouth, Lafayette, Bowdoin, City College of New York, Dickinson, and DePauw.[11] And since 1870, at the least, there has been "a steady stream of serious student protests" in high schools in such cities as New York, Chicago, and Gary, Indiana.[12]

In the United States, however, unlike such countries as Russia, Germany, China, and Japan, young people rarely challenged the legitimacy of their parents', or their university's, or their government's authority. They claimed that authority had been abused or that the wrong people

[8] Peter F. Drucker, *The Age of Discontinuity*, New York: Harper & Row, 1969.
[9] Hasting Rashdall, *The Universities of Europe in the Middle Ages*, New York: Oxford University Press, 1936 edition.
[10] Frederick Rudolph, *The American College and University*, New York: Vintage Books, 1962.
[11] Lewis S. Feuer, *The Conflict of Generations*, New York: Basic Books, 1969.
[12] Alan F. Westin, "Civic Education in a Crisis Age," paper delivered at the Conference on the School and the Democratic Environment, sponsored by the Danforth Foundation and the Ford Foundation, April 10, 1969 (mimeographed).

were exercising it; at times they simply defied authority. They rarely questioned the legitimacy of authority itself.

They are questioning it now! Indeed, they are questioning not only the legitimacy but the very concept of authority. "The most dangerous intellectual aspect of the contemporary scene," the sociologist Robert A. Nisbet states, is the refusal of the young, and of the would-be-young, "to distinguish between authority and power. They see the one as being as much a threat to liberty as the other. But this way lies madness," for "there can be no possible freedom in society apart from authority." Authority, after all, is "built into the very fabric of human association," being rooted in the relationships and loyalties of the members of a group, whether family, church, university, or state, and derived from the function the group or institution performs. Power is necessary to authority only when the function from which it derives has been weakened or when, for whatever reasons, allegiance has been shifted to some other institution.[13]

There are, moreover, many forms of authority besides the ones we generally think of—the state, the church, the school, the university—when we use the term. As Nisbet states, "There is the authority of learning and taste; of syntax and grammar in language; of scholarship, of science, and of the arts. In traditional culture there is an authority attaching to the names of Shakespeare, Montaigne, Newton, and Pasteur in just as sure a sense of the word as though we were speaking of the law. There is the authority of logic, reason, and of genius. Above all, there is the residual authority of the core of values around which Western culture has been formed"—among them, the values of justice, reason, equity, liberty, charity, morality, which until the sixties, conservatives, liberals, and radicals alike recognized. "It was culture and its authority on which minds as diverse as Newman, Spencer, Marx, and even Proudhon rested their causes." Indeed, anarchist that he was, Nisbet writes, "no one could have surpassed Proudhon in his recognition of the necessity of authority in the social order; the authority of the family, the community, the guild; above all the authority of morality that he, as a member of the European community, recognized as the indispensable framework of culture and of social justice."

Contemporary radicals of the over-thirty variety have continued in this tradition. "We are not only free organisms but parts of mankind that has historically made itself with great inspirations and terrible conflicts," Paul Goodman, the contemporary Proudhon, writes, in attacking A. S. Neill of Summerhill fame for his "latitudinarian lack of standards," e.g., his insistence that Beethoven and rock 'n roll are equivalent. "We

[13] Robert A. Nisbet, "The Twilight of Authority," *The Public Interest*, Number 15, Spring 1969.

cannot slough off that accumulation, however burdensome," Goodman adds, "without becoming trivial and therefore servile."[14]

But what the young rebels are trying to do is precisely that—to "slough off" the accumulation of past achievements, creations and discoveries that constitutes contemporary culture and, for the older generation, gives it its authority. Indeed, we cannot understand the crisis in education—the crisis in society and culture as a whole, in the United State and in virtually every other advanced industrial society—except in terms of the fact that many of the young are questioning, and some rejecting altogether, the authority of culture and morality as well as of law. "I can't make clear to a young lady at the Antioch-Putney School of Education," Goodman plaintively reports, "that a child has an historical right to know that there is a tie between Venus and the Sun and thanks to Newton we know its equation, which is even more beautiful than the Evening Star; it is *not* a matter of taste whether he knows this or not."

But the most rebellious among the young insist that it *is* a matter of taste, for they do not recognize the authority of knowledge, of skill, of simple truth; to a frightening degree, they do not even understand the concept. When they question the college administration's authority, say, to make parietal rules or take disciplinary action for infractions of other rules, they are challenging the legitimacy of there being any rules at all. More to the point, when they question the administration's or the faculty's right to make or enforce academic regulations, they frequently are denying that there are, or can be, standards of learning or of scholarship. "The disinterested ideals of science and art are hardly mentioned and do not seem to operate publicly at all," Goodman writes, with only partial exaggeration, "and the sacredness of these ideals no longer exists even on college campuses. Almost no young person of college age believes that there are autonomous professionals or has even heard of such a thing."

It was his experience in teaching a course on "Professionalism" at The New School for Social Research in 1967, in fact, that first made Goodman aware of the degree to which the new generation which he had helped produce did not share—did not even understand—the assumptions about knowledge and society that he took for granted. The professionals whom Goodman brought to class to explain "the obstacles that stood in the way of honest practice, and their own life experience in circumventing them," were uniformly and unanimously rejected by the students, who called them "liars, finks, mystifiers, or deluded," re-

[14] "The Present Moment in Education," *New York Review of Books*, April 10, 1969. This essay and another by Goodman ("The New Reformation," *New York Times Magazine*, September 14, 1969) constitute a most illuminating explanation of the new generation gap.

peating, by way of explanation, what the guests had themselves pointed out. In exploring why the students had not listened, Goodman "came to the deepest truth, that they did not believe in the existence of real professions at all; professions were concepts of repressive society and 'linear thinking.' I asked them to envisage any social order they pleased— Mao's, Castro's, some anarchist utopia—and wouldn't there be engineers who knew about materials and stresses and strains? Wouldn't people get sick and need to be treated? Wouldn't there be problems of communication? No, they insisted; it was important only to be human, and all else would follow." Goodman continues:

Suddenly I realized that they did not really believe that there was a nature of things. Somehow all functions could be reduced to interpersonal relations and power. There was no knowledge, but only the sociology of knowledge. They had so well learned that physical and sociological research is subsidized and conducted for the benefit of the ruling class that they did not believe there was such a thing as simple truth. To be required to learn something was a trap by which the young were put down and co-opted. Then I knew that I could not get through to them. I had imagined that the worldwide student protest had to do with changing political and moral institutions, to which I was sympathetic, but I now saw that we had to do with a religious crisis of the magnitude of the Reformation in the fifteen-hundreds. . . .[15]

. . .

One need only sit in the classrooms, in fact, and examine the texts and reading lists to know that, with the possible exception of mathematics, the curriculum reform movement has made a pitifully small impact on classroom practice. The criteria for deciding what should be in the curriculum, Jerome Bruner of Harvard, one of the chief architects of curriculum reform, has suggested, should be to ask "whether, when fully developed, [the subject or material] is worth an adult's knowing, and whether having known it as a child makes a person a better adult. If the answer to both questions is negative or ambiguous, then the material is cluttering the curriculum."[16]

The answer is negative to both questions for an incredibly high proportion of the elementary and secondary school curriculum. There is a great deal of chatter, to be sure, about teaching students the structure of each discipline, about teaching them how to learn, about teaching basic concepts, about "postholing," i.e., teaching fewer things but in greater depth. But if one looks at what actually goes on in the classroom —the kinds of texts students read and the kind of homework they are assigned, as well as the nature of classroom discussion and the kinds of tests teachers give—he will discover that the great bulk of students'

[15] "The New Reformation," New York Times Magazine, Sept. 14, 1969.
[16] Jerome S. Bruner, The Process of Education, Cambridge: Harvard University Press, 1960. Bruner's book was perhaps the most important and influential to come out of the curriculum reform movement.

time is still devoted to detail, most of it trivial, much of it factually incorrect, and almost all of it unrelated to any concept, structure, cognitive strategy, or indeed anything other than the lesson plan. It is rare to find anyone—teacher, principal, supervisor, or superintendent—who has asked why he is teaching what he is teaching.

ITEM: The students in a sixth-grade English class in a school on a Chippewa Indian reservation are all busily at work, writing a composition for Thanksgiving. The subject of the composition is written on the blackboard for the students (and the visitor) to see. The subject: "Why We Are Happy the Pilgrims Came."

Much of what is taught is not worth knowing as a child, let alone as an adult, and little will be remembered. The banality and triviality of the curriculum in most schools has to be experienced to be believed. The Educational Testing Service's study of secondary school teaching of history and social studies, for example, indicated that the curriculum followed in 1956–66 "does not differ in any striking way from that which has been traditional in the United States for the past twenty-five years." More important, perhaps, the study revealed that even for the students taking college board exams—the top twenty-five percent in terms of academic ability—schools relied heavily on textbooks. Eighty-five percent of the students reported that more than half their reading in a senior American history course came from a single text; some 55 percent did three-quarters or more of their reading in the text. To know what that means, pick up almost any of the texts in widespread use!

The social studies curriculum is even worse at the elementary school level. The obsession with the explorers is one of the mysteries of American schooling; inordinate amounts of time are devoted to their exploits, and the topic may be repeated as many as three times during the elementary years. Disproportionate amounts of time are devoted to the Colonial Period and the American Revolution, too—but with no attempt to relate the ideas and issues of those days to our own time.

.   .   .

III

What happened? Why did a movement that aroused such great hopes, and that enlisted so many disinguished educators, exert so little impact on the schools?

A large part of the answer is that what was initially regarded as the curriculum reform movement's greatest strength—the fact that its prime movers were distinguished university scholars and teachers—has proven to be its greatest weakness. In part because the movement was based in the scholarly disciplines, in part because it grew out of the scholars' revulsion against the vulgarization of progressive education and against the anti-intellectualism that that vulgarization in turn had spawned, the reformers by and large ignored the experiences of the past, and particularly of the reform movement of the 1920s and '30s. They were, therefore, unaware of the fact that almost everything they said had been said before, by Dewey, Whitehead, Bode, Rugg, etc.; and they were unaware that almost everything they tried to do had been tried before, by educators like Frederick Burk, Carleton Washburne, and Helen Parkhurst, not to mention Abraham Flexner and Dewey himself.[17]

One result of this failure to study educational history, particularly the history of progressivism's successes and failures, was that the contemporary reformers repeated one of the fundamental errors of the progressive movement: they perpetuated the false dichotomy that the schools must be *either* child-centered *or* subject-centered. Ignoring the warnings of men like Dewey, Boyd Bode, Harold Rugg, and Carleton Washburne, the progressive reformers had opted for the former; their preoccupation with child-centeredness made them content, in Dewey's phrase, "with casual improvisation and living intellectually hand to mouth." It was this "absence of intellectual control through significant subject-matter," Dewey wrote, "which stimulates the deplorable egotism, cockiness, impertinence and disregard for the rights of others apparently considered by some persons to be the inevitable accompaniment, if not the essence, of freedom."[18]

The reformers of the 1950s and '60s made the same mistake, except that they opted for the other side of the dichotomy. They placed almost all their emphasis on subject matter, i.e., on creating "great compositions," and for the most part ignored the needs of individual children. As Dewey wrote of the progressive educators whose one-sidedness he deplored, the new reformers "conceive of no alternative to adult dictation save child dictation." Reacting against the banality that child-dictated education had become, they opted for adult dictation. They knew what they wanted children to learn; they did not think to ask what children wanted to learn. Some of the reformers, however, now realize their error. Thus it was Zacharias, at the 1965 White House Conference on Education, who made a passionate plea that educators think about children and their needs.

[17] Cf. Lawrence A. Cremlin, *The Transformation of the School* and *The Genius of American Education*; John I. Goodlad, "Curriculum: A Janus Look," *Teachers College Record*, November 1968: J. Stuart Maclure, *Curriculum Innovation in Practice*, Third International Curriculum Conference, Oxford (Her Majesty's Stationery Office, 1968); Patricia A. Graham, *Progressive Education: From Arcady to Academe*, New York: Teachers College Press, 1967; Harold Rugg and Ann Shumaker, *The Child-Centered School: An Appraisal of the New Education*, New York: World Book Co., 1928.
[18] John Dewey, "How Much Freedom in New Schools?", *The New Republic*, July 9, 1930.

Because the reformers were university scholars with little contact with public schools or schools of education, moreover, and because they also neglected to study the earlier attempts at curriculum reform, they also tended to ignore the harsh realities of classroom and school organization. The courses they created were, and are, vastly superior to the tepid and banal fare most students now receive. But without changing the ways in which schools operate and teachers teach, changing the curriculum alone does not have much effect.[19]

To some degree, this error reflected the reformers' innocence and naïveté. Because they had so little firsthand experience with the elementary or secondary school classroom (in contrast to most of the great figures of the progressive movement), they somehow assumed that students would learn what the teachers taught; that is, if teachers presented the material in the proper structure, students would learn it that way. Thus, they assumed implicitly that teaching and learning are merely opposite sides of the same coin. But they are not.

The error reflected academic hubris as well: not content with ignoring the classroom teacher, the reformers, in effect, tried to bypass the teacher altogether. Their goal, sometimes stated, sometimes implicit, was to construct "teacher-proof" materials that would "work" whether teachers liked the materials or not or taught them well or badly. "With the kind of casual arrogance only professors can manage, when they conceived of lower schools," Dean Robert J. Schaefer writes, the curriculum reformers' goal was "to produce materials which permit scholars to speak directly to the child." They viewed teachers, if they thought of them at all, as technicians, and they conceived of the schools, Schaefer suggests, as "educational dispensaries—apothecary shops charged with the distribution of information and skills deemed beneficial to the social, vocational, and intellectual health of the immature. The primary business of a dispensary," Schaefer continues, "is to dispense—not to raise questions or to inquire into issues as to how drugs might be more efficiently administered, and certainly not to assume any authority over what ingredients should be mixed."[20]

The effort was doomed to failure. For one thing, the classroom teacher usually is in an almost perfect position to sabotage a curriculum he finds offensive—and teachers are not likely to have a high regard for courses designed to bypass them. For another, many of the "teacher-proof" curricula have turned out to be more difficult to teach than the courses they replaced; certainly the "discovery method" makes far more demands on

[19] Cf., for example, Blythe Clinchy, "School Arrangements," in Jerome Bruner, ed., *Learning About Learning: A Conference Report*, U.S. Office of Education, Cooperative Research Monograph No. 15. The Clinchy essay is one of thirty in this volume; it is the only one directly concerned with the ways in which schools and classrooms operate.

[20] Robert J. Schaefer, *The School as a Center of Inquiry*, New York: Harper & Row, 1967.

the teacher than does rote drill or lecturing. But insofar as they thought about in-service education of teachers, the reformers tended to assume that the problem was to get teachers to know—to really know—the subject they were teaching. This was crucial, of course, but experience with National Defense Education Act Institutes and the like have made it painfully clear that mastering the subject matter does not begin to solve the problem of how to teach it.

The failure to involve ordinary classroom teachers in the creation and modification of the new curricula, moreover, tended to destroy, or at least inhibit, the very spirit of inquiry the new courses were designed to create. Curriculum designers are not likely to attract students to the life of the mind if they fail to entice the students' teachers as well. "How can youngsters be convinced of the vitality of inquiry and discovery," Dean Schaefer asks, "if the adults with whom they directly work are mere automatons who shuffle papers, workbooks, and filmstrips according to externally arranged schedules?" Since the spirit of inquiry "necessitates a live sense of shared purpose and commitment," the teachers *must* participate in the scholar's search if the effort is to succeed.

The most fatal error of all, however, was the failure to ask the questions that the giants of the progressive movement always kept at the center of their concern, however inadequate some of their answers may have been: What is education for? What kind of human beings and what kind of society do we want to produce? What methods of instruction and classroom organization, as well as what subject matter, do we need to produce these results? What knowledge is of most worth?[21]

. . .

More important, education should prepare people not just to earn a living but to live a life—a creative, humane, and sensitive life. This means that the schools must provide a liberal, humanizing education. And the purpose of liberal education must be, and indeed always has been, to educate educators—to turn out men and women who are capable of educating their families, their friends, their communities, and most importantly, themselves. "Though we cannot promise to produce educated men and women," says the catalogue of the College of the University of Chicago, whose faculty has thought harder about educational purpose than most faculties, "we do endeavour to bring each student . . . to a point beyond which he can educate himself." This must also be the purpose of the public schools.

Of what does the capacity to educate oneself consist? It means that a person has both the desire and the capacity to learn for himself, to dig out what he needs to know, as well as the capacity to judge what is

[21] Cf. especially Lawrence A. Cremin, *The Genius of American Education*, and John I. Goodlad, "Curriculum: A Janus Look."

worth learning. It means, too, that one can think for himself, so that he is dependent on neither the opinions nor the facts of others, and that he uses that capacity to think about his own education, which means to think about his own nature and his place in the universe—about the meaning of life and of knowledge and of the relations between them. "To refuse the effort to understand," Wayne Booth, dean of the College of the University of Chicago, argues, "is to resign from the human race." You cannot distinguish an educated man, he continues, "by whether or not he believes in God, or in UFO's. But you can tell an educated man by the way he takes hold of the question of whether God exists, or whether UFO's are from Mars."[22]

To be educated in this sense means also to know something of the experience of beauty—if not in the sense of creating it or discoursing about it, then at the very least, in the sense of being able to respond to it, to respond both to the beauty of nature and to the art made by our fellow men. "To find and appreciate beauty in the ordinary and the extraordinary is the right of every child," the Ontario, Canada Provincial Committee on Aims and Objectives of Education, has written, "for esthetic experience is a basic need for all men in their universal struggle to add meaning to life. We owe to children the freedom to explore the full range of their senses; to appreciate subtle differences; to be aware of beauty wherever it is found; to see, to touch, to smell, to hear, to taste, so that each in his own way will strive to find and express the meaning of man and human destiny."[23]

To be educated also means to understand something of how to make our intentions effective in the real world—of how to apply knowledge to the life one lives and the society in which one lives it. The aim of education, as Alfred North Whitehead has written, "is the acquisition of the art of the utilization of knowledge." Indeed, "a merely well-informed man is the most useless bore on God's earth."

The schools fail to achieve any of these goals. They fail in another and equally important way. Education is not only a preparation for later life; it is an aspect of life itself. The great bulk of the young now spend a minimum of twelve years in school; with kindergarten attendance, and now preschool programs, becoming more widespread, more and more of the young will have spent thirteen to fifteen years in school by the time they receive their high school diploma.

The quality of that experience must be regarded as important in its own right. A good school, as the English "Plowden Committee" insists

[22] Wayne C. Booth, "Is There Any Knowledge That a Man Must Have?", in Wayne C. Booth, ed., *The Knowledge Most Worth Having*, University of Chicago Press, 1967. Booth's essay and his introduction to the volume represent the best brief statement about liberal education in recent years.

[23] *Living and Learning: A Report of the Provincial Committee on Aims and Objectives of Education in the Schools of Ontario*, Ontario, Canada: Department of Education, 1968.

in its magnificent report on *Children and Their Primary Schools*, "is a community in which children learn to live first and foremost as children and not as future adults."[24] The Committee is exaggerating, to be sure, when it goes on to insist that "the best preparation for being a happy and useful man and woman is to live fully as a child"—an exaggeration from which many American progressive schools of the 1920s and 1930s suffered. "Merely to let children live free, natural, childlike lives," as Carleton Washburne, one of the giants of American progressivism, warned in 1925, "may be to fail to give them the training they need to meet the problems of later life." Thus Washburne insisted on a dual focus. "Every child has the right to live fully and naturally as a child," he wrote. "Every child has the right also to be prepared adequately for later effective living as an adult."[25] In the grim, repressive, joyless places most schools now are, children are denied both those rights.

DISCUSSION QUESTIONS

1. Is the teacher education program being offered to you directed toward producing "a new breed of teacher-educator, educated to self-scrutiny and to serious thought about purpose"?
2. Is it essential for the preparation of teachers that they be given a "a liberalizing and humanizing education" so that they can infuse aims and purposes into their actions?
3. Do you agree with Silberman's evaluation of current schooling as mindless and purposeless?

ROBERT M. HUTCHINS Permanence and Change

*What education must do now is what it
ought to have been doing all along.*

My text is taken from the words of John Dewey in his essay "My Pedagogic Creed." He said: "The only possible adjustment which we can give to the child under existing conditions is that which arises through putting him in complete possession of all his powers. With the advent of democracy and modern industrial conditions, it is impossible to foretell definitely just what civilization will be twenty years from now.

Reprinted, with permission, from the September 1968 issue of *The Center Magazine*, a publication of the Center for the Study of Democratic Institutions in Santa Barbara, California.

[24] Central Advisory Council for Education (England), *Children and Their Primary Schools*, London: Her Majesty's Stationery Office, 1967.
[25] *Progressive Education*, July-September 1925.

Hence it is impossible to prepare the child for any precise set of conditions."

These words were written in 1897. As we look back over the last seventy years and reflect on the changes that have taken place since Dewey wrote, we see that he did not exaggerate. If he were living today, he would feel compelled, I think, to shorten the time interval he mentions. Twenty years is now an eternity.

At a recent meeting of the research committee of the California Commission on Manpower, Automation, and Technology, the man in charge of the training of vocational teachers in the state asked the industrialists present to give him some indication of what vocational education teachers would need to know seven years from now. He was greeted with incredulous laughter. The man from Lockheed said he could not say what kind of training his workers would need seven months from now.

The most obvious fact about education is the one most often overlooked: it takes time.

The most obvious fact about society is that the more technological it is the more rapidly it will change. It follows that in an advanced technological society futility dogs the footsteps of those who try to prepare the child for any precise set of condition. Hence the most impractical education is the one that looks most practical, and the one that is most practical in fact is the one that is commonly regarded as remote from reality, one dedicated to the comprehension of theory and principles.

In the present state of technology, and even more certainly in any future state thereof, the kind of training and information that is central in American education is obsolescent, if not obsolete. Now, the only possible adjustment that we can give the child is that which arises through putting him in complete possession of all his powers.

From a curriculum aiming to make the schools contribute to this result neither training nor information would disappear. But they would be different. The training would be in techniques the child would need under any conditions, in any occupation, at any stage of his life. Such techniques are language and mathematics, which are implicated in everything we do. The information would be such as to confirm, refute, or illustrate the principles under discussion.

If we follow Dewey's prescription, we shall try to get the child ready for anything: if we try to get him ready for something, it may not be there when we have got him ready. About all we can say today is that the one certain calling is citizenship and the one certain destiny, manhood. No occupation—perhaps not even teaching—is immune from technological change. The antibiotics have made the expensively acquired techniques of surgery in certain fields, like mastoiditis, unnecessary. A glance at an automated bakery will convince you that the managing director of Bahlsen's in Germany was right when he said, "Here the skill of the baker dies."

On the other hand, we can never have too many wise citizens or good men. The future of civilization depends on our having a more adequate supply of both. I suggest that the way to get it may be to put all children in complete possession of all their powers.

I repeat "all" children. Admittedly, the effort will carry us beyond the field for which educational administrators are responsible. In the first place, the school cannot do the whole job. Other institutions and agencies have their role. The specific function of education is to help people to become human by helping them learn to use their minds. In the second place, we have good reason to believe now that the environment, particularly the environment of the earliest years, before the child goes to school, decisively affects his performance in school.

The Coleman Report even intimates that all the factors determining a child's success or failure in school are beyond the control of that institution. The Newsom Report, in England, dealing with children of "average or less than average ability," offers evidence in the same direction.

It says of one place it studied, "the children live in back-to-back houses . . . and have no indoor sanitation—four or five families share one public toilet in the middle of the yard. Few of the children here have even seen a bathroom, and in some houses there is not even a towel and soap. All these homes have overcrowded living and sleeping quarters; for example, ten or eleven people may sleep in two beds and one cot. The girls accept drunkenness as part of the normal pattern. Twenty-two per cent of the children in one school have no father, five per cent no mother."

These children are reported to have average or less than average ability. It is amazing they have any ability at all. For what do we mean by ability in school? We mean the ability to compete on even terms in matters literary and intellectual with children from homes in which there are conversation, books, and some sense of the value of education—to say nothing of bathrooms.

All educational standards, no matter how "scientific," are culturally derived. The celebrated Intelligence Quotient, the I.Q., must favor the child who has been fortunate in his early surroundings against one who has lived in the English or American slums. With the best buildings, a permanent staff of the best teachers, and an inspiring curriculum, what hope is there unless the cause of the difficulty, the slum itself is eliminated? And what can the schools do about that?

René Dubos believes that as much as eighty per cent of the genetic potential of most human beings may be repressed by their environment. Neither he nor anybody else would claim that the genetic potential of all human beings is the same; but we can all agree that the child's potential, whatever it is, should, as far as possible, be protected from environmental obliteration.

It used to be assumed that there were different kinds of people, those who could be educated and those who could not be. We know now that man makes himself by making the environment in which he places the newborn. Where racial discrimination inhibits mobility, where poverty suppresses human possibilities, it will be difficult to put any child in complete possession of all his powers.

Our knowledge of the influence of the environment, especially that of the earliest years, upon the educational future of the child cannot excuse the failure of the schools in the ghettos and the slums to do a much better job than they have attempted up to now. The environment can be ameliorated, from the child's point of view, by taking him out of it through part of the day by crèches, nursery schools, and kindergartens. Boarding schools are another possible and perhaps necessary step in the same direction.

Boarding schools, whose quality of education we must now give all children, have been the privilege of the rich. The education designed to put the child in complete possession of his highest powers has, in effect, been limited to those from what are called "good homes." The others, who have confronted an alien culture when they came to school, have been shunted off into vocational training, lower tracks, or the labor market. They have been thought of as ineducable.

As long as they live under adverse circumstances they will not be able to cope with a school that was not built for them. But as Jensen's work at Berkeley shows, their learning ability may be high and, if we spend the money, time, and care necessary to develop it, many of them can conquer the obstacles that have been fatal to their educational careers.

There can be no question that the tracking system as it is employed today in mixed schools of Negroes and whites is a means of perpetuating poverty and racial discrimination. This is not because of ill will or because of any conspiracy. I am confident that in the overwhelming majority of cases children are properly placed in the proper tracks on the basis of adequate tests. I am attacking not the administration of the tracking system, but the system itself. A big rescue job has to be done with pupils who come from the suffocating atmosphere of our slums and ghettos. The first step in rescuing them is to signify to them and everybody else in the school that they are not inferior and that they will receive no fewer educational opportunities than their contemporaries.

Segregation on the basis of color is worse than segregation on the basis of "ability." The ghetto schools have to be improved. Such improvement, to the extent that it is possible, should not be used to justify our failure to break up the ghettos. Open-housing legislation could have a more important influence on education than any educational innovations in the ghetto schools.

We have to abolish the ghettos and slums. Meanwhile, we have to improve the schools that are there. Both these operations will require vast sums of money. I do not need to point out where the money could come from. I need only say that in my judgment thirty billion dollars a year is available, some part of which could be used for the education of our people and for the assistance of the rest of mankind.

An automated society can be a learning society, one in which the object of the community is, as John Stuart Mill suggested, the virtue and intelligence of the people. The question is, what are we going to learn? If we follow John Dewey, we shall hope to put the child in complete possession of his intellectual power, and we shall expect him as he grows up and goes on through adult life to continue the development of that power. This will obviously not be for the purpose of earning a living. The aim must be to become a complete human being, a wise citizen, and a good man, living, as Ortega used to say, "at the height of his times." I do not underestimate training or the acquisition of technical competence. I merely say that where technical competence is required it will, in view of the rapidity of change, have to be gained on the job. On the same job, retraining may have to occur very often. But what we are trying to find out is not how those who need them may learn techniques but how to put all Americans in complete possession of all their powers.

What we are looking for is a new definition of liberal education. We need a definition of it appropriate to the world we are now entering, one characterized by very rapid change, by vast stretches of free time, by the emergence of a world order, and by the urgent demand for wise citizens and good men. We have to make the effort to help everybody achieve this education. The proportions of this effort are indicated by the unanimity with which liberal education has been thought of as the privilege of the few. When what are called "the masses" began to enter the education system, liberal education had to be diluted to the point of insipidity. It is almost nonexistent in this country today. So-called colleges of liberal arts, in which only the name survives, announce that the student is liberally educated when he has accumulated 120 semester hours of miscellaneous credits in his academic account book. As things are today, more than half these credits, and the ones that really count, are those obtained in courses aiming at technical competence in some vocational field.

In the rest of the world liberal education appears to be in retreat, and for the strangest of reasons. The reason is that education is everywhere coming to be recognized as a universal human right. Therefore, everybody is entitled to it. But nobody, so the argument goes, is entitled to any better education than anybody else. Since the great majority of the population is alleged to be too stupid to profit by liberal education, the minority that could profit by it must be deprived of it. These notions have transformed the slogan, education for all, into the idea of inferior education for all. On this point see the current discussion in England in which the Left proposes, instead of extending the benefits of elite "public school" education to everybody, abolishing this kind of education altogether.

No doubt the institutions dedicated to liberal education here and elsewhere were started as elite schools. At a time when every European had a station in life, that to which his parents belonged, and when he was educated, if at all, for that station, it was natural that these institutions, which were designed for the future rulers of the commonwealth, should be limited to the children of the upper classes.

These schools made no pretense of being democratic. They developed a technology of education suited to the background of the pupils they admitted. Pupils with other backgrounds, if they could summon up the courage to scale the battlements of these institutions, found themselves facing an alien culture and a pedagogy designed for that culture. In the ordinary case, they did not try to enter, and when they did enter, they failed.

The remnants of this tradition are scattered all over the place. Socio-economic status, everywhere in the world, determines the length of one's formal education and one's success in it. So when we talk about liberal education today we are plagued by reminiscences and overtones of elitism, aristocracy, and snobbery. It is assumed that something insidiously undemocratic is afoot. But I suggest that true democrats are those who believe that everybody must be educated for freedom, and anti-democrats are those who think there are two kinds of people, those who can be educated and those who can be trained, those who can become human beings and those who are, in Aristotle's phrase, "natural slaves."

The only education worth having in an age of rapid change is liberal education. The formulation of it that we have to discover must meet certain requirements. It must be for all. It must lay the foundations for wise citizenship, the sensible use of leisure, and the continuous development of the highest powers of every human being. It must be the kind of education that will bind men together, not merely in this country but throughout the world; for a world order is emerging.

Harvey Wheeler has said, "In unconsciously creating a unitary industrial world order, man has made his survival depend upon his ability to follow it by a consciously created political order. . . . *Homo sapiens* is everywhere the same. . . . The forces of science, technology, urbanization, industrial development, the mass media, and world integration carry the same imperatives wherever they reach."

An education that tried to assist the formation of the world community would seek to connect rather than divide men; it would seek to do so by drawing out the elements of their common humanity. It would be theoretical rather than practical, because, though men do different things, they can all share in understanding. It would be general rather than specialized, because, though all men are not experts in the same subject, they all ought to grasp the same principles. It would be liberal rather than vocational, because, though all men do not follow the same occupations, the minds of all men should be set free. An education that helps all men to become human by helping them gain complete possession of all their powers would seem to be the only defensible education in a world of rapid technological change; it would seem to be the best for a national community and for the world community as well.

There are no longer any national problems. Or, to put it another way, all national problems are world problems. The United States cannot be an island of power and prosperity in a world of weakness and squalor. That ought to be clear by now. It is equally evident that the United States needs an education that aims not at its own power and prosperity but at the development of the humanity of all mankind. This means dedication to liberal education at home and abroad. The rapidity of technological change, which requires us to take liberal education for all seriously, is a worldwide phenomenon that requires us to take liberal education seriously on a global scale.

We hear a great deal today about relevance and involvement. Education is supposed to be relevant to contemporary issues, and this relevance, it is often suggested, is to be obtained through involvement in action that, it is hoped, will affect contemporary events. I strongly favor relevance and involvement in this sense of these words on one condition, and that is that we recall that education takes time and that we live in a world of very rapid change. Contemporary events and involvement in them are of the first importance if the object is to understand them and through understanding them to refine the principles by which they are understood. However, a curriculum composed only of current events and involvement in them cannot be educational, because by definition current events do not stay current.

I should like to say a word on behalf of critical distance. We see its value easily enough in the matter of language. A child breathes in his mother tongue. He does not understand it, because he does not have to. It is probably fair to say that he never will understand it unless he studies another language. Then he is likely to see for the first time that his own has a comprehensible structure. In the same way, we breathe in the American Way of Life. We assume it is the only way to live because we do not understand it, because we do not understand other ways of life, and because to suggest that the American way could be improved is often regarded as "unpatriotic." But if America is to discharge her responsibilities in a rapidly changing world her citizens have got to be able to appraise her ideals and her performance in terms of standards that can command the respect of mankind. This will involve the effort to discover and comprehend those standards.

This permits me to say a word on behalf of tradition, by which I understand the transmission of our cultural heritage. This is clearly something more than the American way of life. It is the accumulated wisdom of the race. In a rapidly changing world we can recognize it by applying a pragmatic test: it is those works of the mind which illuminate or are likely to illuminate human life under any conditions that may arise.

One way to achieve critical distance is to achieve knowledge of the tradition. If we cannot be sure where we are going, we can at least find out where we have been; we can discover in the reflection of our greatest predecessors suggestions about where we might go and what the advantages or disadvantages of going one way or another may be, and we can try to exert ourselves as intelligently and resolutely as possible in the direction indicated by rational inquiry and debate.

The aim of American education in an age of rapid change should be to do what it can to help everybody gain complete possession of all his powers. As John Dewey says, this is the only possible aim. It is now clear that the only thing we can do is what we ought to have been doing all along.

DISCUSSION QUESTIONS

1. Can an education be truly liberalizing that mandates a certain number of credit hours taken in certain subject areas?
2. How can you undertake to have children learn to learn?
3. Could you sketch an educational design that would promote learning from cradle to grave?
4. Would you agree to the desirability of "an education that helps all men to become human by helping them gain complete possession of all their powers...."? What kinds of learning experiences might bring this about?

JOHN BLACKIE The Character and Aims of British Primary Education

To understand the character and aims of English primary education as it is today, we must know a little of its history. Until 1833 education was provided entirely by the Church or private institutions. In that year the first grant of money (£30,000) was made by the State to aid the Church Schools, but it was not until 1870 that the first schools were started which were independent of the Church and set up and main-

Reprinted by permission of the publisher from Geoffrey Howson, editor, *Children at School: Primary Education in Britain Today.* (New York: Teachers College Press, 1970; copyright 1970 by Teachers College, Columbia University), pp. 1–12.

tained mainly by public money. Even these were not free, the parents having to pay a small sum for their children's education. It was not until 1880 that elementary education became universally compulsory, or till 1891 that it became free.

Until very recently it has been generally believed in England that anyone who can afford it ought to pay for his children's education. The primary schools set up by Church and State in the nineteenth century were intended for the children of the poor, and objections were made to their being used by the rich, though generally speaking they were not the kind of schools that were likely to attract those who could afford something better. The buildings were bare and comfortless, the curriculum very limited, the provision of books meagre, the teaching usually inefficient, the length of stay of the children brief, and the standard of hygiene low.

Few people at that time thought it was possible to cure poverty. It was a Christian duty to relieve it, but that there could ever be a society in which there were no poor people was an idea confined to very few, and generally considered absurd and dangerous. The education of the poor should be limited to what they would need *as poor people* and should not give them ideas 'above their station' in life. The great majority of the poor themselves did not want much education for their children. They were only anxious that they should start earning money at the earliest possible moment. It was only gradually that more liberal ideas spread and education came to be thought of as something which everybody ought to have, and which, for everybody, should be as good as it was possible to make it.

The education that was given in all schools in the nineteenth century, including those attended by the children of the rich, was naturally based upon the ideas then current about children. It was believed that they should be strictly disciplined, severely punished when they were noisy, dirty, naughty or lazy, and that they should learn facts and spellings and figures by heart. There were individual teachers and individual schools in which more enlightened practices were followed, but, in general, strictness, insistence upon sitting still and quiet, endless repetition and the learning of facts were thought to be the only way to teach, and the right one. The story of how this system changed to the freedom and informality of today is tremendously interesting, but too long to be told here. Two of the factors which brought it about may, however, be briefly touched upon.

First there was the influence of educational thinkers. There had always been a few visionaries who were ahead of their time. Even as early as 1570 Roger Ascham had published a book called *The Schoolmaster*, which laid emphasis upon the *love* of learning as an important motive in education; Michel Montaigne (1533–92), in an essay on the teaching of children, had laid stress upon the pleasures of education; but such ideas had little influence on general practice. Jean-Jacques Rousseau in his treatise on education, *Emile* (1762), foreshadowed many modern ideas, notably the education of 'the whole man', though he was working intuitively and had only the slightest practical experience of teaching, at which he was not a success. In the nineteenth century Johann Pestalozzi (1746–1827) first began to observe the behaviour of children systematically, and founded a school in which he could put his ideas into practice, while Friedrich Froebel (1782–1852) was the first to realize the importance of play as a means of learning. John Dewey (1859–1952) emphasized the social aspects of education and the importance of problem-solving. In our own times Jean Piaget (b. 1896) has, through the detailed and systematic observation of children, revealed much about the stages of their learning, some of which the earlier intuitive thinkers had guessed at, and has reinforced much that was already happening in English primary schools and encouraged them to go further.

It is difficult to estimate at all precisely the influence of these thinkers and others like them on English primary education. The complete absence, since 1926, of a centralized curriculum and of what were known in England as Standard (in U.S.A. Grades) and the freedom of the English teacher to frame his own syllabus and follow his own methods, makes such an exercise almost impossible. What is beyond doubt is that it is the principles of Rousseau, Pestalozzi, Froebel, Dewey and Piaget which are most clearly to be found in action in the most advanced primary schools today.

The second factor which brought about the change from formality to informality was the freedom of the teacher, to which I have just referred. This freedom is, so far as I am aware, unparalleled in any other country in the world and it is of such importance that I must deal with it in some detail. In the period of 1862–98 it did not exist. Teachers had to follow a curriculum which had been centrally devised. Their pupils were examined once a year by Her Majesty's Inspectors of Schools, and the amount of salary the teachers received depended in part upon the success of their pupils in this examination. This system was known as 'Payment by results' and anything less free and liberal can hardly be imagined. When the system was abolished in 1898 a process began in which less and less was laid down by the central authority and more and more left to the initiative of the teachers. H.M. Inspectors ceased to be examiners, dreaded and often hated by the teachers, and became increasingly advisers and friends. In 1926, as I have said, the old Standards were abolished and it was left to each individual school to decide what was to be studied in each year and on what principles (age or ability) children were to be promoted.

Since 1926 the responsibility for framing the curriculum, for choosing what subjects it is to include, and what books are to be used, for organizing the school and for deciding what methods are to be employed has been totally removed from the central authority and left in the hands of the teachers. The Education Act of 1944 laid down only two conditions —first that parents should see that their children were educated according to their 'age, ability and aptitude' and secondly, that, subject to a conscience clause, all schools receiving public grants should give religious instruction. The first condition means that there is no obligation of school attendance in England. Nearly all children do of course attend school, but, if a parent can satisfy the authorities that his child is being satisfactorily educated at home, he is within the law; that this is no empty right is shown by a recent case in which the Courts upheld a person who claimed that she was doing just this. To the second condition I shall return later.

If the freedom granted to the teachers is wide, the responsibility is heavy. It may be thought too heavy. The fact that nothing like it is to be found in any other country suggests that the arguments in its favour are not overwhelming. In many countries the curriculum, in all its detail, the books to be used and the methods to be employed, are laid down by the central authority and no deviation from them allowed. The job of the Inspector is to see that the intentions of the authority are put into effect. Even in the United States, where there is no central educational authority and where the authority of the individual state is delegated to numerous smaller units called 'School systems', it yet remains true that the curriculum is drawn up by professional educationalists employed for that puprose and not by the teachers who have to use it.

It is obvious that the centrally devised curriculum has some advantages. It ensures detailed guidance for the weakest teachers even if it limits the initiative of the best. It ensures too that the curriculum and all that is connected with it has been drawn up by experts and that all schools have, if not an equal chance, at least the same material on which to work. It can be, and often is, defended on grounds of social justice. It has, however, according to English thinking, a fatal flaw.

The one essential point in the whole educational system is the point of contact between teacher and child. It is to make this contact as fruitful as possible that everything else—authority, administration, inspection, curriculum exist. If the system fails to work at this point of contact, it fails everywhere. But the contact is a personal one. It is a contact *between persons*, and both the teacher and the pupil must have full scope *as* persons. If the teacher becomes simply a transmitter of other people's ideas and is obliged to follow a scheme of work thought out by somebody else, he ceases to act as a person, because he has not been made, or even allowed, to use his own mind and imagination, to the full extent. The English system does allow him to do this. This means much more than simply allowing him to frame his own syllabus, choose his own books and employ his own methods. It means that he has to work out his own innovations in practice. He is helped in this by his initial training, by the courses he attends after his initial training is finished, by his reading and by the advice and help of colleagues and inspectors, but all has to pass through his own thinking-machine, if the word may be allowed, so that it becomes part of his own personality. Innovation, under such a system, may come more slowly than when it is imposed from above, but it comes more surely because it is initiated by the teacher and based on, and tested by, his own experience.

I would claim further that the English system is much more defensible on grounds of social justice than any other. It allows the teacher to fit all that he does to the needs of the particular children that he is teaching. No centrally devised programme can do this. All children in an age-group must, under such a programme, within narrow limits, follow the same course. This is manifestly unjust, for it makes no allowance for difference in background, ability, choice, taste and state of health. Differences should not be overemphasized, especially those which have a social origin, but to pretend that they do not exist and therefore need not be provided for, is wilful blindness. The English system encourages teacher and child to behave as individuals and each to show initiative and enterprise.

This is a big claim to make and it would be very wrong, in a book written for readers in other countries, to overstate it or to pretend that English primary education is perfect. Perhaps I may claim to know its weaknesses as well as anyone. I do not think that any system is anything like perfect. The ideal of educating an entire population is still a very new one and we all have a great deal still to learn. What I do claim is that a system which allows for the maximum of initiative and imagination at the point of contact between teacher and child will in the end go further than any other.

Go further where? It is time to think about aims. What is English primary education trying to do? It will be obvious at once that the aims of a system which allows so much freedom of choice, can only be stated in very general terms. Such a statement would read something as follows: To allow, and actively encourage, each child to develop his full powers of body and mind (understanding, discrimination, imagination, creation) and to grow up as a balanced individual, able to take his place in society and to live 'in love and charity with all men'. This is very easily said and some would dismiss it as a set of pious hopes and no more. But that is what all educational aims are. It is only when one attempts to realize them that their soundness as well as their feasibility is revealed or disproved. In other words, there must always be a strong element of faith in any statement of educational aims. I hope, in the remainder of this chapter, to show that the aims stated above are genuinely those of many English primary schools and that, however imperfectly, many achieve them.

The first necessity in realizing the aims is to create a physical environment suitable to children. We know, by experience, a lot about this. Children need security. The school building must be safe. It must also not be too large and complicated, for children need security of mind as well as body and little ones can be unhappy and overwhelmed in a vast building. Children need light, air and space, but they also need privacy and small corners and enclosed places. The old kind of school with its row of classrooms, each with rows of desks, and perhaps a hall for assembly and indoor physical exercise, took no heed of the nature of children. The latest English primary schools have no classrooms or desks. They have spaces of varying size, some designed for special purposes, others for general use. There will be a carpeted library for quiet reading and enquiry, one or two studios with tiled floors for painting, modelling, sculpture and craft-work of all kinds, a music room with a variety of musical instruments of a kind which young children can play, places containing mathematical, scientific, historical and geographical material. Out of doors there will be a paved surface for days when the ground is wet, but also plenty of grass, trees to climb, sand to dig in, pools in which to paddle and quiet, sheltered spots in which to sit and talk and daydream. Such buildings, designed in every detail for children and their learning are still exceptional but their number is increasing, because this is the kind of building that a growing number of teachers are demanding.

Children are full of curiosity. They ask endless questions and the equipment of the school provides for this. There are animals, birds and insects to watch and to feed and look after. There are pictures, some chosen simply for their beauty, others to illustrate topics which are being currently studied. But pictures and photographs are not enough. Children love to handle things, little children indeed *must* handle them in order to find out what they are. In addition to toys there are all sorts of things to be handled—shells, stones, bark of trees, leaves, nuts, grasses, feathers, seaweed, textiles—anything that the teachers or children find and bring to school to show the others. Much of England is now urban, and children who live and are brought up in towns know very little about many things which are common and familiar in the countryside, and become very excited when they can see and touch them. When they ask questions they are seldom told the answers. Some boys who asked their Headmaster why bees made their honey-combs in hexagons, received the reply: 'Go and find out for yourselves'. It is no good giving such a reply unless the school is well equipped with the books and apparatus required to find out the answers and unless the children have been trained from the outset in habits of independence. These boys *did* find the answer and it may be agreed that they were fortunate in their teacher as well as in their school, for it is not only a good physical environment that children need but also a good human one.

The human environment is created by the Headteacher and staff, by the example they set and their attitude to the children. This has very little to do with their skill as teachers in the narrow sense. It has to do partly with their knowledge of how children grow and learn, partly with their powers of sympathy and understanding, partly with their temperament and above all with their integrity. A school in which the human relations are good is easily recognizable. The children are friendly and relaxed, obviously happy and confident, kind to each other, usually surprisingly quiet and apparently subjected to no discipline and certainly to no unnecessary rules. It all looks very easy. In fact, of course, it requires endless thought and hard work from the teachers. Yet teachers in such schools seldom look tired or harassed, because the work is so rewarding. The children are not, as they were in the old schools, simply young human beings waiting to be taught or being forced to listen. They are personalities, each with something unique to contribute, each worthy of respect, and learning respect for others and for the differences of others.

It was partly the desire to give children social training suitable to their age which led to an experiment in organization which began in the infant schools (at present 4–8) and which is now beginning to be adopted in the junior schools (8–12). The children, instead of being grouped by age or ability, belong to groups which contain the whole age-range of the school. A child entering the school at, say, 4 years 10 months will join a group which contains 5 and 6 year olds or, in a few cases, 7, 8 and 9 year olds as well. When this organization was first adopted ten or more years ago in a single infant school, many teachers who heard of it thought it utter madness, and of course that is what it would be in a school which used the old formal methods of teaching. With the methods which are now coming into use, to which I shall refer later, and which are discussed in detail in later chapters, it has, however, some obvious advantages. The youngest children find it much easier to settle in when they have not to share their teacher with 30 or more other children of the same age. They receive much help and care from their older companions who themselves learn much from looking after the little ones. It is easier, too, for the teacher when she does not have to cope with a whole group of tiny children, all new acquaintances, who make enormous demands on her time and attention, but has only a small number of these, together with older children whom she has known for two, three, four or five years, with whose capabilities and needs she is familiar, who know her and whom she has trained to work on their own. This organization is known as 'Family Grouping' because it is a large model of a normal family, but it has really existed for many years without anyone thinking it exceptional, in the still numerous though dwindling small village schools with one or two teachers for the whole age-range, in which no other organization was possible. It was the fact that many of these little schools, with their warm, family atmosphere were so good and successful that perhaps first suggested the idea that family grouping might have possibilities in much larger units.

The reader may very likely feel grave doubts about what I have described. He may be ready to concede that under such a system children will be happy and healthy and that the social training may well be effective, but he will say 'What of learning? What of mastering difficulties? What of accuracy? What of the sheer knowledge which is so often needed in life? What of high standards and hard work?' and finally 'What sort of preparation is all this for life in the hard world that follows?' 'Are you not deceiving the children by keeping them in this atmosphere of love and kindness and preparing them for a painful shock when they have to earn their living?'

No system is without its disappointments and failures and no system is proof against misunderstanding or stupidity in those who operate it. The fact that the approach I have indicated makes great demands upon the teacher probably means that, in its most developed form, it is not for everybody, though everybody can learn something from it. There are, however, enough primary schools now in England which conform substantially to the model I have described to make me feel quite confident in making the following assertions.

First, far from the children being inferior either in terms of hard work, accuracy and general achievement, to those taught in a more traditional way, they are markedly superior. They learn from a very early age to act and think for themselves, to use books and to devise experiments in order to find the answers to questions. They perform tasks, not because they are told to, but because their own desires urge them. They are encouraged, indeed they are obliged, to discuss or argue with their teacher, instead of meekly accepting what they are told. They are learning how to learn, not just being taught. When they *are* being taught, more or less perhaps in the old-fashioned way, they know why this particular lesson is being given to them. Very likely they have asked for it themselves. They are, in other words, being educated. And since their education includes all sorts of creative work in art, music, dance and drama and various studies of the world around them, they have a good chance of being educated not only thoroughly but broadly.

One of the marks of an educated man is that he is adaptable. He is accustomed to look objectively at whatever environment he finds himself in and to learn to live in it. The uneducated man is unhappy as soon as he finds himself in strange surroundings. But the educated man is also critical. He does not simply accept what he finds. He may want to alter it. In the last resort he may have to use violence, but he will prefer to proceed by argument and persuasion and will be ready to admit himself mistaken if the argument goes against him and to bow to a majority decision fairly and freely arrived at. It is this kind of man that British primary education aims at producing. He will certainly not fit comfortably into a society ruled by greed, prejudice, hatred and ignorance. In that sense the children in these schools are *not* being prepared for the hard world. They are being prepared for something better by means of experiencing something better in their schools.

There is something else that marks the educated man besides adaptability and a critical mind. He has principles; that is to say he is not convinced that he is automatically right, but has someone or something which he is prepared to admit is a higher authority. England has been a Christian country for over 1,000 years. The number of its people who now, in any sense, practise the Christian faith is not very large, but the Church and the Bible have permeated English life for so long and are so much part of the English scene, that it is still not meaningless to say that England is a Christian country. When the 1944 Education Act laid it down that every school day should begin with an act of corporate worship and that every child should receive religious instruction, unless his parents were conscientiously opposed to it, there was little or no opposition. Even now, when the opposition is stronger and better organized, there is no doubt that the huge majority of English parents want their children to receive religious instruction in school, however little they may give them at home. Such parents, if they were asked what principles they wished their children to follow, would almost certainly reply, 'Christian principles'. If pressed further on what these were, they would probably mention love, kindness, forgiveness, honesty, truthfulness and purity, or, as they might put it, 'leading a decent life'. That none of these virtues, with the possible exception of forgiveness, is exclusively Christian, though all have been consistently upheld by Christianity, would be unknown to them and, if known, would not be thought important. The example of Jesus would be the point on which they would probably insist most. Unlike the Welsh the English are not interested in theology. They are, at heart, pragmatists, that is to say that they believe that if something works it is all right.

The trouble with religious instruction in English primary schools is that it is *not* working. Neither teachers nor children are prepared to accept without question either the literal truth of all the stories in the Bible or many of the dogmas of the faith. The person of Jesus still commands deep devotion, but, generally speaking, religious and moral instruction is a bit shaky and it is incidentally from Christians, not from atheists, that the most searching criticisms of it have come. This, I think, is the weakest part of English primary education at present and the precise place of principles in the education of young children, the basis on which they are to be founded and the form in which they are to be taught and enforced is one of the problems that remain unsolved. Froebel said that all education not founded on religion was unproductive, and the English have given general assent to this view. They would still regard an education which took no account of 'spiritual values' as being incomplete, though the rather vague meaning attached to this term which has hitherto passed muster will not do any longer.

I said just now that the English are pragmatists in religion, that they believe in what worked. This has really always been their approach to education. They have distrusted theories and the experts who thought of them. They were very slow to be influenced by educational thinkers, few of whom were British. Those who were, Rachel and Margaret Macmillan, Susan Isaacs, Nancy Catty and Dorothy Gardner were all practising teachers, and all, it may be observed, women. Rousseau (French), Pestalozzi (Swiss), Froebel (German), Dewey (American), Piaget (Swiss) have perhaps been the most powerful sources of influence, but it was an influence much disguised by being mediated through interpreters. It is probable that few English teachers have actually read any of the books of which these men were the authors. They have put their faith in practical experience; have evolved a system in which practical experience is given the power and have some splendid achievements to record. In future they may have to listen more to the theorist and to the researcher than they have done in the past. Indeed they are already doing this. If they do it with a wary and critical ear they may benefit, but if they ever allow the theorist to take over, they may throw away all that they have gained, and destroy the unique contribution that England has made to primary education, the freedom of the teacher at the point where freedom really matters.

DISCUSSION QUESTIONS

1. Blackie sees English primary education emphasizing the contact between persons, where "both the teacher and the pupil must have full scope as persons." What is the main stress in American education?
2. Evaluate Blackie's statement that the educated man "in the last resort may have to use violence" to alter the social structure which he finds undesirable.
3. Are there any drawbacks to applying the English concepts here?
4. Do you believe that "all education not founded on religion" is unproductive?

CHAPTER 3 Education of the
Culturally Different

Immediately after World War II, the schools of the large urban ghettos throughout the United States became a major social problem. In the period of mass European immigration of the early 1900s, urban schools had accepted and processed large numbers of children. The quality of the education they gave these children is debatable, but the society of the day was amorphous and expansive enough to absorb the school's mistakes. The shocking failure of slum schools cannot now be hidden. Black children who before had been educated in the segregated schools of the rural South, and Spanish-speaking children from Puerto Rico and from the Southwest, present a problem that the schools have bitten off, chewed, but cannot swallow.

Basic to the plight of the schools is the broader social problem of the integration of the newcomers into the social body. Housing patterns and the neighborhood school concept have resulted in "de facto" segregation, northern style. The "Harlems" of America have had schools characterized by old and inferior physical plants, overcrowded classes, underpaid, poorly prepared, and transient teachers, and lack of flexibility of organization and administration, among other ills. This is not to say that other social agencies have been any more capable or visionary in outlook or performance. Taken together, the collective ineptitude demonstrates a deep-seated social breakdown stemming from the second-class citizenship of a large segment of the people.

It might be asked why education is most severely under attack. Perhaps the poor are most angered at the schools because, besides being visible and vulnerable, they are supposed to hold the key to social mobility and eventual affluence. Television has shown the "disadvantaged" what they are lacking; education ought to provide the means for attaining it. Instead, very few are even "making it" out of the ghetto. Education has failed the poor and they are not loath to point the finger of blame.

The poor demand for their children the education that "advantaged" children get. They will be tragically "shortchanged" if they get no more than this. Education for ghetto children will be a mockery until society will no longer tolerate penalizing children for their parents' poverty and the circumstance of their birth. Slum children will become "children" when the ghetto walls, like the walls of Jericho, come tumbling down.

Education for all children calls for bold, new, innovative thinking, deeply rooted in humanity. It must be part of the vision that sees all men joined together as parts of humanity. Only then can democracy be made meaningful. And education is the heart of democracy.

BEATRICE LASKOWITZ GOLDBERG She Is Risen

Ten years ago I lectured to a class
Of Harlem children, come to see the world
Of art made public in a great museum.
I chose, as I had chosen in the past
For ones so young (six or seven years),
A subject for our slow meanderings.
"Let's see the Mother and the Child in art.
Let's see, as artists of the past have seen,
All loving mothers, and their children, here
Upon these walls, inside these frames.
The same, sweet subject, from the far and recent past."

All smiles and romping, as they held the arms
Of sweaters dangling, and the legs of stools,
They said they'd come and follow me around.

More sobered now, with looking, we went by
An Empress with her son upon her knee—
A solemn kingling from the Byzantine.
His nimbus golden, and his sky the same,
He hushed our speaking with his golden eye.

We were more free a hundred years away,
In time proceeding through the Renaissance.
The babies dimpled and the mothers smiled.
The sun shone smiling on the Tuscan hills.
The child stood freely on the balustrade,
Her hand but lightly holding, lest he fall.
And all around were springtime leaves and buds,
Some bursting, as he burst from infancy.
He played with grapes; she would not see. She smiled.
They were not yet the wine of martyrdom.

And so, at last, upon the bright Gauguin,
The final family—mother, child, and friends.
Here was an island brilliant in the sun:
A second Eden, jungled in the light.
Here was the mother, brown and glistening.
Here was the baby, browner on her arm.
"And this is Mary. This is Jesus, here."
I showed the tracings of their halos, drawn
Against the ripeness of the hills and sky.

Reprinted from *Social Education*, January 1969, p. 37. Reprinted with permission of
the National Council for the Social Studies and Beatrice L. Goldberg.

There was a stillness in my audience,
Come down from Lenox Avenue to see
Some beauty in a city lived in stone.

One hand was raised in question—one for all.
One small, brown hand upon a browner arm.

"And that is Mary? That is Jesus, there?"
His eyes were wondered wide with hope and fear.
"They are," I answered, and his brow was knit
Into a trouble, terrible and proud.
I waited, as he stood to make the words
That came so slowly clear: "Is that allowed?"

Where is he now, my visitor, my friend?
What alley; stoop, What furnace room? What school?
What car; what office in the day or night?
Where has he gone? Where will he go—that boy
Who had a Yes, however brief in time,
When he was young, and questioned, and could say:
My love-white Mother could have mothered God.

DISCUSSION QUESTIONS

1. Is it enough for the schools to provide ghetto children with "equal" or compensatory, or even superior education?
2. Is it possible that God is black and a woman?

ROBERT KENNEDY ## A Talk Delivered the Night of the Assassination of Martin Luther King, Jr.

This is a time of shame and sorrow. It is not a day for politics. I have saved this one opportunity to speak briefly to you about this mindless menace of violence in America which again stains our land and every one of our lives.

It is not the concern of any one race. The victims of the violence are black and white, rich and poor, young and old, famous and unknown. They are, most important of all, human beings whom other human beings loved and needed. No one—no matter where he lives or what he does—can be certain who will suffer from some senseless act of bloodshed. And yet it goes on and on.

Why? What has violence ever accomplished? What has it ever created? No martyr's cause has ever been stilled by his assassin's bullet. No wrongs have ever been righted by riots and civil disorders. A sniper is only a coward, not a hero, and an uncontrolled, uncontrollable mob is only the voice of madness, not the voice of the people.

Whenever any American's life is taken by another American unnecessarily—whether it is done in the name of the law or in the defiance of law, by one man or a gang, in cold blood or in passion, in an attack of violence or in response to violence—whenever we tear at the fabric of life which another man has painfully and clumsily woven for himself and his children, the whole nation is degraded.

"Among free men," said Abraham Lincoln, "there can be no successful appeal from the ballot to the bullet; and those who take such appeal are sure to lose their cause and pay the costs." Yet we seemingly tolerate a rising level of violence that ignores our common humanity and our claims to civilization alike. We calmly accept newspaper reports of civilian slaughter in far-off lands. We glorify killing on movie and television screens and call it entertainment. We make it easy for men of all shades of sanity to acquire whatever weapons and ammunition they desire.

Too often we honor swagger and bluster and the wielders of force; too often we excuse those who are willing to build their own lives on the shattered dreams of others. Some Americans who preach nonviolence abroad fail to practice it here at home. Some who accuse others of inciting riots have by their own conduct invited them. Some look for scapegoats, others look for conspiracies, but this much is clear; violence breeds violence, repression brings retaliation, and only a cleaning of our whole society can remove this sickness from our soul.

For there is another kind of violence, slower but just as deadly, destructive as the shot or the bomb in the night. This is the violence of institutions; indifference and inaction and slow decay. This is the violence that afflicts the poor, that poisons relations between men because their skin has different colors. This is a slow destruction of a child by hunger, and schools without books and homes without heat in the winter.

This is the breaking of a man's spirit by denying him the chance to stand as a father and as a man among other men. And this too afflicts us all. I have not come here to propose a set of specific remedies nor is there a single set. For a broad and adequate outline we know what must be done. When you teach a man to hate and fear his brother, when you teach that he is a lesser man because of his color or his beliefs or the policies he pursues, when you teach that those who differ from you threaten your freedom or your job family, then you also learn to confront others not as fellow citizens but as enemies—to be met not with cooperation but with conquest, to be subjugated and mastered.

We learn, at the last, to look at our brothers as aliens, men with whom we share a city, but not a community, men bound to us in common dwelling, but not in common effort. We learn to share only a common fear—only a common desire to retreat from each other—only a common impulse to meet disagreement with force. For all this there are no final answers. Yet we know what we must do. It is to achieve true justice among our fellow citizens. The question is whether we can find in our own midst and in our own hearts that leadership of human purpose that will recognize the terrible truths of our existence.

We must admit the vanity of our false distinctions among men and learn to find our own advancement in the search for the advancement of all. We must admit in ourselves that our own children's future cannot be built on the misfortunes of others. We must recognize that this short life can neither be ennobled or enriched by hatred or revenge. Our lives on this planet are too short and the work to be done too great to let this spirit flourish any longer in our land.

Of course we cannot vanquish it with a program, nor with a resolution. But we can perhaps remember—even if only for a time—that those who live with us are our brothers, that they share with us the same short movement of life, that they seek—as we do—nothing but the chance to live out their lives in purpose and happiness, winning what satisfaction and fulfillment they can. Surely this bond of common faith, this bond of common goal, can begin to teach us something. Surely we can learn, at least, to look at those around us as fellow men and surely we can begin to work a little harder to bind up the wounds among us and to become in our own hearts brothers and countrymen once again.

DISCUSSION QUESTIONS

1. Is, as Robert Kennedy says, the solution to our racial and minority problems to be found only in the hearts of men?
2. Is the fragmentation of America so final and so absolute that the piecemeal steps toward integrating our schools (for example, busing and pairing of schools) are to no avail?
3. Can the schools themselves contribute to healing the breach between diverse groups?

MARTIN LUTHER KING, JR. Letter from
Birmingham Jail

April 16, 1963

MY DEAR FELLOW CLERGYMEN:

While confined here in the Birmingham city jail, I came across your recent statement calling my present activities "unwise and untimely." Seldom do I pause to answer criticism of my work and ideas. If I sought to answer all the criticisms that cross my desk, my secretaries would have little time for anything other than such correspondence in the course of the day, and I would have no time for constructive work. But since I feel that you are men of genuine good will and that your criticisms are sincerely set forth, I want to try to answer your statement in what I hope will be patient and reasonable terms.

I think I should indicate why I am here in Birmingham, since you have been influenced by the view which argues against "outsiders coming in." I have the honor of serving as president of the Southern Christian Leadership Conference, an organization operating in every southern state, with headquarters in Atlanta, Georgia. We have some eighty-five affiliated organizations across the South, and one of them is the Alabama Christian Movement for Human Rights. Frequently we share staff, educational and financial resources with our affiliates. Several months ago the affiliate here in Birmingham asked us to be on call to engage in a nonviolent direct-action program if such were deemed necessary. We readily consented, and when the hour came we lived up to our promise. So I, along with several members of my staff, am here because I was invited here. I am here because I have organizational ties here.

But more basically, I am in Birmingham because injustice is here. Just as the prophets of the eighth century B.C. left their villages and carried their "thus saith the Lord" far beyond the boundaries of their home towns, and just as the Apostle Paul left his village of Tarsus and carried the gospel of Jesus Christ to the far corners of the Greco-Roman world,

Abridgement of "Letter from Birmingham Jail," April 16, 1963, from *Why We Can't Wait*, by Martin Luther King, Jr. Copyright © 1963 by Martin Luther King, Jr. By permission of Harper & Row, Publishers, Inc.

AUTHOR'S NOTE: This response to a published statement by eight fellow clergymen from Alabama (Bishop C. C. J. Carpenter, Bishop Joseph A. Durick, Rabbi Hilton L. Grafman, Bishop Paul Hardin, Bishop Holan B. Harmon, the Reverend George M. Murray, the Reverend Edward V. Ramage and the Reverend Earl Stallings) was composed under somewhat constricting circumstances. Begun on the margins of the newspaper in which the statement appeared while I was in jail, the letter was continued on scraps of writing paper supplied by a friendly Negro trusty, and concluded on a pad my attorneys were eventually permitted to leave me. Although the text remains in substance unaltered, I have indulged in the author's prerogative of polishing it for publication.

so am I compelled to carry the gospel of freedom beyond my own home town. Like Paul, I must constantly respond to the Macedonian call for aid.

Moreover, I am cognizant of the interrelatedness of all communities and states. I cannot sit idly by in Atlanta and not be concerned about what happens in Birmingham. Injustice anywhere is a threat to justice everywhere. We are caught in an inescapable network of mutuality, tied in a single garment of destiny. Whatever affects one directly, affects all indirectly. Never again can we afford to live with the narrow, provincial "outside agitator" idea. Anyone who lives inside the United States can never be considered an outsider anywhere within its bounds.

You deplore the demonstrations taking place in Birmingham. But your statement, I am sorry to say, fails to express a similar concern for the conditions that brought about the demonstrations. I am sure that none of you would want to rest content with the superficial kind of social analysis that deals merely with effects and does not grapple with underlying causes. It is unfortunate that demonstrations are taking place in Birmingham, but it is even more unfortunate that the city's white power structure left the Negro community with no alternative.

In any nonviolent campaign there are four basic steps: collection of the facts to determine whether injustices exist; negotiation; self-purification; and direct action. We have gone through all of these steps in Birmingham. There can be no gainsaying the fact that racial injustice engulfs this community.

. . .

You may well ask: "Why direct action? Why sit-ins, marches and so forth? Isn't negotiation a better path?" You are quite right in calling for negotiation. Indeed, this is the very purpose of direct action. Nonviolent direct action seeks to create such a crisis and foster such a tension that a community which has constantly refused to negotiate is forced to confront the issue. It seeks so to dramatize the issue that it can no longer be ignored. My citing the creation of tension as part of the work of the nonviolent-resister may sound rather shocking. But I must confess that I am not afraid of the word "tension." I have earnestly opposed violent tension, but there is a type of constructive, nonviolent tension which is necessary for growth. Just as Socrates felt that it was necessary to create a tension in the mind so that individuals could rise from the bondage of myths and half-truths to the unfettered realm of creative analysis and objective appraisal, so must we see the need for nonviolent gadflies to create the kind of tension in society that will help men rise from the dark depths of prejudice and racism to the majestic heights of understanding and brotherhood.

. . .

We know through painful experience that freedom is never voluntarily given by the oppressor; it must be demanded by the oppressed. Frankly, I have yet to engage in a direct-action campaign that was "well timed" in the view of those who have not suffered unduly from the disease of segregation. For years now I have heard the word "Wait!" It rings in the ear of every Negro with piercing familiarity. This "Wait" has almost always meant "Never." We must come to see, with one of our distinguished jurists, that "justice too long delayed is justice denied."

We have waited for more than 340 years for our constitutional and God-given rights. The nations of Asia and Africa are moving with jet-like speed toward gaining political independence, but we still creep at horse-and-buggy pace toward gaining a cup of coffee at a lunch counter. Perhaps it is easy for those who have never felt the stinging darts of segregation to say, "Wait." but when you have seen vicious mobs lynch your mothers and fathers at will and drown your sisters and brothers at whim; when you have seen hate-filled policemen curse, kick and even kill your black brothers and sisters; when you see the vast majority of your twenty million Negro brothers smothering in an airtight cage of poverty in the midst of an affluent society; when you suddenly find your tongue twisted and your speech stammering as you seek to explain to your six-year-old daughter why she can't go to the public amusement park that has just been advertised on television, and see tears welling up in her eyes when she is told that Funtown is closed to colored children, and see ominous clouds of inferiority beginning to form in her little mental sky, and see her beginning to distort her personality by developing an unconscious bitterness toward white people; when you have to concoct an answer for a five-year-old son who is asking: "Daddy, why do white people treat colored people so mean?"; when you take a cross-country drive and find it necessary to sleep night after night in the uncomfortable corners of your automobile because no motel will accept you; when you are humiliated day in and day out by nagging signs reading "white" and "colored"; when your first name becomes "nigger," your middle name becomes "boy" (however old you are) and your last name becomes "John," and your wife and mother are never given the respected title "Mrs."; when you are harried by day and haunted by night by the fact that you are a Negro, living constantly at tiptoe stance, never quite knowing what to expect next, and are plagued with inner fears and outer resentments; when you are forever fighting a degenerating sense of "nobodiness"—then you will understand why we find it difficult to wait. There comes a time when the cup of endurance runs over, and men are no longer willing to be plunged into the abyss of despair. I hope, sirs, you can understand our legitimate and unavoidable impatience.

You express a great deal of anxiety over our willingness to break laws. This is certainly a legitimate concern. Since we so diligently urge people to obey the Supreme Court's decision of 1954 outlawing segregation in the public schools, at first glance it may seem rather paradoxical for us consciously to break laws. One may well ask: "How can you advocate breaking some laws and obeying others?" The answer lies in the fact that there are two types of laws: just and unjust. I would be the first to advocate obeying just laws. One has not only a legal but a moral responsibility to obey just laws. Conversely, one has a moral responsibility to disobey unjust laws. I would agree with St. Augustine that "an unjust law is no law at all."

Now, what is the difference between the two? How does one determine whether a law is just or unjust? A just law is a man-made code that squares with the moral law or the law of God. An unjust law is a code that is out of harmony with the moral law. To put it in the terms of St. Thomas Aquinas: An unjust law is a human law that is not rooted in eternal law and natural law. Any law that uplifts human personality is just. Any law that degrades human personality is unjust. All segregation statutes are unjust because segregation distorts the soul and damages the personality. It gives the segregator a false sense of superiority and the segregated a false sense of inferiority. Segregation, to use the terminology of the Jewish philosopher Martin Buber, substitutes an "I-it" relationship for an "I-thou" relationship and ends up relegating persons to the status of things. Hence segregation is not only politically, economically and sociologically unsound, it is morally wrong and sinful. Paul Tillich has said that sin is separation. Is not segregation an existential expression of man's tragic separation, his awful estrangement, his terrible sinfulness? Thus it is that I can urge men to obey the 1954 decision of the Supreme Court, for it is morally right; and I can urge them to disobey segregation ordinances, for they are morally wrong.

. . .

Of course, there is nothing new about this kind of civil disobedience. It was evidenced sublimely in the refusal of Shadrach, Meshach and Abednego to obey the laws of Nebuchadnezzar, on the ground that a higher moral law was at stake. It was practiced superbly by the early Christians, who were willing to face hungry lions and the excruciating pain of chopping blocks rather than submit to certain unjust laws of the Roman Empire. To a degree, academic freedom is a reality today because Socrates practiced civil disobedience. In our own nation, the Boston Tea Party represented a massive act of civil disobedience.

We should never forget that everything Adolf Hitler did in Germany was "legal" and everything the Hungarian freedom fighters did in Hungary was "illegal." It was "illegal" to aid and comfort a Jew in Hitler's Germany. Even so, I am sure that, had I lived in Germany at the time, I would have aided and comforted my Jewish brothers. If today I lived in a Communist country where certain principles dear to the Christian faith are suppressed, I would openly advocate disobeying that country's antireligious laws.

I must make two honest confessions to you, my Christian and Jewish brothers. First, I must confess that over the past few years I have been gravely disappointed with the white moderate. I have almost reached the regrettable conclusion that the Negro's great stumbling block in his stride toward freedom is not the White Citizen's Counciler or the Ku Klux Klanner, but the white moderate, who is more devoted to "order" than to justice; who prefers a negative peace which is the absence of tension to a positive peace which is the presence of justice; who constantly says. "I agree with you in the goal you seek, but I cannot agree with your methods of direct action"; who paternalistically believes he can set the timetable for another man's freedom; who lives by a mythical concept of time and who constantly advises the Negro to wait for a "more convenient season." Shallow understanding from people of good will is more frustrating than absolute misunderstanding from people of ill will. Lukewarm acceptance is much more bewildering than outright rejection.

. . .

I was initially disappointed at being categorized as an extremist, as I continued to think about the matter I gradually gained a measure of satisfaction from the label. Was not Jesus an extremist for love: "Love your enemies, bless them that curse you, do good to them that hate you, and pray for them which despitefully use you and persecute you." Was not Amos an extremist for justice: "Let justice roll down like waters and righteousness like an ever-flowing stream." Was not Paul an extremist for the Christian gospel. "I bear in my body the marks of the Lord Jesus." Was not Martin Luther an extremist: "Here I stand; I cannot do otherwise, so help me God." And John Bunyan: "I will stay in jail to the end of my days before I make a butchery of my conscience." And Abraham Lincoln: "This nation cannot survive half slave and half free." And Thomas Jefferson: "We hold these truths to be self-evident, that all men are created equal . . ." So the question is not whether we will be extremists, but what kind of extremists we will be. Will we be extremists for hate or for love? Will we be extremists for the preservation of injustice or for the extension of justice? In that dramatic scene on Calvary's hill three men were crucified. We must never forget that all three were crucified for the same crime—the crime of extremism. Two were extremists for immorality, and thus fell below their environment. The other, Jesus Christ, was an extremist for love, truth and goodness, and thereby rose above his environment. Perhaps the South, the nation and the world are in dire need of creative extremists.

I had hoped that the white moderate would see this need. Perhaps I was too optimistic; perhaps I expected too much. I suppose I should have realized that few members of the oppressor race can understand the deep groans and passionate yearnings of the oppressed race, and still fewer have the vision to see that injustice must be rooted out by strong, persistent and determined action. I am thankful, however, that some of our white brothers in the South have grasped the meaning of this social revolution and committed themselves to it.

.   .   .

I have heard numerous southern religious leaders admonish their worshipers to comply with a desegregation decision because it is the law, but I have longed to hear white ministers declare: "Follow this decree because integration is morally right and because the Negro is your brother." In the midst of blatant injustices inflicted upon the Negro, I have watched white churchmen stand on the sideline and mouth pious irrelevancies and sanctimonious trivialities. In the midst of a mighty struggle to rid our nation of racial and economic injustice, I have heard many ministers say: "Those are social issues, with which the gospel has no real concern." And I have watched many churches commit themselves to a completely otherworldly religion which makes a strange, un-Biblical distinction between body and soul, between the sacred and the secular.

.   .   .

Before closing I feel impelled to mention one other point in your statement that has troubled me profoundly. You warmly commended the Birmingham police force for keeping "order" and "preventing violence." I doubt that you would have so warmly commended the police force if you had seen its dogs sinking their teeth into unarmed, nonviolent Negroes. I doubt that you would so quickly commend the policemen if you were to observe their ugly and inhumane treatment of Negroes here in the city jail; if you were to watch them push and curse old Negro women and young Negro girls; if you were to see them slap and kick old Negro men and young boys; if you were to observe them, as they did on two occasions, refuse to give us food because we wanted to sing our grace together. I cannot join in your praise of the Birmingham police department.

It is true that the police have exercised a degree of discipline in handling the demonstrators. In this sense they have conducted themselves rather "nonviolently" in public. But for what purpose? To preserve the evil system of segregation. Over the past few years I have consistently preached that nonviolence demands that the means we use must be as pure as the ends we seek. I have tried to make clear that it is wrong to use immoral means to attain moral ends. But now I must affirm that it is just as wrong, or perhaps even more so to use moral means to preserve immoral ends.

. . .

If I have said anything in this letter that overstates the truth and indicates an unreasonable impatience, I beg you to forgive me. If I have said anything that understates the truth and indicates my having a patience that allows me to settle for anything less than brotherhood, I beg God to forgive me.

I hope this letter finds you strong in the faith. I also hope that circumstances will soon make it possible for me to meet each of you, not as an integrationist or a civil-rights leader but as a fellow clergyman and a Christian brother. Let us all hope that the dark clouds of racial prejudice will soon pass away and the deep fog of misunderstanding will be lifted from our fear-drenched communities, and in some not too distant tomorrow the radiant stars of love and brotherhood will shine over our great nation with all their scintillating beauty.

Yours for the cause of Peace and Brotherhood,
Martin Luther King, Jr.

DISCUSSION QUESTIONS

1. Is King's appeal for "love and brotherhood," seeking to touch the hearts of men and affect their actions, so much empty rhetoric in today's America?
2. What immediate steps do you suggest "that will help men rise from the dark depths of prejudice and racism to the majestic heights of understanding and brotherhood"?

NED O'GORMAN The Workers

All I ask of a worker is that he love children, that he will try to learn to love them more, and that he will be ready to be taught by them how to love them and how to teach them.

Beware of this kind of a TEACHER:

The teacher who tells you what children really want, what children are and what children don't want.
The teacher who talks about her lesson plan before she meets her class.
The teacher who talks to the children as if she wanted to make friends with the children. Children are friendly but when they are loomed

over by a creature who is trying to be *nice* they put on an act, hide their feelings, brood, and go "queer."

A teacher who would be a worker must be ready merely to be in a room where there are children. He must wait (often a long time) until children freely open their inner lives to him. A teacher who will be a worker must watch his children and learn how to move *with* them. (I like to think of teachers as workers.)

The lesson plan is in the children.

A radiant, calm, and hopeful patience is the only virtue I'd ask of a teacher. (Not a nervous, hectic patience built on tranquilizers.)

Tend to hire teachers who revere the idea of childhood.

Beware of the teacher who assumes ascendancy over the classroom. There is an air about them, a martial, maitre d' arrogance in the way they sit, in their gestures. Watch how children sit, stand, and look when they're around. They know the gait of a tamer when they see one.

The worker who is a teacher in the cities of the dispossessed is often, alas, a child's only source of discourse and excitement. A worker then must learn how to talk to children about the world. At home there is often no time for such a luxury. In the morning I seek out the children who seem sad and sit with them on the sidewalk and talk about what they had for breakfast, about what they dreamed, and about what goes on around us: the color of cars, the children on their way to school, the dogs and cats that wander along the street; we sing a little and I hold them close to me; we usually laugh a good deal.

A worker ought to be a divining rod.

All the workers in our storefront on Madison Avenue are from the block, or from within two or three blocks from us. None have credentials that could get them a job in Headstart. (Except as a teacher-aide and then they'd be under the thumb of a professional who'd drive them crazy with guidance.)

A child learns about himself and the world in many strange ways. One way is the manner he discovers to move toward other people.

Josephine Lewis knows how to let children come to her, freely, smiling, with their whole selves in whatever state they may be in: sick, angry, terrified, happy. She has learned the tactics of the teacher in a long, suffering, examination of her own life and, as she learned about herself, she learned about children; at the same time the children learned about her.

She is a fine teacher. We were talking one day about Headstart. I was trying to find a word to describe what I had seen in a Headstart classroom that so angered me. She said, "Ned, it's dry."

She knows our children need a loving, reasonable, imaginative, adventurous life. She knows that before alphabets and numbers they need to FEEL the juices and the nerve endings of their "selves." The first thing to happen to children in the public schools will be the fitting on their spirits of the chains and iron masks of system, order, competition, fear, and the "four walls of the SCHOOL."

Minnie Ray, Olivia Day, Bernice Mills, and Lila Mae Carter, Gertrude Safford, Baby Franklin, Geneva Johnson, like Josephine, have come up through the agony, excitement, and awesome troubles and happiness of the streets the children wander through and watch. They know precisely what is to be done with a two year old who cries all day, with a child who bites, with babies who stare out of their cribs as if they were drugged.

They know the dimensions of suffering.

Lesson in observation. Our workers know that children cure each other. Sylvia came in the door her first day in the storefront and cried with such intensity that I thought she'd swallowed a pin. Anthony Day went to her and held her hand. He is five. She is three. She stopped crying. Anthony went about his business. Every morning for a week Anthony held her hand and soon she didn't need to cry in the mornings.

A teacher who doesn't respect the dimensions of suffering would meddle, fuss, and tempt Sylvia to stop crying. ("If I buy you an ice cream will you stop?")

A crying child is almost always crying because he is unhappy; seldom because he's being "naughty."

Lesson in observation. In a classroom the mystery is the mystery of the one and the one and the many: a child alone and a child with a friend, and all the children together. Watch the children fighting. There is fighting that is one against another, and there is some real nastiness in it: scratching, kicking, biting. Then there is fighting that is celebration; a kind of rough dancing. Each child: his peace, bad dreams, joy, tummy ache, and bad temper. Then a class of peace, bad dreams, joys, tummy aches, and bad tempers.

Lesson in observation. Lucy had been registered in the local kindergarten. Someone had taken her out of our school and plunked her down in a strange classroom. The guidance counselor called me: that child is raising hell: fighting, crying, disrupting everyone and everything. She's been put in a "retarded group." I went over and took the child away. How awful to see her in such a state and then to find that the only way the school had to cope with her was to put her in with the children who had been determined retarded.

Millie is four. She has been coming to us for three years. She lives in a five-room flat with twelve other children, three ladies, and from time to time the mothers of some of her cousins—all thirteen are kin.

She is a silent, tiny creature who lives in the fits and starts of her spirit. Life is not easy for her; too many people around, too much noise, not enough room. A contemplative at heart, Millie deceived her psychologist in the local hospital into thinking she was retarded, hostile, regressive, etc., etc. I went to a meeting when Millie was *discussed*. I said, "she is a bright, happy, humorous little girl and if she is silent, etc., etc. with her psychologist it is the fault of the psychologist."

A lot hung on that meeting. If the prognosis was bad she could have been taken from her family. Another child psychologist, who knew something about children, found her to be what I knew she was: bright enough for an average four year old, brighter in fact and acquainted with an extraordinary array of "things."

Our children go on trips three and four times a week. They are aware of the CITY, its zoos, museums, streets, subways, stores, parks, and people. They astonish visitors with their talk about what they have done and what they are going to do. They name things they see as if they were naming worlds. (In an Abilene, Texas, Headstart classroom I saw a teacher sitting at a table with her children handing them cardboard animals and asking them to tell her what they were. A lion. A peacock. An elephant. I discovered there was a zoo in town. What was she doing with cardboard animals?) Preschool classrooms are usually filled with junk: teachers' crutches that kids fall over.

Millie and Lucy are saved for the moment. Lucy returned to school and seems happy and Millie is still with us growing like a wildflower.

They are saved in part because of our workers. Their great gift is their instinct. Public-school teachers lose instinct to bureaucracies, principals, vanity, fear, and loneliness. So many of them have come to me and said that only after years of fear and the dominion of principals and boards of education did they see what a horror the schools were. Most teachers are lonely. The classrooms and the halls of the public schools are armed camps, where teachers are the "generals" and MPs. Children are not ordered and despise order that is based on a fear and contempt for their *disorder (the source of their wisdom and life).*

Our workers are *with* the children all the day, in all kinds of weather. The children come to school (our storefront to them is their *school*) and meet the workers; the workers meet them and they seek out the way the day will go.

No guidelines; the child is the guideline. No rules; the child is the rule. No lesson plan; the child is the lesson plan.

I am in awe of our workers' common sense, of their understanding of what children need, and of their wit, freedom, and ability to remain themselves.

They know that in a child's anger, silence, violence, rage, and strangeness is strength. They revere a child in the spell of his torment and joys. In that "spell" a child discovers the tensions that sing of life and freedom.

Lesson in observation. A junkie had come into the storefront and pushed me against the wall, took a broom handle and tapped it across my eyeglasses threatening to break them. He robbed me of a couple of cents and frightened me. I slipped away and sat on a table. I put my head in my hands and cried. Luis (four) was there and tried to get me to look at him. I couldn't. I didn't want him to see me crying. He went home that night and told his mother I was dead. When he saw me in the morning he said, "Oh, Ned, you not dead, you live."

Jonah is from the south and his whole manner is wild and country and his speech so regional that it is hard to understand most of what he says. (One must be careful too when one tries to change a child's dialect. It is part of his spirit. I praise Jonah's language now. Later on we must try to straighten it out here and there but now it is part of his strength.) He is always on the verge of a fit. In spite of all the hell in his family he is loved and I must never forget how much he is loved. One adds to the love he knows, rectifies it, frees it. I never try to substitute another love for it. *A worker must not deflect love from the parents, no matter how disturbed a child's parents' love may be, how violent that love may be. It is the love upon which the children in the cities of the dispossessed build their survival and their understanding of love.*
The schools could destroy Jonah by trying to convert him into something he is not. We will have to watch him carefully.

The best teachers are those who are ready to be transformed into teachers. No one begins as a teacher; one becomes a teacher. I want a teacher to see each child as the only child in the world. If they work in any storefront school I have anything to do with, I want them to love the streets, the people in them, and the majesty in the cities of the dispossessed that is revolutionary, unique, terrible, and in this world of stereotypes and antiseptic hope, a bright remnant of civilized life.

DISCUSSION QUESTIONS

1. What do you think of O'Gorman's statement, "all I ask of a worker is that he love children, that he will try to learn to love them more, and that he will be ready to be taught by them how to love them and how to teach them"?
2. Should you enter class with a lesson plan? Defend your position?
3. Does a lesson plan interfere with teaching and learning?

JEAN D. GRAMBS The Self-Concept:
Basis for Reeducation of Negro Youth

The human personality is a bundle of dynamic forces about which we have many conjectures and few certainties. Like the inner particles of the atom, which are seen only by the shadows they cast, so we have only the shadows of the workings of the human psyche. We are not always sure, and certainly not always in agreement, as to what these shadows represent. But whatever components there may be to personality, in the words of Park and Burgess, "it is an organization of traits and attitudes of which the individual's conception of himself is central."[1]

There are unresolved differences of opinion among psychologists as to the sources of behavior. Whatever it is that impels an individual to act or not to act, a significant role is played in this determination by what the person thinks about himself.[2] He may be able to tell us something about his view of himself, or he may be able to tell us very little. What he tells us may be what he really thinks, or it may be a selective version for a particular public; on what appears to be safer ground, he may reveal a different version of what he thinks he is. Or he may be completely unaware of what his true feelings about himself are. We are assuming, however, that the person acts and can only act in terms of what he thinks about himself in a given situation, and he cannot assess that situation and its action requirements except in terms of his own view of himself.

Contemporary research in child growth and development has highlighted the central significance of the individual's concept of himself.[3] The way a person views himself is the way he will behave. If he sees himself as successful, as someone whom others like, as good-looking, then his behavior will reflect these views. If the person considers himself to be inadequate, as someone whom others probably won't like, as unattractive, then again his behavior will reflect these valuations. The factual truth of any of these statements is irrelevant. A very beautiful girl may consider herself unattractive; children with adequate intellectual endowment may do poorly in school because they perceive themselves as not able.[4]

The source of one's self-image is, of course, not internal; it is learned. The way a mother responds to her newborn baby—with delight or with weary acceptance—will be apparent in the behavior of the baby before very long. A child whose parents trust and love him will be a loving and trustful individual who will tend to go out to greet the world and its many new experiences.

We have some research insights into the differential treatment that parents accord their children from the very beginning.[5] It is true, too, that different cultures produce different personality types. The ways in which children are reared, the things that they are told to do or not to do, the rewards for various kinds of competencies or their lacks, differ from one culture to another.[6] This produces, as Kardiner has pointed out, what might be termed a basic personality type consistent for a given culture.[7]

Venturing outside the family provides the child with additional clues to his self-worth. As he meets teachers, policemen, and storekeepers, he is told what these powerful persons think of people like him. He learns about himself from other children on the block who report to him how they feel on seeing him and playing with him. Out of countless messages, the individual contrives a picture of who he is.[8]

It is obvious that individuals develop different concepts of themselves and that the concept of self is always in terms of degrees of *adequacy*. Everyone must have some sense of adequacy, no matter how minimal, or he cannot cope with his own existence and then must escape into psychosis or suicide. *"We can define man's basic need, then, as a need for adequacy."*[9] Jersild refines this further: "The needs associated with a person's idea and appraisal of himself include both desires for enhancing his self-esteem and also striving to preserve the integrity or consistency of the self."[10]

There is agreement that the contemporary situation of the American Negro is deplorable. A nationwide, continuing debate is concerned with ways of ameliorating this condition. As educators, we need to develop strategies for change which will aid the individual in achieving more adequate adjustment to and control of his environment. The role of the concept of self in achieving this sense of adequacy thus appears to be central. The questions that must be considered are these:

1. How do Negro children and youth now achieve a sense of who and what they are?
2. What is the role of education in the school in developing this sense of self?
3. What is the potential within the educational setting of achieving a desirable shift in self-image?

These questions can only be answered by further research. Our purpose here is a brief review of the relevant research and speculation.

THE QUESTION OF DIFFERENCES BETWEEN NEGROES AND WHITES

One of the clearest differences between Negro and white is that society in the contemporary United States continually tells the groups that they are different. Not only are the groups different, but the Negro is considered inferior to the white group. This message has been communicated in different ways via different social media ever since the Negro was first brought to America. It is obvious that this kind of differential social communication is going to have a different impact on the personality. As Allport asks:

... what would happen to your own personality if you heard it said over and over again that you were lazy, a simple child of nature, expected to steal, and had inferior blood. Suppose this opinion were forced on you by the majority of your fellow-citizens. And suppose nothing you could do would change this opinion—because you happen to have black skin.[11]

Or, stated in the words of the late President Kennedy:

If an American, because his skin is dark, cannot eat lunch in a restaurant open to the public; if he cannot send his children to the best public school available; if, in short, he cannot enjoy the full and free life which all of us want, then who among us would be content to have the color of his skin changed and stand in his place?[12]

The self-concept of the Negro is contaminated by the central fact that it is based on a color-caste complex. The American color-caste system was evolving at the same time that the brave concepts of the American and French revolutions about human equality were also born. It was thus almost inevitable that the racial situation would cause trouble. The first drafts of the Declaration of Independence contained a clause objecting to the imposition of slavery upon the American colonies by the English power. The clause was stricken from the final version for fear of alienating Southern support. Shades of contemporary political maneuverings over civil rights legislation in Congress!

In order to cope with the obvious discrepancy between Christian beliefs about the oneness of the human family, slaveholders had to resort to the idea of the supposed inferiority of the Negro, preaching in some instances that he really was a subhuman breed of animal. Even today there continue to be strenuous efforts to convince those who require scholarly evidence that the Negro is, in fact, inferior.[13]

The social system that emerged out of the need to rationalize the owning of slaves and, following the Civil War, refusal to accord the Negro full citizen status was a clear development of a caste system. Unlike the caste system of India based on religious beliefs, the caste system in the United States was based on color and on the assumption of inferiority due to color. The Brazilian melting pot, unlike that in the United States, classifies anyone with any amount of white ancestry as white; in the United States, the smallest amount of Negro ancestry classifies an individual as Negro.

In the evolution of institutions, those provided for the Negro in the United States, therefore, had to be *separate*, but also *unequal*. It is possible that there are caste systems in which parallel caste-class groups exist without any presumption of superiority or inferiority for one caste over another; this certainly has not been true in America.[14] Of course, the South had to refuse to provide equal educational opportunity for the Negro; the Negro was *not equal*.

THE IMPACT OF INEQUALITY IN VALUATION

It does not take much imagination to understand what generations of being told one is unworthy do to a group's own valuation of its worth. From the first slave revolts, Negro leaders have continually fought against this self-view; but there have been relatively few leaders, a condition also produced by the effect of inferior caste status. Only in recent decades have there been enough Negroes who have overcome these multiple barriers to challenge the general valuation of the Negro.

To quote Dollard, whose original study of caste first focused general attention on this problem:

Nothing has happened since 1936 [the date of the original study] which has served to unconvince me about what I saw. It seems as real now as then. We are still in the hot water of conflict between our democratic ideals and our personal acceptance of caste status for the Negro. We are still deliberately or unwittingly profiting by, defending, concealing or ignoring the caste system.[15]

Interestingly enough, a recent comprehensive review and evaluation of the research in the area of self-concept does not include any discussion of research that considers race as an aspect of self-concept, though research relating to other factors, such as sex, religious affiliation, social-class status, is discussed.[16] Blindness to, or avoidance of, the implications of the caste system on the self-concept of the Negro, and of the white, which is thus seen to occur at the most- and least-sophisticated levels of society, is symptomatic of the difficulty of dealing with color discrimination in American life and thought.

The Negro personality *cannot* be unmarked by the experience of caste discrimination based upon color.[17] One of the first family learnings of the Negro child has to do with his color. The more white a Negro child is, the more he will be accepted by his family, the greater his opportunity will be to use his talents, the more likely it is that he will be able to make the most of the limited opportunities of his environment. The love that his family will accord him can be calibrated on the same scale as one calibrates color differences. To be most loved as a Negro child, one has to appear least Negro.

In one of their cases, Kardiner and Ovesey describe the reactions of a middle-class Negro woman, herself light, on giving birth to a dark baby. She was sure she had been given the wrong baby; later she tried to bathe it in bleaches of various kinds; she refused to appear in public with it. She reacted almost the same way with a second baby.[18]

In the early drawings and stories and dreams of Negro children appear many wishes to be white. Negro children have a harder time than white children in identifying themselves correctly in terms of race.[19] This identification is also related to color: the darker Negro is able to see himself as a Negro earlier than a light-colored one. In the latter instance, is the nearness to being white such as to make the acceptance of being Negro that much harder?

The self-esteem of the Negro is damaged by the overwhelming fact that the world he lives in says, "White is right; black is bad." The impact on the Negro community is to overvalue all those traits of appearance that are most Caucasian. Evidence is clear that in almost every Negro family, the lighter children are favored by the parents. It is interesting to note that most of the Negro leadership group today are not Negroid in appearance, many being almost completely Caucasian in terms of major physical appearance.

What effect does this have on the child? Of course, his own color becomes extremely important to him. As Dai points out, ". . . the color of one's skin, which does not occupy the consciousness of children of other cultures, is here made an issue of primary importance, and the personality problems thus created are almost as difficult to get rid of as the dark skin itself."[20] The Negro press is replete with advertisements for skin lighteners and hair straighteners. It strikes some Negroes as ironic that, while they strive to become lighter and to make their hair less curly, whites go to great pains to stay out in the sun in order to become darker and spend endless amounts of money on getting their hair to curl! Unfortunately, the efforts of the whites do not assume an acceptance on their part of the features of the Negro which appear to be desirable: darker color and curly hair. But the efforts of the Negro do spring from a deeply ingrained view regarding appearance: it is better to be more white.

One interesting feature of the current Negro revolution has been a small but persistent insistence that the Negro cease trying to make himself white. The Black Muslim group is an almost pure expression of the need to reject all that is white and replace Negro self-hatred with justified hatred of whites, including the dominant white Christian religion.[21] With some Negroes, it is now considered a matter of racial pride to refuse to straighten the hair or to use cosmetics to lighten the skin. It is possible that this movement will reach other Negroes, and with it will come a lessening of the rejection of color and the personal devaluation that this has carried. But unfortunately it hardly seems possible that a reversal of the value system will occur for many, and certainly not for a long time to come.

Thus we see the central ambivalence that makes the world of the Negro so baffling, frustrating, confusing, and demeaning. On the one hand, he is told that white is better, and he relates this to his own social system in which the Negro who is most white, but still a Negro, has highest status. But to *be* white is not good. Whites are not to be trusted; they are, in fact, hated as much as they are feared.

Hatred breeds aggression. Aggression seeks an outlet. A major focus of the hatred of Negroes is the white group, but this group is almost completely protected because of the potency and immediacy of white retaliation.[22] One must remember that the antilynch laws are quite recent. Pictures of burning buses, fire hoses; mounted police with electric cattle prods, and attacking police dogs show only too well that the Negro is still not protected from the quick and vicious reactions of the white group when this power is challenged in any way. Incapable of attacking the white group, the Negro has several psychological alternatives: to hate himself, to act out his aggressive needs within his own group, and to escape into apathy and fantasy. All these paths are utilized, and often by the same individual, depending on the situation. As Combs and Snygg point out, responses to feelings of inadequacy range from the neurotic through perceptual distortions and may result in actual psychosis. The production of "multiple personalities" is, as they see it, one response to feelings of loss of self-esteem.[23] This splitting of the personality in response to the social disvalue placed on being a Negro is graphically stated by Redding:

From adolescence to death there is something very personal about being a Negro in America. It is like having a second ego which is as much the conscious subject of all experience as the natural self. It is not what the psychologists call dual personality. It is more complex and, I think, more morbid than that. In the state of which I speak, one receives two distinct reactions—the one normal and intrinsic to the natural self; the other, entirely different but of equal force, a prodigy created by the accumulated consciousness of Negroness.[24]

As the gifted Negro writer James Baldwin puts it, in commenting on his own childhood:

In order for me to live, I decided very early that some mistake had been made somewhere. I was not a "nigger" even though you [whites] called me one. . . . I had to realize when I was very young that I was none of those things I was told I was. I was not, for example, happy. I never touched a watermelon for all kinds of reasons. I had been invented by white people, and I knew enough about life by this time to understand that whatever you invent, whatever you project, that is you! So where we are now is that a whole country of people believe I'm a "nigger" and I *don't*.[25]

It does not escape the Negro observer that Negro crimes against Negroes are considered far less serious by the law in many areas than similar crimes of whites against whites, and certainly not nearly so serious as Negro crimes against whites. And white crimes against Negroes are the least serious of all. Again, these social symptoms report to the Negro that he is not valued as a person; he cannot, against such massive evidence, counter by his own feelings of self-esteem, since in truth he can typically show little factual support for a contrary view.[26]

CRUCIAL SOCIAL FORCES CREATING THE NEGRO SELF-IMAGE: THE FAMILY AND POVERTY

The potency of the family in producing the culturally approved person has tempted social manipulators since the dawn of history. Sparta intervened at a very early age in the child-rearing functions of the family. Recent attempts to supplant the family have been unsuccessful.

The most enduring such contemporary situation, the Kibbutz of Israel, appears to have produced a rather special kind of person whose social potential can be questioned.[27] So far, no adequate substitute for the family has been found, despite Huxley's predictions.[28]

That there are unique stresses and strains in the modern family is agreed; but the stresses in a Negro family are qualitatively different from those in a white family, even when we hold socioeconomic status constant. The poor have never lived in comfort, and the struggle for material survival has certainly made psychologically adequate survival extremely problematical anywhere in the world. The situation of the Negro family today in the United States is qualitatively different on a number of important counts.

The Negro family is much more likely than the white family to be on the lowest economic rung. Furthermore, we could say that no more than a very small percentage of Negroes is more than one generation removed from abject poverty, so that "Negroes have [a] deeply ingrained sense of impoverishment."[29] It is a rather special kind of impoverishment, too; it is almost inescapable. Although we have seen in recent generations the rise of a Negro middle class, and even a few very wealthy Negroes, most Negroes remain in the "last hired, first fired" category of employment—and if not this generation, their parental generation. Most Negro children, then, inherit a family which is economically insecure from the very start. Most of them live at the edge of survival; and those who have moved a little bit away have a constant fear of a future which may reduce them, too, to desperation.

It is almost impossible for one not reared in a slum to understand its awfulness. Middle-class America flees from a true picture of slum degradation.[30] But as Riessman points out, children reared in these environments will soon constitute 50 percent of all children enrolled in schools in large cities.[31] Most of these children will be Negroes, unless something drastically changes the housing situation which exists in urban centers.

The Negro slum child is far more liable than a white slum child to experience also an unstable home.[32] The self that the Negro child learns early in life is one exposed to the most difficult of all situations for the human being to cope with: an inadequate family living on the edge of economic insufficiency. The impact of family disruption is accentuated by the incapacity of those involved in the rearing of the children to do an adequate job of it because they have had few experiences with family stability and adequacy to guide them.

The circle is indeed a vicious one. The case studies reported by Riese provide appalling accounts of generation after generation of defeat in Negro families.[33] Often neither mother nor father is able to provide the minimum of affection and attention that an infant needs in order to grow into a person able to like himself and others, because, of course, his parents do not like themselves. Too many of these marriages are the result of impulsive escape wishes and lack of a secure base in personal regard for the marital partner.[34] Poignant testimony to the difficulties facing the Negro wife and husband is given by talented Negro singer Lena Horne.[35]

As she describes it, her marriage was an effort to get away from the miseries of being a Negro singer in a white man's world. Yet she was not able to accept her role as a Negro wife. The needs her husband brought home from his work, mainly with white colleagues, she felt quite unable and unwilling to deal with. Not only had she to cope with the ordinary problems of running a home and rearing children, she had to absorb the anger and hurt her husband bore on his job, the countless humiliations and degradations that he, a Negro, experienced daily in his contact with white people.

What Lena Horne tells us provides a needed window into the inner reality of Negro family life. The normal hazards of the working world are multiplied many times over by the pervasive insecurity attendant on almost all of the Negro's economic activities. Not only is the Negro the last to be hired and the first to be fired, but he pays more for insurance premiums, he has a much harder time obtaining home mortgage money and any kind of bank or credit loans. Even the slum store preys upon the poor with higher prices for shoddier stuff. In such an environment, it is hard indeed for the Negro male to achieve a sense of self-worth as a breadwinner and provider for his family.

The woman typically is aggressive and hostile; the man is hostile and dependent. Because his economic situation is so insecure, the husband-father cannot be sure that he will provide the economic base for a family; and in a majority of cases, he is right. He cannot assure his wife of support or his children of food and shelter. Who can feel pride of self in such circumstances, and who can pass on feelings of adequacy to anyone else?

The economic security of the Negro family rests primarily with the mother. This is one outgrowth of slavery, when at least the mother could keep the children with her until they could be physically independent and able to work, while the father was often not even accorded the recognition of paternity. Certainly the family as the white population knew it was prohibited for slaves. The patterns of employment in today's urban centers have continued to make economic stability more available to the women than to the men. The significance of this family situation appears in study after study.

The home life reported in many case studies of Negro youth is one of constant bickering and fighting. One father leaves; a stepfather or father substitute appears. The family conflict continues. Because of death or illness or desertion, children often are left with grandparents or other relatives. If an attachment occurs, it may not last until adulthood. Thus many Negro children have few experiences with stability, warmth, attention—all of the things that are taken for granted as part of the necessary environment for healthy personality development.

The important point, of course, is that while many of the conditions reported are a result of acute and continued poverty, a major ingredient is also the color-caste of the Negro. One of the child's early racial learnings is that he cannot turn to his parents for help and retaliation if he is hurt.

A white man yanked me off a streetcar because I got on ahead of a white woman. He shook me good and tore my clothes. I walked home crying, knowing that my father would do something about it. (But his father could do no more than remark, "You should have known better.")[36]

The denial to a parent of his role in protecting his own child is deeply destructive, not only to the parental feeling but to the possibility that the child will look to his parents as adult models. Nor will the growing child be able to internalize the parental feeling without which having children of one's own is a dangerous enterprise.

What the Negro child is likely to learn is that no one is to be trusted. He is given such small ingredients of affection and attention that he has too meager a hoard to share with anyone else. He learns, too, that his family is only partly responsible for the horrors of his existence; it is the whites who have created this situation, and it is they who keep him in abasement. The burden of hatred for the whites is increased because he is also told that he cannot do anything about that hatred; in fact, he must be particularly careful and watchful in all his relations with whites. These persons hold the key to all that is desirable and good. If only one were white, too!

The earliest learnings, then, of the Negro child, particularly one in the rural or urban slums, is that the family is not a source of basic nurture and support. He seeks his gratifications, therefore, on the street and among peers.[37] But as Kardiner and Ovesey point out, at no time are these relationships such as to produce a feeling of comfort and safety. No one can find in the street a substitute for parental and adult guidance and parental affection. If the child does not necessarily become antisocial, he is asocial.[38]

The damage to the child's self-esteem appears greater for Negro boys than for girls.[39] Though it is debatable whether, in general, it is more or less difficult to grow up as a boy or as a girl in our culture,[40] it seems clear from the evidence that during early childhood and school years, the Negro girl accommodates better to the circumstances of existence. Certainly in school performance the Negro girl exceeds the Negro boy. In most measures of social disorganization, the Negro boy appears to be far more vulnerable. This can be accounted for in part by the fact that the male models available for the growing boy are themselves demoralized. A father who feels defeated by the world is not in good position to give his son a sense of optimism and a feeling that he can achieve something himself. The fact that the father is most likely to be the absent member of the family and often is replaced by a succession of fathers or father substitutes also tends to militate against the establishment of a view of the male as a reliable, responsible individual. If the boy sees around him men who are unable to sustain a consistent and positive social and economic role, it is hard for the youngster to build a different pattern out of his limited experiences.

Recent efforts to equalize educational opportunities for Negroes in the South should not obscure the fact that these efforts are indeed very recent, and still fall far short of providing, even on a segregated basis, an adequate education for all Negro young people. The fact that even today many Negro children and youth have far from adequate schooling, whether they live in the rural South or the urban North, Midwest, West, or Southwest, should not make us forget that, with exceptions, the story of Negro education to this day has been one of gross lacks.[41] As Horace Mann said over a hundred years ago, "No educated body of men can be permanently poor"[42]; and the obverse is that no uneducated group can expect to rise out of poverty.

Although the Ausubels state that "Negro girls in racially incapsulated areas are less traumatized than boys by the impact of racial discrimination,"[43] further evidence is needed to support such a statement. On the surface, Negro girls seem more able to cope with some of the demands of middle-class society: going to school, behaving in school, keeping out of serious trouble with the law, showing responsibility for child rearing, and keeping a job.[44] It is nevertheless possible that the impact of their situation is just passed on to the men in the household. Certainly a mother is a prime source, as we have stated, of the child's self-concept. It is communicated to Negro boys, somehow, that they are less wanted, less able to deal with their world, bound to fail in their efforts to be men. We cannot lay the major blame for the way Negro boys develop on the lack of adequate male models. It is highly probable that the trauma suffered by Negro females is passed on and displaced upon the males in the situation. Certainly the case material of Kardiner and Ovesey shows much personal trouble experienced by female as well as male Negroes.[45] The fact that so many Negroes become contributing and stable members of society is an extraordinary tribute to the resilience of the human psyche.

EDUCATIONAL PROCESSES AND SELF-CONCEPT

It is clear that the life experiences of the Negro child are not such as to aid him in developing a positive sense of himself or of his place in his world. What does this suggest to us? It would seem that a very compelling hypothesis is that *the Negro child, from earliest school entry through graduation from high school, needs continued opportunities to see himself and his racial group in a realistically positive light. He needs to understand what color and race mean, he needs to learn about those of his race (and other disadvantaged groups) who have succeeded, and he needs to clarify his understanding of his own group history and current group situation.*

At the moment, these are missing ingredients in the American public school classroom. Numerous studies of textbooks have shown them to be lily-white.[46] Pictures do not show Negro and white children together; when Negroes appear they are usually either Booker T. Washington, George Washington Carver, or foreign.[47] Neither whites nor Negroes have an accurate picture of the American Negro and his history.[48] One observer noted that a commonly used contemporary civics book had no index entry for *urban renewal, transportation, transit, or Negro.*[49] The lily-white nature of text materials is true also of other visual aids used in the schools. If Negroes appear in school films, they are in stereotyped roles. One film, for instance, showing "community helpers" illustrated the work of repairing the street with a Negro crew and a white foreman. The educational consultant, incidentally, who worked with the film company to produce the film was surprised at his own blindness. This kind of presentation merely reinforces the many communications to children that Negro work is inferior work.

That these materials can and do have a strong impact on the child's perception of himself and others was well documented in the study by Trager and Yarrow. When a story describing a Negro child as a funny savage (*Little Black Sambo*) was read aloud to young children, white and Negro children's feelings were affected, particularly when the white children pointed this out in the schoolyard.[50] The only thing that is surprising about these findings is that educators and others have consistently ignored them. It is interesting that the Trager-Yarrow research report is probably the only study made of the differences in education (textbook) content that is reported in the literature. As a matter of fact, it is claimed by one of the very knowledgeable experts in the field, that *no* experimental study has been done of differences in textbook content, despite the fact that the textbook is the most consistently and constantly used educational aid in the classroom, other than the teacher.[51]

If teaching materials present a slanted view of him and his place in the world to the Negro child, what does the teacher tell him? It is not a very startling piece of news that teachers, too, bear the majority version of the Negro. Studies of their attitudes toward children show that the Negro child is rated lowest in all rankings of groups on a Bogardus-type social-distance scale.[52] The original study was completed thirteen years ago; teachers in training in 1963 give the same responses. Attempts to change teachers' attitudes through human relations workshops and special courses have reached very few. In formulating some guidelines for the education of the culturally disadvantaged, Niemeyer stated:

Our hypothesis is that the chief cause of the low achievement of the children of alienated groups is the fact that too many teachers and principals honestly believe that these children are educable only to an extremely limited extent. And when teachers have a low expectation level for their children's learning, the children seldom exceed that expectation, which is a self-fulfilling prophecy.[53]

Nor is the situation made easier where Negro teachers are employed. The Negro teacher represents a middle-class position, and there is evidence that virulent anti-Negro feelings are expressed by middle-class Negroes for lower-class Negroes. Unfortunately, most Negro children come from lower-class homes. Dai makes the point that, denied access to other rewards in life, the Negro tends to put an overemphasis upon status.[54] The Negro professional, who may have many contacts with white professionals, must even in these professional relationships maintain an etiquette which prevents showing resentment or rage; but this is not necessarily controlled to the same extent when dealing with fellow Negroes. Children, particularly, are available targets of all the displaced self-hatred of the professional middle-class Negro teacher. If they are lower-class children, they typically will demonstrate everything the middle-class Negro most despises about the race from which he cannot dissociate himself. The warmth, welcome, and support which children should find, particularly in the early elementary school grades, and which the Negro child needs in abundance because of so much deprivation at home, is exactly what teachers, Negro or white, as presently oriented, can least provide.

In this necessarily brief discussion of the factors that enter into the development of the self-concept of the Negro, we have utilized only a small sampling of the wealth of research literature and other documentation which bears on this subject. We have merely tried to suggest some of the crucial situations which help to mold the Negro child. It is these of which educational practitioners must be aware.

EDUCATIONAL INTERVENTION

The child with a negative view of self is a child who will not be able to profit much from school. Once a child is convinced that school is irrelevant to his immediate needs and future goals, the task of education becomes almost impossible. As one junior high student said, after having failed all his subjects for two years.

I just don't like it. It seems to bore me. It seems silly just going there and sitting. And most of the time it is so hot and they don't do anything about it and the teachers just talk, talk, and you never learn anything.[55]

Deutsch's research points out that the lower-class Negro child probably received about one half to one third less instructional time in the primary grades than did the white children from the same slum environment: "our time samples indicated that as much as 80% of the school day was channeled into disciplining, and secondarily, into ordinary organizational details. . . ."[56]

. . .

CONCLUSION

If today we note a change of tone, a militancy and impatience on the part of Negro youth, it is not because schools are any different. For the first time, the Negro, via TV, is beginning to see that the world of comfort, luxury, and fun is all around him. He wants some of it, too. As Hayakawa pointed out in a speech at a recent American Psychological Association convention in Philadelphia, the ads that beckon one to join the fun on the picnic do *not* add "for whites only."[57]

But the militancy, welcomed as it may be, cannot erase the burden of self-hatred that has accumulated through so many generations. And many who most need to hear the call to challenge the racial status quo may already be too deeply sunk in despair and apathy. These feelings are so quickly communicated to the infant and child that intervention by the school even as early as kindergarten or the first grade may be too late. But if many older adolescents can respond to a new concept of their role in the world, then certainly the younger child can be reached, too, by deliberate efforts to change the way in which he views himself. These, then, are the challenges we must meet.

REFERENCES

1. Bingham Dai, "Minority Group Membership and Personality Development," in Jitsuichi Masuoka and Preston Valien (eds.), *Race Relations: Problems and Theory*, Chapel Hill, N.C., The University of North Carolina Press, 1961, p. 183.
2. Ruth C. Wylie, *The Self-Concept*, Lincoln, Nebr., University of Nebraska Press, 1961, pp. 1–22.
3. Arthur T. Jersild, "Emotional Development," in L. Carmichael (ed.), *Manual of Child Psychology*, 2d ed., New York, John Wiley & Sons, Inc., 1954, p. 837. "Selective Bibliography on Self," *Childhood Education* vol. 35, October, 1958, pp. 80–81.
4. M. B. Frink, "Self-Concept as It Relates to Academic Underachievement," *California Journal of Educational Research*, vol. 13, March, 1962, pp. 57–62.
5. Robert R. Sears, Eleanor E. Maccoby, and Harry Levin, *Patterns of Child Rearing*, New York, Harper & Row, Publishers, 1957.
6. John W. M. Whiting and Irvin L. Child, *Child Training and Personality: A Cross-Cultural Study*, New Haven, Conn., Yale University Press, 1953.
7. Abram Kardiner et al., *The Psychological Frontiers of Society*, New York, Columbia University Press, 1945.
8. Helen G. Trager and Marian Radke Yarrow, *They Learn What They Live: Prejudice in Young Children*, New York, Harper & Row, Publishers, 1952.

9. Arthur W. Combs and Donald Snygg, *Individual Behavior* (rev. ed.), New York, Harper & Row, Publishers, 1959, p. 46.
10. Jersild, *op. cit.*
11. Gordon W. Allport, *The Nature of Prejudice*, Reading, Mass., Addison-Wesley Publishing Company, Inc., 1954, p. 142.
12. John F. Kennedy, "A Time to Act," an address to the American people, June 11, 1963. Reprinted by Anti-Defamation League of B'nai B'rith, New York.
13. Robert D. North, "The Intelligence of American Negroes," *Research Reports*, Anti-Defamation League of B'nai B'rith, vol. 3, no. 2, November, 1965; Melvin T. Tumin (ed.), *Race and Intelligence: A Scientific Evaluation*, New York, Anti-Defamation League of B'nai B'rith, 1963.
14. John Dollard, *Caste and Class in a Southern Town*, 3d ed., Garden City, N.Y., Doubleday & Company, Inc., 1957.
15. *Ibid.*, p. viii.
16. Wylie, *op. cit.*
17. Abram Kardiner and Lionel Ovesey, *The Mark of Oppression: Explorations in the Personality of the American Negro*, Cleveland, The World Publishing Company (a Meridian Book), 1962.
18. Kardiner and Ovesey, *op. cit.*, pp. 252–253.
19. Kenneth Clark and Mamie P. Clark, "Racial Identification and Preference in Negro Children," in Eleanor Maccoby et al. (eds.), *Readings in Social Psychology*, New York, Holt, Rinehart and Winston, Inc., 1958, pp. 602–611.
20. Bingham Dai, "Problems of Personality Development Among Negro Children," in Clyde Pluckhohn and Henry A. Murray (eds.), *Personality in Nature, Society and Culture*, New York, Alfred A. Knopf, Inc., 1953, p. 560.
21. C. Eric Lincoln, *The Black Muslims in America*, Boston, The Beacon Press, 1961; E. U. Essien-Udom, *Black Nationalism*, Chicago, The University of Chicago Press, 1962; James Baldwin, *The Fire Next Time*, New York, The Dial Press, Inc., 1963 pp. 61–120.
22. Baker M. Hindman "The Emotional Problems of Negro High School Youth Which Are Related to Segregation and Discrimination in a Southern Urban Community," *Journal of Educational Sociology*, vol. 27, November, 1953, pp. 115–127.
23. Combs and Snygg, *op. cit.*, pp. 265–303.
24. J. Saunders Redding, *On Being Negro in America*, Indianapolis, Ind., The Bobbs-Merrill Company, Inc., 1962, p. 12.
25. James Baldwin, "A Talk to Teachers," *Saturday Review*, vol. 46, December 21, 1963, pp. 42–44+.
26. Walter Reckless et al., "Self-concept as Insulator Against Delinquency," *American Sociological Review*, vol. 21, no. 6, 1956.
27. Abram Kardiner, "When the State Brings up the Child," *Saturday Review*, vol. 44, August 26, 1961, pp. 9–11; Albert J. Rabin "Culture Components as a Significant Factor in Child Development: Kibbutz Adolescents," *American Journal of Orthopsychiatry*, vol. 31, 1961, pp. 493–504.
28. Aldous Huxley, *Brave New World*, New York, Harper & Row, Publishers, 1932.
29. Kardiner and Ovesey, *op. cit.*, p. 366.
30. Michael Harrington, *The Other America: Poverty in the United States*, New York, The Macmillan Company, 1963, Chap. 4, "If You're Black, Stay Black," pp. 61–81.
31. Frank Reissman, *The Culturally Deprived Child*, New York, Harper & Row, Publishers, 1962, p. 1.
32. Martin Deutsch, *Minority Group and Class Status as Related to Social and Personality Factors in Scholastic Achievement*, monograph 2, Ithaca, N.Y., The Society for Applied Anthropology, Cornell University Press, 1960; E. Franklin

Frazier, *The Negro Family in the United States* (rev. ed.), New York, The Dryden Press, Inc., 1951; Nathan Glazer and D. P. Moynihan, *Beyond the Melting Pot*, Cambridge, Mass., The M.I.T. Press and Harvard University Press, 1963, pp. 25–85.

33. Bertha Riese, *Heal the Hurt Child*, Chicago, The University of Chicago Press, 1962.
34. Kardiner and Ovesey, *op. cit.*, pp. 345–349.
35. Lena Horne, "I Just Want To Be Myself," *Show*, vol. 3, September 1963, pp. 62–65+.
36. Robert L. Sutherland, *Color, Class and Personality*, Washington, D.C., American Council on Education, 1942, p. 41.
37. David and Pearl Ausubel, "Ego Development Among Segregated Negro Children," in A. Harry Passow (ed.), *Education in Depressed Areas*, New York, Bureau of Publications, Teachers College, Columbia University, 1963, p. 113.
38. Kardiner and Ovesey, *op. cit.*, p. 380.
39. David and Pearl Ausubel, *op. cit.*, pp. 127–128.
40. Walter Waetjen and Jean D. Grambs, "Sex Differences: A Case of Educational Evasion?" *Teachers College Record*, December, 1963.
41. Virgil Clift, Archibald W. Anders, H. Gordon Hullfish (eds.), *Negro Education in America*, New York, Harper & Row, Publishers, 1962.
42. Marjorie B. Smiley and John S. Diekoff, *Prologue to Teaching*, Fair Lawn, N.J., Oxford University Press, 1959, p. 286.
43. David and Pearl Ausubel, *op. cit.*, p. 128.
44. Albert J. Lott and Bernice E. Lott, *Negro and White Youth*, New York, Holt, Rinehart and Winston, Inc., 1963.
45. Kardiner and Ovesey, *op. cit.*
46. Abraham Tannenbaum, "Family Living in Textbook Town," *Progressive Education*, vol. 31, no. 5, March, 1954, pp. 133–141; Martin Mayer, "The Trouble with Textbooks," *Harper's Magazine*, vol. 225, July, 1962, pp. 65–71; Otto Klineberg, "Life Is Fun in a Smiling, Fair-Skinned World," *Saturday Review*, February 16, 1963; Albert Alexander, "The Gray Flannel Cover on the American History Textbook," *Social Education*, vol. 24, January, 1960, pp. 11–14.
47. Lloyd Marcus, *The Treatment of Minorities in Secondary School Textbooks*, New York, Anti-Defamation League of B'nai B'rith, 1961; Jack Nelson and Gene Roberts, Jr., *The Censors and the Schools*, Boston, Little, Brown & Company, 1963.
48. Melville J. Herskovits, *The Myth of the Negro Past*, Boston, The Beacon Press, 1958.
49. Atlee E. Shidler, "Education for Civic Leadership: The School's Responsibility," an address presented to the 68th National Conference on Government, The National Municipal League, Washington, D.C., November 16, 1962, mimeo.
50. Trager and Yarrow, *op. cit.*
51. A. A. Lumsdaine, "Instruments and Media of Instruction," in N. L. Gage (ed.), *Handbook of Research on Teaching*, Chicago, Rand McNally & Company, 1963, p. 586.
52. Jean D. Grambs, "Are We Training Prejudiced Teachers?" *School and Society*, vol. 71, April 1, 1950, pp. 196–198.
53. John Niemeyer, "Some Guidelines to Desirable Elementary School Reorganizations," in *Programs for the Educationally Disadvantaged*, Washington, D.C., U.S. Office of Education Bulletin, 1963, no. 17, p. 81.
54. Bingham Dai, "Minority Group Membership and Personality Development," *op. cit.*
55. Kardiner and Ovesey, *op. cit.*, p. 264.

56. Deutsch, *op. cit.*, p. 23.
57. *Washington Post*, September 10, 1963.

DISCUSSION QUESTIONS

1. Should we absolve the schools from the responsibility of creating a wholesome self-image for the culturally different child, since the school, as a social organism, generally reflects the public conviction of the ghetto child's worthlessness?
2. Are the inadequacies of our slum schools basically rooted in our willingness to have our poor remain invisible and uneducated?
3. How do we educate the public as to what desirable education is and how it is achieved?
4. How do you recruit teachers for slum schools?

JAMES S. COLEMAN Segregation in the
Public Schools

The great majority of American children attend schools that are largely segregated—that is, where almost all of their fellow students are of the same racial background as they are. Among minority groups, Negroes are by far the most segregated. Taking all groups, however, white children are most segregated. Almost 80 percent of all white pupils in 1st grade and 12th grade attend schools that are from 90 percent to 100 percent white. And 97 percent at grade 1, and 99 percent at grade 12, attend schools that are 50 percent or more white.

For Negro pupils, segregation is more nearly complete in the South (as it is for whites also), but it is extensive also in all the other regions where the Negro population is concentrated: the urban North, Midwest, and West.

More than 65 percent of all Negro pupils in the 1st grade attend schools that are between 90 and 100 percent Negro. And 87 percent at grade 1, and 66 percent at grade 12, attend schools that are 50 percent or more Negro. In the South, most students attend schools that are 100 percent white or Negro.

The same pattern of segregation holds, though not quite so strongly, for the teachers of Negro and white students. For the Nation as a whole the average Negro elementary pupil attends a school in which 65 percent of the teachers are Negro; the average white elementary pupil attends a

Reprinted from "Summary Report" of the publication *Equality of Educational Opportunity* (Washington, D.C.: United States Office of Education, Department of of Health, Education, and Welfare 1967), pp. 3, 8, 9, 14, 20, 21, 22, 24, 27, 28, 32, 33. (In the interests of brevity, published tables and references to them have been omitted, in the main.)

school in which 97 percent of the teachers are white. White teachers are more predominant at the secondary level, where the corresponding figures are 59 and 97 percent. The racial matching of teachers is most pronounced in the South, where by tradition it has been complete. On a nationwide basis, in cases where the races of pupils and teachers are not matched, the trend is all in one direction: white teachers teach Negro children but Negro teachers seldom teach white children; just as, in the schools, integration consists primarily of a minority of Negro pupils in predominantly white schools but almost never of a few whites in largely Negro schools.

In its desegregation decision of 1954, the Supreme Court held that separate schools for Negro and white children are inherently unequal. This survey finds that, when measured by that yardstick, American public education remains largely unequal in most regions of the country, including all those where Negroes form any significant proportion of the population. Obviously, however, that is not the only yardstick. The next section of the summary describes other characteristics by means of which equality of educational opportunity may be appraised.

THE SCHOOLS AND THEIR CHARACTERISTICS

The school environment of a child consists of many elements, ranging from the desk he sits at to the child who sits next to him, and including the teacher who stands at the front of his class. A statistical survey can give only fragmentary evidence of this environment.

Great collections of numbers such as are found in these pages—totals and averages and percentages—blur and obscure rather than sharpen and illuminate the range of variation they represent. If one reads, for example, that the average annual income per person in the State of Maryland is $3,000, there is a tendency to picture an average person living in moderate circumstances in a middle-class neighborhood holding an ordinary job. But that number represents at the upper end millionaires, and at the lower end the unemployed, the pensioners, the charwomen. Thus the $3,000 average income should somehow bring to mind the tycoon and the tramp, the showcase and the shack, as well as the average man in the average house.

So, too, in reading these statistics on education, one must picture the child whose school has every conceivable facility that is believed to enhance the educational process, whose teachers may be particularly gifted and well educated, and whose home and total neighborhood are themselves powerful contributors to his education and growth. And one must picture the child in a dismal tenement area who may come hungry to an ancient, dirty building that is badly ventilated, poorly lighted, overcrowded, understaffed, and without sufficient textbooks.

Statistics, too, must deal with one thing at a time, and cumulative effects tend to be lost in them. Having a teacher without a college degree indicates an element of disadvantage, but in the concrete situation, a child may be taught by a teacher who is not only without a degree but who has grown up and received his schooling in the local community, who has never been out of the State, who has a 10th grade vocabulary, and who shares the local community's attitudes.

One must also be aware of the relative importance of a certain kind of thing to a certain kind of person. Just as a loaf of bread means more to a starving man than to a sated one, so one very fine textbook or, better, one very able teacher, may mean far more to a deprived child than to one who already has several of both.

Finally, it should be borne in mind that in cases where Negroes in the South receive unequal treatment, the significance in terms of actual numbers of individuals involved is very great, since 54 percent of the Negro population of school-going age, or approximately 3,200,000 children, live in that region.

All of the findings reported in this section of the summary are based on responses to questionnaires filled out by public school teachers, principals, district school superintendents, and pupils. The data were gathered in September and October of 1965 from 4,000 public schools. All teachers, principals, and district superintendents in these schools participated, as did all pupils in the 3d, 6th, 9th, and 12th grades. First grade pupils in half the schools participated. More than 645,000 pupils in all were involved in the survey. About 30 percent of the schools selected for the survey did not participate; an analysis of the nonparticipating schools indicated that their inclusion would not have significantly altered the results of the survey. The participation rates were: in the metropolitan North and West 72 percent, metropolitan South and Southwest 65 percent, nonmetropolitan North and West 82 percent, nonmetropolitan South and Southwest 61 percent.

All the statistics on the physical facilities of the schools and the academic and extracurricular programs are based on information provided by the teachers and administrators. They also provided information about their own education, experience, and philosophy of education, and described as they see them the socioeconomic characteristics of the neighborhoods served by their schools.

The statistics having to do with the pupils' personal socioeconomic background, level of education of their parents, and certain items in their homes (such as encyclopedias, daily newspapers, etc.) are based on pupil responses to questionnaires. The pupils also answered questions about their academic aspirations and their attitudes toward staying in school.

All personal and school data were confidential and for statistical purposes only; the questionnaires were collected without the names or other personal indentification of the respondents.

Data for Negro and white children are classified by whether the schools are in metropolitan areas or not. The definition of a metropolitan area is the one commonly used by Government agencies: a city of over 50,000 inhabitants including its suburbs. All other schools in small cities, towns, or rural areas are referred to as nonmetropolitan schools.

Finally, for most tables, data for Negro and white children are classified by geographical regions. For metropolitan schools there are usually five regions defined as follows:

Northeast—Connecticut, Maine, Massachusetts, New Hampshire, Rhode Island, Vermont, Delaware, Maryland, New Jersey, New York, Pennsylvania, District of Columbia. (Using 1960 census data, this region contains about 16 percent of all Negro children in the Nation and 20 percent of all white children age 5 to 19.)

Midwest—Illinois, Indiana, Michigan, Ohio, Wisconsin, Iowa, Kansas, Minnesota, Missouri, Nebraska, North Dakota, South Dakota (containing 16 percent of Negro and 19 percent of white children age 5 to 19).

South—Alabama, Arkansas, Florida, Georgia, Kentucky, Louisiana, Mississippi, North Carolina, South Carolina, Tennessee, Virginia, West Virginia (containing 27 percent of Negro and 14 percent of white children age 5 to 19).

Southwest—Arizona, New Mexico, Oklahoma, Texas (containing 4 percent of Negro and 3 percent of white children age 5 to 19).

West—Alaska, California, Colorado, Hawaii, Idaho, Montana, Nevada, Oregon, Utah, Washington, Wyoming (containing 4 percent of Negro and 11 percent of white children age 5 to 19).

The nonmetropolitan schools are usually classified into only three regions:

South—as above (containing 27 percent of Negro and 14 percent of white children age 5 to 19).

Southwest—as above (containing 4 percent of Negro and 2 percent of white children age 5 to 19).

North and West—all States not in the South and Southwest (containing 2 percent of Negro and 17 percent of white children age 5 to 19).

Data for minority groups other than Negroes are presented only on a nationwide basis because there were not sufficient cases to warrant a breakdown by regions.

Facilities

... For the Nation as a whole white children attend elementary schools with a smaller average number of pupils per room (29) than do any of the minorities (which range from 30 to 33). ... In some regions the nationwide pattern is reversed: in the nonmetropolitan North and West and Southwest for example, there is a smaller average number of pupils per room for Negroes than for whites. ... One finds much more striking differences than the national average would suggest: in the metropolitan Midwest, for example, the average Negro has 54 pupils per room—probably reflecting considerable frequency of double sessions— compared with 33 per room for whites. (Nationally, at the high school level the average white has one teacher for every 22 students and the average Negro has one for every 26 students.) . . .

There is not a wholly consistent pattern—that is, minorities are not at a disadvantage in every item listed—but there are nevertheless some definite and systematic directions of differences. Nationally, Negro pupils have fewer of some of the facilities that seem most related to academic achievement: they have less access to physics, chemistry, and language laboratories; there are fewer books per pupil in their libraries; their textbooks are less often in sufficient supply. To the extent that physical facilities are important to learning, such items appear to be more relevant than some others, such as cafeterias, in which minority groups are at an advantage.

Usually greater than the majority-minority differences, however, are the regional differences. . . . 95 percent of Negro and 80 percent of white high school students in the metropolitan Far West attend schools with language laboratories, compared with 48 percent and 72 percent respectively, in the metropolitan South, in spite of the fact that a higher percentage of Southern schools are less than 20 years old.

Finally, it must always be remembered that these statistics reveal only majority-minority average differences and regional average differences; they do not show the extreme differences that would be found by comparing one school with another.

Programs

. . . Just as minority groups tend to have less access to physical facilities that seem to be related to academic achievement, so too they have less access to curricular and extracurricular programs that would seem to have such a relationship.

Secondary school Negro students are less likely to attend schools that are regionally accredited; this is particularly pronounced in the South. Negro and Puerto Rican pupils have less access to college preparatory curriculums and to accelerated curriculums; Puerto Ricans have less access to vocational curriculums as well. Less intelligence testing is done in the schools attended by Negroes and Puerto Ricans. Finally, white students in general have more access to a more fully developed program of extracurricular activities, in particular those which might be related to academic matters (debate teams, for example, and student newspapers).

Again, regional differences are striking. For example, 100 percent of Negro high school students and 97 percent of whites in the metropolitan Far West attend schools having a remedial reading teacher (this does not mean, of course, that every student uses the services of that teacher, but simply that he has access to them) compared with 46 and 65 percent, respectively, in the metropolitan South—and 4 and 9 percent in the non-metropolitan Southwest.

Principals and Teachers

. . . 1 percent of white elementary pupils attend a school with a Negro principal, and . . . 56 percent of Negro children attend a school with a Negro principal. . . . The average white student goes to an elementary school where 40 percent of the teachers spent most of their lives in the same city, town, or country; the average Negro pupil goes to a school where 53 percent of the teachers have lived in the same locality most of their lives. . . . Other characteristics which offer rough indications of teacher quality, [include] the types of colleges attended, years of teaching experience, salary, educational level of mother, and a score on a 30-word vocabulary test. The average Negro pupil attends a school where a greater percentage of the teachers appears to be somewhat less able, as measured by these indicators, than those in the schools attended by the average white student.

Other items . . . reveal certain teacher attitudes. Thus, the average white pupil attends a school where 51 percent of the white teachers would not choose to move to another school, whereas the average Negro attends a school where 46 percent would not choose to move.

Student Body Characteristics

. . . The average white high school student attends a school in which 82 percent of his classmates report that there are encyclopedias in their homes. This does not mean that 82 percent of all white pupils have encyclopedias at home, although obviously that would be approximately true. . . . Clear differences are found on these items: the average Negro has fewer classmates whose mothers graduated from high school; his classmates more frequently are members of large rather than small families; they are less often enrolled in a college preparatory curriculum; they have taken a smaller number of courses in English, mathematics, foreign language, and science.

On most items, the other minority groups fall between Negroes and whites, but closer to whites, in the extent to which each characteristic is typical of their classmates.

Aagin, there are substantial variations in the magnitude of the differences, with the difference usually being greater in the Southern States.

ACHIEVEMENT IN THE PUBLIC SCHOOLS

The schools bear many responsibilities. Among the most important is the teaching of certain intellectual skills such as reading, writing, calculating, and problem-solving. One way of assessing the educational opportunity offered by the schools is to measure how well they perform this task. Standard achievement tests are available to measure these skills, and several such tests were administered in this survey to pupils at grades 1, 3, 6, 9, and 12.

These tests do not measure intelligence, nor attitudes, nor qualities of character. Furthermore, they are not, nor are they intended to be, "culture-free." Quite the reverse: they are culture-bound. What they measure are the skills which are among the most important in our society for getting a good job and moving up to a better one, and for full participation in an increasingly technical world. Consequently, a pupil's test results at the end of public school provide a good measure of the range of opportunities open to him as he finished school—a wide range of choice of jobs or colleges if these skills are very high; a very narrow range that includes only the most menial jobs if these skills are very low.

Table 1 gives an overall illustration of the test results for the various groups by tabulating nationwide median scores (the score which divides the group in half) for 1st-grade and 12th-grade pupils on the tests used in those grades. For example, half of the white 12th-grade pupils had scores above 52 on the nonverbal test and half had scores below 52. (Scores on each test at each grade level were standardized so that the average over the national sample equaled 50 and the standard deviation equaled 10. This means that for all pupils in the Nation, about 16 percent would score below 40 and about 16 percent above 60.)

With some exceptions—notably Oriental Americans—the average minority pupil scores distinctly lower on these tests at every level than the average white pupil. The minority pupils' scores are as much as one standard deviation below the majority pupils' scores in the first grade. At the 12th grade, results of tests in the same verbal and nonverbal

TABLE 1. **Nationwide Median Test Scores for First- and Twelfth-Grade Pupils**

Text	Racial or ethnic group					
	Puerto Ricans	Indian-Americans	Mexican-Americans	Oriental-Americans	Negro	Majority
First grade:						
Nonverbal	45.8	53.0	50.1	56.6	43.4	54.1
Verbal	44.9	47.8	46.5	51.6	45.4	53.2
Twelfth grade:						
Nonverbal	43.3	47.1	45.0	51.6	40.9	52.0
Verbal	43.1	43.7	43.8	49.6	40.9	52.1
Reading	42.6	44.3	44.2	48.8	42.2	51.9
Mathematics	43.7	45.9	45.5	51.3	41.8	51.8
General information	41.7	44.7	43.3	49.0	40.6	52.2
Average of the 5 tests	43.1	45.1	44.4	50.1	41.1	52.0

skills show that, in every case, the minority scores are *farther below* the majority than are the 1st graders. For some groups, the relative decline is negligible; for others, it is large.

Furthermore, a constant difference in standard deviations over the various grades represents an increasing difference in grade level gap. For example, Negroes in the metropolitan Northeast are about 1.1 standard deviations below whites in the same region at grades 6, 9, and 12. But at grade 6 this represents 1.6 years behind, at grade 9, 2.4 years, and at grade 12, 3.3 years. Thus, by this measure, the deficiency in achievement is progressively greater for the minority pupils at progressively higher grade levels.

For most minority groups, then, and most particularly the Negro, schools provide no opportunity at all for them to overcome this initial deficiency; in fact, they fall farther behind the white majority in the development of several skills which are critical to making a living and participating fully in modern society. Whatever may be the combination of nonschool factors— poverty, community attitudes, low educational level of parents—which put minority children at a disadvantage in verbal and nonverbal skills when they enter the first grade, the fact is the schools have not overcome it.

Some points should be borne in mind in reading the table. First, the differences shown should not obscure the fact that some minority children perform better than many white children. A difference of one standard deviation in median scores means that about 84 percent of the children in the lower group are below the median of the majority students—but 50 percent of the white children are themselves below that median as well.

A second point of qualification concerns regional differences. By grade 12, both white and Negro students in the South score below their counterparts—white and Negro—in the North. In addition, Southern Negroes score farther below Southern whites than Northern Negroes score below Northern whites. The consequences of this pattern can be illustrated by the fact that the 12th grade Negro in the nonmetropolitan South is 0.8 standard deviation below—or in terms of years, 1.9 years behind—the Negro in the metropolitan Northeast, though at grade 1 there is no such regional difference.

Finally, the test scores at grade 12 obviously do not take account of those pupils who have left school before reaching the senior year. In the metropolitan North and West, 20 percent of the Negroes of ages 16 and 17 are not enrolled in school, a higher dropout percentage than in either the metropolitan or nonmetropolitan South. If it is the case that some or many of the Northern dropouts performed poorly when they were in school, the Negro achievement in the North may be artificially elevated because some of those who achieved more poorly have left school.

RELATION OF ACHIEVEMENT TO SCHOOL CHARACTERISTICS

If 100 students within a school take a certain test, there is likely to be great variation in their scores. One student may score 97 percent, another 13; several may score 78 percent. This represents variability in achievement *within* the particular school.

It is possible, however, to compute the average of the scores made by the students within that school and to compare it with the average score, or achievement, of pupils within another school, or many other schools. These comparisons then represent variations *between schools.*

When one sees that the average score on a verbal achievement test in School X is 55 and in School Y is 72, the natural question to ask is: What accounts for the difference?

There are many factors that in combination account for the difference. This analysis concentrates on one cluster of those factors. It attempts to describe what relationship the school's characteristics themselves (libraries, for example, and teachers and laboratories and so on) seem to have to the achievement of majority and minority groups (separately for each group on a nationwide basis, and also for Negro and white pupils in the North and South).

The first finding is that the schools are remarkably similar in the effect they have on the achievement of their pupils when the socioeconomic background of the students is taken into account. It is known that socioeconomic factors bear a strong relation to academic achievement. When these factors are statistically controlled, however, it appears that differences between schools account for only a small fraction of differences in pupil achievement.

The schools *do* differ, however, in the degree of impact they have on the various racial and ethnic groups. The average white student's achievement is less affected by the strength or weakness of his school's facilities, curricula, and teachers than is the average minority pupil's. To put it another way, the achievement of minority pupils depends more on the schools they attend than does the achievement of majority pupils. Thus, 20 percent of the achievement of Negroes in the South is associated with the particular schools they go to, whereas only 10 percent of the achievement of whites in the South is. Except for Oriental Americans, this general result is found for all minorities.

The conclusion can then be drawn that improving the school of a minority pupil will increase his achievement more than will improving the school of a white child increase his. Similarly, the average minority pupil's achievement will suffer more in a school of low quality than will the average white pupil's. In short, whites, and to a lesser extent Oriental Americans, are less affected one way or the other by the quality of their schools than are minority pupils. This indicates that it is for the most disadvantaged children that improvements in school quality will make the most difference in achievement.

All of these results suggest the next question: What are the school characteristics that account for most variation in achievement? In other words, what factors in the school are most important in affecting achievement?

It appears that variations in the facilities and curriculums of the schools account for relatively little variation in pupil achievement insofar as this is measured by standard tests. Again, it is for majority whites that the variations make the least difference; for minorities, they make somewhat more difference. Among the facilities that show some relationship to achievement are several for which minority pupils' schools are less well equipped relative to whites. For example, the existence of science laboratories showed a small but consistent relationship to achievement . . . minorities, especially Negroes, are in schools with fewer of these laboratories.

The quality of teachers shows a stronger relationship to pupil achievement. Furthermore, it is progressively greater at higher grades, indicating a cumulative impact of the qualities of teachers in a school on the pupils' achievement. Again, teacher quality is more important for minority pupil achievement than for that of the majority.

It should be noted that many characteristics of teachers were not measured in this survey; therefore, the results are not at all conclusive regarding the specific characteristics of teachers that are most important. Among those measured in the survey, however, those that bear the highest relationship to pupil achievement are first, the teacher's score on the verbal skills test, and then his educational background—both his own level of education and that of his parents. On both of these measures, the level of teachers of minority students, especially Negroes, is lower.

Finally, it appears that a pupil's achievement is strongly related to the educational backgrounds and aspirations of the other students in the school. Only crude measures of these variables were used (principally the proportion of pupils with encyclopedias in the home and the proportion planning to go to college). Analysis indicates, however, that children from a given family background, when put in schools of different social composition, will achieve at quite different levels. This effect is again less for white pupils than for any minority group other than Orientals. Thus, if a white pupil from a home that is strongly and effectively supportive of education is put in a school where most pupils do not come from such homes, his achievement will be little different than if he were in a school composed of others like himself. But if a minority pupil from a home without much educational strength is put with schoolmates with strong educational backgrounds, his achievement is likely to increase.

This general result, taken together with the earlier examinations of school differences, has important implications for equality of educational opportunity. For the earlier tables show that the principal way in which the school environments of Negroes and whites differ is in the composition of their student bodies, and it turns out that the composition of the student bodies has a strong relationship to the achievement of Negro and other minority pupils.

This analysis has concentrated on the educational opportunities offered by the schools in terms of their student body composition, facilities, curriculums, and teachers. This emphasis, while entirely appropriate as a response to the legislation calling for the survey, nevertheless neglects important factors in the variability between individual pupils within the same school; this variability is roughly four times as large as the variability between schools. For example, a pupil attitude factor, which appears to have a stronger relationship to achievement than do all the "school" factors together, is the extent to which an individual feels that he has some control over his own destiny. . . . The responses of pupils to questions in the survey show that minority pupils, except for Orientals, have far less conviction than whites that they can affect their own environments and futures. When they do, however, their achievement is higher than that of whites who lack that conviction.

Furthermore, while the characteristic shows little relationship to most school factors, it is related, for Negroes, to the proportion of whites in the schools. Those Negroes in schools with a higher proportion of whites have a greater sense of control. Thus such attitudes, which are largely a consequence of a person's experience in the larger society, are not independent of his experience in school.

OTHER SURVEYS AND STUDIES

A number of studies were carried out by the Office of Education in addition to the major survey of public elementary and secondary schools. Some of these were quite extensive investigations with book-length final reports; certain of them will be published in full as appendixes to the main report. There will be other appendixes containing more detailed analyses of the public school data than could be included in the main report. Still other appendixes will contain detailed tabulation of the data gathered in the survey so that research workers will have easy access to them.

OPPORTUNITY IN INSTITUTIONS OF HIGHER EDUCATION

The largely segregated system of higher education in the South has made comparison between colleges attended mainly by Negro students and mainly by majority students easy in that region. Elsewhere it has not been possible in the past to make comparison between educational opportunities because of the general policy in Federal and State agencies of not collecting data on race. In the fall of 1965, however, the Office of Education reversed this policy as a result of the interest of many agencies and organizations in the progress of minority pupils in gaining access to higher education. The racial composition of freshmen of all degree-seeking students was obtained from nearly all of the colleges and universities in the Nation.

These racial compositions have been cross-tabulated against a variety of characteristics of the institutions in the report itself. . . . Over half of all Negro college students attend the largely segregated institutions in the South and Southwest. About 4.6 percent of all college students are Negro. . . . Negro students are in colleges with substantially lower faculty salaries. The institutions in the South and Southwest generally pay lower salaries than those in other regions, and the colleges serving primarily the Negro students are at the bottom of this low scale.

Other findings of the study are that—(1) in every region Negro students are more likely to enter the State College system than the State University system, and further they are a smaller proportion of the student body of universities than any other category of public institutions of higher education, (2) Negro students are more frequently found in institutions which have a high dropout rate, (3) they attend mainly institutions with low tuition cost, (4) they tend to major in engineering, agriculture, education, social work, social science, and nursing.

Future Teachers

Since a number of investigations of teacher qualification in the past few years have indicated that teachers of Negro children are less qualified than those who teach primarily majority children, this survey investigated whether there might be some promise that the situation may be changed by college students now preparing to become teachers. To this end, questionnaire and achievement test data were secured from about 17,000 college freshmen and 5,500 college seniors in 32 teacher training colleges in 18 States that in 1960 included over 90 percent of the Nation's Negro population. Some of the findings of this survey are:

1. At both the freshman and senior levels, future teachers are very similar to students in their colleges who are following other career lines. (It should be remembered that these comparisons are limited to students in colleges that have a primary mission in the training of teachers, and is not, of course, a random sample of all colleges.)

2. Majority students being trained at the college level to enter teaching have a stronger preparation for college than have Negro students; that is, they had more courses in foreign languages, English, and mathematics, made better grades in high school, and more often were in the highest track in English.

3. Data from the senior students suggest that colleges do not narrow the gap in academic training between Negro and majority pupils; indeed, there is some evidence that the college curriculum increases this difference, at least in the South.

4. Substantial test score differences exist between Negro and white future teachers at both freshman and senior levels, with approximately 15 percent of Negroes exceeding the average score of majority students in the same region. (This figure varies considerably depending on the test, but in no case do as many as 25 percent of Negroes exceed the majority average.)

5. The test data indicate that the gap in test results widens in the South between the freshman and senior years. The significance of this finding lies in the fact that most Negro teachers are trained in the Southern States.

6. The preferences of future teachers for certain kinds of schools and certain kinds of pupils raise the question of the match between the expectations of teacher recruits and the characteristics of the employment opportunities.

The preferences of future teachers were also studied. Summarized in terms of market conditions, it seems apparent that far too many future teachers perfer to teach in an academic high school; that there is a far greater proportion of children of blue-collar workers than of teachers being produced who prefer to teach them; that there is a very substantial number of white teachers-in-traning, even in the South, who prefer to teach in racially mixed schools; that very few future teachers of either race wish to teach in predominantly minority schools; and finally, that high-ability pupils are much more popular with future teachers than low-ability ones. The preferences of Negro future teachers are more compatible with the distribution of needs in the market than are those of the majority; too few of the latter, relative to the clientele requiring service, prefer blue-collar or low-ability children or prefer to teach in racially heterogeneous schools, or in special curriculum, vocational, or commercial schools. These data indicate that under the present organization of schools, relatively few of the best prepared future teachers will find their way into classrooms where they can offset some of the environmental disadvantage suffered by minority children.

School Enrollment and Dropouts

Another extensive study explored enrollment rates of children of various ages, races, and socio-economic categories using 1960 census data. The study included also an investigation of school dropouts using the October 1965 Current Population Survey of the Bureau of the Census. This survey uses a carefully selected sample of 35,000 households. It was a large enough sample to justify reliable nationwide estimates for the Negro minority but not for other minorities. In this section the word "white" includes the Mexican American and Puerto Rican minorities.

According to the estimates of the Current Population Survey, approximately 6,960,000 persons of ages 16 and 17 were living in the United States in October 1965. Of this number 300,000 (5 percent) were enrolled in college, and therefore, were not considered by this Census Bureau study. Of the remaining, approximately 10 percent, or 681,000 youths of 16 and 17 had left school prior to completion of high school. . . . About 17 percent of Negro adolescents (ages 16 and 17) have dropped out of school whereas the corresponding number for white adolescents is 9 percent. . . . Most of this difference comes from differences outside the South; in the South the white and Negro nonenrollment rates are much the same. . . . Whereas the nonenrollment rate was 3 percent for those 16- and 17-year-olds from white-collar families, it was more than four times as large (13 percent) in the case of those from other than white-collar families (where the head of household was in a blue-collar or farm occupation, unemployed, or not in the labor force at all). Furthermore, this difference in nonenrollment by parental occupation existed for both male and female, Negro and white adolescents.

The racial differences in the dropout rate are thus sharply reduced when socioeconomic factors are taken into account. Then the difference of 8 percentage points between all Negro and white adolescent dropouts becomes 1 percent for those in white-collar families, and 4 percent for those in other than white-collar families. . . . The largest differences between Negro and white dropout rates are seen in the urban North and West; in the nonurban North and West there were too few Negro households in the sample to provide a reliable estimate. In the South there is the unexpected result that in the urban areas, white girls drop out at a greater rate than Negro girls, and in the nonurban area white boys drop out at a substantially greater rate than Negro boys.

Effects of Integration on Achievement

An education in integrated schools can be expected to have major effects on attitudes toward members of other racial groups. At its best, it can develop attitudes appropriate to the integrated society these students will live in; at its worst, it can create hostile camps of Negroes and whites in the same school. Thus there is more to "school integration" than merely putting Negroes and whites in the same building, and there may be more important consequences of integration than its effect on achievement.

Yet the analysis of school effects described earlier suggests that in the long run, integration should be expected to have a positive effect on Negro achievement as well. An analysis was carried out to examine the effects on achievement which might appear in the short run. This analysis of the test performance of Negro children in integrated schools indicates positive effects of integration, though rather small ones.... [I]n every case but one the highest average score is recorded for the Negro pupils where more than half of their classmates were white. But ... often those Negro pupils in classes with only a few whites score lower than those in totally segregated classes.... Those [Negro] pupils who first entered integrated schools in the early grades record consistently higher scores than the other groups, although the differences are again small.

No account is taken in these tabulations of the fact that the various groups of pupils may have come from different backgrounds. When such account is taken by simple cross-tabulations on indicators of socio-economic status, the performance in integrated schools and in schools integrated longer remains higher. Thus although the differences are small, and although the degree of integration within the school is not known, there is evident even in the short run an effect of school integration on the reading and mathematics achievement of Negro pupils.

Tabulations of this kind are, of course, the simplest possible devices for seeking such effects. It is possible that more elaborate analyses looking more carefully at the special characteristics of the Negro pupils, and at different degrees of integration within schools that have similar racial composition, may reveal a more definite effect. Such analyses are among those that will be presented in subsequent reports.

Case Studies of School Integration

As part of the survey, two sets of case studies of school integration were commissioned. These case studies examine the progress of integration in individual cities and towns, and illustrate problems that have arisen not only in these communities but in many others as well. The complete case studies are maintained on file at the Office of Education. In addition, publication of all or some of the reports by their authors will be carried out through commercial publishers.

In the main report, excerpts from these case studies are presented to illustrate certain recurrent problems. A paragraph which introduces each of these excerpts is given below, showing the kinds of problems covered.

LACK OF RACIAL INFORMATION. In certain communities the lack of information as to the number of children of minority groups and of minority group teachers, their location and mobility, has made assessment of the equality of educational opportunity difficult. In one city, for example, after a free transfer plan was initiated, no records as to race of students were kept, thereby making any evaluation of the procedure subjective only. Superintendents, principals, and school boards sometimes respond by declaring racial records themselves to be a mark of discrimination.

A narrative of "the racial headcount problem" and the response to the search for a solution is given in the excerpt from the report on San Francisco.

PERFORMANCE OF MINORITY GROUP CHILDREN.　One of the real handicaps to an effective assessment of equality of education for children of minority groups is the fact that few communities have given systematic testing and fewer still have evaluated the academic performance and attitudes of these children toward education. Yet quality of education is to be estimated as much by its consequences as by the records of the age of buildings and data on faculty-student ratio. A guide to cities now planning such assessment is a pupil profile conducted in Evanston, Ill.

In 1964, the Director of Research and Testing for District 65 gathered and analyzed data on "ability" and "achievement" for 136 Negro children who had been in continuous attendance at either Central, Dewey, Foster, or Noyes school through the primary years. A group of 132 white children in continuous attendance for the same period at two white primary schools was compared. Seven different measures from kindergarten through seventh grade were correlated and combined by reducing all measures to stanines. The excerpt from the Evanston report examines in detail the performance of these two groups of children.

COMPLIANCE IN A SMALL COMMUNITY.　Many large metropolitan areas North and South are moving toward resegregation despite attempts by school boards and city administrations to reverse the trend. Racial housing concentration in large cities has reinforced neighborhood school patterns of racial isolation while, at the same time, many white families have moved to the suburbs and other families have taken their children out of the public school system, enrolling them instead in private and parochial schools. Small towns and medium-sized areas, North and South, on the other hand, are to some extent desegregating their schools.

In the Deep South, where there has been total school segregation for generations, there are signs of compliance within a number of school systems. The emphasis on open enrollment and freedom of choice plans, however, has tended to lead to token enrollment of Negroes in previously white schools. In school systems integrated at some grade levels but not at others, the choice of high school grades rather than elementary grades has tended further to cut down on the number of Negroes choosing to transfer because of the reluctance to take extra risks close to graduation.

The move toward compliance is described in the excerpt from the report on one small Mississippi town.

A VOLUNTARY TRANSFER PLAN FOR RACIAL BALANCE IN ELEMENTARY SCHOOLS. The public schools are more rigidly segregated at the elementary level than in the higher grades. In the large cities, elementary schools have customarily made assignments in terms of neighborhood boundaries. Housing segregation has, therefore, tended to build a segregated elementary school system in most cities in the North and, increasingly, in the South as well, where *de facto* segregation is replacing *de jure* segregation.

Various communities have been struggling to find ways to achieve greater racial balance while retaining the neighborhood school. Bussing, pairing, redistricting, consolidation, and many other strategies have been tried. Many have failed; others have achieved at least partial success. In New Haven, Conn., considerable vigor has been applied to the problem: Whereas pairing was tried at the junior high level introducing compulsory integration, a voluntary transfer plan was implemented at the elementary level. Relief of overcrowding was given as the central intent of the transfer plan, but greater racial balance was achieved since it was the Negro schools that were overcrowded. With the provision of new school buildings, however, this indirect stimulus to desegregation will not be present. In New Haven the transfer plan was more effective than in many other communities because of commitment of school leadership, active solicitation of transfers by door-to-door visits, provision of transportation for those transferring, teacher cooperation, heterogeneous grouping in the classrooms, and other factors.

The original plan provided that a student could apply to any one of a cluster of several elementary schools within a designated "cluster district," and the application would be approved on the basis of availability of space, effect on racial balance and certain unspecified educational factors; that students "presently enrolled" at a particular school would be given priority; and that transportation would be provided where necessary.

DESEGREGATION BY REDISTRICTING AT THE JUNIOR HIGH SCHOOL LEVEL. The junior high schools, customarily grades 7 to 9, have been the focus of considerable effort and tension in desegregation plans in many communities. With most areas clinging to the neighborhood school at the elementary level with resultant patterns of racial concentration, and with high schools already more integrated because of their lesser reliance upon neighborhood boundaries and their prior consolidation to achieve maximum resources, junior high schools have been a natural place to start desegregation plans. Like the elementary schools, they have in the past been assigned students on the basis of geography; but on the other hand, they tend to represent some degree of consolidation in that children from several elementary schools feed one junior high school. Further, parental pressures have been less severe for the maintenance of rigid neighborhood boundaries than at the elementary level.

Pairing of two junior high schools to achieve greater racial balance has been tried in a number of communities. Redistricting or redrawing the boundaries of areas that feed the schools has been tried in other areas. In Berkeley, Calif., after considerable community tension and struggle, a plan was put into effect that desegregated all three junior high schools (one had been desegregated previously). All the ninth graders were sent to a single school, previously Negro, and the seventh- and eighth-graders were assigned to the other two schools. The new ninth grade school was given a new name to signal its new identity in the eyes of the community. The excerpt describes the period following initiation of this plan and the differential success of integration in the different schools.

A PLAN FOR RACIAL BALANCE AT THE HIGH SCHOOL LEVEL.   In a number of communities, students are assigned to high schools on the basis of area of residence and hence racial imbalance is continued. In Pasadena, Calif., a plan was initiated to redress this imbalance by opening places in the schools to allow the transfer of Negroes to the predominantly white high school. A measure of success was achieved but only after much resistance. Of interest particularly in this situation was the legal opinion that attempts to achieve racial balance were violations of the Constitution and that race could not be considered as a factor in school districting. Apparently previous racial concentration, aided by district- ing, had not been so regarded, yet attempts at desegregation were. The school board found its task made more difficult by such legal maneuver- ing. The excerpt describes the deliberations and controversy in the school board, and the impact of the court decision, which finally upheld the policy of transfers to achieve racial balance.

SEGREGATION AT A VOCATIONAL SCHOOL.   The Washburne Trade School in Chicago seems to be effectively segregated by virtue of the practices and customs of the trade unions, whose apprenticeship programs have been characterized by racial isolation. Washburne has presented the same picture since its founding in 1919 after the passage of the Smith- Hughes Act by Congress. That Act provides for the creation of appren- ticeship programs in which skilled workers are trained both in school and on the job. For example, a young man who wishes to be certificated as a plumber may work at his job 4 days a week and attend a formal training program 1 day or more or evenings.

The apprenticeship programs are heavily financed and regulated by the Federal Government through the Department of Labor and the De- partment of Health, Education, and Welfare. In recent years the regula- tions have focused increasingly upon racial segregation within the union structures. One of the causes for this concern has been the rather dis- couraging racial pattern in the apprenticeship schools. Washburne seems to preserve that pattern. In 1960 an informal estimate showed that fewer than 1 percent of the 2,700 Washburne students were Negroes. Half of the apprenticeship programs conducted at the school had no Negroes whatsoever. This excerpt describes the state of racial segregation at Washburne and at Chicago's vocational schools.

RELATION OF A UNIVERSITY TO SCHOOL DESEGREGATION.   Education is a continuum—from kindergarten through college—and increasingly public school desegregation plans are having an impact on colleges in the same area, particularly those colleges which are city or State supported. Free tuition, as in the New York City colleges, has no meaning for members of minority groups who have dropped out of school in high school and little meaning for those whose level of achievement is too low to permit work at the college level. A number of colleges, through summer tutorials and selective admittance of students whose grades would otherwise exclude them, are trying to redress this indirect form of racial imbalance.

In Newark, Del., the pressures for desegregation in the public schools have had an effect on the nearby University of Delaware indicated by the following excerpt:

There are striking parallels in reactions to integration among Newark's civic agencies, school district, and the University of Delaware. Because the university plays such a large part in Newark's affairs, this excerpt examines its problems with school integration.

This section concludes the summary report on the survey; the summary report is the first section of the full report, and it is also printed separately for those who desire only an overview of the main findings of the survey. The full report contains a great deal of detailed data from which a small amount has been selected for this summary. It also contains a full description of the statistical analysis which explored the relationships between educational achievement and school characteristics.

DISCUSSION QUESTIONS

1. What do you consider to be the major findings of The Coleman Report?
2. Which of these can be translated into improved education for the children of the poor and the deprived in America?
3. What resistances do you forsee to the possibilities for change that are implicit in The Coleman Report?

ALICE MIEL and
EDWIN KIESTER, JR.
The Shortchanged Children of Suburbia

At first glance, the community of New Village, not far from New York City, seems an idyllic place for American children to grow up in. The homes are mostly ranged along quiet, winding streets. There are open spaces, greenery, woods to explore. The churches and community

Reprinted from Alice Miel and Edwin Kiester, Jr., *The Shortchanged Children of Suburbia* (New York: The Institute of Human Relations Press, 1967), pp. 10–15, with permission of the publisher.

centers run dances, teen programs and other youth activities. The schools are new and modern, with well-kept lawns and the latest in playground facilities; they boast a curriculum tailored mostly to students headed for college. PTA meeting are among the best-attended events in town.

Yet children miss something in New Village. You do not recognize it at first, but as you drive along the streets, you suddenly realize that all the homes are pretty much of a stripe. None are very lavish, none are very poor. The people are of a stripe, too—almost all of them are white and young or fairly young. You will look long for a dark face or an old one. New Village has many things to offer young people, but diversity is not one of them.

The residents of New Village (which is not its real name) would resent hearing their town characterized as a look-alike suburb. And indeed the community, which began as a cluster of city people's summer cottages, does have a character, individuality and charm of its own that set it apart from other suburbs—even adjoining ones. Just the same, New Village is representative of American's postwar rush to "the country"—with all that is promising and all that is disquieting about that movement. Like hundreds of other new communities, it is made up largely of white middle-income families, clustering together and raising their children in an atmosphere where many of the basic differences among people are fenced out.

In another period of history, this sort of self-segregation might not have mattered. But today Americans cannot afford to shut themselves off from human differences, for these differences are precisely what the chief problems of our times are about. On the domestic scene, the crucial issues of the sixties include the Negroes' drive for equality, the Government's effort to bring a share of prosperity to the impoverished, the nation's concern with the welfare of the elderly, the ecumenical movement in organized religion. On the world stage we see the growing aspirations of the underdeveloped nations, the rise of nationalism and the ascendancy of the colored races. Moreover, hardly anyone believes these prickly questions can be solved during the present generation; our children and perhaps our children's children will have to face up to them as well.

How well is suburbia—the home of vast numbers of Americans, and increasingly the trend-setter for the entire population—preparing the young people of today for such a future? Lacking first-hand contact, how do suburban children learn about human difference, and what do they think about it? How can they acquire respect for persons whom their middle-class society brands less acceptable than themselves? And what can adults—parents, school administrators, classroom teachers, community organizations—do to groom the coming generation for a proper role in a multicultural society?

The Study: Why and How

Some time ago, a group of us—teachers, sociologists and researchers from Teachers College, Columbia University—set out to shed some light on these questions. We focused on New Village as a reasonably typical American suburb.

Of course, we knew that New Village was not a precise counterpart of every suburb. No single community could be, for each has developed according to its own pattern. Some were built on open land, others grew up around an existing community. Some belong almost wholly to one social class, others have at least a small range of socio-economic difference. In some, one faith predominates; in others, religious groups are more evenly represented. Some have stopped growing while others are still increasing in size. Yet, all seem to have a number of characteristics in common. They consist almost wholly of young adults and children. Fathers commute, and mothers dominate the children's upbring. Adults have at least a high-school education and own their homes. Parents are greatly concerned with how their youngsters are raised. In all these respects, we found, New Village strongly resembles suburbs around the country.

Our study concentrated chiefly on the elementary schools as the chief training ground for American children today. We sought to discover how suburban youngsters are taught (or not taught) about human difference, and how their attitudes toward it are shaped and molded. We hoped to find out what opportunities for such "social learning" are available in the schools, and how teachers capitalize on them. We tried to delve into the values and predispositions of parents and teachers, and to guage their awareness of problems connected with group differences. In short, we set out to learn what kind of background a suburb provides for educating children to live in a multicultural society. We also wanted to point up the need for social lessons in schools today, and to suggest how they might be included in the curriculum.

The actual study covered four years. In that time all the teachers in three elementary schools took part in group interviews, and over 200 teachers in seven schools filled out a lengthy questionnaire. Teachers were asked what their pupils seemed to know about human difference, and also how they taught about it. Numerous meetings were held with administrators. One researcher concentrated on the students themselves, using what are known as projective techniques—for example, asking the children to comment on or interpret photographs or imaginary situations. A sociologist on our research team talked to parents of childen in three schools; and two other team members (one of them the study director) conducted a workshop for members of the faculty. In addition, some comparative research was done in urban, suburban and rural localities outside New Village.

The information obtained was then sorted out according to whether it had to do with racial, socio-economic, religious, ethnic or other differences between people. The next few chapters in this pamphlet set out our findings according to the same grouping. In later chapters we outline certain broader attitudes of suburban children (and, incidentally, their elders) that bear on our subject, and discuss the potential role of schools in helping the young get better prepared for life in the modern world. The concluding chapter suggests action programs which should prove useful to educators, parents and community groups in many places besides New Village.

Some General Impressions

The study points up certain troubling aspects of growing up in New Village—and, by extension, in any suburban community. To begin with, it was found that extraordinary effort was required to bring about any encounter between a child of the suburbs and persons different from himself. In big cities today—as in the small towns of the past—youngsters are virtually certain to encounter ethnic, economic or racial diversity, in the course of their school or social life. But the suburban child's life and social contacts are far more circumscribed; in fact they are almost totally controlled by his parents, whether or not the parents recognize this. He depends on his mother to chauffeur him wherever he goes. As a result, he knows little beyond his own home, the very similar homes of friends, the school, and the inside of the family car; he is largely insulated from any chance introduction to a life different from his own.

Second, we observed that children learn to be hypocritical about differences at a very early age. At first, many said things like "I wouldn't care if a person were white or black, I'd play with him if I liked him." But on further probing, it become evident that this supposed tolerance was only skin-deep: when the same children were given any test which involved just such a choice, they almost invariably shied from choosing the Negro. The prejudices of their society were still very much with them, but they had had it drilled into them that it was "not nice" to express such feelings.

Third, group prejudices, of whatever nature, evidently take root early and go deep. Many stereotypes about race and religion cropped up even among the youngest children. Six- and seven-year-olds, for instance, pictured Negroes as poor, threatening or inferior. With such early beginnings, any fight against prejudice is bound to be a difficult uphill struggle.

Fourth, and more hopefully, the study found a good many parents united in desiring more emphasis on certain kinds of human difference. For example, they were greatly in favor of children's learning about nationality differences; many also hoped the schools would help youngsters achieve respect for other faiths and even teach what the beliefs of these were.

Finally, it appears that one area of human difference is almost completely ignored in the American suburb. Many parents and teachers were found eager to bridge religious differences; many recognized, however uneasily, the need for discussion of racial differences. But with a few notable exceptions, neither parents nor schools were facing up to economic inequality. Occasionally, a social-studies class would take up the poor of other nations, or a fund drive would focus attention on the less fortunate in the United States; but the fact that there were impoverished families within a stone's throw of New Village was seldom noted, and how they got there or what kept them impoverished was seldom investigated.

The overall impression one carries away is that something is missing in New Village. People who have moved to the suburbs since the Second World War often say proudly that they did so "for the children." And, of course, the children of communities like New Village do have a host of advantagees, be no means all of them material. But in one aspect of their education suburban children are underprivileged. Though other races, other nationalities, other generations have a great deal to teach them, there is little in their education, formal or otherwise, to familiarize them with the rich diversity of American life.

In this sense, despite the many enviable features of their environment, the children of suburbia are being shortchanged.

BLACK AND WHITE

The average elementary-school child in New Village does not know and has never known a Negro his own age. The school population includes several hundred "non-whites," most of them Negroes, but they are concentrated in one school in the least desirable section of the community and have little or no contact with children outside that section. When our study began, the school in the Negro neighborhood was closed for remodeling, and the pupils were being transported by bus to another, but by the later phases of our work they had been resegregated in their old school.

In one area sampled, all families were white except for one Chinese-American household. When parents were asked if their children had contact with other races, they declared they had indeed—the Chinese family, one Negro teacher and one Negro bus driver. But actually, as the study showed only too clearly, racial ignorance and racial prejudice flourished among the young children there. In fact, throughout New Village, children at the very earliest age had learned to look upon Negroes as different, inferior, undesirable and even violent. Some, as noted above, had learned to be hypocritical and to conceal any such feeling; but it was scarcely difficult to establish its prevalence.

None of this, actually, is surprising, for it clearly mirrors the attitudes of the adult community. When we interviewed the parents of children in the New Village schools, we found that most paid lip service to ideas of racial justice, but admitted to prejudice on closer questioning. Several said candidly that they did not want their children to associate with Negroes. On the other hand, parents agreed that Negroes were "entitled to their rights" and that it was "not nice" to make slurring remarks about them.

DISCUSSION QUESTIONS

1. Are white children educationally shortchanged in our finer suburbs?
2. Is it vital to our nation—and to the world—that our children learn about human difference, as Miel and Kiester state?
3. Do you agree that group prejudices "take root early and go deep"? As a teacher, what is your responsibility for combating such prejudice? How would you go about it in a wealthy suburban school?
4. Are the children of our suburbs likely, when they become adults, to opt for open-housing laws and integrated schools?

FRYE GAILLARD BIA School Target of Severe Criticism

As you follow U. S. Highway 89 into the town of Brigham City, Utah, the Bureau of Indian Affairs' Intermountain Boarding School is on your right—a massive institution, surrounded by a ten-foot chain-link fence and looking very much like the military facility that it used to be. Visitors to the school are supposed to check in at Building 1, the administrative center, but during the slack summer period, you can avoid doing that if you want to and can proceed directly to the classroom buildings or dormitories where a handful of teachers and students may be only too happy to tell you about conditions at the school.

It is quite possible that they will take you to the Intermountain library where you can find a BIA pamphlet entitled "Questions Commonly Asked About Intermountain School." One of the questions concerns the difference between Intermountain and everyday public high schools, and

Reprinted form *Race Relations Reporter*, Sept. 7, 1971, pp. 8–11, with permission of the publisher.

many students and Indian employes at Intermountain find the answer striking.

"The essential difference," says the pamphlet, "is that public schools have the task of preserving the prevailing customs of our society, namely the same language, same costume, same diet, housing, social customs and civic responsibilities. The task of the Intermountain school is to change language, change diet, costume, housing, manners, customs, vocations, and civic duties. Changing people's habits and outlooks is one of the most complex tasks in human affairs."

Implicit in this objective, many Indians feel, is a clear lack of appreciation of the culture and a way of life of the Navajos, whom the school serves exclusively. And there is considerable evidence that throughout Intermountain's history, and particularly in recent times, this lack of appreciation has extended to the Indians themselves and has approached a denial of the humanity of the students in grades 1–12 who attend the school, and of the Indian employes who work there.

When the BIA's new education director, James Hawkins, conceded in May that the Navajos might be better off if the school were closed down, he was acknowledging, something that many Navajos have believed for a long time.

To begin with, Intermountain is nearly 700 miles from the Navajo capital at Window Rock, Ariz. Students are bused to the school in the fall, bused home again at Christmas, bused back after the holidays, and then back home again for the summer. The cost of all this is considerable, and the result is a racially segregated educational institution in which the students lose both the benefit of association with children of other races and the social and cultural support of living in their own communities.

And many of them, like Jody Allen, find Brigham City not only different, but hostile. Jody arrived at Intermountain as a junior high school student. He graduated this year. "It did not take me long," he says with slightly broken English, "to learn that something was bad wrong with this Intermountain place." One of the first things he noticed was that his teachers spoke no Navajo at all, which was a problem because he spoke very little English. He was able to communicate with some of his instructional aides, but even that was difficult because the speaking of Navajo was a punishable offense in those days—both among the students and the aides.

He says there were a number of minor, though very painful, annoyances such as the time he was sitting in class, desperately needing to go to the bathroom, but not being able to communicate the fact to his teacher because his English wasn't good enough yet. But even more discouraging was the fact that he missed a large part of what was taught him in class in those early years, and he was not alone. Most of the students who come to Intermountain have language barriers when they arrive, and the teaching staff is too culturally deprived to do much about it.

But the students' problems do not stop there.

"I remember the first time I was put in jail," says Jody Allen. "I was getting ready to leave the dormitory when my instructional aide asked me to clean my room. I said, 'Man, I would like to clean it when I get back.' But he said, 'Nothing doing,' and he followed me down to the bathroom demanding that I clean the room. When I refused, he hit me and split open my eye. I started to fight back, and some of my friends tried to help me, but they broke us up and put me in jail.'

Another time, Allen says, he came back to campus after purchasing some hair cream at a nearby drug store. His instructional aide (not the one from the previous altercation) insisted on seeing a cash register receipt, and when he failed to produce one, the aide had him jailed on a shoplifting charge.

"And one time after that," Jody continues, "I went AWOL with some friends, and we climbed the mountain behind the school and bought some beer. They caught us, and although we were not drunk, they jailed us because we were underaged. I was 16 then, and the school supported the jailing. These white people who run the school, they always support the jailing of Indian students."

Intermountain's supervisory guidance counselor, Sherman Nay, does not see it quite that way. "Yes, some of our young people have been jailed," he says, "just like young people have been jailed in a lot of other places. The Indian kids are no different. When they are jailed, we send a counselor down to be with them. Usually you'll find it's just a misdemeanor charge, and we try to work out a short sentence. We have a good working relationship with the judge, and we try to arrange it so the kids will miss as little class time as possible. If it's a first offense, usually they will be let off entirely. On the second or third time, a short jail sentence—maybe over the weekend for two or three days, or maybe up to five days—is usually arranged."

Some students who have been jailed don't see the school's role as even that benign. But that may be simply a matter of perspective. What is clear is that an inordinate number of Navajo students are accumulating jail records in Brigham City and unfavorable discipline files at Intermountain.

For example, on a typical weekend in the 1970 school year (as it happened, the weekend of Saturday, May 16), Intermountain records show that seven student were jailed for possession of alcoholic beverages. Three of those jailed were 18; two were 19 and two were 20. There is no record of their causing any disturbance, or even being intoxicated, but they were underaged. The legal age in Brigham City is 21, although if you are a student at Intermountain you can't legally buy liquor or wine or beer at any age.

Intermountain did not try to help the seven jailed students obtain legal counsel. It never does. What it did do, however, was make a record of the arrests to be placed in the permanent file of each student—a file that can be shown to future employers or to future educational institutions that the students may want to attend.

In addition, on that same weekend, 32 other Intermountain students had their permanent records marred by the entry of unfavorable information. School files duly record that seven students were sniffing glue or spray paint, six went AWOL (Intermountain's official term for leaving campus without permission), and 19 were drinking.

There is no record of unruly conduct or clashes between students and Intermountain guidance personnel for the weekend of May 16, but such clashes do occur. And Mrs. Rosa Naranjo, a social studies teacher at the school, is among those who contend that the guidance personnel are often at fault. "Most of the guidance people, like most of the teachers, are non-Indians," she explains. "If the school would hire more Navajo guidance personnel, then they could talk to the Navajo kids in Navajo and calm them down when they are drunk. But the white instructional aides tend to push the kids around, and that makes them mad. And one thing about most of these Navajos—they are not afraid to fight back."

The fights are usually one-sided, and the Navajos usually fare badly —primarily because the white administrators are able to call upon superior weaponry, such as handcuffs, a powerful tranquilizing drug known as Thorazine, and the threat of such humiliating punishment as head-shaving.

"Several employees have secured handcuffs to use in connection with controlling students who are intoxicated and belligerent," said guidance supervisor Sherman Nay in a memorandum to his staff March 31, 1970. "The use of handcuffs is authorized, but employees are cautioned to use them with discretion." Nay did urge the staff to be "as gentle as possible," and he ordered that handcuffs be used only "when other means of control are not practical."

How well the staff has abided by Nay's instructions is an open question, but some students who were handcuffed say the experience was very painful indeed. "It should be pretty damn obvious," contended one student angrily, "that any instructional aide who can't control his students without handcuffing them is not the sort of person who is likely to practice much restraint. There just isn't any way to be humane when what you are talking about is handcuffing kids."

And Lehman Brightman, an Indian civil rights leader from California, told a Senate subcommittee earlier this year that when he visited Intermountain, he found Navajo young people whose wrists are permanently scarred by the use of handcuffs.

Gradually, however, handcuffing appears to have been supplanted by the use of Thorazine. Tom Oxendine, a spokesman for the Bureau of

Indian Affairs, contends the drug is employed only when a student is a danger to himself or the people around him. Oxendine also maintains that the drug is always administered by qualified medical personnel under a carefully scrutinized program, approved by the Indian Health Service of the Department of Health, Education and Welfare.

But the *Physicians Desk Reference,* the standard pharmaceutical guide used by nearly all doctors and based largely on information supplied by the drug manufacturers, offers information that raises questions about the Health Service approval. On page 1,223, the guide lists among conditions under which the use of Thorazine is inadvisable: "the presence of large amounts of Central Nervous System Depressant [such as] alcohol, barbiturates, narcotics, etc." The desk reference also says explicitly, "the use of alcohol with this drug should be avoided," and it explains that Thorazine "prolongs and intensifies the action of C.N.S. depressants." It cautions, in addition, that Thorazine—because it is so powerful—is an extremely dangerous drug if misused.

On top of that, some Intermountain students maintain that Thorazine is often used on Navajo young people who are not particularly unruly. "Yes, I have some friends who were drugged with Thorazine," says Evelyn Reeder, who graduated first in her class this year. "Some of them were unruly, some weren't."

Perhaps the most serious and humiliating punishment yet devised at Intermountain, however, has been the practice of head-shaving. School rules require very short haircuts to begin with, and this traumatic enough for some students. Traditional Navajo hairstyles are long, and many Intermountain students have regarded these styles as an integral part of their culture. Others have not, but the point is that on the reservation the choice is up to them. At Intermountain, it is not.

In addition to the routine haircutting, however, students who (in the judgment of their supervisors) misbehave have often had their hair shaved off at the scalpline—a process which the Intermountain chapter of the National Indian Youth Council sees as alarmingly analogous to scalping. Some sympathetic Indian employees at Intermountain have taken photographs of the head-shaving, and every student interviewed by RRIC was able to list dozens of classmates who were victimized by it.

In March of 1970, Intermountain instructional aide Leonard C. Brown gave this notarized account of one particular head-shaving: "Eddie Livingston [a student] stated that just a week after Christmas when he was coming back from building 328, a boy met him and told him to see Mr. Charles Helseth, instructional aide, immediately. When Eddie got to the building, he was ordered to go to the barber shop in building 44. Mr. Barnett started the cutting, then one of the students, Anderson Toledo, was told to finish what was left on Eddie's head. Since then he [Eddie] attended all classes but refused to go to the dining room for seven days. For the same reason, we have some boys AWOL. I don't think this is right in the Hornor Dorm."

Mrs. Emma Delgarito, an Intermountain instructional aide (who was named Indian Woman of the Year in 1970 by the National Indian Youth Council), explains that many Navajo young people are shy to begin with, "and when they cut their hair off, it is too much for many of them to bear. . . . Some kids cut class. Other go AWOL. And when they do that, sometimes they wind up in jail."

In 1965, one Intermountain student who wound up in jail never came out. Boyd Tsosie Jr., who was 18 at the time, hung himself in his cell with his sweater. Police officials said Tsosie had received "medical attention" at the Intermountain medical center before he was brought in on a charge of being drunk. They told the *Box Elder News*, a Brigham City newspaper, that Tsosie was first seen "lying down and writhing about which is not unusual in such cases." Thirty minutes later, he was dead.

In the context of Intermountain's other problems, many students remember the incident bitterly. But bitterness toward the school is not universal among the young people who attend it, which surprises some observers familiar with its reputation. Tom Sussman, an aide to Sen. Edward Kennedy, says Kennedy's office has received two petitions from Intermountain students—each with approximately the same number of signatures. The first urges Kennedy to investigate the atrocious conditions at the school; the second informs him that the majority of Intermountain students do not support the attempts to despoil the school's reputation.

One of the most ardent student defenders of Intermountain is Frank Lew, the 1970–71 student body president. In a recent interview with *The Navajo Times*, Lew attributed criticism of the school to Indian-power advocates and added, "98 per cent of the students are for progress. The other two per cent are for Indian power." Lew also told the Navajo tribal publication that "outsiders try to rile up the teachers and the administration, and they only hurt the students."

Lew maintains the use of Thorazine can actually be humane, that the reports of hand-cuffing and head-shaving are exaggerated, and that student freedoms are not overly restricted. He contends that all in all, Intermountain is not a bad place to go to school.

Jody Allen and other members of the Intermountain NIYC chapter (which is the student organization most critical of the school) say Lew only says those things to please the administration. Other Navajos— even some members of the tribal school board—believe that Lew is very sincere. And he may well be, for some Intermountain graduates, who are under no apparent pressure to say anything but what they mean, seem to agree with his basic assessment.

"Yes, I am a graduate of Intermountain," says Pearl Hale, a young Navajo girl who now lives near Gallup, N. M. "What did I think of the school? Well, there are good and bad things about every school, but I thing basically it helped me." Reconciling these kinds of comments with the criticisms made of the school has been difficult for many people who have attempted to examine conditions there. But if you talk to Pearl Hale a little longer, the pieces begin to fit together.

When asked point blank what she thought of the rules under which students are compelled to live, Pearl conceded that she found them annoying, often difficult to adjust to, and in some cases downright capricious. She said for example, that she did not like the fact that mail is sometimes opened and inspected by the guidance staff before it is handed out, or the fact that it is distributed only at certain specified times and never on weekends.

"My sister graduated from Intermountain this year," she said, "and the family bought her a new dress to wear at the graduation exercises. We mailed it to her and the package reached the school on the Friday before graduation, which began on Sunday with a baccalaureate service. But they wouldn't let her have it because the mail had already been given out, and they wouldn't make an exception even when she explained the situation to them. I don't like things like that about the school."

Miss Hale says she also did not like the time the principal's wife threw her in the shower just before she was supposed to go out on a date. "Mrs. Kapps ordered me to scrub the shower and bathroom just before I went out," she recalled. "I told her I didn't want to because I had a date and I was ready to go out. So she turned on the water of one of the showers and pushed me under. And then she said, 'There, I guess you are not ready to go out now.' I was very mad, and I pulled her under with me."

The point is that Pearl Hale, whose basic evaluation of Intermountain is positive, is able to cite examples of brutality and senselessness that affected her directly. "A lot of these students don't have anything really to compare Intermountain to," points out Gerald Wilkinson, the executive director of the National Indian Youth Council. "They experience these things at Intermountain, but they think that's just the way schools are. It is not hard for the administrators to make them believe that either, because you can exert a lot of control over young people when you take them 700 miles from home with no one to protect them.

Dan Press, a white attorney for the Navajos DNA legal services agency, agrees. "This is the most frustrating case I have ever worked on," he says, "because at Intermountain they have an incredibly effective interlocking system of repression, intimidation and thought control." Press says he too has been "hung up" at times by the fact that some students continue to praise the school, but he says he has decided that there have been too many complaints of brutality and discrimination, too many official charges and sworn statements, and too much incontestable documentation for him to believe that Intermountain is not beset with severe problems.

It would be a mistake, however, to conceive of the problems solely in terms of physical brutality. Evelyn Reeder, who graduated this year, says her biggest objection to the school was that it didn't teach her anything.

Evelyn is not the only student to complain that course offerings are not challenging enough, but there may be some legitimate problems there. The range of academic achievement is extraordinarily broad, and some teachers say that if courses were made difficult enough to challenge students like Miss Reeder, then slower learners would be left behind.

But Mrs. Rosa Naranjo and a few other teachers believe there are other less legitimate problems. "There are 18 teachers in the social studies department," she says. "Of those, 13 are Mormons and only three are Indians. Most of the teachers bring a very white perspective to their courses, and the textbooks have the same perspective. The result is that the students don't begin to develop a full understanding or appreciation of who they are."

One of the books used by the school is called *Your Country's Story*, published by Ginn and Company. The cover depicts a wagon train crossing Indian territory, and on the title page is a white pioneer holding a rifle. The first chapter is entitled, "Europeans Added a New World to Their Maps," and in the chapter on westward expansion, Indians are discussed only as a threat to the brave pioneers. For example, on page 163 the book reports that, "the area between the Appalachian Mountains and the Mississippi River was fertile, but many hostile Indians lived there."

Course outlines for the 1970–71 school year called for more attention to Indian history and culture, but as Mrs. Naranjo points out, "we have the same white teachers and the same white-washed textbooks." She says she is skeptical of how much change there will be until more Indian teachers are hired, and she maintains there has long been a pattern of discrimination in Intermountain's hiring practices.

One Indian who was definitely not discriminated against, however, was Miss Wilma Victor, a Choctaw from Oklahoma, who was Intermountain's superintendent during the 1960's when controversy over the school began to mount. The outcry peaked in the spring of 1970, and Miss Victor was removed. But to the dismay of her critics, she was promoted to acting director of education for the entire Bureau of Indian Affairs.

She held the post for several months, and then in November of 1970, she was transferred to the BIA's area office in Phoenix, Ariz. She headed the education program there until last March when Secretary of the Interior Rogers Morton selected her to be his special assistant on Indian affairs. Her job is now to advise him about the implementation of the government's entire Indian policy and about the overall operation of the BIA.

Miss Victor told RRIC several months ago that the charges against

Intermountain were "not true at all," and she attributed them to "a group of people who say they speak for Indians but who don't come from an Indian background." She says she does not take such criticisms personally and added, "I have a long record as an educator, and when you get to be my age you just say 'there is my reputation, take your shots at it.'"

Many people have done just that, and they regard Miss Victor's promotion as bitter proof that the government is indifferent. The next issue of the *Race Relations Reporter* will examine the history of the government's response to attempts to change Intermountain, and will assess the prospects for the future which may be brighter.

DISCUSSION QUESTIONS

1. Is it legitimate that minority groups be given the choice of remaining apart if they also are given the choice of integration?
2. What advantages and disadvantages accrue to Indians and other minorities by remaining apart or by being integrated?

ALEXANDER M. BICKEL   Desegregation:
Where Do We Go From Here?

It [was] 16 years this May since the Supreme Court decreed in *Brown* v. *Board of Education* that the races may not be segrated by law in the public schools, and [it will be] six years in July since the doctrine of the *Brown* case was adopted as federal legislative and executive policy in the Civil Rights Act of 1964. Yet here we are apparently struggling still to desegregate schools in Mississippi, Louisiana, and elsewhere in the Deep South, and still meeting determined resistance, if no longer much violence or rioting.

The best figures available indicate that only some 23 percent of the nationwide total of more than six million Negro pupils go to integrated public schools. About half the total of more than six million Negro pupils are in the South, and there the percentage of Negroes in school with whites is only 18.

What has gone wrong? The answer is, both less and a great deal more than meets the eye; it is true both that the school desegregation effort has been a considerable success and that it has not worked.

Reprinted by permission of *The New Republic*, © 1970, Harrison-Blaine of New Jersey, Inc.

The measure of the success is simply taken. Sixteen years ago, local law, not only in the 11 Southern states but in border states, in parts of Kansas, in the District of Columbia, forbade the mixing of the races in the schools, and official practice had the same effect in some areas in the North, for example portions of Ohio and New Jersey. Ten years ago, Southern communities were up in arms, often to the point of rioting or closing the public schools altogether, over judicial decrees that ordered the introduction of a dozen or two carefully selected Negro children into a few previously all-white schools. There are counties in the Deep South that still must be reckoned as exceptions, but on the whole, the principle of segregation has been effectively denied, those who held it have been made to repudiate it, and the rigid legal structure that embodied it has been destroyed. That is no mean achievement, even though it still needs to be perfected and completed, and it is the achievement of law, which had irresistible moral force and was able to enlist political energies in its service.

The achievement is essentially Southern. The failure is nationwide. And the failure more than the achievement is coming to the fore in those districts in Mississippi and Louisiana where the Supreme Court and a reluctant Nixon Administration are now enforcing what they still call desegregation on very short deadlines. In brief, the failure is this: To dismantle the official structure of segregation, even with the cooperation in good faith of local authorities, is not to create integrated schools, anymore than integrated schools are produced by the absence of an official structure of school segregation in the North and West. The actual integration of schools on a significant scale is an enormously difficult undertaking, if a possible one at all. Certainly it creates as many problems as it purports to solve, and no one can be sure that even if accomplished it would yield an educational return.

School desegregation, it will be recalled, began and for more than a decade was carried out under the so-called "deliberate speed" formula. The courts insisted that the principle of segregation and, gradually, all its manifestations in the system of law and administration be abandoned; and they required visible proof of the abandonment, namely, the presence of black children in school with whites. The expectation was that a school district which had been brought to give up the objective of segregation would gradually reorganize itself along other nonracial lines and end by transforming itself from a dual into a unitary system.

All too often, that expectation was not met. The objective of segregation was not abandoned in good faith. School authorities would accept a limited Negro presence in white schools and would desist from making overt moves to coerce the separation of the races, but would manage nevertheless to continue operating a dual system consisting of all black schools for the vast majority of Negro children and of white and a handful of nearly white schools for all the white children. This was sham compliance—tokenism, it was contemptuously called, and justly so—and in the past few years the Supreme Court, and HEW acting under the Civil Rights Act of 1964, determined to tolerate it no longer.

HEW and some lower federal courts first raised the ante on tokenism, requiring stated percentages of black children in school with whites. Finally they demanded that no school in a given system be allowed to retain its previous character as a white or black school. Faculties and administrators had to be shuffled about so that an entirely or almost entirely black or white faculty would no longer characterize a school as black or white. If a formerly all-Negro school was badly substandard, it had to be closed. For the rest, residential zoning, pairing of schools by grades, some busing, and majority-to-minority transfers were employed to ensure distribution of both races through the school system. In areas where blacks were in a majority, whites were necessarily assigned to schools in which they would form a minority. All this has by no means happened in every school district in the South, but it constitutes the current practice of desegregation. Thus among the decrees recently enforced in Mississippi, the one applicable in Canton called for drawing an east-west attendance line through the city so that each school became about 70 percent black and 30 percent white. Elsewhere schools were paired to the same end.

It bears repeating that such measures were put into effect because the good faith of school authorities was in doubt, to say the least, and satisfactory evidence that the structure of legally enforced segregation had been eliminated was lacking. But whatever, and however legitimate, the reasons for imposing such requirements, the consequences have been perverse. Integration soon reaches a tipping point. If whites are sent to constitute a minority in a school that is largely black, or if blacks are sent to constitute something near half the population of a school that was formerly white or nearly all-white, the whites flee, and the school becomes all, or nearly all, black; resegregation sets in, blacks simply changing places with whites. The whites move, within a city or out of it into suburbs, so that under a system of zoning they are in white schools because the schools reflect residential segregation; or else they flee the public school system altogether, into private and parochial schools.

It is not very fruitful to ask whether the whites behave as they do because they are racists or because everybody seeks in the schools some sense of social, economic, cultural group identity. Whatever one's answer, the whites do flee, or try to, whether in a Black Belt county where desegregation has been resisted for 16 years in the worst of faith and for the most blatant of racist reasons; or in Atlanta, where in recent years, at any rate, desegregation has been implemented in the best of faith; or in border cities such as Louisville, St. Louis, Baltimore, or Washington, D.C., where it was implemented in good faith 15 years ago; or in Northern cities, where legal segregation has not existed in over half a century. It is feckless to ask whether this should happen. The questions to ask are whether there is any way to prevent the whites' fleeing, or whether there are gains sufficient to offset the flight of the whites in continuing to press the process of integration.

To start with the second question, a negative answer seems obvious. What is the use of a process of racial integration in the schools that very often produces, in absolute numbers, more black and white children attending segregated schools than before the process was put into motion? The credible disestablishment of a legally enforced system of segregation is essential, but it ought to be possible to achieve it without driving school systems past the tipping point of resegregation—and perhaps this, without coming right out and saying so, is what the Nixon Administration has been trying to tell us. Thus in Canton, Mississippi, a different zoning scheme would apparently have left some all-black and all-white schools, but still put about 35 percent of black pupils in schools with whites.

We live by principles, and the concrete expression in practice of the principles we live by is crucial. *Brown* v. *Board of Education* held out for us the principle that it is wrong and ultimately evil to classify people invidiously by race. We would have mocked that principle if we had allowed the South to wipe some laws formally off its books and then continue with segregation as usual, through inertia, custom, and the application of private force. But substantial, concrete changes vindicating the principle of the *Brown* case were attainable in the South without at the same time producing the absurd result of resegregation.

This argument assumes, however, that the first of the two questions posed above is also to be answered in the negative. Is there, in truth, no way to prevent resegregation from occurring? Approaching the problem as one of straight feasibility, with no normative implications, one has to take account of an important variable. It is relatively simple to make flight so difficult as to be just about impossible for relatively poor whites in rural areas in the South. There is little residential segregation in these areas, and there is no place to move to except private schools. State and local governments can be forbidden to aid such private schools with tuition grants paid to individual pupils, and the Supreme Court has so forbidden them. Private schools can also be deprived of federal tax exemption unless they are integrated, and a federal court in the District of Columbia has at least temporarily so deprived them. They can be deprived of state and local tax aid as well. Lacking any state support, however indirect, for private schools, all but well-to-do or Catholic whites in the rural and small-town South will be forced back into the public schools, although in the longer run we may possibly find that what we have really done is to build in an incentive to residential segregation, and even perhaps to substantial population movement into cities.

On a normative level, is it right to require a small, rural, and relatively poor segment of the national population to submit to a kind of schooling that is disagreeable to them (for whatever reasons, more or less unworthy), when we do not impose such schooling on people, in cities and in other regions, who would also dislike it (for not dissimilar reasons, more or less equally worthy or unworthy?)[1] This normative issue arises because the feasibility question takes on a very different aspect in the cities. Here movement to residentially segregated neighborhoods or suburbs is possible for all but the poorest whites and is proceeding at a rapid pace. Pursuit of a policy of integration would require, therefore, pursuit of the whites with busloads of inner-city Negro children, or even perhaps with trainloads or helicopterloads, as distances lengthen. Very substantial resources would thus be needed. They have so far nowhere been committed, in any city.

One reason they have not is that no one knows whether the enterprise would be educationally useful or harmful to the children, black and white. Even aside from the politics of the matter, which is quite a problem in itself, there is a natural hesitancy, therefore, to gamble major resources on a chase after integration, when it is more than possible that the resources would in every sense be better spent in trying to teach children how to read in place. Moreover, and in the long view most importantly, large-scale efforts at integration would almost certainly be opposed by leading elements in urban Negro communities.

Polls asking abstract question may show what they will about continued acceptance of the goal of integration, but the vanguard of black opinion, among intellectuals and political activists alike, is oriented more toward the achievement of group identity and some group autonomy than toward the use of public schools as assimilationist agencies. In part this trend of opinion is explained by the ineffectiveness, the sluggishness, the unresponsiveness, often the oppressiveness of large urban public school systems, and in part it bespeaks the feeling shared by so many whites that the schools should, after all, be an extension of the family, and that the family ought to have a sense of class and cultural identity with them. And so, while the courts and HEW are rezoning and pairing Southern schools in the effort to integrate them, Negro leaders in Northern cities are trying to decentralize them, accepting their racial character

[1] For instance a UPI dispatch from Oklahoma City dated January 20 as follows:
"Mrs. Yvonne York, mother of a 14-year-old boy taken into custody for defying a federal desegregation order, said today she will take the case to the Supreme Court. US District Judge Luther Bohanon last week ordered the Yorks to enroll their son Raymond at Harding Junior High in compliance with desegregation rulings. The boy had been enrolled at Taft Junior High a few blocks from his home. Harding is four miles from his home. Raymond was taken into custody yesterday by federal marshals when Mrs. York tried to enroll him at Taft. He was detained for a few hours." A city councilman is quoted as saying, "The people of Oklahoma are fed up with forced busing and federal court orders running our schools. We demand an end to this madness."

and attempting to bring them under community control. While the courts and HEW are reassigning faculties in Atlanta to reflect the racial composition of the schools and to bring white teachers to black pupils and black teachers to white ones, Negro leaders in the North are asking for black principals and black teachers for black schools.

Where we have arrived may be signaled by a distorted mirror image that was presented in the Ocean Hill-Brownsville decentralized experimental school district in New York during the teachers' strikes of the fall of 1968. A decade earlier, black children in Little Rock and elsewhere in the South were escorted by armed men through white mobs to be taught by white teachers. In Ocean Hill-Brownsville in 1968, white teachers had to be escorted by armed men through black mobs to teach black children.

Can we any longer fail to acknowledge that the federal government is attempting to create in the rural South conditions that cannot in the foreseeable future be attained in large or medium urban centers in the South or in the rest of the country? The government is thus seen as applying its law unequally and unjustly, and is, therefore, fueling the politics of George Wallace. At the same time, the government is also putting itself on a collision course with the aspirations of an articulate and vigorous segment of national Negro leadership. Even if we succeed, at whatever cost, in forcing and maintaining massively integrated school systems in parts of the rural South, may we not find ourselves eventually dismantling them again at the behest of blacks seeking decentralized community control?

There must be a better way to employ the material and political resources of the federal government. The process of disestablishing segregation is not quite finished, and both HEW and the courts must drive it to completion, as they must also continually police the disestablishment. But nothing seems to be gained, and much is risked or lost, by driving the process to the tipping point of resegregation. A prudent judgment can distinguish between the requirements of disestablishment and plans that cannot work, or can work only, if at all, in special areas that inevitably feel victimized.

There are black schools all over the country. We don't really know what purpose would be served by trying to do away with them, and many blacks don't want them done away with. Energies and resources ought to go into their improvement and, where appropriate, replacement. Energies and resources ought to go into training teachers and into all manner of experimental attempts to improve the quality of education. The involvement of cohesive communities of parents with the schools is obviously desired by many leaders of Negro opinion. It may bear educational fruit, and is arguably an inalienable right of parenthood anyway. Even the growth of varieties of private schools, hardly integrated, but also not segregated, and enjoying state support through tuition grants for blacks and whites alike, should not be stifled, but encouraged in the spirit of an unlimited experimental search for more effective education. Massive school integration is not going to be attained in this country very soon, in good part because no one is certain that it is worth the cost. Let us, therefore, try to proceed with education.

The above article brought a number of comments from New Republic **readers, and Mr. Bickel was moved to write further. Here is further explication of his position, taken from the March 21** New Republic:

A great deal of the critical response to my article on schools has substance as well as fervor, but is not properly addressed to me. Many of my critics see only two positions—theirs, and another that I am supposed to share with Senator Stennis. They are mistaken. They come to their error out of the experience of a decade and a half of fighting Southern segregationists, and out of the memory of how an earlier Reconstruction was defeated and nullified in 1877 by the politically motivated capitulation of the North. The experience is mine also, and I deeply respect those, lawyers and others, who fought and are still fighting as foot soldiers in the trenches, rather than, like myself, as support troops. I recognize, moreover, the danger of another Compromise of 1877. But those who read me more calmly will know that I proposed no capitulation and advocated no equivalent of the notorious Compromise. I had and have distinctly in mind the need to avert both.

Desegregation of Southern schools reached a turning point, I said, about two years ago, when courts and HEW made the transition from the effort to disestablish dual school systems to the active promotion of integration. The Supreme Court has not yet told us that total integration of pupils of both races, in disregard of neighborhood lines and other considerations, is the law of the Constitution. The law is in flux. The question is what it ought to become. The question that I discussed, whatever Senator Stennis may have in mind, is not whether we ought to renege on the desegregation that has been accomplished, or let up in the effort to accomplish it in parts of the South where it is not yet a reality, but where do we go from there?

I agree with Mr. Panetta, with Professor Tyack, with the less temperate Professor Orfield, and with others, whose comments have yet to be published, that desegregation has worked in the South and has produced many stable situations. I would do nothing to disturb this achievement, and I would, as I said, carry the task of desegregation to completion in the South. I agree also that some hopeful attempts at integration —racial dispersal—have been made in special places elsewhere in the country, and I would not disturb these either. But I question any generalization drawn from these few hopeful attempts.

Obviously I make a distinction, as many of the replies to my article fail to do, between segregation and racial imbalance, and a corresponding one between desegregation and integration or racial dispersal. Segregation is the separation of children of different races in the public schools by law or intentional administrative action. Desegregation is the disestablishment of segregation. Racial imbalance is just what it sounds like, and its causes are found in conditions that school law and school administrators have not created and cannot help. Integration, aimed at curing racial imbalance, is the mixing of children of different races in the public school by law or intential administrative action. In order to be satisfied that segregation has been honestly disestablished in a place where it has in the past been imposed by law, it may be necessary to to require some visible mixing of the races in the school. But it remains true that to require integration is quite something else.

I have argued that integration is, under present circumstances, impossible of achievement on a national scale; that attempts to impose it, in the South as elsewhere, often produce the perverse result of resegregation; that a rising segment of Negro leadership no more wants it imposed than do many whites; that it often amounts to the mixing of the black lower class with the white lower class, which is educationally useless, so far as we know, even though the mixing of the lower and middle classes might have some uses; and that, therefore, integration ought not to have the highest priority in the allocation of our human, political, and material resources. That is what I have tried to say—about integration, not desegregation—and I do not believe I have been successfully contradicted. I may add that I am not alone among students of the problem in saying what I do, and that I have myself been saying it for nearly a decade.

I realize that the debate about where to go from here may somehow— any straw will do—enspirit certain unreconstructed Southerners who would like to return to where we started from 15 years ago, and may consequently dispirit Southern moderates, whose fidelity to law in arduous conditions over the same period has been a tremendous national asset. I think, therefore, that the law of desegregation should be reaffirmed by Congress. I believe also that the continuing process of desegregation would benefit from an attempt to stabilize the law and clarify it, so that those who would still resist desegregation cannot make allies by claiming that what will ultimately be imposed is necessarily racial dispersal. To these ends, I have cooperated in drafting a bill with Representative Richardson Preyer of North Carolina, a former federal judge, and one of those Southerners whose career has been marked by fidelity to law and by personal commitment to the moral precepts that the law embodies.

As Professor Charles Hamilton wrote in these pages, government ought to support—not merely permit—the education of children in desegregated situations. And it ought to exert itself to improve the quality of education. The bill I speak of would create a national right for any public school pupil to transfer from a school in which his race is in a majority to one in which his race is in a minority. Transportation, if needed, would be provided at public expense. Secondly, the bill would commit the federal government to the equalization of educational opportunities and facilities. Thirdly, without disturbing the authority of federal courts and of HEW to measure the good faith of a desegregation performance, the bill would define the end result, which, in a term used by the Supreme Court but left by it undefined, is called a unitary school system.

In general, a unitary school system would be achieved either by a genuine neighborhood zoning of school attendance areas or by mixing the races in the schools in a ratio that, within a substantial permissible range, bears a relation to the proportion of one race to the other in the total school population in a district. Voluntary efforts by school boards to achieve better racial balance would, of course, be permitted, as would efforts to forestall resegregation of the schools, and the concomitant hardening of the lines of residential segregation. North or South, once a school system has reached—or has for a half century been in—a unitary state, federal courts and HEW would retain jurisdiction to pursue and cure any measure, however covert, to achieve in whatever degree any forced separation of children in the schools solely on the basis of race.

Segregationists, says Professor Hamilton, "must be fought at every turn. But in our determination to defeat them, let us not devise plans that are dysfunctional in other serious ways. The principle is a free and open society, and we can pursue several realistic routes to its achievement." That is what I believe.

DISCUSSION QUESTIONS

1. Is Bickel a satisfactory spokesman in his explanation of the Administration's integration policies?
2. Do you accept Bickel's arguments for abandoning school integration in favor of better black education?

IVOR KRAFT 1970–The Year of
the Big Sellout on Integration

In 1896 the Supreme Court issued its famous *Plessy* v. *Ferguson* decision, embalming the doctrine of separate but equal treatment for Negro Americans. Knowledgeable observers at the time recognized it for what it was: not a promise of racial equality, but an action that would set

Reprinted from *Phi Delta Kappan*, June 1970, pp. 523–526, with permission of the publisher.

back for generations the ideal of racial justice in our land, by freezing segregation in the public schools and elsewhere. And so it came about.

In 1954 the Supreme Court disembalmed the 1896 decision in *Brown* v. *Board of Education,* affirming that separate education for the races is inherently unequal, unfair, and unjust. Once again knowledgeable observers knew what to predict. They knew that it was not a revolutionary event destined in the matter of a few short years to undo the catastrophic work of decades. It was rather a ringing manifesto, the opening fusillade in a battle that would rage many years before achieving total victory. And so *Brown* v. *Board of Education* has proved itself to be.

Years of bitter struggle ensued. Opponents of integration fought mightily to prevent the will of the Court from prevailing. Supporters of the cause of racial justice fought back, often with great heroism, and here and there the walls of segregation were made to fall.

No one can say for sure how many Negro children are attending integrated schools throughout the country. Mark Twain once quoted Disraeli as saying that there are lies, damn lies, and statistics. A suitable modern paraphrase would be to insert "integration" before "statistics." I would not swear by any statistical rack-ups of our progress on desegregating the schools, but an informed estimate is that we have been desegregating at the rate of around one percent a year. Given a five percent level of integration in the nation's schools back in the early 1950's, we have today about 20 percent to 22 percent of our black children in mixed schools. That is not much, but it is something.

AT THE END OF THE TUNNEL

Until the time of the last presidential election, it looked as if we were about to accelerate the pace of school integration. There were almost hopeless situations in the North (New York, Washington, D.C.), but in small and middle-sized cities, in parts of the South, in rural areas, the die-hard anti-integrationists were beginning to relent; in the federal government there were dedicated teams of battlers for genuine civil rights and racially balanced schools; and the federal courts were beginning to lay down the law in forceful terms.

It began to look as if the extreme white racists were coming to their senses. To be sure, white racism is very much in evidence in our culture —there can be no doubt about that—and it will be around not for a few more years but for a few more generations. But there is white racism and white racism. We can never go back to the callous indifference, the taken-for-granted superiority of the 1940's and 1950's. Just what percentage of Americans are genuinely willing to go along with—never mind whether "in their heart of hearts" they want it or not—real integration of the schools? The Gallup Poll findings of some months back may not be too encouraging, but a March 16, 1970, Harris Poll shows 40 percent opposing the latest Supreme Court rulings with a healthy

48 percent supporting them (there are 12 percent in the "not sure" category). I am inclined to consider this an encouraging result.

But what about the militant community-controllers and the uncompromising black nationalists? Do Negro Americans want separation from white America? It is impossible to come up with a clear assessment of the strength of black separatism, but the fact of the matter is that outright rejection of integration, when that integration is honorable and genuine, is very rare among blacks. As Benjamin E. Mays, president of the Atlanta Board of Education, puts it:

My feeling is that [black separatism] is not strong among the vast majority of black people in this country . . . when a lot of people talk about separatism they are talking about economic and political separatism—where if, you are going to have an entirely black community then black people ought to control their life in it.[1]

In other words, when whites reject and isolate blacks outright, then blacks want to control what they're left with. What could be more reasonable?

In short, despite resegregation patterns in some of our Northern metropolises, up until some months ago it looked as if we might be rounding the bend in the long struggle for public compliance as well as legal and political buttresses to the school integration movement. It even looked as if the white backlash which emerged in 1967 was beginning to spend itself.

Now, suddenly, all seems blighted. Like a huge revolving stage changing scenes before our eyes, desegregation is out and anti-integration is in. Sixteen years after *Brown* v. *Board of Education,* a sell-out on school integration has been mounted. That sell-out is being master-minded in the executive offices of the White House for garden-variety political ends: to win over blocs of right-wing white voters, in the North as well as the South.

THINGS ARE NOT WHAT THEY SEEM

There are those who say that the present administration cannot afford to keep pushing on integration, that it will lead to bad trouble. The administration is portrayed as "realistic," cautious but pro-integration, intent on "bringing us together" but not infuriating the yahoo elements in our midst, and just plain politically smart in backstage maneuvering. None of these justifications will wash.

We live in a nether-nether world of political events, where the Administration's preferred instrument of communication is the forked tongue, and where Alice-in-Wonderland styled definitions are served up

[1] "Integration as a Matter of Heart," *The Christian Science Monitor,* March 21, 1970, p. 11.

as if they were exercises in computer logic. That things are not what they seem is the understatement of the season.

When the administration tells us that it wants to spend more money on educational research, it means that it wants to spend less on those essential programs whose worth cannot be disputed by any amount of additional research. When it tells us, in the words of Presidential adviser John Ehrlichman, that it is a misuse of schools to sponsor changes in "racial make-up" for a purely "social end," this means that schoolmen are being informed that it is O.K. to shift populations so as to preserve or achieve segregation, but it is not O.K. to move pupils so as to promote integration. When the administration declares, through press secretary Ron Ziegler, that the President does not want to "destroy the neighborhood school," this means that the backward-looking voters are being told that in return for their support, de facto segregation can continue as long as they like.

The country is highly sensitive to signals from the White House. Given a pro-integration White House, it is doubtful whether Gov. Claude Kirk of Florida would have made his abortive attempt to take command of the public schools of Manatee County in blatant defiance of a federal integration decree. (A strong federal district judge brought him to his knees within a matter of days, once more revealing the power of the courts to speed integration.) Given a Vice-President whose speeches were clarion calls to racial justice, rather than thinly veiled invitations to defiance of integrationist rulings, is it likely that a mob in Lamar, South Carolina, after viciously attacking two buses carrying terrified black children, would have been received with roars of approval on emerging from a courthouse, free on bail? Given a Justice Department intent on strengthening rather than gutting the 1969 Voting Rights Act (by undermining federal monitoring of Southern voting malpractices), would it have been necessary for 2,000 HEW specialists, in an unprecedented act, to protest their own government's civil rights policies? Given a President who was truly determined to redress the massive grievances of the black man in America, it is unlikely that the White House liberal counselor Daniel P. Moynihan would have dared to advise his chief to pursue a course of "benign neglect" of the needs of Negro Americans.

Actually, the Administration has gone out of its way to insult Negroes. The last-ditch defense of the Carswell nomination for the Supreme Court, and the President's bitter condemnation of the Senate as prejudiced against the South, when his nominee was obviously rejected for incompetence as well as intemperate racism, is merely the most impressive recent evidence of Washington's willingness to betray the black man while wooing the Wallace vote in the South. The designation of Robert C. Mardian—a former campaign aide to Barry Goldwater with an anti-integrationist record—as executive director of the cabinet's desegregation panel chaired by Vice-President Agnew, is another calculated insult to Negroes and a brake on school desegregation. The forced resignation of dynamic Leon E. Panetta from the Civil Rights Office of HEW was a victory for the go-slow coalition of Northern Republicans and Southern Democrats.

Ae review of these and other matters makes it impossible to attribute any sincerity, any political wisdom, to this Administration's wheeling and dealing on racial integration. To date the race record of the Administration is clumsy and appalling. Our leaders in Washington are not healers, they are spoilers.

THE BACKSLIDING OF THE LIBERALS

Particularly to be regretted is the fact that liberals are now throwing in the sponge and joining the separate-but-equal camp. This is the meaning of the recent fracas over the Stennis amendment, a congressional device whose sole purpose was to undermine *successful* processes of integration in the South, on the ground that nothing more should be asked of the South than might be asked of the North. Liberal Sen. Abraham Ribicoff of Connecticut vigorously supported this device, thus showing both white liberals and reactionaries that the doctrine "two wrongs make a right" can be used to justify inaction on integration wherever inaction is convenient. The amendment was defeated, but the anti-integrationist taste of victory remains. It has considerably helped in sweetening Moynihan's doctrine of benign neglect.

The verbal defection of the liberals leads to the active retreat of the moderates. In March the California State Board of Education, without prior notice, repealed state regulations aimed at integrating racially unbalanced schools. This was done despite the fact that in response to an earlier ruling 180 of 190 school districts had already filed reports indicating intent to comply with the integration guidelines. Rochester, New York, with a 33 percent black enrollment, first adopted and then repealed a plan for total integration. Many Southern districts, finally abandoning defiance and moving toward compliance with desegregation rulings, were stopped dead in their tracks on sniffing the new winds from Washington. Desegregation plans well along the way were hastily withdrawn.

The old slanders and myths about integrated schools, gradually expiring, have had new life breathed into them. Even men of good will have been ensnared into subtle denigrations and evasions of the real issues. Professor Bickel of Yale, for example, cavalierly dismisses the results of literally dozens of studies on the successful outcomes of integrated education,[2] saying that "no one is certain" if it is educationally worthwhile.[3]

[2] Meyer Weinberg, *Desegregation Research: An Appraisal.* Bloomington, Ind.: Phi Delta Kappa, 1968.
[3] Alexander M. Bickel, "Desegregation—Where Do We Go from Here?" *The New Republic*, February 7, 1970, p. 22.

He completely distorts the busing issue by feckless reasoning and gratuitous references to "trainloads or helicopter-loads" of school children, as if he did not know that 40 percent of American children are routinely bused to school, and that there are cases on record of Negro children being sent 50 miles from home to attend black schools when there was a white one a short distance away.

Certainly schools experience friction, sometimes severe friction, as the process of integration unfolds and advances. And for a long time to come there will be efforts to "segregate within integration." After 350 years of entrenched racism, it could not possibly be otherwise. But can anyone who knows the history of racism in America seriously suggest that continued polarization and forced separatism is to be preferred to the unavoidable frictions of the era of transition? There is not one shred of evidence to suggest that another 20, or 50, or 100 years in pursuit of the will-o-the-wisp of separate but equal—so that blacks can integrate from a "position of strength" while whites are being "helped to adjust" —will remove the tension and failures along the path to a just multiracial society. We will overcome these risks only by daring to face them.

THE SMOKESCREEN OF AMBIGUITY

To offset temporary setbacks in integrated systems, to keep rallying the people in support of the successful strategies of desegregation—judicious busing, fair zoning, school matching schemes, educational parks, and still other practicable devices—we need forceful moral and political support from Washington. But the President and Vice-President are doing the exact opposite of what one might expect of powerful leaders of a nation beset by conflicting values and weak resolve in the face of massive injustice. Instead of mobilizing the national will, instead of promoting reconciliation and creating a mood of staunch loyalty and respect for those legal and civic forces yielding justice for the black man, our leaders are pandering to the backward elements of the electorate, commiserating with the "plight" of white racists, condemning more outspoken integrationists for their "haste," and capitalizing on every obscurity and ambiguity in the range of choices by opting for inaction.

The 8,000-word Presidential statement on education of March 24, 1970, ostensibly intended to clarify Administration views on education, is a smokescreen of evasions and ambiguities. Even supporters of the statement regret its obscurity. Professor Bickel, for example, wishes that the President had delivered his views "plainly and directly."[4] Having read pronouncements on education authorized by heads of state as diverse as Charlemagne, Bismarck, and Khrushchev, I will say flatly that I have never encountered a national policy statement on education as slippery as that of Richard M. Nixon. Since the President knows how to

[4] *The New Republic*, April 4 and 11, 1970, p. 15.

make blunt and clear statements when he wants to, I conclude that the obscurity of this document expresses its tricky essence, not its innocence.

On the all-important matter of adequate financial support for the schools, it is impossible to know whether the Administration will urge even modest budget increases. Federal school-aid measures now passing through the Congress authorize about $7 billion for public schools in fiscal 1971, going up to about $10 billion in the mid-1970's.But as the Wilson Riles task force report (prepared for HEW) makes clear,[5] double this amount is needed to prevent inner-city schools from falling into decay. But even this low authorized amount will never become reality: In past years, educational monies allocated and spent have been less than half of the amounts authorized.

But what if we are talking, not about preventing decay, but positively upgrading lower-class schools, making them really good institutions—in other words, going to town on "compensatory education"? No one can say how much it will take, other than "a lot," but my rough assessment is that it will cost at least three times what it would require to gain comparable results achievable through integration. We are talking of amounts not on the magnitude of billions, but of tens of billions of dollars. Integration will get us there more quickly and more cheaply. Yet the President—echoed by certain congressmen, schoolmen, and critics like Professor Bickel—despite feeble budgets which make it impossible to follow through on serious efforts in compensatory education, keeps insisting that "improving the schools" rather than integrating them is the answer.

The Presidential statement grows talmudical in spinning out distinctions between de facto and de jure segregation. As a report of the U.S. Commission on Civil Rights makes clear,[6] however, the distinction between dejure and de facto segregation is largely spurious. The basic patterns which impose and perpetuate racial segregation (housing, zoning, inspection standards) all come with strong local and federal sanctions; they can be termed official; they are nearly equivalent to de jure. The courts, if not the government, have the right and even the obligation to draw the line somewhere, and that "somewhere" is logically public education. We need to get into the habit of talking about segregation in terms of its severity, situational peculiarities, alternative strategies available to overcome it, and the like, entirely abandoning the concepts of "de jure" and "de facto."

SLY CALCULATIONS CONCERNING COURTS

With respect to the courts, the Administration has much to say, most of it unclear, on the role of the bench in deciding matters of integration.

[5] "NEA Pushes Riles' Urban School Report Distributions," The Sacramento Bee, April 12, 1970, p. A3.
[6] "Civil Rights Body Scores Nixon's Integration Policy," The Sacramento Bee, April 12, 1970, p. A6.

How are we to tread our way through all these political-legalistic she-nanigans concerning the role of the courts in the struggle for desegregated schools? It will help to keep these factors in mind:

1. The courts possess enormous moral and public-opinion-making powers in addition to their judicial clout. The anti-integrationists want to mute this moral power by keeping key issues away from the liberal courts.

2. Sooner or later—and the later may be 10 or even 20 years hence—the Supreme Court will declare so-called de facto segregation in violation of the law. The anti-integrationists are determined to do their utmost to forestall that ultimate day of reckoning.

3. There is a lack of clarity in the body of decisions on desegregation handed down by the lower federal courts, although the drift is in the direction of challenging racial imbalance whether in the rural or urban context. This means that conservatives must play both sides of the judicial game.

How, then, do we explain the Presidential declaration, in the March statement, that he is willing to rely on the courts and will follow their guidance? This is not a declaration of judicial faith, even though the executive branch has no choice but to obey court directives. It is a gamble, but a sly one. With just a little bit of luck, Mr. Nixon will personally name another three members to the Supreme Bench, and the highest court in the land may become one of the most conservative bastions at his disposal. Under Chief Justice Warren E. Burger, the exhilarating drift toward greater freedom and openness in American society, a hallmark of the Warren court, is being halted with deliberate speed. Although his views did not prevail, Chief Justice Burger's blunt dissents in cases defending the right of welfare clients and juvenile delinquents indicate clearly that he will oppose all attempts to strengthen *Brown* v. *Board of Education*, that he will respect the separate but equal view in the guise of "judical restraint." The healthy 8–1 to 6–3 decisions of the Warren court are emerging as 5–3 decision at this time. Will we, by the mid-1970's, be getting 6–3 decisions favoring the conservative Burger court? It seems likely.

IN THE LONG RUN: INTEGRATED SCHOOLS

For America's responsible and professionally committed schoolmen, these bleak considerations lead to only one conclusion. We must dig in, defend our gains, and oppose any effort to sell out on integration. We have allies. The youth of the nation are with us. Many of the courts are with us. And the responsible, forward-looking citizens—not the defeatists and silent minorities—are also with us. In the long run we shall prevail.

For the destined American way is to establish where they are not established, and to strengthen where they are not strong, basic sectors of service to meet basic human needs—such needs as health, education, and welfare. The services are made available to all Americans, who then are free to choose. Thus, it is not for non-Catholics to tell Catholics that they *must* use the public schools, or for non-Jews to tell Jews that they *must* use the public adoption service, or for non-blacks to tell blacks that they *must* live in neighborhoods where there is integrated housing. But since we begin with the premise that we are Americans without a hyphen first, and minority-Americans second, we can never abandon the task of providing ever more satisfactory basic American services in a multi-racial, open society.

It is this rock-bottom premise in the American way that is now being challenged and crippled by the Nixon Administration. Its minions will make use of any who will aid them in their work of spoilage. Careerist and defeatist liberals, visionary if misled black nationalists, Southern bourbons, tired schoolmen, the always mysterious "silent majority"—there is room for all on the go-slow, turn-back, anti-egalitarian bandwagon.

The decision to all but abandon the struggle for school integration, when we are just on the verge of making real headway in that struggle, is a piece of that work of spoilage. But the alternative to racial integration is the destruction of America. In the last analysis, I believe that white America will abjure destruction. But the present Administration, in breaking the spearhead of the civil rights movement—school integration—is now toying with this alternative. And that, in a nutshell, is the meaning of the somber events now unfolding around us.

DISCUSSION QUESTIONS

1. In your judgment is the alternative to racial integration the destruction of today's America?
2. How can the schools be used to effect social change, as Kraft suggests they be?

SHELDON PTASCHEVITCH STOFF   The Two-Way Street:
A History of the Main Trends in School
Desegregation in the United States

A THEORY OF SOCIAL CHANGE

A study of past school desegregations has convinced me that where racial desegregation of public schools has been brought about in a non-violent manner, either positive action has been taken by persons in

Reprinted from Sheldon P. Stoff, *The Two Way Street* (Indianapolis, Ind.; David-Stewart Publishing Co., 1967), pp. 1–6, 66–68, with permission of the publisher.

leadership positions or specific conditions in the transition communities have precluded the outcropping of violence. In other words, specific factors, events, or deeds are associated with nonviolent school desegregation. This research seeks the isolation and description of these factors.

I have supported a theory of social change that agrees with Professor Kenneth Clark's: "Desired changes in the behavior of individuals and groups can be brought about by a change in the social situation in which they are required to function."[1] He believed that skilled persons, with accurate information, could act so as to vary some community situations, utilize and recognize others, and institute a community situational set which would support nonviolent school desegregation.

A prior claim, now supported by this research, stated that social change in school desegregation could be brought about in a less disruptive, nonviolent manner when there is—

1. Open communication between groups, in good faith working toward common goals.
2. Firm leadership for non-violent desegregation to serve as a unifying force in this direction.
3. Allegiance to the American Creed, upheld and explained.
4. An understanding attitude when implementing change and respect for the dignity of the opposition.

EARLY EFFORTS FOR NEGRO EDUCATION

The early history of the education of the Negro American is characterized by a large zero. Education was denied Negroes by white men. In part, this denial was based on the fear that educated Negroes would not, in all probability, accept their position as slaves. The very structure of slavery would be threatened, which would in turn affect the white man's economic life. As pointed out by Knight and Hall, the denial of education for the Negro was often supported by legal statute. South Carolina imposed a fine of "one hundred pounds current money" on anyone who would "teach, or cause any slave or slaves to be taught, to write, or shall use or employ any slave as a scribe in any manner of writing whatsoever."

This attitude was maintained, with notable exceptions, for years to come. The General Assembly of Virginia, in 1831, prohibited the teaching of slaves, free Negroes, or Mulattoes to read or write. Before and during this time there were also state laws prohibiting the education of Negroes or prohibiting their attendance in public schools in Georgia and Louisiana. Similar prohibitions were enacted in Alabama (1832), South Carolina (1834), Washington, D.C. (1834), Missouri (1847), and Texas (1866). The usual punishment for teaching Negroes was a fine, im-

[1] Kenneth B. Clark, "Desegregation: An Appraisal of the Evidence," *Journal of Social Issues*, 1953, No. 4, p. 72.

prisonment, or lashes; however, a Methodist minister who had taught Negroes was pulled from his pulpit on a Sunday morning by an angry mob and subjected to abuses at the town water pump.

Some of the notable exceptions to this attitude were the early attempts at Negro education which were inspired by religious groups.

An early catechizing school was founded in New York City at Trinity Church in 1704. Instruction was given by Elia Neau regularly until 1712, when blame for a local slave uprising was attributed by some masters to Neau's work.[2]

At this point, he was forced to cease his work. Efforts at educating the Negro were continued by Catholics, and a strong effort was launched by the Quakers. In no Northern states were laws passed against teaching Negroes even though such education was often feared. Still the educational level of Negroes in the North was well below that of their white brethren.

EDUCATION PERMITTED

Following the close of the Civil War, efforts were increased to provide greater educational opportunities for the Negro. The new attempts were usually made within the context of white supremacy and were not aimed at equality of opportunity.

It must be remembered, nevertheless, that violent opposition abated as years passed. Though barriers of caste were to be raised in the New South (1877–1913) as Southern white rule was destroyed, the idea of support for the academic education of the Negro began to receive sympathetic acceptance. By the turn of the century, some communities of the South were giving limited financial support to a segregated Negro education that was controlled by whites, unequally supported, and devoted almost exclusively to elementary or industrial education.[3]

During this period of time increased efforts for the education of the Negro were made in New York, Michigan, Massachusetts, Connecticut, Alabama, Iowa, Louisiana, South Carolina, New Jersey, Pennsylvania, and California. Efforts to provide for segregated education were instituted in Nevada, Georgia, Mississippi, North Carolina, Texas, Virginia, Indiana and Ohio.[4]

EDUCATION AND DESEGREGATION

Many Northerners are surprised to discover that the "separate but equal" doctrine was apparently born in the North rather than in the

---

[2] Virgil A. Clift *et al.* (eds.), *Negro Education in America* (New York: Harper and Brothers, 1962), p. 34.
[3] *Ibid.*, p. 39.
[4] William Brickman and Stanley Leher (eds.), *The Countdown on Segregated Education* (New York: Society for the Advancement of Education, 1960), p. 154.

South. It is interesting that a key court case arose in a stronghold of the abolitionists, Boston, Massachusetts.

Many communities in Massachusetts had abolished racially segregated schools prior to 1849. Then Benjamin Roberts, a Boston Negro, tried to enroll his five-year-old daughter in a white elementary school. Five white schools were closer to his home than the nearest Negro school. His bid was rejected. His attorney contended that the school board had no authority to maintain segregation and "brand a whole race with the stigma of inferiority."[5] He further contended that schools foster understanding, and that separation of the races would lead to bias and ignorance.

Massachusetts State Chief Justice Shaw delivered the unanimous opinion of the court and held that the school board did have the power to enforce segregation. He further held that the legal authority and power in education was "exclusively with them [the board]."[6]

The ruling stated—

The "great principle" that "all persons without distinction of age or sex, birth or color, origin or condition are equal before the law," when applied "to the actual and various conditions of persons in society," does not lead to the conclusion that all persons "are legally clothed with the same civil and political powers." Laws may be enacted that are "adapted" to the respective relations and conditions" of people or classes of people.[7]

This reasoning was later applied to other court cases which strongly supported the "separate but equal" doctrine (in New York, Arkansas, Missouri, Louisiana, and West Virginia). It constituted a precedent for upholding segregated education. And his view was in the fabric of the thinking of white Americans' attitudes in regard to Negroes in all phases of their life, including education.

As the efforts to educate the Negro increased, support for education arose from several quarters. The churches continued their previous efforts. Among them were the American Missionary Association, the Friends Association for Aid to Freedmen, the Presbyterian Church, the Methodist Church, and the Baptist and Episcopal Churches. Wealthy Northerners provided financial aid. Among the leaders were the Peabody fund with a contribution of $3,500,000, the Slater fund with a contribution of $2,000,000, the Carnegie fund with a contribution of $10,000,000, the Rockefeller fund with a contribution in excess of $1,000,000, and the Rosenwald and Jeanes funds. These grants aided school construction, scholarships, endowments, teacher training, and industrial development.[8]

The Southern states also made efforts in this direction, but, before

[5] Milton R. Konvitz, *A Century of Civil Rights* (New York: Columbia University Press, 1961), p. 126.
[6] *Ibid.*, p. 127.
[7] *Ibid.*, p. 127.
[8] Clift, *op. cit.*, pp. 40–42.

1900, many of the efforts were completely inadequate. "The Southern states were spending an average of $4.92 per year on a white child in 1900 and $2.71 on a Negro child."[9]

Under the influence of Samuel C. Armstrong and Booker T. Washington the Negroes were apparently willing to accept segregation in their schools, churches, and industry as long as improvements and a sense of equality could be provided in these areas. To do otherwise in the South, at that time, was unsafe and unrealistic.

The Supreme Court case of *Plessy* v. *Ferguson* in 1896 upholding racial segregation in transportation seemed to settle the issue for a period of time. The question of concern to the court was the reasonableness of the regulation, not the issue of properness of segregation *per se*. The dissenting opinion by Justice Harlan criticized this ruling which seemingly branded Negroes an inferior class of citizens. Here is an excerpt from his decision:

Americans boast of the freedom enjoyed by our people above all other people. But it is difficult to reconcile that boast with a state of the law which, practically, puts the brand of servitude and degradation upon a large class of our fellow citizens, our equals before the law. . . .
Our Constitution is color blind, and neither knows nor tolerates classes among citizens.[10]

The *Plessy* v. *Ferguson* decision enabled states, such as Kentucky, to prohibit mixed schools with the sanction of the U.S. Supreme Court. There was no doubt of Kentucky's position.

It shall be unlawful for any white person to attend any schools or institutions where negroes are received as pupils or receive instruction, and it shall be unlawful for any negro or colored person to attend any school or institution where white persons are received as pupils or receive instruction. Any person so offending shall be fined fifty dollars for each day he attends such institution or school.[11]

Though the promise was "separate but equal," inequality in financial support prevented the Negroes from achieving this equality. The U.S. Supreme Court even held constitutional a Georgia school segregation law providing state funds for white schools although there were no provisions made for Negro schools.

Even with these shortcomings, there was some improvement of Negro schools. But equality was never achieved. In recent years some Southern states have spent from 21 percent to 94 percent as much on their Negro students as on their white students.[12]

[9] *Ibid.*, p. 44.
[10] U.S. Supreme Court Justice Harlan, *Plessy* v. *Ferguson* (163 U.S. 537, 1896).
[11] Acts of the General Assembly of the Commonwealth of Kentucky (1904), pp. 181, 182.
[12] U.S. Dept. of Health, Education and Welfare, Office of Education, *Statistics of State School Systems, Organization Staff, Pupils and Finances 1953–1957* (Washington, D.C.: U.S. Government Printing Office, 1954), Ch. 2, p. 114, Table 48.

During later years there was still a strong carry-over from previous days. There are many recorded reports of threats to white teachers of Negro students, such as the note quoted here:

Mr. Banks we thought we would give you a chance to save yourself one of the worst scourings that a man ever got and you can do so by reading this note and acting upon its contents. You have set up a nigger school in the settlement which we will not allow you to teach if you were a full blooded negro we would have nothing to say but a white skin negro is a little more than we can stand you can dismiss the school immediately or prepar yourself to travail we will give you a chance to save yourself and you had better move instanter.[13]

. . .

FINAL THOUGHTS

In this study some of the variables significantly related to nonviolent desegregation have been identified. Twenty-three variables have been organized into six factors. Examples for most of the variables have been presented.

It is obvious that important differences in community settings did exist between violent and nonviolent public school desegregation situations. The variables significantly associated with nonviolence in public school desegregations in this study were these:

Factor I: Favorable School Leadership
1. The chief school administrator led in the development of a school desegregation plan.
2. The chief school administrator supported the desegregation plan.
3. The school board supported the desegregation.

Factor II: The Opposition
1. There was a lack of active opposition to school desegregation by the governor.
2. There was a lack of active opposition to school desegregation by outside organizations.
3. There was a lack of active opposition to school desegregation by local organizations.
4. There was a lack of opposition to school desegregation by the state education department.
5. There was a lack of opposition to school desegregation by local individuals.

Factor III: The Urban Center
1. Smaller communities (under 50,000 persons) had better success.

[13] *State Journal* (Alabama, 1875); given in E. Knight and Clifton Hall, *Reading in American Educational History* (New York: Appleton-Century-Crofts, Inc., 1951), p. 679.

2. There were no Negroes on the police force.[14]
3. There were no police on duty in plain clothes.
4. Negro and white schools were comparable.
5. Nearby schools desegregated at the same time.

Factor IV: The Practical Community
1. Desegregation was voluntary (not specifically ordered by a court).
2. There was preparation by the white faculty of white students for nonviolent school desegregation.
3. There were nearby desegregated schools.
4. There was a high employment level among the male, nonwhite population.

Factor V. Active Community Support
1. The white clergy supported school desegregation.
2. Respected white community members supported nonviolent school desegregation.
3. School transportation facilities were desegregated.
4. Local newspapers advocated nonviolent school desegregation.

Factor VI: Residual Support
1. There were desegregated labor unions.
2. The state educational agencies supported school desegregation.

It is evident, on the basis of this broad study of school desegregation, that nonviolence does not simply happen. Careful preparation very often precedes its achievement. There are many factors which provide a favorable social set for nonviolent school desegregation. If a favorable social set is to be provided, many forces and individuals in the community must actively fulfill their responsibilities.

It is equally apparent that nonviolent school desegregation can be attained even if many persons in the community do not favor school desegregation. When it is recognized that the present operational issue is violent vs. nonviolent desegregation, those forces favoring nonviolence can act so as to increase the possibility of achieving this goal. One important step is to identify the forces of active opposition and then act so as to mitigate or control their influences.

The related variables identified in this study would indicate that the burden of social action has a certain specificity. But the implications are that every man has an obligation to fulfill. Even in a modern technological society, man is still his brother's keeper.

Some citizens of modern society seem self-condemned to apathy; they think that individual actions don't count or don't matter. Certainly it would be ambitious to seek an answer to that primary question in empirical research. The knowledge that what man becomes is determined

[14] Apparently not substantiated by further in-depth probing and thus discounted.

by his "turning to the other," by the "I-Thou" relationship of mutuality, and the attempt to provide for the worthwhile needs of one's fellow-man, is gained only through inner experience. For those who do not or cannot look within for these answers, this study may provide a statistical basis for action, may demonstrate the broad responsibilities occasioned by interactions between individuals and groups. The examples of individual action which "did count" may indicate guidelines for the responsible citizen in a community in flux.

In an age when we often take social action on the basis of scientific research, studies like this one are necessary, even essential. But if one asked that all his actions be founded only in science, the consequences would be paralyzing. The combination of scientific method, used in this study, and the inner vision of each individual, vital to the development of the balanced person, is for now the best hope for the individual and the community seeking change with dignity, respect, and cohesion.

DISCUSSION QUESTIONS

1. Do you believe that Stoff's guidelines would apply in planning the desegregation of your community?
2. As an educator, do you believe that the responsibilities that Stoff details for educators are a valid charge on the educational profession?
3. Can we insist that small communities desegregate their schools now, while we postpone desegregation and subscribe to "quality segregated education" for ghetto schools, such as those of Harlem?
4. Stoff calls for firm, skilled leadership to bring about reasonable, nonviolent desegregation. Can this be furnished by local civic leadership?

HARRISENE SMALLS A Letter to the Castle

The following letter was written to Dr. Leo Hamalian of the City College of New York by a young woman who is seeking, through his good offices, to find somewhere in the city's educational system an opportunity to train the mind she so obviously possesses. Following the letter there appears a note by Dr. Hamalian.

DEAR DR. HAMALIAN:

Hello again, you wouldn't believe it but I've been penning this letter for weeks. I haven't any excuse but, for the most part, I've been dealing with my immediate problems at hand. My responsibility to my offspring and the daily struggle of life. And, yes, I've started a new job, a meat wrapper at a large store. Adding this job to many others. Forgive me, therefore, for keeping you waiting.

Reprinted from *The Nation*, May 20, 1968, with permission of the publisher.

You asked me to write about myself and why I want to go to school. I'll try to squeeze twenty-six years into these few pages.

Why I Want To Go Back To School. Or should I say why I've got to go back to school.

I was born twenty-six years ago—February 10, 1941— in Morrisania Hospital, the Bronx, six minutes after my twin brother, called Harrison, Jr. I had to be named what else, Harrisene. That was my beginning.

From what I'm told, my father and mother separated when I was 6 months old. I really don't know, I was too young. But, as we grew up my earliest memories were living on Prospect Avenue in the Bronx. I remember my mother raising my two older sisters and a set of twins. I do remember my father wasn't there. Mr. Welfare (ADC) was there: I remember that awful-tasting oatmeal, that was stamped, "Not to be Sold, Gov't Property, Welfare Recipients Only."

My mother, Catherine (Turner) Bailey was murdered soon after. At 26 years old her life was snuffed out. Perhaps it was best, I don't know, for they do say death is peace. I know she died for us, so that we might live but, after twenty years, I still miss her so.

We were taken to one of the children's shelters down by Central Park. There we were to stay, a place so cold and impersonal. I was 6½ then.

Not knowing this would begin many years of disappointment and frustration. But somehow children hold on to something when tragedy strikes. Something deep-seeded in your soul. That something was and still is, hope. My mother left us this something. All she had to leave us, hope, and this came from within herself. And giving of oneself is priceless.

When I was 11½, my father came into our lives again, trying to piece his broken life and family together. We had a stepmother, fourteen years his junior. Somehow in his mind I feel he thought a younger wife could endure raising four children, whose minds were already formed. We had seen practically all of the cruel and seedy side of life, but living with her just added to the misery.

She turned out not to be a true mother; she was an alcoholic and was bisexed and went through my father's hard-earned money, buying liquor and anyone's favors, men, women, even little boys and girls.

One night when my father couldn't endure any more, and knew we could no longer endure starvation or degradation, with all of our worldly possessions wrapped in a spread, we left Nyack, N. Y., and came to Corona, Long Island.

We lived in one room—with use of the bathroom and kitchen. There were four other rooms occupied. This building was formerly a house of ill repute. It was supposed to have been cleaned out; it never was.

I attended Junior High School 16 in Corona. I graduated to Flushing High School but, because of the zoning laws, I had to forget about Flushing and attend Newtown High School in Elmhurst.

This made me very unhappy because I had so wanted to attend Flushing; its curriculum was so much like the school I attended in Nyack. Even though our bellies were empty when we lived in Nyack, the school kind of brought life into our lives. I was now 14. So, with that I went to Newtown. My attitude and my outlook on school were dim, most of all because of the one room, the drunks, the junkies and the apathy. Even the fact that if we didn't work odd jobs—housework on weekends in other people's homes, baby sitting, hauling groceries at the A&P— we would never have had that nickel to go with our bus passes. Breakfast we didn't have and lunch was unheard.

I chose the right way, the hardest way, but in the long run I still had my self-respect. Thus, I worked. I continued school, continuing to survive. Trying to break out reaching up, hoping.

Thus, from the time I was a child I promised my unborn children that they would never hunger for the basic needs in life, which every parent owes their offspring—food, good shoes, books, knowledge and most of all understanding.

When I was 15 I met a boy of 20 years, his name was Robert. He lived down the block from our one room. Robert fed me and my family almost every day. His poor mother's food bill! She worked so hard in the garment district. Robert was attending Manhattan College then, contemplating dropping out. I used to say to him, "I wish I had a mother. I wish I could have gone to school." Knowing then somehow I wouldn't finish school.

I was grateful to Robert, perhaps he felt sorry for me, but anyway I became pregnant. I was 16. I didn't want to get married, so I went away. I worked in a laundry plant eight hours a day, six days a week at 80¢ an hour. This was 1957. I cleaned bungalows and rooms for my room and board. I saved every dime. I was sick; I had just gotten over a spinal operation, a scared kid. Rather than give up I continued to work. All I know is that I had to make it so my baby wouldn't be hungry. I worked until the summer was over, then when the resort closed, I returned home.

Robert still insisted on getting married. Thus, being ill, my spine still open, tired and very much afraid, I agreed. I had returned home September 5, we married September 8, 1957. Kimble Annette was born February 21, 1958; a year later Kendall Anthony was born, February 26, 1959.

Robert continued school. With a teen-age bride, a baby and another on the way, he finished a B-average student. I worked pregnancies. I was to have completed school after helping Robert finish, and go into nursing but it didn't work out that way.

Robert received his B.S. degree in psychology and his commission in the U.S. Air Force. Nine years later he is making it a career. I left Robert almost five years ago. We obtained a legal separation. I won't go into our marriage difficulties; it's a part of my life I would want to leave in back of me.

There I was 22 years old. Seven years of marriage, three children, ages 6 years to 18 months; ten years of schooling. Qualifications: experience in housekeeping, laundry clothes sorter, filing and baby sitting.

Baby sitters were hard to come by, so I had to stay home. I lived in a poverty-stricken area, paying $130 a month for three rooms. It was a dump, I wasn't quite well enough to go to work, with surgery on recent hernia repairs and separation in my stomach muscles, but soon after I found a sitter. Twenty-six dollars a week. I took that out of their support of $300 a month. With the rent, that took care of every cent. I worked as a maid in a motel, cleaning fifteen rooms a day and I worked nights in a real estate office canvassing on the telephone. I worked hard and saved and pinched, to move out of my poverty-stricken area.

The money I receive from their father is theirs. Let's call it the fruits of my labor. I didn't help their father through the hardest years of school to let my children live around apathy, welfare, cat pinto beans and that horrible oatmeal and live in the slums. To let them around dirt, junkies, would be giving them the same inheritance that I had. We owe our children something better.

How can a child think anything of himself if he grows up in a slum? Maybe, moving out of the slum is not the answer. I only know that my children see life different than I did. They do deserve better. I'm not paying the rent here, $150 a month. I couldn't afford it. I couldn't afford it if I wasn't getting this support and I still can't afford it now.

It's funny the Germans, Irish and the Jewish and Italians were in the slums. And somehow my people are still there. Maybe, because it's easier to accept, than to continue to suffer and work hard like my family did and many more of my people to break out of the slums. Obtaining their goals by sacrifice and the sweat of their brows. And still keep their pride.

I've gone to Manpower to ask to be trained and helped to go to school. But one of the stiffest qualifications is to live in a poverty-stricken area. This is what you hear: "I'm sorry Mrs. Smalls, you can take the test, but, there's so little money around, and there's many immediate cases and after all you are getting $300 a month." $3,600 a year for a family of four, are they kidding?

Then on to operation Seek. "This is beautiful" I said Hope again! My son's teacher told me about it, but again another closed door: Requirements high school equivalency and most of all you must live in a poverty-stricken area.

I've had nine jobs in the last four years. Struggling to produce three positive thinking individuals, who will become productive citizens and a credit to their country and their world. Not just to exist and become burdens on any society. But I need help. The Seek program could help me.

Dr. Hamalian, I've just resigned from Creedmore State Hospital, a mental institution. My position there was Grade 6, psychiatric attendant. I worked five days a week. Every weekend, no holidays. I was on the Medical Surgical Ward. Short of help always. Double workload. All aging and incontinent patients. Feedings, dressings, mopping floors with GI mops, lifting poor helpless people. Emptying garbage. Seven months of this slave labor and I cleared $68 a week. Paid a sitter $20 a week, sometimes $25. Physically I'm in no condition, but, most of all cooking, always catching up with housework, the children's studies going down. I had to resign; someone has to be here.

Their father is in Vietnam. He'll be stationed in the Far East for three years. He never had much interest in them anyway. Thus, it is up to me, I am their tree, they are my branches. I must not fall or fail them.

These are some of the reasons why I've got to go back to school; in paving a future for myself it will be for them. I'm scared, not just afraid. I must be qualified. I must get a degree, in order to survive; otherwise I might just as well throw in the towel. Ten years from now I'll be 36. Have a daughter of 20, a son of 19 and a daughter of 15. I'll have so much to give them and to other children.

I'd like to be a teacher in any poverty-stricken area to help children and teach them and most of all give them hope.

If one only could obtain wisdom sooner, rather than take a lifetime. I know what I have to do, I need help, "no man is an island unto himself." If I could just get my toe in the door then I feel confident that I will make it.

I'm working part-time now, to make ends meet and keeping in mind, body and my soul that there is hope. Well, Dr. Hamalian, I've tried to squeeze twenty years into many pages. It wasn't all bleak, it wasn't all dark, life isn't so bad, if you remember to stop and look into the little children's smiling faces.

It could get worse, life I'm referring to, and it has been.

There was no room to take the equivalency test; I'm studying very hard. I haven't fallen asleep over school books in eleven years and it's a good sleep. I'm going to make a good mark on my test in March; when I get the results I'll send them to you.

If you can help me in any way to give me this chance to get back into school I can promise I will not disappoint you: I find that I can't afford the luxury to put my books down.

I'll close now. God bless you and your family.

I remain
Sincerely,
/s/ *Harrisene Smalls*

One night about two months ago, Harrisene Smalls, high school drop-out, amateur actress, mother and main support of three children, started out from her home in Queens Village to seek advice from me about the possibility of attending The City College either as a non-matriculant or as a Pre-Bacc student (see Leonard Kriegel's "Headstart for College," *The Nation*, February 26). On her way to the college she was attacked in St. Nicholas Park by a knife-wielding hood. She now thinks that she may have saved herself from rape by refusing to "freeze up." Instead, she knocked her attacker off balance with a swift blow and fled for the safety of the college library up on Washington Heights.

When she had recovered her composure, she started out for my office. She was accosted a second time by the same assailant and once more managed to escape him ("Hard work keeps this mother in shape"). She reached my office only to find that through a misunderstanding we had missed connection. Had Harrisene Smalls decided at that moment that not even a degree from City College was worth repeating the experience she had just endured, no one could have blamed her.

But Harrisene Smalls is tough and she called to arrange another appointment. We met this time, and as I questioned her about her educational background, she told her story, calmly, even cheerfully. I asked her to put it down on paper so that I could pass it on to the proper authority for evaluation. I hardly expected her to do so and after I read the account, I knew I would have to bring it to the attention of other readers as well.

Harisene Smalls is not asking for much: merely the opportunity to give dignity and purpose to her life. In this land where people who wish to attend school are given a second, third, and sometimes fourth crack at college, she is requesting a first real chance to educate herself up to her intellectual capacity. If she has the intelligence and motive to absorb higher education, then this request is neither idle nor arrogant.

Perhaps we have to establish immediately a unit in the City University or State University where there are *no prerequisities of any kind*, where adults long on intelligence but short on information will be afforded an opportunity to apply that intelligence arduously. That a Harrisene Smalls is 26 years old means only that her powers of perception have been heightened by her suffering, her appreciations broadened by experience, and that they both are likely to be further sharpened by the discipline and direction of a rigorous education which she is now ready to accept with joy.

Leo Hamalian

DISCUSSION QUESTIONS

1. Should all students who have the desire be admitted to college on an open-admissions basis?

2. Would open admissions make it necessary to compromise the colleges standards, thus making a degree worthless?
3. Is it possible for colleges to offer black ghetto students a new and relevant curriculum built to their concerns and their strengths? How would you define such a curriculum if you believe it feasible?

JAMES KILPATRICK It's Time To Teach Self-Help

Washington—The thought occurs, and can no longer be repressed, that it's time for some of us who write for a living to stop writing so nicey-nice about this summer's riots and the Negro leadership. This is a summer of outrage, scored for kettle drums of violence; but such is our sense of genteel restraint that most of us have been playing our typewriters pianissimo. We have settled for murmuring my-my and oh-oh, and they certainly do have grievances, don't they.

Well, nuts. There comes a time when the law-abiding majority of this country, imperfect as it is, ought to put a hard question to large elements of the Negro community: When in the name of God are you people going to shape up? One is tempted to exempt from the thrust of that question many thousands of Negro citizens who have played no active part in the recent violence and indeed have been victims of it. They can't be left out. Who has given sanctuary to the Negro snipers? Fellow Negroes, They share in the guilt.

What's the matter with the Negro leadership? Since the first torch was put to Newark, one has waited—and waited in vain—for some high-level expression of shame, apology, contrition. Non est. Perhaps nothing was to be expected from H. Rap Brown; his theme is "Get you some guns and burn this town down." The sullen Stokely Carmichael yearns "to kill the whites first." But what of Roy Wilkins, Whitney Young, Martin Luther King? They are full of excuses, and in King's case, something more. It's all the fault, he says, of "the policy-makers of white society." He proposes strikes and sit-ins to "dislocate" the cities without actually destroying them. He will do this "lovingly."

At every hand, the cry goes up for crash spending programs in the slums. Most of the money would go toward jobs and housing. The *New Republic* tells us what kind of jobs—not merely jobs for "black waiters, dishwashers and busboys, but jobs that will restore Negro self-respect."

What's wrong with being a waiter, a dishwasher, or a busboy, if one qualifies for the work? Hundreds of thousands of white men and women

Reprinted from *Newsday*, August 23, 1967, with permission of the copyright owner, the Washington Star Syndicate, Washington, D.C.

perform these humble but essential labors. What's the matter with a teenager's starting as a bootblack? It's an honest trade.

And what of "jobs that will restore Negro self-respect"? Employers increasingly are searching for Negroes as sales clerks, bank tellers, draftsmen, technicians. They may not be overcome with altruism; it may be only the Equal Employment Opportunity Commission breathing down their necks. But the jobs are there. Where are qualified Negro applicants to fill them?

The excuse is that the "ghetto schools" are so bad, and the Negro teenagers so "insufficiently motivated," that they drop out. It's a feeble excuse. Many a middle-aged American looks at some of these "ghetto schools" and is dimly reminded of the elementary schools of his own unfair nonage. The opportunity for an education lies within them. What's asked of the Negro? Ambition. Hard work.

The cry is that "ghetto housing" is so bad. Okay. Some of it is awful. Some of it is not. But there are twice as many poor whites as poor blacks; the poor colored neighborhoods of Watts and Detroit have their counterparts—and their rats—in poor white neighborhoods across the land. The blunt truth is that self-help could cure at least a part of the ills. If some of Jesse Gray's complainers would spend more time with a dollar rake or a 50-cent broom, and less time with a $2 pint of gin, maybe a sense of mutual respect would start to grow. Heresy, one supposes, to say such things. But they need to be said.

DISCUSSION QUESTIONS

1. Kilpatrick asks of the Negro that he be ambitious and work hard, if he wishes to get an education. How reasonable is his request?
2. What contribution do you think Kilpatrick's arguments will make in bridging the ever-widening gap between blacks and whites in America?
3. Can society sit back and wait for the "disadvantaged" to become "advantaged"?

KEITH WHEELER Integration Vendetta
in a Northern Town

Until five years ago New Rochelle—the town saluted in George M. Cohan's *Forty-five Minutes from Broadway*—was about as typical as a suburb of New York City could get. A patriarch of a place, with archives stretching back to French Huguenot refugees and their Negro slaves around 1688, it had grown up to be mostly a pleasant and prosperous

Reprinted from *Life*, May 6, 1966, with permission of the publisher.

small city though its older sections were sliding into slums. Then, all at once, New Rochelle saw itself both unique and notorious; it became the first northern city forced by the courts of the United States to desegregate a public school which had become virtually all Negro.

Half a decade has gone. Now it is possible to look back and see how New Rochelle made out in first, obeying the court, and second, enduring the consequences. New Rochelle is not likely to welcome the scrutiny, for the town—as full of prejudice, fair-mindedness, compassion and cussedness as any other—has already had more painful publicity than it wants. A place which likes to call itself the "Queen City" cannot be expected to enjoy the memory of having been also called the "Little Rock of the North."

But a backward look, although possibly wounding, can be useful to all of us. New Rochelle furnishes the pioneer northern case history of an attempt to make cold law mesh with hot blood and passion. Every large urban place outside the South—from Boston to Gary to Los Angeles— is either already face-to-face with something like New Rochelle lived through, or soon has to be.

In New Rochelle the aftermath of the court's order to desegregate sent the public schools through a special kind of hell and, until just recently, they were still suffering it. In the process (1) the board of education was harassed and coerced, (2) teachers were tormented, (3) school discipline went to pot, and (4) most important of all, the business of education—which is the only legitimate endeavor schools are in—was crippled. Only now that New Rochelle's ordeal has finally eased are the schools convalescing satisfactorily.

Full desegregation of all the nation's public schools has been law since 1954. And that concept has been propped and buttressed since by a whole series of remarkable and enlightened court decisions. But law is one thing, the quirky human animal another. Old grievances and old suspicions die in a slow and wretched way. In New Rochelle it was man, not the law, that went sour. And—it has to be said—the spirit of the Negroes, hot at being winners after 100 years of monotonous losing, was such that many could not see—or were damned if they would admit —that having equality carries as heavy a responsibility as the obligation to fight for it.

It was incongruous that the trouble should have come to the New Rochelle schools. For years the town's senior high has maintained one of the highest academic ratings in the country. And the graduates of its college preparatory program haven enjoyed a warm welcome at the choosiest colleges and universities in the land.

The order to desegregate struck New Rochelle as both ironic and insulting. In the way a town looks at itself, New Rochelle has considered its public school system entirely integrated ever since 1889, when the last deliberately segregated Negro school was closed down.

In 1960 there were 12 elementary schools, two junior high schools and one senior high for a city population of 77,000. From first through sixth grades, a child went to the elementary school in the district where he lived—to his "neighborhood school," words which these days mean either sacred institution or tool to destroy human dignity, depending on who is speaking. Above sixth grade, everybody merged. The hitch in New Rochelle was one old school—Lincoln Elementary. By all the pressures which bear upon American society, Lincoln had become 94% Negro—that is, "*de facto* segregated," another epithet in the modern social lexicon. This was not entirely by chance. Former school boards had created the district so that Lincoln would serve New Rochelle as a segregated elementary school.

The situation takes various forms in urban areas, but the basic problem remains the same. It is most baffling in bigger cities where the difficulties and confusions of integration are bound to increase. Most large northern urban centers will have nonwhite majorities within a decade. Washington is already more than half Negro; Detroit, Chicago, Cleveland will get there by 1980.

In May 1960, New Rochelle's citizens approved a referendum to tear down Lincoln Elementary, which was 62 years old and decrepit—and to build a new $1.3 million school in the same area. A proposal to build a new Lincoln had been put to vote three years earlier but was turned down. This defeat focused attention on the issue and whites and Negroes alike joined in debate over the need for a new school. By 1960 the proposal had such widespread support that it easily passed. Only in the Lincoln district did the voters, most of them Negroes, oppose the referendum—by a ratio of 1.36 to 1. While some Lincoln parents apparently wanted a new school and others didn't appear to care, many believed that it would serve only to continue segregation. They felt that the education their children were getting at Lincoln didn't amount to much and the only way to improve matters was to get them out of there.

"I went to Lincoln as a kid and I guess I was happy there," a Negro insurance man has recalled. "But I suspect I was shortchanged on education. I doubt if the teachers *wanted* to stunt us, but they asked only a low level of performance. They used to have us sing *Old Black Joe* and *Swanee River* at assemblies. You had to get to high school to find out how much you didn't know."

When the fall term began in 1960, a small group of Negro parents and their children formed themselves into an all-or-nothing wedge to force their way out of Lincoln. They showed up at eight elementary schools with preponderantly all-white enrollment, demanding to register their children. They were refused. After a sitdown at one school they were given summonses for loitering. Within a few days the school board's attorney filed neglect charges against the strikers for "failing to send their children to school in accordance with the compulsory attend-ance law."

Now it was everybody's issue and it soon developed into a war of every person's fears, convictions and prejudices. An NAACP leader told a meeting of white parents that, unless Negro children were taken into white schools, he would "come through you like a bulldozer." A Negro woman principal was repeatedly called "Aunt Jemima" for supporting the referendum because she felt that the Negroes in the Lincoln School did not have the socio-economic background to compete with the stu-dents in the north end of town. PTA meetings in the all-white sections turned into yelling matches where the clearest sounds to be heard were soaring exchanges of "bigot" and "Communist," "fascist" and "fat-head."

Matters might have tapered off in mere vituperation if it had not been for the dedicated involvement of an outsider. He was Paul Zuber, a tall, tough, articulate young Negro lawyer who had already won a civil rights dispute with the New York City school board. Zuber, representing the Negro parents who challenged the Lincoln proposal, has learned to wel-come any tool and so the split among the whites interested him. But he did not count upon the split for really substantial strategic help.

"Of course we get support from white liberals," Zuber said. "But it tends to fade off when they realize integration could also get to *their* street. One white woman thought it over and told me, 'I really don't see what our Children can have in common. We take ours to Florida for Christmas.' "

Zuber, a gentle and friendly man in private but a battering ram in matters concerning Negro civil rights, knew exactly how he intended to fight his fight in New Rochelle.

"We'll get them into court," he said. "Demonstrations are for babies. You can go out there and march up and down with placards and sing *We Shall Overcome* till you fall down. The other side comes out and yells 'Two, Four, Six, Eight, We don't wanna integrate!' . . . a Mexican standoff. But in court only one man can talk at a time and one man in front of a judge is just as big as a whole damn school board."

He couldn't have been more right. On Jan. 24, 1961, U.S. District Judge Irving Kaufman—rendering a landmark decision—found down the line for the plaintiffs. The New Rochelle board of education, he ruled, had gerrymandered the Lincoln district to keep the Negroes in and, by pursuing the "neighborhood school policy," it had violated the constitutional rights of Lincoln pupils under the 14th Amendment.

The judge ordered the board to offer a plan for desegregation of the school. But the board, which had ignored the racial overbalance at the school in the past and the fact that over an extended period white pupils —but no Negroes—had been allowed to transfer from Lincoln to other schools, kept up its fight for the "neighborhood school" concept. In a stubborn refusal to accept the Kaufman decision, the board decided to carry their argument to higher courts. Three of the nine board members voted against appeal, but the board petitioned all the way to the U.S. Supreme Court—and lost all the way.

That was the end of Lincoln Elementary. Within two years the school was torn down. All that remained was a place where Negro children still assemble in the morning to board their buses for schools all over town.

Lincoln Elementary was dead but the effect of its passing was only beginning to spread through town. Like every other northern city, New Rochelle and its schools would have felt the impact of the drive for Negro equality even without the fight over the school. But the legacy of Lincoln made a difference. An angry minority, battling for its civil rights, had taken on the local establishment and beaten it hands down. And an establishment, once beaten, can be beaten again.

The question was how would the momentum of this new force be directed in New Rochelle? In the next five years, it seemed to be guided more by a severe case of bitterness over old wounds than by any newly acquired sense of responsibility for the welfare of the community as a whole.

In the five-year period New Rochelle's board of education, appointed by the mayor ("When you talked, they made jokes and didn't hear," a Negro leader said of the board) had 10 changes of membership. The turnover in the school administration itself was even more telling. There were three different principals of the senior high school. There were three school superintendents. One superintendent heard from a civil rights militant, "We brought you and we can send you away."

Individuals were able to borrow from the massed vigor. One outraged Negro mother, whose daughter had been sent home for getting into a fight, took the little girl to school the next morning and marched into the principal's office to announce, "I've brought T——— back; she's going to stay back or I'll break your neck." The child stayed.

But the most painful inheritance from Lincoln Elementary was the climate created for the children. In the beginning the struggle had been an adults' contest. But now the children took over from their elders and carried the challenge to constituted authority into the classroom—to nobody's benefit. So began a siege on campus, fought mainly in the junior and senior high schools.

"These kids come in here with a chip on the shoulder," said a faculty member. "They're primed to take offense. You can't keep telling a kid at home that he's the victim of discrimination and expect him not to look for discrimination—and find it whether it's there or not."

The defiant students, aware of the distemper of their elders, knew they could count on adult support when they needed it. And they soon learned that, under pressure, authority—the faculty and the board of education—would back down.

The board itself, ready to acknowledge concern over affairs in the nation's schools generally, shied away from admitting that these problems were particularly pressing at home. Said the board on one occasion: "Throughout the country, parents, teachers and school administrators are becoming increasingly concerned with the maintenance of law and order and respect for adult authority . . . in our public schools. The present unrest and the problems of maintaining good attendance and conduct at our own high school should be viewed in this perspective. Disturbing as it is to us, the behavior of a very small percentage of the New Rochelle students, both white and Negro, is not peculiar to this city."

Some teachers began to agree with the students that the administration was caving in under pressure. A young woman teacher who was cussed at by a pupil in the hall marched him off to his guidance counselor. The boy admitted his profane outburst while the counselor frowned his disapproval and said nothing. The boy shrewdly regarded both teacher and counselor, then with a grin simply turned and walked out, leaving the teacher to sputter her indignation.

"What can you do?" the counselor shrugged. "That's the way *they* are. Let's not make waves."

Student discipline began to deteriorate and, along with it, faculty morale. "School master" is an old and honorable title; but New Rochelle's teachers began to feel they were no longer masters in their own schools.

Faculty members found themselves involved in incidents that might have passed as ordinary breakdowns in discipline—except that too often they took on racial complications. Although the more outrageous acts of defiance and law-breaking were committed by a relatively small group of easily identified hooligans, the example they set encouraged hundreds of other students to disobedience and infected the whole school.

▶ An 18-year-old boy, an 11th grader, swore at a teacher who was trying to herd him and others into their homeroom. Then he disappeared. Around noon the same day he was found and taken to the principal's office. There was liquor on his breath; the boy slouched down in his chair and stared back at the principal.

"Where were you?" the official asked. "Home, sick," the boy said.

"No, you weren't. I called your mother. Where were you?"

The boy lounged deeper, thought a while, then spoke. "If you're so damned smart, you tell me where I was." And so the boy was suspended for five days—the legal limit without board of education sanction.

The boy's mother asked CORE for help. CORE representatives met with school officers three times to discuss the case. Finally, the principal showed them the boy's past record, with 28 teacher complaints about his behavior. At least one CORE representative thought the use of the boy's past record was unethical.

"You're prejudiced, aren't you?" the delegate said.

▶ At a high school football game, a coach spotted a boy in a sweat-shirt stolen from the school's athletic supplies. The coach grabbed the youngster, but was immediately surrounded by other boys, yelling at him to get his hands off the offender. The situation teetered on the edge of explosion until the coach marched the boy away and told him to turn in the pilfered shirt the next day. But when the boy failed to appear, the coach went for advice to a faculty friend, who asked, "Does this involve race?" The coach said "no, it involved school property." "Negro?" he was asked. "Yes," said the coach.

"Drop it," the faculty member said. "If you try to get that shirt back, you'll be alone."

The coach appealed to the boy's assistant principal, anyway, and asked him to recover the shirt. A few days later the assistant principal called to say that he had had the boy in his office. "He admits he took the shirt," the assistant principal told the coach. "But he won't give it back." And with that the administrator simply hung up.

▶ Two white girls rushed into the senior high principal's office and reported that some Negro girls were brandishing knives in one of the lavatories. The principal, a custodian and a teacher took stations outside the door and, with the custodian holding it open, ordered the occupants out. After some scurrying and laughter, a dozen girls, Negro and white, appeared. The white girls were allowed to leave, but the Negroes were taken to an adjacent room, where a teacher searched their purses. She got three knives and a partly filled bottle of liquor. The police were called but made no arrests. Later the girls were suspended.

Prompt protest came from civil rights leaders. The principal's phone began ringing; his callers accused him of invading the girls' lavatory, of searching them personally, of invading their civil rights. The principal later admitted he had been "tactless" in having only the Negro girls searched. A demand for a public apology was sent to the superintendent. The Negro girls' defenders explained that the girls needed the knives to protect themselves when they walked home, past a nearby car-wash emporium whose attendants were forward.

As they have in so many places in recent years, home football games became occasions of such hazard that New Rochelle police and faculty "goon squads"—as they described themselves and getting $10 each for extra duty—were needed to stop gate-crashing and prevent all sorts of violence and abuse during and after the games. The principal, with binoculars, always surveyed the scene from the roof of a nearby school building and at game's end an assistant principal patrolled the field on the jump seat of a cop's motorcycle.

Student outlawry ran through most of the forms young and active imaginations devise. There were cases of extortion by big kids from little ones; most of the demands were petty but a few involved large sums of money. ("Give, or I'll use this can opener on you! Jump up and down and jingle and I'll know how much you have!") The lavatories especially took a beating—from vandals, from fights, from fires, from cherry bombs. "They finally took all the mirrors out; mirrors are dangerous," a student said. A mother, who moved away from New Rochelle because of the school situation, said: "The toilets are where they can get hurt. I trained my kids not to go to the toilet at school; they can wait until they get home."

The students' favorite form of eluding authority—and education at the same time—was to reach school late or not at all. One senior homeroom of 30 members recorded 320 cases of lateness or absence between school opening and Christmas, and one student showed up only twice all semester. Senior high absenteeism ran up to 600 cases a day—the past average had been around 250—and the school racked up a record of 23,000 students late or absent in the 1964–65 school year.

Teachers were treated with insolence often, ignored frequently, defied on occasion. Seldom were they actually assaulted, but there were exceptions. An elderly male teacher entered a classroom just in time to see a strange Negro boy getting ready to heave a heavy wastebasket at one of the students. He yelled and then grappled with the boy, who dropped the basket and began hammering his fists into the teacher. The racket brought a guidance counselor and several women teachers. The boy was finally wrestled into the hall and to an assistant dean's office. The dean, charged with student discipline but conscious of previous experience, listened to a description of the incident and announced that the boy would be sent home. The outraged teachers demanded that the boy be prosecuted for assault. He was brought to trial on a charge of assault and disorderly conduct. The assault charge was later dropped and the boy, already on probation under a four-year suspended sentence for robbery, pleaded guilty to disorderly conduct. He was given the maximum sentence of 30 days.

Some of the hell-raisers enjoyed distinct advantages. One white pupil, brought to book for school arson, stood mute before an assistant principal. His father, he said, had instructed him that if he ever got into trouble he should refuse to talk until he had his own lawyer. Next day the boy's father telephoned to let the school know that, if the authorities intended to press the matter, he himself would testify that his son hadn't even been in school the day of the fire.

On a basis of proportion it rings oddly that the hoodlums in New Rochelle's school population could have disconcerted the process of education as much as they did. New Rochelle is a concentrated system with 2,900 in the senior high, 1,800 in one junior high, 1,050 in the other. The genuine malefactors were relatively few. And they were not all Negroes by any means; they scarcely could be in a school population where Negroes numbered less than one-fifth. Faculty, who had to deal with the rebels estimated that the senior high contained only about 100 really hard-core incorrigibles. But those 100 were active and—worse—they attracted the hero worship of many others who were too eager to experiment with slightly milder forms of outlawry.

The vast majority of the school population—white and Negro alike—remained law-abiding citizens, as intent upon getting an education as any other group of individuals. But the hooligans levied a price upon the lawabiding. The first and most obvious damage to all was that the faculty became so preoccupied with maintaining order that the teachers' real function—teaching—had to suffer. One faculty member who finally gave up in frustration commented in her resignation, "I studied to teach English; if I had wanted to be a social worker, I'd have studied that."

"I try to handle every case as an individual and never as a matter of race," another teacher said. "But it won't work when the kid involved is a Negro. Land on a Negro pupil and the civil rights people land on you. I'm a teacher; part of what I'm supposed to teach is that order is essential to civilization. But am I teaching that—if I see kids raising hell in the halls and I have to stop before cooling it off and wonder whether I'm setting off a race crisis?"

In the autumn of 1963 the board of education had installed a new principal in the senior high. He was Dr. John Kelley, a peppery, no-nonsense educator who spent 23 years in public schooling and had an enviable reputation as an administrator. For a while Dr. Kelley felt that things were going well and that, within a couple of years, he could overcome the discipline problem and restore the school to its former place as "one of the finest secondary schools in the country." But early in the next school year, a Negro faculty member warned Dr. Kelley that, by his outspoken firmness, he had offended the civil rights activists and they intended to "get" him. It took time, but in the end Dr. Kelley was "got."

Over a span of five months, 26 students—12 white, 14 Negro—were suspended for various misdeeds. A delegation called the Westchester Joint Committee on Equal Opportunity—representing CORE, the NAACP and four other Negro organizations—decided to act and went to the board of education with a call for Dr. Kelley's "immediate removal."

The group caused to be read a statement resounding with such phrases as: ". . . treatment which minority-group children receive in public schools tends strongly and tragically to be, in effect, not only 'separate' but not 'equal' either . . . board has the immediate responsibility of removing the unwilling and ineffective administrative personnel . . . actions of Dr. Kelly (sic) are arbitrary and capricious . . . serious breaks in his [Dr. Kelley's] judgment. . . . Dr. Kelly's handling is punitive and retaliatory . . . when 75% of disciplinary problems are designated by Dr. Kelly as coming from Negroes, who are less than 17% of the school population, then there is critical need for review of the teachers' obvious failure to motivate and understand their students . . . our strong and unyielding opinion that his unsatisfactory and unprecedented performance as principal mandates his replacement. . . ."

The statement also included this passage: "We find also . . . the presence of unfounded and irrational fear, shown by white teachers, of well-developed, physically fit, attractive, well-dressed young Negro male adolescents, particularly when they are expressive and assertive."

Against this assault, Dr. Kelley got impressive support. The faculty, which included 11 Negro teachers, and all the custodial staff, largely Negro, signed a statement of support that ran in the daily New Rochelle *Standard Star*.

The high school paper, the *Huguenot Herald*, commented: "His [Dr. Kelley's] loss to the high school would be incalculable. . . . To tamper with this [the power to suspend] would be to create so chaotic a situation that learning and living at New Rochelle high school would be impossible. . . . Students who are not capable of living in the school environment should not be permitted to disrupt it for the majority. . . ."

But this support did Dr. Kelley little tangible good. Within 14 weeks he was out, ostensibly after a voluntary resignation—which few really believed.

"We got him. We could get another if we needed to," a CORE activist said later.

Even before Dr. Kelley left, the lack of effective discipline and rehabilitation attempts was deliberately dramatized at a special board meeting in a confrontation between a group of teachers, on the one hand, and the board and the then superintendent, on the other.

A teacher staged this interrogation of Dr. Kelley:

TEACHER: Dr. Kelley, isn't it true that we have had students found with knives in this school?
DR. KELLEY: Yes.
TEACHER: Isn't it true that we have had students found intoxicated in this school?
DR. KELLEY: Yes.
TEACHER: Isn't it true that certain students assaulted other students in school in the presence of witnesses?
DR. KELLEY: Yes.
TEACHER: Isn't it true that these students are back in school?
DR. KELLEY: It would be accurate to say they never left.

In such an atmosphere of "getting" and being "got" there were no winners, but losers abounded. And it was a distasteful paradox of his and the school's condition that the New Rochelle youngster who needed education most—the so-called "disadvantaged child"—lost most.

The term "disadvantaged child" seems to have been manufactured to avoid giving offense in a climate where many stand more than ready to take offense. The way things are, the "disadvantaged child" today is most frequently Negro. The nature of his disadvantagement varies with the individual; but, in practice, it most often means a Negro child from an impoverished, broken-home background, where hopelessness and bitter resentment are the large character-shaping influences. This is a youngster whose only real chance hitherto came through some miracle of luck or pluck.

How ironic, then, that the very pressure of the civil rights drive sometimes worked to the further disadvantage of the already disadvantaged. Swept up in the movement—with its legitimate hunger for full equality, right now, in American society—the people could not tolerate an admission that many of its children were not as ready for existing educational systems as their counterparts from fuller backgrounds.

In New Rochelle the civil rights militants preferred to blame the school system alone for failing to overcome the fundamental social and economic disadvantages of many Negro children. They appeared to feel that a conspiracy in the system was deliberately designed to betray the Negro child.

"There is a definite, conscious intent to keep the Negro male ignorant," declared a Negro minister in New Rochelle. "It is fine for him to play football, but he is encouraged to take the line of least resistance. They [the white establishment] want him so he can't go to anybody's college.

"Education is often slanted for the advantaged child," said a Negro woman psychologist there. "More attention must be given to the children the school doesn't seem able to reach. . . . The teachers must be creative enough to motivate these kids.

"Along with the problems [the Negro child] brings from home are the new problems he encounters in his teachers. Many [teachers] are definitely prejudiced. They seem to ask, 'What can be expected of him?' There is a basic contempt for the Negro child among some teachers."

And it was on this point that constructive dialogue in New Rochelle seriously broke down. "They will never understand that the school is looking for talent, not trying to stifle it," a teacher said. "How the hell am I supposed to motivate a kid I never see more than three time between school opening and Christmas?"

The suspicions, coupled with the common parental inclination to push a child too soon and too hard, often plunged the Negro student in over his head. And then, too often, he sank.

"A man in my job used to carry a lot of weight," said one guidance counselor in New Rochelle. "His function was to analyze a student's needs and capacities. He had the student's school record, his test scores and personal interviews to work with. Then, along with department heads, he would advise the student what courses he ought to take—and, in most cases, that's what he would do.

"It doesn't work that way any more. For instance, Negro girls shy away from home economics; they suspect you're trying to trap them into being domestics. Negro boys don't much want vocational school. The pressure is on them to shoot for white-collar jobs—that is, the ones who are serious about school at all. So the parents and civil rights people insist that a child go into the college preparatory program, the toughest regimen the school has to offer. And that, by golly, is where he goes.

"This is fine—if . . . if he has soaked up enough education to handle it. But if he isn't ready for CP, he soon discovers they might as well be speaking Sanskrit for all he understands. He's flabbergasted and left with nothing much to do but stare at the blackboard or start cutting classes. By the end of the semester, he's ready to be a dropout."

One Negro mother of 10 wanted to send her oldest son through the high school business course; but, suspicious that the school would prejudge him as unqualified, went to the school and "really sat on" the boy's guidance counselor: "They didn't want to give him a chance. Wanted to say ahead of time that he couldn't pass the course."

The counselor surrendered and the boy went where his mother wanted him to go. But he didn't stay long. The mother's explanation: "He was bored. The teacher didn't try to get him interested. He would rather stay in his room and play records. Then he dropped out of school. But he's back now. The Army was going to draft him if he wouldn't go to school."

When asked what had gone wrong to bring her fight for her sons's rights to this sorry end, she said, "I don't know. The children are confused, the parents are confused, the teachers are confused. It just makes a big mess."

Confusion over how to reach a workable, livable, acceptable and fruitful human condition in the nation's schools is hardly limited to New Rochelle. It is only that New Rochelle has had longer and, because of the exacerbation of Lincoln Elementary, possibly more intense experience with the struggle. (Mount Vernon, a cheek-by-jowl Westchester County neighbor of New Rochelle's is right now at the point of anger and bitter no-compromise that New Rochelle was in five years ago. The measure of the bitterness in Mount Vernon was reached a few weeks ago when an enraged CORE spokesman railed at his neighbors that Hitler didn't kill enough of them.)

But in New Rochelle, forced to be a pathfinder in the North, there are beginning to be reasons to rejoice, to nourish hope that, given time, the matter can be resolved. It has not been easy, but progress has been made.

The board of education has created a human relations committee and given it a franchise to hunt out avenues of inter-racial communication.

A government "Headstart" program has been instituted within the school system; the idea is to catch children young—under kindergarten age—and demonstrate to them early that education is the thing that must be got.

The PTAs have concluded that they were going at their mission backwards. "Regular meetings get the regular customers. Same people, same speeches, same agenda," a PTA leader said. "We weren't getting anywhere near the people we really needed to reach. Some people are uncomfortable, feel out of place in a big PTA meeting, and some people had never even heard of PTA. We had to go out and get them."

Using the techniques of a door-to-door brush salesman they began to attract more parents. The newcomers were invited to small, intimate kaffee-klatsches in private homes.

"I enjoy those little meetings," a Negro mother said. "No speeches to listen to. I've heard so many speeches I can tune them out, the same way my kids tune me out when they don't want to listen. But in these little groups you can find out things about the schools—and about kids—that are of some use to you."

A group of New Rochelle women started a Volunteer Tutoring Program. These women went into the schools and with advice from the teacher of those students who were having trouble, both academically and emotionally, went to work on them on a one-to-one basis. To prepare themselves, the women had to take courses in the new math and, because the schools were crowded, they sometimes found themselves holding class in the boiler room. The tutors' program eventually had 65 members handling a case load of 136 kids, 103 of them Negroes, from grades 1 to 12.

The high school faculty has agitated to modernize the curriculum for the approximately 12% of the student body who are unable or unwilling to cope with the vocational, business or college preparatory courses. They have also lobbied for a remedial reading program, special classes for the emotionally out-of-kilter and psychological help for those in need of it. These have been tentative steps—and well short of the need—but they have been steps and there has been detectable positive response from the civil rights side of the fence.

"Things are better," Paul Dennis, head of the New Rochelle NAACP chapter, said recently. "Now we have a school board that will listen—not just a stone wall. And there are other improvements in the town and outside the schools. We're getting jobs for Negroes, jobs that were never open to us before."

Even a year ago nobody among the civil rights activists could have afforded to admit that the burden for order and education could rest anywhere but on the schools. Even that has changed—a little.

"The children do have to fight for their rights. They're entitled to that and they're bound to do it," one formerly uncompromising leader said.

"They have to strike back when they're discriminated against. But also I know they have to learn respect for the institution, the school system itself. That begins at home."

It may have begun. In the last few months the school system, which for too many years was intimidated by the civil rights pressures, has gradually been putting its house in order. Discipline is now being enforced more stringently and consistently. Two new disciplinary officers have been appointed. Students away from their classes are required to carry cards certifying their right to be abroad. Some of the most lawless have been suspended or expelled. Among those kicked out were several of a kind once considered "untouchable"—including the son of a civil rights leader. No organized protests have been brought in their behalf.

At its essense, the ordeal that the New Rochelle schools underwent, and from which they are now painfully emerging, was a crisis of human relations—the unwillingness and inability to understand, the unwillingness and inability to take responsibility. If the Negro community was defiant in its striving for its civil rights, the white community was complacent in the face of social change.

It may be that the community's best hope lies in the students themselves. Though they fought the system, they never did fight one another except in odd and isolated instances. Students, after all, are what the schools are all about—they and the kind of education they get or don't get. An essential element of that education is, again, human relations. The youngsters of New Rochelle, with the example of the struggle their elders had waged, were offered on a silver platter an invitation to wage race war inside the schools. But they have ignored that invitation.

"Once in a while somebody will yell 'Paleface' or 'Whitey' and mean it nasty, but not often. Or somebody will write hate-Negro stuff on a toilet wall," said a Negro student who is a class officer. "Or a Negro girl will say you are a snob because you have white friends, too. But those are exceptions. I have as many white friends as Negro, and some of the whites I'm more comfortable with than *some* of the Negroes."

There it is—the dividend: the kind of practicing humanity that too many adults are too old and ornery to take upon themselves.

DISCUSSION QUESTIONS

1. Was the confrontation of Negroes and whites in New Rochelle and the conflicts growing out of this confrontation an inevitable step in the development of relationships between Negroes and whites in our society?
2. What preparatory courses of action would you suggest the Board of Education and the Administration of the schools might have taken so that the confrontation might have been made on a different level?
3. Evaluate the steps the school eventually took to accommodate and meet the needs of its Negro children in terms of their cost, adequacy, and timing.
4. Do you agree with the author's estimate of Dr. Kelley's leadership in his crisis role?

CHAPTER 4 Religion

Religion is an integral part of our culture and our history. The drama of the founding of the colonies has religionists as its protagonists: Protestants in New England, Catholics in Maryland, Quakers in Pennsylvania, and a host of others elsewhere.

From the beginning, education in the colonies served the cause of religion; the first schools were church schools, established to give religious education. Thayer say of the Massachusetts Educational Act of 1647 that "it reflected more the determination of colonial officials to insure orthodoxy in religion than the stirrings of a democratic conscience."[1]

Education in colonial times "attempted no more than to develop 'an ability to read and to understand the principles of religion and the capital laws of the country.' "[2] Today, while religious education still claims large numbers of adherents, the nature of education is predominantly secular. Pragmatic themes, status, wealth, and vocational preparation looming largely among them, are of major concern.

Perhaps as a reaction to the narrowness and sterility of modern life, young people have become increasingly disenchanted with the affluent society. Many have turned to political activity, out of high ethical and moral principle. Others have joined Vista and the Peace Corps. There are evangelical overtones in the fervor and the dedication of their commitment to render service to mankind. The values displayed are the deep

---

[1] V. T. Thayer, *Formative Ideas in American Education*, Dodd, Mead, & Co., Inc., New York, 1965, p. 4.
[2] *Ibid.*

concern of education, but they are part too of the religious sentiment and tradition that has always been present in American life. Education is never far from religion; the question may be raised whether religion is, or should be, part of education.

Should the state provide financial support for religious schools, to insure and to strengthen religion's contribution to American life? Would such aid be divisive and destructive of the American social fiber? Exactly what does separation of church and state mean? The issue of religion and education is by no means settled, as a reading of the latest Supreme Court decision and any local paper at Christmas time will make obvious. The doubt arises that it ever will be.

SAM DUKER The Public Schools and Religion

The Supreme Court of the United States occupies a unique role in our society. No parallel to this role can be found in any other time or place. Nine men, appointed for life by the President with the consent of the Senate, have the responsibility for setting social policy in many areas without authority to do so except insofar as this social policy is determined by their legal interpretation of the laws and the Constitution of the United States in the light of present-day needs. Unless the Court itself reverses its ruling in a later case, an event which happens very rarely, there is, in the last analysis, only one appeal from a Supreme Court decision and that is to the process of amending the Constitution. This process is long, difficult, and infrequently successful. The word of the Supreme Court is, therefore, in most cases the final one. It must be accepted, graciously or ungraciously as the case may be, by all other components of American society.

It is not at all surprising that many of the major constitutional decisions of the Supreme Court are unpopular when one considers that it is almost invariably a minority that seeks the protection of its constitutional rights. It is worth noting that in each of the 12 cases excerpted it was a minority group that brought about the Court's decision. Because the protection of the minority so frequently involves the majority, there is often a pained outcry. While the Supreme Court proceeds with great caution and seeks to avoid meeting any issue except when it becomes necessary, it has always been the view of this body that no entering wedge shall be allowed in the matter of a clear violation of a constitutional right.

REVIEW OF THE CASES EXCERPTED

In *Meyer* v. *Nebraska* the issue presented was the validity of a state law prohibiting the teaching of foreign languages in the nonpublic elementary schools. Clearly, it was the majority sentiment in those states passing such laws that Americanization would be promoted by such laws. As has been previously noted, no direct religious question was raised, but actually the schools involved were almost all religiously supported and operated. The Supreme Court held these laws to be beyond the constitutional powers of a state and thus preserved the rights of private schools, whether religiously oriented or not, to determine the content of their curricula. This decision did not imply any impotence on the part of the state in the matter of requiring inclusion of material in that curriculum but dealt solely with exclusion.

In *Pierce* v. *Society of Sisters,* the law requiring all children to attend public school had been adopted by a clear majority of the voters of the State of Oregon. While it is true that this law did not single out religious schools, it was clear to all concerned that religiously oriented schools were the target. Here, as in the *Meyer* case, no mention was made either in the arguments or in the Court's decision of the First Amendment, but in later cases the point is made over and over again that because of this case there is no justification for religious instruction or exercises in the public school classroom.

The only cases decided by the Supreme Court that concern the question of "free exercise" and the schools are those involving compulsory saluting of the flag. Once more it was an expression of the majority will that brought about the adoption of laws and regulations requiring all public school pupils to participate in giving the Pledge of Allegiance to the Flag. The members of the Jehovah's Witnesses sect who found participation in this ceremony to be in conflict with their religious beliefs represented a very small sector of our population. A sharp difference is found between these cases and the *Engel* and *Schempp* cases. Here the Supreme Court held that excusing the objecting children from participation was all that was required, but in the subsequent cases involving devotional exercises the Court held that excusal did not serve to adequately protect the rights of the minority group. The reason for the different holdings clearly lies in the fact that the flag salute cases involved the Free Exercise Clause of the First Amendment while the prayer cases turned on an interpretation of the Establishment Clause.

Just an excusal was held insufficient protection of constitutional rights in the later prayer cases, so in *McCollum* excusal was held not to properly protect the rights of the small minority who did not wish to participate in sectarian religious instruction given in the public school classroom during school hours. The *Zorach* case also involved the appeal of a minority but in this case the ruling was in favor of the majority when the Court held dismissal from school for the purpose of attending sectarian religious instruction elsewhere during school hours to be constitutionally unobjectionable.

The *Cochran* case which did not turn on the First Amendment and the *Everson* case which the Court used as an occasion for its most thorough analysis of the Establishment Clause established the important principle of "child-benefit." It is, of course, obvious that any help, financial or otherwise, given to a parochial school child tends directly or indirectly to aid the parochial school itself as this then becomes a service that that school need not render. By the same token, when the government assumes an expense that would otherwise be a parental one, the parochial school is benefited at least indirectly by the resulting greater share of parental resources available to it. It is, however, exceedingly difficult to draw the line between a governmental expenditure on behalf of the child and one on behalf of the parochial school. Extremes are easily interpreted but in the middle group this becomes an exceedingly sticky question. A few more words will be said about the child-benefit theory later in this chapter.

The last four cases excerpted here deal with devotional exercises in the public school classroom. *Engel* v. *Vitale* stirred the most controversy but actually the decision in that case was the mildest and most restricted of the four. Considerable doubt existed for a year after the decision as to whether the Court would or would not extend the doctrine of that case. *Engel* turned largely on the fact that the prayer in question had been composed by a state agency and there was no intimation one way or another as to the Court's views on Bible reading or on prayers not composed by state agencies.

Schempp and *Murray* squarely presented the Court with the validity of Bible reading and praying in the public school classroom. The Court unequivocally held such activities violative of the Establishment Clause of the First Amendment. Surprisingly, the reaction to the decision in these cases was not nearly so furious and volatile as the reaction had been to *Engel*. This does not imply that it was a popular decision or that the groups reacting unfavorably to *Engel* had been won over.

The *Chamberlin* case presented many issues about which there had been and still are great uncertainties, but in the last analysis the final decision dealt only with prayers and Bible reading and thus did not extend or restrict the *Schempp* ruling in any way whatsoever. The principal point of interest in this case lies in the byplay between the Florida Supreme Court's anxiety to display its deep-seated disagreement with the Supreme Court of the United States' interpretation of the Establishment Clause and the Supreme Court's summary disposition of the case on two separate occasions.

The 12 cases included in this book show the result of a chain of reasoning in which, to a remarkable degree, each case gives support to the decision in the following one. It must be borne in mind, however, that the view contrary to the one adopted by the Court was upheld by learned counsel and almost invariably by one or more members of the Court itself. To say that these decisions were foreordained as an indisputable matter of logic or reasoning would be rash indeed.

It can be argued that the series of decisions tends to have a unifying effect on society in that diversity of opinion is respected and protected. It can also be argued that these decisions have had the effect of polarizing the viewpoints of the factions of society holding varying points of view as to the proper relationship between religion and the public school. Time will have to pass before a fair judgment can be made as to which of these arguments has the most validity. We are now too close to the events to gain the necessary perspective.

CRITERIA EMPLOYED BY THE COURT

Everson, the released time cases, and the prayer cases all rest on the Court's interpretation of the Establishment Clause of the First Amendment which states: "Congress shall make no law respecting an establishment of religion." A great portion of the decisions in these cases deal with attempted analysis of the intentions of the "Founding Fathers" when they inserted this provision into our Bill of Rights. There certainly is no incontrovertible evidence available as to exactly what these intentions were. It is clear that at the time of the drafting and the adoption of the Bill of Rights there was considerable concern lest the newly created federal government usurp greater powers than its constituents intended to bestow upon it. It is also evident that there was strong feeling against the formation by that federal government of a state church supported by taxes and imposed on an unwilling populace.

There had been a great deal written about the intended strength of the concept referred to as the "wall of separation" between church and state, if indeed at the time that concept was generally accepted—which seems very doubtful. From extensive reading in this area one can only conclude that most of our Founding Fathers, if not all of them, would have been amazed at the interpretation now placed on this phrase. This does not mean, however, that they would necessarily be out of sympathy with this construction in the light of present-day conditions. It seems highly likely that men of the strong practical views of Madison and Jefferson would enthusiastically agree that the language of the Constitution should be interpreted in the light of existing conditions and current societal needs. The point would seem to be that the strongest support for the decisions in question does not necessarily come from the intentions of the framers of the Bill of Rights even if those intentions could be ascertained with any degree of certainty.

Similarly, without questioning the desirability of the interpretation given the Due Process Clause of the Fourteenth Amendment, it seems futile to seek historical evidence that its framers meant to incorporate the First Amendment's guarantees of religious freedom in the clause.

It is perfectly clear from the ruling of the Court on the five cases dealing with the Establishment Clause that there is no question about the interpretation of its meaning. There is an unequivocable and consistent view in these opinions to the effect that this clause demands an absolute separation between church and state. It seems most unlikely that the Court will, in the foreseeable future at least, depart to any extent from this view. The question that remains open is only whether a given activity impinges on this separation. In this respect it is not at all impossible that, in time, varying shades of interpretation may arise.

DISCUSSION QUESTIONS

1. Do you agree with the trend of the Supreme Court decisions concerning religion and education?
2. Should the basis for educational decision-making in matters affecting religion in the schools be pragmatic, ethical, or legal? Are these mutually exclusive?

PHILIP BURTON Public Funds for Public Schools Only

Many Roman Catholic proponents of tax-subsidized religion are engaging in intricate verbal exercises to invert the meaning of the Constitution's First and Fourteenth amendments and use them against their opponents. Faced with dilemmas posed by expanding population, galloping inflation and canon law imperatives, they are claiming—with amnesiac blandness toward clear dicta of Supreme Court decisions blocking tax-supported religion—that refusal of such support is an unconstitutional limitation of parental rights and religious liberties.

No advocate of tax support for parochial school denies that such schools are a religious enterprise. *Extra ecclesium nulla salus* is the rationale that accounts for their establishment and compels Catholic parents to use them. Beyond ensuring their right to exist (upheld by the Supreme Court in 1925), the government's obligation toward them is identical with its obligation to the churches themselves. As the Supreme Court has made clear, parochial schools are legally precluded from any tax support whatsoever. If they were to receive such support, the government would thereby acquire the right to regulate them in the same way it regulates public schools, and under such circumstances no religion could be taught in them.

I

Traditional Roman Catholic opposition to public aid to education in general has been modified in recent years by growing anticipation of sharing in larger benefits for public education at public expense. In 1930 the U.S. Supreme Court drew a distinction between child benefits and aid to religion, and rendered a decision permitting parochial school pupils to share in free textbook distribution. Religious school pupils were in some places being transported at public expense even before any legal clarification by the Supreme Court. The Everson case, which came before the court in 1947, culminated in one of the court's most notable verdicts. By a slim majority of one the court adhered to a precedent, drawn first in the 1930 textbook case, distinguishing between child benefits and aid to religion. On this basis it made public transportation of children attending parochial schools permissible. Four members of the court rejected the distinction and declared such use of tax funds violative of the Constitution. And the whole court concurred in the judgment that the First Amendment erects an impregnable wall of separation between church and state and absolutely precludes publicly supported religion. The reasoning of the dissenters was adopted in the McCollum case the following year in an 8–1 decision outlawing the teaching of religion in public classrooms. Taken together, these two Supreme Court decisions settle by a clear negative any real questions as to whether government can subsidize religion.

Comprehensive as this answer seems, those who seek public support for religious enterprises remain undaunted. The extent of their anticipations can be surmised from the nature of the denunciations that have been hurled at the Supreme Court following the Everson and McCollum decisions. The court is charged with departing from tradition and misinterpreting the Constitution. The Constitution, say the accusers, does not prohibit nonpreferential tax support of religion; the court ignores history, logic and law by imposing a novel interpretation upon the First Amendment. They further argue that there is no wall of separation between church and state except an imaginary one in the minds of smokers of secular opiums. The misinterpretations the court imposes reject the honored tradition of liberty, deny parental rights and violate freedom of religion. So goes the argument of the proponents of tax-supported religion.

The substance of this argument was articulated last summer by Bishop Lawrence J. Shehan, chairman of the department of education of the National Catholic Welfare Conference. Preaching on August 28 at a Red Mass held at the National Shrine of the Immaculate Conception, Washington, D.C., and attended by three Supreme Court justices (including Chief Justice Earl Warren) and many members of the American Bar Association, Bishop Shehan bluntly posed the question whether the financial burdens of those who send their children to religious schools is an unconstitutional limitation of parental rights and violation of freedom of the practice of religion. While Bishop Shehan put the matter in question form, his own answer was obvious—and clearly contrary to that already established in law by the Supreme Court decisions. Beneath his arcane language is to be found a different concept of the proper relationship between church and state than that which informs the Constitution and guides Supreme Court decisions.

The bishop's logic obviously identifies the Constitution's concern to protect parental and religious rights with a nonexistent governmental duty to incur parents' expenses deriving from exercise of such rights. This kind of logic betrays confusion in the minds of those who invoke its aid. The Constitution upholds the right of parents to send their children to the church of their choice, but maintenance of these legal rights carries no concomitant obligation for the government to, say, pay pew rent in the church chosen. If such a principle were constitutionally valid, legal consistency could claim that the government incurs the obligation to pay any and all expenses involved in a citizen's exercises any one of his constitutional privileges. No claim could be more patently absurd. The financial burden of parochial schools is a private religious problem; nothing relevant to constitutional questions of rights is involved. A clear violation of the Constitution would be perpetrated if the government were to honor the plea for tax support implicit in the presuppositions behind the bishop's question.

II

Bishop Shehan's approach was not born full grown of his homiletic travail last August 28. Inherent in it is Cardinal McIntyre's notion of circumventing the wall that separates parochial schools from the federal treasury by a ruse to gain funds for such schools through scholarship awards to parents of children attending them. Included also is a conception of child welfare benefits that would include everything from erecting religious school plants to stopping leaky toilets in them. Obviously such grab-bag expenditures could be made to cover the major costs of parochial religious education. This method of breaching the wall of separation between church and state is assumed by its proponents to have no constitutional complications and to nullify the Supreme Court's clearest interpretations of the First Amendment. They imply that the government's refusal to adopt some such way of nullifying Supreme Court decisions blocking direct or indirect tax support of these schools is equivalent to violation of Catholics' constitutional rights. The assumption ignores the fact that *no person has constitutional rights to religious education at public expense.* Any citizen possesses the legal right to acquire religious education for himself and his children; these rights have been as fully upheld for Roman Catholic citizens as for others. Obviously it is fallacious to confuse legal rights with private economic problems.

Roman Catholic citizens have the legal right to make use of public schools but are prevented by dicta of their church from doing so. The government does not infringe upon their right to act on the insistence of their church's authorities that they send their children to religious schools not entitled to tax support. The germane core of the point at issue here lies in the fact that Roman Catholics accept for themselves an extralegal position that constrains them to go beyond what the government requires and assume for themselves extra educational costs. This is the crux of the dilemma of dual loyalties upon which the government approach to educational responsibility has in many countries foundered.

Contrary to the view of the Roman Catholic hierarchy, the economic disabilities of those required by their churches to assume the burdens incident to religious education are not in any way the result of government discrimination. They are instead incidental costs of the actualization of rights ensured under the First and Fourteenth amendments. The same amendments which set forth these rights prohibit the government from collecting taxes to subsidize the individual's exercise of such rights. The government is not a church and cannot act as one in order to collect church school fees. By due process of law the government collects taxes from all its citizens; it treats Roman Catholic citizens on equal terms with all others. If they complain that they are victims of double taxation without representation, they cannot in good conscience lay blame upon the government. If they refuse to accept their share of what the government provides for all on equal terms, the refusal is not one for which the government is responsible.

Advocates of tax-supported religion increasingly recognize the futility of securing direct tax support and tend to cloak their claim for public support under the guise of proposals that speak of child welfare benefits. Their hopes lie in the dubious distinctions discussed herein and appealed to by the slim majority of one which in the Everson case ruled in favor of free transportation of parochial pupils. The dissenting minority of four in that case saw no such distinctions, and in the 1948 McCollum case their reasoning was adopted as the basis for an 8–1 decision outlawing the teaching of religion in public classrooms.

III

When proponents of tax support for religious schools accuse the court of rejecting the tradition of religious liberty, they have in mind the precedents based on dubious distinctions. Carried to logical conclusions, this recent tradition might open the way for vast public expenditures for religion. Such was not the tradition from which James Madison reasoned when he protested federal compensations for chaplains in the House and Senate on the ground that they are unconstitutional. Madison knew more intimately the intent of the tradition that informs the First Amendment than do some of those who now appeal to tradition against that amendment! Madison knew of no tradition of nonpreferential aid to religions; he did know that the authors of the Constitution countenanced neither preferential nor nonpreferential aid to religions at public expense. And he knew of no tradition using "benefits to children" as a subterfuge for extending tax support to religious institutions. In the McCollum case the court was wisely sensitive to the tradition known to Madison and others of his day.

Bishop Shehan cites the government's providing chapels and chaplains for the armed forces and special veterans' programs as the kinds of measures needed to facilitate religious freedom. As a matter of fact, the constitutionality of tax-supported chaplaincies and chapels is highly debatable. Madison opposed them as unconstitutional. One can only wait until the Supreme Court takes on and decides a case involving the issue to be certain of its opinion. It is not inconceivable that the practice might be found illegal. As for special programs for veterans, their purpose was not motivated by any concern either to facilitate or hinder practice of religious freedoms. Much less was their purpose to solve the financial dilemmas of administrators of religious schools! That such was the incidental effect in some instances is hardly to be questioned; it is not certain, however, that all aspects of the administration of the programs could pass a constitutional test.

Such problematic cases may yet provide the occasion for future litigations and decisions; nevertheless the fact remains that the kinds of expenditures uppermost in the minds of advocates of tax support for religion are clearly precluded by law. The law which prohibits teaching of religion in a public classroom cannot be bent to accommodate ruses encompassing scholarship awards, child welfare benefits and loans which would in fact constitute financial aid to religion. The answer to questions presupposing that denial of such requests is an unconstitutional violation of parental rights and freedom of religion is contained in these words by Justice Hugo Black (in the Everson decision): "No tax in any amount . . . can be levied to support any religious activities or institutions." Words could not be clearer!

DISCUSSION QUESTIONS

1. How tenable is the distinction drawn in the Everson case between child benefits and aid to religion?
2. Is Burton's distinction between the legal rights and the private economic problems of Roman Catholic citizens borne out in constitutional law?
3. How much justice is there in the complaint of double taxation without representation on the part of parents of children in both public and independent schools?

ROBERT M. HUTCHINS Aid to Church Schools

Federal aid to education is an absolute necessity. But a political argument over funds for parochial schools, masquerading as a constitutional issue, bars the way. Unfortunately President Kennedy, while calling for $5.3 billion in aid to education over a period of years, is himself guilty of jeopardizing aid to all schools by perpetuating the masquerade.

The President and many others, especially liberals, tell us aid to church-school pupils is a constitutional question. They say there is a wall of separation between church and state forbidding any kind of assistance, direct or indirect, to an educational institution operated under the auspices of a church.

In fact, the Constitution says nothing of separation and makes no mention of a wall. The words of the First Amendment are: "Congress shall make no law respecting an establishment of religion, or prohibiting the free exercise thereof. . . ." The Supreme Court has held that the Fourteenth Amendment makes these words applicable to state legislatures as well as to Congress. Nothing in the words necessarily leads to the conclusion that every form of aid, direct or indirect, to educational institutions under religious auspices in unconstitutional.

We owe the wall not to the Constitution but to a letter from Thomas Jefferson to the Baptist Association of Danbury, Connecticut, in 1802, replying to a complimentary address. Jefferson wrote, "Believing with you that religion is a matter which lies solely between man and his God, that he owes account to none other for his faith or his worship, that the legislative powers of Government reach actions only, and not opinions, I contemplate with sovereign reverence that act of the whole American people which declared that their legislature should 'make no law respecting an establishment of religion, or prohibiting the free exercise thereof,' thus building a wall of separation between church and state."

The letter shows that what Jefferson was interested in was freedom of religion. He did not want the Government telling people how or whom or whether they should worship—first, because of the nature of religion, and second, because of the nature of government. Religion was a matter between a man and his God; government should not, if only because it could not, attempt to control the thoughts of men.

The wall Jefferson erected in the name of the First Amendment rose no higher than was necessary to wall off the religious opinions and practices of citizens from interference by government. His letter does *not* suggest that he would have opposed public expenditures that might benefit schools under religious management. And the record shows that he recommended procedures by which students at the University of

Reprinted from the *Saturday Evening Post*, June 8, 1963, with permission of the author.

Virginia, supported by the state and founded by Jefferson, might receive religious instruction.

Jefferson's wall disappeared into the mists of history for 77 years. Then it came back into view when the Supreme Court held that the First Amendment did not protect polygamy among the Mormons. It came back, that is, with a hole in it, through which the Government marched against a practice defended in religion's name. In justifying legislative condemnation of a church's action, Chief Justice Morrison Waite, who wrote the opinion of the court, used the Jefferson doctrine that legislative powers should be limited specifically to regulation of actions.

All was quiet along the wall for 62 years. Then, in 1951 it reappeared, but with another large hole in it, through which a school board in New Jersey drove buses carrying some children to parochial schools. The action was authorized by state law. In 1947 its constitutionality was *upheld*. The majority opinion said, "The First Amendment has erected a wall between church and state. That wall must be kept high and impregnable. We could not approve the slightest breach. New Jersey has not breached it here."

For the last 15 years, whenever there has been a case involving church and state, almost every Supreme Court justice has felt constrained to bow before the wall. The psalms sung in its behalf have grown more eloquent and more moving. It has become one of our more popular figures of speech. But the only effect of the wall on the decisions of the court has been to confuse the opinions of the justices.

The wall is used indiscriminately as a jumping-off point in all cases in which the religion clauses of the First Amendment are invoked. These cases are in general of three quite different kinds: those in which a public agency has used public money in a way benefiting private schools indirectly; those in which a public agency has authorized a program of "released time" for religious instruction in public schools or in connection with public schools; and those in which a public agency has instituted religious exercises in public schools.

Released time and religious exercises put the power of the state behind religion and raise the question of public pressure, direct or indirect, on the consciences of individuals and the consequent limitation of the exercise of their religious freedom. Indirect financial aid to schools under religious auspices does not raise this question. Such aid may actually help the aided pupils to exercise their religious freedom; it cannot be seriously argued that it restricts the religious freedom of those who are not assisted.

For all its talk of the wall, the fact is that the Supreme Court has never held aid to pupils in religious schools unconstitutional. As the court sustained New Jersey in providing transportation for pupils in Catholic schools, so it sustained Louisiana in providing textbooks for children in all schools. The theory in both cases was the same: an overriding public purpose was to be served—the education of the children in the state. The fact that some benefit might incidentally accrue to a private school or to the religious organization that managed it was not significant.

The tax exemption of church schools has never been challenged. Neither have the numerous Government programs of grants, loans, scholarships and tax benefits under such laws as the GI Bill of Rights, the College Housing Act, the School Lunch Act, and the Surplus Property Act, all of which have been available to church-supported institutions. The Kennedy Administration has sonorously opposed Federal aid to church schools. Yet it finds no logical difficulty in recommending in its present bill appropriations to facilitate the recruitment of teachers by parochial as well as by public schools.

My conclusion is that Federal aid to pupils in parochial schools is not a constitutional issue. It is a political issue, a real and important one. It may be stated this way: Will the general welfare be promoted by including parochial-school pupils in a national program of education, or will it be promoted by leaving them out?

In 1961 five and a half million children received education in Catholic elementary and secondary schools. That is a little more than an eighth of all schoolchildren in these categories. If the Constitution does not require us to leave one eighth of our children out of a national program of education, why should we do so?

In the New Jersey bus case, the court said, "It [the state of New Jersey] cannot exclude individual Catholics, Lutherans, Mohammedans, Baptists, Jews, Methodists, Nonbelievers, Presbyterians or the members of any other faith, *because of their faith, or lack of it*, from receiving the benefits of public welfare legislation."

The children in schools supported by religious denominations should not be excluded because of their faith from the benefits of a national program of education. And we can hardly have a national program unless these children are involved in it.

Rep. James J. Delaney of New York has reintroduced a bill to authorize a two-year program of Federal aid to all elementary and secondary school-children in all the states. The bill provides that $20 shall be allotted annually to each pupil to defray part of the cost of his education. Pupils who did not record their intention or desire to attend a private school would be presumed to be destined for a public school, in which case the allotment would be paid to the public educational authority in their community.

This is a GI Bill of Rights for Children in elementary and secondary schools. Over a two-year period it would add $1.7 billion to the resources of these schools. Something more than $100 million a year would go to church-related schools.

Legislation of this sort would quiet the fears of those who are alarmed at the prospect of Federal control. It should calm those who believe that aid to church-related schools means the destruction of the public schools. It should satisfy everybody, except those who hold that a church-related school is the same thing as a church. They might say that legislation authorizing payment of $20 of taxes to a church school was the same as giving a citizen $20 of taxes to put in the plate on Sunday. They might argue that such payments were neither constitutionally possible nor politically wise.

But a school is not an assembly for worship. It does not perform ecclesiastical functions. Payments to a pupil for his education are not payments for the support of worship, of ecclesiastical functions or of the propagation of the faith. The object of education is the development of the mind. This may be conducted under religious auspices, but it is not the same as the development of religion or of the spiritual life. The Supreme Court would not have allowed New Jersey to pay for buses to carry worshipers to church.

A sensational shift in public opinion has been going on over the past two years on the subject of Federal aid to all schools. In March, 1961, the Gallup Poll showed that 57 percent of those interviewed thought Federal aid should go only to public schools; in February, 1963, only 44 percent of those polled were of this opinion. Apparently the common sense of the American people is winning over the pedantry of their leaders.

DISCUSSION QUESTIONS

1. Do you agree with Hutchins that federal aid to parochial schools is a political rather than a constitutional issue revolving around the question of whether or not it is in the national interest to render the independent school such aid? What is the basic constitutional issue, if any?
2. Discuss Hutchins' statement, "the development of the mind may be conducted under religious auspices, but it is not the same as the development of religion or of the spiritual life."
3. What would be the effect of the $100 million a year available to church-related schools under the Delaney bill?

TRACY EARLY The School Aid Question

The American Jewish community is engaged in a major reassessment of its position on government aid to religious schools. In the past, Catholics trying to get aid for parochial schools met almost unanimous op-

Reprinted from *The Catholic World*, June 1971, with permission of the publisher, The Paulist Fathers.

position from Jews. Now they find a considerable segment of the Jewish community allied with them, and others beginning to move in that direction.

The most notable indication of the change appeared this past January when Rabbi Harold I. Saperstein delivered his presidential address to the annual meeting of the New York Board of Rabbis. Billing itself as "the world's largest representative rabbinic body" serving "the world's largest Jewish community," the Board embraces all three branches of Judaism—Orthodox, Conservative, and Reform.

"I believe that the time has come for a reevaluation of our position," said Rabbi Saperstein, leader of a Reform synagogue in suburban Lynbrook, Long Island. "There is need for an intensified search for means by which a measure of aid can be given within the framework of our Constitution and without violating the principle of separation."

Not all Jews agreed with Rabbi Saperstein, and a number of Jewish organizations immediately declared their continuing opposition to government aid. But although the address did not constitute an official policy change of the New York Board, it was something more than just one rabbi's personal opinion. He had discussed the idea with several Board officials and found sufficient support to go ahead with his proposal for restudying. On the day following his address, furthermore, the Synagogue Council of America, which represents all three branches of Judaism on a national basis, called for a conference of its constituent groups to "reassess our present stand," an indication that the mood is widespread.

In an interview, Rabbi Saperstein listed among the immediate reasons for the changing attitude the intensified financial crisis confronting parochial schools. Where the Jewish community was not particularly impressed with Catholic complaints that maintaining their schools was burdensome, the prospect of the parochial school system being destroyed by financial pressure is something else.

He also noted that the critical needs of the nation make it necessary for Jews to support quality education for every child, whether in public school or parochial, a point echoed by Rabbi Marc Tanenbaum, interreligious affairs director for the American Jewish Committee. "For the sake of its future our country needs all its brains," says Rabbi Tanenbaum, a Conservative. "It is ethically callous, almost suicidal, to be indifferent to what is happening to the millions of kids in religious schools." Another reason for the changing attitude, Rabbi Tanenbaum observes, is the new ecumenical climate that has developed since Vatican II and its historic declaration on the Jews.

On the basis of past experience, Jews had seen the Catholic Church as a threat to religious liberty. For the state then to use tax money to support Catholic institutions would mean Jews were compelled to finance the enemy, with the possibility that it would become oppressive in the United States as it had been in Europe. Now that the Catholic Church has taken a more positive attitude toward Judaism as a living faith, says Rabbi Tanenbaum, and "the bugaboo of the threat to religious liberty is no longer a salient factor," that feeling has subsided.

In the changed atmosphere, some Jewish officials are saying, Catholics and Jews can be of help to each other with their special problems. As Jews look to their Catholic friends for support on such matters as the security of Israel, says Dr. Joseph Lichten, national director of intercultural affairs for the Anti-Defamation League of B'nai B'rith, so Jews are concerned when Catholics face a special problem like the financing of their schools.

The battle is shifting to another front. Where Jews, as members of a minority religion, were afraid of one religious body coming to dominate, says Rabbi Saperstein, the battle now is one of all religious forces against the indifference of a culture that tends to ignore religious values. In that fight, Judaism and the Church are allies.

Parallel to the new view of where the point of conflict lies is a rethinking in the Jewish community about its own need for religious schools. In his address calling for a restudy of school aid, Rabbi Saperstein discussed a number of other issues. Among them was intermarriage, which he said "threatens to undermine the very future of the Jewish community," and another was maintaining the loyalty of Jewish youth. "We must be frank in admitting that the best of them are in large measure being lost," he said. In response to both issues he called for greater emphasis on Jewish education, a point especially notable coming from a Reform rabbi since the Reform group has tended to accent integration into American society.

Orthodox Jews, on the other hand, have stressed maintenance of the traditional patterns of Jewish life, and in furtherance of that goal have been operating an extensive and growing system of day schools for some time. That experience has made the Orthodox community aware that the operation of schools on anything like an acceptable standard is extremely difficult without government help.

Some Jewish opponents of aid express support for the idea of day schools but insist the Jewish community should finance them without government assistance. "The Jewish federations and welfare agencies should put Jewish education near the top of their priorities rather than near the bottom," says Rabbi Ronald Sobel of the Reform Temple Emmanu-El on New York's Fifth Avenue. "The Hebrew day schools could be adequately supported if they were given one tenth of what is spent on lavish bar mitzvahs," says Rabbi E. E. Klein of the Stephen Wise Free Synagogue, a Reform congregation on New York's West Side. Whatever the theoretical validity of such remarks, however, those Jews actually operating the schools find that the Jewish community is not in fact providing adequate support. So they have been campaigning for government financing of the nonreligious part of their program.

The impression that Jews were virtually unanimous on the subject of aid to religious schools has been misleading for several years now. "We deplore that an incorrect image has been foisted upon the American public of the Jewish position on this issue . . . stemming from statements by certain secularist Jewish leaders and Reform clergy," said Rabbi Morris Sherer of Agudath Israel, an Orthodox organization, in an appearance before a House Education and Labor subcommittee in 1961. He has since been working in alliance—"discreetly," he says—with Catholic officials for both state and federal aid. He notes, however, that their positions differ on one point: Orthodox Jews are not saying they will close their schools if they do not get aid; they are determined to continue and it is just a matter of what quality of education they can offer in secular subjects.

"I was the first Jew to testify for federal aid to religious schools," Rabbi Sherer recalls. "We had just been struggling along and not doing much to get aid, but when a new federal program was being planned, we realized we would have to get aid too if we were going to keep up with the public schools." When federal aid became a reality in 1965, two Orthodox bodies—the Union of Orthodox Jewish Congregations of America and the Rabbinical Council of America—withdrew from the more or less united Jewish front against government aid.

As passed, the federal aid program allows religious schools to get funds for such things as Head Start and remedial reading, and the Hebrew day schools have participated in many of those activities. In New York they also get some state funds through programs that help religious schools in matters such as bus transportation, textbooks, and the maintainence of administrative records required by the state.

A noteworthy point is that whereas opponents of government aid often warn of the dangers of government control, the people actually operating the schools have no such fear. "The least of our problems," says Rabbi Sherer. And Dr. Alfred L. Schnell, an educational consultant to Torah Umesorah, the Hebrew Day School Association, reports that government officials have always been cooperative in allowing for the special requirements of their schools.

The increase in Jewish support for the principle of government aid has notably paralleled the increase in day schools. Though New York had a Hebrew day school as early as 1730, the growth of the system did not really get underway until after World War II. Torah Umesorah, which represents only Orthodox schools, reported a total of 378 schools with 75,000 pupils in the United States last year. That was an increase from 323 schools and 63,500 pupils in 1965, and 49 schools with 10,000 pupils in 1945.

Conservative Jews did not begin establishing schools, called Solomon

Schechter Day Schools after a distinguished Conservative educator, until 1965. But they now have thirty-four schools, with four or five more scheduled to open next September. Though the Conservative organization—United Synagogue of America—still opposes government aid, important voices within the Conservative group favor a change.

Reform Jews have not yet begun establishing schools. But the subject was among the topics discussed at the last biennial meeting of their national body, the Union of American Hebrew Congregations.

A change in Conservative and Reform thinking would be especially important for the public debate because their traditional opposition to government aid has meant the opposition of the Jewish public affairs organizations, which they have generally dominated.

The American Jewish Congress—regarded as an "extremist group" by Rabbi Sherer, as he would perhaps be regarded by the AJC—has been a center of resistance to any breach in the wall of separation between church and state. Advocating a strict interpretation of the First Amendment, it continues to fight even those forms of federal and state aid that have already established. When Rabbi Sherer appeared before the Congressional subcommittee in 1961, the *New York Times* published excerpts from his remarks. But alongside them was the opposing statement that had been given to the subcommittee by Leo Pfeffer, then general counsel of the AJC and still serving the agency on a part-time basis. Representing the AJC, Mr. Pfeffer has been one of the most prominent courtroom opponents of government aid on legal and constitutional grounds. The AJC has also led in the work of the Committee for Public Education and Religious Liberty (PEARL), a coalition of twenty-nine organizations opposing moves in New York State to aid religious schools.

The American Jewish Committee, which promotes a philosophy of integration into American society, has likewise been opposed to aid, and its New York chapter is a member of PEARL. But the Committee is currently involved in an internal debate, Rabbi Tanenbaum reports, over whether it should not revise its position.

Rabbi Sherer dismisses much of the support for aid now coming from Reform and Conservative Jews as merely an attempt to be "with it" in a changing climate of opinion. Whether there is any truth in that or not, it is still necessary to ask why the climate has changed so that support for aid has become an acceptable position. Beyond the factors already mentioned and on a somewhat different plane, in some sense underlying the intangible shift of mood, is a growing disenchantment with the public school—and that perhaps nowhere more acute than in the New York area where the Jewish community is concentrated.

Jews have tended to be liberal in their political outlook, and liberals have viewed the free public school as the place where children of all races, religions, and economic levels would learn to live together according to the ideals of American democracy. For Jews who had suffered discrimination in other countries, the neutral stance of such public institutions was a welcome change. And on the more practical side, the public school was the means through which poor immigrant Jews qualified themselves for successful participation in American society.

Much of the opposition to government aid for religious schools is still phrased not so much in terms of the reluctance to support somebody else's religion—though that is not omitted—as in terms of what it will do to the public schools and the opportunities they represent for the poor. "We are confident that the voters of this state do not wish to punish the public schools by giving sorely needed funds to the private schools," says a statement issued by PEARL. "Nor do voters wish to weaken or destroy the public school system by encouraging the proliferation of private and parochial schools. . . ."

And always looming in the background is the issue of race. Joseph B. Robinson, successor to Mr. Pfeffer as counsel of the AJC, puts the question in terms of this dichotomy: "Should we accept the obligation to educate black underprivileged children? Or should we abandon the poor and simply rescue our own children from the educational hazards they are increasingly encountering in the cities—by removing them to suburban public schools or to urban non-public schools?"

If aid is given to private schools, opponents argue, the middle class will desert the public schools and they will then become nothing but a "dumping ground for the disadvantaged," with even less support than at present. The opponents often mention the efforts of some Southern whites to establish private schools as a way of avoiding integration. With rather strong feeling, Dr. Schnell and Rabbi Sherer deny that what they are doing is analogous to that. Hebrew day schools are restricted to Jews, and since few blacks are Jews, the schools have only an occasional black student. But the reasons for maintaining the schools are purely religious, they insist, and in no sense racist.

But anyway, idealistic talk about the public school teaching all groups how to live together in democratic harmony sounds rather hollow today. "I would have appreciated that in 1930 or 1940," says Rabbi Sherer, who received part of his own education in public schools, "but now the public schools have become havens of hostility." If they are abandoned, he adds, it will not be because of religious schools, but because of "inner decay."

In New York, at least in some sections, people who can afford it tend to feel that getting their children out of the public schools is not only desirable but mandatory. However liberal and idealistic, they reluctantly decide that private schools are essential if their children are to get high quality education in an atmosphere free from disruption, ethnic tensions, and even violence. And in New York the black-white tensions often become specifically black-Jewish tensions since Jews are predominant in the public school teaching and administrative staff.

That situation, together with various other factors, has led to some rethinking of American pluralism. What is the place of group identity within a democratic society? Not only Jews but also other groups are giving new thought to that question. Some Catholic liberals, for example, who formerly criticized church schools as divisive are now becoming more concerned about the possible effects of a government monopoly on education.

During the years when integration was the sacrosanct word for liberals, group identity was disparaged. But now when many blacks, as well as other minorities, are deciding they do not want to be homogenized into the rest of society, and in some cases prefer to have their own institutions under their own control, and, in particular, want schools that will pass on their distinctive ethnic culture, the whole question opens up again. In 1954, the Supreme Court decided that segregated schools for blacks were inherently inferior. But would any white liberal today dare to tell black militants that a school operated by blacks and for blacks is inherently inferior?

Among Jews a group self-consciousness somewhat like that of other minorities, but no doubt resulting more from the impact of the state of Israel, is growing. Many Jews are thinking maybe they should work a little less on integrating into American society and more on maintaining their Jewish culture. Like blacks demanding black studies, militant Jewish youth confront their elders with demands for more support of Jewish education. "I wouldn't like to see all Jews in religious schools," says Rabbi Saperstein, "but many leaders now think they are needed to train a committed religious elite that is essential for the future of the Jewish faith."

And if for Jews, who not for all groups? And if for the leaders, really why not for all if they so choose? And if this is desirable social policy, why should not the government make it economically possible for all who want it? For the first time the poor would have the choice the affluent have had all along of going to either a public or a religious school.

Since what ultimately is at stake is a decision about public education policy, continuing to bandy about the phrase "separation of church and state" seems to confuse thought rather than clarify it. Nobody in this country is arguing for a state church, so we might well put the phrase into retirement, at least for a time. The Jews who favor aid have not come to the point of saying that, however. In setting forth their position they always include an expression of their devotion to "separation of church and state," but just go on to argue that aid to religious schools does not violate it.

The question, however, is not how we should exegete the First

Amendment, and is not ultimately one that should be decided by the Supreme Court. Rather it is the public policy question of what a continuation and possible increase of separate schools for groups within the society will mean both for those groups and for the society as a whole. Do the religious communities want and need special schools through which to transmit their distinctive teachings and orientation? Or do they want their children to get their general education alongside children of other groups, with the religious teaching given through home, church, and synagogue?

Then, members of all groups must decide whether as citizens of the nation they want a society with perhaps a dozen or more competing school systems, dividing every community by religion and perhaps also by race, political ideology, and economic class. Apart from its social effects, is this educationally sound? The Jewish community has not reached a consensus on these questions. But while some Catholics are deciding the parochial school is not so essential as once was thought, many Jews are wondering if perhaps it is not more important than they had recognized.

DISCUSSION QUESTIONS

1. Should public funds be allocated to religious schools in order to perpetuate religious diversity in the United States?
2. Can the Constitution be stretched to give religious school aid without violating the principle of separation of church and state?
3. In your opinion, will aid to private schools of any kind, religious or secular, result in a weakening of education?
4. Can religion be taught after school hours or must it permeate the entire life of a school and home?

SHELDON PTASCHEVITCH STOFF ## How Can the Public Schools Manage Religious Issues?

The Supreme Court ruling against Bible-reading and recitation of the Lord's Prayer in public schools as part of required classroom exercises should cause educators and laymen to evaluate the relationship between religion and the public schools. This Supreme Court ruling is not anti-

Reprinted from *The Clearing House*, Vol. XXXVIII, No. 5 (January 1964), pp. 271–274, with permission of the publisher.

religious. It is consistent with the basic ideal of a separation of church and state so that both may flourish. It is consistent with past Supreme Court statements in the Zorach case: "We are a religious people whose institutions presuppose a Supreme Being. We guarantee the freedom to worship as one chooses. We make room for as wide a variety of beliefs and creeds as the spiritual needs of man deem necessary. . . . Government may not finance religious groups nor undertake religious instruction nor blend secular and sectarian educators, nor use secular institutions to force one or some religion on any person."[1]

What then should be the role of the public school in the area of religion? It would be wishful thinking to believe that the issue is now clearly resolved. The religious influence in the schools is far deeper than simply Bible-reading and the recitation of the Lord's Prayer. Basic moral and educational implications must be dealt with.

In many parts of our nation the Christmas season is heralded by emotional controversies regarding certain practices in the public schools. Religious issues become the subjects of heated debate during a period of time in which thoughts of good will are supposed to dominate. For many decades this season of the year has brought forth decorations, trees, crosses, plays, hymns, and nativity scenes for the Christmas celebration in our public schools. This outward display of religious observance quickly brings forth cries for the separation of church and state, and for the public disestablishment of religious favoritism. The results are tears, suspicion, discord, and no concrete solution.

With or without conflict or controversy, the situation is not being properly managed. The Constitutional view is further classified by the Supreme Court in *Zorach* v. *Clauson*: "The government must be neutral when it comes to competition between sects. It may not thrust any sect on any person. It may not make a religious observance compulsory. It may not coerce anyone to attend church, to observe a religious holiday, or to take religious instruction."[2]

The public schools, functioning with compulsory attendance laws in a pluralistic society, cannot justify any religious participation and ritual on public property. Religious services and celebrations should be conducted in the home, church, synagogue, or church-supported school. Religious observance should not enter into a pluralistic public forum supported by public funds.

On the other hand, such observances of Christmas celebration cannot often be completely removed from the schools without initiating strong public clamor. The public observance of Christmas has become firmly entrenched in much of our national culture, and many of the population expect its preservation.

[1] *Zorach* v. *Clauson*, 343 U.S. 306, 1952. Mr. Justice Douglas delivered the opinion of the Court.
[2] *Ibid.*

A dilemma? Partially, but a third alternative does exist that should satisfy the majority, conform to the Constitution, safeguard minorities, and strengthen the ability of the schools to perform a basic role of enriching and disseminating the culture and enabling the student to grow, mature, and broaden his horizons. Justice Douglas' statement that "We are a religious people" is completely supported by the U.S. Census (95 per cent of those polled classified themselves into one of our three major religious groupings),[3] by *The Catholic Digest* (95 per cent of those interviewed stated that religion was either very important or of medium importance to them),[4] and by statements by every President of the United States (as detailed by James Keller in *All God's Children*).[5] This religious facet of our lives cannot be ignored without distorting the world culture as it is presented in our schools. It is equally important to remember that it is not the function of the schools to indoctrinate religious dogma. We are historically a nation of many backgrounds and beliefs and we have thrived on this principle. The rights of the religious and the nonreligious should be respected.

The school cannnot and should not try to decide whether the religious need has an answer and, if it does, which one it must be. The school is only obliged, if it would inform its students, to remind them that men have made and lived out a variety of answers. . . .

No man can be regarded as informed, awakened, and free unless he has learned as much as he can about himself and about the examples of others like him in history. No man can call himself educated unless he knows what his religious potentialities are, no matter how unreal, foolish or otherwise objectionable he judges them.[6]

This statement by Professor Harper can be practically applied to our public school situation by assigning the education for a particular religious orientation to the home or church and encouraging the schools to perform the function which neither is performing. I am referring to teaching comparative religion in a specialized course of study. Through this democratic approach, in keeping with our nation's pluralistic and cultural heritages, the school would open students to a broader understanding of life rather than indoctrinate them with specific religious dogma or even force them into a general religious orientation.

The program presented here, to manage the controversy over religious practices in public education, is both practical and educational. It was developed after communication with religious leaders from each of the

[3] U.S. Bureau of the Census, *Current Population Reports*, Series No. 79 (Washington: Government Printing Office, 1958), p. 20.
[4] B. Gaffin and Associates, "Who Belongs to What Church," in *The Catholic Digest* (January, 1953), p. 5.
[5] James Keller, *All God's Children* (Garden City, New York: Hanover House, 1953), p. 237.
[6] Ralph Harper, "Significance of Existence and Recognition for Education," in *Modern Philosophies and Education*, N. Henry, ed. (Chicago, Illinois: The National Society for the Study of Education, 1955), p. 248.

six religions concerned. A sincere effort was made to meet their recommendations and also meet the general goals many desire for public education.[7] In the development of the program it was desirable to set goals which were compatible with the basic aims of the schools and the nation's Constitution. The goals are these:

1. A greater understanding of other people by the student.
2. A more mature development of the student.
   a. An enriching process for the student because of the broad spectrum of ideas explored.
   b. A more significant insight by the student into his own life, which could lead to a deeper character development.

The basic program is divided into two areas. The first (Part A) could be adopted by the schools immediately. It involves no great expense and would help resolve the pressing issues which have gained the most notoriety. The implementation of the second (Part B) involves the teacher training institutions cooperating with the schools in an attempt to meet their responsibilities in this vital area.

PART A. IMMEDIATE ACTION

The proposals in this phase center on the celebrations of religious holidays in the schools. Christmas is the most notable example. In our society, the schools cannot defend holding religious celebrations on public property. For the most part, Christmas observance cannot be eliminated from the schools without causing considerable public clamor. This total separation should not be attempted. Instead of promoting a religious view by one religious celebration, the schools should seriously consider the several major religious holy days of the world's great religions as resources for the dissemination of knowledge and understanding. The dogma, the ritual, the affirmation is to be avoided; the educational message is to be promoted.

The question which most quickly comes to mind is: "How do you accomplish this education without indoctrination?"

At this preliminary stage in the program I would suggest that a qualified social studies teacher make the presentation to a general assembly or lead a panel discussion in which the "why" of the holy day should be considered. As material becomes more available in the future, dramas could be added to this type of presentation.[8]

We need not have ritual at Christmas in the public schools, but the

---

[7] Approval on the part of these religious leaders for this program is not here suggested or rejected.

[8] Some sources of material are:

The National Conference of Christians and Jews, Inc. 43 West 57th Street, New York 19, New York.

message inherent in Christmas can be explored. The holy days of Hinduism, Judaism, Buddhism, and Islam could be explained and "respected" in their turns. If the emphasis is placed on promoting broad knowledge and understanding instead of narrow ritual, even the atheist cannot be offended.

A brief understanding of the world's religions is made possible without favoritism, by overcoming existing provincialism. The views of other local religions which are not already represented by the aforementioned should also be considered.

The schools would then have the power to outgrow localism. They could continue to fulfill their basic responsibility—education—in the full knowledge that people must learn to live with, and respect, their neighbors.

PART B. THE LONG-TERM SOLUTION

The proposal in this part centers on the role of the school. It is the job of the school and all structures of society to disseminate and enforce that which is beneficial in the culture. The school has responsibilities in the area of knowledge about religion that no other agency can render as well. In outgrowing a concentration on local practices, beliefs, and attitudes, the schools have deep obligations to meet.

Course Content

This proposal advocates that a specific course dealing with the religions of mankind be taught in the social studies area of our senior high schools. It would be taught by a specifically trained teacher. The prime content of the course would be concerned with the study of six major religions: Islam, Buddhism, Catholicism, Judaism, Protestantism, and Hinduism. In areas where other religions are present, they would also be explored.

The study of these religions should concern itself with:

A. History and leaders
B. Ethics
C. Rituals and customs
D. Present application

The material for each of the religions under discussion should be provided by or acceptable to the individual religions.

Buddhism: Dr. Kurt F. Liederker, 306 Caroline Street, Fredericksburg, Virginia; Washington Friends of Buddhism, Washington, D.C.
Islam: The Islamic Foundation of New York, One Riverside Drive, New York 23, New York: Diyanet Isleri Reisligi, Ankara, Turkey.
Hinduism: Ramakrishna-Vivekananda Society, 17 East 94th Street, New York, New York; Vedanta Society, 34 West 71st Street, New York, New York.
For Buddhism, Catholicism, Protestantism, Hinduism, Islam, Judaism: *Great Religions of Modern Man* (6 volumes), published by George Braziller, New York.

Religious Practices

No religious practices would enter into the curriculum. No religious dogmas would be inculcated. This course could develop a broad area of enlightenment and understanding. No one religion would be favored. No expression of faith would be asked of the student. There would be no worship or ritual. The separation of church and state would be maintained as constitutionally intended.

Role of the Teacher

The teacher would be sympathetic to each religion as it was studied. He would help his students gain a knowledge and appreciation of each. In the classroom he would not be a partisan supporter of any individual faith.

Teacher Training

The teacher should be specifically trained for this task. His training would be in the area of social studies, with a major concentration in the area of comparative religion. Specific knowledge of each of the religions would be included in this training program. The program offered by the Department of Religious Education of New York University could well provide a guide in this area.

CONCLUSION

The above proposal is both practical and far reaching. Interested persons could well take immediate steps toward action. Part A needs no elaborate preparation. Part B would require strong support in order to be executed. This program would help fill a void in present public school curricula. It is designed to present six of the world's great religions as a part of the total world's culture. Some will view this proposal as a program charged with risks. Most certainly some risk is involved. Most steps forward require daring, but the greatest risks are those of inaction. Ignorance should not be preferred to an honest, careful attempt at understanding.

The Supreme Court decision of June 17, 1963, may yet awaken educators and the general public to this serious void existing in much of the American educational system.

DISCUSSION QUESTIONS

1. What is the difference between teaching religion and teaching about religion?
2. What difficulties do you perceive in Stoff's recommendations?
3. What benefits?
4. Do you agree with Stoff that "the greater risks are those of inaction"?
5. Do the schools have any obligations to religion? To the religious?
6. What course of action do you recommend for the schools to take in providing for religion and education?

Education Is Always Religious

> *From the first, education was the American religion.*
> *It was and is—in education that we put our faith:*
> *it is our schools and colleges that are the peculiar*
> *objects of public largesse and private benefaction;*
> *even in architecture we proclaim our devotion,*
> *building schools like cathedrals.*

. . .

> *In a personal statement, written in 1930, John*
> *Dewey said philosophy should "focus about*
> *education as the supreme human interest in which,*
> *moreover, other problems, cosmological, moral,*
> *logical, come to a head."*
>
> Henry Steele Commager

> *If we have any ground to be religious about*
> *anything, we may take education religiously.*
>
> John Dewey

> *The essence of education is that it be religious.*
>
> Alfred North Whitehead

Everyone knows that plants turn their leaves and flowers toward the sun, from its rising to its setting. Men only seem to be less heliotropic. The sun is the great fact of cosmic weather for mankind. When we awaken we want to know: where is the sun? One might even say, *how* is the sun? Is it full and warm, or pale and distant? Will it rule the day, or be overlaid and withdrawn from us? Weather from the cosmos is the background of all our living. Though we may forget it later in the day when lesser questions temporarily preoccupy us, we come back to it in many moments. The sun sets the tone of our earth-experience.

What the sun and the sun-filled atmosphere are to our feeling for each day, some conception of divine or ideal being is to our feeling for life as a whole. We can forego the latter as little as the former. We are quite as heliocentric with regard to it. No man gladly takes hold of life until he senses that his existence is lighted and warmed by spiritual sunlight. The heart always asks after the inward weather and the inward weather is always ruled by an ideal sun: that highest value which gives meaning to existence and which blesses it to fruitfulness. It is the value which makes life livable by making lovable what it touches.

This comparison of inner to outer sunlight may help to illustrate what is meant when one maintains, as we do, that mankind is religious *sui generis:* is inveterately and inalienably religious: is religious as the

Reprinted from "Towards a Truly Public Education: A Philosophy of Independence for Schools," *Proceedings No. 18*, The Myrin Institute, Inc. for Adult Education.

growth of a plant is always heliotropic, or the orbit of a planet is always heliocentric.

Men delude themselves with sophistries when they imagine that they have dispensed with religion. As long as they remain men they will never cease to draw from above and beyond themselves their enthusiasm for living, their power to improve life, their strength and guidance for moral decisions. Men may have different theories about the nature of the sun they see, and these differences may lead to fairly important consequences in action; but sun they will and must see. Dethrone one sun and another rises to take its place by the force of the whole depth of human nature. Behind all the imperfectly visualized suns shines the primordial sun-power itself. Destroy this objective power in the man and you destroy the man fundamentally.

It is possible for an observer on earth to mistake a firefly for a comet, an airplane light for a planet, or a planet for a star. But what is sought and felt, even in mistaken judgments, is still part of the true seeking and feeling, which are matched by truth somewhere. Sunlight shines through diffusely to the seaweeds below the surface of the ocean. Mushrooms are not organized to make the most of light. But even seaweed and mushrooms live toward the sun.

"The sun shines into the eye of an adult, but into the eye and heart of a child," said Emerson. If the grown man needs the sun of the ideal to bring for his best and deepest, a child is still more dependent. He is more open, more all-one in his devotion.

The child's very existence is trust, hope and belief. He confides himself trustingly to the world because he naturally believes the best of it. He still sees the world in God. People and things are for him still radiant with the invisible light. They yet bear the signature of the divine. They seem as newly coined as he himself from the *fons et origo* of being.

Of course, the religious feeling which is the ground-tone of every normal child's attitude does not direct itself toward abstractions. It is his actual environment that excites the child's wonder. It is his actual father, mother and teacher whose hand he takes in loving trust. He sees the ideal *in* people and things, and *as* people and things, and will not begin to conceive it apart from these until childhood ends. Then the actual will sink to a more prosaic level of reality and the ideal will be sublimated from it. His instinctive love of persons will transform itself into the conscious love of ideal reality: of truth, beauty and goodness as such; the second form of love being strong in proportion to the first.

Grownups need to live with religious awareness, aspiration and discipline, but children need religion still more. If we see this clearly, we are ready to perceive a fundamental truth about education and the institutions of education which are the focus of every modern child's existence from the age of four or five to sixteen or eighteen and beyond. We can perceive that we have been on the wrong track in imagining that a school can ever exclude religion from its teaching. Every school that satisfies children is religious. Through curriculum, methods and attitudes it cultivates a religious life.[1]

We should not let ourselves be deceived by the fact that public schools are supposed to be neutral about religion. Neutral they are not. By the necessity of the nature which pulsates and breathes in pupils, teachers, and parents as human beings, every school fosters some form of devotion. The religion that inspires a public school, despite the neutrality taboo, will be one of the traditional faiths, or a crusading zeal for social reform, or some other holy cause.

American public schools are divided chiefly between those which are still rooted in the Protestant Christian impulse that quite consciously and acceptably motivated most of them a century ago, and those which, pressed by changes in the population they serve, have substituted for this religion a new one. The new ideal is generally society-centered; the new faith is called Democracy. It might also be called The American Way of Life. This faith has its hierarchy of power, its credo, its hymn-singing, ceremonies and ritual. It has been brought forward (always with the close support of science, a second sacred cause) to satisfy seeking hearts. Citizenship in the democratic society is increasingly represented as the goal of life. Studies need focus and the preparation for life needs an incentive. These are being found in the earthly paradise which men hope to create.

We have said, then, that education is always religious, in the public school as in a church school. And we have said that the religion which is now coming to the fore with ever-increasing strength in public schools, the sun around which school life is ordered and toward which all eyes are again and again directed with religious feeling, is that of the Ideal.

Society is commonly thought of as a socialized form of democracy in the industrial American image. That these two characterizations are not without support may be seen in the following quotations.

Why should we longer suffer from deficiency of religion? We have discovered our lack: let us set the machinery in motion which will supply it. We have mastered the elements of physical well-being; we can make light and heat to order, and can command the means of transportation. Let us now put a similar energy, good will, and thoughtfulness into the control of the things of the spiritual life. Having got so far as to search for proper machinery, the next

[1] Looking at the matter from quite another point of view I stated the conviction in an earlier article on *Religion and Science in the Waldorf School* that "the religious life cannot be successfully developed by the family and church alone, apart from the school. The time to learn *how* to view the creation as God's handiwork is when created things are being studied for the first time. This occurs in school. Every fact will then speak from its beauty and immediacy the language of God—or none will. And if the school has presented the detail of Nature materialistically, it may be beyond the power of pastor or parents thereafter to bring Deity into a fully credible relationship with the natural order."

step is easy. Education is the modern universal purveyor, and upon the schools shall rest the responsibility for seeing to it that we recover our threatened religious heritage.

. . .

So far as education is concerned, those who believe in religion as a natural expression of human experience must devote themselves to the development of the ideas of life which lie implicit in our still new science and our still newer democracy . . . In performing this service, it is their business to do what they can to prevent all public educational agencies from being employed in ways which inevitably impede the recognition of the spiritual import of science and of democracy, and hence of that type of religion which will be the fine flower of the modern spirit's achievement.

If one inquires why the American tradition is so strong against any connection of State and Church, why it dreads even the rudiments of religious teaching in state-maintained schools, the immediate and superficial answer is not far to seek . . . The cause lay largely in the diversity and vitality of the various denominations . . . But there was a deeper and by no means wholly unconscious influence at work. The United States became a nation late enough in the history of the world to profit by the growth of that modern (although Greek) thing—the state consciousness.

John Dewey

Doubtless many of our ancestors would have been somewhat shocked to realize the full logic of their own attitude with respect to the subordination of churches to the state (falsely termed the *separation* of Church and State): but the state idea was inherently of such vitality and constructive force as to carry the practical result, with or without conscious perception of its philosophy.

. . .

In such a dim, blind, but effective way the American people is conscious that its schools serve best the cause of religion in serving the cause of social unification; and that under certain conditions schools are more religious in substance and in promise without any of the conventional badges and machinery of religious instruction than they could be in cultivating these forms at the expense of a state-consciousness.

John Dewey

Democracy, therefore, is not limited to political, governmental, or economic arrangements. It is a personal, school and civilization ideal . . . Democracy, reconceived, is that quality of experience which pervades social life, and in so doing contributes to the attainment of the fullest possible growth of all toward qualitative ideals. So defined, democracy is a conception about an esthetic-religious affair.

Democratic public education is that form of education which provides this sort of religious experience . . . This esthetic-social objective is one of developing competence in shared qualitative and theoretical intelligence that will enable men to move toward the religious ideal that is democracy.

Francis T. Villemain and Nathaniel L. Champlin
writing on behalf of Dewey's educational philosophy in *The Antioch Review*, Fall, 1959

As long as the assumed neutrality of the public schools toward religion masked the situation, one could not see that education is always religious. And one could not go on to draw the inevitable conclusion as regards the proper relation of schools to the state. But the religious nature of public schools is slowly coming at last to be recognized by more and more people who are thoughtful and close to the realities of education. And the time is coming when we shall have to draw conclusions from our observations.

My own conclusion may be expressed as a syllogism:

A. *The state must be neutral with respect to religious institutions.*

The First Amendment to the Constitution of the United States has laid down this true and necessary principle: "Congress shall make no law respecting an establishment of religion. . . ."

B. *Schools are religious institutions.*

An education that is not decisively religious is neither serious nor effective. On the other hand, a religious attitude toward life which tries to establish itself only through the influence of church and home, leaving the school out of account, will either fail or will create within the mind, the heart and the will of children a most painful schism. For the sake of education we need religion and for the sake of religion we need education: the two are fundamentally inseparable.

C. *Therefore, the state must become neutral with respect to the support and control of schools.*

Since all serious educational institutions are at the same time religious institutions, the spirit of the First Amendment requires us to realize that the state power must keep hands off the schools as it does the churches. The state schools must eventually—of course by due process, by many small steps, and, as a matter of harmonious evolution—be "disestablished" as state churches have been.

The situation that should arise with regard to schools need not by any means by exactly analogous to the present situation of churches in our culture. But, improbable as it may sound to our ears at the moment, the state school as an ideal must be progressively supplanted by the ideal of full independence for all schools.

DISCUSSION QUESTIONS

1. Does Gardner's description of democracy as a religion stand up in America today?
2. Gandhi believed that religion is an individual experience bringing one face to face with reality. Does Gardner share this concept?
3. What implications do you see for the schools in Gardner's belief in the interrelationship between religion and education?

CHAPTER 5 The Financing of Education

The history of federal aid to education predates the Constitution. Yet, ever since the inception of such aid, it has been received in an atmosphere of distrust and suspicion. Today, when federal assistance to education is viewed by many as a matter of the greatest national urgency, its propriety and legality are questioned in an atmosphere suggestive of a rural, isolated America of a time long passed.

From our own point of view, there is little need to document the tremendous inequalities of economic ability and well-being among the fifty states and in the educational subdivisions within the states. To the range in capacity to pay for education must be added an equally broad divergence in willingness to do so, so that the extent and quality of a child's education becomes a concomitant of the economic wealth and the dedication to education of his place of birth.

The proportionately enormous growth in the last few years in the federal effort to bring about some degree of equalization of educational opportunity for America's children merely highlights the magnitude of the task facing us. Our efforts and expenditures are still the proverbial drop in the bucket; if we mean for education to be successful we must commit to it the necessary national resources. We need to rethink through our priorities. Then the question whether states and localities should be permitted to spend on education what they wish to spend or can provide out of their own resources is seen in its proper perspective. In the national interest, we must balance the risks attendant upon massive federal intervention in education against the loss of immediacy of action and involvement that local control and financing are said to insure.

BERNARD BARD # Do We Really Care About Our Public Schools?

This is the age that has discovered early childhood education as the key to success in school. Yet 17 American states give no public funds to support kindergartens.

This is the age that has become shock-proof to teacher militancy, almost anesthetized to the impact of teacher walkouts (elsewhere). Yet the average starting salary for teachers, $5,940, is still less than police and firemen receive, $6,555 and $6,200, respectively, without having to go to college.

This has been called the "Education Age," with the inner workings of the schools amplified into the public consciousness with unprecedented volume.

And yet, last year witnessed a $1.5 million school standing empty in Grand Ledge, Mich., because voters three times rejected the budget necessary to staff it.

A money shortage at about the same time forced East St. Louis, Ill., to eliminate kindergarten classes; decided Oakland, Cal., school officials to halt painting of all schoolhouses; impelled Decatur, Ill., to drop 65 of its thousand teachers; and prompted 125 high school students in Oyster Bay, New York, to march three miles with a banner that said, "Give us the tools that we may build a 21st Century"—after taxpayers for the fifth time in four years turned down a high school bond issue to end split sessions.

In Champaign, Ill., last year teachers had to be paid in "scrip," which local banks agreed to cash on the assumption that eventually the school district would sell enough bonds to redeem the vouchers.

And Youngstown, Ohio, which closed all its schools for a month in an incident that captured national attention, took that dramatic step only after trying to maintain financial solvency by first abandoning all kindergarten classes, freezing all textbook purchases, and shutting down all extra-curricular activities. It didn't work.

The "crisis in American education" has by now become a cliché. All are calloused by the phrase, fatigued by the components: Inner-city schools, the litany goes, "fail" the poor. Suburban schools "bore" the middle class. Teachers must work by the light of the moon to see financial daylight. Taxpayers are in "rebellion." School expenses go up; innovations fall down. Teachers lack "imagination" and their administrators are "martinets."

Reprinted from the New York State Federation of Teachers *Teacher News*, November, 1970, with permission of the copyright owner, The United Teachers of New York State.

The "crisis in American education" is real, of course, and it has to do with money. Having said that, some chroniclers of the "crisis" seek to turn around the indictment and aim it at the American people. The people don't "care" about the schools, it is sometimes said, otherwise they would put their money where their mouthings about education are. They would pay teachers more than construction workers, instead of the other way round. They would take the guidance office out of the broom-closet. They would see to it that calculus was offered in all high schools, instead of only 40.3% as of last count (Dr. James Bryant Conant's). And they would insist on pre-school opportunities for all children from low-income families, instead of only a fortunate one out of three (the estimate of Wilbur Cohen, Former Secretary of Health, Education and Welfare).

Any broadside intended to excoriate the American public for "not caring" about the state of its schools, for not expending enough of its substance for public education, is probably off the main target.

If the people have been derelict, it is for tolerating a system of school finance that dooms the public education system to never-ending crisis.

The schools of this country—separated into 20,440 local schools dis-tricts—must lean for most of their support on the local property tax, and it is the weakest tax-strut of all. Where the assessed valuations of real estate remain static—and the incomes of people living in it nearly so—the schools are in trouble.

"I never saw so many old people helping one another up the polling place steps to go in and vote no," said a school official in Champaign, Ill., where voter resistance to a tax increase forced teacher salary pay-ments in scrip.

"Property taxes are exhausted," said Joel Cogen, assistant to the mayor of New Haven, Conn., "you can't raise them any more."

And the schools—threatened by financial strangulation and dependent on overburdened local property taxes—are perhaps the only agency of government that must put their operation to an annual popularity con-test, the budget vote. This means that taxpayers, without a voice on any other taxes, may take out all their tax resentments on school budgets. They do. Schools last year in the state of Washington took "the worst beating" in ten years in budget referendums, according to the Washing-ton Education Association.

The largest tax most people pay, federal income tax, is "progressive" (based on ability to pay) and is designed to pour an avalanche of dollars into the federal treasury during periods of economic growth and infla-tion. And the schools' proceeds from this tax are relatively minute.

Federal aid to elementary and secondary education this year is ex-pected to total no more than $4 billion, compared to about $80 billion for defense. The federal government today pays only about 8¢ of every dollar it costs to run the public schools, a figure which the most conservative among federal-aid reformers say ought to be at least doubled. Bolder critics, such as economist Leon Keyserling, say the federal contribution to public schools must be quintupled by 1977 if there is to be "a minimum nationwide standard" of "educational excellence."

"The very unequal distribution of economic and financial capabilities among regions and states, the fact that progress must be so much faster in some regions and states . . . and the immense relative advantages enjoyed by the federal government in the raising of revenues make it desirable that by 1977 the state and local share in the total $70.1 billion cost of public school education . . . be reduced to 61% or $42.8 billion," said Dr. Keyserling in a recent study for the American Federation of Teachers.

Governor Nelson A. Rockefeller has defined what he calls "an acute fiscal squeeze" confronting state and local efforts to finance education this way:

"Washington collected 64% of all tax revenues in the nation, while state governments collect only 19%, and local governments 17%. And the tax which is most responsive to economic growth, the personal income tax, is securely dominated by Washington, which collects 92.6% of all personal income taxes paid in this country.

"Contrast Washington's vast income-gathering power with the growing income needs at the other two levels of government. Between 1950 and 1966 federal domestic spending rose 142%. But in the same period, spending by state governments shot up 247% and local governments experienced a 245% increase.

"State and local governments are clearly in an acute fiscal squeeze, caught between higher expectations from their citizens and inadequate resources to meet these growing demands. The federal government, not deliberately, but nevertheless, decisively, accentuates this squeeze through its fiscal policies."

If the schools receive stingy treatment at the hands of the federal government, as many education analysts have charged, the treatment they receive at the local and state level is nothing short of chaotic. In some states, schools draw more than 2/3 of their funds from the state, while in others the figure is as low as 6%, according to Dr. James B. Conant, president emeritus of Harvard University and generally considered the nation's most influential critic of public education.

According to *School Management*, a magazine for education administrators, 1968–69 expenditures per pupil varied greatly. They ranged from a high of $682 per elementary pupil in the Middle Atlantic region (New York, New Jersey and Pennsylvania) to a low of $327 in the south–central states (Alabama, Mississippi, Tennessee and Kentucky). On the West Coast, the average teacher was earning $11,800 after 13 years on the job; in the southwest, he earned only $6,912 after 15 years.

Because of the fragmented American school system, and its crazy-quilt system of financing, the disparities among public schools are wide. What this means, in a nation so mobile that one of every five Americans moves every year, is that a child who receives a poor education in one state may wind up as a public ward in another state. One state's economies on education become another state's welfare payments, unemployment compensation, and crime rate.

Former U. S. Education Commissioner Harold Howe II pinpointed the price of educational Balkanization this way:

"Local control of education has given us some remarkably fine elementary and high schools. But it has also given us some abysmally bad ones. . . .

"Almost every school offers some kind of science instruction. But in many districts, local voters decide through their support for bond issues and levels of taxation whether the local high school will offer physics and biology as well as chemistry.

"They decide whether the school library, if there is one, will add new books every year, or whether it will have to make do with the Five-Foot Shelf donated by the mothers' auxiliary back in 1930. They determine whether the history teacher will have extra time to prepare for class or whether he will have to double as gym instructor. . . ."

Howe offered his remarks at a Governor's Conference on Education in New Jersey. He called for a stronger state role in education, even at the cost of diminished local control. "I do not believe that any locality should have the 'freedom' to impose a poor education on any of its children because of civic apathy," said Howe, "or out of the dangerous notion that the children of the poor must suffer because their fathers do not make a proportionate contribution to the public purse. Nor do I believe that any locality should be forced to short-change its children on education because it has not the tax base to assure them a minimum opportunity to develop their abilities."

But local tax bases are eroding, especially in the face of spiraling education costs that rise at a rate of about 10% a year. "Local taxes are at a peak, yet the budget gap is greater than ever," notes Edward J. Logue, president of the New York State Urban Development Corp. Chicago this year was expecting tax revenues to fall $48 million short of requirements for its 580,000 public school system, was threatening a cutback of 6,000 teachers from its current staff of 22,000. In Cincinnati, School Supt. Paul Miller said—after three defeats in three bids for higher school taxes— "Our backs are against the wall, there's no denying that."

Decades of cumulative financial neglect have caught up to schools— in big city and small town alike. When Chicago Schools Supt. James F. Redmond took office in 1966 he found a system of $19 million in the red. He accepted that deficit budget so that his teachers could have a raise. "There was no question but that they were entitled to it. But there were only vague references to sources of revenue to meet the commitment," said Redmond, whose prospects for relief are still ephemeral.

And in Vancouver, Wash., (enrollment only 16,000) the budget pinches just as tight. "We just cannot operate modern, forward-looking educational systems on archaic and woefully inadequate structures of fiscal support," said Supt. R. C. Bates.

The magazine *Education News* interviewed 746 school superintendents in the fall of 1968. The poverty they described is of a pattern that has blunted the sensibilities of a generation calloused by now to educational crisis. "Teacher desires for better pay will clash with a limited budget." "Statutes limit budgets to 4% increase. An increase to improve your education is *not* permitted!" "We lost out last referendum and had to dismiss 15 teachers to stay within our financial means." "We pay too little; there is poor housing, nothing to hold people in the community. This is a stepping stone for teachers."

The relation between money and education is direct. A study was made of graduates of Teachers College, Columbia University, to find out whether they were still in teaching; and if not, why not. Of 658 alumni polled, some 200 had left for better-paying fields (thereby increasing their pay an average of 25%). Virtually all those who abandoned the education profession were "mentally superior" to those who remained teachers.

In education—as in any other enterprise—the customer would appear to get what he pays for.

Every generalization ever made about the quality of life in the American school house might well be measured against the findings of that Columbia survey. The chief pediatrician for the Head Start program was forced to resign last spring after assailing the "deadening atmosphere" of regular school. Charles E. Silberman, head of a Carnegie Corp. study of American schools, says the schools destroy spontaneity and joy, the entire enterprise is marred by "mindlessness . . . nobody's encouraged to think about the purpose of his work, why he's doing what he does."

If those characterizations are harsh, they are no less damning than the observations of the U.S. Office of Education which has concluded its first assessment of the teaching profession, required under the Education Professions Development Act. It found:

No other profession has a higher dropout rate. Some 30% of those trained to teach never teach; of those who go into the profession, at least 60% call it quits after five years.

Teachers come, for the most part, from "middle-ranking" students in both ability and performance.

More than 80% of the nation's teachers are trained at colleges rated on "C" or "D" on the American Association of University Professors scale of faculty salaries. Fewer than 4% come from colleges with an "A" rating. While the cost of preparing dentists or physicians may range from $5,000 to $12,000 a year, teacher training averages less than $1,000 a student.

The profession is not getting its fair share of "the bright, the talented, the doers."

And, despite tons of literature on new educational technology and innovation, the profession still approaches children in the same old ways. "We know better," said Dr. Don Davies, associate commissioner in charge of the Bureau of Educational Personnel Development (which ran the assessment), "but we don't have personnel geared to perform otherwise, and we don't have the setting that lends itself to other approaches. What is in the literature cannot solve the problems of educating the disadvantaged. What is in the heads and hearts of education personnel can. Yet we haven't nearly enough school people with the kinds of attitudes that can make a difference."

If, as has been charged, there is not enough challenge and excitement in the classroom, the victims would appear to be the middle-income as well as the "disadvantaged."

A hundred 11th and 12th graders at Lake Oswego, Ore., High School spent six months studying and dissecting every facet of their school's operations—the role of the school board, the curriculum, the budget, the performance of individual teachers. They said in their summary:

"The students should be held more responsible for getting themselves to school and working towards goals. But before this will work, the schools will have to become more interesting. This means the schools will have to attract a greater number of teachers who can make classroom work interesting, understandable and challenging to students.

"We realize you would have to pay much higher salaries to attract the type of teacher we are talking about."

"And where does the money come from?" asked a parent at a public hearing on the students' evaluation in the school auditorium.

"Our committee believes some of the additional money for higher teacher salaries should come from the federal level," answered Anita Skralskis, a brunette with finely-chiseled features.

But the "federal level" is a very thin reed indeed in the field of education—notably so in the crucial pre-primary years. Early childhood education has come to be called "the educational Cinderella of the decade" because of the awesome research findings that demonstrate profound education growth is possible in the years before a child enrolls in school.

Benjamin Bloom of the University of Chicago has concluded that half of all growth in human intelligence takes place between birth and age four, another 30% between ages four and eight, and the balance between eight and seventeen. In other words, half a child's intellectual development takes place before the school ever sees him. These, and similar findings by other researchers, produced the thrust to bring the child into school much earlier, and so was born Head Start.

But the most recent statistics from the U. S. Office of Education (Oct.,

1968) show that of 12,242,000 children ages three to six, only 31.6% were in any kind of pre-primary program. Head Start accommodated only 218,000 in year-round programs, and an additional 475,000 three-to-five year olds were in other pre-school programs under Title I of the Elementary and Secondary Education Act. The balance were in kindergarten.

Millions found no place in kindergartens (or in Head Start) because of crowded facilities or long waiting lists. And, paradoxically, kindergarten attendance was most common among children from white-collar families (75.2%), lowest among farm families (46.3%). Those most likely to be in kindergarten were from families with incomes of $10,000 or more. The most deprived child, the one in greatest need of pre-school, was found to be the least likely to get such help.

Money again was at the root of the problem. As far as ESEA was concerned, "tens of thousands" of childen were left out of its programs, the Office of Education told Congress in a report on Title I's second year of operations, because in many communities the cash was spread too thin.

As for kindergarten, many states either regard it as a luxury item or just don't have the funds to help local school districts pay the bills. The roster of states that gave no kindergarten aid as of the fall of 1968 was: Alabama, Arizona, Arkansas, Georgia, Idaho, Kentucky, Mississippi, Montana, New Hampshire, New Mexico, North Carolina, North Dakota, Oklahoma, Oregon, South Carolina, Texas and West Virginia.

John Dunworth, dean of Teachers College at Ball State University, Muncie, Ind., reported, after a survey of kindergarten and nursery school programs for the Office of Education, "budget is always a factor." But he warned that communities (and presumably states as well) that refused to underwrite kindergartens had their priorities askew:

"Kindergarten," said Dunworth, "is one of the finest educational investments that can be made. In my judgment, any community that fails to provide kindergarten in its publicly supported educational system is shortchanging its citizens by denying thousands of children the opportunity for directed learning during one of the most formative years of their lives."

But the schools do, of course, shortchange the very young—as well as older children, and the teachers who serve them. They are all victims of a continuous austerity budget—even when the budget passes. Amid the reports of the critics, and the demands for sweeping change in U. S. education, the schools find they can't even spare the money on research to find out what they are doing right and what they are doing wrong. Dr. John M. Stalnaker, president of the National Merit Scholarship Corp., noted some years ago that "no activity involving so many people and so much money (the schools) has done so little to find out about itself, the nature of its raw material, the effectiveness of its processing and the quality of its finished product."

More recently, a group of top business leaders and educators said pretty much the same thing. The Research and Policy Committee of the Committee for Economic Development said only a tiny fraction of 1% of the nation's investment in education went for research, evaluation and innovation. "The schools suffer severely because of this neglect," said the CED. "No major industry would expect to progress satisfactorily unless it invested many times that amount in research and development."

It found schools and school systems were often handicapped by outmoded organization. Too many classrooms were overcrowded and too many schools understaffed, with pupils receiving little personal attention. Individualized instruction, said the group, is rare even for the handicapped or the gifted.

The 75-page report of the Committee for Economic Development drew prominent display in newspapers and professional journals. Yet, nothing really has changed. Take the word of Girard D. Hottleman, who recently told it as it presumably is, in *Today's Education*, published by the National Education Association. His report was titled "Our Curriculum Is As Solid as A Mausoleum."

Hottleman, the director of educational services for the Massachusetts Teachers Association, tells about "curriculum reform" as seen from the inside of most American school systems. Most school systems, he finds, manage to turn loose a handful of teachers over a summer for curriculum development. But there hardly ever is a year-round study committee to pinpoint curriculum weaknesses that exist, to make sure the summer committee is working on the right things, says Hottleman. Nor is a follow-up committee named in the fall to make sure the summer's work is implemented.

"Curriculum directors? . . . We've got one. In fact, he's a crackerjack. He's so good at his job that he can coordinate the entire school system and still have time to make out the school budget for the superintendent, arrange the school bus schedules, run the evening school program, and supervise all the principals That's pretty good when you consider that he never had any special training for all this, but by dint of many years of experience, he's gotten a good 'feel' for it."

Hottleman observes that industry spends between 20 and 30% of its income on research and development, employs "highly paid teams of men who do nothing but research, analyze, evaluate and modify" the product. Sarcastically, he adds, "what shocking waste! You'll be happy to know that none of this is true in education. We spend less than 1% of our budget on research and development.

"We don't fool around with expensive analysts, consultants, pilot studies, and all those other tax dodges. No sir. We've got a curriculum. It's basically the same as when we went to school and in many cases it's the same as when our mothers and fathers went to school."

It would seem that the educators and the educational researchers are trying to tell America something.

They are not asking whether we care about the public schools, for that is another way of asking whether we care about the children in them. And such a question, of course, would be insulting.

Presumably America cares about what happens in its schools. The questions would seem to be: Do we care enough to see to it that all children are treated equally—in their once-in-a-lifetime chance at a public education? Do we care enough to overhaul the grotesque and lopsided ways state governments and local school systems manage (and mismanage) school finance? And do we care enough to *demand* that the federal government—whose taxes we pay automatically, without a referendum—begin to repay some of its riches to the children of America?

Dr. Harold Taylor, former president of Sarah Lawrence College and co-founder of the National Committee for Support of the Public Schools, said America is cutting school budgets and holding down teachers' salaries even as it commits $70 to $90 billion to defense, seems willing to spend $10 billion to perfect supersonic travel, and watches television programs of men in space orbit and athletes who are paid $50 to $100 thousand a year.

The way we spend our money, he said, is the "arithmetic of commitment."

By this measure, America does not appear to take very seriously the education of the young. Not so far.

DISCUSSION QUESTIONS

1. What does it mean when teachers are low-paid and schools lack financial support?
2. If the statement is to be accepted that "the customer gets what he pays for," how would you assure adequate support for education?
3. How would you raise the quality of people entering teaching?
4. How would you commit people to the cause of education?

GENE I. MAEROFF School Districts:
Why They Are Inherently Unequal

Manhasset and East Meadow, two bedroom communities in suburban Nassau County, are separated by a mere 15-minute stretch of expressway, but the distance between what they spend on their children's education is measured in light years.

In Manhasset, the per pupil expenditure is $1,721; in East Meadow, the figure is $968. The difference is a function of the economics of the two, and of the manner in which they, as well as thousands of other communities across the nation, pay their school bills.

Manhasset and East Meadow are both school districts, among the 17,000 such administrative units responsible for operating America's public schools. For the most part, educational funds in the districts are raised by levying property taxes.

But East Meadow has no special tax base, while Manhasset boasts the famous, tax-yielding Miracle Mile row of luxury shops and specialty stores. Thus, Manhasset can spend nearly twice as much per pupil on a property tax rate only two-thirds that of East Meadow.

The system giving rise to such disparities has often been accused of being inequitable, most recently by a group of parents in Los Angeles County who went to court to change it. The Superior Court dismissed the suit on the ground that the parents lacked legal standing; but last week, the California Supreme Court reversed that finding and, in the process, raised the possibility that the nation's school-financing procedures may be in for some drastic changes.

For the court went beyond the ruling on legal standing to comment that California's method of financing public schools through property taxes "makes the quality of a child's education a function of the wealth of his parents and neighbors." And it appeared to leave no doubt that it considered the present system in violation of the equal protection clause of the 14th Amendment to the United States Constitution.

A verdict in favor of the parents' group in California would not, of course, be legally binding in other states. But it is expected to set a precedent for similar suits elsewhere. A measure of the importance of such a change is the fact that local property taxes, gathered by school districts, generate 51 per cent of the $42-billion spent annually on the nation's public elementary and secondary schools. (The states provide 43 per cent; the Federal Government, 6 per cent.)

At issue in the California case, as in the discrepancy between Manhasset and East Meadow, is the disparity in the value of taxable property among school districts. For example, the construction of a shopping center or a large factory on one or the other side of a street dividing two districts may determine the quality of the education received by the districts' children.

This is not to say that individual states, New York among them, do not attempt to inject a measure of equalization. In New York, for instance, the state's contributions to local school districts are based on a complicated formula that takes into account average daily attendance and the value of taxable property in each district. Every school district in New York gets at least $310 per child from the state, and the neediest districts can get as much as $860 per child.

But as Dr. James E. Allen Jr., a former New York Commissioner of

Education and later United States Commissioner of Education, points out: "There is still an enormous amount of discrimination in the amount of money behind each child in New York, as well as in other states." The California ruling, he says, was a "landmark" because equalization of educational opportunities is "virtually impossible" under the present patterns.

"There would be more equity for each child and for each taxpayer if the school funds were allocated to local districts from a central source," says Dr. R. L. Johns, director of the National Educational Finance Project, a Federally supported study being conducted from Gainesville, Fla. "Allocations from the central source wouldn't just be on a flat per pupil basis. There would have to be more money per child for each one who is physically handicapped or culturally disadvantaged because it is more expensive to educate such children.

"Equal funding would not mean equality. Some children need more money spent on them than others do in order to equalize educational opportunities."

Authorities such as Dr. Johns are careful to point out that the attitude of the California court, even if it were to become the law of the land, would not mean the end of the property tax. Their assumption is that it would be more fairly imposed and, presumably, would be collected and redistributed by the state, rather than by local governments.

Many questions would have to be answered, though, before a central authority could assume control over local property taxes—if, indeed, such a step ever wins the approval of the courts and/or the legislatures.

A redistribution of tax wealth so that more money could be spent on children in tax-poor districts would be one thing, but there would be a huge outcry if, suddenly, less money per child were available in the richer districts.

Also, it would have to be determined whether local school districts would retain the power to raise revenues on their own, aside from what they would receive from a central authority. And, if such power were retained, what would prevent the inequities from reappearing?

Finally, the problem of unequal wealth among the school districts of any given state cannot be dismissed without some attention to the similar problem that exists from state to state. New York's average expenditure per child is $1,370, while Mississippi's is $521. That, of course, would be a job for the Federal Government.

DISCUSSION QUESTIONS

1. Is it fair or reasonable that some communities are able to spend double the money of that spent by other communities on public education?
2. How would you resolve the matter of public support for education?

ANDREW H. MALCOLM Football Escapes
                   Philadelphia School Ax

When the financially hard-pressed Board of Education here announced
a range of serious spending cuts last May, including an end to 600 teaching jobs and all extracurricular activities this year, the statement was
met with a citywide chorus of cynical yawns.

It was, after all, the fourth consecutive year the board had warned of
financial disaster.

But when September came and the city suddenly realized these economies also meant the end of varsity football, the uproar rivaled the
screams of a Super Bowl crowd.

The threat to high school football touched off dozens of protest meetings, talk of a mass march and a lawsuit against the school board by
teen-age football players. But now, under the prodding of a mayoralty
candidate, Frank L. Rizzo, the Philadelphia Eagles have rushed in with
enough money to save the season, and football practice has begun.

Philadelphia's angry football fans seem placated. But the 600 teaching
jobs have not been restored and school officials still face a $30-million
budget gap.

"What this says," remarked Dr. Mark R. Shedd, the Philadelphia
school superintendent, "is that the people who make the noise have a
distorted sense of values."

The sometimes bizarre series of events began last May when the
board—faced with increased costs and staggering debt payments—drew
up what one member called "a baloney budget" of $360-million, al-
though it knew it would receive only $330-million in revenues and
needed $394-million just to maintain last year's level of operation.

Among the items slashed from the budget was $4.5-million for all
extracurricular activities, including $79,000 for varsity football. The rest
covered other sports, drama, art, music, school yearbooks and student
newspapers.

On Sept. 1, when football training was to begin, the coaches and 18
teams were physically barred from the fields and Philadelphia became
the first major city in the country to eliminate high school sports—at
least temporarily.

"My God," said one aroused parent, "they just can't do that." Similar
feelings were expressed throughout the city.

Bob Caesar, Lincoln High's football coach, asked, "When a student
gets to high school, are reading, writing and mathematics more important than extra curricular activities?"

The Philadelphia Federation of Teachers had already threatened a strike and had gone to court in an attempt to halt the cuts. Mayor James Tate said the school board should not have "a prevalence of stuffy people who are antisports."

On Sept. 3, Dr. Shedd told the school's 22,000 employes that the academic year would end four weeks early next May 24. The teachers' union urged the Mayor to remove any board member who failed to support a full sports program.

C. Carson Conrad, head of the President's Council on Physical Fitness, arrived in town, found the situation "deplorable" and vowed to do everything possible to help, short of providing money.

Then four football players and a cheerleader sought an injunction in United States District Court to halt the board's cutbacks. And Jack McKinney, a local college coach, reported: "Everywhere I travel, people are laughing at us. They can't believe this is happening."

Most speakers expressed concern over the possible effect of the cutback on the city's 285,000 public school students, 60 per cent of whom are black. The lack of activities would encourage drug use, dropout and juvenile gangs, contended the Public League Coaches Association, whose members each stood to lose up to $1,800 a year in supplementary income.

Sports, on the other hand, teach teen-agers leadership, team spirit, self-sacrifice and "the give-and-take of life," the coaches said.

Coach Caesar said that 94 per cent of the 2,000 seniors in varsity sport here last year stayed in school to graduate, and 57 per cent went on to college, many on athletic scholarships.

On Sept. 8, 500 persons attended a rally sponsored by parents, coaches, students, the Veterans of Foreign Wars and the Philadelphia Labor Committee, a Socialist group. The group decided to march downtown two days later.

MORE ECONOMIES URGED

But events were moving swiftly as the cuts became a political issue. Both mayoral candidates were on record as favoring restoration of all extracurricular activities.

Thacher Longstreth, the Republican candidate and a former football player at Princeton, said the schools could close even earlier in May to save money. He also suggested closing the city's Civil Defense Office, thus freeing those funds for sports.

Mr. Rizzo, the Democratic candidate and former police commissioner, demanded more economies by school officials. He was particularly angered by a $900 desk for Dr. Shedd.

According to current versions, on Sept. 7—two days before classes resumed—Mr. Rizzo telephoned Leonard Tose, the owner of the Philadelphia Eagles, who had donated $55,000 to the school system from the proceeds of the Aug. 16 game against the Buffalo Bills.

Mr. Rizzo asked Mr. Tose to donate another $24,000. At a news conference the next day, Mr. Tose produced a check and said: "Mr. Rizzo has told me $79,000 will get the kids back on the [football] field. Let's start the game!"

But the school board's acting president, the Rev. Henry H. Nichols, said that he would accept the money and restore all extracurricular activities, including football, only if Mr. Rizzo would guarantee that, if elected, he would provide whatever funds the schools needed to finish the full year. Mr. Rizzo agreed, providing he could audit the board's books first.

Mr. Longstreth agreed, too, and last Monday the board ratified the deal.

FIRST GAMES SEPT. 30

Football practice began after the next day's classes, two weeks later than usual. The first games were pushed back to Sept. 30.

For Central High's star halfback, Kenny Anderson, the decision to restore extracurricular activities had a special significance. He lives for football practice, he said, adding: "I love the game and I want to play it."

He has received feelers from a half a dozen colleges about a scholarship, which he says is the only way his family could afford higher education for their children.

For Dr. Shedd, the larger issue "is whether the urban schools will survive or not."

"I object," he said, "to people who get hysterical just because the great American pastime isn't going to happen here, but don't say a single word about the 600 teaching positions wiped out. It's a question of priorities."

He remained skeptical, too, of the entire football deal. "We are operating on the political promises of two mayoral candidates," he said, "and that's a lot of fluff. I want to see the color of the cash."

Another education official said:

"Even though campaign promises are tenuous, at least one of these guys will be mayor when our annual spring crisis comes up, and we'll have someone to go to. It's not money in the bank, but it's a lot more than we've had in the past."

DISCUSSION QUESTIONS

1. How important is football to public education?
2. Is the present method of funding public education rational, reasonable, and in the best interests of students and taxpayers?

EDNA LONIGAN # Federal Aid to Education

In the last session, Congress rejected two major programs for Federal "aid" to education—the Democratic proposal for general subsidies and the Republican compromise which was limited—at the start—to subsidies for school construction only.

Now the struggle has moved to the Congressional districts. The "educationists" want a more docile Congress. They will fight to re-elect the members who voted with the education lobby, and to defeat those who dared to vote against their wishes.

They know the next session of Congress may decide the issue for all time. They know that once a bill for Federal assistance passes Congress, it is never rescinded but rather grows and grows like a banyan tree.

One curious aspect of the voting on education aid in Congress is that members of Congress from the states which would have received the largest grants above their share of taxes were against the bills. The states which would have paid the largest amounts in taxes were most aggressive in support of the bills. Why?

The United States Chamber of Commerce has prepared a table, from United States Office of Education figures, listing the costs and benefits to each state of Federal funds for education. In 10 states the margin of Federal payments over taxes would exceed $2 million a year apiece. They are Virginia, North Carolina, South Carolina, Georgia, Alabama, Mississippi, Louisiana, Arkansas, Texas, and Tennessee. In these states 87 out of their 88 Representatives in Congress voted against the Federal funds for schools.

On the other hand, 17 states would have paid most of the bill for new Federal expenditures for schools, but 15 out of 17 of them voted for Federal aid. Only Ohio and Florida voted to hold down new expenditures.

One key to this curious lineup of votes is what might be called the "legislative interlock." Bills for Federal welfare spending in the states grant multiple powers. Some of these powers can be discovered by reading the bill at hand. Some can be discovered only by reading the fine print in quite separable bills in many diverse fields.

Legislative proposals for area redevelopment, community facilities, sewage control, juvenile delinquency, and revival of the Civilian Conservation Corps, all have these interlocking provisions. For example, area redevelopment bills amended the urban renewal acts, so that housing appropriations could be used for industrial construction as well as residential. Also, the dangerous provision for "back door financing," by which some Federal agencies print bonds and "sell" them to the Treas-

Reprinted from *Human Events*, Vol. XVII, No. 41 (October 13, 1960), with permission of the publisher.

ury, was ostensibly taken out of the bill, but it was, in fact, left in, because the Area Redevelopment Agency could use funds from urban renewal appropriations, which can still be raised by "back door" borrowing.

Earlier drafts of the area redevelopment bills openly permitted the Federal Government to move workers from their own communities to other cities or states for "retraining." But this would permit the Federal Government—as some of the earlier witnesses frankly admitted—to move Negroes from the South to other states. The idea was that whites and Negroes ought to be relocated until every community had a "fair share" of Negroes. This is like the ruling of the New York City Board of Education which compelled white children to go to schools distant from their homes so every school and classroom could have a "proper" mixture of Negro and white children.

Federal funds for school construction make it possible for the executive branch to rule that no money be paid to states unless their schools are forcibly integrated, according to the planners' new doctrines of "Constitutionality," and law enforcement with the use of Federal troops.

It is true that Representative Adam Clayton Powell tried to put such a provision into the legislative draft and was opposed by its supporters on the ground that it would kill the bill.

Does that mean that the planners in the executive branch do not intend to use school subsidies to enforce segregation or keep any other promise, to get mass votes? Not at all. It is simpler to impose reforms by executive ruling than by legislative consensus, and there is virtually no appeal from directives of the executive branch. Why put it in the law?

The states which stood up against the trend to Federal aid for schools were those in which the mass pressure groups, like CIO-PAC and NEA —are not strong. The states which voted—against their own self-interest —to subsidize the taxpayers of 33 other states, are those in which the mass pressure groups, which lead the fight for centralization, are strongest.

Now the appeal has been transferred from the old Congress to the new one. Every effort will be made to defeat the "reactionaries." We shall hear more of the little tots who have no seats in the classroom. The truth is that state and local boards of education have built new classrooms for ten million students and replaced obsolete classrooms seating another four million. The war-stimulated increase in population passed its peak in 1955, and the picture is getting constantly brighter, because local school construction remains high.

The real issue is this—Federal funds mean Federal control. The centralizers intend to control American education and American children. City fathers and boards of education are to be tempted by "aid" for school construction. Teachers will hear the siren promise of higher salaries. Administrators will be promised more funds for administration and services. Of course nothing is said about the tax bite which will be necessary to pay for all this—when the bills are rendered.

The NEA and their friends will say they do not want Federal control. But no Federal official may pay out Federal money unless he knows the money will be used for the purposes stated in the law. With Federal money go the Federal auditor, the Federal advisor committee, the Federal requirement for "approved plans" before a penny is allotted, and the skill of the Federal bureaucrats in conveying to state and local officials how foolish it is to bite the hand that feeds you. People who say Federal "aid" will not mean Federal control are either not very honest or not very bright.

The "educationists" have told us frankly what the trouble is. We have in this country some 20,000 local boards of education, under citizen control, the fruit of our deep-rooted belief that government, where necessary, should be as close to the people as possible. But it is difficult business for the educationists in Washington to control 20,000 citizen groups scattered over the whole United States. Such independent bodies can delay, obstruct, or openly oppose plans to make all our schools into one monolithic system managed by control panels, with push-buttons hidden deep in the Federal bureaucracy.

Myron W. Leiberman, in "The Future of Public Education," has frankly explained why 20,000 boards of education are anathema to the planners. School boards cater to parents and taxpayers. You know, of course, if you have been reading educational literature, that the influence of parents and taxpayers over American children and their schooling must be ended.

Once the camel's nose is in the tent, we can predict the rest. Ten to fifteen billion a year, higher teachers' salaries, higher expenses for buildings, services, overhead. The 20,000 school systems will turn to Washington, first for money, then for "standards." The educationists will know how to coordinate them into one monolithic system. They will feel the irresistible pull to identical content, professional standards, buildings, supervision.

How will the protesting parent, the dissenting teacher, or the local parent, express his disagreement? He won't. That is the point. Federal "aid" is Federal politicalization of education, but a politicalization in which only the opinions of the "managers" will be heard. The notion that dissent is a healthy safeguard will pass from memory. The 20,000 local boards of education will probably be kept as exhibits of "democracy," but they will be shorn of their only strength, the power of the purse.

Do we want a monolithic educational system in the United States, even if it is a good one? Do we want a monolithic system following the blueprints of the NEA, the AFL-CIO, and their allies, with left-wing doctrinaire "intellectuals" at the control panels? The fight is the same whether it is waged over relief, social insurance, health, farm aid, or education. Only the simple-minded can believe Federal "aid" to education will be "different."

Behind the curious division in Congress over Federal subsidies for schools, we can see, then, the hardening of the lines between the collectivists who already occupy so many of the positions of power in American life and the Constitutionalists who believe in local self-government, self-help, and the power to dissent from orders from Washington.

The states which voted against Federal school grants, though they would have gained millions of dollars a year, were voting against the forces bringing all our local agencies into the Federal monolith with its simple control panels at the center.

The states which voted for Federal aid, though they would pay for the subsidies for 33 other states, voted to carry us further along the road to the Federal monolith in which education and all the other responsibilities of states and local governments are collectivized.

Each of the separate welfare programs has its own mass pressure groups to urge its cause. But in the contests for Congress, all these groups interlock, in the congressional districts, to elect their friends and to punish their enemies.

The NEA, the CIO-PAC, the ADA, and the rest, will work as one coordinated whole. They will bring all their influence to bear on the ballot box. Will conservatives work as hard to defend Constitutional government and to reward the men who have defended it for them?

DISCUSSION QUESTIONS

1. Do you agree with Lonigan that "People who say Federal 'aid' will not mean Federal control are either not very honest or not very bright"?
2. Does federal aid result inevitably in "politicalization of education," as Lonigan charges?
3. Are independent local school boards sounding boards for the resolution of disagreements and dissent for parent and for teacher, as Lonigan states?
4. Is it possible to have, at the same time, local control of education and equalization of educational opportunity?

HENRY M. LEVIN The Failure
of the Public Schools
and the Free Market Remedy

The American public schools have been severely criticized in recent years, and no schools more so than those responsible for educating "disadvantaged children" in urban areas. The utter failure of traditional

Reprinted from *The Urban Review*, Vol. II, No. 7 (June 1968), pp. 32–37, with permission of the publisher, the Center for Urban Education.

schooling to impart even basic reading skills to substantial numbers of youngsters has stimulated a barrage of proposals, from educators and noneducators alike, to change the educational system.

While some critics suggest that changes within the present structure would cure the impotence of the inner-city schools, others see a necessity for much more radical changes in the structure itself. Among the former group are proponents of new instructional techniques and remedial programs, while some of the latter group would turn over the schools to the community and others would dismantle the present system of public schools altogether, replacing them with private schools that would be—in part—publicly financed.

The aim of this article is to explore those proposals which would replace the public schools with a free market strategy for elementary and secondary schooling. The discussion will be based upon the assumption that basic education yields two types of benefits—those to the student (private benefits) and those to society-at-large (social benefits)—and that any proposal for educational change should be judged on the basis of both criteria. My analysis suggests that the free market approach is likely to increase the private returns of schooling, but that these gains would be largely offset by social costs higher than those received from the present schools or other feasible alternatives. Accordingly, I shall construct a balance sheet that will present both the losses and the gains inherent in replacing our present system with a market scheme. Finally, I shall outline several plans that would implement competition among schools without a framework that might foster both the private and the social goals of education.

Whatever the causes, wherever the blame may be, it seems clear that the traditional public schools are failing to meet the needs and the expectations of vast numbers of their clientele.[1]

In the light of their records of failure in educating the disadvantaged, how is it that these institutions have survived? How is it that even when schools do try to adapt to the educational needs of the poor, the major efforts are so limited and unimaginative?

For example, most efforts at compensatory education place principal emphasis on the largely conventional approaches of reduced class size and the addition of specialized remedial services. In the first instance, a typical reduction in class size from 30 students to 20 is very expensive (increasing per pupil expenditure about one-third); yet its effectiveness has yet to be shown in improving educational outcomes for disadvantaged children. On the other hand, remedial services are likely to be helpful to a few individual students, but they are not capable of improving a situation which calls for massive efforts, not minor repairs.

[1] A terse, but skillful, description of the "organizational sclerosis" that characterizes the slum schools is found in Christopher Jencks, "Is the Public School Obsolete?" *The Public Interest*, winter 1966, pp. 18–28.

In the main, the continued existence of these schools derives from the fact that they do not have to be effective to survive. In most cases they perform for a captive audience. Pupils are assigned to them for better or for worse, and each school can retain most of its students because the majority of pupils have no other alternatives.

A MARKET FOR SCHOOLING

The proponents of the market approach believe that by giving students and their families a choice of schools, and by requiring schools to compete for students, massive increases in educational effectiveness and output would result. For, if schools had to compete for students, they would likely be much more responsive to the particular needs of their clientele. That is, the private schools—in order to achieve goals of profit, or in the case of nonprofit ones, capacity enrollments—must provide what appears to be good schooling in order to attract students.

The father of this approach is the Chicago economist, Milton Friedman, and it is Friedman's basic scheme that dominates the proposals of others who would also replace the public schools with a market of choices.[2] Before outlining the Friedman plan, however, it is important to point out that all of the advocates of the market approach view basic schooling as a public function. They do so because at the very least, " . . . a stable and democratic society is impossible without widespread acceptance of some common set of values and without a minimum degree of literacy and knowledge on the part of most citizens. Education contributes both."[3] Thus, because of the social benefits derived from a citizenry which has received some basic level of schooling, the responsibility of paying for this education is considered to be a social burden rather than an individual one. But Friedman would separate the financing, which would be public, from the management and operation of schools, which would be private.

Government could require a minimum level of education which they could finance by giving parents vouchers redeemable for a specified maximum sum per child per year if spent on 'approved' educational services. Parents would be free to spend their sum and any additional sum on purchasing educational service from an 'approved' institution of their own choice. The educational services could be rendered by private enterprises operated for profit, or by nonprofit institutions of various kinds.[4]

---

[2] Christopher Jencks has also endorsed the Friedman plan in the work previously cited. The fact that the "new left" (Jencks) and the "old right" (Friedman) can concur on the same educational palliative is reason enough to consider the market approach to education as a serious alternative to the present system.

[3] Milton Friedman, "The Role of Government in Education," in Robert A. Solo, ed., *Economics and the Public Interest*, New Jersey: Rutgers University Press, 1955, pp. 124–125.

[4] *Ibid.*, p. 127.

The result would be that:

... Parents could express their views about schools directly, by withdrawing their children from one school and sending them to another to a much greater extent than is now possible.[5]

Indeed, the scheme is based upon the plausible premise that:

Here as in other fields, competitive private enterprise is likely to be far more efficient in meeting consumer demands than either nationalized (publicly run) enterprises or enterprises run to serve other purposes.[6]

It is interesting to note that almost two centuries before Friedman, Adam Smith asserted that while the public should pay some of the costs of teaching children of the working class the 3 R's, the teachers would soon neglect their responsibilities if they were fully paid out of public funds.[7]

In summary then, the government would provide families with a voucher for each school-age child, which would guarantee a maximum specified sum of money which could be paid as tuition to any "approved' school. Nonpublic schools would compete among themselves— and perhaps with the public schools—for students by offering a variety of educational choices.[8] Freedom of entry by schools into the market— provided that they met minimum qualifications—would insure efficiency in the production of schooling, and students and their families would be given a market of educational alternatives in place of the present rigid assignment practices. Moreover, such competition would induce innovation and experimentation in that each school would try to obtain competitive advantages over the others. Thus, the operation of the market would provide far more choices and a greater degree of efficiency in the schooling of all students, especially those pupils who are presently confined to slum schools.[9]

[5] *Ibid.*, p. 129.
[6] *Ibid.*
[7] More specifically he stated that:

> The public can facilitate this acquisition (of reading, writing, and arithmetic among children of the poor) by establishing in every parish or district a little school, where children may be taught for a reward so moderate, that even a common labourer may afford it; the master being partly, but not wholly paid by the public; because, if he was wholly, or even principally paid by it, *he would soon learn to neglect his business.* (Emphasis provided.)

Adam Smith, *The Wealth of Nations*, Modern Library Edition, New York: Random House, Inc., 1937, p. 737.

[8] Friedman has suggested that under certain conditions it might be desirable to have a mixed system of both public schools and private alternatives. Parents who did not wish to use the public institution would receive a tuition voucher the maximum sum of which would be equal to the cost of educating a child in a government school. See, "The Role of Government in Education," *op. cit.*, p. 130.

[9] Jencks, "Is the Public School Obsolete?" *op. cit.*

PRIVATE AND SOCIAL BENEFITS

I have already noted that there are two types of benefits associated with basic (elementary and secondary) schooling: private benefits and social ones. The private benefits represent those which accrue to the individual (and his family) tangibly in the form of higher earnings, and intangibly in the form of heightened appreciation, awareness and insights, and so on. If all of the returns to basic education were private ones, a strong case could be made for letting the market determine the production and allocation of schooling among the population.

Yet, as Friedman recognizes, the very reason that basic schooling is considered to be a public responsibility is that it also yields benefits to the society as a whole. In this social context, there are at least two roles which elementary and secondary schooling are supposed to fulfill:

1. Provision of minimum levels of literacy, knowledge, and understanding of our common heritage which are necessary for the functioning of a stable and democratic society, and

2. reduction of disparities in incomes and opportunities presently associated with race and social class.

What, then, are the probable effects of the market approach on the production of both private and social benefits?

In terms of private benefits, it is likely to be true that any measure of competition among schools would lead to increases in their effectiveness. The motive for success—profit maximization—would require that a school meet the need of its students better than its competitors for any given cost. The fact that existing policies would have to be re-examined in the light of their educational contributions would probably engender thorough changes in the administration of the schools. By increasing the number of decision-making units, the probability of schools innovating to gain competitive advantages would be far greater than under the present system. While many examples of such change can be envisioned, a notable one would be the introduction of those new curricula and instructional aids which showed great promise relative to their costs. Most of the existing public institutions have been loath to adopt any but the most modest changes in their educational strategies.

Another fruit of competition among schools might be more imaginative recruitment policies for teachers. At present, teachers are hired on the basis of a single-salary schedule, one which fixes the teachers' salary on the basis of how much schooling he has had and the amount of his teaching experience. Such factors as the quality of his schooling, his actual teaching ability, his expected performance as reflected in his pre-service teaching and personality traits or his field of specialization have no effect on his salary. Under this system, the more imaginative persons —who are often able to reap greater returns outside of teaching—either do not enter the schools or leave after short periods of time. On the other hand, those who have few alternatives in the labor market remain in the schools, protected from dismissal by life-long tenure contracts after only three years of experience. Thus, while there are some exceptions, the single-salary schedule fosters mediocrity in teacher selection and retention.

Furthermore, it leads to shortages of teachers with training in some specialties and surpluses of teachers with other training. That is, while mathematics and science majors receive higher starting pay in the market-at-large, they receive the same salaries as do other specialists in the schools. It comes as no surprise, then, to find that schools show a shortage of teachers properly trained in science and mathematics and a surplus of social studies and male physical education teachers.[10] As a result, of course, the social studies and physical education teachers are then often assigned to teach secondary courses in mathematics, physics, chemistry, and other shortage areas. Competitive schools would have to hire on the basis of the realities of the market place rather than on the basis of rigid salary schedules.

Moreover, competitive schools would be more likely to adopt a policy of flexible class size depending upon subject matter, grade level, and type of student, which is a more sensible goal than maintaining uniform class sizes. There would also be more willingness to differentiate staffing by substituting teacher aides, curriculum specialists, and other specialized personnel for classroom teachers wherever accompanied by increases in efficiency *ceteris paribus*. Most important of all, individual differences among teachers might be utilized as an asset in the educational process by enabling teachers to pursue their own teaching styles and approaches in place of the present attempts of the schools to standardize curricula, syllabi, and pedagogy along narrow guidelines.

These are some of the changes that we might realistically envision among competitive schools, changes that are not now feasible given the institutional rigidities of the typical public school system. Since Friedman might leave the public schools as an alternative, only the best of them—those which could compete effectively—would survive over the long run. That is, competition would keep the remaining public schools on their toes.

In short, it is likely that Friedman is correct in asserting that the market approach is a more efficient device for satisfying the educational preferences of consumers than is the traditional, highly-centralized public school system. Under a competitive market, we could probably expect that greater educational benefits would accrue to students and their

---

[10] See Joseph Kershaw and Roland McKean, *Teacher Shortages and Salary Schedules*, New York: McGraw-Hill, 1962. I have also developed an extensive set of data on this phenomenon which will be published in the future.

families. Yet, increases in private benefits do not necessarily yield similar increases in social benefits.

THE EDUCATION MARKET PLACE AND SOCIAL BENEFITS

Our schools shoulder the primary burden for satisfying at least two social goals: Those of imparting minimum levels of literacy, knowledge and the common values necessary for a stable democracy; and of decreasing disparities in incomes and opportunities associated with race and social class.

Friedman considers only the first of these social objectives. Under his plan, schools would be required to meet minimum standards—such as a common content in their programs—much as restaurants are required to ". . . maintain minimum sanitary standards."[11] But Friedman's analogy is a bad one, for requiring a common content in school programs is more like requiring uniform nutritional offerings in restaurants, not just cleanliness. Who would decide what minimum content was, and how would it be assessed? Would the traditional sequence of courses be considered minimal? Would teachers be required to satisfy certain criteria, or could anyone be hired to teach? All of these issues would have to be reconciled, and it is likely that the common content requirements to which Friedman alludes would lead to far more extensive regulation than he suggests. And obviously the greater the requirements which are imposed, the more alike schools would be; and in the extreme, the very animal which we wish to replace might merely be disguised in the new trappings of a highly regulated private industry.

Beyond the social responsibilities of assuring minimal literacy and basic skills, there is also the responsibility of exposing children to fellow students who are drawn from a variety of social, economic, and racial groups. It has also been asserted that slum children become more highly motivated and are likely to develop greater aspirations when they are exposed to children from the middle-class. Our present system of segregating school populations according to the neighborhoods in which they are located does little to achieve the goal of mixed-class schools. Friedman's approach, however, makes no provision for insuring that students attend schools in racially and socially diverse environments. Indeed, it is likely that social segregation—one of the by-products of the neighborhood school—would increase under the market proposal. For, experience with private schools suggests even greater segregation of student bodies on the basis of religious, ethnic, racial, economic, and other social criteria.

The significance of the probability of increased socioeconomic segregation under a free market system is that such a result would work directly against the second social responsibility of the schools—the equali-

[11] Friedman, "The Role of Government in Education," *op. cit.*, p. 127.

zation of opportunity for all racial and social groups. Friedman asserts that: "the widening of the range of choice under a private system would operate to reduce . . . stratification;"[12] and Jencks agrees with him, but neither gives any evidence to support this contention.

It is interesting to note that at least two Southern states, Virginia and Louisiana, adopted tuition plans to circumvent the court edict requiring them to integrate their public schools. In particular, then, how have the poor fared in the market place?

THE POOR AND THE MARKET PLACE

If the public sector has failed the poor in the efficient production and allocation of social services, the private market can hardly claim a greater degree of success in satisfying their needs. For example, a recent study of the Federal Trade Commission showed that goods purchased for $1.00 at wholesale sold for an average of $2.65 in stores located in poor neighborhoods, but only $1.65 in stores located in the "general market."[13] Geographic mobility, education, income, access to capital (credit)—the very things which the poor lack and the middle class possess—are the characteristics that enable one to operate most successfully in the private market. The failure of the market to give rich and poor equal access to privately produced goods and services should, in itself, make us skeptical about applying it to education.

First, while the private market would likely provide many educational alternatives to middle-class children, there would probably be far fewer sellers of educational services to the children of the poor. It is important to note that schooling must be consumed at the point of purchase; therefore geographical location of schools becomes a salient feature of the market place. But if the previous experience of the slums can be used for prediction, few if any sellers of high quality educational services at competitive rates will locate in the ghetto. Not only is there no Saks Fifth Avenue in Harlem; there is no Macy's, Gimbels, Korvettes, or Kleins.

In part the disparities between the slum markets and markets in other areas are the result of differential costs. Those firms or agencies which did elect to build schools in the "inner cities" would face higher land prices, construction costs, and even teacher costs than those in less congested areas.[14] Thus students attending schools in the slums would re-

---

[12] *Ibid.*, p. 130.
[13] Leonard Downie, Jr., "FTC Chief Testifies the Poor Pay More," *The Washington Post*, January 31, 1968, p. A1. Other evidence is provided in David Caplovitz, *The Poor Pay More*, Glencoe, Ill.: Free Press of Glencoe, 1963.
[14] At the same salary level, the inner-city schools appear to obtain teachers of lower quality than do schools in middle-class areas. This phenomenon is probably the result of the fact that most teachers prefer middle-class schools to those in the ghetto. See my *Recruiting Teachers for Large-City Schools* (Brookings Institute, in process).

ceive less education per dollar than those attending schools in other areas.

In addition, the fact that many families could increase their expenditures on schooling beyond the maximum provided by the state would also tend to bid schooling resources away from the ghettos, particularly in the short run. Not only do the poor lack the incomes to add private expenditures to the proposed public vouchers, but on the average they also have more children to educate. Consequently, public funds will be all they will have to spend on the schooling of their children. Given this situation, the schools which now serve the poor could not hope to obtain the better teachers since such personnel would probably prefer to teach for more money in a middle-class school rather than for less money in a ghetto school.

Even if the slum children were accepted at private schools located outside the ghetto—a highly dubious eventuality given the history of private schools—the poor would have to bear the costs of transportation to such institutions. While the monetary costs of transportation represent only part of such a burden, even $5 a week represents $180 over a school year.[15] Thus, the ghetto resident is likely to face a higher cost of educational services whether he sends his child to a school in or out of the inner city.

Jencks asserts that private schools would spring up to serve Negro children if only money equal to what was spent in the public schools were provided for tuition.[16] Unfortunately, experience with this very approach has suggested that such optimism is probably unwarranted. In order to defy the desegregation order provided by the 1954 Brown decision, Prince Edward County, Virginia, abolished its public schools in 1959 and provided tuition grants to students so that they could attend privately operated schools. While a system of private schools did emerge to serve the needs of white students, no private alternatives became available to black pupils. As a result, those Negro children who could not be sent to relatives or friends in other districts received no regular education at all.[17]

The fact that education as a good is difficult to define or measure also violates an important premise of the competitive market. There is no clear concept of what should be considered "educational output," and data purporting to measure even partial outputs are not wholly satisfactory. Indeed, when schools are referred to as "good" or "bad," such

[15] Compare this amount with the average estimated current expenditure per pupil for all educational services in 1967–68 (except capital) of $619. See *Estimates of School Statistics, 1967–68*, Research Report 1967-R18, National Education Association, 1967.

[16] Jencks, "Is the Public School Obsolete?" *op. cit.*, p. 26.

[17] Robert Collins Smith, *They Closed Their Schools: Prince Edward County, Virginia, 1951–1964*, North Carolina: University of North Carolina Press, 1965.

judgments ordinarily reflect the characteristics of the student body, school expenditures, or some other set of input measures rather than measures of output. Or, when "output" measures are utilized, they are generally based upon absolute performance levels of students on standardized tests or the proportion of students who go on to college or win scholarships. But all of these measures are largely a function of the social class of the student body. A more appropriate measure of a school's success would be the "value-added" to the student body along certain cognitive, attitudinal, and other behavioral dimensions. No measures of these are available.

Given the fact that even professional educators have no objective way of rating schools, how are the parents of the poor going to compare them? Friedman has suggested that they will emulate the rich, for "The rich are always the taste makers, and that is the method by which the standards of society are raised."[18] Those of us who have observed the criteria by which families select colleges for their offspring might find this assumption difficult to accept. But even if we were to accept it, and its normative undertones, one might question whether the youngster in Harlem and his counterpart in Great Neck and Scarsdale have the same schooling needs. Further, the only way that the poor could emulate the rich in purchasing education would be if the poor possessed the resources of the rich, as well as their exalted tastes. Indeed, it is the discrepancy in the initial income distribution which is likely to raise the greatest difficulties in a market approach to education.

Friedman tacitly assumes that the initial distribution of income among households is appropriate, and he proposes that individual households should consume educational services according to their own demand functions, rather than by requiring all households to accept the formal schooling allocated by the political process. Friedman considers that a "major merit" of the voucher system is that parents with higher incomes and greater desires for education could add their own monies to the standard tuition grant provided by the government.[19] That is, the middle and upper classes—having higher incomes and fewer children—could purchase much better educations for their offspring than could the poor.

This argument ignores completely the crucial role which has been given education in increasing the future opportunities and incomes of youth. True equality of opportunity implies that—on the average—an individual of any race or social class has the same opportunity to achieve a given income or occupation as a member of any other race or class. Of course, it is sham to assert that any such situation exists today; but under the market approach to education, the disparity in income distri-

[18] Quoted from Robert C. Maynard, "The Ultimate Solution Recommended for Schools," *The Washington Post*, November 12, 1967.
[19] Milton Friedman, "A Free Market in Education," *The Public Interest*, spring 1966, p. 107.

bution among rich and poor and among Negroes and whites would probably increase.

Educational expenditures represent investment in "human capital," investment that raises the potentialities and increases the future incomes of those receiving the schooling. By increasing the difference in educational investment between rich and poor, middle- and upper-class children would experience even greater advantages over lower-class children than their parents enjoy at the present time. That is, rather than schooling being utilized as a device for equalizing opportunity, the market would enable it to widen the present disparity between the opportunities afforded the privileged and the disadvantaged.[20]

Even on certain grounds of social efficiency, an unmitigated free market approach to basic schooling might not be desirable. Middle-class children receive a great deal of "educational investment" from their parents and communities prior to and during their formal schooling. The privileged child begins his formal schooling with a far higher level of "educational capital" than does the poor child and he receives greater stimulation and support from his home during the schooling process. Further, it is *a priori* reasonable to believe that the law of diminishing returns is applicable to investment in basic schooling. Since disadvantaged pupils begin their schooling with a smaller amount of "capital" invested in them, it is likely that the marginal returns in future productivity from investing in the schooling of the poor will be greater than those which might be derived from spending the same amount on basic schooling for the advantaged.[21]

Thus, the social goal of maximizing future economic growth—for any given level of educational investment—would imply spending greater amounts on the formal education of the poor than on the rich. Moreover, the goal of future equality of opportunity among groups would also imply greater expenditures on the schooling of the disadvantaged than on the advantaged. Unfortunately, the distribution of expenditures on elementary and secondary education, if left to the free market, would probably yield exactly the opposite results.

Thus the free market remedy as Friedman has proposed it would probably have greater private benefits than does the present system. Even the poor might experience some improvement in their schooling

[20] For a discussion of the distribution of educational resources and equality of opportunity, see Samuel S. Bowles, "Towards Equality of Educational Opportunity?" *Harvard Educational Review*, spring 1968.

[21] Evidence which would appear to confirm this phenomenon is the fact that achievement levels of Negro students seem to be far more sensitive to differences in school resources than are achievement levels of white students. See James S. Coleman *et al.*, *Equality of Educational Opportunity*, Washington, D.C.: U.S. Dept. of Health, Education, and Welfare. Office of Education, 1966, Chapter III. This finding has been confirmed in reanalysis of the Coleman data by Samuel S. Bowles of Harvard.

from a market which gave them alternatives to their present schools. Yet offsetting these private gains are the social costs imposed by a system which would tend to change the relative distribution of schooling alternatives in such a way that the present disparities in income and opportunities among social and racial groups would increase. Moreover, the free market approach would probably lead to greater racial and social segregation of pupils among schools than presently exists. These are tremendous costs to inflict upon a society which is preaching equality on the one hand and on the other hand is reeling from urban riots that are largely attributable to the frustration of unequal opportunity.

A SIMPLE MODIFICATION

The Friedman approach might nevertheless be modified to avoid some of its deleterious consequences while taking advantage of the benefits of a competitive system. Since we are particularly concerned with the educational deficiencies of the inner-city schools and their disadvantaged clients, we might inquire into how the market approach might be adapted to the specific needs of ghetto children. The simplest way to implement the market approach without putting the poor at a disadvantage would be to grant tuition payments which are inversely related to family income and wealth. Disadvantaged children might be given vouchers which are worth two or three times the value of the maximum grants given children of the well-to-do. Such a redistributive system of grants would overcome many of the initial market handicaps faced by slum families. Thus, differences in tuition would be based upon relative educational needs, costs, and the family resources for fulfilling those needs.

However, since it is unlikely that this differential voucher plan would ever be adopted by the electorate, we ought to consider other market proposals. One of the most meritorious of these is the plan recommended by Theodore Sizer, dean of Harvard's Graduate School of Education. Sizer would have the state provide tuition payments—and thus schooling alternatives—only for children of the poor. These family allowances ". . . would allow that one section of our population that suffers most seriously from segregated schooling—the poor—to move, at their own initiative, and if they want to, into schools of their choice outside their neighborhoods."[22] This specific application of the Friedman proposal appears to be politically feasible and it is likely to spawn both the private and social benefits that we discussed above.

The voucher plan is not the only way of instituting some measure of competition among schools. James S. Coleman has suggested that school districts might contract with private firms for specific educational serv-

[22] Theodore Sizer, "Reform and the Control of Education," 1967, p. 14. (Mimeo.)

ices such as arithmetic and reading instruction, and the firms would be reimbursed on the basis of their performances in imparting skills to students as measured by standardized tests.[23] These reading and arithmetic programs would be located throughout the city, and they would represent alternatives to those which are presently offered within each school. "Each parent would have the choice of sending his child to any of the reading or arithmetic programs outside the school, on released time, or leaving him wholly within the school to learn his reading and arithmetic there. The school would find it necessary to compete with the system's external contractors to provide better education, and the parent could . . . have the . . . privileges of consumer's choice."[24]

While this proposal deserves serious consideration, it would have to overcome two obstacles First, full consumer choice among schooling programs might lead to similar or even greater social, racial and economic segregation among schools than presently exists. Coleman suggests that "One simple control . . ." would solve this problem. "No contractor could accept from any one school a higher proportion of whites than existed in that school, nor a higher proportion of students whose parents were above a certain educational level than existed in the school."[25]

Such a quota system is neither simple (administratively), nor would it tend to reduce segregation. If a student from a school which was 100 per cent white wished to enroll in a particular reading program, the contractor could always accept that student, since undoubtedly no more than 100 per cent of the students in his reading program would be white. That is, whites coming from virtually segregated white schools could enroll in virtually segregated white special programs under Coleman's "open school" criterion. Indeed, even if the quota system were workable, it would tend to perpetuate the existing stratification of students along racial and social class guidelines.

Further, the crudeness of present test instruments and their admitted cultural biases do not suggest that standardized tests should be the only basis on which contractors would be rewarded. Indeed, the Coleman Report found that its "ability" tests appeared to measure achievement far better than its achievement tests did.[26]

Moreover, to the degree that there are educational goals which should be implemented into instructional programs but do not necessarily coincide with changes in test performances *per se*, we might find contractors pursuing goals which are so narrow that they are deleterious to the

[23] James S. Coleman, "Towards Open Schools," *The Public Interest*, fall 1967, pp. 20–27.
[24] *Ibid.*, p. 25.
[25] *Ibid.*
[26] The Coleman Report's extensive analysis of the determinants of *verbal achievment* is based upon the standardized tests of *verbal ability* provided by Educational Testing Service. See Coleman *et al.*, *Equality of Educational Opportunity, op. cit.*, pp. 292–295.

imparting of broader learning skills. After all, a contractor who is rewarded on the basis of tests results has a strong incentive to prepare the student *only* for the limited dimension of the performance to be tested.

COMMUNITY SCHOOLS AND THE MARKET

Recent emphasis on improving the public education system has focused on community involvement in the public schools. The premise on which the community approach rests is that a school should serve the particular needs of its clientele rather than some general set of requirements which are defined at a highly centralized level. Several efforts have been made to initiate individual community-run public schools in the large cities; but the boldest overall move in this direction is that recommended for the New York City schools by the Mayor's Advisory Panel on School Decentralization. The Bundy Report—as the New York study is commonly called—proposes that some 60 or so largely autonomous school districts be set up in New York City, each representing a distinct community or set of communities.

Such community school districts would carry out most of the educational functions for their residents and would—in addition—"promote coordination in the planning and operation of health, recreation, and other human resource programs in the city."[27] Responsiveness to the particular educational needs of local resident would be insured by Community School Boards composed of 11 members: "six selected by a panel elected by the parents of children who attend schools in the district; five selected by the Mayor from lists of qualified persons presented by the central education agency after consultation with parents and community organizations."[28]

Given community schools and the promise that they appear to hold in adapting to the special needs of their students, it is possible to suggest a method by which they, too, can benefit from the competitive market. Communities could plan their educational requirements and solicit bids from private industry, universities, and nonprofit groups for fulfilling these needs. Educational contractors would compete for the particular educational services that the community wished to buy, and the most promising proposals would be selected. Contrasts could be awarded to the same groups if the community were satisfied with their performances; or they could be turned over to the other firms whose probable performances would be superior to those of the present contractors. Thus, the groups selling educational services to the community schools would have an incentive to perform well or else chance losing a customer.[29]

[27] *Reconnection for Learning—A Community School System for New York City*, Report of the Mayor's Advisory Panel on Decentralization of the New York City Schools, 1967, p. 16.
[28] *Ibid.* p. 18.
[29] Both Jencks and Sizer have endorsed this approach.

The purchasing of educational services on the private market by community schools holds particular promise at the present time, for many firms which have been developing educational programs and technology over the last decade have not really had a chance to test their products in a "natural" environment. Such firms appear to be very anxious to show that their approaches are worthy of implementation. Indeed, the potential rewards to be reaped by educational contractors who can show successful implementation are likely to be enormous. Accordingly, the contractor's motive to demonstrate the effectiveness of his approach to educational buyers would operate to make competition among sellers keen. In such a market, there is much to be gained by those firms who succeed; there is much to lose for those firms who do not.

A SUMMARY

The replacement of the existing system of publicly operated schools by a market of private ones—supported by government vouchers—would probably yield mixed results. On the one hand, some parents would have greater choices among schools and some schools would have to be productive in order to survive in the competitive framework. The increase in consumer choice and the resultant competition among schools would be likely to lead to greater educational benefits for many students and their families (private benefits) than those which they receive under the present monopolistic system.

On the other hand, the schools are also expected to fulfill certain social functions. It is in these that a market approach to schooling is likely to yield poor results. For example, basic schooling represents the primary device for equalizing opportunities among racial and social groups. Yet, advantaged children would probably receive far better schooling under the market proposal than would disadvantaged ones, and it is likely that this disparity would lead to larger future inequalities in opportunity between the children of the middle class and those of the poor. Further, it is not clear that a set of largely autonomous schools could provide the common set of values and knowledge necessary for the functioning of a democratic society. Finally, it is likely that the market proposal would increase racial and social stratification of students among schools. Whatever the success of the market in meeting consumer preferences, it would be offset by the market's failure to satisfy the social goals of basic schooling.

Fortunately, we are not limited to choosing between the traditional educational bureaucracy on the one hand or an unmitigated free market for educational services on the other. There are several ways to create competition within a public school system. Jencks, Sizer, and Coleman have suggested particular plans based upon the competitive framework, and the proposal for community schools represents a more general framework in which the competition of the market place might be used to advantage. The time is ripe to experiment with at least one of these plans for the children of the ghetto. Do we have any buyers?

DISCUSSION QUESTIONS

1. In an open-market setting, Levin states, schools would compete for students "by offering a variety of educational choices." What are these choices? Who would offer them? How would they be paid for? Would the same amount be allocated for each child's education?
2. How would the competition among a variety of schools resulting from an open-market strategy contribute to the resolution of our educational problems? In what ways might the Detroit design of industrial competition be unsuitable to the educational process?
3. What do you think would be the reaction of Albert Shanker (head of the United Federation of Teachers in New York City) to the free-market approach to the provision of education?

FRED M. HECHINGER   The Problem Is To Separate
Aid from Control

Three years ago, the Educational Policies Commission, the ideological voice of the National Education Association and the American Association of School Administrators, dropped a bombshell when it urged educators to throw their support behind "categorical" Federal aid to education. These powerful organizations had always demanded general aid —money which the states and local school districts could spend as they wished—and had rejected Federal subsidies with "categorical" strings attached, such as the requirement that funds be used to aid the disadvantaged or to improve science instruction.

Last week, during the annual convention of the N.E.A. in Minneapolis, the commission returned to its pre-1964 stand. It denounced categorical aid as a form of Federal control and urged that Washington henceforth strengthen the public schools with dollars to be used as the states see fit.

The 1964 reversal was born of political realism. President Kennedy's efforts to enact general aid had turned into a fiasco, as had 40 years of similar efforts. The combination of the Roman Catholic parochial school supporters' threat to torpedo such public-schools-only aid and Southern opposition to any move that might increase the Federal role and press for desegregation seemed unbeatable.

MANY VICTORIES

On the other hand, categorical aid had a history of triumphs. It has long supported vocational education, school transportation and lunches, created the land-grant colleges and provided the G. I. Bill of Rights. During the Eisenhower Administration, the National Defense Education Act of 1958 (N.D.E.A.) was as categorical a measure as anyone could devise. It reacted to the first Soviet Sputnik by trying to put American mathematics, science and foreign languages in orbit.

Though expedient, the 1964 line was never popular with school administrators who are trying hard to remain the power base of the N.E.A. Last week the commission, perhaps submitting to that power, said: "Categorical grants have been accepted by the educational community as a means of getting a flow of Federal funds established." And so, it went on, the time is ripe "to increase reliance" on general aid.

The flow referred to was the Elementary and Secondary Education Act of 1965 which provides aid in such categories as the support of disadvantaged children, remedial instruction, after-school centers, school libraries and teaching materials. That flow is now estimated at about $3-billion annually.

Perhaps the commission's desire to get back to aid-without-strings was fanned by the recent battle in Congress over just this issue. Representative Albert H. Quie of Minnesota, as a spokesman for the Republican attack on President Johnson's categorical aid legislation, called for $3-billion in direct grants to the states, with most of the categorical qualifications removed. The proposals, however, were defeated, although some of the existing Federal prerogatives were modified.

What are some of the major controversies tackled in the commission's policy statement, "Federal Financial Relationships to Education"?

The commission charged that "special-purpose Federal aid . . . is in itself a form of Federal control of education." It cited the N.D.E.A. as "an indirect but nevertheless powerful influence . . . upon what is taught; how it is taught; and the priority of resources, time, and money allocated to it."

Those who reject this view say that the professional educationl leadership, over a considerable period of time, failed to establish priorities attuned to the needs of the nation. For example, those who hold this view recall that educators virtually struck foreign language study from the list of essential academic subjects and permitted a majority of students, including highly gifted ones, to leave school without instruction in physics.

FAILURE SEEN

The commission said "state and local educational authorities tend to view such [categorical] aid as a conglomeration of projects rather than as fundamental parts of a coherent educational program." It warned that this destroys the "essential unity of the educational enterprise, to the detriment of the educational program and the individual child."

Those who oppose this view reply that the Federal Government sensed an emergency exactly because the local and state experts had failed to evolve coherent programs. Far from working to the detriment of the individual child, this argument goes, the biggest item of the 1965 aid measure was aimed specifically at the individual child in the slums who had been ignored by the "essential unity of the educational enterprise." They suggest that special aid for a difficult school in the slums does, in fact, offer some of the benefits of general aid by freeing regular funds for the normal support of local schools.

Moreover, Secretary of H.E.W., John W. Gardner, in criticizing the commission's statement, charged that the anti-urban sentiments of the state capitols force the cities to rely on special aid from Washington.

The commission, while calling the enforcement of civil rights legislation "desirable and necessary," said categorical aid has had "limited success in reducing the problems of school desegregation."

The other side says that the combination of such aid with the desegregation guidelines has been responsible for most of the desegregation in the South.

Possibly the most serious flaw of local and state controlled American education in the past has been its leadership's failure to oppose, moderate and eliminate prejudice and inequality of opportunity. Much of the need for categorical aid is the direct result of that failure.

. . .

Perhaps the most convincing argument against categorical aid put forth by the commission is that it too often comes only sporadically and therefore adds uncertainty to local school budgets. An objection even more basic is the fuzzy language which has created considerable legal doubt whether some of the funds now going to children who attend parochial schools are not in reality a subsidy of church-related institutions—and this in violation of the Constitution.

The extent of the controversy involved in the Policy Commission's reverse was underlined by a rare statement of dissent. Dr. John H. Fischer, president of Teachers College, Columbia University, and former school superintendent of Baltimore (where he insisted on school desegregation before the advent of categorical aid), agreed that some present categorical programs "are less than perfect." But he added: "The commission's position would be more tenable if one might safely assume that as the 50 states pursue their own interests the national interest will automatically be served. Long experience, to say nothing of recent events, will not support that assumption. . . ."

In fiscal terms, what does the commission propose? It seems to support a phasing out—though not a drastic elimination—of categorical aid, while general aid would be provided either through no-strings Federal grants-in-aid to the states or through tax-sharing, i.e., the return of a certain percentage of Federal income taxes to the states.

The Policies Commission said last week: "Indeed, there is good reason to believe that most local school systems, if not arbitrarily constrained, are both responsive and responsible to the public's quest for the best in education."

In reality, large segments of the public pointing to past educational history, deny that. They—along with many educational dissenters—have called in the Federal Government as a policy-influencing partner for just that reason.

The commission warns of the political intrusions by the Federal Government, while admitting that many state education authorities are weak. Yet the chief state education officers in 22 states continue to be politically elected and thus to be more political than the Federal authorities.

Ideally, Federal aid should come to the schools with as few Federal strings attached as possible. The road to that ideal will have to be paved with growing confidence that the public school leadership has its eyes on national goals as well as on local needs. Only such a program among state education authorities can confine Washington's role—sometimes excessive and ill-considered—to that of a balancing, mediating and guiding force. Perhaps this is when the Policy Commission could best play its part.

DISCUSSION QUESTIONS

1. Do you favor general or specific federal aid to education?
2. Do you see federal control as the big issue in the aid controversy?

CHAPTER 6 Control of Education

From the beginnings of mass public education in the United States, control has resided in local boards of education. The concept of local control seems to be uniquely American, growing out of the rural, Jacksonian democracy of the first half of the nineteenth century. The arrangement was fortuitous; the Constitution did not provide for a federal system of education so that is was quite natural for the states, under the states' rights doctrine, to move into the vacuum.

Massachusetts, led by Horace Mann, offered an outstanding example of the capacity of the state to influence and to direct education. But state departments, in general, have been cast in an advisory and regulatory role. They have too often been understaffed, underfinanced and politically oriented. Their ineffectuality has allowed local school boards practical autonomy. Traditionally, control has been one step away from the local citizen.

Prior to Sputnik (1957), there was very little contact between the federal educational authority and state and local levels. The Office of Education gathered statistics on the state of American schools and published resource materials. The Commissioner of Education was Washington's unknown man, and the position was considered a major step on the road to oblivion.

The federal role in education has changed radically since Sputnik. Education, formerly a branch of the Federal Security Agency, has grown to cabinet status, in the new Department of Health, Education and Welfare. Federal aid to education has become massive and pervasive; Washington has moved into virtually every school building in the land.

Proponents of local control have reacted to the federal presence with alarm. The issue of aid to education is seen as the desire for control of education. The dollar sign and dominance are directly associated.

The power and authority of local boards of education are under fire from two other sources, increasingly militant teachers and sometimes even more militant parents. Teachers, unified in power blocs and stimulated by the competition between rival organizations, have moved beyond routine union matters to demand a voice in shaping school policy. Militant black parents, lacking representation on large city school boards and faced with their children's educational failure, are demanding complete control of their local schools.

On the college level, students have disrupted and immobilized entire campuses in their insistence upon a redistribution of responsibility and control.

The locus of control must be resolved once more. An active and persuasive federal authority, a growing and broadening base of teacher power, aroused and vehement parents and radical students have created a revolutionary process for America's schools. Tomorrow's schools will be different from today's.

MELDRIM THOMSON, JR. Federal Control of Schools:
Myth or Fact

> *The true purpose of this bill [The Elementary and Seconday Education Act of 1965] is to authorize general aid without regard to need, and the clear intent is to radically change our historic structure of education by a dramatic shift of power to the Federal level.*
>
> *In terms of our structure of educational control, to say nothing of public policy, this progression of Federal influence in the sciences to Federal influence in the social sciences is a quantum leap toward a centralized, standardized, uniform national school system.*
>
> From Minority Views on Elementary and Secondary Education Act of 1965, House Report No. 143, 89th Congress, 1st Session.

IF

If you believe that local control of your schools is vital to an independent and vibrant educational system;

If you wonder whether there is another side to the story of Federal control of our schools, other than the one of innocence and rich gifts told by the professional educator;

And, if you oppose Federal scheming for the minds of your children;

Then you might find that a few minutes spent in reading this pamphlet could alert you to some unbelievable truths about the dangers confronting your local school.

FEDERAL CONTROL OF SCHOOLS

Danger Ahead

Few voters in New Hampshire realize the speed with which Federal controls are invading their schools. The invasion is not confined to public schools; a snare of controls awaits the unwary private school lured by the bait of Federal aid. Even fewer persons recognize the revolutionary changes in policy structure of which these controls are but the outward manifestations.

Fortunately, for those who believe that one of the supporting pillars

Reprinted with permission of the author, Meldrim Thomson, Jr., as privately circulated by him.

of our Republic rests on the bedrock of local control of public schools, a fresh breeze of independence is blowing out of the north country.[1]

From Colebrook southward voters in six school districts had, as of January 1, 1966, rejected more than $30,000 in Federal funds for fear of Federal control.[2] Since very little has been written or said about the entrapments behind these Federal gifts, most of these rejections were prompted by an inherent fear on the part of the voter of Federal controls.

So lethargic has been the voter interest that in some school districts in New Hampshire these co-called entitlements have been accepted by voters where school board members constituted a majority of the persons voting.

The passage on April 11, 1965, of the Elementary and Secondary Education Act of 1965, Public Law 89–10, signalled a dramatic shift of power to the Federal level of our historic concept of local control of education.[3]

This Act was described in Congress as full of loopholes. "It presents a virtual bulldozer for Federal bureaucracy to overrun our long-established policy regarding local control of our schools."[4]

Even one Congressman who voted for P.L. 89–10 expressed, with money witnesses, a real concern over the possibility that this Act might be administered in an unconstitutional manner in some local programs.[5]

Under this Act vast power has been placed in the Office of Education in the Department of Health, Education and Welfare. There are $1.06 billion available to implement the Act. Of this huge sum $2.5 million are allocated to New Hampshire for the current fiscal year. That is about equivalent to the state aid our school districts receive in one year. And out of this $2.5 million more than $100,000 will be used to administer the program in our state.

Jubilant bureaucrats in the Office of Education were recently reported as saying their office now has a life of its own. "It has billions to disburse, and the commissioner is in charge. The Federal commitment can not help but get bigger."[6]

With this enormous fund it should be easy to shackle Federal controls on local schools, reasons the Washington bureaucrat. Thus, money becomes the weaponry in the battle to shift control over our public schools to Washington.

[1] *The New Hampshire Sunday News*, January 2, 1966. The arguments used by those opposed to accepting Federal school funds were described as "typical New England arguments" by Commissioner of Education, Paul E. Farnum.
[2] *Ibid.*
[3] Minority Views, House Report No. 143, 89th Congress, 1st Session.
[4] Congressman Ashbrook, *Congressional Record*, March 26, 1965, p. 5918. "Its pitfalls will trouble educators, boards of education, and, indeed, communities for years to come."
[5] Congressman Scheuer, House Report No. 143, *ibid.*, p. 80.
[6] *National Observer*, December 27, 1965.

Expanding Federal Controls

THE ISSUE. Like the forked tongue of a snake, the issue is twofold. Is the Federal government really reaching into our communities to run our schools; and if so, would Federal control be good or bad for us?

The issue under Title III of the Act is "between (1) our historic pattern of local public education controlled locally under state law and (2) the establishment of a separate public education system financed and administered by a Federal agency."[7]

Recently an official of our State Department of Education was quoted as saying "There's no particular measure of control" under Title I of the Elementary and Secondary Education Act of 1965.[8]

Schools boards that have been in touch with the offices of their school superintendents know that all through the recent fall months their superintendents experienced a very real measure of control in the long hours of tedious labor exacted to prepare the mountain of forms required under Title I of the Act.

We can understand the position of the professional educator even if we do not sympathize with it. "Unfortunately, all too many educators take the position that as long as some money is being spent, they are for it and will accept it regardless of any erosive effect it may have on the future of education."[9]

CONTROLS UNDER PRIOR ACTS. We have accepted Federal funds under such prior Federal acts as the National School Lunch Act, the National Defense Education Act, and various vocational education acts. Because of this fact, educators are prone to equate Public Law 89–10 as just another grant of Federal funds to our schools.

Inevitably, whenever Federal funds were given to schools, the money carries with it controls. In the beginning controls were gentle, subtle and quiescent. Under these earlier acts the threat of control was ever present, but gloved; and so we lived with it while large and less palatable doses of control were quietly being prepared for us. The stinger was there but generally sheathed. Occasionally, a school district was stung.

Our Department of Education has admitted that even under the National School Lunch Program there was a little red tape or control.[10]

Department of Education officials, with Federal funds available to implement the vo-ag program, recently indicated to the Orford School Board that about three thousand dollars would not be forthcoming this

---

[7] House Report No. 143, *ibid.*, p. 76.
[8] The *Valley News*, December 29, 1965.
[9] Congressman Ashbrook, *ibid.*
[10] "We are confident that few Federal programs have as little 'red tape' or 'controls' as this program exercises for the benefits received." Letter to all New Hampshire School Board Chairmen, dated December 22, 1965.

year, because among other things, the vo-ag curriculum was not changed as directed.[11]

BATTLE PLAN FOR THE BIG GRAB. The shadow that we see clearly today often portends the substance of the reality of tomorrow. So it was with a 56-page booklet entitled "A Federal Education Agency for the Future," issued in 1961 by the Department of Health, Education and Welfare.[12] This was the Federal blueprint for control of our local schools. This plan for the big grab of our schools stressed Federal participation and control in formulating educational policies. It urged Federal review of teacher preparation, curriculum and textbooks. It even proposed to have the Office of Education implement international educational projects in cooperation with UNESCO in the United Nations.

One important new role which the Washington educational bureaucrats planned to add to the Office of Education was designated in the 56-page report as "extensive involvement in formulation of national policy."

According to this battle plan, the Office of Education "must also prepare itself to assume larger responsibilities in carrying out Federal policy through the administration of operating programs. It must assume a new role, speaking within the Federal government for the long-term interests of education. And it must render assistance in the development of public educational policy."

This revealing report stated that "curriculum will have to undergo continual reshaping and upgrading, and new techniques and tools of instruction will have to be developed"; also, "teacher preparation, textbooks, and the curriculum in the subject fields must be improved in the decade ahead."

Judged by their own words, these Federal educators are ambitious men. In the area of international education, their report provided that, "the responsibilities of the Federal government in this effort are marked. Not only is it the constitutional responsibility of the Federal government to conduct the foreign affairs of the nation: it is almost equally evident that national observers are especially well qualified to assess the international deficiencies of our domestic educational system."

Certainly enough has been said in the Office of Education's own blueprint about the future role of that power-hungry agency to demonstrate conclusively that Federal aid without controls is a myth.

If there is any lingering doubt that Federal control of our public schools is just around the corner of Capitol Hill, then bear constantly in mind this ominous warning from the report: "The Committee foresees an extension of the active Federal role in education."

[11] Letter September 21, 1965, from New Hampshire Division Vocational-Technical Education.
[12] *Congressional Record*, July 18, 1961.

THE RUTHLESS GRAB. It took the Federal educators only four years to implement their grandiose battle plan. In 1965 it was made effective, in large measure, by Public Law 89–10, and particularly by Title I of that Act.

Seldom has a law been so ruthlessly steamrolled through the Congress.

When Public Law 89–10 was before the House for consideration it was pushed through quickly by the raw power of the majority. One Congressman stated, "I have seen debate cut off with no opportunity to present views on vital amendments. In one instance the Chairman of the Education and Labor Committee moved that debate close in 5 minutes. He then took the entire 5 minutes himself!

"On one occasion he even flouted custom and refused to allow the minority leader to speak for an additional 5 minutes. On one occasion, he moved to close debate before it had even started, but fortunately the long-standing rules of the House required at least one speaker address himself to the matter before the motion could be made.

"It is only appropriate that these tactics brought the American people a bill so badly drafted and so tied together by sealing wax that no amendment could be accepted regardless of merit, lest the political support for the bill by various groups who put the coalition together be withdrawn."[13]

IN BATTLE ARRAY. The high command in the camp of the Federal educators has been expanded and strengthened.

Harold Howe II, described as an "eager innovator" was recently made U.S. Commissioner of Education. The former commissioner, Francis Keppel, was promoted to Assistant Secretary for education in the Department of Health, Education and Welfare. With the Secretary of the Department, John W. Gardner, a specialist in education, this "triumvirate provides the strongest educational leadership ever exerted from Washington—for the political battles that lie ahead."[14]

Thus, equipped with some of the best command talent in the nation, loaded with three billions of taxpayers' dollars, and with a battle plan designed to take over the operation of our local schools, the Federal educators have begun the fight in thousands of school yards all over the country. Initially, the battle will be waged through the exercise of Federal controls funneled through state agencies.

SOME EXAMPLES OF CONTROLS. To qualify for an entitlement, that is to say, Federal monies, a school board makes application through the State Department of Education for a "basic grant or a special incentive grant" under Title I of the Act. It must make several determinations, under

[13] Congressman Ashbrook, *Congressional Record*, March 26, 1965, p. 5918.
[14] *National Observer, ibid.*

section 205 of the Act, which, in the language of the statute, must be "consistent with such basic criteria as the Commissioner may establish." It would be difficult to imagine any better language to effectuate controls than that used in the statute.

"At first reading, this bill appears to leave approval of local programs to the State education agency, where the power belongs. However, there is inserted (hidden, almost) a power in the U.S. Commissioner of Education to require that such approval be consistent with basic criteria formulated by him. This effectively robs the State agency, or the local schools for that matter, of any real authority to shape the programs. This centralization of power in the U.S. Post Office of Education runs throughout the bill."[15]

There are eight determinations a school board must make under section 205 of Public Law 89–10. Citation of two of these should be sufficient to illustrate the type of controls the Act establishes.

Under par. (5) of section 205, a school board must find "that effective procedures, including provision for appropriate objective measurements of educational achievement, will be adopted for evaluating at least annually the effectiveness of the programs."

And under par. (8) a school board must determine that "effective procedures will be adopted for acquiring and disseminating to teachers and administrators significant information derived from educational research, demonstration, and similar projects, and for adopting, were appropriate, *promising educational practices* developed through such projects."[16]

Under paragraph (5) we open the school door to the administration of all kinds of tests on the nod of a Federal educator. These could include the obnoxious personality questionnaires in which the pupil must check out such prying statements as—

My father is a tyrant.
I wonder if I am normal in my sexual development.

Pupils in grades 4 through 7 could be required to take one of the so-called Wishing Well tests in which they check off such statements as—

I wish my parents did things that would make me feel more love toward them.

Under paragraph (8) we throw open our schools to the wildest forms of pedagogical experimentation. Conceivably, we could be required to give sex education, instructions in how to overthrow the United States Government, or a course in some Chinese dialect if the Federal educator found them to be "promising educational practices."

These possibilities may sound far fetched. But it has been said that under Title II of the Act, "if a text used in a single school district should

[15] House Report No. 143, *ibid.*
[16] Italics supplied.

depict one racial or national group as inferior, or leave the clear inference that a President or other public figure was a traitor, or covertly adopt a Marxist interpretation of history, Federal funds could be used to supply that text to every child in the State."[17]

CONTROLS IN ACTION. According to the administrator of the Title I program in New Hampshire, "Washington is not doing anything but allocating the funds and providing the mechanics of how they are administered to the districts."[18]

This sounds quite innocent. No evidence of control here; but does this statement square with the facts?

Following complaints last fall of racial discrimination in the schools of Chicago, $30 million in Federal funds were summarily withheld on orders from Washington. Later the funds were released upon direction from the White House.[19]

Last November Dr. Carl Hansen, superintendent of schools in Washington, D.C., admitted that controls did exist. He said, "despite soothing assurances that local schools are to remain fully independent in their management of Federal funds, the evidence is that controls are being imposed even at the early stages of the new programs."[20]

Vanishing Local School Powers

For decades the strength of our nation was taprooted in the soil of local institutions. On the anvil of local public forums, with the issue at cherry heat, were hammered out the decisions that fashioned our nation's greatness.

Through their locally elected school trustees, New Hampshire voters control the education and thus the destiny of their children. They have the last word in such vital areas as hiring teachers, approving curriculum, purchasing textbooks, and determining discipline.[21]

Curriculum and textbooks are the arteries to our educational system. Expose these to the Federal educators and the transfusion to a centralized, national school system will be swift and certain.

We have seen by their own battle plan published in 1961 that Federal educators would gain control over curriculum and textbooks. We have noted that the Office of Education is equipped with superior talent in the struggle to establish supremacy over local schools. And we have observed that the supply depots of the Federal educators are bursting with taxpayers' dollars with which to assert their ascendancy.

If our state laws on education can be circumvented through the administration of Public Law 89–10, and they can be; and if our voters

[17] House Report No. 143, *ibid.*, p. 74.
[18] *New Hampshire Sunday News, ibid.*
[19] *U.S. News & World Report*, Oct. 18, 1965.
[20] *U.S. News & World Report*, Nov. 8, 1965.
[21] N.H. RSA sections 189: 10, 189: 15, 189: 16, 189: 39.

and their representative school board members lost control over curriculum and textbooks, then local authority will be reduced to a caretaking role of the schoolhouses. Centralization will then be complete, and possibly some computer monster in Washington will even issue the report cards to our children.

Late Is the Hour

The hour is late, but not too late! You can reverse the onward sweep of Federal control over our schools.

If your school district has not yet voted to accept current Federal funds under Title I of Public Law 89–10, you can work to decisively reject these funds. A strong demonstration at the grass-root level that local voters want no part of Federal control, would show our representatives in Congress, more emphatically than words or letters, that we do not want our tax dollars spent on further appropriations under Public Law 89–10. Instead, let us keep these dollars at home and controls on Washington.

Unless amended, Public Law 89–10 will remain effective until 1968. To keep it operative, Congress will have to appropriate new funds each year. If your school district is one of many which accepted Federal funds under this Act, possibly because voters were unaware that control did accompany the funds, then you will have an opportunity to vote against accepting this aid at your next annual school district meeting. To avoid special school district meetings, convened by court order, school boards in New Hampshire will probably include a Federal aid item under Public Law 89–10 in their 1966–67 school budget.

If you are alarmed about Federal control of your school, then by all means attend your next school district meeting and vote against accepting Federal funds under the Elementary and Secondary Education Act of 1965.

DISCUSSION QUESTIONS

1. Should local school districts refuse federal aid for fear of federal control?
2. If poor districts reject federal aid, where will they get the financing to meet their needs? Are the alternatives offered either federal control or inadequate education for children?
3. Must control inevitably follow after dollars? Is federal control necessarily invidious? Is local control necessarily good?

MYRON LIEBERMAN **Local Control of Education**

One of the most important educational trends in the next few decades is likely to be the decline of local control of education. Such a development is long overdue. Local control of education has clearly outlived its usefulness on the American scene. Practically, it must give way to a system of educational controls in which local communities play ceremonial rather than policy-making roles. *Intellectually*, it is already a corpse. At least, I propose to treat it as such in this book. The proper way to treat a corpse is to conduct an autopsy upon it and then bury it promptly. Having done this, we can better understand the rationale for the school system which will emerge from the present chaos in education.

An autopsy of local control reveals several reasons for its demise. In the first place, mobility and interdependence have completely undermined the notion that local communities ought to have a free hand in educating their children. Second, national survival now requires educational policies and programs which are not subject to local veto. Third, it is becoming increasingly clear that local control cannot in practice be reconciled with the ideals of a democratic society. Finally, local control is a major cause of the dull parochialism and attenuated totalitarianism that characterizes public education in operation.

Let us analyze these reasons briefly. In order to do so, consider carefully the following question: *Who* should decide whether the children in a given community should be required to learn to read and write?

Some persons would undoubtedly argue that parents should have the right to raise their children as illiterates if they wish to do so. Most people would probably feel that the public ought to have the right of final decision in this matter. Still, there are many publics: local, state, regional, national, international, and even publics which are not defined geographically. Which of these publics should be authorized to have the last word in the matter?

Until a short time ago, every state had a compulsory education law. These laws took the power to decide our hypothetical question out of the hands of parents and local communities. Recently, however, some states have passed standby legislation which would enable them to abolish compulsory education in order to avoid racial integration in their public schools. States cannot be prevented by the federal government from abolishing public education. There is no way that the federal government can force a state legislature or local community to appropriate money to operate public schools. But what about our basic question—should the decision as to whether children shall learn to read and

Reprinted from Myron Lieberman, *The Future of Public Education* (Chicago: University of Chicago Press, 1960), pp. 34–50, with permission of the publisher and author. Copyright © 1960 by the University of Chicago Press.

write be properly regarded as one for local communities or even governments to make?

The reasons why the power to make this decision was taken away from parents and later from local communities will help us to answer this question. One reason was based upon the concept of fair play for the individual child. There was growing acceptance of the belief that a child's chances in life should not depend upon whether his parents or his local community were willing and able to educate him.

Should a child's chances depend upon whether he lives in a state which is willing to educate him? Certainly not as long as we adhere to the concept of an open society, one in which the individual's chances are not determined by fortuitous factors. As far as the individual child is concerned, the extent to which his state government is willing to provide him with an education is as much a fortuitous matter as the socioeconomic status of his parents or the educational values of his local community.

Consider the problem from a social standpoint instead of an individual one. We are an extremely mobile people. Most of us eventually move away from the community in which we received our education. In the year ending in April, 1958, 30,800,000 Americans changed their residence. Over 11,000,000 moved from one county to another; about half this number moved to a different state. Thus, on the average, every American moves to a different state two times during his life. Under these circumstances, does it make sense to insist that the citizens of one state have no right to insist upon literacy for the children of other states? Today, we plead for federal aid to education in order to equalize opportunities between states. Tomorrow, we could hardly contend that the federal government must stand by idly while a state legislature compounded the inequity by depriving children of an education altogether.[1]

As an abstract proposition, it has always been clear that it is undemocratic to permit educational opportunity to be determined by circumstances of race, geographical location, or economic status. It has also been clear that our national welfare was dependent upon the extent to which individual talents were able to flourish, regardless of their social, economic, racial, or geographical origins. Neither the ideal of equality of opportunity nor the fact of our interdependence is new. What is new is the urgency of these things. Proposals for federal aid to education in order to equalize educational opportunities between states have been

[1] My argument treats control of education by the states as local control of education. Fundamentally, this identification is sound although people do not now think of control at the state level as local control. It is only a matter of time before they do so, and then the control of education at the state level will go the way of control at the parental and community levels. In point of time, the decline of community control over broad educational policy will precede the decline of state control over it, but the same forces that undermine the one will eventually undermine the other.

ignored by Congress for generations. The same proposals, advanced as a counterpoise to Russian scientific progress, are now regarded as insufficient by panic-stricken congressmen who never supported them on equalitarian grounds.

Some idea of the bankruptcy of local control of education may be seen in the statistics concerning selective service registrants disqualified for failure to pass mental tests. In 1956 the lowest rate of rejection for failure was in Montana, where 2.5 per cent of the registrants failed these tests. The highest rate was in Mississippi, where 44.9 per cent of the registrants failed the tests. In ten states, fewer than one out of every twenty registrants failed to pass; in eleven other states, one or more out of every four registrants failed to pass.[2]

The vast differences among the states in the rate of disqualification are not due solely to the differences in the quality of their school systems. A registrant educated in Montana might take his selective service tests in Mississippi or vice versa. The statistics on rejection include the failures to pass because of inherited mental deficiency, and there are other causes for such failure over which the schools have no control. Nevertheless, the differences between the states cannot be explained solely by noneducational causes. Because some states and communities provide a decent minimum education for only a small minority of their children, we must, in all states, draft persons who, for family or occupational reasons, ought not to be in the armed service at all. This is only a small part of the exorbitant price we are paying for local control of education. The intellectual smog that has obscured our grasp of this fact is being cleared away once and for all by such dramatic events as the riots in Little Rock and the Russian conquests of space.

LOCAL CONTROL AND TOTALITARIAN CONTROL

The prevailing point of view is that anything but local control of education, with perhaps a few concessions made to control at the state level, would be a step toward totalitarianism. This view is profoundly mistaken. Our present system of local control is far more conducive to totalitarianism than a national system of schools would be. I know that this statement is not acceptable to the overwhelming majority of the American people, including the teachers, but I am willing to stand on it.

The assertion that our educational system tends toward totalitarianism seems absurd on its face. A totalitarian system is one which develops a massive uniformity of outlook. It is based upon a policy of intellectual protection for a point of view that cannot stand the test of free discussion. We have a multitude of schools of all denominations or no denomination at all. Among the teachers and students in our public schools,

[2] NEA Research Division, *Research Bulletin*, XXXVI, No. 1 (February, 1958), 29.

there are adherents to every major political, economic, and religious point of view. What could be further from totalitarianism than this?

In most states the purposes and the content of education are left to local school boards to determine. Undoubtedly, there are some constitutional limits to the purposes for which communities may operate public schools. However, these limits have never been spelled out, and there is great latitude in what a community might require of its schools. Since the purposes of education are set forth locally, the predominant groups in the community tend to establish purposes which accord with their particular religious, political, economic, or social points of view. As a practical matter, therefore, local control results in the same kind of intellectual protectionism that characterizes schools in totalitarian countries.

The basic problem is not that communities define the purpose of education to be the acceptance of the Protestant faith or unswerving devotion to the single tax or the inculcation of the tenets of the Democratic party. Some communities have not blinked at adopting purposes as sectarian as these, but this is not where the problem lies. Even where a community accepts the most liberal educational purposes for its public schools, its interpretation of what intermediate objectives and what educational programs fulfil these purposes may have the same stultifying effect as outright adherence to a sectarian purpose. Every pressure group is for the general welfare, but each has its own version of what measures do in fact promote the general welfare. Similarly, every pressure group is for a liberal or a democratic education, but has a special version of what intermediate objectives and what educational programs lead to this result.

What is crucial is that, at the local level, it is relatively easy for a preponderant group to enforce a policy of intellectual protectionism for its sacred cows. Thus the white majorities in Southern communities exclude instruction that is critical of racial segregation. Communities in which fundamentalist sects predominate exclude instruction critical of evolution. Some communities have prohibited the study of the United Nations or of UNESCO. Ours is a heterogeneous country, but in most communities the predominant racial, religious, economic, or political groups are able to veto whatever in the school program displeases them.

Looking at our system as a whole and seeing the existence of public schools teaching diverse doctrines, one might infer that our schools are free. We do not readily recognize the totalitarianism implicit in our situation because not all schools protect the same dogmas. Nonetheless, a diversity of schools based upon intellectual protectionism for different dogmas does not constitute a "democratic school system." At least, it does not do so if "democratic" refers to the education actually provided in these schools instead of to the legal structure which encourages a variety of one-sided programs.

The diversity of our undemocratic schools is not the only factor which maintains the fiction that we have a democratic school system. No matter how successful a group may be in excluding certain facts and ideas from the public schools, television, radio, and other mass media are almost certain to expose students to these facts and ideas. The power structure of American society is such that no single group is able to enforce or to indoctrinate its dogmas on the population as a whole. People look at this situation and say "Our schools have kept us free." They should say "Our freedoms have survived our schools."

THE MYTHOLOGY OF LOCAL CONTROL

Many persons believe that public education was not made a federal responsibility in the Constitution because the founding fathers feared the potentialities for dictatorship in a federal school system. Actually, education was not included as a federal function in the Constitution because the idea of free public education had not even occurred to the founding fathers. At the time of the American Revolution, the concepts of universal public education was receiving attention for the first time and then only from a few frontier thinkers. Our decentralized school system was not an inspired stroke of genius but a historical accident, resulting from the fact that the ideal of free public education for all became widely accepted only long after the American Revolution.

Our schools have never been an important foundation of our free society. Our freedom is partly due to a separation of powers which enables us to transact public business reasonably well while avoiding excessive subjection to government officials. Perhaps for this reason we tend to regard the diffusion of power over our schools as an essential element of our free society. But adherence to the general principle that we must avoid excessive concentration of power does not automatically justify every separation or diffusion of it. Everything depends upon the circumstances—what powers are involved, who is to wield them, and so on. It is preposterous to think that merely because their political genius was expressed through a constitution embodying a remarkably successful separation of powers, the founding fathers would align themselves today with the supporters of local control of education.

People are seldom aware of the non-public character of public education. They tend to regard it as a legal concept and to neglect it as an educational concept. However, the ideal of public education means more than having some governmental unit—local, state, or federal—provide the funds to operate schools. Public education has a referent in the quality of education as well as in its financial basis. The qualitative referent is an education in which the search for truth is carried on regardless of what empires topple, interests collapse, or heads roll. Without this, public education is a delusion, as dangerous as the notion that mere government ownership of the means of production will automatically result in their operation for the public welfare instead of for private interests. The socialization of a service at any level of government is no automatic guarantee that the service will be performed in the public interest. The "new class" should have ended all of our illusions on this score.

Public schools, then, are not necessarily infused with a public spirit. Likewise, the fact that a school is privately controlled does not mean that its program is necessarily sectarian in character. The program of some privately controlled institutions such as Harvard is more free of parochial limitations than the programs in most publicly controlled institutions. In short, we cannot assume anything about the educational program of a school merely from a knowledge of whether the school is publicly or privately controlled.[3] Nor can we infer that the educational program of a school is undemocratic merely because the school is locally controlled or that it is democratic merely because the schools are part of a national system. The relationship between the legal status of a school and the quality of its educational program is never one of strict logical implication.

The system of legal controls under which schools operate is only one factor which serves to shape their educational programs. However, it is an extremely important factor. Because a national system of controls is more likely to broaden the purposes of education and to preserve the professional autonomy of teachers, it is much more likely to provide a truly liberal education than a multitude of totalitarian systems under local control. It is a striking fact that in England, which has a national system of education, the teachers are on record as being opposed to local control of education precisely because they fear that it would undermine their professional autonomy.[4] Meanwhile, teachers in the United States, who lack any substantial measure of professional autonomy, continue to act as if local control must be maintained inviolate lest academic freedom (which they do not possess) be imperiled.

The decentralization of our schools is often justified by an appeal to the experimental nature of this situation. We supposedly have fifty state school systems, each of which is free to try something different from the others. Each state has delegated considerable power to local school

[3] The notion that private education per se is superior to public education is assiduously cultivated by private school interests at all levels. It is a myth insofar as it pretends to be a generalization or even a statement of probable tendency. This myth results in outright tragedy at the elementary and secondary levels if parents assume that exorbitant fees automatically purchase educational advantages not available in the public schools.

[4] Educational leaders in England are very outspoken in their view that any trend toward giving local boards of education increased control over the financing of education would be a threat to the freedom of the teaching profession. See Sir Ronald Gould, "The Teaching Profession," *The Concept of Professional Status* (London: College of Preceptors, 1957), p. 42.

boards, which supposedly multiplies the experimental possibilities. This is thought to make for progress, since each state and each system is not only free to try something new but is free to benefit from the experience of other systems.

There is no doubt that some change for the better occurs in this way. Nevertheless, such enormous decentralization cannot be justified on the grounds that the different school systems constitute a vast pool of educational experimentation. The different schools do not constitute experiments except in the loosest sense of the word. They do not operate under conditions carefully controlled for purposes of analysis and comparison. They just operate.

Much of the experience of different systems is valuable only on the premise that education should be a state or local responsibility. A school board may indeed be interested in how another community put over a school bond campaign. But if funds came from the federal government, the experience of this or that school system in raising money would be academic.

The truth is that local control of education has obstructed rather than facilitated educational research. By and large, only large urban systems allocate funds to research. Even in these cases, the research is generally limited to problems that are of local concern. Very few school systems support any research that is even theoretically of more than local interest.

Educational research is supposed to be a function of our universities, but they also have a tendency to concentrate on local problems. Thus a university will make a study of population trends in a nearby community which desires to know where to build its new schools. Few universities devote any substantial effort to research on teaching and learning which would be of universal interest.

Educators have not learned from the development of industrial research. In industry, most research is conducted by corporations with a monopoly or near monopoly of the market for a particular product. These firms can support research intended to have a national impact because they stand to benefit from it. On the other hand, little research is conducted from private funds on products whose ownership is diffused. For example, individual farmers are generally unwilling to support research from their private funds because they would be adding substantially to their own cost of operation, while the results of the research would be immediately available to all farmers whether they had contributed to it or not.

We have much the same problem in education. Why should a particular school system support research which is for everyone's benefit? If we do not expect an individual farmer to support basic agricultural research from his own funds, neither should we expect him to support an educational research program in his local schools from local funds. The federal government supports basic research in agriculture because of the clearly evident futility of waiting for the small operator to do so. The same policy can and should be followed in education.

The U.S. Office of Education, a branch of the Department of Health, Education, and Welfare, has conducted research on certain administrative problems for many years. However, it was not granted funds for research in the art and science of teaching until 1956. In that year, $3,000,000 was made available by Congress for grants in various fields of education. The National Defense Education Act passed by Congress in August, 1958, included an appropriation of $18,000,000 over a four-year period for research on the educational use of radio, television, and audiovisual aids. It is likely that larger amounts for educational research will be appropriated by Congress in the future. But as long as education is primarily a state and local responsibility, educational research will never receive the support it ought to have. Local communities and state governments will never adequately subsidize research which is clearly universal in application.

How much money ought to be spent on educational research? Public education is a $15,000,000,000 enterprise [1960]. Enlightened practice in large-scale industry and government is to spend 3 to 6 per cent of the total budget for research. In education, this would call for an expenditure of from $450,000,000 to $900,000,000 annually. In fact, it is unlikely that the country is spending more than $25,000,000 a year from all sources for educational research.

The suggestion that it is realistic to think in terms of a twentyfold increase in expenditures for educational research will be considered a pipe dream by most educators. Nevertheless, such an increase would still leave expenditures for educational research at a conservative level even if we are now spending only $25,000,000 annually for this purpose. Those who blanch at my proposal should remember that we are currently spending well over $300,000,000 annually for medical research. A report submitted to the Secretary of Health, Education, and Welfare in the summer of 1958 by a distinguished advisory committee of medical educators and research executives calls for increasing our expenditures for medical research to the point where the nation will be spending a billion dollars a year for such research by 1970. Foundations which are currently supporting educational research might well support studies and action programs designed to develop more adequate sources of funds on a national basis. It does not take such studies, however, to realize that educational research has been neglected under our system of local control of education.

In this connection, it is interesting to note that one of the most persistent and most pathetic arguments against a national school system is that such a system would not permit experimentation in the schools. The assumption seems to be that centralized administration is necessarily non-experimental or that it necessarily insists upon uniformity down to every detail. Actually, several federal departments which have centralized administration also subsidize programs of research which dwarf anything we have ever seen in education. The departments of Defense and Agriculture illustrate the possibilities.

If the present structure of American education is not conducive to the support of research, it is well designed to obstruct the utilization of it. On this subject, we need only to compare the lag between the discovery and the application of knowledge in education and the lag in other professions.

In the legal profession, important developments such as Supreme Court decisions are taken into account by all lawyers within a very short period of time. When the Bureau of Internal Revenue makes a ruling which affects a substantial number of tax returns, the accountants generally absorb it within a matter of months. Everyone is familiar with the short period of time between the discovery of an effective polio vaccine and its use by doctors everywhere. In education, however, the lags between discovery and practice are scandalous. These lags are reflected in what is taught as well as in how teachers teach their subjects.[5]

The average person is little aware how long it takes for important new knowledge to be reflected in the public school curriculum. The diffusion of teacher education and of the curriculum is so great that it often takes decades before teachers realize the need to add or delete a subject or to make radical changes in the content of an accepted subject. Even after this hurdle has been passed, tens of thousands of school boards must be persuaded that these changes are desirable. "Go ye therefore and persuade all those who are affected by the decision"—thus reads the Word in textbooks on school administration. The Curriculum Committee of the PTA, the school board, the parents, the students—all must have a voice in a decision which affects them. An infinite number of banana peels lie between the professional decision to modify the curriculum and actual practice in the school.

THE BREAKDOWN OF LOCAL SUPPORT FOR PUBLIC EDUCATION

The case against local control of education becomes more compelling when we consider the practical problems involved in introducing basic changes that require heavy expenditures. In recent years, our high schools have been severely criticized for their real or alleged neglect of science. For the sake of argument, suppose that we required every high-

---

[5] The need for drastic revision in the mathematics and physics curriculum of the public schools is discussed in Howard F. Fehr, "The Mathematics Curriculum for the High School of the Future," *Teachers College Record*, LIX (February, 1958), 258–67, and the articles on the Physical Science Study Committee in *Science Teacher*, XXIV (November, 1957), 316–29; and *Harvard Educational Review*, XXIX (Winter, 1959), 1–36.

school student who has the ability to do college work to take three years of physics during his high-school career. At this point, consider only the practical problems involved in implementing this recommendation. How would we get from the status quo to a situation in which all these high-school students take three years of physics? Regardless of whether this particular change is desirable, consider its implementation solely from the standpoint of the difficulties of making any basic curriculum reforms under the present system.

There are over 21,000 high schools across the country. In 1956, only 12,000 of these schools offered one full year's work in physics. As late as 1954, 50 per cent of all schools having tenth-grade pupils did not offer physics at all. These were usually the smaller schools, but it is interesting to note that only one-fourth of all high-school students in 1954 took as much as one full year of physics before graduation. We are thus confronted by thousands of school boards which have seen fit to offer one year's work or none at all in physics.[6] Each board must now be persuaded, one by one, to make drastic changes in its curriculum. Since it is unlikely that the additional work in physics will simply be added to the present curriculum, each board must make its own decision about what subjects shall be reduced or eliminated. Each board must decide what to do with the teachers in subjects to be eliminated.

Even assuming that most school boards could be convinced that more work in physics is desirable, can they be persuaded to implement such a change? If a school is to offer three years of physics instead of one or none, extensive remodeling would almost invariably be required. There would have to be substantial expenditures for new laboratory equipment and supplies. Just how substantial these would have to be is evident from a survey made in March, 1957, by the NEA's Research Division, which covered the needs for instructional equipment in high-school science and mathematics classes. More than half the schools responding to the inquiry from the Research Division reported that they did not even have direct electric current in their physics laboratory. Less than 15 per cent of the schools reporting had a calculator available for mathematics courses. Only one school in five had a graph board in every mathematics classroom; about two out of every five did not have a graph board in any mathematics classroom. The report indicated that 57 cents was the average per pupil expenditure for supplies and consumable equipment in science classrooms.[7]

Before most high schools could offer three years of physics, local

---

[6] I do not mean to suggest that there is one school board for each high school. Actually, the number of school districts is over twice as large as the number of high schools, even though many districts include more than one high school.

[7] NEA Legislative Commission, *The Hidden Need: Basic Instructional Equipment for Schools* (Washington, D.C.: National Education Association, n.d.). See also n. 8 below.

school boards would have to adopt salary schedules much more attractive than the prevailing ones. Even though physics is now offered for only one year in the majority of schools which offer it at all, there is already a large and growing shortage of physics teachers.[8] It would be pleasant to think that school boards which have heretofore balked at making minimal expenditures for physics instruction will suddenly be inspired to vote the necessary taxes for an adequate program. Unfortunately, the odds are overwhelmingly against such a development.

Under our present system of financing education, the states and local communities supply over 95 per cent of the funds for public education. Our nation spent a total of $14,827,550,000 for public education in 1957–58. Of this total, about 3 per cent came from federal sources, 40.8 per cent from the state governments, and 56.2 per cent from local sources. On a state-by-state basis, there are wide variations in the relative amounts supplied by local, state, and federal sources. In Alaska, 14.7 per cent of the total expenditures for public education came from the federal government, whereas only 0.5 per cent of the total spent in New Jersey were from this source. Also in 1957–58, Delaware raised 88.2 per cent of its school revenues at the state level and 10.3 per cent at the local level. At the other extreme, Nebraska raised 6.9 per cent of its school revenues from state sources and 89.5 per cent from local sources.[9]

In general, the trend has been for local sources to provide a decreasing percentage of the total expenditures for public education. Expenditures by the state governments tend to constitute a much larger percentage of the total, while the percentage from federal sources has been increasing but at a much slower rate than that coming from the state governments. There are several reasons why this structure is not working and can never be made to work.

In the first place, some states have four to five times as much taxable wealth, on the average, as other states. The differences between school districts are even greater; some school districts have several hundred times as much taxable wealth as others. Ability to support education has also been studied in terms of what educators call "personal income payments per pupil enrolled," that is, the total income received by the residents of a state divided by the number of pupils enrolled in its public schools. In 1956–57, "personal income payments per pupil enrolled" amounted to $17,432 in Delaware and $3,754 in Mississippi. Needless

---

[8] The National Defense Education Act passed by Congress on August 23, 1958, provided an appropriation of $300,000,000 over a four-year period for science equipment. It will be interesting to see how long it takes for Congress to recognize the futility of waiting for local school boards to institute salary schedules high enough to attract reasonably competent science and mathematics teachers.

[9] Data from Research Division, *Estimates of School Statistics* (Washington, D.C.: National Education Association, 1959).

to say, there were even greater differences between the richest and the poorest school districts.

For many years, authorities on school finance have pointed out that the poorest states and school districts usually devote a higher proportion of their resources to education than do the wealthier ones. Theoretically, one might argue that this is not very significant because all states and school districts should be making a greater effort to support education. However, this argument overlooks many important considerations relating to our tax structure.

One such consideration is the competitive aspect of state and local taxation. In New York City, there is a concentration of high incomes unequaled anywhere in the country. Nearly 20 per cent of all internal revenue is collected in New York State. Thus it would appear that New York City, which is permitted to levy an income tax but does not [it does now], and New York State, which does levy an income tax, could easily have the very best schools in the nation. The difficulty is, however, that many high-income persons and corporations would move if tax rates were raised substantially. This is why it is often fallacious to criticize states and communities for not raising taxes; if they did so, they would lose people and businesses to areas less concerned about education. The need for, and justice of, federal taxation for education would thus remain even if there were substantial equality in wealth and revenues among all states and school districts. The fact that a federal tax cannot be evaded at the expense of children in a particular school district is one of the most compelling reasons why we must move toward an educational system financed by the federal government.

Still another factor makes it very unlikely that an adequate educational system could be financed without massive federal support. School districts have been forced to raise most of their funds (54 per cent in 1953–54) by means of the property tax. Unlike most other taxes, property taxes must usually be submitted to popular vote. As is usual in this type of situation, the people who are badly hurt by a substantial tax increase are more effective politically than the diffuse majority which benefits from the increase. The result is that an increasing number of bond issues for school funds are being defeated in communities sympathetic to public education. Here is some indication of the rising (and often justified) tide of resentment against such discriminatory taxation.

The need for federal support of public education, if not for a federal system, is also related to the way in which the federal government supports non-educational activities. In the new highway program, for example, the federal government will spend $9.00 for every dollar appropriated by the state governments. Obviously, this will result in a bigger share of the state dollar being spent on highways. And, in general, states are tending to appropriate funds for projects which will receive substantial support from the federal government. Thus the only way that education can compete for funds, even at the state level, is for the federal government to assume a much larger share of the educational budget.

DISCUSSION QUESTIONS

1. Is local control of education as inadequate, stultifying, and undemocratic as Lieberman charges? Do you agree with his thesis that our freedoms have survived in spite of our schools?
2. What dogmas were given intellectual protection in the schools you attended? What, in your experience, contradicts Lieberman's description of the narrow parochialism of the public schools? Would American teachers have greater professional autonomy under a federal system of education?
3. Does local control of education give little attention to educational research and stifle the utilization of it, as Lieberman states?
4. Do you accept as inevitable federal financing of education and a national system of schools? Would you oppose these vigorously?

THE PROGRESSIVE LABOR PARTY **We Must Rule**
EDUCATION COMMITTEE[1] **the School**

What kind of life is ahead for our boys and girls who go to public school in New York?

Our boys and girls are on a slow boat to nowhere. There are a few good teachers and good classes, but these are for the middle-class children—mostly white. The working-class children get such bad schooling that they can hardly even read.

Even the Board of No Education says that most of our boys and girls are years behind. The end of the line for them will be a low-pay job, or maybe no job, or learning to kill other working people in Vietnam.

Now, why is this? Can we do anything about it?

Every school system in history has been the front man for the ruling power of the country. The schools aim to train people to serve the rulers' interests.

The New York City Board of No-Education is no different. This Board represents those who control this society: the ruling class. It "educates" people to fill the economic needs of our ruling class. Today

Reprinted with permission of the publisher, the Progressive Labor Party, Manhattanville Post Office Station, New York, N.Y. 10027.

[1] The Progressive Labor Party asks that its present position be emphasized: that it is demanding "a better curriculum, smaller class sizes, more and better teachers, better lunches, crossing guards [and] for [its] children to be able to read. . . ." Community control, the Party states, is a phrase used to divert parents from their goals, since "there can never be real community control under U.S. capitalism. . . ."

they need a small group of intellectuals to teach, service and act as "spokesmen" for the people; a group of scientists and technicians to organize industry; a large mass of working people to run that industry; and a large group of unemployed unskilled workers to serve as "competition" for the employed labor force.

The rich ruling class[2] wants *service*. They want unthinking workers who will be forced to work in low-pay jobs. They want soldiers. They don't want to give our boys and girls good schooling—they want them to have just enough to put them in a bad job or the army. And the rich ruling class doesn't want to spend money on schooling the working class—they would rather spend billions on the army and police who keep working-class people down, here and around the world.

Of course, they have some good jobs which need better schooling. They want to give these jobs to "their own kind." The good public schooling goes to people whom the ruling class can trust to keep their robbery system going smoothly. These are the middle-class families—mostly white, plus a few other educated mis-leaders who will help to sell out and oppress their own people.

So let's look at the New York "school problem," the way the ruling class looks at it. All of a sudden it makes some sense. The middle-class parts of the city have the better schools. Manhattan and the south Bronx and the Brooklyn ghettos—all the sections where working-class people are crowded in—have the worst, most overcrowded schools. *These boys and girls just aren't taught.*

For instance, at P.S. 176, at 12th Avenue and 68th Street in Brooklyn, which is a white working-class neighborhood, the ethnic breakdown is:

Black	Puerto Rican	White
5.2%	1.5%	93.4%

The reading level for the 6th grade, as given out by the Board of Education, is 6.2; the level should be 6.8.

At P.S. 68 at 127th Street between 7th Avenue and Lenox Avenue in Manhattan, the ethnic breakdown is:

Black	Puerto Rican	White
96.9%	3.1%	0.0%

The reading level for the 6th grade is 4.9.

At P.S. 81 at Riverdale Avenue and 255th Street, a white upper-middle-class school, the ethnic breakdown is:

[2] We use the term "ruling class" here to describe the group of bankers, bosses and landlords who own the large industrial plants, factories and farms, and buildings. They actually determine who will be president, governor, mayor, police chief, judge, etc. This class of rich people that run this country are the exact opposite of us and are our enemy and as long as they run the country we will never be free!

Black	Puerto Rican	White
1.7%	2.6%	95.7%

The reading level for the 6th grade is 9.4.

These figures show that while the worst schools are in Harlem, the white working-class is not being taught either, and the children who are being taught by the Board are those who live in upper-middle-class areas like Riverdale.

Most upper-class children, of course, never go to public school. In case a middle-class family sends a child to public school, they have the "track" system. That means that inside these jail-houses that they call "schools" there are a few good classes—and if you come from a middle-class home, you will be "tracked" into these classes. That is, inside the public school system they have "private schools" for the middle class.

But if you are working-class Black or Puerto Rican, *You will not be educated*. If they educated you, would you work for the low pay they want to give you? Would you fight their wars when you could go to college instead? They know you wouldn't. That's why they don't improve the schools.

FIGHT FOR CHANGE

This book will try to show just what changes we need in our schools. But it won't do you any good to say "That sounds good. I'll send a copy of this book to the Mayor and the Board of Education." The Mayor and the Board of No-Education belong to the ruling class.

Working people will get what they need only by fighting for it. We have to get the parents and students together, join hands with any sincere teachers who really put the children's needs first, and say to the government:

We know you need this kind of school system to keep the country going the way you want it. But *we want* our boys and girls to grow up and be proud of their own people and ready to look any man in the eye. And any schools here are going to be, we're going to make you run them our way.

We want our youth to know enough to be able to do anything they want—maybe even reading and writing and planning about how to change the whole U.S. imperialist system so that our people don't get cheated all their life. We know that you rulers are afraid that workers—especially Black and Puerto Rican workers—will learn how to organize and fight harder for their own people. That is why you won't teach the real history—the fighting working-class history, the fighting Afro-American history, the fighting Hispanic-American history—in public schools today.

But there is no tomorrow for these old schools, because we are going to fight until we win our right to a full and proud education.

DISCUSSION QUESTIONS

1. Is there a "conspiracy" to deprive the poor of the kind of education that would break down social and economic barriers? Who are the "conspirators"?
2. Do the reading scores cited buttress the "conspiracy" arguments? How do you explain these scores?
3. Are middle-class children "tracked" into good classes? Are poor children "tracked" into inferior classes?

SHELDON PTASCHEVITCH STOFF   New Directions for Education: Humanize the Dehumanizer

In advocating new direction for education one must assume at least the following: A structure which was appropriate at an earlier point in history may not be appropriate today, and a structure which was wrong at an earlier time in history may not be wrong today. One must judge solely on the basis of merit, ignoring the binds that tradition may hold for us.

One must be prepared to ask fundamental question such as: Is the educational system under question accomplishing that which it was instituted to accomplish? If not:

1. Minor changes within the system may be in order.
2. The structure of the system itself may be of such a nature as to constitute a contribution to failure. In fact, it may be a prime cause for failure, and the system may require major change in order to now succeed.
3. One may even see the system as beyond salvage and thus a new structure or system must evolve.

I assume that the structure of the system must fundamentally change if success is to be achieved.

A presentation prepared for the New York State Commission on the Quality, Cost, and Financing of Elementary and Secondary Education, February 1971.

THE SYSTEM

I assume that any monolithic school system, such as we have at present, is a dehumanizer because it restricts both the teacher and the taught, seeking conformity to an ideal imposed by authority rather than confirming major responsibility on themselves. The system that demands conformity and acceptance deprives us of variety and grace.

Any government or school official, offering "the way" for the future of education, is a dehumanizer in that he takes this responsibility out of the hands of teachers, students, and parents. What strange concept of "individuality" mandates that everyone be part of a monolithic system? It is only an individuality to dance to the piper's melody, one on a long list of hit tunes, each destined to fall by the way as it is replaced. Woe to the man who does not wish to dance to the current tune. He is looked upon as a "traditionalist," obstructionist, or worse.

For example, in recent years we have seen major attempts at rejuvenating education. These include at least the following:

Team teaching
Programmed instruction and teaching machines
Modular-time programming
New math
New sciences
New social studies
Sensitivity training
Computer assisted learning
Community control
Professional control
The discovery method
The open classroom
The open school
The free school

Any one-dimensional solution assumes that all teachers and all students must follow the same track. But why shouldn't democracy and free choice exist in education? If college students are given some degree of democracy in selecting their schools why should not this basic right be extended into the secondary school and the elementary school? Why doesn't pluralism exist as a working ideal of democracy in education?

If the ideal of pluralism and democracy in education were offered as a contrasting ideal to a monolithic system, let us explore what it has to offer.

It assumes that, in financing, a government must obligate itself to the support of education for all children. It assumes this burden of the government, but it does not assume that the government has the right to call the tune and completely dictate the kind of education offered.

For example, I assume that the government has the obligation to provide assistance to the aged, but no right to demand how they spend their money. Pluralism advocates the philosophy of the G.I. Bill, which supported many thousands of students through college, but did not challenge *their* choice of college. It only asked that the college be accredited. No government has the right to ask more of any student. The government must demand that firm, comprehensive standards, designed and supervised by independent professional sources, be established. But it must not seek conformity by control.

To be free, students must, at least, have freedom of choice and a minimum of government interference in their selection of schools. No government should exert the kinds of restrictions over choice in education that we are forced to live with today. Freedom of choice is sacred, but it must involve ability and capacity to choose if it is to have meaning. This cannot exist unless we have an open government committed to school support without preference![1]

What benefits might accrue from such a pluralistic system?

FOR THE TEACHER

The teaching occupation will begin to take on the aspects of professionalism. Teaching and teacher-training will take on a new excitement. Rather than taking a teacher-training program eclectically styled, each student will have the choice of programs, each one designed to prepare him to teach with a different commitment.

Education courses in the colleges will have greater substance because differences in philosophy, psychology, and methods will constitute education for different school systems—system built around ideals rather than conveniences. The young college student will be able to select a program based on his ideals. The school he eventually elects to teach in will stand for this ideal. It might be modeled after Dewey or Buber or the open classroom or Conant or Hutchins.

It will surely stand for something. Teachers of like mind will gather together to teach there and a commonality and continuity of purpose will exist which will generate quality. This certainly could begin immediately with schools within schools in existing public schools, each articulating the ideals of its teachers, and each standing for something. The independent schools have already made a start in this direction, a movement toward an open marketplace in education.

FOR THE STUDENT

Imagine the power we will give to students, a balance of what we have previously afforded teachers. The teachers will control the destiny

[1] Safeguards, in terms of desegregation, etc., are welcome and expected.

and philosophy of their schools and the students will have full responsibility for selecting the kind of school they wish to attend. For the younger children it will mean that the parents will have a choice. They will have to review what schools are offering and make a selection.

For older pupils it will mean that they must evaluate the significance of their education and make meaningful choices. They will not be simply pawns in a system. They will create the system by attendance, or doom it by withdrawal. I believe that they will select that which will provide nourishment for them. Isn't this freedom of choice what democracy is all about?

FOR SOCIETY

There is one additional effect that pluralizing education could have, and in the long run it could be the most important reason for pluralization. If the United States can accept the ideal of democracy in education, the ideal that no government has the right to dominate and control education, an important step toward world peace may have been taken.

This vital ideal might well be the real American contribution to peace in our time. Imagine the implication if other nations followed our example, if their school systems were removed from government control. One can envisage international systems devoted to the ideals of a Dewey or a Buber or a Neill, and fewer devoted to nationalism or pedantry. Sterility in education would decline. One can expect that, essentially, parents and students would choose wisely. Those schools offering little would attract few. That which is meaningful would grow.

There will be education with a difference. Ideas will flow in education. Our government will support, not dictate. Other governments might follow, thus building a firmer basis for international brotherhood.

DISCUSSION QUESTIONS

1. Do you believe that Stoff is justified in providing for free choice of schools for parents and students? Will students choose wisely?
2. Is the balance of power between teachers and students a reasonable division?
3. What might be the worldwide results of a separation between government and education?

JAMES MICHENER   # Kent State:
What Happened and Why

The Threat to Education

If events like those which overtook Kent State were to continue to occur either at Kent or elsewhere, American advanced education would be in the gravest peril. Society would react with revulsion and would rebel against giving any further moral or financial support to education beyond the high school level, and the whole grand superstructure of advanced learning as we have known it would come crashing down. It is impossible to believe that this would benefit the United States or that it would be anything but a tragedy of enormous dimension, but there are many in our society who want to see it happen.

We must understand how it could happen, and anyone who was present at Kent during the summer and autumn of 1970 saw only too clearly how this could have been accomplished. Here are three scenarios that observers feared.

SCENARIO ONE.   At the opening of school in early October a cadre of committed revolutionaries, nameless successors to the more peaceful radicals who had once dominated the Haunted House and the place on Ash Street, would declare war on society by either dynamiting a building or shooting a policeman. It was not necessary to look to university students for such action, because a message from the underground, purporting to have come from Bernardine Dohrn, had publicly threatened that the national revolutionary movement would soon dynamite Kent.

Regardless of who committed the act, the reaction would be the same. The student body, almost unanimously, would condemn this violent action, but to no avail, for the Ohio legislature in Columbus would demand immediate and excessive reaction, and the local authorities in Portage County would feel free to close the university down again, this time perhaps for a couple of years. Also, with the first intimation of trouble on campus, vigilante groups from the surrounding countryside would arm themselves and begin a private cleaning-up of anyone with long hair or habits offensive to them. There would be open gunfire, which would be responded to by those students who had managed to smuggle weapons onto campus. The students would lose. Because of Kent's symbolic significance across America, there would be anguished responses from other student groups in other universities, and one by one our great educational institutions would close . . . the list would grow each day. And some would stay closed for a year or more.

SCENARIO TWO. It was quite possible, in October, 1970, that violent disruptions in any college or university could have served as the spark for general student unrest. If the educational community at Wisconsin kept an eye on Kent, fearful of what might happen there, it was equally true that people in Kent were watching Wisconsin, and Colorado, and Michigan, and a dozen other schools. Any spectacular student rioting in any of those institutions would have ignited the entire student population of this country to the flash point. Suppose that some insane incident at Wisconsin, following in the wake of the August bombing there, had inflamed both the townspeople and the student body, with resulting confrontations and bloodshed. Surely the consequences would have reverberated around this nation, and students in Kent might well have reacted. From that point on, the counter-reactions of society would be the same as before, with similar results.

SCENARIO THREE. This is the most mournful, because it is the most likely, and it is likely because it grows not from some one insane act committed by some addle-pated idiot, but from the daily life and desperations of thoughtful students. It is this possibility that must be carefully considered.

The degree of radicalization that occurred at Kent State on May 4 when the guns went off is almost impossible to describe. Jocks who saw girls gunned down began to talk like revolutionaries. Greeks whose houses were invaded needlessly by police and who were gassed while sitting on their front porches sounded like YSA members of two years before. Students who had thought of themselves as straight suddenly found themselves discussing what they called 'the repressive nature of the police state.' And thousands of white students who had never paid much attention to black student demands began to say to one another, 'Maybe they have legitimate complaints.'

Colin Neiburger was standing on a train platform in Cleveland shortly after the shooting when a sorority girl from Kent rushed up to him, embraced him fervently, and cried, 'Colin! I should have listened to you last year.' One of the researchers had the opportunity of meeting with sixty fraternity men at Kent, the straightest group on campus, and came away in a state of near-shock. 'They talked like flaming radicals!' he reported. 'They despise Vietnam. They discuss openly whether they should flee to Canada to avoid the draft. They believe we're destroying our natural resources. And they claim that neither the university nor the national administration will listen to them. If parents in middle America believe that it's only the long hairs who are demanding action, they ought to listen to their conservative children.'

Now suppose that this large body of sensible students, already partially radicalized by events of the past two years, become convinced that there is no hope of modifying society through normal channels. Suppose they come to believe that their best professors are being intimidated by the FBI, or spied upon by the army. Suppose they grow increasingly resentful at the rumored presence of informers in the classroom. Suppose they feel, correctly or not, that they have no recourse at the administration level. Suppose our national leaders continue to belabor them publicly while diminishing economic support. And then suppose that the Vietnam war drags on interminably, with sporadic escalations and no diminution in the killing or no escape from the draft.

Is it not possible that students might interpret some otherwise trivial thing as the final indignity and overrespond to it? There would be mass protest of some kind, harsh reaction from the police, an irresponsible act by some student, and the quick mobilization of vigilantes. From there on, the descent is clearly marked out.

. . .

The end result of the three scenarios is the same. A substantial number of centers of higher education throughout the United States would be immediately closed down. This must not be taken as a remote possibility. State legislatures and local governing bodies are itching for a chance to do this, 'to teach those snot-nosed kids and smart-aleck professors a lesson.' The important thing is not the temporary disciplining of the universities, for they could absorb that, but what might happen next.

As soon as the universities were closed, legislatures would take steps to emasculate the state-supported schools. The right of professors to criticize society would be abolished. Many departments would be eliminated permanently. Student enrollments would be cut 40 percent. Graduate schools would be dropped from many universities, and emphasis would be placed upon vocational education. Courses like The New Family, Karl Marx and Nineteenth Century Thought, The New York School of Action Painting, and The Protest Novel would vanish, and any professor brave enough to teach sociology, English or philosophy would be supervised by constantly running tape recorders whose contents would be reviewed not by university personnel but by civil authorities not connected with the university. The result would be the passing of stern laws prohibiting the enrollment of students from out of state; these would be popular with voters for two reasons. They see no reason why as citizens of State A they should pay for the education of students from State B; and they are convinced that it is outsiders, especially Jewish students from New York, who cause local disruptions, in spite of the fact that most of the known agitation has moved from west to east and involved only as many Jewish students as the percentage of Jews in the general population would have provided.

It is entirely possible that in each state certain state-supported institutions, especially those which had caused irritation in the past, might be closed permanently and their vast investment of campus and building diverted to other uses. Thus Kent State in Ohio and Temple University in Philadelphia, to take only two schools who have battled long and well for certain principles, might be shut down forever. Had a plebiscite been taken in Portage County in the summer of 1970, it is likely that the voters would have elected to get rid of Kent State once and for all. As late as October, when school had peacefully resumed, researchers for this book attended a series of informal dinner parties at which well over 80 percent of those present, responsible citizens all, were in favor of abolishing the university and turning its physical plant over to some other social use.

Nor would private institutions be exempt from such discipline. Boards would be pressured both from within and without to terminate all aspects of university life which cause trouble. Alumni, battered emotionally by what they had been witnessing over the past three or four years, would withhold contributions until such time as corrective measures were taken, and in the long run the private university might be in a more perilous position than the public, in that a legislature might be quicker to respond to public demand for reinstitution of some form of public education than a private board might be.

It would be very tempting to close major educational institutions, but for a democracy to do so would be insanity This complex industrial democracy could not function if even one generation of its trained personnel were lacking. Who would plan the sewer systems? Who would design the new Pontiac cars? Who would invent the better plastic or print the better books? High school graduates cannot provide the medical and dental services required nor the leadership in law and engineering—and to believe that they can is preposterous.

More important, the constant study and evaluation of society which is required if a nation is to remain healthy can be carried on only in the university. Trained minds are essential for the understanding of where we are and where we are heading. Universities are needed more today than ever before, if only because the need for response to new problems is accelerated.

Two examples illustrate this condition. One of the subjects which most infuriates the outside observer is sociology. Of a hundred professors whom the laymen of this country would like to silence, a vast majority would be from this field, yet in no area of exploration is professional guidance more needed. The American system of courtship and marriage is undergoing the most violent change. Young people have struck out in bold new directions, and the trial marriage, which so infuriated Americans when Judge Ben Lindsely and philosopher Bertrand Russell first proposed it, is now commonplace, and in the very families of those whose parents objected most strenuously when the idea was first suggested. Communal living, new plans for rearing children and new attitudes toward the care of elderly people must all be studied, dissected and judged. The professor who directs his microscope to such subjects is not popular with the general public, but his work is essential and he must be protected while he carries it out.

The second example comes from a less inflammatory field. The great Penn Central railroad combine, one of the largest corporations in America and one of the important symbols of our business history, has for the past fifteen years been going quietly broke. Vast changes were under way in American life, and these produced sharp repercussions in the transportation industry, but the managers of the Penn Central seemed not to be aware of this. Because of the vital significance of railroading to this nation, there ought to have been in universities like Penn, Columbia and Chicago, to name only those in the major cities affected by the collapse of this particular railroad, college professors who were philosophically analyzing the nature of railroads in our democracy and issuing warnings that if the Penn Central continued the way it was going, it would soon be broke. Had there been such professors, and had they issued their warnings a decade ago, it is obvious that business leaders would have castigated them as meddlers and warned them to return to the campus and not interfere with real life. It is the job of the university to put all of real life under the microscope of reason and investigation. To consign the university to a lesser role would be stupid, for to do so would be to insure the collapse of this society.

The question, then, in this twilight age when great institutions may be closed for shorter or longer periods, is this: How can we have a disciplined university whose behavior conforms to generally accepted standards and at the same time preserve the freedom of investigation and discussion? If the universities cannot insure the former, then society will not provide the latter. And if free investigation vanishes, then this democracy will also vanish.

If we did close our schools, we could continue for a while without apparent loss, but soon we would no longer be able to maintain a creative society here at home, and we would fail in our competition with Russia and China abroad. Our industries would find themselves lagging behind those of Germany and Sweden. Our music and theater and magazines would begin to wither, and what imagination we had in television would vanish. Public services would begin to falter and there would be no inventions to keep factories alive. Worst of all, the yeast of ideas which makes life palatable would no longer operate and a terrible drabness would overtake us all, for the intellectual leadership which a modern society requires would be lacking.

We need education. We need intelligence. We need the inspiration and the fire of the young. And if we believe, even in moments of frustration and despair, that we can get along without them, we are trying to do what no other creative civilization in history has been able to do: function without trained minds. It is our job to restudy the role of education in a free society so that the historic functions of the university can continue after its weaknesses have been corrected.

. . .

Recommendations of the committee are far-ranging, and are accompanied with a warning that the committee will be visiting each campus six months hence to check on what the universities have done to police themselves. Students are to be expelled or suspended for 'misconduct involving moral turpitude, drug abuse or persistent misconduct, whatever its gravity.' Faculty members are warned that the committee has heard of instances in which 'faculty members had condoned or actively encouraged disruptive activities by students and had even participated in such activities, had failed to teach the scheduled course content, had failed without excuse to meet scheduled classes, had made unwarranted and repeated use of obscene language in open class, and before other students had ridiculed and degraded students holding political and social opinions opposed to their own.' Appended to this list was the recommendation: 'The code of faculty conduct and discipline should provide that whether an offender is tenured or not is irrelevant to the imposition of appropriate sanctions for misconduct.' Administrators are chided for having surrendered so many of their prerogatives to faculty and student committees and are urged to take them back: 'In part, such committees represent administrative surrender to increasingly clamorous demands by faculty and students for control of university affairs. It was pointed out that such committees frequently deal with matters beyond the experience or competence of some or all of their members, and require weeks and even months to reach decisions which a competent administrator might make in a matter of hours or days.'

From these samples it can be seen that many changes are going to be forced upon public education, some of them draconian; after a brief experience the most repressive will be ignored by both the legislature and the university. Others will persist and some of them will be salutary. Let us see what the necessary changes might be, remembering that they apply only to public universities; private colleges have their own special problems.

REGENTS AND TRUSTEES. Both the public and the legislature will demand a higher level of performance from appointed boards, who will have to exercise more control than in the past. The senseless proliferation and duplication of fields of specialization ought to end. In a state like Ohio, or a region like the Rocky Mountains, where population is not concentrated, institutions should reach an agreement that each would do what it can do best. Libraries, staffs and students should be concentrated at the effective point and other institutions in the area should not try to compete in the same field.

Boards must insist that the universities get back to the problem of teaching and stop trying to be all things to all people. Specifically, research on military matters should not be conducted on university campuses nor subsidized by the military or industry. The many institutes of questionable teaching value—although of unquestioned investigative importance—should be removed from the university and located elsewhere. Balance between teaching and research must be achieved, and freshman and sophomore students should have at least some contact with full professors, for they are in their most formative years and would profit most from such teaching.

The question of open admission to the university must be reconsidered. Kent State is cluttered with students who have no vocation to be on campus. The young man whose previous education has not prepared him to read, write, figure or grapple with abstract ideas and who lacks the capacity to acquire those skills has no place in a university. He is destined, from the moment he sets foot on campus, to a life of frustration; too often he will become radicalized, and with bad luck, could become a revolutionary, for he knows that the university cannot fulfill his needs. For the poorly prepared student who does have a capacity to learn, the state should provide some kind of pre-university experience which enable him to catch up; after two years or more of such educational therapy, the successful learner should enter the sophomore year with the probability that he will succeed.

Serious consideration should be given to a plan whereby a large system like Ohio's is broken down into three different kinds of universities. The first would specialize in technical training, with emphasis upon skills; every effort would be made to make this type of education respectable. . . . The second would specialize in granting the bachelor's degree in all fields, the master's in some, and the doctorate in a highly selected few. Emphasis would be upon teaching, with the faculty required to keep abreast of research being done throughout the nation. The third would be the traditional, full-fledged university competing with great schools like Harvard and Chicago. It would offer a complete roster of research and would contain law and medical faculties. Once a decision was made as to the kind of institution a given university was to be, regents and trustees should be watchful in protecting it against encroachments which would divert it from its responsibility; it should not be allowed to slip unobtrusively back into the sloppy tradition whereby each university, regardless of its capacity, tried to be everything to everybody. Obviously, a university of the third type ought not to permit open admission, because its curriculum and teaching would be so advanced that only the more literate high school graduate could profit. But there should be a fairly free interchange of students after the sophomore year, for by then students would have gained a clearer understanding of their interests and capabilities.

When such a proposal was discussed in Ohio, one knowing resident cautioned, 'It would never work. Ohio State University wouldn't enroll enough football players to retain its pre-eminence. And that the legislature would not allow.'

ADMINISTRATION. In the next decade American advanced education is going to make a grave mistake, but there seems no way to prevent it. Regents and legislatures will call for appointment of administrators from outside fields like business or the military in the mistaken idea that they will know how to run a university. Fortified by automatic laws like House Bill 1219 and the proposed Oregon statutes, these men will be able to keep the lid on for a while, but the outcome can only be second-rate education and a constant deterioration of that. University administrators are best when they come up through the ranks and have an intellectual competence, for they deal not only with buildings and budgets but also with young minds and the future of this nation. There is no 'administrative type'; there is only the trained educator who has a gift for administering complex organizations. If he is difficult to find in the local universities, Ohio must look elsewhere, and then start quickly to develop its own crop, for one such man, properly placed, can inspire the young people of an entire state.

During all but the last crisis, the administrators of Kent State performed well and no blanket condemnation can be justified by the facts. However, the legislative committee is correct when it recommends that every administration in Ohio recover to itself the basic functions of administration. Too many boards and committees have been allowed to grow up and to siphon off the responsibilities of the administrator. Faculty and students are entitled to representation on such boards as are decided upon, but a complex of such boards must not be allowed to stultify action.

It is regrettable that a university today must have a crisis plan, but if this is an age of crisis, not to be prepared is preposterous. Ths distinction in military circles between line and staff—those who are responsible for command and those whose job it is to see that command has the materials to do the job—is an admirable one. On every campus it should be clearly understood where the line of command runs and upon whom it devolves when swift decision is required.

Universities probably make a mistake when they place too much emphasis and hope on campus police. In Ohio, the pendulum has swung much too far in the direction of an armed guard poised to sweep down on evildoers; it is frightening to realize that under the new laws any one of these quasi-policemen has the power to arrest either a student or a faculty member and thus cause his instant suspension for a year or his loss of enrollment or job for life. This is much too close to the old Japanese and German systems which caused such vigorous and ill-advised countermeasures after the last war. The university would be better served by calling in outside police and reserving for its campus force various caretaking and supervisory jobs.

FACULTY.   Tenure for professors should be abolished. It is abused by men of little dedication, protects mainly the incompetent, does not protect the young who are on the firing line, and has no parallel in the adult life of a democracy except in the lesser jobs in civil service, where its principle produces even greater evil. It is an affront to those who best support education in that they enjoy no tenure. Its place should be taken by a guaranteed-employment contract renewable after review at ten-year intervals (or seven) with tenure till retirement after thirty years of satisfactory service.

Although it is preposterous to think of a university not founded on a basis of scholarship, and although major faculty emphasis must continue to be the search for truth and new understandings of it, there ought to be an equal opportunity for professional advancement for those members of the faculty who bear the major teaching load. Indulgent smiles used to greet those who proposed dividing the faculty into two categories, 'the scholars and the teachers,' for it seemed obvious that one became a scholar in order to teach and that no one had a right to teach unless he was a scholar, but many critics of the university are now satisfied that advanced research has become so highly specialized that the old belief is no longer viable. There is a place for the man who specializes in instruction, and no interview was more gloomy than the one in which a young graduate assistant confessed, 'When I reported to Kent for my job, the head of the department told me, "You have two responsibilities, teaching and research, and you must not get your priorities confused. It will take you at least two years to get your degree, but unless you maintain a 3.5 average your first year, you won't be invited back. Therefore, apply yourself to the courses you are taking and learn to get by in the courses you are teaching." '

The more that restrictive legislation hampers the traditional role of the professor, the more dedicated he must become. His impartial wisdom is needed now more than ever. As changes are forced upon the university, his experience and precaution are essential. And as our nation faces new problems, it requires the counsel of the best brains available. In recent years there have been harsh attacks on professors; to them there is only one reply: 'Could this intricate nation exist for one year without the help of trained intelligence?' Professors are more valuable now than ever before, more essential to the national well-being. They must continue as bastions of freedom, for this may be their finest contribution to America.

We spent many hours listening to a debate which confronts all large universities. Should teaching fellows and graduate assistants be made a formal part of the faculty? We have heard every reason why they should not, for example: 'They are too immature to have the best interests of the university at heart.' But not one counterbalances the overwhelming fact that much of the instruction first- and second-year students receive comes from these unattached young scholars. If they are not absorbed into the general faculty, they ought at least to be handled differently from the way they now are. To do otherwise is to lay the university open to the charge of employing sweated labor.

STUDENTS. Society is going to demand that students comport themselves more responsibly; if they don't, they are going to be thrown out of the university. Insofar as behavior is concerned, the new rules impose no added hardship on the young person who wants an education. For the most part they enforce laws already on the books, laws which the majority of society accepts but which in recent years have been overlooked where students were concerned. Arson is arson, and persons guilty of it should go to jail. Inciting to riot has been a felony for many years. And the enticing theory of sanctuary was never acknowledged in law .

While students should volunteer to respect accepted modes of behavior, they must not allow themselves to be muzzled in speech nor put in blinders intellectually. The university is a place for investigation, and the years from eighteen through twenty-five are a time for broad questioning. Political activity on the campus ought to continue as vigorously as in the past, for our democracy depends upon a constant inflow of young people committed to politics. All aspects of our political, social, economic and moral life ought to be subjected to scrutiny. Indeed, there is a greater need for the questing student now than there was ten years ago, for the rate of change has accelerated. But the excesses of recent years, when intellectual investigation led to physical violence, must be halted, and every sensible student acknowledges that.

In a time when the stress is on what students must not do, it may be helpful to remember what they should do. They attend a university to gain an education, and this presupposes intellectual, social and political participation. Our nation has prospered in part because so many of our young people have learned at university the full range of their capabilities, and any effort now to diminish the breadth of that experience would be folly, for it would impoverish our nation twenty years from now. Specifically, in addition to studying, students ought to (1) participate in the governance of the university; (2) help set rules of behavior; (3) help determine what is to be taught; (4) help evaluate their teachers; (5) help establish university priorities; (6) help in the political organization of the student body along democratic lines; (7) assume some responsibility for good relation with the surrounding community of which they will be a significant part for four years.

In the 1970's it is especially difficult to be a responsible student, because as the university relinquishes its role of *in loco parentis* and accords the student freedoms no previous students have known, he is obligated to use that freedom intelligently and with some restraint; behavior and speech patterns which accomplish only the alienation of the general community are counterproductive. Society is not yet wise enough to solve the marijuana problem, but when infraction of present rules can bring down upon a student three non-concurrent jail terms of twenty to forty years, prudent behavior is necessary until society does clarify its thinking. It is impossible to condone the decision of those students who believe that the only escape from American pressures is to emigrate either to Canada or Sweden; if the existing alternatives are judged to be morally unacceptable, a jail term in the United States would seem preferable. Finally, the breadth of the gap between parents and children seems greater now than in previous generations, and young people are obligated to do what they can to diminish this distance. If student life is more complicated now, it also seems more exciting and potentially rewarding. It is hard to muster sympathy for the recurring statement, 'Who cares? We may all be dead tomorrow.' That is not a legitimate student posture.

Finally, the student must identify his major goals and must not expect the university to fulfill those which it is not competent to handle. The student whose life goal is 'the complete restructuring of society' or 'the immediate abolishment of capitalism' or 'the end of racism in America' cannot reasonably demand that the university solve those problems. Kent enrolled many students in the years 1968–70 who sought from it not an education but a social revolution; they were frequently brilliant young people and often the most likable, but the university was not where they should have been fighting their battles; it would have been justified in asking them to leave.

. . .

If we had one major criticism of the Kent State student body, it would be that its most promising scholars had been so diverted by politics that they were ignoring those basic studies which have been the very foundation of political action. One did not find the young man whose mind was ablaze with the ideas of Immanuel Kant or the social theories of J. J. C. L. Blanc; he did not meet young women enraptured during their fall quarter with Palestrina and about to transfer their affections in winter quarter to the soaring work of Le Corbusier. There seemed to be a lack of dedication to knowledge, as if societies or lives could be held together without it. We were especially disturbed by the lack of formal knowledge on the part of the young radicals; they seemed not to know that men like Marx and Lenin studied endlessly before they developed their ideas and that Americans like Thomas Jefferson and

Sam Adams were patient scholars before they became revolutionary leaders. They were irritated when we pressed for specific answers as to what they would do if their revolution succeeded; Abbie Hoffman's famous reply can be considered amusing. 'Abolish pay toilets, man, that's the goal of our revolution. Eternal life and free toilets.' Such a wisecrack has a place in any movement, for it jollies up the debate, but to accept it as a substitute for the hard, bitter analysis that men and movements require is to accept rubbish. The university is a gold mine from which the student can dig whatever ore he requires, but he must do the digging.

DISCUSSION QUESTIONS

1. Michener sees the university threatened by the irrational forces that lie close to the surface of American life. How widespread and powerful are these forces? Do they imperil the university? Do they restrict freedom of thought and expression by creating a climate of fear and silence?
2. Michener's brief for the importance of the role the university plays in the American scene is essentially pragmatic in orientation. Are there more important reasons that would make the continuance of the university vital to a free and open society?
3. Do you accept Michener's thesis that we must "have a disciplined university whose behavior conforms to generally accepted standards"?

BRUNO BETTELHEIM The Anatomy of
Academic Discontent

While history does not repeat itself, and while the present situation in the United States is radically different from that of pre-Hitler Germany, some similarities between the present student rebellion in this country and what happened in the German universities to spearhead Hitler's rise to power are nevertheless striking. Politically, of course, the German student rebels embraced the extreme right, while here the dissenters embrace the extreme left, but what is parallel is the determination to bring down the establishment. In Germany the philosophy which gained the rebels a mass following was racist and directed against a discriminated minority (the Jews), while here the radical students intend to *help* a discriminated minority. This is an important difference, but it does not change the parallel that universities then and now were forced to make decisions with respect to the race of students, rather than on the basis

By permission of the author.

of disregard of racial origin. To use only one example, German universities began to cave in when students coerced faculties to appoint professorships in *Rassenwissenschaft*; that is, professorships devoted to teaching the special aspects, merits and achievements of one race as opposed to others, rather than teaching the contribution to knowledge, whatever the origin of the contributors.

Professor Walter Z. Laqueur (*Young Germany*, Basic Books, 1962) says, "National Socialism came to power as the party of youth." Its cult of youth was as pronounced as that of Italian fascism whose very hymn was called "Youth" (Giovenezza). Hitler insisted all along that his movement was a revolt "of the coming generation against all that was senile and rotten with decay in German democratic society." Professor Peter Gay (*Weimar Culture: The Outsider as Insider*, Harper and Row, 1968) stresses the prevalence in pre-Hitler days of an ideology that pitted sons against fathers and insisted that the generations cannot understand each other, that they are deadly enemies; in short, an ideology that said exactly the same thing in this respect that our rebellious students, who insist that nobody over thirty is trustworthy, say today. Then, as now, the student rebels were pictured as the new generation, disgusted with the complacency of their parents, fighting courageously for a better world. And what were then the mass media often depicted them as idealists, as young people concerned with the real issues of society. They were, in their time, the wave of the future. And leftist student activists in 1968 burned books they did not like in the same manner and at the same place—Berlin—as did Hitler's youthful followers in 1933.

Then, as now, these youthful followers of the extremists were antiintellectual, resting their case on convictions based on their emotions. They were fascinated with violence. Their favorite technique was to disrupt meetings, not just because they were not to their liking, but more as a demonstration of their power; and they created disorder which then was claimed to demonstrate that the establishment was unable to function, and hence had to be replaced by one based on their creed.

Having stressed these parallels, one must also recognize the vast differences between the present American student rebelliousness and that of pre-Hitler Germany. It is these differences which should permit us to work toward an entirely different outcome. If I read the signs of the time correctly, I do not think that the rebellious students in and by themselves are a serious danger to this country, although they are a real danger to the universities. The danger, I fear, is rather an opposite one: that the disgusting behavior of a very small group of students—the overwhelming majority of our students are sound and wish nothing more than to take advantage of the opportunities higher education offers them—will arouse a severe counterreaction, so much so that their leftist radicalism may lead to a fascist type of backlash. This is the greatest danger inherent in their efforts to create chaos. To prevent chaos, and in desperation—and the rebels do succeed in creating desperation—repressive measures might be embraced which would be dangerous to our democratic institutions. Because of this danger, student rebellions must be dealt with in the best interest of all society, including that of the rebelling students themselves. But they can be dealt with intelligently and constructively only if the measures adopted are designed to eliminate the causes of the widespread discontent.

To understand this discontent, one has to realize first that many more young people go to college today than ever before, and hence many more are much less prepared for it. Taking advantage of college and being satisfied with the experience, rather than being defeated by it, requires a considerable amount of self-discipline and a high degree of satisfaction with developing one's intellect. Present-day education, both at home and in school, teaches very little self-discipline compared to even very recent times. The expectation now is that education can hand over knowledge and skills, and nearly instantly; there is a widespread feeling that if students do not do well in school, then this is the failing of the educational system, not the result of a lack of personal application. With each year in school, this feeling becomes stronger in those who do not do well academically. And with it, the system becomes the enemy which deliberately withholds from them what they believe it could so easily give; hence their hatred of the system.

To understand why pressures erupt in adolescence on a growing scale nowadays, and why society's controls seem to grow weaker, we must recognize that adolescent revolt is not a stage of development that follows automatically from our natural makeup. What makes for adolescent revolt is the fact that our society keeps the younger generation too long dependent in terms of mature responsibility and a striving for independence. Years ago, when formal schooling ended for the vast majority at the age of fourteen or fifteen and thereafter one became self-supporting, married and had children, there was no need for adolescent revolt. Because while puberty is a biological given, adolescence as we know it with its identity crises is not. All children grow up and become pubertal; but by no means do they all become adolescents. To be adolescent means that one has reached, and even passed, the age of puberty, is at the height of physical development—healthier, stronger, even handsomer than one has been or will be for the rest of one's life; but to be adolescent also means that one must nevertheless postpone full adulthood long beyond what any other period in history has considered reasonable. And the educational experiences in home and school prepare well only a small minority of young people for such a prolonged waiting, for being able to control their angry impatience while waiting.

It is this waiting for the real life that creates a climate in which a sizeable segment of college students can at least temporarily be seduced into following the lead of small groups of militants. It seems to give them a chance to prove themselves as real men. Thus it is the empty wait for real life which makes for student rebellions. This can be seen from the fact that most of the rebellious students, here and abroad, are either undergraduates, are studying the social sciences and the humanities, or both. There are few militants among students of medicine, engineering, the natural sciences; they are busy doing things that are important to them: they are working in the laboratory and at their studies. It is those students who do not quite know what they are preparing themselves for and why, those students who sit around waiting for examinations rather than doing active work, who form the cadres of the student rebellion.

One example may stand for many. In a class I am presently teaching, a student who was close to the activitists gave me, at first, a very hard time in class. Two months later he was one of my most interested, co-operative students. I asked him what happened. He answered: "A few weeks ago I got a job which interests me, and I also began to be interested in my classes; that did it."

There are today far too many students in college who essentially have no business there. Some are there to evade the draft; many others are there out of a vague idea that it will help them to find better paying jobs, although they do not know what jobs they want. And many go to college simply because they do not know what better to do and because it is expected of them. Their deep dissatisfaction with themselves and their inner confusion is projected first against the university, and second against all institutions of society, which are blamed for their own inner weakness.

To make matters worse, our institutions of higher learning have expanded much too rapidly; under public pressure for more education for everybody, they have increased enrollment beyond reason. The result is classes which are too large, and which are often taught in our large universities by teaching assistants, some of whom, out of their own inner dissatisfaction and insecurity, tend to side with the rebellion. All this leads to the anonymity, the impersonal nature of student-faculty contacts, about which many students rightly complain. And since many of them are essentially not interested in the intellectual adventure, the knowledge which the faculty can convey to them is not what they want. What they do want, essentially, is group therapeutic experiences to help them to mature, to be secure, to find themselves. But since colleges are not mass therapeutic institutions, they disappoint the students where their greatest need lies.

Because of the vast expansion in numbers, moreover, the old methods to lend coherence to the college experience, and to offer students a life geared to the needs of late adolescence, have disintegrated. This the fraternities and sororities used to do by offering group homes to ease the transition from family to society at large. But they no longer can contain the large proportion of students. The demand of some black students for separate black housing should therefore be understood, at least in part, as the consequence of their feeling lost in the anonymous mass of students. Indeed, most white students are similarly lost until they find themselves in their work and study experiences. The old rituals which enhanced student life and bound students both to each other and to their college—the football rallies, the homecomings—have lost most of their meaning and have been replaced by nothing equalling the excitement which the sit-ins and protests provide. The spirit of intimate comradeship—important as at no other time in life—that used to prevail in the fraternity house is now found by all too many students in their demonstrations, where they feel closely bound together, doing things which they deep down know they do also for the emotional satisfaction of simply being together, whatever high sounding issues they think are motivating their actions. Nor should the symbolic meaning of students invading the dean's or president's office, whether violently or non-violently, be overlooked; big in age and size, they inwardly feel like little boys, and hence they need to play big by sitting in papa's big chair. They want to have a say in how things are run, want to sit in the driver's seat, not because they feel competent to do so, but because they cannot bear to feel incompetent.

It is unnatural to keep large numbers of young people in dependency and attending school for some twenty years. This was the way of life for that small elite which always in the past went to universities, but never did they represent more than a small percentage of the youth population, the vast majority of which actively met life early and proved itself as men and women, as real and strong human beings. Now, however, the tremendous push to send everybody to college has brought into the university an incredibly large number of young people who do not find their self-realization through study, or through the intellectual adventure. Yet, still needing to find their early manhood, they try to change the university into something in which they can find it by engaging in an active, sometimes violent, battle against the existing order or all of society. Their victory would change the university into an institution no longer dedicated to the intellectual virtues, to the frontiers of knowledge, but dedicated, rather, to the belligerent reshaping of society; and this is exactly what the militants want—not to engage in study and research, but in political battles. The reason we didn't have student revolts of this kind and this scope before is partly because only those went to college who wanted to be educated, and partly because those student who had to put themselves through school proved their early manhood—at least to some degree—by the very fact that they could do so. I think many of the rebellious students today are essentially guilt-ridden individuals. They feel terribly guilty about all their advantages, including their exemption from the draft, which is a serious guilt. Unable to bear living with their inner guilt, they try to destroy society or certain of its institutions rather than deal with it.

Since all too many students who now go to college have little interest, ability and use for what constitutes a college education, they would be better off with a high-level vocational education closely linked to a work program to give scope to their needs for physical activity and visible, tangible achievement. The complaint of many of these students is that nobody needs them. They view themselves as parasites of society, and therefore come to hate the society which they think makes them feel this way. Here we should learn from the communist countries where studies are combined with work in factories and in the fields. This, I believe, would be a much better arrangement for those students who do not feel a deep commitment to the intellectual enterprise (that is, study and research), and those who are so committed will never constitute more than a relatively small segment of youth.

I would, in fact, urge the creation of a government program of a couple of years' duration—a civilian Peace Corps—in which young people would work on socially significant projects while earning pay for it, and simultaneously receive higher vocational training. After such service and training, only those who really wish to do so would enter the universities, while the rest would feel a much greater stake in a society they helped to rebuild; at the least, they would be well-prepared for permanent jobs. Such a program should be an alternative to the draft. Only those young men who volunteer should serve in the armed forces. And I am convinced that if every able-bodied person were required to serve two years in national service of some kind, there would be no scarcity of volunteers for the armed forces, particularly if military servicemen received advantages in pay or other special advantages at the end of their service. This would also eliminate the draft exemption of college students which, in connection with the war in Vietnam, is behind so much of the student unrest. *If I am exempt from service when others are not, I can live in peace with myself only if convinced this is a vile war.*

In calming the dissent that is so widespread on our campuses now, we should concentrate our efforts on separating the ready followers from the small group of rebellion leaders. Were it not for the widespread discontent, protest leaders would find a scant following, and if they should break the law without such followers, they could be readily dealt with. It is the mass following they can arouse because of the widespread malaise which alone makes them dangerous.

There has always been a small percentage of persons bent on destroying society and on fomenting revolution. In earlier generations there were the Wobblies; later there were the campus communists. But the present brand of campus revolutionaries, who are of anarchist and nihilist persuasion, are much more dangerous because they can point to success after success with their disrupting tactis. And nothing succeeds like success. Two hundred years ago Immanuel Kant warned that we shall never be able to control violence if it is rewarded. "It is far more convenient," he wrote, "to commit an act of violence, and afterwards excuse it, than laboriously to consider convincing arguments and lose time in listening to objections. This very boldness itself indicates a sort of conviction of the legitimacy of the action, and the God of success is afterwards the best advocate."

The greatest danger presently, then, is the readiness with which violence is excused, and the seemingly convincing arguments which are brought forth to justify it before and after the act. Worst and most dangerous of all, there seems to be a tendency in our society to legitimize the results of violence so that, as Kant put it, the God of success afterwards serves as advocate for the violent action that preceded it, and suggests its future use. On our campuses, those committed to violence (to quote Kant again) "lose no time on considering arguments, or on listening to objections." They refuse to be rational about their grievances and, by violent means, insist on having their way, no matter what. And if they get it, as Kant knew, their success then legitimizes their disruptive actions.

The rebels gain their success by arousing a sizeable number of students through the tactic of confrontation, and by the universities' fear of confrontation. Confrontation has one important aim—to use the reaction of the provoked to generate a new unity among the demonstrators. In its most direct form, militants have stood in front of policemen and denounced them as pigs until the men in uniform hit out. The art of demonstrating then lies in ensuring that the blows are directed against the less-committed demonstrators and, if possible, against completely uninvolved persons. This provides the mass following required for success.

Of the small group of leaders of the radical left, it has been observed that most come from well-educated, very liberal families. Of those whom I know, I would say, too, that they have had their intellectual abilities developed very highly at much too early an age, at the expense of their emotional development. Although often very bright, emotionally some of them remained fixated at the age of the temper tantrum. It is this discrepancy between great intellectual maturity and utter emotional immaturity which is so baffling, often even to the universities, where some members of the faculty fail to see behind the obvious intelligence the inability to act rationally, and most of all, the inability to act responsibly. It is one of the weaknesses of university professors that, as persons committed to value intellectual ability most highly, they are captivated by the intelligence of these students to the degree that they are ready to excuse or brush aside the students' disruptiveness and intellectual arrogance.

As for the discontented students themselves, psychologically I always found them hating themselves as intensely as they hate the establishment, a self-hatred they try to escape by fighting *any* establishment. They need help in overcoming their emotional difficulties, and punishment is hardly the answer. If we bring them to the universities, we should provide facilities for helping them. It is their emotional immaturity that explains both their call for immediate action, and the retreat of the dropout and the hippy into utter non-action; each masks the inability of very intelligent young people to take time to think things out. The militants must want to destroy the universities because they do not want to be students, for to be a student means to prepare oneself to do something more worthwhile in the future. The militant student's cry is for action now, not preparation for action later. In this sense, he is no longer a student at all, since he clearly rejects knowledge as a precondition of a meaningful activity. Truth, moreover, is no longer sought but "revealed"; the contempt for free speech and free thought is demonstrated as much by his actions as by his words. Were he ever to capture the university, it would cease to be a university.

In their inability to delay action for thought, both right and left extremists, the militants of all colors, are brothers under the skin. This is among the reasons why historically it has happened before that the young followers of the extreme right have become those of the extreme left, or the other way around. The mainspring of the rebels' action is more their wish to prove themselves strong—and less any particular political conviction—superimposed on self-doubt and hatred of a society which they feel has left them out in the cold. In Germany the National Socialists and the Communists voted together and worked together to bring down the democratic Weimar government, and in the same context, it is not so surprising that former Nazis easily involved themselves in the communistic government of East Germany.

But there are also good reasons why it is mainly the children of leftist parents who become hippies or student revolutionaries in our society, just as in other places and other times the children of conservative parents, under similar emotional conditions, spearheaded rightwing radicalism. It was the children of conservative German parents, for example, who first embraced the Emperor's War and enthusiastically went to their death because they felt a need to lay their bodies on the line for ideas their parents had only lukewarmly held; for thus they proved themselves strong, while at the same time proving their parents weak, wishy-washy and unworthy of true respect. They felt, too, that this was a means of rebirth, a way to revitalize an ossified society, to create a new society; with little patience for the voice of reason, they asked for authenticity and confrontation. All these were the main tenets of Hitler's academic youth, as they are now those of our own student left.

Thus, while the emotional constellations which make for very different student revolts are strangely similar, the specific political content of a student revolt depends to a large degree on the beliefs of the students' parents. For in many ways rebellion represents a desperate wish by youth to do better than their parents in exactly those beliefs in which parents seem weakest. In this sense, rebellion also represents a desperate desire for parental approval, but even more it represents a desperate wish that parents had been stronger in their convictions. So many of our radicals embrace Maoism and chant "Ho, Ho, Ho Chi Minh" much as another generation chanted at football rallies. These are strong father-figures with strong convictions who powerfully coerce their "children" to follow their commands. While consciously the students demand freedom and participation, unconsciously their commitment to Mao and other dictatorships suggests their desperate need for controls from the outside, since without them they are unable to bring order into their inner chaos. Such controls, however, must not be imposed punitively, nor for the benefit of others. They must be controls that clearly and definitely benefit the individual, so that he will eventually make them his own.

The inability of militant students to wait and work hard for long-range goals marks them as emotionally disturbed; so does their hatred for their parents who failed to give them direction and set them against the world by exposing their immature minds to criticism of all that could have given meaning to their lives. Indeed, it is their hatred of society that makes it so easy for the militant student leaders to make common cause with another small group that provides temporary leadership for some of the rebellions: outright paranoid individuals. The proportion of paranoids among students is no greater than in any comparable group of the population. But they are more dangerous because of their high intelligence, which permits them to conceal more successfully the degree of their disturbance. And student revolt permits them to act out their paranoia to a degree that no other position in society permits. How understandable, then, that all paranoids who can, do flock into the ranks of the militants. Unfortunately, most non-experts do not know how persuasive paranoids can be, at least until they are recognized. The persuasiveness of a Hitler or a Stalin is now regarded as the consequence of his own paranoia and his unconscious appeal to the vague paranoid tendencies among the immature and disgruntled. I have no doubt that the ranks of today's militants contain some would-be Hitlers and Stalins.

Paranoids make a persuasive appeal to any group in the population which rightly or wrongly feels persecuted, and they seek out such groups because they are most likely to view their own paranoia as true understanding of a persecuted group's particular predicament. Which brings me to the special problems of some of our black students who, fortunately, seem to recognize more and more that SDS is using them rather than helping them. (They are not quite as successfully seeing through the motives of some of the paranoid student leaders.)

The overwhelming majority of black students desires exactly the same as does the overwhelming majority of white students: a rightful place in society. Only a very small minority of black and white students wishes to destroy it. Thus if the blacks could be convinced that there is a good place for them in society, their attitude would change and they would part ways with SDS, as many of them have already done. But the difficulty is that many black students, because of the nature of the commitment of the university, do not feel that being a student is necessarily the best way for them to find their rightful place in society. It is here that our wish and theirs, that they should become part of the elite, runs afoul of what for many of them is their reality. Many black students in our colleges are often ill-prepared academically and lacking in the skills required for academic success. At the same time, they have been imbued with the notion that it is the fault of the establishment that they are disadvantaged. While this is true to some degree, awareness of such truth offers an easy way out if one does not succeed. All students find the transition from home to college difficult. In past times the student placed the blame for this on himself, and most students therefore tried to do something about themselves and sooner or later succeeded. Today both white and black students tend to blame the faculty for the difficulties they encounter in adjusting to a different way of life and study. The demand for black-study programs originated, not only in the justified feeling that one must be familiar and proud of one's own background, but to a large degree in the feeling that such studies would be easier, and that the faculty would have greater understanding.

The fact is that the preparation of some black students who are induced to go to college is inferior to that of the white majority of the college population. While the faculty is ready to make allowances for this, compensation runs counter to the self-respect of the black student, who rightly does not wish to be treated as a second-class citizen. But if he cannot compete successfully with his fellow students who have had so many educational and social advantages, he is in a terrible conflict. Brought to college to do as well as the other, when he fails his background does not permit him to accept that fact of failure because of his lack of preparation; to do so would make him feel second-class, a position he is seeking to escape by obtaining a college education. Although intellectually able, he has difficulty in adjusting, and he comes to feel that the very place which promised to make him equal fails to do so. Disappointed, he rages against the institution which once more makes him feel inferior, and special programs of assistance only make his feelings of inferiority even deeper. The many black students who are well able to hold their own with the best feel they must not desert their fellow black comrades, and in times of protest, they make their comrades' burden their own.

If we want to bring a large number of black students into our universities, as we should, we must start much earlier than college. From high school on, it will be necessary to educate a larger number of blacks, together with white youngsters from culturally deprived backgrounds, in true prep schools to permit them to enter college as well prepared academically and socially as the more advantaged students.

There is today a fascination in society with sex and violence, with drugs and insanity, which both influences the student militants and provides them with a noteworthiness which they exploit to the full. If students protest in an orderly and rational fashion, they receive little public attention. But if they shed their clothes and walk around naked, this makes news all over the nation, whatever case they may or may not have had; it is part of a dangerous fascination with youth and its extreme positions. What passes for modern literature which these youngsters read in junior high school intoxicates their minds with the appeal of drug-induced madness, with sexual acting out and with violence.

The universities, because of their intellectual prestige, give the student activists a platform for their revolutionary claims which they otherwise would never have. For example, for days not more than some twenty to thirty students recently occupied the administration building of the University of Chicago. They got headlines every day and were prominently featured on radio and television. Had thirty people demonstrated in any other place, they would have received no attention whatever. This SDS knows, and this is why it aims at the universities. The contrast between an institution devoted to the highest achievements of reason, and the obscenity and violence perpetrated there, makes it all the more fascinating, a fascination on which SDS tries to build its revolutionary success.

An idea in itself may amount to next to nothing, but it becomes news by interfering with something else which is considered to be of public importance. In themselves, a couple of hundred demonstrators somewhere in New York or Chicago would amount to very little; but when fifty students march into a lecture hall, seize control of the podium and broadcast their claims and philosophy to people who came to hear something quite different—then they have made news. If someone advocates urinating on graves (as the Fugs did), or if a few girls dress up as witches and put curses on professors (as they did in Chicago), if they did so without reference to politics, people would rightly wonder about their sanity. But when they do so as a condemnation of the Vietnam war or in the name of some progressive cause, they win the support of many older liberals and enlightened radicals who invariably consider it all very socially significant. When a teen-ager wrestles with the police for the sake of the moral superiority of a future social order, he cannot fail to obtain the sympathetic attention of radio and television editors, if not psychiatrists. The ritualistic invocation of ideology is thus both an alibi and a defense.

Perhaps it all has made too many headlines, perhaps it has been talked about too much for people to accept the fact, but the truth of the matter is that these rebellions can and do paralyze our universities. Not only are classes interrupted and buildings occupied, but faculty members must devote their energies to calming things down. Even more importantly, the time and energy which should be devoted to more lasting achievements are drained away on plans to forestall new confrontations. A last comparison with pre-Hitler days. In Germany at that time, as Professor George L. Mosse (*The Crisis of German Ideology*, Grosset and Dunlap, 1964) puts it, "professors tended to be either scholars who withdrew into their own specialty, taking scant notice of the world around them, or men who attempted to play the role of prophets. The first kind of academic wanted only to be left in peace. . . . The professor as prophet, with very few exceptions indeed, was to be found on the side of the revolting students" Of the students of that time he says, "They had found a basis for action that opposed existing authority yet remained independent of any political movement directed by their elders." And the faculties, he says, "failed to provide any opposition, failed to use administrative powers and failed to organize effective alternative groups of students. At best they displayed a detached passivity . . . at worst they joined in the harrassment."

In our universities today we have faculty members who are trying to remain aloof from it all, and others who are trying to anticipate even the most radical student demands so as to avoid confrontations. Worse, though, there are few efforts being made to organize effective alternative groups of students. Worst of all, many professors are so intimidated that they cave in even before the students exercise pressure. It is the continuous worry about what the militant students may do next, the anxious efforts to give them no offense, which saps the universities of their strength to the point of paralysis. And this anxious avoidance of taking a firm stand gives not only these militants, but also many non-committed students, the feeling that they have the faculty on the run.

If the colleges and universities would take a determined stand against coercion and intimidation—though always open to, indeed inviting, reasonable and non-coercive discussion about much-needed reform—then student rebellions could be reduced to the point where they would no longer threaten either the universities or society. The university must strengthen its will to resist disruption and coercion. If it succeeds, it will have little need to take recourse to punitive measures, beyond setting into practice the principle that those who do not wish to have any part of our universities should have their will: they should not be permitted to be, live or work in a place they hate, not as a punishment, but because to remain in a place they hate and despise serves no good purpose and is detrimental to their emotional well-being.

DISCUSSION QUESTIONS

1. Do you agree with Bettelheim's belief that disruptive students "should not be permitted to be, live or work in a place they hate"?
2. Is it true that "the inability of militant students to wait and work hard for long-range goals marks them as emotionally disturbed"?
3. Is Bettelheim's insight correct in observing "as for the discontented students themselves, psychologically I always found them hating themselves as intensely as they hate the establishment, a self-hatred they try to escape by fighting *any* establishment"?
4. How would you decide which areas of activity within the university should be subject to control.

TOM HAYDEN "Two, Three, Many Columbias"

The goal written on the university walls was "Create two, three, many Columbias"; it meant expand the strike so that the U.S. must either change or send its troops to occupy American campuses.

At this point the goal seems realistic; an explosive mix is present on dozens of campuses where demands for attention to student views are being disregarded by university administrators.

The American student movement has continued to swell for nearly a decade: during the semi-peace of the early '60s as well as during Vietnam; during the token liberalism of John Kennedy as well as during the bankrupt racism of Lyndon Johnson. Students have responded most directly to the black movement of the '60s: from Mississippi Summer to the Free Speech Movement; from "Black Power" to "Student Power"; from the seizure of Howard University to the seizure of Hamilton Hall. As the racial crisis deepens so will the campus crisis. But the student protest is not just an offshoot of the black protest—it is based on authentic opposition to the middle-class world of manipulation, channeling and careerism. The students are in opposition to the fundamental institutions of society.

The students' protest constantly escalates by building on its achieve-

Reprinted from *Ramparts*, June 15, 1968, p. 40. Copyright *Ramparts Magazine*, 1968. By permission of the editors.

ments and legends. The issues being considered by seventeen-year-old freshmen at Columbia University would not have been within the imagination of most "veteran" student activists five years ago.

Columbia opened a new tactical stage in the resistance movement which began last fall: from the overnight occupation of buildings to permanent occupation; from mill-ins to the creation of revolutionary committees; from symbolic civil disobedience to barricaded resistance. Not only are these tactics already being duplicated on other campuses, but they are sure to be surpassed by even more militant tactics. In the future it is conceivable that students will threaten destruction of buildings as a last deterrent to police attacks. Many of the tactics learned can also be applied in smaller hit-and-run operations between strikes: raids on the offices of professors doing weapons research could win substantial support among students while making the university more blatantly repressive.

In the buildings occupied at Columbia, the students created what they called a "new society" or "liberated area" or "commune," a society in which decent values would be lived out even though university officials might cut short the communes through use of police. The students had fun, they sang and danced and wisecracked, but there was continual tension. There was no question of their constant awareness of the seriousness of their acts. Though there were a few violent arguments about tactics, the discourse was more in the form of endless meetings convened to explore the outside political situation, defense tactics, maintenance and morale problems within the group. Debating and then determining what leaders should do were alternatives to the remote and authoritarian decision-making of Columbia's trustees.

The Columbia strike represented more than a new tactical movement, however. There was a political message as well. The striking students were not holding onto a narrow conception of students as a privileged class asking for inclusion in the university as it now exists. This kind of demand could easily be met by administrators by opening minor opportunities for "student rights" while cracking down on campus radicals. The Columbia students were instead taking an internationalist and revolutionary view of themselves in opposition to the imperialism of the very institutions in which they have been groomed and educated. They did not even want to be included in the decision-making circles of the military-industrial complex that runs Columbia: *they want to be included only if their inclusion is a step toward transforming the university.* They want a new and independent university standing against the mainstream of American society, or they want no university at all. They are, in Fidel Castro's words, "guerrillas in the field of culture."

How many other schools can be considered ripe for such confrontations? The question is hard to answer, but it is clear that the demands of black students for cultural recognition rather than paternalistic tolerance, and radical white students' awareness of the sinister paramilitary activities carried on in secret by the faculty on many campuses, are hardly confined to Columbia. Columbia's problem is the American problem in miniature—the inability to provide answers to widespread social needs and the use of the military to protect the authorities against the people. This process can only lead to greater unity in the movement.

Support from outside the university communities can be counted on in many large cities. A crisis is foreseeable that would be too massive for police to handle. It can happen; whether or not it will be necessary is a question which only time will answer. What is certain is that we are moving toward power—the power to stop the machine if it cannot be made to serve humane ends.

American educators are fond of telling their students that barricades are part of the romantic past, that social change today can only come about through the processes of negotiation. But the students at Columbia discovered that barricades are only the beginning of what they call "bringing the war home."

DISCUSSION QUESTIONS

1. Do you agree with Hayden's characterization of the social order as one of "manipulation, channeling, and careerism"?
2. Is Hayden performing a valuable social service in demanding the reformation of what he sees as a sterile and corrupt society?
3. Is he justified in his radical attempts "to stop the machine if it cannot be made to serve humane ends"?

TOM POWERS Autopsy on Old Westbury

THE POLITICS OF FREE-FORM EDUCATION

By 1966 American college officials had sensed they were an *ancien régime* threatened by revolutionary discontents. In that year the State University of New York, hoping to avoid the troubles besetting her sister university in California, announced plans for a new four-year college with "an almost unrestricted opportunity for innovation" in which students would have "full partnership." In 1967 Harris Wofford, a former director of the Peace Corps in Ethiopia and a Kennedy civil-rights aide, was appointed president of the new college, to be called the State University at Old Westbury.

For nearly a year Wofford invited suggestions from students, academics, and prophets of the new youth culture, including four Diggers from San Francisco who stopped by on their way to the march on the Pentagon in October 1967. Wofford's ambitions for the school were high. "It shouldn't be called Old Westbury," he told one of the first people he hired, "because it's going to be a school of the world."

A fire on the original Old Westbury, Long Island, campus forced the school to move to a 409-acre estate in nearby Oyster Bay, a town of staggering affluence about an hour from New York City. In September 1968, the first eighty-five students arrived in Oyster Bay for two years of experiment before the "real" students, eventually to number 5,000, arrived at the "real" campus still under construction at Old Westbury. During the next eighteen months, while the academic world watched closely, the following entirely typical events took place:

At a meeting the first night, the students spent four hours arguing whether all, some, or none of the school's bathrooms should be co-ed. No conclusion was reached.

A girl spent one entire semester polishing a four-foot-high piece of bark.

Perhaps one thousand proposals were met with the objection, "What's new about that?"

A course on the oppression of women turned into an activist group that mothered the entire Women's Liberation movement on Long Island.

Two campus buildings were burned, and bomb scares repeatedly emptied classrooms.

All students received grades of "pass" or "no credit," but grades of "no credit" were not recorded.

Students and faculty failed to agree on anything except the urgent necessity of Wofford's resignation.

This agreement was about to be formally voiced at an open meeting in the spring of 1970 when Wofford insisted on speaking first and then announced, with regret, that he was leaving. State University officials in Albany, picking up echoes of these events, appointed a five-man committee, named for its chairman, Clifford Craven, to assess the school's progress. The Craven Committee, whose members believed in courses, departments, and grades, spent two days on the Oyster Bay campus and then submitted a report that amounted to an academic counterrevolution. The result was a decision to close the college in Oyster Bay and start again this fall with a new president, John D. Maguire, a theologian, on the rebuilt campus in Old Westbury.

Wofford left to become president of Bryn Mawr. A black anthropologist was appointed acting president of the Oyster Bay campus for a final year, and the school became, for two brief semesters, one of the best undergraduate colleges in America, a fact not as widely recognized in academic circles as the now infamous piece of polished bark.

The State University at Old Westbury had been intended as a response to the discontent expressed in the Free Speech Movement slogan, "I am a student—do not fold, spindle or mutilate." It was not to be a "multiversity" turning out technicians for corporate America, but a "free" institution in which students would direct their own education in "relevant" subjects. Ever since the school was closed as a failure, the enemies of academic experiments have cited Old Westbury as reason for leaving things alone. In fact, however, the failure of the school had little to do with the experiments, and a lot to do with the divisions in American society.

SYMBOL OF WHITE AMERICA

For a college determined to face the American Crisis, locating itself on a Long Island estate that might have been Jay Gatsby's was surprising and, as things turned out, something of a mistake. The three main factions at the school—white radicals, hippies, and the Non-White Caucus—arrived on the campus in an apocalyptic mood, in the fall of a year dominated by assassination, riot, and street fighting. No one was prepared for the lush physical beauty of the environment where a rich marine insurance broker had spent forty years creating one of the finest arboretums in America. The geodesic domes that housed the school were surrounded by Siberian crab apple trees, Japanese maples, Austrian pines, purple beech, and Camperdown elms. Coe Hall, a Victorian-Gothic building named after the estate's former owner, was closed the first year, but students used to sneak in and wander admiringly through the enormous rooms.

Frank Miata, a leader of the white radicals, was stunned the first time he saw the campus. Miata, who spent a year as an SDS regional organizer in upstate New York before he came to Old Westbury, had grown up on Long Island's South Shore, where affluence is paid for on time, and the Ruling Class, for those who believe in it, is an abstraction. At Old Westbury, Miata discovered that the Ruling Class lived next door. He saw its members coming home from Wall Street in the evening in rented helicopters. He passed their gate cottages and their long tree-lined driveways. In 1969 Miata married another Old Westbury student, Pat Sweeney, in Coe Hall. When Pat and her father, a working man from Chicago, drove up to the campus he asked, "What is this? A forest preserve?" A friend of Pat's, Deborah Leavy, did a research project on the membership of Oyster Bay's 100-year-old Sewanakah-Corinthian Yacht Club. What she found was a corporate world as tightly bound by blood, marriage, and money as the city-states of Renaissance Italy. White radicalism at Old Westbury was not weakened by the knowledge that the Coe estate was once *one man's home*.

The effect of the school's location was equally arresting to other students. The hippies took one look and decided that Old Westbury ought to be a liberated zone where youth culture could flourish in magnificent isolation. A distinct minority, they spent their days in a dreamy state known as "grooving in the grass." The bark-polishing devotee, a former high-school cheerleader, later designed a course that she called "Poetry of Life" and described as follows:

Now I hear beautiful music. Then I paint a mind picture. Later I walk in the wood. Reverently I study my wood, know it. Converse with a poet meaningful to me. Make Love.

For the hippies, Old Westbury was the Enchanted Wood. In their spiritual enthusiasm, they neglected to remember that eventually the State University would give them B.A.s in Life Poetry and send them back to Queens and Brooklyn. They wanted to retreat from the society collapsing around them, a notion that brought them into immediate and continuing conflict with the rest of the school.

For the Non-White Caucus, the Oyster Bay campus was final proof that America was indeed two nations, separate and unequal. Blacks were regularly reminded that they were new to the town of Oyster Bay, and not altogether welcome. When one black girl tried to cash a state check at a local bank, the teller refused. She produced a driver's license, an Old Westbury student card, and other identification. He still refused. She asked why. "Well," he said, "you could have stolen it." The bank finally accepted the word of a school administrator. Oyster Bay was a hostile *white* environment, and black students responded by depending on each other. Black-white couples were resented, and political coopera-tion between the races was cautious, when it occurred at all. While the white radicals saw Old Westbury as a living reminder of the Class Enemy, and the hippies saw it as a refuge, the Non-White Caucus saw it as a symbol of everything white America had reserved for itself. Black students did not altogether trust the motives of those who had brought them to Old Westbury, and were determined not to forget the reality of the world they had temporarily left behind.

NO PATHS TO MODERATION

The first (1968–69) academic year at Old Westbury was intensely political. The three factions had definite ideas about how to save America and were inclined to view disagreement, much less resistance, as reactionary obstructionism. Everyone felt time was running out, and was correspondingly short-tempered. Nobody gave anybody the benefit of the doubt. As a result, all disputes created a maximum of bitterness.

The sharpest fight of all naturally centered on who was in charge. Students understood "full partnership" to include everything, not only the free election of courses but determination of what courses the school would offer, the hiring of faculty to teach them, the sort of grades to be recorded, the allotment of money for field projects, even the overall purpose of the school. At the same time, they did not want to limit the right of students in later years to decide the same questions all over again.

The struggle for control of Old Westbury was sharpened by the experience of some of the students on field projects in New York City. Wofford and his planners had decided that part of the year would be spent in urban field work, a plan immediately opposed by some blacks, who objected that they had just *left* the city, and by most of the hippies, who liked sitting around on the grass. That fall, during New York City's prolonged teachers' strike, the white radicals decided to take sides with the community and teach in Bedford-Stuyvesant, one of the country's worst ghettos (a decision reached only after a week of agonized argument about the propriety of crossing picket lines). Students who began with the idea of creating a Brooklyn "Summerhill" of loving spontaneity were shocked by the poverty and what it had done to the kids they were trying to teach. The daily contrast between Bedford-Stuyvesant slums and Oyster Bay elegance did nothing to encourage political moderation.

In some ways Old Westbury relived in a matter of months the history of political activism in the Sixties, which began with the rediscovery that rich and poor live side by side in America. The classic effect of such an experience is radicalization, the willingness to take extreme measures to correct social wrongs. There is no morally valid argument why the rich should be happy in Oyster Bay and the poor miserable in New York. That morality is beside the point is a truism learned only over a period of time. Old Westbury radicals did not know what to do about the things they saw during second semester field projects, but they returned to Long Island in May with an angry determination to do *something*.

Another issue that split the school still further was a proposal to bring the faculty and student body to an even 50-50 balance between blacks and whites, a proposal eventually defeated in a referendum. Even before the referendum, however, Wofford had announced that he would veto the 50-50 plan no matter how many people favored it. This and other arbitrary acts focused the prevailing discontents on the question of campus control, which resulted in a struggle for power as bitter and resolute as if a nation had been at stake. On May 19, 1969, the school began a two-week "evaluation session" to sum up the Old Westbury experiment thus far. The session opened with a picnic to which white radicals pointedly brought two large cakes in celebration of the birthdays of Ho Chi Minh and Malcolm X. A collision was rapidly approaching. When Mrs. Annabelle Bagdon, Wofford's secretary, left the president's office that day, she wondered whether she ought to lock the files.

She hesitated, then decided, "That's not what Old Westbury is all about," and left them open.

Wofford formally opened the evaluation session in the old carriage house, with a lofty speech quoting Robert Frost and Gandhi. Most of the students sat in stony-faced silence. Finally Frank Miata got up and said, "This is obscene. We've been listening and listening. I'm not going to listen anymore." He turned, stumbled over a chair, and marched out, followed by the rest of the white radicals and most of the Non-White Caucus. The ensuing one-week sit-in ended any real possibility of reconciliation, particularly after the white radicals went through Wofford's files and learned that a lot of people had been making a good thing out of Old Westbury. A consultant, for example, had apparently been paid in advance for 150 days of consulting at $100 a day but had yet to do any consulting. The range in salaries also came as a shock. One hardworking secretary was paid only $4,700 a year, while a professor made $22,000.

The disenchantment extended to Wofford himself. The public Wofford was a man of passionate intellectual idealism. His correspondence suggested to the radicals that he was still concerned with questions of political power and position—as might well be expected of any former associate of the Kennedys. And the possibility that Wofford might have political ambitions of his own struck the radicals as somehow deeply improper. None of them ever called him by his first name again.

During one period, Miata and Wofford had often discussed their political differences. Wofford freely admitted what he hoped Old Westbury would do to young radicals like Miata. "I really believe in this system," Wofford told him one day, "and I want to co-opt you into it as far as I can." When Miata finally turned against the school, it was with a sense of having been almost personally betrayed. By the time the sit-in ended, the white radicals had decided Old Westbury was as corrupt as the rest of the country. The promises had all turned out to be lies, they felt, and the ideals a sham. They were even beginning to suspect that Old Westbury had been founded principally to isolate radicals from the rest of the State University system.

While making a final break with the administration, the white radicals also cut themselves off from much of the rest of the student body. On the first day of the sit-in they announced to the large group of students crowded into Wofford's office, "There are people here who are not our friends." The nonfriends were expelled. If this is not quite Stalinism, it is not exactly participatory democracy, either. Politics, in short, was allowed to discredit the educational experiment at Old Westbury.

Given a student body deliberately recruited for its interest in educational experiment and social change, power conflicts were inevitable, especially since the "full partnership" idea was never well defined. Power seemed to be there for the taking, and everybody reached at once.

Old Westbury's problems can be traced back to Berkeley where the Free Speech Movement in 1964 gave birth to organized student activism. In 1966, shortly before Old Westbury entered its planning phase, the slogan "Student Power" was adopted by the SDS at their national convention in Iowa. (The group was fascinated by the phrase "Black Power," which Stokely Carmichael had coined during the Meredith march through Mississippi in early June.)

There has been a tendency to tar all educational experimentation with the brush of student excesses. In fact, the SDS frankly considered student power solely as an organizing tool; they did not really plan to take over schools, and quickly abandoned educational issues for larger political questions. By the end of 1967 the SDS had turned against student power as evasion of the real problems of American society, which it was beginning to see in traditionally Marxist-Leninist terms. In the meantime, however, other elements in the university community sensed that higher education was on the verge of breaking down. Educators realized that something had to be done to give students a sense of participation in their own lives, and one of the tentative solutions proposed was to give them a voice in running the schools they attended.

On its surface, student power in this sense had considerable appeal. It seemed a simple extension of the democratic process in a country that prided itself on democracy. At the same time, student power evoked immediate opposition by academics jealous of their power over appointments, curriculum, grades, and related matters. This was not simply old fogeyism, but a reflection of genuine doubts about how scholarship would fare under the control of passionate laymen. Old Westbury was only one of many attempts to resolve these dilemmas.

At Old Westbury as on many other campuses, there were two broad factions: a group of what might be called disciplinarians, who sought academic excellence and felt that teachers, the presumed experts, are entitled to exercise a certain authority over students; and a group of libertarians, who believed that learning thrives in conditions of freedom and teachers are there to guide students toward the things they want to learn. Old Westbury's educational struggle was colored by Wofford's admiration for the Great Books program at St. John's College in Maryland, which, in effect, put him in the camp of the disciplinarians. He envisioned a school centering on what he considered to be the three great divisions of Western intellectual life: law, medicine, and theology. One of Old Westbury's original student planners, more sensitive to the times, said that would be fine as long as it meant crime, disease, and heresy.

Few students or teachers took any interest in Wofford's experiment. He had a real love for Greek intellectual ideals, he believed in Socratic dialogue as mental exercise, even as a way of life. If the dialogue did not answer pressing questions, well, answers might come later. Students at Old Westbury were suspicious of large ideas that tended to overlook the actual state of things. The central experience of their generation, after all, had been that American democracy in theory and in fact were two quite different things. During one seminar Wofford spoke eloquently about law as the fundamental principle of human society. A skeptical black student asked, "But what about the laws that let big corporations evade taxes?" "That's not the kind of law I'm talking about," Wofford answered. Old Westbury students, however, were interested in exactly that sort of law. Wofford's set of the Great Books remained in his office, rarely used, while the rest of the school pursued a fiercely contemporary course of study.

The passionate struggles for control of Old Westbury and the effort to involve students in the problems of their time were barely alluded to in the Craven Committee's report. The committee was primarily concerned with standards, of which it found few during its two-day study of the school. This did not necessarily mean that nothing of value was taking place at the school, but it did mean that the results were difficult to evaluate. In its report, the committee diagnosed the problem this way: "There appears to be a philosophy at Old Westbury which deliberately seeks to guard against the possibility that the quality of a student's work as a whole might jeopardize his status." In other words, it was impossible to *fail*.

The school's badly outnumbered disciplinarians, openly doubtful if not contemptuous, objected to nonacademic courses like "The Craft of Sewing," "Candlemaking," "Guitar Country Blues," "Afro Dances," and "Verbal and Non-Verbal Conversation." They believed in standards: in right and wrong answers, in good and bad work, in valid and invalid arguments.

The disciplinarians frequently cited Luis Camnitzer, a South American artist who was reluctant to tell students what he wanted them to do. As a result, they often did nothing. Occasionally, however, he would set problems for the class, such as asking them to create something that would change their psychological environment. The class finally made a huge papier mâché boulder and hung it over the entrance to the dining hall. Everyone agreed that it added an air of doom to the campus. On another occasion, Camnitzer's class cut eye holes in paper bags and put them on. The students drew faces on each other's bags (which the wearer, of course, could not see) and then carried on conversations that seemed significant because of the contrast between the speaker's mask and what he was saying. The disciplinarians did not view this sort of thing as education, and more than a few students found that Old Westbury's freedom left them confused and depressed. Everything was so indefinite; by the time a class had decided what to study and how to study it, the year might be half over.

Next to educational anarchy, the disciplinarians most disliked educational polemics. There was, naturally, an extensive offering of courses on Marxism, the Cuban revolution, the war in Vietnam, American foreign policy, and similar subjects. The Craven Committee cited a course in "Domestic Imperialism" that consisted entirely of movies about welfare agencies, OEO projects, SDS community organizing, and other attempts to solve American social problems. The description of the course in the 1970 *Spring Curriculum* said students would receive only two credits, "because for the first eight weeks we will be simply sitting in our ivory tower, gasping at American atrocities in America." The Craven Committee clearly felt that two credits were two too many.

RELEVANCE IS HARD TO ASSESS

The libertarians are ready to admit that Old Westbury never found a way to measure its progress, but they insist it was an educational success anyway. Donald Bluestone, who left Roosevelt University in Chicago because he wanted a freer relationship with his students, invited open discussion at Old Westbury. Although he was singled out for criticism by the Craven Committee, which apparently felt his course in nineteenth-century American history amounted to an anti-American bull session for credit, there was, in fact, a reading list of thirty books; Bluestone's students were conscientious, and the seminar generally stuck to the point. If the tone of the course was critical, that was because it centered on slavery and Reconstruction, not exactly happy themes in American history. Short of attending the course, however, there was no way for the Craven Committee to have known what it was really like. Bluestone admits the committee might have formed a different impression if he had graded his seminar students or given an A-plus to one particularly brilliant paper by Pat Sweeney. On the other hand, Bluestone feels, giving grades would have made his seminars cautious and dull, and if Pat Sweeney had been more interested in an "A" than in her argument, her argument inevitably would have suffered.

The question of grades was not taken lightly at Old Westbury. The disciplinarians were convinced that nothing else could keep students honest. Libertarians like Bluestone felt that grades interfered with learning, and were painfully aware of a grade's relationship to a student's standing in the draft. Zonia Krassner, who taught a tightly organized course in the life sciences, wonders how grades could have recorded what *she* learned. Her students, for example, convinced her that eugenics could never be neutral, that every conceivable standard for the control of human breeding would inevitably contain racial and cultural biases. This kind of exchange makes education a human process, Mrs. Krassner feels. The Craven Committee failed to take note of it.

Another thing the committee did not assess was Old Westbury's attempt to provide an education that students would find socially and politically relevant. Wofford's paradigm of the Peace Corps was predictably out of phase with the harsher student radicalism of the late Sixties, but the students experimented with other techniques of social change that had real effects. The Young Lords, an activist party of Puerto Ricans in New York's Spanish Harlem, grew out of discussions that began at Old Westbury.

Radicals also point to a course in the oppression of women organized by students in the fall of 1969. At the end of the first semester, students at a local high school invited members of the course to speak on Women's Liberation. When the Old Westbury students also handed out leaflets, including one on "The Myth of the Vaginal Orgasm," the high school's principal protested and the incident was reported in local papers. The result was a steady stream of invitations from other Long Island high schools and colleges.

That spring the group held a conference on Women's Liberation that led directly to the organization of more than twenty other groups. When the Cambodian invasion and the Kent State killings in May 1970 sparked a nationwide student strike, the women's group used its extensive contact list to organize the strike throughout Long Island. The success of the course in moving beyond academic subjects to an active role in society is indisputable, but the State University's response was naturally ambivalent. Radicals argue that it was successes like these which led Albany officials to close Old Westbury.

The least discussed part of the Old Westbury experiment was the attempt to recruit black and Puerto Rican students from ghetto schools. Cultural differences between the races emerged immediately. The white students had a sentimental regard for the blues-singing Southern Negroes of the early civil-rights movement but felt distinctly uneasy around loud-talking ghetto blacks in leather caps and chartreuse pants who stayed up until three in the morning. A more important, but even less freely acknowledged, cause of black-white tension was white fear of black violence, a fear not entirely unfounded. During one heated argument at an open student meeting, a frustrated black suddenly grabbed a white by the throat and shouted, "You're stalling us! We've been stalled for three hundred years!" When a white student broke a ban on drugs by giving LSD to an unprepared Ethiopian student, blacks threatened to "ice" him if he ever returned to Old Westbury. He conferred with a dean (off campus) and transferred to another school.

By Old Westbury's third and last year, relations between white and black students relaxed. The Non-White Caucus was never formally disbanded, though it ceased to function. Luis Elisa, a black student who was active in running the school, found race at Old Westbury comparatively muted after several semesters at New York Community College, where a professor had once stated that black Africans had never made a single contribution to Western civilization. At Old Westbury, Elisa found, teachers were prepared to accept blacks as people. He doubts whether he could have graduated from any other school.

NEVER ANY COMPROMISE

Of the four experiments at Old Westbury, only one, "full partnership," was a clear failure. The attempt to include blacks was, in the end, a success; the concern with urban problems was a partial success; the granting of near-total academic freedom was, at worst, inconclusive. Old Westbury's freedom and sense of community, even when it was a community at war with itself, were both unique. The school was something new in the world, and everyone connected with it fears that it may be gone for good. The State University is committed to going ahead with a reorganized school on the new campus, but the old willingness to take a chance may no longer be there.

Old Westbury had the bad luck to open at a moment when political passions throughout the country were unrestrained. In retrospect, disputes at the school are generally described in terms of lofty principle, but, at the time, they were touched with passionate irreconcilable animosities. Hippies called radicals fascists, blacks called whites racists, faculty members called each other anarchists and reactionaries. It was even argued on one occasion that student control of faculty appointments meant (if carried to its logical limits) the end of Western civilization. The bomb scares during the school's second year and a steady rise in thefts at the student-run bookstore helped reinforce such fears. Few now like to remember the time when hundreds of thumbtacks were carefully set out point up on a stairway in the administration building, or the morning when a secretary discovered human feces smeared across her desk.

The struggle for power at Old Westbury did not end until the State University announced the closing of the school. The effect of that decision was an instant clearing of the air. Meetings, for the first time, began coming to the point, ending before midnight and reaching conclusions. Factions began to blur and bitterness faded. Few of the experiments at Old Westbury were incompatible with a strong central administration exercising clearly defined powers for a clearly defined purpose. If any lesson can be drawn from the whole chaotic experience, it was probably this: campus conflict is inevitable as long as the question of ultimate control remains open. Old Westbury proved that students could be granted enormous freedom in choosing what they wanted to study. It also proved that running a school and getting an education are not easily reconciled, although President Maguire's administration fervently hopes to avoid the pitfalls of the past.

The final graduation party was held at the very height of spring, on May 22, 1971, when the air was heavy with the scent of flowering trees and new-mown grass. The school's impending death naturally put everyone in an elegiac mood. Wofford was only a memory, and the old battles, lost and won, no longer made any difference. Students and faculty who had left a year or two before returned to see friends and former enemies a final time. Don Bluestone read a poem and Russell Ellis, who came all the way from Berkeley, spoke about the unique bond that joined people who had both loved and hated each other. Students presented a well-liked administrator with a plaque that read, "In the beginning God created Old Westbury and it was good." If there were sharp words, they were all directed at state officials in Albany. Nevertheless, some of those present felt that it had been not the state, but they, who had killed the school.

Along with the good feelings, inevitably, there were reminders of the way things had been. Two unpopular professors came but left after a few awkward minutes. Some people only nodded. Certain subjects were not discussed. Three years of struggle had taught people to be delicate with each other. On its final day in Oyster Bay, Old Westbury practiced the one virtue it had always lacked—forbearance.

DISCUSSION QUESTIONS

1. Was Old Westbury's fate inevitable in terms of the historical development of free-form education in the United States?
2. Is it true that Old Westbury's demise was attributable to the fragmentation of American society, rather than to any malaise within the institution itself?
3. Might the two positions "disciplinarian" and "libertarian" be thought of as the extremes of a continuum? If so, where do you place yourself on this schema?
4. Was Old Westbury an educational success? A political success?

LEONARD BUDER Look to Stars,
Says School Chief

Educators and guidance counselors should use "every art and science," including astrology, to know their pupils better, predict behavior and individualize instruction, Isaiah E. Robinson, the president of the city Board of Education, said yesterday.

Speaking at a forum held by the Public Education Association, Mr. Robinson said that "if astrology is correct," the reason some pupils pose behavior problems in class was not because they were emotionally disturbed but because their "birth signs" conflicted with those of other children or, perhaps, those of the teacher.

He told his audience of 75 persons, which included members of the education association and representatives of other organizations:

"I have been able through the ancient science of astrology—some call it a superstition—to just about peg people and know how they will act just by their birth signs."

The 47-year-old board official later told newsmen that he had been interested in astrology and hypnosis since the nineteen-fifties. He conceded that his views on astrology might be controversial, but said he felt that schools should take all matters affecting pupils into consideration, including the "position of the moon and the planets".

He added that he was born under the sign of Aquarius (his birthday is Feb. 17) and that "Aquarians get along well with most people but are hard to know."

Webster's New International (Second Edition) defines astrology, in part, as a "pseudoscience which treats of the influences of the stars upon human affairs."

Astrology believers hold that birth signs, coupled with the positions of the moon and planet, can influence and foretell human behavior.

In the course of his one-hour address to the P.E.A., Mr. Robinson covered a wide range of school topics. He then answered questions for another hour. The session was held at 20 West 40th Street.

Some of his criticisms of present educational practices and school deficiences evoked applause from the audience. There was no discernible reaction to his references to the possible value of astrology to the educational process and no questions were asked on this subject although Mr. Robinson again brought up the matter while responding to a query on another topic.

Attacking what he described as the present "lockstep method of education," Mr. Robinson charged that despite all the money spent on education and the many new programs introduced, "the product is getting worse and worse."

"INFINITY IS ABILITY"

He said that stereotyped expectations of pupil ability had restricted growth and harmed many youngsters, and declared:

"We must broaden the concept of innate ability. We should believe that for every human being, without physical or mental malady, infinity is his ability."

Mr. Robinson said that it was possible "to seed the mind of a child to the extent of man's knowledge" in a matter of two years. After the session, he explained that this could be done through hypnosis but emphasized that he was not advocating this in the schools.

"If we utilize the new sciences—psychiatry, the mental sciences, astrology even," he told the audience, "we can begin to look at the human being, can begin to talk about individualized instruction. Now we are just talking the game of instruction while still teaching to a group."

He decried the fact that most of the recent outcry over the school budget cut focused on the loss of teaching jobs, not on their effects on pupils.

Mr. Robinson said he was not as concerned about the fiscal problem as he was with how the money that was available was being spent.

He said that since 1965 more than $500-million in Federal Title I funds had gone to the city to help improve the education of disadvantaged children and during this time, "the affluent became more affluent" and the number of underachieving pupils increased.

DISCUSSION QUESTIONS

1. Do Robinson's views on astrology and hypnosis disqualify him from the presidency of the New York City Board of Education, in your judgment?
2. Is it possible that some youngsters pose behavior problems in class because their "birth signs" conflict with those of other children or their teacher?
3. Is human ability infinite, as Mr. Robinson states?
4. How would you spend $500 million to improve the education of "disadvantaged" people?

CHAPTER 7 Looking at Teaching and Learning

In surveying education today, what impresses most is how greatly change is needed and how slowly and haltingly it occurs.

Until Sputnik, America seemed secure in the advantage her educational system gave her over the rest of the world. Sputnik shocked the nation and upset the American educational establishment. One immediate reaction was the pooling of our mathematical and scientific talents in revising and strengthening these disciplines. Belatedly, the national feeling of emergency created a new, active role for the federal government in education in supporting the competition with the Soviets for world supremacy in technology.

Recent curriculum revision has responded to consideration of the method, structure, and process of the various disciplines. Along with this movement has come a reemphasis on the power, the economy, and the retentiveness of inductive learning, though it be called "the discovery process" or any other name.

Among the psychologists who have studied cognition, the Frenchman, Jean Piaget, is especially noteworthy for having returned learning and teaching to its proper focus on the object of all education, the child. Piaget's research is directed toward a startling insight, the child's view of his universe. His procedures and findings are filled with warmth and feeling and compel recognition of the commonality of childhood everywhere.

Americans have only recently begun to know and appreciate Piaget's work. The English, who have known it longer, have found in it the rationale for the remaking of their primary schools, to the point where one-third are Piagetian in outlook and function, one-third are affected by him, while the reminder continue in the traditional pattern.

American education has changed little in form and structure although there is increasing recognition of the need to individualize instruction and to break out of rigid organizational molds. One attempt to provide an alternative to the age-grade format, the nongraded school, has too often resulted in more efficient "tracking" rather than in the flexibility of movement and fluidity of grouping that would offer the child a genuinely individual program. In fact, the very concept of individualized instruction must be brought under rigid scrutiny.

Programmed learning has been suggested as an answer to the problem of individualizing instruction and giving the teacher greater mobility. However, a model for learning based on stimulus, response, and selective reinforcement raises in many minds thorny questions concerning teachers, children, and the goals of education.

The mass media have entered into active competition with the schools as instruments for learning. The nonschool environment is saturated with them to the point where, jointly, they are coming to create an all-inclusive, wraparound presence of sight and sound. The schools of the twenty-first century must learn to utilize the media—both singly and in a variety of combinations—without being overwhelmed by them.

The lack of responsiveness of the schools to change can only be fully comprehended when one views the society of which they are a part, a society so chaotic, so violently agitated, in such flux that the old established roles are no longer identifiable. What does it mean to be a teacher, a student, a parent? What is a school? What is education? What does it mean to be a human being?

To be armed for today with what McLuhan calls a rear-view mirror mentality is to attack space projectiles with peashooters. To fail to see things whole is to court doom. The revolution we confront is a revolution of rising expectations, born of an affluent society, with television as the midwife. The crisis arises out of denial of what is most deeply human, of decency, integrity, wholeness, manhood—a crisis brought about by man's inhumanity to man. It is remediable only by a return to humanness. Weston LaBarre speaks of "The Human Animal," and Desmond Morris of "The Naked Ape"; both remind us of man's origins and his limitations when acting in animality.

Education is the means whereby children learn their humanness; it is necessarily an interaction suffused with sentiment. Education begins when the child asks, "Am I Loved?" It ends when the answer is, "No."

ROBERT T. SIDWELL   Cooling Down the Classroom:

Some Educational Implications of the McLuhan Thesis

When Nietzsche's Zarathustra announced the death of God, the people continued to laugh and dance. Concluding that his inauguration of the period *post mortem Dei* was somewhat premature, the prophet retired once more to his mountain. Nietzsche (and his alter ego, Zarathustra) was, as he somewhere wryly conceded, born posthumously. Our modern seer, Marshall McLuhan, on the other hand, announced the death of the mechanical technology and was awarded the Albert Schweitzer professorship of a $100,000 chair in the humanities at Fordham University. "The times," as Bob Dylan sings "they are a-changin'."

Søren Kierkegaard describes a scene wherein a clown is called upon to announce a fire in a theater. He was greeted with laughter and applause (the melancholy Dane suggested that such would probably be the popular reaction to the end of the world). Laughter and applause have, by and large, been the reaction to Professor McLuhan's revolutionary thesis (in addition to outright bewilderment), possibly because he too tends to play the clown at times. In our admiration, amusement (or bewilderment), however, let us not lose sight of the fact that the McLuhan thesis *is* a revolutionary document, particularly for the educational profession.

Unlike Marx and Engels, McLuhan does not call for a revolution; he in fact describes one that is to a large degree a *fait accompli*. McLuhan's description is of a technological revolution, the replacement of the mechanical age by the electronic age. This is the content of the revolution, and, as such, is scarcely very exciting news to anyone over the age of twenty. The McLuhan thesis, however, does not rest on this obvious transformation from mechanical media to electronic media. The new medium of electric technology, suggests McLuhan, treated formally, is itself (like any medium) a "message" quite divorced from the sum of its contents. As a matter of fact, a preoccupation with the content of any medium or process is, from McLuhan's perspective, to ignore the message of that medium *qua* medium. As he has so catchingly phrased it, "the medium is the message."

McLuhan's contention that not content but the medium itself is the message is predicated upon his belief that "any technology creates a

Reprinted from *The Educational Forum*, Vol. XXXII, No. 3 (March 1968), pp. 351–358, with permission of Kappa Delta Pi, an Honor Society in Education, owners of the copyright.

totally new human environment."[1] It, in fact, introduces a change of scale, or pace, or pattern into human affairs.[2] The real "message" of any medium, then, is to be found in those changes in perceptual patterns or sensual ratios that it, *qua* medium, engenders. That such changes *are* made, says McLuhan, is due to the fact that technological media represent an extention (or amputation) of some human faculty—psychic or physical.[3] Thus, the wheel is an extension of the foot, the book an extension of the eye, clothing an extension of the skin, etc. Furthermore, ". . . such extension demands new ratios or new equilibriums among the other organs and extensions of the body."[4] One cannot avoid these adjustments or accommodations. Media alter the environment and evoke in us, willy-nilly, ". . . unique ratios of sense perceptions. The extension of any one sense alters the way we think or act—the way we perceive the world. When these ratios change, men change."[5]

Although we cannot avoid these changes, we can, since McLuhan, be intelligently aware of them and of their implications.

"There is absolutely no inevitability as long as there is a willingness to contemplate what is happening."[6] As Father John Culkin notes, "Such influence [of media] are deterministic only if ignored."[7]

McLuhan's contention of an intimate relationship between technological process and modes of societal perceptions and sensual ratios has been shared by a number of other thinkers, usually in less explosive terms and with a more peripheral emphasis. Husserl, for example, noted that

The scientific abstraction from concreteness, the quantification of qualities which yield exactness as well as universal validity, involve a specific concrete experience of the *Lebenswelt*—a specific mode of seeing the world.[8]

To put this into McLuhan's terminology, the "specific concrete experience" is provided by the technological media of that world, and the "specific mode of seeing the world" is the "message" of the media.

Herbert Marcuse has provided a similar analysis of the "message" of the science of Galileo, when he observed it ". . . is the science of methodical, systematic anticipation and projection . . . that which experiences, comprehends, and shapes the world in terms of calculable, predictable relationships among exactly identifiable units."[9]

[1] Marshall McLuhan, *Understanding Media: The Extensions of Man* (New York: McGraw-Hill, 1966), p. vi. (Cited hereafter as McLuhan, *Understanding*).
[2] *Ibid.*, p. 8.
[3] McLuhan and Quentin Fiore, *The Medium is the Massage* (New York: Bantam Books, 1967), p. 26. (Cited hereafter as McLuhan and Fiore, *Massage*).
[4] *Ibid.*, p. 45.
[5] *Ibid.*, p. 41.
[6] *Ibid.*, p. 25.
[7] John M. Culkin, S.J., "A Schoolman's Guide to Marshall McLuhan," *Saturday Review*, March 18, 1967, p. 51.
[8] Herbert Marcuse *One-Dimensional Man* (Boston: Beacon Press, 1966), p. 164.
[9] *Ibid.*

In reducing matter to quantifiable qualities, Marcuse suggests, science (Galilean) provided a new mode of seeing the world. This new perceptual framework tended to relate men to one another "in accordance with quantifiable qualities. . . ."[10]

McLuhan himself has devoted a considerable number of words to a description of the "message" of the media of the past age—the highly literate and mechanized age. The revolutionary impact of the McLuhan approach lies in his assertion that that is a *past* age. To glimpse some of the significant implications of the McLuhan thesis for education, it is necessary to look briefly at *The Gutenberg Galaxy,* which was ". . . intended to trace the ways in which the *forms* of experience and of mental outlook and expression have been modified, first by the phonetic alphabet and then by printing."[11]

Pre-alphabet man was predominately an auditory creature—the ear was the dominant sensory organ. He lived in "acoustic" space—undifferentiated, intuitive, total. His medium of communication was speech, and its "message" was a specific patterning of perception and sensual ratios. In this (auditory) patterning, action and reaction were simultaneous and demanded a total involvement. McLuhan's term for this modality of life is "mythic," by which he means a ". . . mode of simultaneous awareness of a complex group of causes and effects."[12] The mythic dimension that characterized pre-alphabetical life has been maintained in literate cultures (as the Chinese) which uses a nonphonetic (ideographic) script that ". . . enables them to retain a rich store of inclusive perception in depth of experience. . . . For the ideogram is an inclusive *gestalt,* not an analytic dissociation of senses and function like phonetic writing [as such, it] . . . invests each ideogram with a total intuition of being and reason that allows only a small role to visual sequence as a mark of mental effort and organization."[13]

That pre-alphabetical man's perceptual patterns *were* radically different has been eloquently demonstrated by S. Giedion's studies of spatial conception in prehistoric are. He concludes that:

The distinguishing mark of the space perception of primeval art is the complete independence and freedom of its vision. . . . In our sense there is no above and no below, no clear distinction of separateness from an intermingling, and also, certainly, no rules of proportional size. . . . All is within the continual present, the perpetual interflow of today, yesterday, and tomorrow.[14]

Dorothy Lee has concluded that "The given as undifferentiated con-

[10] *Ibid.,* p. 157.
[11] Marshall McLuhan, *The Gutenberg Galaxy* (Toronto: University of Toronto Press, 1962), p. 1. (Cited hereafter as McLuhan, *Gutenberg*).
[12] McLuhan and Fiore, *Massage,* p. 114.
[13] McLuhan, *Understanding,* pp. 84–85.
[14] S. Giedion, "Space Conception in Prehistoric Art," in Edmund Carpenter and Marshall McLuhan, eds., *Explorations in Communication* (Boston: Beacon Press, 1960), pp. 85–86. (Cited hereafter as Carpenter and McLuhan, *Explorations*).

tent is implicit in the nominal categories of the Wintu. . . . To the Wintu, the given is not a series of particulars . . . the given is unpartitioned mass. . . ."[15] Again, with regard to Malinowski's well-studied Trobrianders:

Events and objects are self-contained points in another respect; there is a series of beings, but no becoming. There is no temporal connection between objects. . . . There is no arrangement of activities or events into means and ends, no causal or teleologic relationships. What we consider a causal relationship in a sequence of connected events is to the Trobriander an ingredient of a patterned whole.[16]

This totality of tribalistic involvement without differentiation of pre-alphabetical man (as reflected in his art and language) is the basis of the *Gemeinschaft* (community) so well delineated by Toennies—an organic rather than a mechanical formation.[17]

Then came the phonetic alphabet—its message, as McLuhan has so well shown, was devastating to the all-at-once-ness organicity of pre-alphabetical man's world.

The alphabet is a construct of fragmented bits and parts which have no semantic meaning in themselves, and which must be strung together in a line, bead-like, and in prescribed order. Its use fostered and encouraged the habit of perceiving all environment in visual and spatial terms—particularly in terms of a space and of a time that are uniform, c,o,n,t,i,n,u,o,u,s, and c-o-n-n-e-c-t-e-d.[18]

Man became linear, his activities fragmented, his thoughts sequential and departmentalized. From an undifferentiated all-at-one-ness, the phonetic alphabet encouraged a perceptual awareness of a sequential one-at-a-time-ness. Man became individualized (de-tribalized)—an individual and unrelated atom at large in sharply differentiated visual space.

Phonetic culture endows men with the means of repressing their feelings and emotions when engaged in action. To act without reacting, without involvement, is the peculiar advantage of western literate man.[19]

The integral wholeness of pre-alphabetical man's world underwent a radical departmentalization—his sensual, emotional, imaginative facets were delineated and disassociated from the "whole," while he himself was individualized, detribalized and specialized.

Such a world view is the *sine qua non* of applied knowledge and technology. Printing, McLuhan notes, is merely an extension and intensifica-

[15] Dorothy Lee, "Linguistic Reflections of Wintu Thought" in Carpenter and McLuhan, *Explorations*, pp. 12–13.
[16] Lee, "Lineal and Nonlineal Codifications of Reality," in *ibid.*, p. 141.
[17] Ferdinand Toennies, *Gemeinschaft und Gesellschaft*, quoted in Talcott Parsons, Edward Shils, Kaspar D. Naegle, Jesse R. Pitts, eds., *Theories of Society* (New York: Free Press, 1961), 2 Vols., I 192.
[18] McLuhan and Fiore, *Massage*, p. 44.
[19] McLuhan, *Understanding*, p. 86.

tion of the visual orientation. David Riesman noted that "Print may be said to mark the epoch of the middle class—the time-attentive, the future oriented, the mobile. . . . If oral communication keeps people together, print is the isolating medium par excellence."[20] Many a wife may have shared this feeling while staring at the back of her husband's morning paper at the breakfast table.

The supreme quality of print, McLuhan feels, is the simple fact of its repeatability—it is "a ditto device."

This fragmenting process of mechanized handicraft produced the "division of labor." Noting the detribalizing effects of this fragmented and linear perceptual pattern, Marx ". . . interpreted the division of labor as the social expression of self-alienation."[21] It would be interesting to hear what that dedicated rebel would have made of a recent newspaper item headed "Ten Specialists Required to Reset Phone Button."[22]

Another item in this same edition serves to demonstrate what may well be the epitome of a visually dominated sensorium. Dr. Edward E. Burns, of Texas A&M, is therein credited with the statement that "People eat with their eyes." SEE what I mean?

The education of typographic man has been a faithful reflection of the "message" of his media—it too has been linear, fragmented, non-participatory and sequential. Even the fragmented learning space (classroom) reflects this bias.

Print meant the possibility of uniform texts, grammars and lexicon visually present to as many as asked for them. The classroom, as we know it, was entirely the by-product of print.[23]

The typographic extension of man brought in, among other things, universal literacy and education—homogenized and uniform. So much is past history. Enter the age of electric technology and *its* unique message.

If all media are extensions of some human faculty, then electric circuitry is the penultimate extension of man—an extension of his central nervous system. As such, its message is totality, not fragmentation; a cluster configuration rather than the sequential, linear configuration of print. Electric circuitry is SPEED, the acceleration of information. "At the high speeds of electric communication, purely visual means of apprehending the world are no longer possible; they are just too slow to be relevant or effective."[24] The electric world demands an involvement of the total sensorium for its apprehension. Meaning is altered by ac-

[20] David Riesman, "The Oral and Written Tradition," in Carpenter and McLuhan, *Explorations*, pp. 113–114.
[21] Robert C. Tucker, *Philosophy and Myth in Karl Marx* (New York: Cambridge University Press, 1961), p. 185.
[22] *The New York Times*, March 29, 1967.
[23] Marshall McLuhan, "The Effect of the Printed Book on Language," in Carpenter and McLuhan, *Explorations*, p. 129.
[24] McLuhan and Fiore, *Massage*, p. 63.

celeration, and the totality of electric simultaneity demands a totality of perception which sounds the death-knell for fragmented, serial, one-at-a-time-ness. It is a world of all-at-once-ness. The electric extension of the central nervous system constitutes, as Father Culkin has aptly put it, ". . . a single instantaneous and coexistant field of experience."[25] As such, the media demand an involvement and participation in depth of the whole being, a mythic dimension. Segmented, individualistic typographic man is being "retribalized" by his media; the atomistic *Gesellschaft* of visual space is being "massaged" by the media into an organic, universal *Gemeinschaft*. A glance at some of the strange (to a typographic perception) goings-on among the students at our higher institutions of learning reveals, if nothing else, the mythic demands of the electric age student for involvement, participation, organic role. The attraction of such participatory activities as the Peace Corps, Civil Rights, etc., are precisely their mythic qualities—an organic *rôle* rather than a linear *position*.

The church has its *aggiornamento* (up-dating) movement—an attempt to establish new (organic) relationships between the fragmented two cities of Augustine—a realization of the demand for the restoration of a mythic dimension in religion. The transcendent God of the fragmented typographic world has surely died; the electric world demands immanentism not transcendent aloofness. "If anything characterizes the modern temper," writes theologian Gabriel Vahanian, "it is radical immanentism."[26]

Easter Sunday, 1967. A group of some 10,000 young people gather in New York's Central Park for a "Be-In." "We wanted it to be an active celebration of being alive, of having that experience in the park," says Mr. James Fouratt, one of the organizers. "People in New York don't look at each other, don't see each other, don't talk to each other."[27]

Mexico City officials report that the Sunday afternoon band concerts became amazingly popular since jazz numbers were added to the traditional fare. The unprecedented crowds were "humming, clapping and shouting."[28] They were involved and participating because jazz is, in McLuhanese, a "cool" medium (one that is of low definition and demands participation or completion by the audience). The electronic age is cool, as illustrated by the TV screen which presents the audience with some three million "dots" of which only a few dozen are selected by the participant to form his visual image. As a product of these cool media of participation, the electronic age learner is a new breed of cat; he is involved and oriented to involve himself in depth, to live mythically. When this new learner is put into a linear, fragmented school environment

[25] Culkin, *op. cit.*, p. 70.
[26] Gabriel Vahanian, *The Death of God* (New York: George Braziller, 1961), p. 188.
[27] *The New York Times*, March 27, 1967.
[28] *Ibid.*

(the creation of the typographic media) of low participation and high definition (as is print—a "hot" medium)—enter one big educational problem.

The youth of today live mythically and in depth. But they encounter instruction in situations organized by means of classified information—subjects are unrelated, they are visually conceived in terms of a blueprint. . . . The student find no means of involvement for himself and cannot discover how the educational scheme relates to his mythic world of electronically processed data and experience that his clear and direct responses report.[29]

The implications of the McLuhan thesis are enormous for the educational profession (and threatening for linear educators). The student of the electric world is a participant in discovery and not the passive recipient of neatly pre-packaged linear learning. The linear, analytic, and irrelevantly fragmented bits of information make increasingly less sense to the products of the electronic media. "Young people are looking for a formula for putting on the universe—*participation mystique*. They do not look for detached patterns—for ways of relating themselves to the world, *à la* nineteenth century."[30]

Actually, McLuhan suggests, the T.V. child in a social and educational world that is visually oriented is an "underprivileged cripple."[31]

Apparently one reason why Johnny can't read is that he tries to apply the set of perceptual patterns of his cool electronic media (involvement in depth of *all* senses) to a hot (print) medium which demands an isolated and extended *visual* sensuality rather than a unified sensorium. This seems much like attempting precise target shooting with a shotgun.

How then are we to cool off the classroom in order to get in phase with our media?

Education, it would appear, in order to reflect the message of the electronic media, must begin to dismantle its linear organization pattern on all fronts. It would have to become more "formal" and synthesizing, and less analytic and instructional.

In our time John Dewey worked to restore education to its primitive, pre-print phase. He wanted to get the student out of the passive role of consumer of pre-packaged learning. In fact, Dewey in reacting against passive print culture was surfboarding along on the new electronic age.[32]

If, in fact, our school audiences have been massaged by their media to take a participatory rôle in the learning process, all is not as dark and linear in the educational world as it might seem. As Father Culkin has observed, the current educational innovations display an interesting similarity—a break with the linear, print-oriented pattern: team teach-

[29] McLuhan and Fiore, *Massage*, p. 100.
[30] *Ibid.*, p. 114.
[31] McLuhan, *Understanding*, p. 332.
[32] McLuhan, *Gutenberg*, p. 144.

ing, audio-lingual language training, multi-media learning situations, seminars (cool and participatory as opposed to hot, passive lectures), individualized learning (learning responsibility shifting from teacher to student).[33] The mythic (not mystic) East would certainly appear to be a topic of increased interest to educators attempting to totalize learning; the teacher who introduces Haiku poetry and the Zen koan to the elementary grades might be surprised at what the electric age learner can do with these forms of mythic experience.

Clearly, the message is involvement, not "scholarly" detachment; synthesis of knowledge and experience, not fragmented analysis; wholeness and convergence, not sequential linearity. From a position of a curricular luxury, the arts ". . . now become a dynamic way of tuning up the sensorium and of providing fresh ways of looking at familiar things"[34] "The arts," of course, include non-western as well as western sources. The "empty" spaces in classical Chinese painting, for example, should prove quite comfortable to the young products of the participatory electronic media (although their teacher may feel a linear annoyance at the "incompleteness" of the undifferentiated aesthetic continuum). In terms of educational theory, the multi-disciplinary and cross-cultural emphases of such theorists as Theodore Brameld are very much in phase with the totality of electronics.

It is regrettably true that in the sharply linear groves of Academe, the pre-electrical perceptual pattern that resulted in fragmentation of knowledge, has been virtually reified in academic departmentalization. This (arbitrary) pattern of segmentation has acquired all of the sacrosanct qualities of an immutable natural law, a "ghostly objectivity" to borrow the apt phrase of Georg Lukács. That the reality is "ghostly" and merely the hypostatized human delineation is painfully obvious to the students of the electric age, who constantly complain that course x bears absolutely no relationship to the activities in courses y and z (and none seem to bear much relationship to their increasingly mythic *Lebenswelt*).

If the McLuhan thesis is indeed the message (commercial?) on the screen ("handwriting on the wall" seems too downright typographical to apply to McLuhan), the educational implications are clear enough. The electronic age pupil requires an educational environment that does not ask him to consume a carefully weighed bundle of pre-digested and pre-packaged knowledge, that allows him a maximum participation in discovery, that will relate and synthesize rather than linearly f/r/a/g/-m/e/n/t knowledge. Not "rite words in rote order," but the unified all-at-once totality of instant automation.

"Paradoxically," McLuhan claims, "automation makes liberal education mandatory."[35] Should education persist in moving into the future

[33] Culkin, *op. cit.*, p. 72.
[34] *Ibid.*
[35] McLuhan, *Understanding*, p. 357.

looking steadfastly to the rear, continue the present fragmented unrelatedness of its curricular offerings, it will insure a future citizenry wholly alienated from the cybernetic world in which they will be living. "Control over change would seem to consist in moving not with it but ahead of it. Anticipation gives the power to deflect and control force."[36] Such anticipation may be seen in, for example, the new three-year college (tentatively named "Ben-salem") which was to open its doors at Fordham University in July, 1967. Perhaps this experimental college will be the archetype of future experiments in providing student participation in matters of curriculum.[37]

If education must be the "civil defense against media fallout," it must become aware of the message of the media—the depth and interrelation of the new world of electronic organization.

Perhaps the best understanding of the message of the electronic media for education is presented in the advertisements for the Berlitz Language Schools—"total immersion."

DISCUSSION QUESTIONS

1. How can the schools help man to become "whole" if they accept McLuhan's premises?
2. Which of his educational ideas do you find most stimulating and provocative?
3. With which do you agree?

JAMES HERNDON The Stream of Life

When I got back the school had a new program. The junior high school assumes that it was invented in order to bridge the gap between elementary and high school, but it is always uncertain which way it ought to lean. In our case, Spanish Main had started out leaning toward the elementary side, but by the time I got there it was definitely taking a hard line toward high school, telling the kids stuff like you have grow up, take responsibility, get along with more than one teacher. But over that summer someone had had second thoughts, it seemed, and recognized that in the school there were a number of kids who didn't take to the hard-line high school approach. It was decided to call these kids "immature" and deal with them in a self-contained classroom, for one

Reprinted from James Herndon, *How To Survive in Your Native Land* copyright © 1971 by James Herndon. Reprinted by permission of Simon and Schuster.

[36] *Ibid.*, p. 199.
[37] *The New York Times*, April 6, 1967.

year, "to make their transition easier." There were only a couple such classes. Apparently the one thousand or so other kids weren't immature.

It seems to me now that that was the beginning (at SM) of two tactics used by public schools to win their battle for existence; first, to establish special groups of kids in various categories ranging from "immature" through neurologically or emotionally or educationally "handicapped" to "deprived" to the marvelous, blatant "non-achiever," and second, to take teachers who wish to teach in some odd way and let them teach those odd kids. For all the terms for special kids really just mean kids who can't or won't or don't do things the way the school thinks they ought to be done; once labeled as special, the school can pretend that there is a *normal* group which is well served by the custom of the school. The school's obvious inability to satisfy many children can then become natural, since the kids are "special" and *shouldn't* be satisfied by any normal procedures and the school does not need to change its ways at all, has only to create some arrangements on the outskirts of the school to keep them special kids and special teachers out of the way.

I wasn't thinking of that at the time. Frankly, the first few days I was besieged by parents who wanted to know if their kids were in some sort of dumb class. What the parents instinctively knew was that any special arrangement probably meant the school considered their kids to be dumb or goofy, and in any case, didn't think they would be going to Harvard. They wanted to know how their kids happened to get in this class and they wanted it understood that their kids weren't dumb, and if it *was* a dumb class they wanted their kids out of it and promised to cooperate by making them do homework, forbidding TV, and so on. Well, I ended up telling the parents what the school told me, which was that the kids were supposed to be "immature" rather than dumb, that in fact they were probably a brighter group than most, that the school was not selling them out of Harvard, and in any case I wasn't. That satisfied almost everyone. Immaturity was O.K. with them.

I tried to think then why it was that these kids were supposed by the school to be immature. Now, I decide to isolate the quality of stubbornness. I know that it is only in the terms of the book that I say so. It is simply that the kids as I remember them demonstrated no other particular quality which they might be said to hold in common. Some were very smart, some were not smart; some did lots of school work, some did very little. Some had broken homes, some didn't. Some were minorities, some weren't. Some couldn't get along with other kids, couldn't accept criticism or conform; some could. Hal Smith was a stout blond kid who got all A's, did the work, and had his life planned; he was going to enter the Coast Guard like his father and pilot those boats across the bar. He had a notebook full of *Life* magazine pictures of tremendous waves roaring up at the mouths of Oregon rivers, of small Coast Guard boats battling them. Charles Ford was a witty child of stern Lutheran parents, who did nothing right except school work, who would only catch baseballs one-handed with a right-handed glove on his left hand and who wrote cynical and satiric papers about fairytales á la *Mad* magazine. Rosie was a girl who spent all day reading books, crouched down in her desk, which she moved to a corner, and her afternoons out of school with fruit flies, upon which she made endless experiments. Ray had already given up on school work because he couldn't do none of it, add, read, or write, and wanted to spend his days cleaning up; taking roll, investigating what other kids were doing and putting up good stuff on the board. Howard was a science-mad kid from Canada whose cum folder remarked that he, while an excellent student, wouldn't participate in sports; he was the only kid in the class who played hockey in some junior league—of course the school had no hockey league to play in. Lucy and Sally were beautiful giggly girls who wanted to interact (as we say) with me all day long. After school they sat on my car, defying me to go home. Susan was an Italian girl of great social consciousness, full of clear and accurate notions about the injustice of the world. Eileen and Rosa were Catholic girls whose main concern was their mothers' wish that they attend Catholic high school, who didn't want to do it, who kept trying to keep out of trouble in order that their mothers wouldn't have some objective reason to send them there, who knew they were going there anyway (and they did) but who wanted to make sure that there could be no reason like bad grades or bad citizenship which their mothers could call upon as justification for their actions—that their mothers would just have to say in the end, I just am going to send you there because I want to, and then they, Eileen and Rosa, would win the battle. There was Robert Chow, a fat lump of a Chinese kid who wouldn't do anything at all in school, but who was later discovered by Rosie to have been raising (or growing) fresh-water clams in various tanks in his house since he was seven or eight, a feat which, so said Rosie, was thought almost impossible by the experts she was always reading.

Well, there were obviously some twenty-five or so others, too—I imagine I remember more kids from that class than from any other I've had—none of them alike, all different people as to desire, need, aspiration, even though the school had decided to classify them as being all the same, i.e., immature. Perhaps the school had hoped I would figure out some lessons aimed specifically at immaturity, that I would either cure them of immaturity or, if incurable, figure some way to teach them in spite of it; or perhaps the school only hoped I'd keep them out of everyone's hair for a year. Obviously that wasn't my concern. I hadn't invented immaturity nor been consulted about it by the school and so I could ignore it except to wonder occasionally why it was that these particular kids (and by implication, I myself) were chosen to be immature.

Considering my recent past, the New World and all that, I could have brooded about the gulf between something called *learning* and something called *achieving in school*, about the teacher as authority or entertainer or provider of work—about the razor's edge you must walk, between the expectation of the kids (one to which they cling firmly, even though they may despise it) about what school *is* and your own conviction that most of that is worthless at best. In fact, though, I slipped into the year, the class, as easily as a fish into water without (as I feel) much thought about it, without trying to reform the school and the world, following the kids' leads and offering mine for them to follow, feeling good about coming to work and living easily in the classroom. Everything followed *naturally*, is what I want to say; only now, in retrospect, do I want to write down something about the way we lived in and out of school with the purpose of taking a look at that razor's edge and how you may walk it if it appears during your journey that you must.

For if we are talking about what the school wants kids to do, we are talking about seventh grade spelling books with twenty words to spell and define each week for thirty-six weeks, talking about math books with per cent problems to do and interest and decimals and review of add-subtract-etc., talking about social studies with Egypt and the Renaissance and talking about science with water cycle and gravity and health-vitamin-germs-Pasteur-don't-smoke. (The school changes textbooks; in math besides the above now it is commutative and associative to define; in science DNA and ecology and don't-take-drugs; in language it is watered-down and crude linguistics. Egypt remains.) I you feel that what the school calls learning is bullshit shall you inform your students of that and forbid them to do the school work? If you feel that what the school calls learning is bullshit shall you inform the kids of that and still make them do it? If you feel that what the school calls learning is bullshit ought you to pretend that you don't feel that? Pointless questions. Arrogant questions, besides; you forget that the kids really know the score, know that no matter what you, some nutty individual teacher with whom they've been saddled for no reason of their own, think about it, they've their parents and future teachers and their cum folders and the high school counselors and achievement tests and four years of high school and college and grade school and the Coast Guard to satisfy. They have lives to lead, something which is often forgotten (I had, too, a fact which became rather obtrusive around this time), and for many kids the school was only a gambit to be achieved in some way within those lives—part of them, important perhaps, but not a point of philosophy, nothing relevant, crucial only in that it shouldn't get messed up and be allowed or forced to intrude. Still, I was affected by the New World. I couldn't say that the school work was learning. I couldn't judge the students on the basis of whether they did it or not, did it well or O.K.

or lousy. Still the students were waiting for me to give out the course of study in all those academic disciplines—language, social studies, science and math—so that they could deliver another year's performance according to their own lights. So that Hal could establish another leg on the way to the Coast Guard, so that Charles could satisfy his notion of what he ought to do before doing what he liked, so that Eileen and Rosa could have something to use against their mothers, so that Rosie could have something to not-do, so that Ray could have something going on to observe and approve and disapprove (he was of course the greatest judge and moralist of school work, as are most kids who get F's in school). What—should I refuse the kids this staple of their existence? Refuse them an item they had good use for? Not likely. On the other hand, was I going to indicate a serious attachment to this bullshit? Not likely either. I got in all the textbooks the school had, in all the subjects, got the supplementary books, the high, average and low readers, math puzzles, Lifes in Syrias (tangential to Egypt), Negro histories, Clouds and Bugs, Flax and Other Products, Atlases, and so on. I put up on the board segments of each to be done (read and questions answered about) each week or (in the end) each month, according to a simple schedule which would allow for the completion of this work in these books by the end of the year, supposing some kid wanted to complete this work in these books by the end of the year. I made ditto sheets of my own about form classes in the new grammar, about why Egyptians showed both feet pointing the same way, about "The Rocking Horse Winner," about why ice is lighter than water.

Only I refused to pretend that I had to "teach" any of that stuff. We all knew it was stuff to do, rather than anything which had to be learned or even could be learned. I knew that most of the kids could already do it if they wanted or needed to do it, and that some of the kids couldn't do it because they really couldn't read or figure it, which was because it was against the principles of their lives to do it. It is the old German notion of apprenticeship; this year you get a nail, the next year you get a hammer, the next you get to hit the nail with the hammer. I know that is crazy and the kids know it is crazy and the Germans know it is crazy but we also know that is how things are, even if we don't know how they got that way or who decided it. If we want to be carpenters or enter the Coast Guard we'll hold still for this craziness, knowing that it has nothing at all to do with whether or not we become good carpenters or with how we will finally encounter the breakers off the Oregon coast, for that is entirely up to us at that point in the river where everything narrows, the game narrows, and it is up to our individual courage as men, women, girls, and boys.

But look what happens when you do that. You don't have to stand up in front of the class and make everyone shut up and listen to you as you explain the assignment, demonstrate how to work equations, point out what metaphors are . . . you don't have to pretend that order and silence have to do with learning (or even with doing school work!) and you don't have to pretend that no one can produce work without your lecture, and in short you don't have to be a contemptible ass and that is good. What you can do then is to say loudly every Monday morning that You (you students) *already know* this, *already know* what the school intends to teach you this year and any other year, that the means to produce this and satisfy the school and the Coast Guard is *already in your hands*—you get to say Quit asking me if this or that is right or if this or that ought to be capitalized or if such and such is a noun or class I word—you get to repeat (as teacher) all that kind of information is already in your heads, you only have to reach in there and get it out—you get to say I'm not playing that particular school game with you, where I start explaining and you start not-paying attention (since you don't need or can't use the explanation) and talking or fucking around and then I'm supposed to say Pay Attention and you're supposed to say I am (while you're not, since it's not necessary and therefore obligatory that you don't, while obligatory to me as teacher that you pretend you are)—you get to say: "And then went down to the ship, / Set keel to breakers, forth on the godly sea, and / We set up mast and sail on that swart ship, / Bore sheep aboard her and our bodies also . . ." and so get going with the day, the week, the journey. . . .

You get to arrive at school in your car and go drink coffee and smoke and talk (if you've someone to talk to) until the bell rings and then begin another smoke and go to the bathroom and get another cup of coffee to take to class and when you arrive late the kids are settling into the day and the room, someone is taking roll and the lunch count with some shouts about who is really here even if they aren't really *here* yet, and when you come in several kids rush you with urgent requests about going to the library or to their lockers or to phone their moms or get some other kid's homework out of a third kid's locker and you can agree or forbid or stall them, saying Wait until I have a little coffee, a number of other kids are sitting around drinking their Cokes and eating doughnuts which they've just bought on their ways to school. . . .

But you don't have to stand in front of the class and give out some lesson and explain things which no one needs explained to a restless group who have a lot of other things on their minds and who (as soon as you finish explaining) will ask you questions about what you just clearly explained. There's time, you can say to yourself; and when the first urgent group is dealt with and given passes and gone you can talk to the next group of kids who just want to talk, about what's going on today or what their moms said or their brother did or what outrage is being served for lunch or do you want some gum? You can have all the roll slips and lunch-count slips and hall passes and library passes and the slips for ordering movies and prints and film strips and supply-order forms available in your desk for the students to fill out and order and go get and (since they understand the bureaucracy of the school at least as well as you do) you can be assured that they will keep your desk straight and order stuff on time and keep the room well supplied with three-hole lined paper and ditto paper and paper clips and staples and take inventory of the books from time to time (faking reports for losses or stolen just as well as you will) and getting the couple of kids who have spent some diligent time learning to forge your initials do all the signing on all these slips and notify the class of assemblies and dances and games and threats from the administration and clean up the room on occasion and put up the assignments on the board and check off the papers according to who has done what of the regular work and get the mop from the custodian when paint is spilled. . . .

And then sometime during the day if it looks like the time is right or you just feel like it or indeed anxiety tells you you must do it, you can get around to getting up and standing there and telling everyone to shut up and then sum up what's going on in science or remind everyone that today we decided to read everyone's stories or say I want everyone to be careful with the goddamn paint and sometimes that is just the right thing and everyone wants to be drawn together and be a group (and sometimes it's not and you can either forget it or get tough and make everyone, if that's what you really feel like, which it sometimes is) . . . but quite possibly it will be Janet instead who has dreamed up the idea of *Culture Hour*, what this class needs is some *Culture!* (I teach her the word *Kultur,* which she likes very much) standing up there, a little blond chick yelling Shut up for Culture Hour! and an uproar of laughing and griping and sitting down because everyone really knows Janet is going to *have* Culture Hour no matter what and they might as well get it over with and besides everyone really likes the grand bullshit of the idea, and Janet then reads Robert Browning or "Hiawatha" or *The Nonsense Book* or something of her own or some other kids' stories so long as they are cultured and everyone scoffs and makes uncultured remarks and has a grand time. . . .

And while teachers are complaining they haven't any *time* you see that you have all the time in the world, time to spend with Lucy and Sally telling them they got glue on their heads and threatening them about what you're going to do if they get on the hood of your car again until they are satisfied, time with Eileen and Rosa, who have discovered that if they get caught a couple of times smoking in the bathroom their mothers will react most satisfactorily, time to talk with Howard, who has discovered simultaneously a real woods out in back of the drive-in and The Byrds and is trying to make sense out of both (the woods have foxes and a skunk and a red-tailed hawk flying overhead and some kind of marvelous purple moss which the Museum of Science don't know about and who would have thought that right here in this prototype [his word] of suburban developments there would be a real woods, and here too that is just what The Byrds are singing about)—every day there are going to be kids who want to spend some time talking to you, as adult, as teacher, as whatever you are, wanting to relate their adventures and troubles and excitements and miseries and aspirations and confusions or hoping perhaps to get some clear idea of the world they live in through you. At the same time there are going to be a lot of kids in the room who don't want to talk to you at all, that day, just want to be left alone with their school work (it may happen) or eats or books or drawings or models or to talk to each other or get mad and begin fights or arguments, they can get along very well without you, it seems, and you can let them. Then you will even have time to go round to Ray or whoever else it is and teach them something that they really need to know, not only in order to get along in the school but in order to be *equal* in America—get Ray some book to read and sit down with him awhile and read it together and *teach* him, get Robert to pull himself together enough to attempt the mystery of dividing and teach *him*, go around later on to Ray and say you *can* read, now read me some. You can teach some kids something that they need and want to know, so long as you have the time, including of course showing some kids how to do the week's or month's official work if they want to do it and are having trouble with it (if they want to be official achieving seventh graders, which oddly enough many kids want to be) or talking with kids about what they might do otherwise if they don't want to be those same official seventh graders but are interested in writing or drawing or painting or making empty gallon cans of ditto fluid cave in for Science. You have time to protect some kids and get mad at others, you have time to answer over and over again questions about what kind of cigarettes you smoke and when did you start to smoke, are you married, how many kids do you have, would you let your kids smoke, let them grow long hair, do you think Robert is really smart? what would you do if your kids cut school, got an F, smoked in the bathroom, what kind of car, what was the war like, did you get in any fights, can you dance, did you like girls when you were thirteen, don't you think the PE teacher is unfair about giving out checks, Mrs. so-and-so said this yesterday, do you agree with that? Time to talk about all that, without worry, since the official part of the school work is going on, or not going on, without your total involvement in it. Time to read your book in there too, look at the want ads in the paper if you feel like it, telling everyone to leave you alone, time to cut out of the class and go visit the shop or the art room or some other class to see what's going on, knowing everyone will get along while you're gone. . . .

Time to live there in your classroom like a human being instead of playing some idiot role which everyone knows is an idiot role, time to see that teaching (if that is your job in America) is connected with your life and with you as a human being, citizen, person, that you don't have to become something different like a Martian or an idiot for eight hours a day. Time to deal with serious concerns of the kids and time to deal with put-on concerns and time to fuck around and time to get mad either seriously or not seriously . . . but you can only live that kind of life in there if you are willing to realize that the dicta of the school are crazy but that at the same time the kid's life is connected to the school in complicated ways and you'd better offer him the chance to take any part of it he wants or has to. These dicta do not exist in themselves. *One is not Duchess one hundred yards from a carriage.* They too are part of what Dewey would call the continuum of existence. I prefer Wittgenstein's words—the stream of life.

DISCUSSION QUESTIONS

1. Do schools really take highly disparate youngsters and put them in a created category where they are supposed to hold some nonexistent trait in common? What are the categories presently in vogue?
2. Can children make the distinction between "stuff to do" and "what had to be learned and even could be learned," as Herndon states?
3. Do you accept Herndon's explanation of the idiocy of school and how children and teacher can act in such a way as to preserve the sanity and decency of both?
4. How many of us could fulfill the vision that Herndon has of the teacher as a human being in the classroom?

IVAN ILLICH Why We Must Abolish Schooling

Many students, especially those who are poor, intuitively know what the schools do for them. They school them to confuse process and substance. Once these become blurred, a new logic is assumed: the more treatment there is the better are the results; or, escalation leads to success. The pupil is thereby "schooled" to confuse teaching with learning, grade advancement with education, a diploma with competence, and fluency with the ability to say something new. His imagination is "schooled" to accept service in place of value. Medical treatment is mistaken for health care, social work for the improvement of community life, police protection for safety, military poise for national security, the rat race for productive work. Health, learning, dignity, independence, and creative endeavor are defined as little more than the

Reprinted with permission from *The New York Review of Books.* Copyright © 1970 NYREV, Inc.

performance of the institutions which claim to serve these ends, and their improvement is made to depend on allocating more resources to the management of hospitals, schools, and other agencies in question. Not only education but social reality itself has become "schooled."

It costs roughly the same to school both rich and poor in the same dependence. The yearly expenditure per pupil in the slums and in the rich suburbs of any one of twenty US cities lies in the same range—and sometimes is favorable to the poor.[1] Rich and poor alike depend on schools and hospitals which guide their lives, form their world view, and define for them what is legitimate and what is not. Both view doctoring oneself as irresponsible, learning on one's own as unreliable, and community organization, when not paid for by those in authority, as a form of aggression or subversion. For both groups the reliance on institutional treatment renders independent accomplishment suspect. The progressive underdevelopment of self- and community-reliance is even more typical in Westchester than it is in the Northeast of Brazil. Everywhere not only education but society as a whole needs "de-schooling."

Welfare bureaucracies claim a professional, political, and financial monopoly over the social imagination, setting standards of what is valuable and what is feasible. This monopoly is at the root of the modernization of poverty. Every simple need to which an institutional answer is found permits the invention of a new class of poor and a new definition of poverty. Ten years ago in Mexico it was the normal thing to die in one's own home and to be buried by one's friends. Only the soul's needs were taken care of by the institutional church. Now to die at home has become a sign either of poverty or of special privilege. Dying and death have come under the institutional management of doctors and undertakers.

Modern poverty is not necessarily the consequence of inferior treatment. It can, of course, be associated with fewer years of school attendance or cheap schooling; but it can also accompany more costly schooling such as the higher than average per capita expenses of "compensatory education" in slums and "rehabilitation" behind bars. Modern poverty is not necessarily the result of less treatment, but of different treatment with inadequate results. A certificate attesting to four years of attendance in adult, reformatory, or remedial education is a doubtful recommendation, although the costs of financing the institution in question may be very high indeed.

The poor have always been socially powerless. The increasing reliance on institutional care adds a new dimension to their helplessness: psychological impotence, the inability to fend for themselves. Peasants on the

[1] Penrose B. Jackson, *Trends in Elementary and Secondary Education Expenditures. Central City and Suburban Comparisons 1965 to 1968*, US Office of Education, Office of Program and Planning Evaluation, June 1969.

high plateau of the Andes are exploited by the landlord and the merchant—once they settle in Lima they are, in addition, dependent on political bosses, and disabled by their lack of schooling. Modernized poverty combines the lack of power over circumstances with a loss of personal potency. This modernization of poverty is a world-wide phenomenon, and lies at the root of contemporary underdevelopment. Of course it appears under different guises in rich and in poor countries.

It is probably most intensely felt in US cities. Nowhere else is poverty treated at greater cost. Nowhere else does the treatment of poverty produce so much dependence, anger, frustration, and further demands. And nowhere else should it be so evident that poverty—once it has become modernized—has become resistant to treatment with dollars alone and requires an institutional revolution.

Today in the US the black and even the migrant can aspire to a level of professional treatment which would have been unthinkable two generations ago, and which seems grotesque to most people in the third world. For instance, the US poor can count on a truant officer to return their children to school until they reach seventeen or on a doctor to assign them to a hospital bed which costs $60.00 per day—the equivalent of three months income for a majority of the people in the world. But such care only makes them dependent on more treatment, and renders them increasingly incapable of organizing their own lives around their own experiences and resources within their own communities.

The poor in the US are in a unique position to speak about the predicament which threatens all the poor in a modernizing world. They are making the discovery that no amount of dollars can remove the inherent destructiveness of welfare institutions, once the professional hierarchies of these institutions have convinced society that their ministrations are morally necessary. The poor in the US inner city can demonstrate from their own experience the fallacy on which social legislation in a "schooled" society is built.

Supreme Court Justice William O. Douglas observed that "the only way to establish an institution is to finance it." The corollary is also true. Only by channeling dollars away from the institutions which now treat health, education, and welfare can the further impoverishment resulting from their disabling side effects be stopped.

This must be kept in mind when we evaluate federal aid programs. As a case in point, between 1965 and 1968 over three billion dollars were spent in US schools to offset the disadvantages of about six million children. The program is known as Title One. It is the most expensive compensatory program ever attempted anywhere in education, yet no significant improvement can be detected in the learning of these "disadvantaged" children. Compared with their classmates from middle-income homes, they have fallen further behind. Moreover, in the course of this program, professionals discovered an additional ten million children laboring under economic and educational handicaps. More reasons for claiming more federal funds are now at hand.

This total failure to improve the education of the poor despite more costly treatment can be explained in three ways:

1. Three billion dollars are insufficient to improve the performance of six million children by a measurable amount; or
2. The money was incompetently spent: different curricula, better administration, further concentration of the funds on the poor child, and more research are needed and would do the trick; or
3. Educational disadvantage cannot be cured by relying on education within the school.

The first is certainly true so long as the money has been spent through the school budget. The money indeed went to the schools which contained most of the disadvantaged children, but it was not spent on the poor children themselves. These children for whom the money was intended comprised only about half of those who were attending the schools that added the federal subsidies to their budgets. Thus the money was spent for custodial care, indoctrination, and the selection of social roles, as well as education, all of which functions are inextricably mingled in the physical plants, curricula, teachers, administrators, and other key components of these schools, and, therefore, in their budgets.

The added funds enabled schools to cater disproportionately to the satisfaction of the relatively richer children who were "disadvantaged" by having to attend school in the company of the poor. At best a small fraction of each dollar intended to remedy a poor child's disadvantages in learning could reach the child through the school budget.

It might be equally true that the money was incompetently spent. But even unusual incompetence cannot beat that of the school system. Schools by their very structure resist the concentration of privilege on those otherwise disadvantaged. Special curricula, separate classes, or longer hours would only constitute more discrimination at a higher cost.

Taxpayers are not yet accustomed to permitting three billion dollars to vanish from HEW as if it were the Pentagon. The present Administration might believe that it can afford the wrath of educators. Middle-class Americans have nothing to lose if the program is cut. Poor parents think they do, but, even more, they are demanding control of the funds meant for their children. A logical way of cutting the budget and, one hopes, of increasing benefits is a system of tuition grants such as that proposed by Milton Friedman and others. Funds would be channeled to the beneficiary, enabling him to buy his share of the schooling of his choice. If such credit were limited to purchases which fit into a school curriculum, it would tend to provide more equality of treatment, but would not thereby increase the equality of social claims.

It should be obvious that even with schools of equal quality a poor child can seldom catch up with a rich one. Even if they attend equal schools and begin at the same age, poor children lack most of the educational opportunities which are casually available to the middle-class child. These advantages range from conversation and books in the home to vacation travel and a different sense of oneself, and apply, for the child who enjoys them, both in and out of school. So the poorer student will generally fall behind so long as he depends on school for advancement or learning. The poor need funds to enable them to learn, not to get certified for the treatment of their alleged disproportionate deficiencies.

All this is true in poor nations as well as in rich ones, but there it appears under a different guise. Modernized poverty in poor nations affects more people more visibly but also—for the moment—more superficially. Two-thirds of all children in Latin America leave school before finishing the fifth grade—but these *"desertores"* are not therefore as badly off as they would be in the US.

Few countries today remain victims of classical poverty, which was stable and less disabling. Most countries in Latin America have reached the "take off" point toward economic development and competitive consumption, and thereby toward modernized poverty: their citizens have learned to think rich and live poor. Their laws make six to ten years of school obligatory. Not only in Argentina but also in Mexico or Brazil the average citizen defines an adequate education by North American standards, even though the chance of getting such prolonged schooling is limited to a tiny minority. In these countries the majority is already hooked on school, that is, they are schooled in a sense of inferiority toward the better schooled. Their fanaticism in favor of school makes it possible to exploit them doubly: it permits increasing allocation of public funds for the education of a few, and increasing acceptance of social control by the many.

Paradoxically, the belief that universal schooling is absolutely necessary is most firmly held in those countries where the fewest people have been and will be—served by schools. Yet in Latin America, different paths toward education could still be taken by the majority of parents and children. Proportionately national savings invested in schools and teachers might be higher than in rich countries, but these investments are totally insufficient to serve the majority by making even four years of school attendance possible. Fidel Castro talks as if he wanted to go in the direction of de-schooling when he promises that by 1980 Cuba will be able to dissolve its university since all of life in Cuba will be an educational experience. At the grammar school and high school level, however, Cuba, like all other Latin American countries, acts as though passage through a period defined as the "school age" were an unquestionable goal for all, delayed merely by a temporary shortage of resources.

The twin deceptions of increased treatment, as actually provided in the US—and as merely promised in Latin America—complement each other. The northern poor are being disabled by the same twelve-year treatment whose lack brands the southern poor as hopelessly backward. Neither in North America nor in Latin America do the poor get equality from obligatory schools. But in both places the mere existence of school discourages and disables the poor from taking control of their own learning. All over the world the school has an anti-educational effect on society: school is recognized as the institution which specializes in education. The failures of school are taken by most people as a proof that education is a very costly, very complex, always arcane, and frequently almost impossible task.

School appropriates the money, men, and good will available for education and in addition discourages other institutions from assuming educational tasks. Work, leisure, politics, city living, and even family life depend on schools for the habits and knowledge they presuppose, instead of becoming themselves the means of education. Simultaneously both schools and the other institutions which depend on them are priced out of the market.

In the US the per capita costs of schooling have risen almost as fast as the cost of medical treatment. But increased treatment by both doctors and teachers has shown steadily declining results. Medical expenses concentrated on those above forty-five have doubled several times over a period of forty years with a resulting 3 percent increase in life expectancy in men. The increase in educational expenditures has produced even stranger results; otherwise President Nixon could not have been moved this spring to promise that every child shall soon have the "Right to Read" before leaving school.

In the US it would take eighty billion dollars per year to provide what educators regard as equal treatment for all in grammar and high school. This is well over twice the thirty-six billion dollars now being spent. Independent cost projections prepared at HEW and the University of Florida indicate that by 1974 the comparable figures will be $107 billion as against the forty-five billion dollars now projected, and these figures wholly omit the enormous costs of what is called "higher education," for which demand is growing even faster. The US, which spent nearly eighty billion dollars in 1969 for "defense" including its deployment in Vietnam, is obviously too poor to provide equal schooling. The President's committee for the study of school finance should ask not how to support or how to trim such increasing costs, but how they can be avoided.

Equal obligatory schooling must be recognized as at least economically unfeasible. In Latin America the amount of public money spent on each university graduate is between 350 and 1,500 times the amount spent on the median citizen (that is, the citizen who holds the middle ground between the poorest and the richest). In the US the discrepancy is smaller, but the discrimination is keener. The richest parents, some 10 percent, can afford private education for their children and help them to benefit from foundation grants. But in addition they obtain ten times the per capita amount of public funds if this is compared with the per capita expenditure made on the children of the 10 percent who are poorest. The principal reasons for this are that rich children stay longer in school, that a year in a university is disproportionately more expensive than a year in high school, and that most private universities depend—at least indirectly—on tax-derived finances.

Obligatory schooling inevitably polarizes a society; it also grades the nations of the world according to an international caste system. Countries are rated like castes whose educational dignity is determined by the average years of schooling of its citizens, a rating which is closely related to per capita gross national product, and much more painful.

The paradox of the schools is evident: increased expenditure escalates their destructiveness at home and abroad. This paradox must be made a public issue. It is now generally accepted that the physical environment will soon be destroyed by bio-chemical pollution unless we reverse current trends in the production of physical goods. It should also be recognized that social and personal life is threatened equally by HEW pollution, the inevitable by-product of obligatory and competitive consumption of welfare.

The escalation of the schools is as destructive as the escalation of weapons but less visibly so. Everywhere in the world school costs have risen faster than enrollments and faster than GNP; everywhere expenditures on school fall even further behind the expectations of parents, teachers, and pupils. Everywhere this situation discourages both the motivation and the financing for large-scale planning for non-schooled learning. The US is proving to the world that no country can be rich enough to afford a school system that meets the demands this same system creates simply by existing: because a successful school system schools parents and pupils to the supreme value of a larger school system, the cost of which increases disproportionately as higher grades are in demand and become scarce.

Rather than calling equal schooling temporarily unfeasible we must recognize that it is, in principle, economically absurd, and that to attempt it is intellectually emasculating, socially polarizing, and destructive of the credibility of the political system which promotes it. The ideology of obligatory schooling admits of no logical limits. The White House recently provided a good example. Dr. Hutschnecker, the "psychiatrist" who treated Mr. Nixon before he was qualified as a candidate, recommended to the President that all children between six and eight be professionally examined to ferret out those who have destructive tendencies, and that obligatory treatment be provided for them. If necessary their re-education in special institutions should be required. This memorandum from his doctor the President sent for evaluation to HEW. Indeed, preventive concentration camps for pre-delinquents would be a logical improvement over the school system.

Equal educational opportunity is, indeed, both a desirable and a feasible goal, but to equate this with obligatory schooling is to confuse salvation with the Church. School has become the world religion of a modernized proletariat, and makes futile promises of salvation to the poor of the technological age. The nation-state has adopted it, drafting all citizens into a graded curriculum leading to sequential diplomas not unlike the initiation rituals and hieratic promotions of former times. The modern state has assumed the duty to enforce the judgment of its educators through well-meant truant officers and job requirements, much as did the Spanish kings who enforced the judgments of their theologians through the conquistadors and inquisition.

Two centuries ago the US led the world in a movement to disestablish the monopoly of a single church. Now we need the constitutional disestablishment of the monopoly of the school, and thereby of a system which legally combines prejudice with discrimination. The first article of a bill of rights for a modern, humanist society would correspond to the first amendment to the US Constitution: "The State shall make no law with respect to the establishment of education." There shall be no ritual obligatory for all.

To make this disestablishment effective, we need a law forbidding discrimination in hiring, voting, or admission to centers of learning based on previous attendance at some curriculum. This guarantee would not exclude performance tests of competence for a function or role, but would remove the present absurd discrimination in favor of the person who learns a given skill with the largest expenditure of public funds or —what is equally likely—has been able to obtain a diploma which has no relation to any useful skill or job. Only by protecting the citizen from being disqualified by anything in his career in school can a constitutional disestablishment of school become psychologically effective.

Neither learning nor justice is promoted by schooling because educators insist on packaging instruction with certification. Learning and the assignment of social roles are melted into schooling. Yet to learn means to acquire a new skill or insight, while promotion depends on an opinion which others have formed. Learning frequently is the result of instruction, but selection for a role or category in the job market increasingly depends on mere length of attendance.[2]

[2] For detailed exposition of the language here used see: Everett Reimer, *Alternatives in Education*, report on a seminar in Cuernavaca, 1968/70. This can be ordered free from CIDOC, APDO 479, Cuernavaca, Mor, Mexico.

Instruction is the choice of circumstances which facilitate learning. Roles are assigned by setting a curriculum of conditions which the candidate must meet if he is to make the grade. School links instruction—but not learning—to these roles. This is neither reasonable nor liberating. It is not reasonable because it does not link relevant qualities or competences to roles—but rather the process by which such qualities are supposed to be acquired. It is not liberating or educational because school reserves instruction to those whose every step in learning fits previously approved measures of social control.

Curriculum has always been used to assign social rank. At times it could be prenatal: karma ascribes you to a caste and lineage to the aristocracy. Curriculum could take the form of a ritual, of sequential sacred ordinations, or it could consist in a succession of feats in war or hunting, or further advancement could be made to depend on a series of previous princely favors. Universal schooling was meant to detach role assignment from personal life history: it was meant to give everybody an equal chance to any office. Even now many people wrongly believe that school ensures the dependence of public trust on relevant learning achievements. However, instead of equalizing chances the school system has monopolized their distribution.

To detach competence from curriculum, inquiries into a man's learning history must be made taboo, like inquiries into his political affiliation, church attendance, lineage, sex habits, or racial background. Laws forbidding discrimination on the basis of prior schooling must be enacted. Laws, of course, cannot stop prejudice against the unschooled—nor are they meant to force anyone to intermarry with an autodidact—but they can discourage unjustified discrimination.

A second major illusion on which the school system rests is that most learning is the result of teaching. Teaching, it is true, may contribute to certain kinds of learning under certain circumstances. But most people acquire most of their knowledge outside school, and in school only in so far as school, in a few rich countries, has become their place of confinement during an increasing part of their lives.

Most learning happens casually, and even most intentional learning is not the result of programmed instruction. Normal children learn their first language casually, although faster if their parents pay attention to them. Most people who learn a second language well do so as a result of odd circumstances and not of sequential teaching. They go to live with their grandparents, they travel, or they fall in love with a foreigner. Fluency in reading is also more often than not a result of such extracurricular activities. Most people who read widely, and with pleasure, merely believe that they learned to do so in school; when challenged, they easily discard this illusion.

But the fact that a great deal of learning even now seems to happen casually and as a by-product of some other activity defined as work or leisure does not mean that planned learning does not benefit from planned instruction and that both do not stand in need of improvement. The strongly motivated student who is faced with the task of acquiring a new and complex skill may benefit greatly from the discipline now associated with the old-fashioned schoolmaster who taught reading, Hebrew, catechism, or multiplication by rote. School has now made this kind of drill teaching rare and disreputable, yet there are many skills which a motivated student with normal aptitude can master in a matter of a few months if taught in this traditional way. This is as true of codes as of their encipherment; of second and third languages as of reading and writing; and equally of special languages such as algebra, computer programming, chemical analysis, or of manual skills like typing, watchmaking, plumbing, wiring, TV repair; or for that matter dancing, driving, and diving.

In certain cases the acceptance into a learning program aimed at a specific skill might presuppose competence in some other skill, but it should certainly not be made to depend upon the process by which such prerequisite skills were acquired. TV repair presupposes literacy and some math, diving, good swimming, and driving very little of either.

Progress in learning skills is measurable. The optimum resources in time and materials needed by an average motivated adult can be easily estimated. The cost of teaching a second Western European language to a high level of fluency ranges between $400 and $600 in the US, and for an oriental tongue, the time needed for instruction might be doubled. This would still be very little, compared with the cost of twelve years of schooling in New York, which is a condition for acceptance of a worker into the Sanitation Department—almost $15,000. No doubt, not only the teacher but also the printer and the pharmacist protect their trade through the public illusion that training for it is very expensive.

At present schools pre-empt most educational funds. Drill instruction which costs less than comparable schooling is now a privilege of those rich enough to bypass the schools, and those whom either the army or big business sends through in-service training. In a program of progressive de-schooling of US education, at first the resources available for drill training would be limited. But ultimately there should be no obstacle for anyone at any time of his life to be able to choose instruction among hundreds of definable skills at public expense.

Right now educational credit good at any skill center could be provided in limited amounts for people of all ages, and not just to the poor. I envisage such credit in the form of an educational passport or an "edu-credit-card" provided to each citizen at birth. In order to favor the poor, who probably would not use their yearly grants early in life, a provision could be made that interest accrues to later users of cumulated "entitlements." Such credits would permit most people to acquire the skills most in demand at their convenience, better, faster, cheaper, and with fewer undesirable side effects than in school.

Most of the skills which are in demand and which require human teachers have already been acquired by a great many of the people who use them. They are now discouraged from sharing them with others by teachers who monopolize the license and by unions who protect the trade interest. Skill centers which would be judged by customers on their results, and not on the personnel they employ or the process they use, would open unsuspected working opportunities, frequently even for those who are now considered unemployable. Indeed, there is no reason why such skill centers should not be at the work place itself, with the employer and his work force supplying instruction as well as jobs to those who choose to use their educational credits in this way.

In 1965 there arose a need to teach Spanish quickly to several hundred teachers, social workers, and ministers from the New York Archdiocese so that they could communicate with Puerto Ricans. My friend Gerry Morris announced over a Spanish radio station that he needed native speakers from Harlem. Next day some two hundred teen-agers lined up in front of his office, and he selected four dozen of them—many of them school dropouts. He trained them in the use of the US Foreign Service Institute (FSI) Spanish manual, designed for use by linguists with graduate training, and within a week his teachers were on their own—each in charge of four New Yorkers who wanted to speak the language. Within six months the mission was accomplished. Cardinal Spellman could claim that he had 127 parishes in which at least three staff members could communicate in Spanish. No school program could have matched these results.

Skill teachers are made scarce by the belief in the value of licenses. Certification constitutes a form of market manipulation and is plausible only to a schooled mind. Most teachers of arts and trades are less skillful, less inventive, and less communicative than the best craftsmen and tradesmen. Most high-school teachers of Spanish or French do not speak the language as correctly as their pupils could after half a year of competent drills. Experiments conducted by Angel Quintero in Puerto Rico suggest that many young teen-agers, if they are given the proper incentives, programs, and access to tools, are better than most school-teachers at introducing their peers to the scientific exploration of plants, stars, and matter, and to the discovery of how and why a motor or a radio functions.

Opportunities for skill-learning can be vastly multiplied if we open the "market." This depends on matching the right teacher with the right student when he is highly motivated in an intelligent program, without the constraint of curriculum.

Free and competing drill instruction is a subversive blasphemy to the orthodox educator. It dissociates the acquisition of skills from "humane" education, which schools package together, and thus it promotes unlicensed learning no less than unlicensed teaching for unpredictable purposes.

There is currently a proposal on record which seems at first to make a great deal of sense. It has been prepared by Christopher Jencks of the Center for the Study of Public Policy and is sponsored by the Office of Economic Opportunity. It proposes to put educational "entitlements" or tuition grants into the hands of parents and students for expenditures in the schools of their choice. Such individual entitlements could indeed be an important step in the right direction. We need a guarantee of the right of each citizen to an equal share of tax-derived educational resources, the right to verify this share, and the right to sue for it if denied. It is one form of a guarantee against regressive taxation.

The Jencks proposal, however, begins with the ominous statement that "conservatives, liberals, and radicals have all complained at one time or another that the American educational system gives professional educators too little incentive to provide high quality education to most children." The proposal condemns itself by proposing tuition grants which would have to be spent on schooling.

This is like giving a lame man a pair of crutches stipulating that he use them only if the ends are tied together. As the proposal for tuition grants now stands, it plays into the hands not only of the professional educators but of racists, promoters of religious schools, and others whose interests are socially divisive. This discrimination in favor of schools which dominates Jencks's discussion on refinancing education could discredit one of the most critically needed principles for educational reform: the return of initiative and accountability for learning to the learner or his most immediate tutor.

The de-schooling of society implies a recognition of the two-faced nature of learning. An insistence on skill drill alone could be a disaster: equal emphasis must be placed on other kinds of learning. But if schools are the wrong places for learning a skill they are even worse places for getting an education. School does both tasks badly, partly because it does not distinguish between them. School is inefficient in skill instruction especially because it is curricular. In most schools a program which is meant to improve one skill is chained always to another irrelevant task. History is tied to advancement in math, and class attendance to the right of using the playground.

Schools are even less efficient in the arrangement of the circumstances which encourage learning for learning's sake, for which I will reserve the term "education." The main reason for this is that school is obligatory and becomes schooling for schooling's sake: an enforced stay in the company of teachers, which pays off in the doubtful privilege of more such company. Just as skill instruction must be freed from curricular restraints, so must liberal education be dissociated from obligatory attendance. Both skill learning and education can be aided by institutional arrangement but they are of a different, frequently opposed nature.

Most skills can be acquired and improved by drills, because skill implies the mastery of definable and predictable behavior. Skill instruction can rely, therefore, on the simulation of circumstances in which the skill will be used. Education in the exploratory and creative use of skills, however, cannot rely on drills. Education can be the outcome of instruction, though instruction of a kind fundamentally opposed to drill. It relies on the relationship between partners who already have some of the keys which given access to memories stored in and by the community. It relies on the critical intent of all those who use memories creatively. It relies on the surprise of the unexpected question which opens new doors for the inquirer and his partner.

The skill instructor relies on the arrangement of set circumstances which permit the learner to develop standard responses. The educational instructor is concerned with helping matching partners to meet so that learning can take place. He matches individuals starting from their own, unresolved questions. At the most he helps the pupil to formulate his puzzlement since only a clear statement will give him the power to find his match, moved like him, at the moment, to explore the same issue in the same context.

Matching partners for educational purposes initially seems more difficult to imagine than finding skill instructors and partners for a game. One reason is the deep fear which school has implanted in us, fear which makes us censorious. The unlicensed exchange of skills—even undesirable skills—is more predictable and therefore seems less dangerous than the unlimited opportunity for meeting among people who share an issue which for them, at the moment, is socially, intellectually, and emotionally important.

The Brazilian teacher Paulo Freire knows this from experience. He discovered that any adult can begin to read in a matter of forty hours if the first words he deciphers are charged with political meaning. Freire trains his teachers to move into a village and to discover the words which designate current important issues, such as the access to a well or the compound interest on the debts owned to the *patron*. In the evening the villagers meet for the discussion of these key words. They begin to realize that each word stays on the blackboard even after its sound has faded. The letters continue to unlock reality and to make it manageable as a problem. I have frequently witnessed how discussants grow in social awareness and how they are impelled to take political action as fast as they learn to read. They seem to take reality into their hands as they write it down.

I remember the man who complained about the weight of pencils: they were difficult to handle because they did not weigh as much as a shovel; and I remember another who on his way to work stopped with his companions and wrote the word they were discussing with his hoe on the ground: "*reforma*." My friend Freire since 1962 has moved from exile to exile, mainly because he refuses to conduct his sessions around words which are preselected by approved educators, rather than those which his discussant bring to the class.

For years now Monsignor Robert Fox has shown that the same method can work in Spanish Harlem. Fox uses photographs of the neighborhood and gathers his adult pupils to interpret them. He conducts his program called "mansight" exploring the meaning of the words used to design their relationship to the trash cans, graffiti, policemen, and children in the picture. The effect of such sessions of psycho-social group analysis is liberating, and surprising for non-Puerto Ricans. More than once I saw them lead to the celebration of a fiesta on the sidewalk. Fox, of course, can count less and less on the support of either Church or city hall or federal programs. He matches people to gain insight, instead of helping society to get control over them.

The educational matchmaking among people who have been successfully schooled is a different task. Those who do not need such assistance are a minority—even among the readers of serious journals. The majority cannot and should not be rallied for discussion around a slogan, a word, or a picture. But the idea remains the same: they should be able to meet around a problem chosen and defined by their own initiative. Creative, exploratory learning requires peers currently puzzled about the same terms or problems. Large universities make the futile attempt to match them by multiplying their courses, and they generally fail since they are bound to curriculum, course structure, and bureaucratic administration. In schools, including universities, most resources are spent to purchase the time and motivation of a limited number of people to take up predetermined problems in a ritually defined setting. The most radical alternative to school would be a network or service which gives each man the same opportunity to share his current concern with others motivated by the same concern.

Let me give, as an example of what I mean, a description of how an intellectual match might work in New York City. Each man, at any given moment and at a minimum price, could identify himself to a computer with his address and telephone number, indicating the book, article, film, or record on which he seeks a partner for discussion. Within days he could receive by mail the list of others who recently had taken the same initiative. This list would enable him by telephone to arrange for a meeting with persons who initially would be known exclusively by the fact that they request a dialogue about the same subject.

Matching people according to their interest in a particular title is radically simple. It permits identification only on the basis of a mutual desire to discuss a statement recorded by a third person, and it leaves the initiative of arranging the meeting to the individual. Three objections are usually raised against this skeletal purity. I take them up not only to clarify the theory that I want to illustrate by my proposal—for they high-light the deep-seated resistance to de-schooling education, to separating learning from social control—but also because they may help to suggest existing resources which are not now used for learning purposes.

The first objection is: Why cannot self-identification be based also on an *idea* or an issue? Certainly such subjective terms could also be used in a computer system. Political parties, churches, unions, clubs, neighborhood centers, and professional societies already organize their educational activities in this way and in effect they act as schools. They all match people in order to explore certain "themes"; and these are dealt with in courses, seminars, and curricula in which presumed "common interests" are prepackaged. Such theme-matching is by definition teacher-centered: it requires an authoritarian presence to define for the participants the starting point for their discussion.

By contrast, matching by the title of a book, film, etc., in its pure form leaves it to the author to define the special language, the terms and the framework within which a given problem or fact is stated; and it enables those who accept this starting point to identify themselves to one another. For instance, matching people around the idea of "cultural revolution" usually leads either to confusion or to demagogy. On the other hand, matching those interested in helping each other understand a specific article by Mao, Marcuse, Freud, or Goodman stands in the great tradition of liberal learning from Plato's Dialogues, which are built around presumed statements by Socrates, to Aquinas's commentaries on Peter the Lombard. The idea of matching by title is thus radically different from the theory on which the "Great Books" clubs, for example, were built: instead of relying on the selection by some Chicago professors, any two partners can choose any book for further analysis.

The second objection asks. Why not let the identification of match seekers include information on age, background, world view, competence, experience, or other defining characteristics? Again, there is no reason why such discriminatory restrictions could not and should not be built into some of the many universities—with or without walls—which could use title-matching as their basic organizational device. I could conceive of a system designed to encourage meetings of interested persons at which the author of the book chosen would be present or represented;

or a system which guarantees the presence of a competent adviser; or one to which only students registered in a department or school have access. Or one which permits meetings only between people who define their special approach to the title under discussion. Advantages for achieving specific goals of learning could be found for each of these restrictions. But I fear that, more often than not, the real reason for proposing such restrictions is contempt arising from the presumption that people are ignorant: educators want to avoid the ignorant meeting the ignorant around a text which they may not understand and which they read *only* because they are interested in it.

The third objection: Why not provide match seekers with incidental assistance that will facilitate their meetings—with space, schedules, screening, and protection? This is now done by schools with all the inefficiency characterizing large bureaucracies. If we left the initiative for meetings to the match seekers themselves, organizations which nobody now classifies as educational would probably do the job much better. I think of restaurant owners, publishers, telephone answering services, department store managers, and even commuter train executives who could promote their services by rendering them attractive for educational meetings.

At a first meeting in a drugstore, say, the partners might establish their identity by placing the book under discussion next to their cup. People who take the initiative to arrange for such meetings would soon learn what items to quote to meet the people they seek. The risk that the self-chosen discussion with one or several strangers leads to a loss of time, disappointment, or even unpleasantness is certainly smaller than the same risk taken by a college applicant. A computer-arranged meeting to discuss an article in a national magazine, held in a corner drugstore on Fourth Avenue, would obligate none of the participants to stay in the company of his new acquaintances for longer than it takes to drink a cup of coffee, nor would he have to meet any of them ever again. The chance that it would help to pierce the opaqueness of life in a modern city, and further new friendship, self-chosen work, and critical reading is high. (The fact that a record of personal readings and meetings could be obtained thus by the FBI is undeniable; that this should still worry anybody in 1970 is only amusing for a free man, who willy-nilly contributes his share in order to drown snoopers in the irrelevancies they gather.)

Both the exchange of skills and matching of partners are based on the assumption that education for all means education by all. Not the draft into a specialized institution but only the mobilization of the whole population can lead to popular culture. The equal right for each man to exercise his competence to learn and to instruct is now pre-empted by certified teachers. The teachers' competence in turn, is restricted to what may be done in school. And, further, work and leisure are alienated from each other as a result: the spectator and the worker alike are supposed to arrive at the work place all ready to fit into a routine prepared for them. Adaptation in the form of a product's design, instruction, and publicity shapes them for their role as much as formal education by schooling. A radical alternative to a schooled society requires not only new formal mechanisms for the formal acquisition of skills and their educational use. A de-schooled society implies a new approach to incidental or informal education.

Incidental education cannot any longer return to the forms which learning took in the village or the medieval town. Traditional society was more like a set of concentric circles of meaningful structures—while modern man must learn how to find meaning in many structures to which he is only marginally related. In the village, language and architecture and work and religion and family customs were consistent with one another, mutually explanatory and reinforcing. To grow into one implied a growth into the others. Even specialized apprenticeship was a by-product of specialized activities, such as shoemaking or the singing of psalms. If an apprentice never became a master or a scholar, he still contributed to making shoes or to making church services solemn. Education did not compete for time with either work or leisure. Almost all education was complex, lifelong, and unplanned.

Contemporary society is the result of conscious designs, and educational opportunities must be designed into them. Our reliance on specialized, full-time instruction through school will now decrease, and we must find more ways to learn and teach: the educational quality of all institutions must increase again. But this is a very ambiguous forecast. It could mean that men in the modern city will be increasingly the victims of an effective process of total instruction and manipulation, once they are deprived even of the tenuous pretense of critical independence which liberal schools now provide at least for some of their pupils.

It could also mean that men will shield themselves less behind certificates acquired in school and thus gain in courage to "talk back" and thereby control and instruct the institutions in which they participate. To ensure the latter we must learn to measure the social value of work and leisure by the educational give-and-take for which they offer opportunity. Effective participation in the politics of a street, a work place, the library, a news program or hospital is therefore the best measuring stick to evaluate their level as educational institutions.

I recently spoke to a group of junior high school students in the process of organizing a resistance movement to their obligatory draft into the next class. Their slogan was "participation—not simulation." They were disappointed that this was understood as a demand for less rather than for more education, and reminded me of the resistance which Karl Marx put up against a passage in the Gotha program which—one hundred years ago—wanted to outlaw child labor. He opposed the proposal in the interest of the education of the young, which could happen only at work. If the greatest fruit of man's labor should be the education he receives from it and the opportunity which work gives him to initiate the education of others, then the alienation of modern society in a pedagogical sense is even worse than economic alienation.

The major obstacle on the way to an educational society was well defined by a black friend of mine in Chicago, who told me that our imagination was "all schooled up." We permit that State to ascertain universal educational deficiencies of its citizens and establish one specialized agency to treat them. We thus share in the delusion that we can distinguish between what is necessary education for others and what is not—just as former generations established laws which defined what was sacred and what was profane.

Durkheim recognized that this ability to divide social reality into two realms was the very essence of formal religion. There are, he reasoned, religions without the supernatural and religions without gods, but none which does not subdivide the world into things and times and persons that are sacred—and others that as a consequence are profane. Durkheim's insight can be applied to the sociology of education, for school is radically divisive in a similar way.

The very existence of *obligatory* schools divides any society into two realms: some time spans and processes and treatments and professions are "academic" or "pedagogic," and others are not. The power of school thus to divide social reality has no boundaries: education becomes unworldly and the world becomes noneducational.

Since Bonhoeffer contemporary theologians have pointed to the confusions now reigning between the biblical message and institutionalized religion. They point to the experience that Christian freedom and faith usually gain from secularization. Inevitably their statements sound blasphemous to many churchmen. Unquestionably, the educational process will gain from the de-schooling of society even though their demand sounds to many schoolmen like treason to the enlightenment. But it is enlightenment itself that is now being snuffed out in the schools.

The secularization of the Christian faith depends on the dedication to it on the part of Christians rooted in the Church. In much the same way, the de-schooling of education depends on the leadership of those brought up in the schools. Their curriculum cannot serve them as an alibi for the task: each of us remains responsible for what has been made of him even though he might not be able to do more than accept this responsibility and serve as a warning to others.

DISCUSSION QUESTIONS

1. Summarize Illich's view on education and evaluate it.
2. Does Illich offer a reasonable and viable alternative in education? Comment in detail.

ROLAND S. BARTH   # So You Want To Change to an Open Classroom

Another educational wave is breaking on American shores. Whether termed "integrated day," "Leicestershire Plan," "informal classroom," or "open education," it promises new and radical methods of teaching, learning, and organizing the schools.[1] Many American educators who do not shy from promises of new solutions to old problems are preparing to ride the crest of the wave. In New York State, for instance, the commissioner of education, the chancellor of New York City schools, and the president of the state branch of the American Federation of Teachers have all expressed their intent to make the state's classrooms open classrooms. Schools of education in such varied places as North Dakota, Connecticut, Massachusetts, New York, and Ohio are tooling up to prepare the masses of teachers for these masses of anticipated open classrooms.

Some educators are disposed to search for the new, the different, the flashy, the radical, or the revolutionary. Once an idea or a practice, such as "team teaching," "nongrading," and (more recently) "differentiated staffing" and "performance contracting," has been so labeled by the Establishment, many teachers and administrators are quick to adopt it. More precisely, these educators are quick to assimilate new ideas into their cognitive and operational framework. But in so doing they often distort the original conception without recognizing either the distortion or the assumptions violated by the distortion. This seems to happen partly because the educator has taken on the verbal, superficial abstraction of a new idea without going through a concomitant personal reorientation of attitude and behavior. Vocabulary and rhetoric are easily changed; basic beliefs and institutions all too often remain little affected. If open education is to have a fundamental and positive effect on American education, and if changes are to be consciously made, rhetoric and good intentions will not suffice.

There is no doubt that a climate potentially hospitable to fresh alternatives to our floundering educational system exists in this country. It is even possible that, in this brief moment in time, open education may have the opportunity to prove itself. However, a crash program is dan-

Reprinted from *Phi Delta Kappan*, October 1971, with permission of the publisher.

[1] For a fuller description of this movement, see Roland S. Barth and Charles H. Rathbone, annotated bibliographies: "The Open School: A Way of Thinking About Children, Learning and Knowledge," *The Center Forum*, Vol. 3, No. 7, July, 1969, a publication of the Center for Urban Education, New York City; and "A Bibliography of Open Education, Early Childhood Education Study," jointly published by the Advisory for Open Education and the Education Development Center, Newton, Mass., 1971.

gerous. Implementing foreign ideas and practices is a precarious business, and I fear the present opportunity will be abused or misused. Indeed, many attempts to implement open classrooms in America have already been buried with the epitaphs "sloppy permissivism," "neo-progressive," "Communist," "anarchical," or "laissez-faire." An even more discouraging although not surprising consequence has been to push educational practice further away from open education than was the case prior to the attempt at implementation.

Most educators who say they want open education are ready to change *appearances*. They install printing presses, tables in place of desks, classes in corridors, nature study. They adopt the *vocabulary:* "integrated day." "interest areas," "free choice," and "student initiated learning." However, few have understanding of, let alone commitment to, the philosophical, personal, and professional roots from which these practices and phrases have sprung, and upon which they depend so completely for their success. It is my belief that changing appearances to more closely resemble some British classrooms without understanding and accepting the rationale underlying these changes will lead inevitably to failure and conflict among children, teachers, administrators, and parents. American education can withstand no more failure, even in the name of reform or revolution.

I would like to suggest that before you jump on the open classroom surfboard, a precarious vehicle appropriate neither for all people nor for all situations, you pause long enough to consider the following statements and to examine your own reactions to them. Your reactions may reveal salient attitudes about children, learning, and knowledge. I have found that successful open educators in both England and America tend to take similar positions on these statements. Where do you stand?

ASSUMPTION ABOUT LEARNING AND KNOWLEDGE[2]

INSTRUCTIONS

Make a mark somewhere along each line which best represents your own feelings about each statement.

Example: School serves the wishes and needs of adults better than it does the wishes and needs of children.

| strongly agree | agree | no strong feeling | disagree | strongly disagree |

I. ASSUMPTIONS ABOUT CHILDREN'S LEARNING

Motivation

Assumption 1: Children are innately curious and will explore their environment without adult intervention.

| strongly agree | agree | no strong feeling | disagree | strongly disagree |

[2] From Roland S. Barth, "*Open Education*," unpublished doctoral dissertation, Harvard Graduate School of Education, 1970.

Assumption 2: Exploratory behavior is self-perpetuating.

strongly agree   agree   no strong feeling   disagree   strongly disagree

Conditions for Learning

Assumption 3: The child will display natural exploratory behavior if he is not threatened.

strongly agree   agree   no strong feeling   disagree   strongly disagree

Assumption 4: Confidence in self is highly related to capacity for learning and for making important choices affecting one's learning.

strongly agree   agree   no strong feeling   disagree   strongly disagree

Assumption 5: Active exploration in a rich environment, offering a wide array of manipulative materials, will facilitate children's learning.

strongly agree   agree   no strong feeling   disagree   strongly disagree

Assumption 6: Play is not distinguished from work as the predominant mode of learning in early childhood.

strongly agree   agree   no strong feeling   disagree   strongly disagree

Assumption 7: Children have both the competence and the right to make significant decisions concerning their own learning.

strongly agree   agree   no strong feeling   disagree   strongly disagree

Assumption 8. Children will be likely to learn if they are given considerable choice in the selection of the materials they wish to work with and in the choice of questions they wish to pursue with respect to those materials.

strongly agree   agree   no strong feeling   disagree   strongly disagree

Assumption 9. Given the opportunity, children will choose to engage in activities which will be of high interest to them.

strongly agree   agree   no strong feeling   disagree   strongly disagree

Assumption 10. If a child is fully involved in and is having fun with an activity, learning is taking place.

strongly agree   agree   no strong feeling   disagree   strongly disagree

Social Learning

Assumption 11: When two or more children are interested in exploring the same problem or the same materials, they will often choose to collaborate in some way.

strongly agree   agree   no strong feeling   disagree   strongly disagree

Assumption 12: When a child learns something which is important to him, he will wish to share it with others.

strongly agree   agree   no strong feeling   disagree   strongly disagree

Intellectual Development

Assumption 13: Concept formation proceeds very slowly.

strongly agree	agree	no strong feeling	disagree	strongly disagree

Assumption 14: Children learn and develop intellectually not only at their own rate but in their own style.

strongly agree	agree	no strong feeling	disagree	strongly disagree

Assumption 15: Children pass through similar stages of intellectual development, each in his own way and at his own rate and in his own time.

strongly agree	agree	no strong feeling	disagree	strongly disagree

Assumption 16: Intellectual growth and development take place through a sequence of concrete experiences followed by abstractions.

strongly agree	agree	no strong feeling	disagree	strongly disagree

Assumption 17: Verbal abstractions should follow direct experience with objects and ideas, not precede them or substitute for them.

strongly agree	agree	no strong feeling	disagree	strongly disagree

Evaluation

Assumption 18: The preferred source of verification for a child's solution to a problem comes through the materials he is working with.

strongly agree	agree	no strong feeling	disagree	strongly disagree

Assumption 19: Errors are necessarily a part of the learning process; they are to be expected and even desired, for they contain information essential for further learning.

strongly agree	agree	no strong feeling	disagree	strongly disagree

Assumption 20: Those qualities of a person's learning which can be carefully measured are not necessarily the most important.

strongly agree	agree	no strong feeling	disagree	strongly disagree

Assumption 21: Objective measures of performance may have a negative effect upon learning.

strongly agree	agree	no strong feeling	disagree	strongly disagree

Assumption 22: Learning is best assessed intuitively, by direct observation.

strongly agree	agree	no strong feeling	disagree	strongly disagree

Assumption 23: The best way of evaluating the effect of the school experience on the child is to observe him over a long period of time.

strongly agree	agree	no strong feeling	disagree	strongly disagree

Assumption 24: The best measure of a child's work is his work.

| strongly agree | agree | no strong feeling | disagree | strongly disagree |

II. ASSUMPTIONS ABOUT KNOWLEDGE

Assumption 25: The quality of being is more important than the quality of knowing; knowledge is a means of education, not its end. The final test of an education is what a man *is*, not what he *knows*.

| strongly agree | agree | no strong feeling | disagree | strongly disagree |

Assumption 26: Knowledge is a function of one's personal integration of experience and therefore does not fall into neatly separate categories or "disciplines."

| strongly agree | agree | no strong feeling | disagree | strongly disagree |

Assumption 27: The structure of knowledge is personal and idiosyncratic; it is a function of the synthesis of each individual's experience with the world.

| strongly agree | agree | no strong feeling | disagree | strongly disagree |

Assumption 28: Little or no knowledge exists which it is essential for everyone to acquire.

| strongly agree | agree | no strong feeling | disagree | strongly disagree |

Assumption 29: It is possible, even likely, that an individual may learn and possess knowledge of a phenomenon and yet be unable to display it publicly. Knowledge resides with the knower, not in its public expression.

| strongly agree | agree | no strong feeling | disagree | strongly disagree |

Most open educators, British and American, "strongly agree" with most of these statements.[3] I think it is possible to learn a great deal both about open education and about oneself by taking a position with respect to these different statements. While it would be folly to argue that strong agreement assures success in developing an open classroom, or, on the other hand, that strong disagreement predicts failure, the assumptions are, I believe, closely related to open education practices. Consequently, I feel that for those sympathetic to the assumptions, success at a difficult job will be more likely. For the educator to attempt to adopt practices which depend for their success upon general adherence

[3] Since these assumptions were assembled, I have "tested" them with several British primary teachers, headmasters, and inspectors and with an equal number of American proponents of open education. To date, although many qualifications in language have been suggested, there has not been a case where an individual has said of one of the assumptions, "No, that is contrary to what I believe about children, learning, or knowledge."

to these beliefs without actually adhering to them is, at the very least, dangerous.

At the same time, we must be careful not to assume that an "official" British or U.S. government-inspected type of open classroom or set of beliefs exists which is the standard for all others. Indeed, what is exciting about British open classrooms is the *diversity* in thinking and behavior for children and adults—from person to person, class to class, and school to school. The important point here is that the likelihood of successfully developing an open classroom increases as those concerned agree with the basic assumptions underlying open education practices. It is impossible to "role play" such a fundamentally distinct teaching responsibility.

For some people, then, drawing attention to these assumptions may terminate interest in open education. All to the good; a well-organized, consistent, teacher-directed classroom probably has a far less harmful influence upon children than a well-intentioned but sloppy, permissive, and chaotic attempt at an open classroom in which teacher and child must live with contradiction and conflict. For other people, awareness of these assumptions may stimulate confidence and competence in their attempts to change what happens to children in school.

In the final analysis, the success of a widespread movement toward open education in this country rests not upon agreement with any philosophical position but with satisfactory answers to several important questions: For what kinds of people—teachers, administrators, parents, children—is the open classroom appropriate and valuable? What happens to children in open classrooms? Can teachers be *trained* for open classrooms? How can the resistance from children, teachers, administrators, and parents—inevitable among those not committed to open education's assumptions and practices—be surmounted? And finally, should participation in an open classroom be *required* of teachers, children, parents, and administrators?

DISCUSSION QUESTIONS

1. Is "the structure of knowledge personal and idiosyncratic"? Comment and discuss the implications.
2. Comment on the statement: "The final test of an education is what a man is, not what he knows." Can this sort of distinction logically be made?

MAX RAFFERTY # Classroom Countdown:
Education at the Crossroads

(1) *"The aim of education is to work joyfully and find happiness."*
No. It isn't.

The aim of education is to give young people the intellectual tools that the race over the centuries has found indispensable in the pursuit of truth. Working joyfully, finding happiness, making a million dollars, trapping a sexually attractive mate—all these consummations are, I suppose, devoutly to be wished and have in fact occupied a considerable fraction of human interest and ingenuity down the ages. But none of them has much to do with the main goal of education, which is the equipping of the individual with the arsenal he will need throughout life in his combat against the forces of error. Happiness is a by-product of education, not its be-all and its end-all. Education does not guarantee happiness. It merely enables one to be more discriminating in his quest for the elusive butterfly.

(2) *"Make the school fit the child."*

But will life in later years recast its iron imperatives to fit the individual? And isn't the school supposed to be, in the large, divine, and comfortable words of the Dewey Gospel, a microcosm of life, or at the very least a preparation for it?

If we deceive the child into thinking that life is going to adapt itself to him through all the vexing decades ahead, then surely we are lying to him in the most cynical and scoundrelly fashion. More, we are sowing the dragon's teeth of disillusion and defeat for every youngster who goes through his formative years swaddled in a cotton-batting environment of sweetness and light only to have the ugly fact of reality thrust suddenly into his at the age of eighteen.

Sooner or later, a human being must come to an understanding with the world around him. Either he adjusts to it, or by dint of personality, intelligence, and force of will he shapes a small corner of it more closely to his heart's desire. In either case, he will be ill-fitted for the task if his teachers have convinced him since nursery school that the universe is going to accommodate itself to him.

The school must meet individual needs and differences, true enough. It should help the child in every possible way to prepare himself for life in a world diked and plowed by two hundred generations of men past. The school should be just. It should be kindly. It should by all

---

From the book *Classroom Countdown: Education at the Crossroads*, by Max Rafferty, pp. 49–54. Copyright © November 1970 by Max Rafferty. Reprinted by permission of Hawthorn Books, Inc., 70 Fifth Avenue, New York 10011.

means be as interesting as possible. But it should not and it cannot "fit" every child.

The Progressive Educationists conceive the school as Proteus. It isn't. It's Atlas holding up the centuries of human thought. Somehow the children of each generation must come to terms with the Titan.

(3) *"The absence of fear is the finest thing that can happen to a child."*

In Heaven, yes. On our imperfect earth, certainly not. It's one of the worst things that could possibly happen to a child.

One wiser than Dewey has said, "The fear of the Lord is the beginning of wisdom." This is one kind of fear, and a necessary one for sheer salvation's sake. On another level altogether, children should be taught to fear all sorts of earthly evils—from ant paste to sex perverts—if they are to grow up at all. Survival is the password here.

Assuredly the school cannot be an updated version of Dotheboys Hall, with assorted Squeers-instructors wielding terror weapons against panicked pupils. Fear as a motivation for learning is little better than no motivation at all. But fear as an ingredient of existence is as necessary for the survival of the species as is pain. Like pain, too, it has been a fellow traveler with man since the very beginning. When man ceases to be healthily afraid, he will be extinct.

The *unnecessary* fears are those that the schools should war against unceasingly. Ghosts, werewolves, witches, broken mirrors, skin a different color from our own—these chimeras should indeed be exorcised instructionally. On the other hand, live wires, drunken drivers, venereal disease, atomic fallout—fears of these all-too-actual menaces had better be encouraged by the schools, not discouraged, or presently there will be no more pupils to instruct, or schools to instruct them, for that matter.

And so it goes. The common denominator in all those misconceptions is the inability of education to make people *want* to do what's obviously good for them. Education can give Americans the facts. It can teach them how to organize those facts. It can even build up certain desirable work habits and patterns of stimulus-response. But it cannot merely by holding up the good, the beautiful, and the true to its captive audience every day necessarily make that audience hanker after these fine old attributes.

What a lot of folks fail to realize is that the schools are up against some pretty stiff and even unprecedented competition these days.

Novels tell the world in four-letter words that every hero is in reality a villain, and vice-versa. This is a big help.

The stage today glorifies the "un-man"—the spiritual amputee—the adult crybaby who blubbers about the twentieth century without having the gumption to try to improve it.

The movies—many of them—are as sniggeringly and tastelessly vile as a stag party after the guests have become maudlin enough to hiccup barnyard quips at the overweight and somewhat jaundiced stripteaser.

And much of television should be commented on only by an authority on the mentally retarded.

We educators, in short, are doing our darnedest to maintain an oasis of values in a vast desert of sometimes sparkling and occasionally seductive slop. But it would be unreasonable to expect us unilaterally to reclaim the entire Sahara.

There are somethings education *can* do, however, and do it better than we have been doing, especially in regard to the teaching of attitudes. One of these is the highly important but generally overlooked little four-letter word "Love."

The self-appointed Pied Pipers of today's youth have been making a big thing out of hate. Hate is what is wrong with the world, they tell everyone who will listen: hate in Vietnam, hate in Alabama, hate among the right-wingers. If we could somehow just substitute big, wonderful love for all this hate, they say, everything would be real cool.

Maybe they've got something. Of course, I'd like to be around—though at a safe distance—the first time our bearded and sandaled friends tried selling the virtues of love as opposed to hate to that eminent peace-lover Mao Tse-tung. And I'm reasonably certain that the ghosts of the butchered Hungarian Freedom Fighters of a few years back would have a few things to say about the practical difficulty of loving Communist tank crews while they are busy crushing you to a jelly.

However, let's concede that our activist friends have a point. As the late Father Divine used to say: "Peace, it's wonderful." And so is love, of course. Which makes me wonder why, in all this talk about the positivism of love and the negativism of hate, no one ever seems to want to talk about love of country.

The official magazine of the Knights Templar recently discussed the results of two polls given to young Americans, one at the New York World's Fair, and one among the Big Ten universities. In both, 84 percent of the students questioned denied the importance of patriotism and described it as unnecessary.

I know this isn't necessarily the future speaking. The heroism and dedication of our young men fighting today in the slaughterhouse of Southeast Asia gives sufficient lie to any such contention as to make any feeble words on my part unneeded.

But there were other interesting findings in these polls. Sixty-one percent of the pollees rejected the profit incentive. More than half were for government ownership of the nation's industries. Seventy-one percent would deny an accused person the right to face his accuser.

Just as an aside to some of our creepier national newspaper columnists and editorial writers who have been doing their best in recent years to create a congenial climate for this point of view, 41 percent of the kids favored canceling freedom of the press altogether!

But it's the black eye hung on love that nonpluses me. That's all patriotism is, you know: just love. And with all the blackguarding and downgrading of hate that's going on these days, I should have thought that hate's opposite—love—would begin at last to come into its own. Apparently not, or at least in only its more trivial and superficial manifestations, to be found in any pad.

Perhaps a clue can be found in the recent statement of one young teacher who declined to lead his students in saluting the American flag.

"The pledge of allegiance mentions freedom and justice for all," he mused profoundly, "and I don't believe we have achieved freedom and justice in this country yet."

So we haven't attained perfect freedom yet. Your mother didn't give you perfect freedom either, did she? But did that prevent you from loving her? And telling her so? And being loyal to her?

Ideal justice admittedly is still somewhere in the dim future. Does your wife always treat you justly? And if, being human, she doesn't, are you going to stop telling her you love her? You'll have a fine, rewarding marriage, my friend. Just as you'll be a fine, rewarding citizen.

The schools should teach their pupils that it's good to seek after perfection. The very search cannot but ennoble those who take part in it. But the schools should also teach that to demand divine faultlessness as a prerequisite to love, or to the public expression of that love, is to banish love effectively from human affairs.

America is human, created by humans, populated by humans. As such, she will fall short of perfection. But with all her faults, she is still preeminently the fairest and the freest and the finest of all the countries of the world. She needs your love, and she needs to hear about it from you, even as your own loved ones do.

Why not tell her once in a while?

I have said that the old question "Does Education have a future?" has given way of late to a newer, more frightening query, "Does America have a future?" Given the knowledge that education has always been the indispensable mentor and handmaiden of the Great Republic, the escalation of the original question was inevitable.

I'd like to record my present answer to both questions as "Yes." When my profession clears its head and starts thinking hard once more instead of reacting impulsively to outside stimuli, it is capable of breaking through the iron paradoxes of the Misconceptions. Until it thinks more and emotionalizes less, it will continue to be held prisoner behind their rigid bars. The same thing is true of our country in this, the final third of the twentieth century.

The precious and unique function of the educator is to spur men on to think. And this we cannot do until we clear our minds of cant and see the causes of our present discontent clearly and without protective coloration. When we have done this as a profession, we will have earned our salt. Quite incidentally, we may also in the process have provided our country with a future that seems so darkened and so dim today but which education alone can so grace and illuminate.

DISCUSSION QUESTIONS

1. Compare Rafferty and Barth, listing similarities and differences.
2. How do Rafferty and O'Gorman deal with "love" as an ingredient in education?

JOHN F. GARDNER   # The Experience of Knowledge

> To me . . . the real crisis in the life of our society is the crisis of the life of the imagination. Far more than we need an intercontinental missile or a moral rearmament or a religious revival, we need to come alive again, to recover the virility of the imagination on which all earlier civilizations have been based: Coleridge's "synthetic and magical power" by which 'the whole soul of man' may be brought to activity, and knowledge may be known.
>
> Archibald MacLeish, "The Poet and the Press"

One of my chief duties during the last twelve years has been to interview all students applying for admission to the Waldorf School of Adelphi College. There comes a time in every interview when the student leaves my office to be seen by the appropriate teacher, and I am alone with his parents. I generally ask, "Why have you brought your child to *this* school?"

The answers are varied and often vague. I am told that the school is known to have high standards, to provide an enriched curriculum, to work for the all-round development of the child. There is said to be an atmosphere of warmth and idealism in our school; art is much cultivated; French and German are taught through the elementary grades. One hears that our teachers give attention to the individual student;

Reprinted from John F. Gardner, *The Experience of Knowledge* (Garden City, N.Y.: The Myrin Institute, Inc., Adelphi University, 1962), pp. 5–9 and 35–38, with permission of the author and publisher.

gifted students are challenged; the maverick has a chance to find himself. . . ."

While all of these allegations are actually true, none of them serves clearly to distinguish the Waldorf style of education from others. I feel duty-bound eventually to point this fact out to parents, but as soon as I do so, of course, the tables are turned. Now it is I who must answer questions: "How *does* the Waldorf School differ from other schools? What can I expect my child to receive here that he would not get somewhere else?"

It might seem easy to reply, provided there *is* anything distinctive about Waldorf education, and yet it is not easy. While it does appear sometimes that schools make their reputation with a specialty such as strict discipline, emphasis on creative arts, high academic standards, the international exchange of students, an exceptional athletic program, or a particular religious attitude, Waldorf schools have no specialty of this kind. The emphasis they place upon the arts is well known yet the stress they lay on science is equally strong and deserves equal attention. They have developed a unique twelve-year curriculum, involving a great number of new methods of teaching the various subjects, yet no subject or particular method can be singled out as most important. Curriculum and methods are, in any case, subject to evolutionary change, and they derive from something more basic than themselves. To answer an inquirer's simple question, therefore, with an equally simple answer—or as the request is usually phrased, 'in a few words'—is very difficult, even impossible, for anyone intimately acquainted with the scope of the educational undertaking known as a Waldorf school.

Perhaps not all Waldorf educators would simplify matters in the same way, but when I face the necessity of choosing according to my own preference from among the possible ways of describing what we are trying to do in The Waldorf School of Adelphi College, I come back invariably to our belief that *knowledge should be fully experienced.*

Ordinarily, the knowledge with which education confronts the child consists of facts that are to be observed and ideas that are to be thought. Such observations and thoughts certainly use a part of the human capacity for experience, but not the larger part. They leave out both the feeling and the active sides of a child's inner nature. Arithmetic, spelling, grammar, science, geography, and history, as these are generally taught in school, make no contribution to a student's desire to be inwardly touched and moved.

What we call natural scientific method has influenced education as it has all of culture, and this method has seemed to demand suppression of the feelings that naturally rise in the scientific observer and thinker. Waldorf education, however, supports Rudolf Steiner's concept of a spiritual science of the future. Such a science calls for the transmutation of feeling and will into thinking, rather than their elimination from it.

It would purge irrelevancies from one's psychological reaction, but not psychological reaction from one's objective study of the world.[1] The special effort of Waldorf education, therefore, is to strengthen, clarify, and articulate the student's capacity to feel, his readiness to unfold inward movement, by letting every percept and concept awaken its appropriate experience.

Waldorf teachers believe that nuances of feeling and inward gestures belong to each perceived fact quite as objectively as does a certain concept. Just as the fact awakens thoughts in an observer and these thoughts reveal something about this fact; so, if we do not arbitrarily prevent it from doing so, this same fact will awaken, with equal necessity, configurations of feeling; it will stir the observer in his will. Such inward stirrings and feelings also reveal something about the fact. They are signs that one is dealing with the whole fact, not just its external body.

We become aware of the higher, deeper, or truer aspects of nature and the world-process at first as obscure stirrings within ourselves. If we encourage the whole man to respond to the complete phenomenon, and if we are patient, we can expect that what starts in subjective obscurity will gradually rise to objective consciousness as surely as bubbles will form at the bottom of a pot of boiling water, out of the water itself, and will rise at last to join the upper air.

Waldorf schools bear ever in mind, besides, that when a student allows facts and events to engage his attention completely, the world not only begins to confide its secret life to him; its effect upon him is also penetrating, and therefore thoroughly educative. The pursuit of knowledge becomes a true *discipline* for him. He is transformed, as well as informed, by the knowledge he acquires.

. . .

CREATIVE ABILITY OPENS THE DOOR TO PRACTICAL LIFE

The impracticality of minds that pass for practical has thus far contrived a technological civilization in which it seems that the steps forward are matched by steps backward: where those who save most time actually have least; where those who cover more space see less; where creature comforts engender dissatisfaction and restlessness; where crops grow big while nourishment shrinks; where such an all-purpose advance as the use of atomic energy endangers the safety and health of every living thing on earth.

We need a practicality that *is* practical. We need successes that really

---

[1] "I believe that some of the worst confusions in contemporary thinking and doing arise from the general failure to realize that there is as great an 'objective within' as there is an 'objective without.'" Laurens van der Post, *The Dark Eye in Africa*, William Morrow and Co., Inc., New York, 1955.

do succeed. Human society today more than ever before needs creative artists in the shaping of economic, political, legal, medical, agricultural, educational affairs.

The main distinction between a theorist and one who actually shapes events, aside from the difference in sheer energy flowing through them, is that the theorist approaches life from outside. He comes as a stranger, seeking to impose his good ideas on wayward reality. The practical artist, however, approaches from within life. He is at one with events. His good ideas rise directly from the ripening of his experience of fact. His ideals are not hatched all too predictably out of abstract logic on the one hand, or personal ambition on the other. Rather, they are learned by him, perhaps unexpectedly and to his surprise, as he follows the metamorphoses of real events. Such ideals gradually emerge from reality itself, albeit with the help of his thought and of his hand.

Why does a theorist so often stumble against reality? Of theoretical minds we feel that they do not learn properly from life. They work from and toward generalities. The theorist thinks out principles, but has difficulty with their application. He does not know precisely where to place his feet, as it were. It is likely that his timing will be off, or his approach will offend. He may well become discouraged in his attempts to improve the world, because "hard facts" seem to fight him. All this is because he tends to draw his original conception from the air, from his own head, from a book, rather than from reality. The difficulty is that, even when facts are straight and his ideas appropriate, reality will have taught only his head. Until his knowing becomes an experience of the whole man, reality will not also give power to his heart, and ability to his hands.

PRACTICALITY OPENS THE DOOR TO PEACE

Nearly everyone wants peace today. But unless schools educate men who are more practical to occupy leading positions in society, there is no telling whether the universal desire for peace will actually succeed in bringing to an end the succession of wars that has thus far characterized our century.

We have mentioned the paradoxical nature of modern technological progress. Starting from the wish to make land more fertile, we continue to reduce its natural fertility and so find ourselves chained to the necessity of ever bigger doses of fertilizer to maintain the status quo. Starting from the idea of destroying bacteria and bugs, we call into being new strains of frightening virulence. Starting from the presumably sincere wish to reduce the farm surplus, or the federal deficit, one administration after another finds itself watching their continued growth. And starting from the desire to do something to uplift the little man, socialistic big government shows signs that it could end by crushing him altogether.

The results of cold-blooded intelligence may seem scientific, but in practical life they will always be paradoxical, which really means, in the end, impractical. For every one-sidedness calls out its opposite. Cold blood calls forth hot; an overdose of rationalism calls forth an upsurge of the irrational—whether revolutionary, criminal, psychotic, mystical, or "beat." As these opposites collide inside the individual, they engender frustration, paralysis, and atrophy; or they break out of him in violence and destruction. Colliding in society, they bring about warfare, cold or hot. Only a whole intelligence, maturing from complete experience, well centered and in harmony with itself, can actually do what it sets out to do. Only such an intelligence can so master the extreme paradoxicality of modern life as to achieve peace.

An intelligence that matures from experience, that shares in the life of nature, that is creative and practical, fufills itself. It finds satisfaction in properly human pursuits. Not at war with nature or with itself, it does not project war into human society. Waldorf schools aim to develop this kind of intelligence, for in it they see the only prospect for freedom and peace in the world.

DISCUSSION QUESTIONS

1. Do you agree with Gardner that not "... facts to be observed and ideas that are to be thought" but "... the feeling and active sides of a child's inner nature" are "... the larger part of the human capacity for experience"?
2. Should the child be "transformed, as well as informed, by the knowledge he acquires"?
3. Is it possible and practical to build a pedagogy that recognizes that "nuances of feeling and inward gestures belong to each perceived fact quite as objectively as does a certain concept"?
4. Is the Waldorf approach to education applicable to the public schools?
5. Might independent Waldorf schools, available to all who wish to attend, be a reasonable alternative to the public schools? What proportion of the public, do you think, would send its children to such schools? How might they be financed?

CARL R. ROGERS The Interpersonal Relationship in the Facilitation of Learning

> ...It is in fact nothing short of a miracle that the
> modern methods of instruction have not yet entirely
> strangled the holy curiosity of inquiry; for this delicate
> little plant, aside from stimulation, stands mainly in

From Robert R. Leeper (ed.), *Humanizing Education: The Person in the Process*, (Washington, D.C.: Association for Supervision and Curriculum Development, 1967), pp. 1–18. Reprinted with permission of the Association for Supervision and Curriculum Development and Carl R. Rogers. Copyright © 1967 by the Association for Supervision and Curriculum Development.

> *need of freedom; without this it goes to wrack and*
> *ruin without fail.*

Albert Einstein

I wish to begin this paper with a statement which may seem surprising to some and perhaps offensive to others. It is simply this: Teaching, in my estimation, is a vastly overrated function.

Having made such a statement, I scurry to the dictionary to see if I really mean what I say. Teaching means "to instruct." Personally I am not much interested in instructing another. "To impart knowledge or skill." My reaction is, why not be more efficient, using a book or programmed learning? "To make to know." Here my hackles rise. I have no wish to *make* anyone know something. "To show, guide, direct." As I see it, too many people have been shown, guided, directed. So I come to the conclusion that I *do* mean what I said. Teaching is, for me, a relatively unimportant and vastly overvalued activity.

But there is more in my attitude than this. I have a negative reaction to teaching. Why? I think it is because it raises all the wrong questions. As soon as we focus on teaching, the question arises, what shall we teach? What, from our superior vantage point, does the other person need to know? This raises the ridiculous question of coverage. What shall the course cover? (Here I am acutely aware of the fact that "to cover" means both "to take in" and "to conceal from view," and I believe that most courses admirably achieve both these aims.) This notion of coverage is based on the assumption that what is taught is what is learned; what is presented is what is assimilated. I know of no assumption so obviously untrue. One does not need research to provide evidence that this is false. One needs only to talk with a few students.

But I ask myself, "Am I so prejudiced against teaching that I find no situation in which it is worthwhile?" I immediately think of by experience in Australia only a few months ago. I became much interested in the Australian aborigine. Here is a group which for more than 20,000 years has managed to live and exist in a desolate environment in which a modern man would perish within a few days. The secret of his survival has been teaching. He has passed on to the young every shred of knowledge about how to find water, about how to track game, about how to kill the kangaroo, about how to find his way through the trackless desert. Such knowledge is conveyed to the young as being *the* way to behave, and any innovation is frowned upon. It is clear that teaching has provided him the way to survive in a hostile and relatively unchanging environment.

Now I am closer to the nub of the question which excites me. Teaching and the imparting of knowledge make sense in an unchanging environment. This is why it has been an unquestioned function for centuries. But if there is one truth about modern man, it is that he lives in an environment which is *continually changing*. The one thing I can be sure of is that the physics which is taught to the present day student will be outdated in a decade. The teaching in psychology will certainly be out of date in 20 years. The so-called "facts of history" depend very largely upon the current mood and temper of the culture. Chemistry, biology, genetics, sociology, are in such flux that a firm statement made today will almost certainly be modified by the time the student gets around to using the knowledge.

We are, in my view, faced with an entirely new situation in education where the goal of education, if we are to survive, is the *facilitation of change and learning*. The only man who is educated is the man who has learned how to learn; the man who has learned how to adapt and change; the man who has realized that no knowledge is secure, that only the process of *seeking* knowledge gives a basis for security. Changingness, a reliance on *process* rather than upon static knowledge, is the only thing that makes any sense as a goal for education in the modern world.

So now with some relief I turn to an activity, a purpose, which really warms me—the *facilitation of learning*. When I have been able to transform a group—and here I mean all the members of a group, myself included—into a community of *learners*, then the excitement has been almost beyond belief. To free curiosity; to permit individuals to go charging off in new directions dictated by their own interests; to unleash curiosity; to open everything to questioning and exploration; to recognize that everything is in process of change—here is an experience I can never forget. I cannot always achieve it in groups with which I am associated but when it is partially or largely achieved then it becomes a never-to-be-forgotten group experience. Out of such a context arise true students, real learners, creative scientists and scholars and practitioners, the kind of individuals who can live in a delicate but ever-changing balance between what is presently known and the flowing, moving, altering, problems and facts of the future.

Here then is a goal to which I can give myself wholeheartedly. I see the facilitation of learning as the aim of education, the way in which we might develop the learning man, the way in which we can learn to live as individuals in process. I see the facilitation of learning as the function which may hold constructive, tentative, changing, process answers to some of the deepest perplexities which beset man today.

But do we know how to achieve this new goal in education, or is it a will-of-the-wisp which sometimes occurs, sometimes fails to occur, and thus offers little real hope? My answer is that we possess a very considerable knowledge of the conditions which encourage self-initiated, significant, experiential, "gut-level" learning by the whole person. We do not frequently see these conditions put into effect because they mean a real revolution in our approach to education and revolutions are not for the timid. But we do find examples of this revolution in action.

We know—and I will briefly describe some of the evidence—that the initiation of such learning rests not upon the teaching skills of the leader, not upon his scholarly knowledge of the field, not upon his curricular planning, not upon his use of audio-visual aids, not upon the programmed learning he utilizes, not upon his lectures and presentations, not upon an abundance of books, though each of these might at one time or another be utilized as an important resource. No, the facilitation of significant learning rests upon certain attitudinal qualities which exist in the personal *relationship* between the facilitator and the learner.

We came upon such findings first in the field of psychotherapy, but increasingly there is evidence which shows that these findings apply in the classroom as well. We find it easier to think that the intensive relationship between therapist and client might possess these qualities, but we are also finding that they may exist in the countless interpersonal interactions (as many as 1,000 per day, as Jackson [1966] has shown) between the teacher and his pupils.

What are these qualities, these attitudes, which facilitate learning? Let me describe them very briefly, drawing illustrations from the teaching field.

REALNESS IN THE FACILITATOR OF LEARNING

Perhaps the most basic of these essential attitudes is realness or genuineness. When the facilitator is a real person, being what he is, entering into a relationship with the learner without presenting a front or a facade, he is much more likely to be effective. This means that the feelings which he is experiencing are available to him, available to his awareness, that he is able to live these feelings, be them, and able to communicate them if appropriate. It means that he comes into a direct personal encounter with the learner, meeting him on a person-to-person basis. It means that he is *being* himself, not denying himself.

Seen from this point of view it is suggested that the teacher can be a real person in his relationship with his students. He can be enthusiastic, he can be bored, he can be interested in students, he can be angry, he can be sensitive and sympathetic. Because he accepts these feelings as his own he has no need to impose them on his students. He can like or dislike a student product without implying that it is objectively good or bad or that the student is good or bad. He is simply expressing a feeling for the product, a feeling which exists within himself. Thus, he is a person to his students, not a faceless embodiment of a curricular requirement nor a sterile tube through which knowledge is passed from one generation to the next.

It is obvious that this attitudinal set, found to be effective in psychotherapy, is sharply in contrast with the tendency of most teachers to show themselves to their pupils simply as roles. It is quite customary for teachers rather consciously to put on the mask, the role, the facade, of being a teacher, and to wear this facade all day removing it only when they have left the school at night.

But not all teachers are like this. Take Sylvia Ashton-Warner, who took resistant, supposedly slow-learning primary school Maori children in New Zealand, and let them develop their own reading vocabulary. Each child could request one word—whatever word he wished—each day, and she would print it on a card and give it to him. "Kiss," "ghost," "bomb," "tiger," "fight," "love," "daddy"—these are samples. Soon they were building sentences, which they could also keep. "He'll get a licking." "Pussy's frightened." The children simply never forgot these self-initiated learnings. Yet it is not my purpose to tell you of her methods. I want instead to give you a glimpse of her attitude, of the passionate realness which must have been as evident to her tiny pupils as to her readers. An editor asked her some questions and she responded: " 'A few cool facts' you asked me for. . . . I don't know that there's a cool fact in me, or anything else cool for that matter, on this particular subject. I've got only hot long facts on the matter of Creative Teaching, scorching both the page and me" (Ashton-Warner, 1963, p. 26).

Here is no sterile facade. Here is a vital *person*, with convictions, with feelings. It is her transparent realness which was, I am sure, one of the elements that made her an exciting facilitator of learning. She does not fit into some neat educational formula. She *is*, and students grow by being in contact with someone who really *is*.

Take another very different person, Barbara Shiel, also doing exciting work facilitating learning in sixth graders.[1] She gave them a great deal of responsible freedom, and I will mention some of the reactions of her students later. But here is an example of the way she shared herself with her pupils—not just sharing feelings of sweetness and light, but anger and frustration. She had made art materials freely available, and students often used these in creative ways, but the room frequently looked like a picture of chaos. Here is her report of her feelings and what she did with them.

I find it (still) maddening to live with the mess—with a capital M! No one seems to care except me. Finally, one day I told the children . . . that I am a neat, orderly person by nature and that the mess was driving me to distraction. Did they have a solution? It was suggested they could have volunteers to clean up. . . . I said it didn't seem fair to me to have the same people clean up all the time for others—but it *would* solve it for me. "Well, some people *like* to clean," they replied. So that's the way it is (Shiel, 1966).

I hope this example puts some lively meaning into the phrases I used

[1] For a more extended account of Miss Shiel's initial attempts, see Rogers, 1966a. Her later experience is described in Shiel, 1966.

earlier, that the facilitator "is able to live these feelings, be them, and able to communicate them if appropriate." I have chosen an example of negative feelings, because I think it is more difficult for most of us to visualize what this would mean. In this instance, Miss Shiel is taking the risk of being transparent in her angry frustrations about the mess. And what happens? The same thing which, in my experience, nearly always happens. These young people accept and respect her feelings, take them into account, and work out a novel solution which none of us, I believe, would have suggested in advance. Miss Shiel wisely comments, "I used to get upset and feel guilty when I became angry—I finally realized the children could accept *my* feelings, too. And it is important for them to know when they've 'pushed me.' I have limits, too" (Shiel, 1966).

Just to show that positive feelings, when they are real, are equally effective, let me quote briefly a college student's reaction, in a different course. ". . . Your sense of humor in the class was cheering; we all felt relaxed because you showed us your human self, not a mechanical teacher image. I feel as if I have more understanding and faith in my teachers now. . . . I feel closer to the students too." Another says, ". . . You conducted the class on a personal level and therefore in my mind I was able to formulate a picture of you as a person and not as merely a walking textbook." Or another student in the same course,

. . . It wasn't as if there was a teacher in the class, but rather someone whom we could trust and identify as a "sharer." You were so perceptive and sensitive to our thoughts, and this made it all the more "authentic" for me. It was an "authentic" *experience*, not just a class (Bull, 1966).

I trust I am making it clear that to be real is not always easy, nor is it achieved all at once, but it is basic to the person who wants to become that revolutionary individual, a facilitator of learning.

PRIZING, ACCEPTANCE, TRUST

There is another attitude which stands out in those who are successful in facilitating learning. I have observed this attitude. I have experienced it. Yet, it is hard to know what term to put to it so I shall use several. I think of it as prizing the learner, prizing his feelings, his opinions, his person. It is a caring for the learner, but a non-possessive caring. It is an acceptance of this other individual as a separate person, having worth in his own right. It is a basic trust—a belief that this other person is somehow fundamentally trustworthy.

Whether we call it prizing, acceptance, trust, or by some other term, it shows up in a variety of observable ways. The facilitator who has a considerable degree of this attitude can be fully acceptant of the fear and hesitation of the student as he approaches a new problem as well as acceptant of the pupil's satisfaction in achievement. Such a teacher can accept the student's occasional apathy, his erratic desires to explore by-roads of knowledge, as well as his disciplined efforts to achieve major goals. He can accept personal feelings which both disturb and promote learning—rivalry with a sibling, hatred of authority, concern about personal adequacy. What we are describing is a prizing of the learner as an imperfect human being with many feelings, many potentialities. The facilitator's prizing or acceptance of the learner is an operational expression of his essential confidence and trust in the capacity of the human organism.

I would like to give some examples of this attitude from the classroom situation. Here any teacher statements would be properly suspect, since many of us would like to feel we hold such attitudes, and might have a biased perception of our qualities. But let me indicate how this attitude of prizing, of accepting, of trusting, appears to the student who is fortunate enough to experience it.

Here is a statement from a college student in a class with Morey Appell.

Your way of being with us is a revelation to me. In your class I feel important, mature, and capable of doing things on my own. I want to think for myself and this need cannot be accomplished through textbooks and lectures alone, but through living. I think you see me as a person with real feelings and needs, an individual. What I say and do are significant expressions from me, and you recognize this (Appell, 1959).

One of Miss Shiel's sixth graders expresses much more briefly her misspelled appreciation of this attitude, "You are a wounderful teacher period!!!"

College students in a class with Dr. Patricia Bull describe not only these prizing, trusting attitudes, but the effect these have had on their other interactions.

... I feel that I can say things to you that I can't say to other professors ... Never before have I been so aware of the other students of their personalities. I have never had so much interaction in a college classroom with my classmates. The climate of the classroom has had a very profound effect on me ... the free atmosphere for discussion affected me ... the general atmosphere of a particular session affected me. There have been many times when I have carried the discussion out of the class with me and thought about it for a long time.

... I still feel close to you, as though there were some tacit understanding between us, almost a conspiracy. This adds to the in-class participation on my part because I feel that at least one person in the group will react, even when I am not sure of the others. It does not matter really whether your reaction is positive or negative, it just *is*. Thank you.

... I appreciate the respect and concern you have for others, including myself. ... As a result of my experience in class, plus the influence of my readings, I sincerely believe that the student-centered teaching method does provide an ideal framework for learning; not just for the accumulation of facts, but more important, for learning about ourselves in relation to others. ...

When I think back to my shallow awareness in September compared to the depth of my insights now, I know that this course has offered me a learning experience of great value which I couldn't have acquired in any other way.

... Very few teachers would attempt this method because they would feel that they would lose the students' respect. On the contrary. You gained our respect, through your ability to speak to us on our level, instead of ten miles above us. With the complete lack of communication we see in this school, it was a wonderful experience to see people listening to each other and really communicating on an adult, intelligent level. More classes should afford us this experience (Bull, 1966).

As you might expect, college students are often suspicious that these seeming attitudes are phony. One of Dr. Bull's students writes:

... Rather than observe my classmates for the first few weeks, I concentrated my observation on you, Dr. Bull. I tried to figure out your motivations and purposes. I was convinced that you were a hypocrite. ... I did change my opinion, however. You are not a hypocrite, by any means. ... I do wish the course could continue. "Let each become all he is capable of being." ... Perhaps my most disturbing question, which relates to this course is: When will we stop hiding things from ourselves and our contemporaries? (Bull, 1966).

I am sure these examples are more than enough to show that the facilitator who cares, who prizes, who trusts the learner, creates a climate for learning so different from the ordinary classroom that any resemblance is, as they say, "purely coincidental."

EMPATHIC UNDERSTANDING

A further element which establishes a climate for self-initiated, experiential learning is empathic understanding. When the teacher has the ability to understand the student's reactions from the inside, has a sensitive awareness of the way the process of education and learning seems *to the student*, then again the likelihood of significant learning is increased.

This kind of understanding is sharply different from the usual evaluative understanding, which follows the pattern of, "I understand what is wrong with you." When there is a sensitive empathy, however, the reaction in the learner follows something of this pattern, "At last someone understands how it feels and seems to be *me* without wanting to analyze me or judge me. Now I can blossom and grow and learn."

This attitude of standing in the other's shoes, of viewing the world through the student's eyes, is almost unheard of in the classroom. One could listen to thousands of ordinary classroom interactions without coming across one instance of clearly communicated, sensitively accurate, empathic understanding. But it has a tremendously releasing effect when it occurs.

Let me take an illustration from Virginia Axline, dealing with a second grade boy. Jay, age 7, has been aggressive, a trouble maker, slow of speech and learning. Because of his "cussing" he was taken to the principal, who paddled him, unknown to Miss Axline. During a free work period, he fashioned a man of clay, very carefully, down to a hat and a handkerchief in his pocket. "Who is that?" asked Miss Axline. "Dunno," replied Jay. "Maybe it is the principal. He has a handkerchief in his pocket like that." Jay glared at the clay figure. "Yes," he said. Then he began to tear the head off and looked up and smiled. Miss Axline said, "You sometimes feel like twisting his head off, don't you? You get so mad at him." Jay tore off one arm, another, then beat the figure to a pulp with his fists. Another boy, with the perception of the young, explained, "Jay is mad at Mr. X because he licked him this noon." "Then you must feel lots better now," Miss Axline commented. Jay grinned and began to rebuild Mr. X. (Adapted from Axline, 1944.)

The other examples I have cited also indicate how deeply appreciative students feel when they are simply *understood*—not evaluated, not judged, simply understood from their *own* point of view, not the teacher's. If any teacher set herself the task of endeavoring to make one non-evaluative, acceptant, empathic response per day to a pupil's demonstrated or verbalized feeling, I believe he would discover the potency of this currently almost nonexistent kind of understanding.

Let me wind up this portion of my remarks by saying that when a facilitator creates, even to a modest degree, a classroom climate characterized by such realness, prizing, and empathy, he discovers that he has inaugurated an educational revolution. Learning of a different quality, proceeding at a different pace, with a greater degree of pervasiveness, occurs. Feelings—positive and negative, confused—become a part of the classroom experience. Learning becomes life, and a very vital life at that. The student is on his way, sometimes excitedly, sometimes reluctantly, to becoming a learning, changing being.

THE EVIDENCE

Already I can hear the mutterings of some of my so-called "hard-headed" colleagues. "A very pretty picture—very touching. But these are all self reports." (As if there were any other type of expression! But that's another issue.) They ask, "Where is the evidence? How do you know?" I would like to turn to this evidence. It is not overwhelming, but it is consistent. It is not perfect, but it is suggestive.

First of all, in the field of psychotherapy, Barrett-Lennard (1962) developed an instrument whereby he could measure these attitudinal qualities: genuineness or congruence, prizing or positive regard, empathy or understanding. This instrument was given to both client and therapist, so that we have the perception of the relationship both by the therapist and by the client whom he is trying to help. To state some of the findings very briefly it may be said that those clients who eventually showed more therapeutic change as measured by various instruments, perceived *more* of these qualities in their relationship with the therapist than did those who eventually showed less change. It is also significant that this difference in perceived relationships was evident as early as the fifth interview, and predicted later change or lack of change in therapy. Furthermore, it was found that the *client's* perception of the relationship, his experience of it, was a better predictor of ultimate outcome than was the perception of the relationship by the therapist. Barrett-Lennard's original study has been amplified and generally confirmed by other studies.

So we may say, cautiously, and with qualifications which would be too cumbersome for the present paper, that if, in therapy, the client perceives his therapist as real and genuine, as one who likes, prizes, and empathically understands him, self-learning and therapeutic change are facilitated.

Now another thread of evidence, this time related more closely to education. Emmerling (1961) found that when high school teachers were asked to identify the problems they regarded as most urgent, they could be divided into two groups. Those who regarded their most serious problems, for example, as "Helping children think for themselves and be independent"; "Getting students to participate"; "Learning new ways of helping students develop their maximum potential"; "Helping students express individual needs and interests"; fell into what he called the "open" or "positively oriented" group. When Barrett-Lennard's Relationship Inventory was administered to the students of these teachers, it was found that they were perceived as significantly more real, more acceptant, more empathic than the other group of teachers whom I shall now describe.

The second category of teachers were those who tended to see their most urgent problems in negative terms, and in terms of student deficiencies and inabilities. For them the urgent problems were such as these: "Trying to teach children who don't even have the ability to follow directions"; "Teaching children who lack a desire to learn"; "Students who are not able to do the work required for their grade"; "Getting the children to listen." It probably will be no surprise that when the students of these teachers filled out the Relationship Inventory they saw their teachers as exhibiting relatively little of genuineness, of acceptance and trust, or of empathic understanding.

Hence we may say that the teacher whose orientation is toward releasing the student's potential exhibits a high degree of these attitudinal qualities which facilitate learning. The teacher whose orientation is toward the shortcomings of his students exhibits much less of these qualities.

A small pilot study by Bills (1961, 1966) extends the significance of these findings. A group of eight teachers was selected, four of them rated as adequate and effective by their superiors, and also showing this more positive orientation to their problems. The other four were rated as inadequate teachers and also had a more negative orientation to their problems, as described above. The students of these teachers were then asked to fill out the Barrett-Lennard Relationship Inventory, giving their perception of their teacher's relationship to them. This made the students very happy. Those who saw their relationship with the teacher as good were happy to describe this relationship. Those who had an unfavorable relationship were pleased to have, for the first time, an opportunity to specify the ways in which the relationship was unsatisfactory.

The more effective teachers were rated higher in every attitude measured by the Inventory: they were seen as more real, as having a higher level of regard for their students, were less conditional or judgmental in their attitudes, showed more empathic understanding. Without going into the details of the study it may be illuminating to mention that the total scores summing these attitudes vary sharply. For example, the relationships of a group of clients with their therapists, as perceived by the clients, received an average score of 108. The four most adequate high school teachers as seen by their students, received a score of 60. The four less adequate teachers received a score of 34. The lowest rated teacher received an average score of 2 from her students on the Relationship Inventory.

This small study certainly suggests that the teacher regarded as effective displays in her attitudes those qualities I have described as facilitative of learning, while the inadequate teacher shows little of these qualities.

Approaching the problem from a different angle, Schmuck (1963) has shown that in classrooms where pupils perceive their teachers as understanding them, there is likely to be a more diffuse liking structure among the pupils. This means that where the teacher is empathic, there are not a few students strongly liked and a few strongly disliked, but liking and affection are more evenly diffused throughout the group. In a later study he has shown that among students who are highly involved in their classroom peer group, "significant relationships exist between actual liking status on the one hand and utilization of abilities, attitude toward self, and attitude toward school on the other hand" (1966, p. 357–58). This seems to lend confirmation to the other evidence by indicating that in an understanding classroom climate every student tends to feel liked by all the others, to have a more positive attitude toward himself and toward school. If he is highly involved with his peer group (and this appears probable in such a classroom climate), he also tends to utilize his abilities more fully in his school achievement.

But you may still ask, does the student actually *learn* more where these attitudes are present? Here an interesting study of third graders by Aspy (1965) helps to round out the suggestive evidence. He worked in six third-grade classes. The teachers tape-recorded two full weeks of their interaction with their students in the periods devoted to the teaching of reading. These recordings were done two months apart so as to obtain an adequate sampling of the teacher's interactions with her pupils. Four-minute segments of these recordings were randomly selected for rating. Three raters, working independently and "blind," rated each segment for the degree of congruence or genuineness shown by the teacher, the degree of her prizing or unconditional positive regard, and the degree of her empathic understanding.

The Reading Achievement Tests (Stanford Achievement) were used as the criterion. Again, omitting some of the details of a carefully and rigorously controlled study, it may be said that the children in the three classes with the highest degree of the attitudes described above showed a significantly greater gain in reading achievement than those students in the three classes with a lesser degree of these qualities.

So we may say, with a certain degree of assurance, that the attitudes I have endeavored to describe are not only effective in facilitating a deeper learning and understanding of self in a relationship such as psychotherapy, but that these attitudes characterize teachers who are regarded as effective teachers, and that the students of these teachers learn more, even of a conventional curriculum, than do students of teachers who are lacking in these attitudes.

I am pleased that such evidence is accumulating. It may help to justify the revolution in education for which I am obviously hoping. But the most striking learnings of students exposed to such a climate are by no means restricted to greater achievement in the three R's. The significant learnings are the more personal ones—independence, self-initiated and responsible learning; release of creativity, a tendency to become more of a person. I can only illustrate this by picking, almost at random, statements from students whose teachers have endeavored to create a climate of trust, of prizing, of realness, of understanding, and above all, of freedom.

Again I must quote from Sylvia Ashton-Warner one of the central effects of such a climate.

... The drive is no longer the teacher's, but the children's own. ... The teacher is at last with the stream and not against it, the stream of children's inexorable creativeness (Ashton-Warner, p. 93).

If you need verification of this, listen to a few of Dr. Bull's sophomore students. The first two are mid-semester comments.

... This course is proving to be a vital and profound experience for me. ... This unique learning situation is giving me a whole new conception of just what learning is. ... I am experiencing a real growth in this atmosphere of constructive freedom. ... The whole experience is very challenging. ...
... I feel that the course has been of great value to me. ... I'm glad to have had this experience because it has made me think. ... I've never been so per-

sonally involved with a course before, especially *outside* the classroom. It's been frustrating, rewarding, enjoyable and tiring!

The other comments are from the end of course.

... This course is not ending with the close of the semester for me, but continuing. ... I don't know of any greater benefit which can be gained from a course than this desire for further knowledge. ...

... I feel as though this type of class situation has stimulated me more in making me realize where my responsibilities lie, especially as far as doing required work on my own. I no longer feel as though a test date is the criterion for reading a book. I feel as though my future work will be done for what *I* will get out of it, not just for a test mark.

... I have enjoyed the experience of being in this course. I guess that any dissatisfaction I feel at this point is a disappointment in myself, for not having taken full advantage of the opportunities the course offered.

... I think that now I am acutely aware of the breakdown in communications that does exist in our society from seeing what happened in our class.

... I've grown immensely. I know that I am a different person than I was when I came into that class. ... It has done a great deal in helping me understand myself better. ... Thank you for contributing to my growth.

... My idea of education has been to gain information from the teacher by attending lectures. The emphasis and focus were on the teacher. ... One of the biggest changes that I experienced in this class was my outlook on education. Learning is something more than a grade on a report card. No one can measure what you have learned because it's a personal thing. I was very confused between learning and memorization. I could memorize very well, but I doubt if I ever learned as much as I could have. I believe my attitude toward learning has changed from a grade-centered outlook to a more personal one.

... I have learned a lot more about myself and adolescents in general. ... I also gained more confidence in myself and my study habits by realizing that I could learn by myself without a teacher leading me by the hand. I have also learned a lot by listening to my classmates and evaluating their opinions and thoughts. ... This course has proved to be a most meaningful and worthwhile experience. ... (Bull, 1966).

If you wish to know what this type of course seems like to a sixth grader, let me give you a sampling of the reactions of Miss Shiel's youngsters, misspellings and all.

... I feel that I am learning self ability. I am learning not only school work but I am learning that you can learn on your own as well as someone can teach you.

... I have a little trouble in Social Studies finding things to do. I have a hard time working the exact amount of time. Sometimes I talk to much.

... My parents don't understand the program. My mother say's it will give me a responsibility and it well let me go at my own speed.

... I like this plan because thire is a lot of freedom. I also learn more this way than the other way you don't have to wate for others you can go at your on speed rate it also takes a lot of responsibility (Shiel, 1966).

Or let me take two more, from Dr. Appell's graduate class.

... I have been thinking about what happened through this experience. The only conclusion I come to is that if I try to measure what is going on, or what

I was at the beginning, I have got to know what I was when I started—I don't. . . . So many things I did and feel are just lost . . . scrambled up inside. . . . They don't seem to come out in a nice little pattern or organization I can say or write. . . . There are so many things left unsaid. I know I have only scratched the surface, I guess. I can fell so many things almost ready to come out . . . maybe that's enough. *It seems all kinds of things have so much more meaning now than ever before.* . . . This experience has had meaning, has done things to me and I am not sure how much or how far just yet. I think I am going to be a better me in the fall. *That's one thing I think I am sure of* (Appell, 1963).

. . . You follow no plan, yet I'm learning. Since the term began I seem to feel more alive, more real to myself. I enjoy being alone as well as with other people. My relationships with children and other adults are becoming more emotional and involved. Eating an orange last week, I peeled the skin off each separate orange section and liked it better with the transparent shell off. It was jucier and fresher tasting that way. I began to think, that's how I feel sometimes, without a transparent wall around me, really communicating my feelings. I feel that I'm growing, how much, I don't know. I'm thinking, considering, pondering and learning (Appell, 1959).

I can't read these student statements—6th grade, college, graduate level—without my eyes growing moist. Here are teachers, risking themselves, *being* themselves, *trusting* their students, adventuring into the existential unknown, taking the subjective leap. And what happens? Exciting, incredible *human* events. You can sense persons being created, learnings being initiated, future citizens rising to meet the challenge of unknown worlds. If only one teacher out of one hundred dared to risk, dared to be, dared to trust, dared to understand, we would have an infusion of a living spirit into education which would, in my estimation, be priceless.

I have heard scientists at leading schools of science, and scholars in leading universities, arguing that it is absurd to try to encourage all students to be creative—we need hosts of mediocre technicians and workers and if a few creative scientists and artists and leaders emerge, that will be enough. That may be enough for them. It may be enough to suit you. I want to go on record as saying it is *not* enough to suit me. When I realize the incredible potential in the ordinary student, I want to try to release it. We are working hard to release the incredible energy in the atom and the nucleus of the atom. If we do not devote equal energy— yes, and equal money—to the release of the potential of the individual person, then the enormous discrepancy between our level of physical energy resources and human energy resources will doom us to a deserved and universal destruction.

I'm sorry I can't be coolly scientific about this. The issue is too urgent. I can only be passionate in my statement that people count, that interpersonal relationships *are* important, that we know something about releasing human potential, that we could learn much more, and that unless we give strong positive attention to the human interpersonal side of our educational dilemma, our civilization is on its way down the drain.

Better courses, better curricula, better coverage, better teaching machines, will never resolve our dilemma in a basic way. Only persons, acting like persons in their relationships with their students can even begin to make a dent on this most urgent problem of modern education.

I cannot, of course, stop here in a professional lecture. An academic lecture schould be calm, factual, scholarly, critical, perferably devoid of any personal beliefs, completely devoid of passion. (This is one of the reasons I left university life, but that is a completely different story.) I cannot fully fulfill these requirements for a professional lecture, but let me at least try to state, somewhat more calmly and soberly, what I have said with such feeling and passion.

I have said that it is most unfortunate that educators and the public think about, and focus on, *teaching*. It leads them into a host of questions which are either irrelevant or absurd so far as real education is concerned.

I have said that if we focused on the facilitation of *learning*—how, why, and when the student learns, and how learning seems and feels from the inside, we might be on a much more profitable track.

I have said that we have some knowledge, and could gain more, about the conditions which facilitate learning, and that one of the most important of these conditions is the attitudinal quality of the interpersonal relationship between facilitator and learner. (There are other conditions, too, which I have tried to spell out elsewhere [Rogers, 1966b]).

Those attitudes which appear effective in promoting learning can be described. First of all is a transparent realness in the facilitator, a willingness to be a person, to be and to live the feelings and thoughts of the moment. When this realness includes a prizing, a caring, a trust and respect for the learner, the climate for learning is enhanced. When it includes a sensitive and accurate empathic listening, then indeed a freeing climate, stimulative of self-initiated learning and growth, exists.

I have tried to make plain that individuals who hold such attitudes, and are bold enough to act on them, do not simply modify classroom methods—they revolutionize them. They perform almost none of the function of teachers. It is no longer accurate to call them teachers. They are catalyzers, facilitators, giving freedom and life and the opportunity to learn, to students.

I have brought in the cumulating research evidence which suggests that individuals who hold such attitudes are regarded as effective in the classroom; that the problems which concern them have to do with the release of potential, not the deficiencies of their students; that they seem to create classroom situations in which there are not admired children and disliked children, but in which affection and liking are a part of the life of every child; that in classrooms approaching such a psychological climate, children learn more of the conventional subjects.

But I have intentionally gone beyond the empirical findings to try to take you into the inner life of the student—elementary, college, and graduate—who is fortunate enough to live and learn in such an interpersonal relationship with a facilitator, in order to let you see what learning feels like when it is free, self-initiated and spontaneous. I have tried to indicate how it even changes the student-student relationship—making it more aware, more caring, more sensitive, as well as increasing the self-related learning of significant material.

Throughout my paper I have tried to indicate that if we are to have citizens who can live constructively in this kaleidoscopically changing world, we can *only* have them if we are willing for them to become self-starting, self-initiating learners. Finally, it has been my purpose to show that this kind of learner develops best, so far as we now know, in a growth-promoting, facilitative, relationship with a *person*.

REFERENCES

Appell, M. L. "Selected Student Reactions to Student-centered Courses." Mimeographed manuscript, 1959.

Appell, M. L. "Self-understanding for the Guidance Counselor." *Personnel and Guidance Journal* 42 (2): 143–48; October 1963.

Ashton-Warner, S. *Teacher*. New York: Simon and Schuster, 1963.

Aspy, D. N. "A Study of Three Facilitative Conditions and Their Relationship to the Achievement of Third Grade Students." Unpublished Ed.D. dissertation, University of Kentucky, 1965.

Axline, Virginia M. "Morale on the School Front." *Journal of Educational Research* 38: 521–33; 1944.

Barrett-Lennard, G. T. "Dimensions of Therapist Response as Causal Factors in Therapeutic Change." *Psychological Monographs*, 76, 1962. (Whole No. 562.)

Bills, R. E. Personal correspondence, 1961, 1966.

Bull, Patricia. Student reactions, Fall 1965. State University College, Cortland, New York. Mimeographed manuscripts, 1966.

Emmerling, F. C. "A Study of the Relationships Between Personality Characteristics of Classroom Teachers and Pupil Perceptions." Unpublished Ph.D. dissertation, Auburn University, Auburn, Alabama. 1961.

Jackson, P. W. "The Student's World." University of Chicago, Mimeographed, 1966.

Rogers, C. R. "To Facilitate Learning." In: Malcolm Provus, editor. NEA Handbook for Teachers, *Innovations for Time To Teach*. Washington, D.C.: Department of Classroom Teachers, NEA, 1966a.

Rogers, C. R. "The Facilitation of Significant Learning." In: L. Siegel, editor. *Contemporary Theories of Instruction*. San Francisco, California: Chandler Publishing Co., 1966b.

Schmuck, R. "Some Aspects of Classroom Social Climate." *Psychology in the Schools* 3: 59–65; 1966.

Schmuck, R. "Some Relationships of Peer Liking Patterns in the Classroom to Pupil Attitudes and Achievement." *The School Review* 71: 337–59; 1963.

Shiel, Barbara J. "Evaluation: A Self-directed Curriculum, 1965." Mimeographed, 1966.

DISCUSSION QUESTIONS

1. Compare Rogers' views on the facilitation of learning with those of Skinner and of Taylor.

2. How do your own learning experiences bear out Rogers' exegesis?
3. Has every child in our schools the right to ask that his teachers respect him, his language, his "style," his background?
4. What changes would be mandated upon our teacher-education institution were they to become "Rogerian" in outlook and practice?

RUDOLF STEINER   Educational and Spiritual
Impulses for Life
in the Twentieth Century

Yesterday I pointed out how the longing of the young today is permeated by something Janus-headed. Certainly, this appears to be permeated by enthusiasm which comes from opposition. But however strongly, at the beginning of the century, this feeling breathed of the present, whoever has now had experience of it no longer finds the opposition in its full measure. Many do not yet admit this impartially, particularly among the young themselves. Yet it indicates something very significant.

The generation which at the beginning of the twentieth century confronted world-evolution in such a way that "facing Nothingness" was a most profound experience—this generation was quite new upon the scene in human evolution. But this feeling must reckon with many disappointments prepared out of its own depths.

The full spread of the sails as it was some twenty years ago is no longer there. Not only the terrible event of World War I has deflated these sails, but certain experiences working outward from within have arisen in young people and modified their original feeling. One such experience became evident, at the beginning of the twentieth century, in the feelings of those who had grown older in years but were not inwardly old. It was not clearly expressed in words, but in other than the literal words there was in the young something which pointed to a responsive tiredness.

Here I am placing before you an idea difficult to describe accurately, because what I really mean is only fully intelligible to those who have experienced the youth movement with a certain awakeness, whereas a great part of humanity has been asleep to this youth movement. When one speaks to people in the way I have during the past days, it is as if one were talking of something quite foreign to them, something they

Reprinted from Rudolf Steiner, *The Younger Generation* (New York: Anthroposophic Press, Inc.) by permission of the publisher. Copyright © 1967 by Anthroposophic Press, Inc. pp. 83–95.

have slept through and towards which even today they adopt an extra-ordinarily sleepy attitude.

Responsive tiredness, I called it. In ordinary life organic existence requires not only activity but also after accomplished work the accompanying state of tiredness. We must not only be able to get tired, we must also from time to time be able to carry tiredness around within us. To pass our days in such a way that we go to sleep at night simply because it is customary to do so, is not healthy; it is certainly less healthy than to have the due amount of tiredness in the evening and for this to lead in the normal way into sleep. So too, the capacity to become tired-out by the phenomena meeting us in life is something that must be.

When education, for example, has been discussed, I have often heard it said that there must be an education which makes learning a game for children; school must be all joy for the child. Yes, those who speak like this should just try how they can make school all joy for the children, so that the children laugh all the time, so that learning is play and at the same time they are learning something. This is the very best possible educational principle for ensuring that nothing at all is learnt.

The right thing is for teachers to be able to handle what does not give the child joy, but perhaps a good deal of toil and woe, in such a way that the child as a matter of course submits to it. It is very easy to say what should be given to the child. But childhood can be injured through learning being made into a game. For it is essential that we should also in our life of soul be made tired by certain things—that is to say, things should create a responsive tiredness. One must express it thus, though it sounds pedantic. Triedness existed among the young in earlier times, too, when they had to strive towards something living, a certain science, a certain kind of knowledge. I mean times when those possessing a certain amount of knowledge were still able to stand before the young, who wanted to acquire it, as an embodied ideal. Tiredness certainly existed even then.

My dear friends, there may be some here who take the above statement with mild scepticism. There are many people today who would take it with scepticism, for when it is claimed that those who knew something stood as a kind of ideal for those anxious to learn, this idea appears to many as unrealizable. For, at the present time, it is almost incredible that anybody should be regarded as a kind of embodied knowledge, embodied science, that is striven for as we strive for a personal ideal.

Yet, leaving out ancient times, this feeling was still present in a high degree even in the later Middle Ages. Those wonderful and inspiring feelings of reverence, permeating life with real recreative forces for the soul in the later Middle Ages, have to a great extent been lost. And because the urge that once existed was no longer there, the young could no longer get tired from what they were destined to experience. To give this concrete expression I should have to say: Science—I mean science at is was actually pursued, not what frequently goes by the name of science—could be stored up, something that is not in the heads of human beings but in the libraries. Science gradually was not really wanted any more. Hence it did not make people tired. There was no feeling of being overcome by an urge for it; it no longer made one tired. There was no longer any possibility of getting tired from a knowledge that was acquired with difficulty.

And from this, what permeated the young, at the turn of the nineteenth century, derived a quite special character—the character of the life-force in a human being who goes to bed at night before he is tired and keeps turning and twisting about without knowing why. I do not want to imply anything derogatory, for I am not of the opinion that these forces, which are there at night in the human being when he turns and twists about in bed because he is not tired, are unhealthy forces. I am not calling them unhealthy. They are quite healthy life-forces, but they are not in their proper place; and so it was, with those forces which worked in the young at the turn of the nineteenth century. They were thoroughly healthy forces, but there was nothing to give them direction. The young had no longer the urge to tire these forces by what was told them by their elders. But forces cannot be present in the world without being active, and so, at the time referred to, innumerable forces yearned for activity and had no guiding line.

And these forces appeared, for example, in the academic youth. And then one noticed things which I have indicated during these lectures, but which must receive more careful consideration if we want to understand ourselves.

Since the first third of the fifteenth century, all man's striving for knowledge has, out of intellectuality, taken on a character pre-eminently adapted to science, which hardly touches the human being at all. People no longer feel how the human element holds sway in writings of the twelfth or thirteenth century, for instance. This does not imply that we have to return to the twelfth or thirteenth century, to implicit belief in all we find there. We shall certainly not comply with the demands of certain churches in this direction.

But because of the indifference with which people study nowadays what is to be found in a chapter of modern biology—or of some other subject—it is impossible to understand what Albertus Magnus wrote. In that way we do not get to know what he wrote at all. We must take the book and sit down to it as if we were sitting down in front of another human being, because what he says cannot be taken with indifference, or objectively as one says; the inner being, the life of soul, is engaged, it rises and falls, and is quickened to movement. The life of soul is at work when we read even the driest chapter written at that time, by an Albertus Magnus, for instance. Quite apart from the fact that in these writings there is still the power of pictorial expression for what appear abstract things, there is always something in the general ideas which gives us a feeling of movement that we might be working with spade and shovel—from the point of view of our life soul, that is—everything is brought in to splendid human activity; through the pictures we are given we sense that the one who possesses this knowledge has full confidence in what he is imparting.

For such people it was not a matter of indifference if they discovered something of which they thought that in the eyes of God it could be either pleasing or displeasing. What a difference there is between the picture given, let us say, by Albertus Magnus, as the great scholar of the Middle Ages, and one of the eminent minds of the nineteenth century, as, for example, Herbart—one could name others but Herbart had a great influence on education up to the last third of the nineteenth century—whoever realizes what a difference there is must see it like this: Albertus Magnus seems to come before us as a kind of fiery luminous cloud. What he does when he devotes himself to knowledge is something that lights up in him or becomes dim. We feel him as it were in a fiery, luminous cloud, and gradually we enter this fire, because if one possesses the faculty of getting inside such a soul even if for the modern soul it is antiquated, in steeping oneself in what is moral, writing about it, speaking about it, or only studying it, it is not a matter of indifference whether in the eyes of a divine-spiritual Being one is sympathetic or antipathetic. This feeling of sympathy or antipathy is always present.

On the other hand, if according to the objective scientific method, Herbart discusses the five moral ideas: good-will, perfection, equity, rights, retribution—well, here we have not a cloud which encircles us with warmth or cold but something that gradually freezes us to death, that is objective to the point of iciness. And that is the mood that has crept into the whole nature of knowledge and reached its climax at the end of the nineteenth century.

And so knowledge gradually became something to which people devoted themselves in a way that even outwardly was quite remarkable. It was only at the lecture-desk that one got to know those represented as men of knowledge. I do not know if others as old as myself have had similar experiences. But in the nineties of last century I was always having cause for annoyance. At that time I used to be mixing in all kinds of learned circles, and there I had much reason to rejoice, and was eager to discuss many questions. One could look forward to such conversations and say to oneself: Now we shall be able to discuss, let us say, "the difference between epigenesis and evolution"—and so on.

Yes, one might begin like that but very soon one heard: No, there is to be no "talking shop." Anything that savored of talking shop was taboo. The man who knew his subject was only heard from the platform and when he left it he was no longer the same person. He took the line of speaking about everything under the sun except his own special subject. In short, life in science became so objective that those with a special subject treated this too very objectively, and wanted to be ordinary men when not obliged to deal with their subject.

Other experiences of a similar kind could be related. I have said this just for the sake of elucidation. But I will tell you the real point in another way. We may find that the teacher hands on to the young things he has only half learnt. We find here or there, for example, those who teach standing before their class with a note-book, or even a printed book by someone else—for all I know, the note-book too may contain things written by other people, but I will not assume that—and boldly setting to work to give his lesson out of this book. By such a procedure he is presupposing that there is no supersensible world at all. How it is that people give their lessons from a note-book or some other book, thus presupposing that no supersensible world exists?

Here too Nietzsche had one of his many interesting flashes of insight. He called attention to the fact that within every human being another is hidden. This is taken to be a poetic way of speaking, but it is no such thing. In every human being another is hidden! This hidden being is often much cleverer than the one to be seen. In the child, for example, this hidden being is infinitely wiser. He is a supersensible reality. He is there within the human being, and if we sit in front of a class of say, thirty pupils, and teach with the help of a book or a note-book, we may perhaps be able to train these thirty pupils to regard this, in their visible selves, as something natural, but—of this we can be quite certain—all the thirty invisible human beings sitting there are judging differently. They say. "He is wanting to teach me something that he has first to read. I should like to know why I am expected to know what he is reading. There is no reason for me to know what he is only now reading for himself. He doesn't know it himself, otherwise he wouldn't be so uncertain. I am still very young and am expected to learn what he, who is so much older, doesn't know even yet and reads to me out of a book!"

These things must be taken concretely. To speak of a supersensible world does not mean merely to lose oneself in phantastic mysticism and to talk of things which—I say this in inverted commas—are "hidden" from one; to speak of supersensible worlds means in the face of life itself to speak about actual realities. We are speaking of actual realities when we speak as the thirty invisible children about the teacher of the thirty visible ones who perhaps on account of discipline were too timid to say this aloud. If we think it through, it does not seem so stupid; the statements of these thirty invisible, supersensible beings are, in fact, quite reasonable.

Thus, we must realize that in the young individuality sitting at the feet of someone who is to teach or educate, much goes on that is entirely hidden from outer perception. And that was how there arose deep aversion to what came in this way. For naturally one could not have a great deal of confidence in a man who faced the hidden being in one in such a way that this job of his had become as objective as the approach to knowledge generally at the end of the nineteenth century. So a deep antipathy was felt; one simply did not try to take in hand what should have carried one through life, and consequently could not get tired from it. There was no desire to have what would have made one tired. And nobody knew what to do with the forces which could have led to the tiredness.

Now one could also meet on other ground those who were in the youth movement at the turn of the nineteenth century. Often they were not young physically—mostly very old. They were to be met in movements like the theosophical movement. Many were no longer young, yet had a feeling towards what contemporary knowledge gave them similar to the young. They did not want this knowledge, for it could no longer make them tired. Whereas the young, as the result of this incapacity to get tired, raged,—forgive the expression—many theosophists were looking in their theosophy for a kind of opiate. For what is contained in theosophical literature is to a great extent a sleeping draught for the soul. People were actually lulling themselves to sleep. They kept the spirit busy—but look at the way in which they did so. By inventing the maddest allegories! It was enough to drive a sensitive soul out of its body to listen to the explanations given to old myths and sagas. And oh! what allegories, what symbols! Looked at from the biology of the life of soul, it was sheer narcotics! It would really be quite good to draw a parallel between the turning and twisting in bed after spending a day that has not been tiring and the taking of a sleeping draught in order to cripple the real activity of the Spirit.

What I describe are not theories but moods of the age, and it is imperative to become familiar with these moods by looking from every angle at what was there. This incapacity to get tired at the turn of the nineteenth century is extraordinarily significant. Yes, but this led to the impossibility of finding anything right, for human evolution had arrived at a point where people said with great enthusiasm: "We shall allow nothing to come to us from outside; we want to develop everything from within our own being. We want to wander through the world and wait until there comes out of our own inner being what neither parents, nor teachers, nor even the old traditions can give us any longer. We want to wait for the New to approach us."

My dear friends, ask those who have spoken in such a way whether this new thing has come to them, whether ready-prepared it has dropped into the laps of those who have had this great longing. Indeed the intoxication of those times is beginning in some degree to be followed by the "morning after" headache. My only aim is to characterize, not to criticize. The first thing that arose was a great rejection, a rejection of something which was there, which man could not use for his innermost being. And behind this great rejection there was hidden the positive— the genuine longing for something new.

But this genuine longing for what is new can be fulfilled in no other way than by man permeating himself with something not of this earth. Not of this earth in the sense that when man only lets soul and body function as they do, nothing can come with the power really to satisfy. The human being unwilling to take in anything is like a lung which finds no air to breathe. Certainly a lung which finds no air to breathe may first, before it dies, even if only for a moment, experience the greatest thirst for air. But the lung cannot out of itself quench this thirst for air; it has to allow for the air to come to it. In reality the young who honestly feel the thirst of which we have been speaking, cannot but long for something with which to be in harmony, that does not come only out of himself like the science that has grown old and is no longer wholesome for the soul to breathe in.

That was felt in the first place but far too little that a new, young science must be there, a new spiritual life, able once again to unite with the soul.

Now what belongs to present and future ages must link itself with older phenomena of human evolution. The difference consists in these old phenomena of human evolution arising from a life of soul that was full of pictures and dream-like, whereas the life of soul we bear within us and towards which we are still striving, must become fully conscious. But we must in many respects go back to older contents of the soul.

Now I should like to turn your mind's eye to a constitution of the Spirit prevailing in old Brahmanism in the ancient East. The old Brahmin schools spoke of four means to knowledge on the path of life. And these four means for gaining knowledge are—well, it is difficult to give ancient thoughts in a suitable form considering we are living not only centuries but thousands of years later—but, in order to get somewhere near the mark, I will depict these four means to knowledge in the following way. First, there was that which hovered, as it were, midway between tradition and remembrance, something connected with the Sanscrit root s-mr-ti[1] which at present man only has as idea. But it can be described. Everyone knows what remembrance, personal remembrance is. These people did not connect certain concepts with personal remembrance in the rigid way we do, where the idea I have here in mind was concerned. What they remembered out of their own childhood became one with what their fathers and grandfathers had told them. They did not distinguish between what they themselves remembered and what they received through tradition. If you were to practise a more subtle

[1] s-mr-ti—Tradition, Remembrance.

psychology, you would notice that actually these things flow together in what lives in the soul of the child, because the child takes in a great deal that is based on tradition. The modern human being sees only that he acquired it as a child. The ancient Indian did not see this. He paid much more heed to its content, which did not lead him into his own childhood but to his father, grandfather and great-grandfather. Thus tradition and personal remembrance flowed into each other indistinguishably. That was the first means of acquiring knowledge.

The second means for acquiring knowledge was what we might describe as "being represented", (not a "representation" as the word is applied in ordinary intercourse today, but literally—an "appearing before the eyes")—what we call "perception."

The third means to knowledge was what we might call thinking that aims as synthesis.

Thus we could say: remembrance with tradition, observation, and the thinking that aims at synthesis.

But a fourth means for acquiring knowledge was also taught with all clarity in ancient Brahmanism. This can be described by saying: Having something communicated by other human beings.

So I ask you to notice that in ancient Brahmanism tradition was not identified with having something communicated by other human beings. This was a fourth means for the attainment of knowledge. Perhaps this will be clearer if we link it up with what is tradition and at the same time of the nature of remembrance. Where tradition is concerned, the human being did not become conscious of the way in which it came to him, he was conscious only of the content. But in man's remembrance he had in mind that it had been communicated to him by someone else. The fact of having received something from others was an awakening force in knowledge itself.

Today many of those who are true sons of the nineteenth century are shaking their heads, if we count this "what is told us by others" as one of the means of acquiring knowledge. A philosopher who dabbled in thinking that aimed at synthesis and regarded what he was told by others as a means to knowledge would never get through with his thesis nor be accepted as a university lecturer. At most he might become a theologian, for theology is judged in a different way. What is at the bottom of all this? In olden times men understood the experience of having something kindled within them in mutual intercourse with another human being. They counted somebody else telling them what they themselves did not know among the things needed for life. It was reckoned so emphatically as one of the factors necessary for life that it was considered equal to perception through eyes and ears.

Today people will naturally have a different feeling—that it is splendid for a human being to tell another what the other does not know, and the world calls for this. But it has nothing to do with the essence of things. What is essential is for observations and experiments to be made and for the results to be clearly expressed. The other has nothing to do with the essential nature of knowledge. Today it will be natural to feel this. But from the human standpoint it is not correct. It is part of life that man should be permeated in soul and spirit by what I described yesterday as a necessary factor of the social life, namely, by confidence. In this particular domain, confidence consists in what one human being tells another, thus becoming for the other a source of experience for soul and spirit.

Confidence must above all things be evoked in the young. Out of confidence there must be found that for which the young are thirsting. Our whole modern spiritual development has moved in the opposite direction. Even in theoretical pedagogics no value is attached any longer to the fact that a human being might have something he would like to tell another which the latter did not know. Theoretical pedagogics was thought out in such a way that as far as possible there was only presented to the young what could be proved in front of them. But that could not be a comprehensive proof. In this regard people have remained at a very infantile stage. Pedagogy envisaged: How can I give the children something under the assumption that they do not believe me? How can I introduce a method which perceptibly proves? No wonder that there came the corresponding echo and that it was henceforth demanded of teachers: Yes, now prove that for me! And now what I am going to say may sound antiquated, my dear friends. But I do not feel it at all antiquated; I feel it as something really young, even as part of the youth movement.

Today when someone stands there before a number of young people who are to be taught, it is as if there sounds towards him out of the young souls even before he is in their presence: "Prove that for me, prove that for me; you have no right to ask us to believe you!" I feel it as tragic—and this is no criticism—that the young should suffer from having been educated by the old so that they have no longer the ability to receive what is necessary for life. And so there arises a tremendous question, which we shall be considering in the next few days. I should like to give you a graphic description of it.

Let us imagine the youth movement progressing and taking hold of younger human beings—finally mere infants. We should then get an infant youth movement, and just as the later youth movement rejects the knowledge that can be given to it, so will the infants who ought still to be at their mothers' breasts, say. "We refuse it, we refuse to receive anything from outside. We don't want our mothers' milk any longer; we want to get everything out of ourselves!"

What I have here presented as a picture is a burning question for the youth movement. For the young are really asking: "Where are we to obtain spiritual nourishment?" And the way in which they have asked hitherto has been very suggestive of this picture of the infants. And so in the coming days we shall consider the question of "the source of life", after which Faust was striving. The question I have put before you as a picture is intended to stimulate us to contribute towards a solution, but a solution which may mean something for your perception, for your feeling, even for your whole life.

DISCUSSION QUESTIONS

1. Should a teacher strive to be an Albertus Magnus, coming to the students as a "fiery luminous soul"?
2. What reaction would you expect students to have toward a teacher who disseminates information that "he has only half-learnt"? Does this statement indicate anything about the current condition of education?
3. Do you agree with Steiner that "this genuine longing for what is new can be fulfilled in no other way than by man permeating himself with something not of this earth"?
4. Do you believe that "the young are really asking: Where are we to obtain spiritual nourishment"?
5. Does Steiner provide the student with the encounter of a "significant other"? What of O'Gorman, Rafferty, and Gardner?

HARIETTE SUROVELL Most Girls Just Pray

The High School Women's Coalition was formed several years ago to unite girls from high schools all over New York City. The members of the coalition were primarily concerned with issues relevant to girls in high schools. After meetings and discussions about what life is like for high school girls, we unanimously concluded that our curriculum was severely lacking in a topic of vital concern to a large percentage of high school students; namely, contraception.

Hygiene is a required course in high school. It is, however, outdated. Kids are purchasing heroin in the back of the room as the teacher shows a film about Nebraskan teenagers smoking marijuana at a hippie party. When we get around to discussing venereal disease, a disease which has reached crisis proportions among New York City's young people, we are shown a film about some wholesome 1956 teenage boy who takes a "loose woman" clad in tight pedal pushers to a motel room. He con-

Hariette Surovell is a sixteen-year old senior at John Bowne High School in Queens. These are excerpts from her testimony before the National Commission on Population Growth and the American Future.

tracts V.D. and subsequently infects Sally, the nice girl next door, who wanted to please him because he took her to the expensive country club dance. She breaks out in a rash, sees the doctor, and in a few days her parents are notified. It is a tragic ending with parents and child crying hysterically in the doctor's office.

Because contraception is not included in the high school curriculum, I made a special request to my hygiene teacher that we discuss it. For one day, the teacher wrote on the blackboard all the methods that she knew. "What method would you recommend to a sixteen-year-old girl," asked the students. "Sleep with your grandmother," she replied. Is this an appropriate answer in a climate where thousands of high school girls are getting pregnant each year? (Incidentally, one of the girls in my hygiene class had a baby approximately ten months later.)

The following day I brought in ten birth-control handbooks to distribute among the girls in the class. They went over so well that the next day about twenty girls asked me for more copies for their friends. But I couldn't bring them: The head of the gym department had told my teacher to inform me that it was illegal to give them out.

At our April meeting we asked the Board of Education to institute a birth control and V.D. information and referral programs in all of the city high schools. We submitted a formal proposal to them and also submitted approximately 3,000 signatures in support of this program.

Some time last year a "rap room" was opened in my school. It was created so that students with problems could discuss them with one of their peers. I worked there two periods a day. Because the Students' Rights Handbook mandates that students can give out literature in their schools as long as it does not contain material that is obscene or racist, I launched my own pilot project and distributed birth-control leaflets that my group had written. I also dispensed birth-control handbooks and leaflets concerning pregnancy testing, a diagram of the female reproductive organs and Planned Parenthood literature. As soon as word got around the school, it went like hot cakes. Every morning I would bring stacks of literature and by the end of the school day it had disappeared.

I was barraged with questions. In my experience with girls I came across, I would find that many of those who were sexually active were using withdrawal as a method of contraception and almost as many were using nothing at all.

It is not irresponsibility that causes this, it is ignorance. How can high school girls be expected to be responsible about using birth control when all knowledge is gotten on the street? Many don't even have a clear picture of how babies are made. "Oh, I thought you couldn't get pregnant if he only comes one time," a girl once told me. "You can only get pregnant right after your period," said another. And then there are others who knew about the pill so that they took their mother's, sister's and friend's pills or they took a pill before they had sex or after they had sex. Most girls just pray.

It is obvious that the answer to this problem is not to tell the teenagers to stop having sex. The solution is that we be taught methods of birth control and where to obtain contraceptives. This does not mean that every teenager must use birth control. If a girl wants to get pregnant that should be her option.

In the New York City Department of Education Syllabus on Sex Education for 1971, which incidentally makes no mention of contraception, they say that "irresponsible sexual behavior may invoke conflicting feelings, lead to health hazards and result in premarital pregnancy." The High School Women's Coalition submits that it is the Board of Education that is irresponsible and not the students.

DISCUSSION QUESTIONS

1. How relevant, would you think, is the curriculum in the hygiene course? Has Surovell suggested meaningful improvements? Does either position understand an I-Thou relationship and its implications in curriculum or sexual relations?
2. Does this article present a reasonable view of the relevancy of school curriculum and its detractors? Comment in deail.
3. Was your high school curriculum relevant? How would you construct one that is relevant?

GEORGE K. RUSSELL **Vivisection and the True Aims of Biological Education**

> If ... [a man] has been touched by the ethic of Reverence for Life, he injures and destroys life only under a necessity which he cannot avoid, and never from thoughtlessness. So far as he is a free man he uses every opportunity of tasting the blessedness of being able to assist life and avert from it suffering and destruction. Devoted as I was from boyhood to the cause of the protection of animal life, it is a special joy to me that the universal ethic of Reverence for Life shows that sympathy with animals, which is so often represented as sentimentality, to be a duty which no thinking man can escape.
>
> Albert Schweitzer, *Out of My Life and Thought.*

As a young child I once spent two or three weeks during the summer at Loon Lake in the Adirondack Mountains. One day as I was walking

Reprinted from the *American Biology Teacher*, Vol. XXXI, No. 4 (April 1972), with permission of the publisher and author.

by myself, I noticed a school of tadpoles swimming near the edge of the lake. Many of the tiny creatures had little legs and were well on their way to becoming adult frogs. A miraculous transformation was taking place right in front of my eyes, and the feelings of wonder and amazement which awoke in me at that time were overwhelming. I spent a good part of every day for the next two weeks watching the tadpoles and marvelling at an experience which for me was unforgettable. Very rarely during eight years of study at undergraduate college and graduate school did I have any feelings of wonder or admiration or respect even remotely similar to my earlier experience of the tadpoles. I learned a great deal of factual material, modes of analytical thought, and advanced techniques of research, but the actual experience of living creatures as living creatures was not part of my education.

It seems that biology, to a large extent at least, has forgotten that organisms are alive. The study of life is in many cases an investigation of "components and processes of living system," but the description itself suggests the emphasis on mechanisms and mechanical principles. Many factors contribute to this approach, but I would like to examine only one, the use in high schools and colleges of vivisection for experiments on animals. In my opinion, the value of these studies is negligible and the feelings which they product in the students required to perform them are ones of disgust, disrespect, and alienation. Many students of my aquaintance have stated emphatically that they would never continue their study of biology because they were forced to kill animals in high school.

Several arguments are usually advanced to justify the use of vivisection in education. Many well-meaning teachers favoring the development of experiential learning hold the view that teaching is enhanced by providing "living material" for the use of students. As a general proposition this may well be true, but in actual practice it would depend entirely upon how the organisms were used and the attitude which the instructor adopted toward them. An experiment in which the brain of a frog is destroyed in order to study the spinal reflexes of the animal demonstrates very little which could not be found in any elementary textbook and is a gruesome experience for a student with even modest sensitivities. One can learn a surprisingly large amount about a frog by quietly observing its rate of respiration, feeding habits, the structure of its tympanic membrane, etc. A film loop I have used in class concerning the feeding preferences of a toad has never failed to stimulate interest and wonder. In addition, an imaginative teacher could make good use of transparent organisms (various species of fish and invertebrates) to demonstrate *living* processes in *living* animals. It seems to me that one must always keep firmly in mind what the experiment is supposed to be demonstrating. Does the end result in any way justify the agonies inflicted on a sentient creature?

A common complaint about vivisection in classroom exercises is that the experiments very often do not work because the teacher is untrained and inexperienced. The net result of an hour or two of work is a heap of dead animals, a class of students filled with emptiness and distaste, and another "unsuccessful experiment." A long-standing disgust in myself for earthworms originated in a mishandled high school experiment and was corrected only years later when I witnessed the incredible role that earthworms play in reducing leaf compost to soil. But my point is more than this. Even if the teachers had the best possible training, and even if the experiments were always successful and were always carried out in the most humane way possible, the destructive effect of the experience on the student, in my view, would simply not be worth it. My opposition to vivisection is based both on a concern for the humane treatment of animals and an equal concern for the emotional and mental health of the students.

The psychological effects of vivisection upon the personality of the individual cannot be overemphasized. In no way does vivisection make a man better, more capable or more humane. Every time a person kills an animal he becomes increasingly insensitive, callous, and cruel. Experimentation of this kind leads to a systematic and progressive crippling of an individual's capacity for feeling and produces changes of personality which, in my opinion, are noticeable even to someone with no formal training in human psychology or psychiatry. An individual able to inflict suffering on defenseless animals will certainly be capable of doing the same to his fellow human beings. We live in an age of sadism and criminality. Is it asking too much for biology to try to awaken respect for life and to develop love and admiration for living things? The future of the world may depend on it.

In many courses which I took as a student, various animals were used more or less as reagents in chemistry experiments. The instructions in the laboratory manual invariably state, "sacrifice the animal . . .," but one could easily have scratched out the word "sacrifice" and substituted "use" or "kill." In no sense was a sacrificial mood present in either the students or the teacher. Most of the experiments we performed could have been illustrated with short films or reading assignments, and we could have spent our time observing living fish in aquaria, amphibians and reptiles in terraria, or any living organism in its natural habitat.

The use of living animals in experimentation has been justified by its contribution to the advancement of human knowledge. The developments in medicine through the use of vivisection, for example, are very great indeed, but the question under consideration here is whether high school or college students derive any benefit whatsoever from studies of this kind. No single experiment in high school or college advances the forefront of human knowledge in the slightest. The well known naturalist and literary critic, the late Dr. Joseph Wood Krutch, has called attention to the cruel and pointless nature of many so-called investigations in which animals are starved, infected, inoculated, and abused in a variety of ways simply so that students can witness at first hand the effects of experimental procedures and manipulations, the results of which are already known in advance. One biological supply house provides eight different deficiency diets and appropriate test animals so that students can observe various forms of malnutrition.

By now it is as well know that a rat will sicken and die without certain minerals and vitamins as it is that he will die if given no food at all. Would anyone learn anything by poking out the eyes in order to prove that without them animals can't see? . . . Taught by such methods, biology not only fails to promote reverence for life, but encourages the tendency to blaspheme it. Instead of increasing empathy it destroys it. Instead of enlarging our sympathy it hardens the heart.[1]

In actual fact these studies are not experiments at all, but are simply demonstrations. In no way do they give the student a true experience of research or the joy of discovery.

Vivisection is included in premedical curricula as a prerequisite for later medical studies and as a means for developing manipulative skills. In my view, undergraduate premedical education would be performing a far greater service by developing veneration and compassion for life. In an age of specialization when many physicians are more interested in the disease than in the welfare of the patient, compassion is needed as much as diagnostic, therapeutic, and technical skills. The dramatic increase in psychosomatic illnesses calls for physicians with a great deal of understanding and compassion.

Lest I be accused of arguing against all forms of experimentation with animals, let me point out that there are numerous experiments which can be performed with living animals or with the students themselves as subjects, which illustrate a wide variety of physiological phenomena. Isometric and isotonic muscle contraction, muscle fatigue, the rate of nerve impulse transmission, respiration studies, experiments in sensory physiology, and countless other experiments can be carried out either with living or with student subjects. In most if not all cases it is simply unnecessary to destroy an animal to study a given physiological process. An imaginative teacher could use every means at his disposal to employ living animals to illustrate the points under consideration. In addition, students are always eager to engage in physiological studies and learn just as much as they would through vivisection. As newer forms of educational equipment become available, the range of these experiments should expand considerably.

[1] Joseph Wood Krutch, *The Great Chain of Life*, New York, Pyramid Books, 1956, p. 142.

It may seem that I have overemphasized the role of education in fostering the development of the life of feeling, for education is supposed to be concerned with the training of intellect. It is essential, however, that students feel inwardly connected with the material they are studying. A student can begin to understand the "personality" of a species of bird or insect from patient observations of its life habits without even knowing the common name of the animal. Only when he has some basis of familiarity founded on devotion and a sense of kinship can he pursue a true course of intellectual study. Many students of biology have very little aquaintance with living plants and animals, and what concerns me greatly is that vivisection severs the tenuous connection which does exist and makes real learning impossible. A student will eagerly learn the names, parts and processes of plants and animals for which he feels admiration and respect.

I was once asked to cite an example to illustrate how one could teach in a manner which stimulated a sense of wonder in students. I replied by describing a study involving the Manx Shearwater, a shorebird inhabiting the west coast of Great Britain. The Shearwater was flown by airplane across the Atlantic and released in Boston. Twelve days later the bird had successfully flown the Atlantic and was back in its nest. Through some mysterious fashion the homing instinct of the bird had guided it across 2800 miles of ocean. The questioner's response was that the wonder experienced by the students was in direct proportion to the inexplicibility of the example. The students were awed by the Shearwater because there was no easy "explanation" available. "But," the questioner continued, "how would you teach about ordinary phenomena for which there *are* explanations in a way which developed reverence?" A great deal of what passes for scientific explanation, especially in the teaching of biology, is actually a set of abstractions having little to do with the phenomena themselves, and more to do with theoretical models and mechanisms abstracted from the phenomena. The more one analyzes the parts and processes of an organism, the more one becomes removed from the life of the animal. Only by experiencing the animal as a living, sentient, responding creature can one begin to awaken the faculties of comprehension needed to understand life. A sense of wonder can be developed in *any* circumstance if the observer confronts the living organism itself and sets aside the tangled web of explanations and mechanisms which deter him from experiencing the living creature.

Dr. Franz E. Winkler, physician and author of the book, *Man, the Bridge Between Two Worlds,* has suggested that children, whose minds are unencumbered with intellectual explanations, are much closer to direct awareness and comprehension of the living world. Because of this they can truly experience a sense of wonder.

As a matter of fact, the more intellectual we become, and the more we learn about details and mechanisms, the further we remove ourselves from the comprehension of the whole. The child feels this immediately and counters abstract "explanations" with a most sensible response, an endless series of "Whys". Usually the conversation ends with mutual resentment and frustration. Yet it is not difficult to answer the child's question provided we keep in mind that he is closer than we to a grasp of causality, and merely requests a translation of his intuitive comprehension into intellectual terms.[2]

In his book he divides cognition into two constituent faculties, intellect and intuition. Intellect analyzes, dissects, and describes: intuition synthesizes and comprehends. Earlier peoples knew about the healing properties of herbs, had great skill in mathematics and architecture, and had an understanding of natural processes with very little modern scientific knowledge. Dr. Winkler attributes these abilities to powers of intuitive comprehension, which he feels modern man has largely lost. Intuitive powers are akin to creative faculties and must be stimulated and nourished by compassion and love. They have much more to do with appreciation of the whole then with analysis of the parts. The central role of intuition in scientific discovery is well known and has been amply described by Poincaire, Kekulé, Gauss, Heisenberg and numerous others.[3] In my opinion, modern education with its emphasis on components and mechanisms and the deadening of sensibility which results from this, will ultimately lead to paralysis of the very faculties of intuition upon which the progress of science depends. If it were possible to develop this faculty, as Dr. Winkler suggests in his book, and bring it into balance with analytical intellect, many secrets of nature might be revealed through intuitive comprehension rather than through the endless dividing and subdividing of parts, which characterize a good part of modern science. Biological education ought to concentrate on developing understanding and devotion for animals and life: intuitive faculties will never develop in students who cannot truly love all living creatures.

Science is the leading force in modern life. In the future it will be more and more the scientists who determine the course of world events. Science itself is neither good nor bad, but is an extremely powerful institution either for the destruction or salvation of mankind. The power and prestige of scientists make them almost immune to correction or control by the public. So far their performance has been doubtful and ominous, for scientists of the twentieth century have been more inclined to invent destructive weapons than to find truly constructive benefits for humanity. The fate of our civilization may well depend upon the way in which we educate our future scientists. Unless we train them from the very beginning to respect and uphold the beauty and integrity of creation, they will ultimately misuse their ever-increasing powers. The power

[2] Franz E. Winkler, *Man, the Bridge Between Two Worlds*, The Myrin Institute, 521 Park Ave., New York, New York 10021.
[3] See Arthur Koestler, *The Act of Creation*, New York, Dell Publishing Co., 1967, pp. 112–120.

of science without the control of compassion and admiration for life is too immense to be applied merely for the satisfaction of scientific curiosity. If biology were taught in a manner which developed a sense of wonder and reverence for life, and if students felt inwardly enriched from their study of life, these students would formulate as a lifelong goal the steadfast determination to protect and preserve all life and would bring healing to a world desparately in need of it.

DISCUSSION QUESTIONS

1. Should the sciences be "taught in a manner which developed a sense of wonder and reverence for life"?
2. Should all subject matter be experienced "in a manner which developed a sense of wonder and reverence for life"?
3. How would you apply the concept of "reverence for life" in your field of study?

NATHAN ISAACS Piaget and His Work as a Whole

1. THE MAN AND HIS WRITINGS

First of all, then, Piaget himself. He is a French-Swiss genetic psychologist, born in 1896. He started with a training in biology, and still carries this with him, but he soon became more and more interested first in the philosophy and then in the psychology of knowledge, which in fact became his main lifework. For he had come to see in genetic psychology the key to the growth of the human capacity for knowledge and understanding as such. This meant for him, in essence, the growth of logical, mathematical and scientific thinking, and everything to which they have led. And by the age of 25 or so, he had worked out a great plan of experimental enquiry into the processes of intellectual development in children from their beginnings to maturity. Together with a large team of collaborators and pupils, he has been realising this plan ever since.

From the early 1920's onward he published a series of volumes on the language and thought of children, their judgment and reasoning, their ideas of causality and their notion of the physical world. These were followed by an illuminating excursion into the development of moral

Reprinted from Nathan Isaacs, *New Light on Children's Ideas of Number* (London: Ward Lock Educational Limited), pp. 4–7, by permission of the publisher. Copyright 1967 by Ward Lock Educational Limited.

judgment in the child. Then came an intensive study of his own three infants from birth onward, recorded in two remarkable volumes: *The Origin of Intelligence in the Child,* and *The Child's Construction of Reality.* After that he poured forth studies of *Play, Dreams and Imitation in Childhood;* of the growth of the notions of number, physical quantity, space, time, movement and speed; of the development of the child's logic and capacity for abstract thought, etc., etc. As his findings took full theoretical shape, he also published some more general works on the psychology of intelligence and on logic, and furthermore a three-volume treatise called *An Introduction to Genetic Epistemology,* which is a comprehensive analysis of the development of the main type of knowledge in both the race and the individual. A number of his books has not been translated yet, or anyway has not yet appeared in translation. Unfortunately also much of Piaget's work is at best not too easy to read, whether in the original or in its English rendering, and in one or two cases the latter has not served its author too well.

I should add here that in the opinion of some of us the first group of writings, though very stimulating, was open to deep-reaching criticisms. However, Piaget subsequently modified his procedure in the light partly of these criticisms, but still more of his intensive study of his own children and of all he learnt from them; and his later results in my view carry substantial conviction. The book on Number belongs to this later period. It was first published in French in 1941; the English translation came out in 1952. It is only fair to say that whilst the latter shows Professor Piaget as sole author, the French original joins with him a colleague, Mlle. Alina Szeminska, whose name should equally have appeared in the translation. However, it remains true that the theoretical inspiration was obviously Piaget's, as part of his total research plan, which had already gone on for many years. And he had always mobilised the labours of a considerable number of helpers, above all experimental; that in fact is one of the important sources of strength of his work. Their contribution have thus been material and should not by any means be underated. (One of them, Mlle. Inhelder, is now a permanent close colleague who speaks with an authority second only to Piaget's own.) Yet the master-plan remains his and he stays the true architect of the great structure of new knowledge and insight linked with his name. I shall therefore continue, if only for simplicity's sake, to refer solely to him.

2. HIS OVERALL VIEW OF MENTAL DEVELOPMENT: ACTION AS THE KEY EVEN TO MATHEMATICAL AND LOGICAL THOUGHT

If now we look at his work as a whole, the first point to note is that we have here a vast series of ingenious and searching experiments, spread over more than a generation and over most major aspects of intellectual, development, all leading to mutually supporting results. The general viewpoint which Piaget formulated at an early stage has in fact, in the further course of his labours, been steadily confirmed, elaborated more fully, and again confirmed.

The essence of that view is this. The starting-point and crux of the child's intellectual growth is not—as it was long the fashion to assume —sensory perception or anything else passively impressed on him from outside, but *his own action*. And action in the most literal, physical sense of the term. From the beginning it is patterns of active behaviour that govern his life. Through these he takes in ever new experiences which become worked into his action-patterns and continually help to expand their range and scope. It is through actively turning to look or listen, through following and repeating, through exploring by touch and handling and manipulating, through striving to walk and talk, through dramatic play and the mastery of every sort of new activity and skill, that he goes on all the time both enlarging his world and organising it. His own physical activity thus enters from the outset into his whole world-scheme and indeed fashions it, supports it and provides the master-key to it.

In effect thought itself is now simply an internal version or development of outward action. It is action which becomes *progressively* internalised through the child's acquisition of language and his growing use of imagination and representation. It then goes on expanding under the guidance partly of social life, partly of the physical world, till it culminates in a great organised scheme of mental *operations*. This is governed by certain rules of *mobile* equilibrium that allow us to make the most flexible use of our knowledge and to regulate our thought-life to our utmost adaptive advantage. These rules form themselves into two closely related patterns, intimately interacting with one another and probably at bottom one, which we call logic and mathematics respectively. Their operation represents our intelligence at its most effective level. They can both be clearly seen at work in those great notion-systems whereby we order all our experience: space—time—objects—causality, and so on. Piaget traces the development of each of these systems from its beginnings until it becomes fully operational. And the key all the way, up to the *most abstruse forms of logical and mathematical thought*, remains *action*. The child stays an organism or person continually interacting with his environment and striving by ever more complex procedures partly to fit himself into his world, partly to fit it to himself, physically and socially.

So condensed a sketch may not convey overmuch at the present stage; but it is only intended as a first backcloth and I hope will gather further meaning as we go along. I should only make clear again that I am not putting Piaget's work forward as *fully* established but rather as a point of view which is tremendously worth following through, at least as a working hypothesis. And since over most of its range it has strong experimental support, we should either have to find some major flaw in this, or else be ready to treat it as something with which we must come to terms.

I should add here, regarding the view taken of Piaget's work by contemporary British psychologists, that it is still somewhat early days for any definite summing-up. Only within the last few years has widespread attention been brought to bear on this work, and active scientific research focused on it. There had previously been a tendency to treat it as interesting, but rather off the main line of advance of modern psychology. It was criticised as too philosophic or not sufficiently scientific, not properly standardised and controlled, not satisfactorily presented and badly lacking in any statistical foundation, etc. Some of the latter criticism is not to be gainsaid, as I shall note. However, in spite of all this, the sheer calibre and weight of the steadily mounting work has more recently begun to win through. In a number of places experimental psychologists have seriously started checking up on Piaget's findings, repeating this or that part of his investigations, organising closely related researches, and so on. Much of this work is still uncompleted, or unreported, or anyway unpublished. However, it can be said that several broad confirmations of his results, both as regards number and in other fields, have already been obtained. One particularly interesting instance is an enquiry recently carried through at Aden on the number-ideas of local schoolchildren representing the most diverse races, where the investigator was fascinated to obtain from Arab and Somali children just the same kind of responses as Piaget has reported on his European, that is Genevan subjects.

The broad confirmations found do not exclude points of difference, and it may well emerge that both his concrete findings and his theory need some qualification, above all in the direction of greater flexibility. On the other hand there is still much misconception about the meaning and effect of some of his views. Once this is corrected, I think one can fairly sum up that such confirmation as has already accrued, together with the cumulative and cross-checking force of Piaget's own evidence, has now established his work as a development of major importance that demands the closest attention.

DISCUSSION QUESTIONS

1. Summerize Piaget's position on action and learning. What implications do you see for education?
2. How do Gardner and Barth differ from Piaget in their application of the action principle in education?